W9-ABK-989

ASSIGNMENT IN UTOPIA

BY EUGENE LYONS

THE LIFE AND DEATH
OF SACCO AND VANZETTI

MOSCOW CARROUSEL

SIX SOVIET PLAYS (*ed.*)

WE COVER THE WORLD (*ed.*)

ASSIGNMENT IN UTOPIA

Eugene Lyons

Harcourt, Brace and Company · New York

Third printing, October, 1937

PRINTED IN THE UNITED STATES OF AMERICA
BY QUINN & BODEN COMPANY, INC., RAHWAY, N. J.
Typography by Robert Josephy

To Billy and Genie

Contents

BOOK 1. *Prelude to Moscow*

BOOK 2. *Hallelujah!*

BOOK 3. *Doubt*

BOOK 4. *Disillusionment*

BOOK 5. *Rededication*

BOOK I

PRELUDE TO MOSCOW

I. Revolt Against Ugliness

IN AMERICA we still romanticize the glories of a hard, poverty-ridden youth. Our rags-to-riches legends and literature overlook the fact that Tony the Bootblack ends up as a hod-carrier or a gangster more often than a millionaire. They overlook the more vital fact that when he does achieve wealth he generally carries the scars of the unequal struggle on his mind and spirit forever. He can rarely attain the mellow quality of the full, cultured existence of those whose rise was more orderly, less desperate. Our up-from-the-gutter type of true, or nearly true, story is written by the few who did creep out of the quagmires of want and its endless degradations. The many who were swallowed up, or who emerged broken in body and spirit, do not write autobiographies or make after-dinner speeches.

On the East Side of New York, where I grew up, we knew hardship and fear in their less romantic guises. Our streets teemed with crowded, chaotic life like the underside of a moss-grown stone. Our tenements were odoriferous garbage heaps where the same over-abundant life proliferated. We knew coarseness, vermin, want, so intimately that they became routine commonplaces. The affluence, the ease, the glimpse of ordered beauty were distant and unreal, like stories in books. Only the ugliness and sweat and unrelenting tussle were close and terribly familiar.

The idealization of poverty as "the university of hard knocks" seemed to me insult added to injury as early as I was able to think at all. The be-furred ladies who came into the social settlements of our slums to assure us patronizingly of the blessings we were enjoying infuriated me. They fascinated me too, with suggestions of incredible far-off splendors in their sleekness.

I was presiding at a Boy Scout meeting at the Educational Alliance one evening when just such a lady, trailing clouds of radiance from her up-town world, came into the room. Her intrusion offended some vague sense of fitness in me, so that when she asked me an innocent question I ordered her sharply not to interrupt our meeting. The reward of my impertinence was an invitation, several days later, to call on her at a West End Avenue address. I had never seen such elegance at close range (though it was only an ordinary apartment), and passed through the interview in numb bewilderment. I remember the softness of the rugs, like lush grass, and the loveliness of a little boy who called my hostess "mother"—the word "mother" somehow did not jibe in my experience with glossy, care-free, nicely-upholstered women; it had always meant harassed, overworked and slovenly women. But what I carried away chiefly was a burning humiliation because the lining of the overcoat I gave up to the valet was in tatters. In my confusion, when I retrieved the coat, I slipped my arm into the torn lining instead of the sleeve, and the glamorous lady herself helped me to extricate myself. The shame of it rankled for months.

Poverty was only half of our routine ordeal. The other half was an acute awareness of being aliens and intruders in a nation of Americans. Between the world of our text-books and movies and newspapers and the other world of our homes and parents there was a deep gulf: different interests, preoccupations, ideals, languages. On the threshhold of your home you removed your American self like an overcoat, and you put it on once more when you left home. We lived this double existence so continuously that the idea of an integrated life, in which home and out-of-home activities were part of the same pattern, was beyond our imagination.

The school principal, Dr. Kottman, talked casually in my hearing one day about playing baseball with his son. The implication of a father who talked the same language and played the same games as his son, I can still recall, struck me as bizarre.

No American with deep roots in the American soil can understand the nostalgic homelessness of immigrant children, the pathos of second-generation aliens. *Land where our fathers died, land of the Pilgrims' pride*—sung in the assembly hall by several thousand Jewish, Russian, Italian, other foreign boys and girls whose fathers had never heard of the Pilgrims. We were "Americanized" about as gently as horses are broken in. In the whole crude process, we sensed a disrespect for the alien traditions in our homes and came unconsciously to resent and despise those traditions, good and bad alike, because they seemed insuperable barriers between ourselves and the adopted land.

We were caught and tangled in a mass of people for the most part resigned to their fate, sodden with hopelessness, and in a stupor of physical exhaustion. For the average boy it was easier to burrow deeper into the heap, taking the aroma and the drabness of the East Side into his soul, than to attempt the Gargantuan job of escaping. The Americanism that he acquired and dragged into the writhing heap was the loud, vulgar, surface—the slang, the sporting page, the crude success ideals of the movies and yellow journals—and nothing of the grandeur at the core of America.

But when the urge to escape does enter into the blood of a slum denizen, it is a feverish thing that drives him with whips of fire. "Success" is never a pale beckoning star. It is a flaming ball that blots out nearly everything else in the boy's firmament. Elsewhere it may be mere self-fulfillment. On our East Side it was that and more—a species of defiance and revenge against the clinging squalors and the smugness of the lucky ones and, above all, against the social system that breeds such plague spots.

Whatever the expression of that pitiless ambition, it is always shot through with hatred for the *status quo*. Sometimes it is openly defiant of restraints and carries the jungle law of dog-eat-dog competition to its logical conclusion in crime, gangsterism. At other times, the predatory technique is kept within the safer bounds of legality. Whether the exceptional boy revolting against putrescent surroundings turns into an unprincipled criminal or an unprincipled businessman is often simply a question of the proportions of courage and cleverness in his make-up.

And occasionally, as in my own case, the clamoring protest transcends the personal. The driving ambition widens out to embrace all the disinherited and exploited. It becomes a conscious protest against ugliness and injustice as such, and embraces passionately whatever formula of social revolt is closest to hand. There is a vast and unbridgeable difference between the radicalism that is accepted at second-hand, from the outside, through the mind, and the revolt that is nurtured in one's very bones. Those of us who were—or thought ourselves—"socialists" instinctively, through spontaneous hatred for the reality as we savored it, could never quite get over a certain distrust of "converts" to the cause from other social strata.

2

I thought myself a "socialist" almost as soon as I thought at all and years before I had heard of the *Communist Manifesto*. Congressman Meyer London, the shrill personification of the East Side yearning for Justice, loomed much larger on my horizon than Karl Marx. Long before I learned the standardized proofs that capitalism is doomed, I knew for a certainty that the whole world was one battle ground, contested between fat-bellied Capitalists and downtrodden Workers, and that victory for the Workers, for my side, was inevitable. The coming triumph was at most a matter of chronology, and life's one duty was to bring the date nearer. The class struggle was not an academic formula or a political slogan. It seemed to me as real as my friends and school and the burden of the monthly rent and gas bills. It was something much too obvious to need explaining or defending, let alone proving.

My memory can conjure up no one moment of thunderous illumination when the rightness and certainty of the socialist future of eternal justice and equality were revealed to me. In our multifarious world of dreams and ugliness, a boy soaked up a social faith, if he was built that way, as naturally and imperceptibly as his schoolmates and blockmates soaked up the tough-guy philosophy or the success-at-any-price philosophy. By a sort of social osmosis.

As a child, down in a stinking steerage hole full of vermin and vomit, in one of the foul ships which, at that time, dumped cargoes of bewildered immigrants on the American shores, I treasured a vision of the fairyland called America. I shut my eyes and saw it clearly—the glittering streets, the happy faces, the new shiny land stocked with beauty. That lovely vision broke sickeningly on the garbage cans of the Corlears Hook section of New York. The specters of "slack" seasons, of strikes for a living wage, of illness that cut off all earnings for a large family—the sight of my father's cadaverous face after a long day at the machine (it was a curiously handsome and sensitive face under the mask of bottomless fatigue)—these were less horrible when viewed as aspects of the perpetual class hostilities and as prelude to an ineffable triumph.

Our ant-heap was infested with street gangs. But I found myself somehow enrolled in a "Socialist Sunday School" on East Broadway, run by the Workmen's Circle. The hymns we chanted were *Arise, ye prisoners of starvation, Arise, ye wretched of the earth!*, and *The people's flag is deepest red.* One May Day I stood on a platform and recited a lugubrious poem about a beggar boy which began:

> Alone in the cold and dreary street,
> With my torn old clothes and bare cold feet.

Among those who heard me was a beautiful child of seven, with curls to her shoulders. I was all of thirteen, with the weight of suffering humanity on my thin shoulders and a volume of Dostoievsky under my arm. Ten years later this girl became my wife. Twenty-four years later, because the sad rhymes about the beggar boy had become a tradition in the family, our daughter made me recite them in the inappropriate setting of the Ethical Culture School.

From the Socialist Sunday School I graduated naturally into the "Yipsels," the Young People's Socialist League, where we debated weighty questions and took courses in Marx and Spencer and distributed leaflets for socialist candidates without the slightest hope of their election.

The highest reach of anxious parental hope in homes like mine was to turn sons into doctors and lawyers and to marry off daughters to doctors and lawyers. In affectionate moments, proud relatives, impressed by my seriousness and report cards, tried the prefix "Dr." before my name, and, miraculously, it always fitted nicely. The sacrifice involved in sending me to high school, and then to college, rather than into the factory, practically made my eventual emergence as a physician or lawyer a duty—a very onerous duty. The fact that neither calling stirred me to enthusiasm made me feel a good deal of an ingrate towards my parents and towards my elder brother, who, since the age of thirteen, had been among the sweated legions bending over sewing machines. But I had no stomach for the professional respectability to which they aspired for me. Ostensibly I was being primed for the law. But my dreams were of writing, not as a means of making a living, but as a weapon on my side of the class war.

My parents' sacrifices consisted in dispensing with my potential contribution to the family income and in providing me with food, clothing and shelter. But it could not easily be extended to include bugaboo items of carfares and occasional expenses. By working after school hours, I managed to earn these myself. At one tragic juncture, internal politics ousted me from a night job at the Educational Alliance and the lack of a single dollar a week threatened to cut short my high school career. That sum, advanced for ten weeks running by Adolph Nash, my Scoutmaster, helped a little to patch up the faith in social work which the ouster had shattered.

By the end of the ten weeks, I was earning three dollars a week as "assistant professor" to a teacher of English in the hurry-up preparatory schools for adults. My function was chiefly the correction of examination papers on literary subjects about which I knew precisely nothing. One night I would remain up, hurriedly digesting *As You Like It* in preparation for a set of test papers; another night it might be *Hamlet* or *Silas Marner*. This "professorship" I retained for two or three years, despite profound ignorance of the subjects my employer taught and even deeper ignorance of certain alarming predilections on his part which he described as "hedonism." I looked up the word in dictionaries and warded off his occasional experimental sallies in my direction (luckily his hedonism was not insistent) but I did not understand what it was all about until many years later. This brand of hedonism was one of the few weeds that did not find root in our slum soil.

3

The Russian revolution, in March, 1917, was, for most of the boys in my college freshman classes, just one more headline in a time replete with startling news. For a few of us, it was the rapturous harbinger of that Great Change in the glow of which we had warmed our spirits. Kerensky, Lvov, Miliukov, fraternization between Russian and German soldiers, the rise of Soviets—great names and great events, amidst the fumes of inspired rhetoric.

Even the confusion was heart-warming, because it sparkled with words and phrases learned in the socialist Sunday schools, shouted in the Meyer London campaigns, debated in the Yipsel circles. Our intimate, esoteric language suddenly holding the center of the world stage! The exultant realization that our thinking and dreaming had become history so soon! We hummed the new Russian *Hymn to Freedom* and we hummed the *International* at socialist lectures and dances, blissfully unaware that the two melodies were locked in life-and-death combat.

Then came yet greater names and greater events: Lenin, Trotsky, Zinoviev, Smolny Institute, the battleship *Aurora,* the surrender of the Winter Palace. The Bolshevik seizure of power in the name of the Soviets seemed confirmation of the new era born eight months before. We envied the men and women who lived and fought within the circles of light shed by the heroes of the triumphant class war. We decked the revolution in the opalescent raiment of our visions. A Fatherland at last, and a focus for our hopes!

Our New York lives seemed hatefully prosaic by contrast with the poetry of victorious revolution. The draft . . . slackers . . . Liberty Bonds . . . Liberty cabbage. . . . Give until it hurts. . . . *Good-by, Broadway, hello, France.* . . . It all seemed a stupid burlesque in the blinding light of events in Russia. Stupidest of all were the college classes, the marching and saluting and bayonet drills of the Students Army Training Corps into which we had been herded.

For some of us Armistice, for all the hysteria and noise, was an anti-climax, because there had been Brest-Litovsk.

Soon after I was demobilized and presented with an honorable discharge, I heard Norman Thomas speak. I can recall neither the occasion of the meeting nor what he said, but only my inner excitement. I carried away the revelation that the Russian revolution had no boundaries, since it was the initial stage of the world revolution. The fight against capitalists in America, the battle to restore freedom to political prisoners and conscientious objectors, were just part of the world-wide defense of the Russian revolution. I am not certain that Thomas said these things. More likely they were my private deductions from the fervor with which he depicted the capitalist injustice around us.

On the very day when I removed my army uniform, I wrote my first publicity story for the Workers Defense Union, organized by Elizabeth Gurley Flynn, with offices at the Rand School. Day after day, I composed these stories, destined for the New York *Call* and other radical publications, recounting the sufferings of I.W.W.'s and other political prisoners, the depredations of the Department of Justice on a rampage, the havoc being wrought by the American Legion. It was a time of raids on radicals, "Treat-'em-rough!" hooliganism, and mass deportations. Tales of horror poured in upon our Workers Defense Union.

Our work seemed to me an intrinsic, inseparable part of the civil wars being fought out then in the land of the Soviets. It was all part of the Russian revolution and was, despite the cruelty and the suffering, curiously exhilarating—like the exhilaration of war. And when I left my parents' home in Brooklyn for a shabby furnished room on lower Second Avenue, that, too, seemed part of the imminent world revolution. Society and I were coming of age at the same time! The world was casting off its capitalist shackles and I was casting off the shackles of home and school at the same time. The coincidence, of course, was a marvel of marvels, even if no one realized the mystic significance of that conjuncture of events except myself. The thrill of seeing my name in print, secretly cherished, was no selfish indulgence as with some of my literary friends, since *my* writing was for the cause. Such is the towering egotism of youth, even in its most altruistic poses.

There was that May Day in 1919, a day of blood and terror and the excruciating pain, of helpless anger. Workers' parades were smashed, radicals were brutally mauled, jails were crowded. The telephone rang continuously to apprise us of more raids, more brutality, more arrests. Late that afternoon the patriotic marauders swarmed through the Rand School, clambering up fire-escapes. A metal workers' union shared our offices. I can still see the burly workman with an iron weight in his hairy fist waiting tensely at the door for the first Legionaire who forced it open. Only the accident that they overlooked our room prevented another serious casualty.

Yet that appalling day was touched with rapture. We felt ourselves in the thick of a great struggle for Justice, only a few of us, but pitting our faith against something monstrous. We had just emerged from another battle and the lull was sweet.

There was a separate rapture for me. The others in the office may have been aware of her—"Little Sunshine," one of the men nicknamed her. But in my eyes she was the loveliest thing ever created. She came to the office that evening in a middy blouse and a red tam, and she remembered how I had recited *Nobody's Child* centuries ago. She was now nearly fifteen, radiant and electrically vivacious, and picked out on the typewriter words more wonderful than anything Shakespeare or Goethe had ever put together:

"Dear Comrade Eugene: I like you. Do you like me? Yours truly, Billy."

II. The Clowning Called Justice

THE next two years were so full, so rich, so tight-packed with sharp impressions and enthusiasms that they seem in retrospect a whole lifetime. I worked briefly on several newspapers, among them the Erie, Pa., *Dispatch*, and *Financial America* on Wall Street, and wrote copy for some months in the publicity departments of two motion picture companies. I succeeded in getting several high-pitched effusions into arty little magazines. I became habituated to the thrill of my name in print. These things, however, were secondary. First place belonged to the exciting friendships and activities in the radical movement.

There was Elizabeth Gurley Flynn, the most brilliant woman I had ever met. A veteran of the front trenches in the labor struggle since fifteen, she was, at thirty, attractive, winsomely Irish in her wit and her savor of life, with a remarkably cool intelligence behind her fiery oratory and personality. In the Mesaba Range strike, the Paterson and Lawrence strikes, her eloquence and courage and sweetness had won her tens of thousands of worshipful friends among the workers. And there was Carlo Tresca, big, bearded, boastful, life-loving, and as unlike the embittered anarchist of popular tradition as possible. Priest-baiting and spaghetti were among his chief passions, and his hairbreadth escapes from enemy bullets everywhere from Abruzzi to the copper empire of Montana were ample proof of his charmed life. And Fred Biedenkapp, the most Latin and temperamental German that ever lived. And the soft-spoken Vincent St. John—"the Saint" to "Wobbly" fellow-workers—full of mature class-war wisdom, tales of prospecting for gold, and off-color stories. He was a compact little man who conveyed a sense of immense concentrated strength in reserve—the kind of man who needed only a first-rate revolution to win him immortality. And scores of other I.W.W.'s, anarchists, socialists, American lumberjacks, Jewish clothing workers, Russian intellectuals, Italian terrorists, Hindu nationalists—even liberals with creases in their pants and Harvard accents were not taboo.

I had entered the American radical *milieu* in the twilight of its brief Golden Age, which had reached its high noon just before the war. United-front slogans had not yet become sources of disunion. Differences of opinion were sharp enough, but they remained essentially a family affair. As against the rest of the world, which meant everyone from J. P. Morgan to Matthew Woll, there was a solid front.

And the symbol of that unity after 1917 was the Russian revolution. The fact that shiploads of assorted deportees, with every shade of radical philosophy represented, sailed towards Russia without the slightest misgivings about the revolution and its course, is proof of the vitality of that symbol.

In the autumn of 1919, the Workers Defense Union sent me to Tulsa, Oklahoma, to cover the trial of Charles Krieger, an I.W.W. organizer accused of dynamiting the home of a Mr. Pew, a Standard Oil official. I stopped in Kansas City and was met at the station by the I.W.W. attorney in the case, Fred H. Moore, and Ella Reeves Bloor, that grand old lady of the American labor movement who then, as now, was known affectionately as "Mother" Bloor. Moore, rather sinister-looking under his broad-brimmed Western hat (a few years later, as defense lawyer for Sacco and Vanzetti, he was to become the most hated man in Massachusetts) took in my hundred-odd pounds of scrawny youthfulness, my poetic haircut, the bohemian untidiness of my clothes, in one scowling inspection. He did not trouble to hide his disgust.

"And I thought Gurley was sending us a man!" he said.

Despite this inauspicious reception, we were close friends almost immediately and remained friends until his death a few years ago. Books about the American labor and radical movements have not done justice to Moore. A brilliant lawyer, quixotically devoted and self-sacrificing, he was handicapped by a genius for non-conformity. He had started in the Northwest as attorney for the railroads, but just on the brink of precocious success, had scrapped it and begun anew in Los Angeles. One day in 1912, he was called on the phone by a casual I.W.W. acquaintance who had been arrested in a free speech fight in San Diego. Fred took his hat and his revolver.

"I'm running over to San Diego," he told his law associates, "to see what I can do for this fellow. I'll be back soon."

He returned some twelve years later.

From one labor fight to another he drifted, taking on the cases that could not afford the more publicized attorneys, the hopeless, desperate cases in the labor struggle. Many of those legal battles have become famous in American labor history—the Ettore-Giovanniti case; the Spokane free speech fight; the Everett, Wash., case; the Bisbee, Arizona, case; the Wichita I.W.W. case—but no share of this fame accrued to him. Always he quarreled with the defense committees or the clients or got himself into some private emotional scrape and lost the laurels of victory. Even in the Sacco-Vanzetti case, to which he gave four years—and there probably would have been no such case if Moore had not taken hold of it and turned it to a *cause célèbre*—a well-paid capitalist lawyer in the end reaped the credit and the fame.

The dynamiting charge against "Big Boy" Krieger, a tall, raw-boned Pennsylvania Dutchman, was so palpably a frame-up that no one even pretended it was anything else. The average citizen of Tulsa, which was then ruled by a vigilante Committee of One Hundred, merely had a sporting interest in whether the Standard Oil crowd could make their fantastic invention stick. The case was the last stage of a determined effort of the oil interests to drive I.W.W. union agitation, which had been making considerable headway, out of the state. Organizers had been beaten, tarred and feathered, ridden out on rails. But they kept coming back like so many pesky flies. One night someone set off dynamite under the Pew porch, where Mrs. Pew normally slept. She wasn't there, it happened, and not much harm was done. But the press promptly headlined it as Red Terror and the authorities proceeded to round up every known and suspected I.W.W. in Oklahoma.

The police were considerably chagrined when it appeared that not one of the men taken into custody had been in or near Tulsa the night of the explosion. After the recent tar-and-feather parties, the Wobblies had apparently kept at a distance from the city. But that little detail did not checkmate patriotic ardor. The Red Terror, the police decided, had been applied by absent treatment.

The gangling Pennsylvania boy, Charlie Krieger, had passed through Tulsa three days before the dynamiting and had stopped overnight at a hotel. The state now charged that he had hired three notorious yeggs, the renowned John Hall and two of his young desperadoes, to blow up Pew, and that he had done so at the express order of Big Bill Haywood in Chicago. By the time the trial came up, Hall had been committed to Leavenworth Penitentiary for some Federal crime, but his lieutenants, who were in an Oklahoma jail, were ready to plead guilty to the Pew dynamiting as Krieger's agents.

That dynamiting had not been the only dirty work that night. About the same time a post-office had been broken into, its safe blown, and the contents carried off. The two thugs had originally been arrested in connection with the post-office job. The dynamiting of public buildings carried a fifty years' prison sentence. The dynamiting of private dwellings carried only a ten years' rap. They knew enough arithmetic to prefer responsibility for the lesser job, particularly when the bargain won them some influential friends. They were ready to plead guilty to the Pew job as agents of the I.W.W. monster. It was a neat and amusing story. Its transparency only added to the joy of the occasion.

The prosecution was prepared for everything—except Fred Moore. The trial, lasting ten weeks, was the longest in the history of Oklahoma at that time. Every now and then, the court recessed for a few hours and disposed of some minor matters like murder cases. Flint Moss, hired by Standard Oil, ostensibly assisting the public prosecutor, actually was in complete control. Humiliated by his virtual expulsion from the case, the prosecutor tipped us off occasionally on Flint's plans. The judge, a decent fellow and uncomfortable under the Standard Oil pressure, sometimes called Moore and myself into his chambers; we talked about life and literature, but now and then His Honor let fall a hint or two that helped Moore pull the props from under the frame-up. Even a court stenographer, being also stenographer for the vigilantes, telephoned one midnight to warn us that a formal decision had been reached that evening to run Moore and the other Reds out of town.

Why the decision was not carried out, and why we were not riddled by bullets that tense afternoon when Flint Moss, under the guise of a summation to the jury, all but incited the tensely hostile crowd in the courtroom to settle us right there and then, amazed us. Not until afterward did we find out that we had been under the sharp-eyed protection of a little army of private gunmen, under orders to shoot down the first man who touched us. But even if we were sadly ignorant of this invisible and unsolicited defense, the vigilantes had been apprised of it.

The orders had been issued by the picturesque three-hundred-pound dictator of a nearby town. He was perhaps the last of the oil barons, the only great "independent" operator in that vicinity, and he hated Standard Oil even as Standard Oil hated Reds. Anyone accused of an attempt to erase a Standard Oil official automatically rated the support of his private army, recruited from the prisons of the Southwest under laws permitting the parole of prisoners who could show respectable jobs waiting for them. The hulking oil man explained it all to us after the trial, as he sat on the huge butcher's block in his refrigerator, oblivious to the cold while the rest of us congealed slowly into icicles. He was disappointed at Fred Moore's assurances that Krieger was innocent and that private terror was no part of the I.W.W. code. Haywood's movement there and then lost a potential millionaire recruit.

"Sure," he said, "my men were all around the courtroom, with their fingers on the trigger. The Standard Oil bastards knew that if anyone let loose there'd be hell to pay. Yeh, I'm respected in these parts, I am."

He laughed till the immense meat block shook.

The trial, as I said, dragged for many weeks. Every time Moore demolished an essential sector of the state's flimsy case, the prosecution got a brief adjournment and when court opened again there it was, with brand-new witnesses to bolster up the blasted sector. It was most amusing, and Tulsa chuckled. The two rat-faced yeggs testified in low voices, with downcast eyes, how Krieger had hired them and Hall to pull the Pew dynamiting job. They were very convincing in describing how they had stolen the dynamite but rather vague on the dynamiting itself.

Haywood's defense committee in Chicago was chronically short of funds. Besides, more important legal battles had a prior claim. Our burdens of perjured witnesses, murderous public hostility, and a frankly unfriendly jury were therefore complicated by financial distress. I recall the morning when we all turned our pockets inside out to find that the pooled resources would barely cover coffee and doughnuts. As we chewed the doughnuts, wondering when we would eat again, we smiled over a local eight-column streamer headline "revealing" that a million-dollar fund was at the disposal of the Red agitators defending Krieger.

The dangers and hardships of our situation drew us closer together. They added a tang of high adventure to the routine business of defending another Wobbly in another frame-up. Besides Moore and myself, there were the handsome Lola Darroch (during the Sacco-Vanzetti case in Boston she became Mrs. Moore); Caroline Lowe, a sweet spinsterish lady lawyer driven by her social conscience to defend deportees and I.W.W.'s and to intrude herself precisely where her primness seemed most out of place; a poverty-ridden local attorney named George Bonstein, a Jewish pioneer of the Indian country with the temerity to tackle the whole Standard Oil caboodle; and a number of roughneck Wobblies whom Moore had saved from jail or the noose at various times and who hung around like faithful dogs in the hope of serving him. These latter were not too fastidious about the nature of the service, nor was Moore himself too finicky. He had no inhibitions about using the same weapons as the other side, when necessary. The fact that Standard Oil officials tried to buy him into their service before he left Tulsa, is some measure of his equipment.

2

The most melodramatic episode in that unequal battle, perhaps, centered around the enigmatic John Hall, a desperado in the best Jesse James tradition. The state made no effort to bring him from Leavenworth, preferring to rest on the testimony of his underlings. Moore's problem was whether to bring him in as a defense witness. It was hazardous business. If our own witness were to support the other two in their cock-and-bull story, Krieger's fate would be sealed. Moore interviewed Hall in his cell but elicited only a non-committal smile. "What I'll say is my own business," Hall told him.

"That fellow's a straight-shooter," Moore reported back to us. "He's no rat. I'd stake my life on his telling the truth."

But he hesitated to stake Krieger's freedom on his impression. Caroline Lowe listened. A light flared in her meek eyes. She announced that she, too, wanted to talk to Hall before a decision was made. She did, and returned to confirm Moore's impression. There was a warmth in her report that made us nudge one another. For years after this Leavenworth meeting, the schoolteacherish Miss Lowe and the notorious killer maintained a correspondence. Up until her untimely death, she tried to obtain his release. At least she was spared the sorrow of his end. John Hall was, I believe, the second man to die in the famous lethal chamber experiments in Arizona.

But she had her moment of rapturous pride when Hall, calm, self-possessed and a little contemptuous, was brought into the Tulsa courtroom as a defense witness.

It was a courtroom made for paradox. The judge puffed a big cigar under the "No Smoking" sign crusted with smoke. Spectators with revolvers in their holsters threw "howdy" to their friends in the jury box. Moore was completely in the dark as to what Hall's testimony would be. The prosecution had the post-office job as a spur to the witness's memory. But Hall, black as his record was, did not seek safety at the expense of an innocent stranger. I have never seen human creatures tremble and wilt as did the two yeggs when confronted with their gang leader. He withered them with one slow accusing scrutiny and never once looked again in their direction. Hall confirmed their story of the stealing of the dynamite, but denied ever having seen Krieger before the latter's arrest. He denied any knowledge of the Pew explosion. No, he knew nothing of the post-office job either.

"Why did you need dynamite?" Flint Moss hammered at him hour after hour.

"Oh, I just wanted to blow some stumps out of the road."

"What did you do with the dynamite?"

"I blew up those stumps. They annoyed me."

He stuck to the story, unsmiling, calm, while spectators guffawed.

Excessive physical courage is not my chief vice. The threat of a tar-and-feather party or worse under which we worked occasionally sent undignified thoughts of retreat through my head. In that week before the trial started, for instance. Perhaps by way of punishing me for being so young and scrawny when he had expected a full-sized man, Moore had sent me ahead into Tulsa to investigate the state of mind of the community. I decided to investigate first of all the state of mind of the spiritual leaders of Tulsa. I listed all the clergymen in town and started on my rounds. The first of these men of God was a bulky, red-faced cow-puncher in appearance. He listened to my story, then leaned over and gripped my shoulders. There was nothing remotely affectionate about that grip.

"Young man," he said, "I have only one piece of advice for you. Take the next train out of town, or we'll hang your hide on a fence!"

In no less picturesque forms the equivalent advice was proffered by seven or eight other muscular vicars of the Lord in Tulsa. That Sunday I was the text of a sermon in one church, I learned from Monday's papers. Only the Catholic priest showed any friendliness or any sane resentment against the local Red baiting. I have had a soft spot in my heart for Catholic priests ever since.

Eventually, I took the stand and quoted the high-minded advice of the Lord's anointed, swear-words and all. We did not get the change of venue we demanded, but we did have the satisfaction of seeing one of the clergymen squirm in his seat. It was the same clergyman who preached sermons to the jury on Sundays, since jurors could not be denied the solace of spiritual uplift, on themes as remote from the case in court as patriotism and foreign agitators.

Scream headlines out of Centralia, Washington, on Armistice Day, when the trial was at its height, did not sweeten the atmosphere for us. They told how I.W.W.'s had "murdered" American Legion paraders, making it clear that Krieger and his friends were part of the same homicidal fraternity. They merely failed to make clear that the I.W.W. boys had shot in defending their union hall against violent invasion by over-stimulated patriots.

My reports of the trial, a little late for lack of telegraph tolls and much too full of indignant adjectives, appeared in the New York *Call*, in the Butte *Bulletin*, and in four or five other labor papers. A sizzling summary entitled, with a flash of superb originality, *Tulsa: a Study in Oil*, appeared under my signature in the *I.W.W. Monthly*. An audience heard the story from me at the Rand School. Then the case entered the limbo of forgotten minor sensations. But in my own mind it remained as sign and symbol of the clowning that goes by the name of justice.

The jury reported eleven to one for conviction. The one recalcitrant juror emerged with visible proofs that the arguments used on him were the kind that left marks on the body. We learned later that he had had a personal grudge against Standard Oil in some matter connected with a pipe-line on his farm. His insistence on Krieger's innocence apparently had no more to do with the evidence than the others' insistence on Krieger's guilt.

In a second trial, which I did not attend, the whole case collapsed and Krieger was freed. The last I heard he was settled down in his home town as a law-abiding plumber with a taste for solid respectability.

III. On the Eve of Fascism

IN THE autumn of 1920, Italian workers seized the metal plants in Milan and ran up the red flag. Hope of world revolution, dimmed by reverses elsewhere, flared up once more. And since I thought the impending Italian revolution needed its John Reed out of America no less than its Russian precursor, I was soon in the steerage of an Italian liner bound for Naples. I was equipped with credentials from the Federated Press, a struggling labor news agency, and the *Liberator;* one cardboard suitcase half-stuffed with paper to keep my worldly belongings from rattling; and that week's salary from *Financial America* by way of sinews of war.

The long hand of Italian anarcho-syndicalism (via a well-placed word from Carlo Tresca) reached down into the bowels of the ship and yanked me up into the comforts of officers' quarters. On deck I struck up an acquaintance with a slim, shy fellow a few years my senior, Norman Matson by name. He, too, was inclined to push the ship along for fear of missing the revolution. For a day or two, we pretended to be the plenipotentiaries of respectable capitalist journals. Then we looked one another straight in the eyes, laughed, and laid our cards—that is to say, our press credentials—on the table. He, too, was exclusive and authenticated correspondent for the Federated Press and the *Liberator,* and a candidate for the role of Italy's John Reed. Norman and I shared a room, our deficits, and our soaring thoughts in the next six months, and discovered that Italy was brimming over with potential John Reeds, all representing the Federated Press and the *Liberator.*

If the Italian proletariat failed to live up to our expectations, at least Italy did not. Naples was an extravagant dream come true. We explored its narrow streets and smelly cafés and stuffy music halls. We hunted up comrades at Socialist Party headquarters and wrote reams of "first impressions" which, alas!, never got printed. We helped a scared and bungling secret service man, assigned to shadow us, to make out his report and treated him to black coffees. We mixed with Neapolitans in a daze of intoxication that blended the Bay of Naples and *Viva Lenin e Trotsky!*, Pompei and socialist mass meetings, everything exotically old and desperate, with the Soviets around the corner.

Then came Rome and the Pension Dinesen and socialist Deputies and Roman girls who exchanged Italian and kisses for English and kisses. We went into homes in crowded side-streets where grimy children answered to the name of Lenin and Trotsky and Karl Liebknecht and Rosa Luxembourg—thousands of these little Lenins and Liebknechts were destined to be hurriedly re-christened after the fascist March on Rome. We watched fist fights on the floor of Parliament and saw the earlier castor-oil episodes in the rebirth of the glory that was Rome. How I managed to pay the rent and board at the *pension* is a miracle somewhat blurred in memory. A few articles in the *Nation* helped; a dollar went a long way when turned into inflated *lire*.

Fred Moore, by the time I left for Italy, was in full command of an obscure case in Boston involving a fishmonger named Bartolomeo Vanzetti and a shoemaker named Nicola Sacco. He had given me explicit instructions to arouse all of Italy to the significance of the Massachusetts murder case, and to hunt up certain witnesses and evidence. The Italian labor movement, however, had other things to worry about. An ex-socialist named Benito Mussolini and a locust plague of blackshirts, for instance. Somehow I did get pieces about Sacco and Vanzetti into *Avanti!*, which Mussolini had once edited, and into one or two other papers. I even managed to stir up a few socialist *onorevoles*, like Deputy Mucci from Sacco's native village in Puglia, and Deputy Misiano, a Sicilian firebrand at the extreme Left. Mucci brought the Sacco-Vanzetti affair to the floor of the Chamber of Deputies, the first jet of foreign protest in what was eventually to become a pounding international flood.

Norman and I went to Livorno to witness the epochal congress of the Socialist Party, which saw the birth of a Communist Party and the tragic splintering of the Left forces that opened the road to Mussolini's legions. We consorted only with the communist wing, of course, and sang paeans of praise for Terracini and Bombacci and the other leaders. Nothing less than immediate revolution suited our fervor and theirs. The excessive caution of the parliamentarians and timid evolutionists, we were convinced, had nipped a Soviet revolution in the bud when the metal workers took over the factories. Resentment against the lost opportunity smoldered in our hearts and flamed into oratory from the Left. We had on our side, moreover, the weight of the triumphant Russian proletariat whose agents were in Livorno to guide and inspire. What matter if the Bolshevik faction was a minority in this conference, since it spoke with the voice of the Third International, not to mention History and Humanity?

Only one argument directed against the Left baffled its orators. It was hurled at them by Serrati from the Center and Modigliani from the Right. In the light of subsequent Italian history that argument seems irony at its most tragic.

"A dictatorship may be possible in Russia," the Left was repeatedly admonished, "but surely, comrades, it is unthinkable in our country. We Italians are individualists, anarchists, by nature. Discipline, blind obedience? *Ma che!* When an Italian sees a 'No Smoking' sign in a tramcar or theater, it reminds him to light up. To talk of organized restraint and dictatorship in our land is foolishness!"

Even the communists could not deny anything so axiomatic. They said that in Italy, maybe, the new social order would be established without the need for dictatorial methods. A little more than a year later the fascist dictatorship was in force. . . .

Though we posed as correspondents, the Livorno congress was no mere "story" for Norman and me. We felt it to be an extension of the civil warfare over in Soviet Russia, a local sector on the widening front of an international class struggle. We cheered and booed at the proper points along with communist sympathizers in the six steep galleries of the Teatro Goldoni.

But the Associated Press correspondent, come from Fiume for the occasion, took the proceedings less seriously. He was never quite sure who was Left or Right or why. Nothing in his training as a Pittsburgh, Pennsylvania, police reporter had prepared him to record an epoch-making split in the Italian socialist ranks. Indeed, his private summary of the talk-fest was remarkable both for its simplicity and comprehensiveness. Strolling between Norman and myself after a stormy session, he confided it to us:

"Just look at 'em! Karl Marx and the other guy with the alfalfa on his chin whose pictures are on the wall, and Bombacci, Serrati, Modigliani!"—he called off the leaders of all the factions who happened to wear beards—"just a lot of Jews!"

The other guy with the alfalfa, of course, was Friedrich Engels, as Germanic as Bismarck. Bombacci, the eccentric communist leader, was an ex-priest. Only one or two of the other leaders in the limelight were Jews, and in Italy the anti-Semitic issue was never a serious factor. But for a Pittsburgher whiskers are whiskers.

The exigencies of the Sacco-Vanzetti defense took me to the southern olive and grape provinces, into Sacco's native village of Torremaggiore. I found that his elder brother, Sabino Sacco, was the socialist *sindaco* (mayor) of Torremaggiore. Red flags were flying over the municipal building and the coöperative store, and nearly every infant born since November, 1917, was named for some Bolshevik deity. I even saw a baby "Soviet" peacefully sucking her mother's breast. Rumors of the blackshirt *camions* rumbled even through Puglia, and occasionally violent incidents were reported from larger towns. But the suggestion that a fascist regime was in the offing would have sounded like gibberish to Torremaggiore and a thousand other villages gesturing with red flags and Russian catch-phrases.

Sacco-Vanzetti matters also sent me into the Marchesan hills, beyond Jesi, to a sleepy, mud-colored village called Santa Maria Nove. I tracked down an anarchist deportee from Massachusetts, whose yellow-haired wife wept for the vanished glories of life in a New England shoe town, snatched from her by the ardor of Mitchell Palmer's agents. The man's shelves were lined with brochures on the home manufacture of bombs and he professed himself a terrorist of the Galleani school. So deep, however, had the fear of American law and police entered his heart that it needed a week of pleading and threatening and pressure by Merlino, the grand old man of the anarcho-syndicalist movement, to bring this terrorist to the point of signing an innocuous affidavit in support of Sacco's alibi.

No sooner had I descended from the Marchesan heights, though, than he recovered his magnificent courage. It expressed itself in a colored picture post-card addressed to me at my prim Danish *pension* and showed an anarchist iconoclast hurling a smoking bomb at a row of gods. My standing with the Roman police must have been greatly improved by this belated boldness at my expense. It was not the only time I was to meet bomb-throwing bravado masking abject cowardice.

Already, in the civil strife between blackshirts and communists or socialists, the casualties were too numerous for the newspapers to report in full. Daily tallies of the number of Reds and Blacks killed all over the country had to suffice, and the preponderance of communist over fascist deaths increased rapidly. The legend which pictures the March on Rome as a bloodless seizure of power ignores the ferocious blood-letting which preceded it.

2

Panic spread in the Italian labor ranks. Almost overnight it seemed, after the Livorno split, the sense of confidence and faith in their own strength departed from the revolutionary elements. An influx of communist refugees from Hungary, after the collapse of Bela Kun's government, deepened the gloom in the Italian circles with which I was in contact. Norman and I smuggled a few of these homeless, penniless refugees into our hotel room for a period and heard hair-raising tales of torture in Horthy's prisons. One boy bared his back and chest by way of illustration. They were thickly sown with tiny raw wounds. "Cigarette burns," he explained, "a favorite Hungarian amusement."

I followed the news out of Russia with anxious and intimate concentration. Every defeat of some interventionist or counter-revolutionary general, every advance of the Soviet forces into Poland, was a personal triumph. There came a day when the Soviet drive was turned back at the very gates of Warsaw, and the bottom seemed to drop out of my own life.

I remember pacing the roof of our *pension* with Norman, discussing that blow. It seemed to us that the fate of all history, of the whole human race, was in the balance. If Soviet Russia were beaten, we decided, the darkness of reaction and barbarism would settle over the universe for centuries (we reckoned glibly in centuries in our idealistic trance of those days).

The only bright spot in the encroaching gloom was the arrival of Vorovsky as Moscow's first Ambassador to Italy, and the opening of the Soviet Embassy. It fired anew my half-conscious ambition to reach Soviet Russia. I seized eagerly at the suggestion of a Soviet attaché that he might use me as secret courier to Moscow—an American would be a safer messenger across the more dangerous stretches between Rome and the Kremlin. Arrangements to this end were in swing at the time I was arrested and expelled from Italy. Chagrin over the spoiling of those plans was, in fact, the bitterest ingredient in my expulsion.

It was while about to depart for a town in central Italy, after the second bell had been sounded and the locomotive strained at its leash awaiting the final signal, that half a dozen detectives piled into my coupé and took me into custody.

A tall, thin, mysterious and rather dandified Balkan fellow—I never did ascertain whether he was Montenegrin or Serbian or Bulgarian—who was my traveling companion was arrested at the same time. I had met him in Italy through anarchist acquaintances and listened in fascinated horror to his boastful stories of revolutionary exploits. Pulling off fingernails to extract ransom money for the cause from bloated landlords and capitalists was, I recall, among his routine procedures. None of the money, at the moment, was in his pockets and the ease with which I parted from my few *lire* was evidently my chief recommendation to him. On my part I felt compensated by the atmosphere of recondite mystery and adventure that surrounded him.

When Moore wrote me emphasizing the critical importance of obtaining the photograph of an Italian criminal who, as nearly as I could figure out, may have been mixed up in the crime for which Sacco and Vanzetti were being tried, I naturally turned to my Balkan friend for assistance. We were about to embark on the important mission of stealing a photograph from the home of that criminal's parents in central Italy when the law took us in hand.

We were separated and I never saw the man again. To this day I do not know whether I was picked up on his account, or he on mine. From questions in the course of that day's intensive grilling I surmised that in the eyes of the Italian police, at least, my companion was a terrorist of some importance. But my own brief record of amateur dabbling in revolution was not unknown to the police either.

On the *commissario's* desk, when I was ushered into his presence, was a dossier in which I caught glimpses of my articles in *The Nation* and other publications and what looked like copies of my private mail. In my pockets and baggage nothing more incriminating than a few Sacco-Vanzetti pamphlets and letters in Billy's childish scrawl were discovered.

By the end of the day, after I had been formally presented with a paper ordering me to leave the country in twenty-four hours, the *commissario* had achieved a paternal attitude towards his American charge. At twenty-two I looked eighteen and weighed a hundred-odd pounds. Although a few hours before he had threatened to turn me over to the fascisti for a castor-oil purge, he now draped his arm around my shoulders in the most fatherly manner.

"I am a Sicilian, my son," he said, "and we Sicilians have a proverb. It's a good proverb and I recommend it to you. *Ammazza, ammazza, é tutta una razza.* (Kill, kill, it is all a race.) Stop bothering with the Saccos and Vanzettis and the socialist dogs, and take care of your own interests."

He fumbled among the confiscated contents of my pockets and found the picture of the wide-eyed little girl whose letters he had read.

"Go home," he said, "marry this beautiful girl and come back here for a honeymoon."

Nearly ten years later I did bring the girl to Rome. As we walked and drove through the streets, I kept hoping unreasonably that the *commissario* would suddenly appear. Perhaps he was among the hundreds of men in black shirts who were operating on his Sicilian proverb.

The intercession of my friends among the socialist deputies won me a few additional days of grace. Then I was escorted to the French frontier. The escort, in civilian clothes, watched until I was safely on the French side of the turnstile at the border station.

I was literally without a penny when I stepped off the train in Paris, but by evening was installed in that sanctuary of impecunious American newspapermen, the *Paris Herald*. I lied about understanding French in order to obtain the job, and rewrote items out of the French paper largely by intuition during the month I survived on the job. The intuition played me false on occasion and Americans on the Continent, I fear, were given some strange versions of French current events. By the end of the month I received a check from America just big enough to pay my way home.

Just big enough, with a few francs to spare for the trip. Unluckily my ship needed some repairs and kept the passengers waiting in Havre. The few francs paid for a bed in a sailors' hotel but left nothing for food. It was a very hungry young man, a little groggy from weakness, who fell to when at last we were permitted to board the boat and taste its fare. It was a delightful trip, devoted to reading and flirting, its beauty somewhat marred by two circumstances. First, because I had no money for cigarettes, and could not bring myself to sponge on others, I pretended that I did not smoke. Second, despite all that a rubber eraser could do, my collar and cuffs grew dingier and their owner more embarrassed every day; I lacked a clean change.

Shamefacedly I borrowed a nickel from a fellow passenger to take me from the pier to my parents' home in Brooklyn. Two checks awaited me, one from *The Nation* and another from *The Freeman*. Never before or since has money looked bigger. The whole European adventure seemed fantastic and wasteful to my family, which still cherished a slight though fast-fading hope that I would "succeed" despite my penchant for strange friends and strange travels. I did not attempt to explain or justify myself. Instead, I betook myself to a department store, bought a collection of foreign-looking trinkets and presented them nonchalantly as gifts from Paris.

May they forgive me the deception when they read these words!

IV. I Defend Sacco and Vanzetti

BEFORE the end of that week I was on a boat bound for Boston, where Sacco and Vanzetti had already been condemned to death. Billy, whose picture had struck a paternal spark from a Sicilian heart, was on the boat with me, uninvited, but gloriously welcome. She was nearly seventeen now and magically ripened to womanhood during my long year of absence. Her beauty seemed to me to transcend even the high promise of her loveliness as a child which had captivated me just ten years before. The mysterious half-realized attraction touched by adolescent embarrassment which had drawn us together across the chasm of six years' difference in age suddenly acquired a name: love. In a few weeks we were married.

Our fourteen months in Boston were hectic with excitement, as an obscure and seemingly dull murder case expanded into a worldwide *cause célèbre* unparalleled since the Dreyfus affair. They were filled, too, with the bitterness of defeat and frustration, as we bruised ourselves against the unyielding granite of laws and precedents and prejudice in the sanctimonious robes of formal justice.

But they were months edged with the ecstasy of young love. We were pleased to find a small, inexpensive apartment right in Back Bay. Gradually, reading newspaper reports of police raids on adjoining houses, it dawned on us that we had settled in a "red light" district. Far from being distressed, the discovery provided a fillip of amusement to the enchantments of our young marriage.

A Supreme Court Justice, though he knew nothing about it, solved the great problem of furniture for our two-room home. Mrs. Elizabeth Glendower Evans, the hundred arms of whose mothering instinct embraced everything young and helpless in sight, had become aware of the problem. She had the key to the Brookline cellar where Justice Brandeis had stored some old furniture on moving to Washington. We selected everything that an impecunious couple could desire to feather their nest. When I met Justice Brandeis at his Cape Cod summer home the following year and confessed the theft, I discovered that Mrs. Evans had not overestimated his generosity.

The arrest of Nicola Sacco and Bartolomeo Vanzetti on May 5, 1920, was not mentioned outside the local press. Their conviction on July 14, 1921, rated exactly seven and a half inches on an inside page of the New York *Times*. Their execution six years later, on August 23, 1927, received five full pages in the same newspaper, several of them recording the sorrow and anger of millions of men and women in every country in the world.

A thousand different factors contributed toward that extraordinary growth of the case. The obscurity of the simple, uncouth protagonists; the unctuous smugness of the Brahmin New England which rallied against them; the fury of Red-baiting in America in the post-war years—everything combined to give the drama and the players a heightened significance. The protracted struggle achieved a peculiar symbolic quality for all men in their own lives. It challenged their institutions and tested their professed ideals. It ripped the varnished surface off American life and revealed the deep fissures of class and race antagonisms underneath. A simple murder case, it evolved into a complicated and terrifying sacrificial rite.

In a book called *The Life and Death of Sacco and Vanzetti*, published immediately after the men were electrocuted, I wrote:

> These aliens by a strange chance combined in their obscure persons all the things that most offended and frightened a smug New Englander. In a section where family pride and an ingrown sense of racial superiority flourished, Sacco and Vanzetti were from the lowest social layer of wops and hunkies and polaks. At a time when Bolshevism gave householders nightmares, Sacco and Vanzetti were by their own confession reddest of the Reds. With the textile industry drifting to the South and the shoe industry to the West, in a period of strikes and discontent, Sacco and Vanzetti were self-confessed labor agitators. Amidst a raging blood-fed patriotism, they were slackers. In Puritan New England they were atheists.
>
> It required no special effort or apparatus to generate fear of and hatred for the two men. They attracted the fears and hatreds already

in full play. The belief of some that agents of the Department of Justice and of the State of Massachusetts got together and decided to electrocute them, innocent or guilty, is naive.

It was not a frame-up in the ordinary sense of the word. It was a far more terrible conspiracy: the almost automatic clicking of the machinery of government spelling out death for two men with the utmost serenity. No more laws were stretched or violated than in most other criminal cases. No more stool-pigeons were used. No more prosecution tricks were played. Only in this case every trick worked with a deadly precision. The rigid mechanism of legal procedure was at its most unbending. The human beings who operated the mechanism were guided by dim, vague, deep-seated motives of fear and self-interest.

It was a frame-up implicit in the social structure. It was a perfect example of the functioning of class justice, in which every judge, juror, police officer, editor, governor and college president played his appointed role easily and without undue violence to his conscience. A few even played it with an exalted sense of their own patriotism and nobility.

Many of those who were outraged by the deaths of Sacco and Vanzetti resented this interpretation. They preferred to regard it as a deliberate "plot to railroad two workers," and themselves as the heroic if unsuccessful rescuers. But their hero-and-villain pattern seemed to me false and petty against the reality of vast inchoate forces at play on both sides. To me the whole thing shaped up not as melodrama but as epic tragedy.

2

Though I did not formulate it in these terms until I had attained the perspective of time, I think that I sensed the epic quality from the first. All of us who defended the two Italians were wholly and deeply convinced of their innocence. Yet it was profoundly right that the question of innocence and guilt should become, as it did, of secondary importance to both sides, because the issues involved were wider than the character or destiny of two men. Those who rallied to our side, a relatively small and despised group at first, did so as inevitably and often as irrationally as the others who leagued against us. The case, I felt, was a catalytic agent that crystallized forces until then held in a deceptively unified social solution.

Fred Moore was at heart an artist. Instinctively he recognized the materials of a world issue in what appeared to others a routine matter. A socialist newspaperman spent a few days in Boston and returned to New York to report that "there's no story in it . . . just a couple of wops in a jam." Not one of the members of the defense committee formed immediately after the men's arrest suspected that the affair was anything larger than it seemed. When the case grew into a historical tussle, these men were utterly bewildered. But Moore saw its magnitude from the first. His legal tactics have been the subject of dispute and recrimination. I think that there is some color of truth, indeed, to the charge that he sometimes subordinated the literal needs of legalistic procedure to the larger needs of the case as a symbol of class struggle. If he had not done so, Sacco and Vanzetti would have died six years earlier, without the solace of martyrdom.

With the deliberation of a composer evolving the details of a symphony which he senses in its rounded entirety, Moore proceeded to clarify and deepen the elements implicit in the case. And first of all he aimed to delineate the class character of the automatic prejudices that were operating against Sacco and Vanzetti. Sometimes over the protests of the men themselves he cut through legalistic conventions to reveal underlying motives. Small wonder that the pinched, dyspeptic judge and the pettifogging lawyers came to hate Moore with a hatred that was admiration turned inside out. He was not "playing the game" according to their sacred rules.

Perhaps his most difficult task, and therefore his most creative achievement, was to show the two Italians as types and symbols of workmen everywhere. Labor elements in other countries recognized Sacco and Vanzetti as their own long before American workers consented to this identification. American labor, and especially the portion organized into conservative trade unions, at first rejected violently the implication that these two foreigners—self-confessed anarchists, internationalists, atheists—were in any sense representative American workers. Their social views were "un-American." To accept them as brothers was to throw doubt on the middle-class delusions of the *bona fide* labor movement.

Vanzetti had worked as an unskilled laborer, peddled fish and taken some part in local strike agitations. Sacco was a skilled shoe worker. But as anarchists they neither sympathized nor coöperated with the organized American labor movement, which they regarded as simply a part of the apparatus of capitalist enslavement. Despite this, American labor in the end was obliged to overcome its first revulsion and accept the Sacco-Vanzetti case as in large measure its own. Moore had slashed through the many layers of outer differences to the core of identity between Sacco and Vanzetti and all other workmen. To accomplish this, he did not hesitate to use any and all instrumentalities of publicity. On the one hand, the labor records of the two men were "built up" and emphasized; on the other, the attitudes of the prosecution were exposed as essentially anti-labor.

By the time I arrived on the scene, John Nicholas Beffel and others had already done the groundwork, under Moore's guidance, in this connection. Because my presence, in 1921-22, happened to coincide with the period when the case exploded into world significance, I received at the time more credit (or blame, depending on the point of view) than I merited. A series of articles in the old New York *World* by Samuel Spewack, in particular, sensationalized and exaggerated my role. I figured in his version as one of three men—an Italian, a Spaniard and a young American—who sat at their typewriters in a chilly little office in Boston and incited the whole world to protest. This journalistic simplification infuriated me. As a matter of fact, Felicani, Lopez and I, writing articles and news stories in Italian, Spanish, and English, respectively, were very minor factors in a situation that had outgrown all of us by that time and was rolling along on its own momentum.

It is a curious fact that Sacco and Vanzetti, whose names are linked inseparably, saw one another very rarely in the seven years between their arrest and electrocution. Sacco was kept in the county jail at Dedham, Vanzetti in Charlestown Prison. Only on those rare occasions when some new hearing or empty formality brought them into court did they meet, embrace, and chat briefly. Several times, almost a year elapsed before they met again. By the time their cold bodies were laid out on adjoining marble slabs in the death chamber, they had become almost strangers.

Of the same race, the same political faith, their destinies intertwined, they were yet men of the most contrasting temperaments and minds. Sacco was the Latin at his most impetuous, a man of emotion rather than logic, driven literally to madness on at least two occasions by the ordeal of imprisonment and waiting. The separation from his pretty red-headed wife and his two children, from friends and work, consumed his flesh and shook his reason. A week of incarceration for a man like Sacco was more terrible than a year for the more phlegmatic and contemplative Vanzetti. Sacco was a caged and raging animal; Vanzetti seemed a monk in calm seclusion. Under the ferocious Italian mustaches which gave him a look of fierceness in the eyes of the ordinary American, the fishmonger from Piemonte had ascetic features and eyes of a tenderness that haunted one.

With every year of imprisonment Vanzetti seemed to grow calmer, gentler, more philosophic. His was the consolation of genuine martyrdom in which there was no rancor but an ever-deepening understanding. Where Sacco had acquired his anarchist beliefs at second-hand, more attracted by its harsh code than its philosophy, Vanzetti had read and studied the poets and prophets of his faith. His mind was crystal clear and expanded immensely in the enforced leisure of his seven years' isolation. Some of his letters and speeches from the prisoners' cage have the ring of enduring literature—this despite his use of English, an alien, half-apprehended tongue. Certainly the scene while he was being strapped into the electric chair, when he proffered his forgiveness to those who were about to snuff out his life, belongs among the high moments in the history of the human spirit.

3

I saw Sacco and Vanzetti frequently, either in the company of Moore or alone. But in the fight that reverberated through all the nations and made their linked names a familiar word, their own roles were passive. They merely waited. My day-to-day contacts were with members of the defense committee, zealous Puritan ladies, visiting reporters, lawyers, wrathful anarchists, conniving communists, distressed liberals, local newspapermen and the extraordinary assortment of men and women drawn together by a common interest in freeing the two men.

In the final year of the case five years later, the liberal intellectuals rushed belatedly and flamboyantly to the rescue. But at this juncture the affair had not yet become respectable or sufficiently notorious. The enlightened attorneys, poets, novelists, columnists, educators who were to hold the spotlight in the last frenzied months of the futile fight in 1927 were with few exceptions blissfully oblivious to the affair in 1921-22.

It was a motley and colorful and rather high-pitched company that gathered around the defense at this stage. Some were moved by an undiluted urge to save two innocent men, others were interested primarily in the propagandist value of the case, still others got an emotional kick out of the battle. At one extreme were hot-headed and desperate Italians and Spaniards distrustful of all law, bitterly sarcastic about the hocus-pocus of motions and affidavits, and often refusing on principle to coöperate with their own lawyers. At the other extreme were men and women of old New England stock chiefly concerned with saving the Commonwealth of Massachusetts from the stigma of an ugly miscarriage of justice. I can recall vital meetings in which a snarling, red-headed little Italian exponent of direct action argued some question of policy with a benign pacifist like Mrs. Evans. It was Moore's delicate job to reconcile these people and placate their idiosyncrasies.

Because we all worked under great tension, in a ceaseless ferment of hope and despair, we moved in a strangely electrical atmosphere, surcharged with emotion and at moments touched with hysteria. Lack of funds forced a great many of the group to live very closely together in one narrow house on Rollins Place, and that scarcely helped matters. If anyone could record that house, its people, its complicated cross-currents of conflicting political philosophies, the erotic overtones characteristic of nervous strain, what an incredible novel it would make!

Commonplace stenographers accidentally drawn into this intense atmosphere developed into flaming radicals. Roughneck detectives sprouted a social conscience. Cautious A. F. of L. officials hobnobbed with foreign firebrands. A milk-white, golden-haired little poetess swept like a tornado through the defense group, working havoc among the harassed men and spreading despair among their wives and sweethearts; she dominated the lives of a writer, a strike leader, a lawyer and a Boston newspaperman in quick succession, with forays into the domestic preserves of half a dozen others, while composing soulful verses in defense of the accused Italians. A gawky, half-savage boy lured from the Maine woods to plead with his mother, a crucial identification witness, to retract her perjured testimony, had to be forced, literally, to take a bath; soon he blossomed into a spick-and-span U. S. Marine. One of the closest comrades and most ardent defenders of Sacco fell hopelessly in love with Sacco's wife (he married her after Sacco's execution). Within the larger drama of the case, there developed complicated cycles of lesser dramas of private emotion.

Of the reporters who had covered the trial for local newspapers and the great press agencies, not one believed that the foreigners had been proved guilty. A few of them, on the contrary, were deeply convinced of the men's innocence, so that several prominent Boston newspapermen, like Sibley and Folsom, sided openly with the defense. The newspapers themselves, however, were a solid phalanx against us.

I had a privileged inside view of their attitude. In one of the frequent periods when the defense committee went completely broke, I got myself a job on the Boston *Telegram*, a scandal-monger sheet now happily out of existence and unmourned. It occurred to no one on the staff, fortunately, to connect me with my notorious namesake at defense headquarters. I enjoyed the ticklish sensation of seeing my Sacco-Vanzetti publicity releases kicked into the waste-basket with a growl of distaste while feature stories under my signature were being published in the paper; and of writing inflammatory defense literature on the *Telegram's* time and typewriter. I attended to many an assignment by the city editors on the telephone from the Sacco-Vanzetti office.

The rigmarole of legalistic gestures unrolled slowly and dully. More motions for a new trial based on new evidence, confessions of perjury by state witnesses, exposés of other state witnesses as criminals—and every motion matched by a denial from the self-righteous Judge Webster Thayer. All the forms of justice were preserved, only the spirit was absent. Many years later I wrote: "Sacco and Vanzetti were given all their legal rights. They were deprived only of their liberty and their lives."

V. Working for the Soviets

JUST before the birth of my daughter, in November, 1922, I returned to New York. I had been away more than two years, in Europe and then in Boston, and was unaware how completely the revolutionary *milieu* in the metropolis had changed. I had simply been too engrossed in the specific job of defending the two Italians—one of the few issues on which all factions agreed—to gauge the depth of the new hatreds among yesterday's comrades. What had been a many-sided radical movement had disintegrated into so many sects. The Golden Age of American radicalism was ended.

Unhesitatingly I cast my lot with the communists. I devoted the next five years largely to Soviet activities. For a year I edited the first popular American magazine about Russia, the *Soviet Russia Pictorial*, and for four years thereafter, until the day I sailed for the U.S.S.R., I worked for the official Soviet news agency, Tass.

I did not join the Communist Party and consequently was never on the inside of its involved and embittered political life. Such close-ups of the internal party machinery as I had by reason of my everyday work strengthened my obstinacy in resisting solicitations to join up. In any organization which rests on absolute discipline, there is no intermediate role between leadership and blind obedience. I had not the slightest taste for one and a definite distaste for the other. This incapacity for organization and discipline I counted a defect in my character. My instinct was always to undertake specific tasks and to carry them through as best I could, whether it happened to be the preparation of a strike leaflet or the contribution of a newspaper column.

My entire social environment in those years, however, was communist and Soviet. In a loyalty to the Russian revolution which outweighed in my mind all considerations of past friendship or present advantage, I broke relations with most of my old acquaintances who were still in the Socialist Party. Enthusiastically, I contributed my share to the rancor directed against that party. Its members were Mensheviks, Social-Democrats, henchmen of Germany's Scheidemanns, Noskes, and Eberts, and therefore, in Bolshevik and near-Bolshevik eyes, more despicable by far than capitalists. They were deserters, "renegades."

The legions of the damned grew apace in those years, as radicals of divers denominations failed in the decisive test of their political morals by casting doubt on any phase of the Soviet experiment. It did not occur to me to examine the statements of people who went to Moscow to pray and emerged to scoff, since the process of investigation would have implied blasphemous doubts. The fact that Emma Goldman, Alexander Berkman, many other deportees from America abandoned the Soviet land, preferring a capitalist exile, was for us a commentary on these people rather than on the Soviets.

We did not content ourselves with impugning their sanity, but tarred them as knaves, liars, self-seeking betrayers. A lifetime of exemplary devotion to the cause of the revolution did not save an anarchist, socialist or I.W.W. from the hot pitch of our epithets; on the contrary, the more impressive the culprit's record the more urgent was our compulsion to level him with the dust.

I was among the more temperate in this respect, yet I know the anger that flared in my heart against those who attacked the Soviets. If they were bourgeois journalists, middle-class tourists, even milk-and-water liberals, their blasphemy could be explained along orthodox class lines and discounted. But if they were workers, socialists, active radicals, they must be marked with the mark of Cain and sent wandering in the wilderness of bourgeois turncoats.

Soviet Russia Pictorial was the progenitor of the many illustrated magazines about Russian achievements now on the American news stands. It was at the time the mouthpiece of the Friends of Soviet Russia and its primary purpose was to help raise funds for famine relief. Far from concealing the horrors of the Volga famine and the incapacity of the young workers' republic to cope with the disaster, we spread the facts on record as gruesomely as possible in text and picture to stimulate charity from the Left. The horrors, however, were amply balanced by panegyrics for the Soviet leaders and their works. If the wounds of the civil wars were still raw and painful, the romance and elation likewise were fresh. The mere fact that a Socialist Soviet State was in existence was a miracle to halo each new day.

All the giants of the revolution were still alive and in active control. Lenin, Trotsky, Zinoviev,* Kamenev,* Rakovsky,† Radek,† Dzherzhinsky—flaming names to light new vistas of history. We knew the warmth that only people who possess a private pantheon can know. The circumstance that infidels regarded our gods as devils merely testified to the awesome significance of our deities and attested our position as a chosen and anointed people. Trotsky, Zinoviev, and others destined to be expelled from the pantheon, figured so heroically on our pages, in fact, that by 1928 a bound volume of the magazine which I brought into Moscow seemed a counter-revolutionary document. The volume was borrowed by Olga Kameneva, sister of Trotsky and wife of Kamenev, and never returned. To the best of my recollection we did not have occasion to use Stalin's picture once while I edited this Soviet publication—an interesting commentary on how grievously American communists underrated him as late as 1923.

My associate on the editorial staff who, if the truth be told, did the major part of the work, was a man of encyclopaedic knowledge with whom the accumulation of recondite facts, figures, dates, and anecdotes was a grand passion, one Max Podolsky.‡ The deep-dyed cynicism of Max's well-stocked mind made him proof against the lush enthusiasms in which those around him wallowed. He had been active in the revolutionary movements of at least half a dozen European nations, had sampled prisons in most European capitals, and had known many of the Bolshevik gods before their apotheosis. He proceeded on the assumption that all heroes have clay feet and that power is a dangerous narcotic even for revolutionaries. His support of the Soviet system was therefore leavened with large mental reservations. He worked loyally enough but with a distinctly counter-revolutionary twinkle in his eyes.

* Executed in August, 1936.

† Imprisoned in 1937.

‡ Better known as Max Nomad, author of *Rebels and Renegades* and other significant books.

2

The Soviet news agency, at the time I entered its service as general assistant to Kenneth Durant, the American director, was called Rosta. Later the name was changed to Tass. It operated on an agreement for exchange of facilities with the United Press and had its headquarters in one of the United Press offices in the old *World* Building. Our job was to report the news of the entire Western hemisphere as it poured over the U.P. wires.

While we naturally emphasized aspects of the social and economic struggle, and went in for earnest analysis of political conditions everywhere from Canada to Cape Horn, our dispatches were as realistic and uncolored as we could make them. It was Durant's theory that Moscow needed a truthful picture of affairs on this side of the Atlantic—whether it found it politic to publish the picture was its own affair. At no time, in the years that I worked under him, did he knowingly permit the picture to be touched up to please the wishful thinking of communists here or abroad.

Thus, while communist politicians in America, partly through the ardor of their hopes and partly to magnify their own importance, fed the Kremlin empty promises of American recognition and apocryphal communist victories, our news service provided the antidote of unadulterated facts. Not infrequently the reports of American party functionaries on some local situation and our report gave totally different accounts.

I was decidedly under the spell of Durant's personality during our years of collaboration. He was a man of sharp mind and dour disposition, whose rapier of malice was sheathed in a scabbard of pervasive charm. In one mad jump, he had cleared the immense social territory between Rittenhouse Square and Sovietism. I say Sovietism rather than communism advisedly. It was communism as a functioning and ruthless system, backed by armies and secret services, I think, that fascinated him rather than communism as a philosophy of human emancipation. I was to meet others from the upper social strata who are thus captivated by a distant proletariat, triumphant and regnant, but feel not the faintest kinship for the flesh-and-blood proletarians all around them. Kenneth's frank dislike of all American communists flowed from his natural aversion to the "lower" social orders, though he would have denied this most vehemently.

Tall, thin, with aristocratically ascetic features and a ruthless wit, Kenneth had the intolerance of a recent convert. Unconsciously he tried to make up for his advantages of social and educational background, for the fact that he was a foreigner in the adopted land of revolution, by harshness toward non-believers in general and backsliders in particular. In full eruption against a political renegade, Kenneth was a magnificent and disquieting spectacle. Those who offended him personally (and every real or imagined slur on the Soviets he counted a personal affront) became the objects of his anxious, brooding, and patient attentions. The maze of his character was a subject of discussion among those of us under his spell. I recall Joseph Freeman remarking in one such discussion that Kenneth, given the scope, had the makings of a Torquemada. He had a nose for heresy which did not often mislead him and a bloodhound persistence in following the trail.

Emotionally and professionally I lived close to the new Russia. I read all the books on Russia, saw its motion pictures, befriended some of its emissaries, discussed it with returning tourists or American communists, defended it against detractors, steeped myself in its legends and lingo. For months at a stretch, when Durant was visiting Russia or ill, I conducted the Tass bureau, and corresponded with Jacob Doletzky, the head of the organization, or Constantine Umansky, then its foreign editor, or others whom I was to meet before long in Moscow. This direct relation with the center of world revolution, though limited to the routine of news dispatches and cable tolls and technical news-gathering problems, surrounded the work with an aura of importance. It gave me a precious sense of nearness to the one thing that counted above all other things in the modern world.

As an employee of a Soviet organization, it was impolitic, of course, for me to participate openly in the radical movement in America. But from time to time I was sucked into its vortex all the same. As long as Moore remained in Boston, I maintained an active interest in the Sacco-Vanzetti defense, writing occasional articles, or helping at the New York end on matters of evidence or fund-raising. Vanzetti's strictures on the Soviet system from his vantage point of philosophic anarchism were a painful embarrassment, particularly since communists here and abroad were the most active spokesmen for the case. In publicity material these views of Vanzetti were carefully soft-pedaled, but in his voluminous correspondence with sympathizers in all parts of the country he did not conceal them.

During the communist-led strike of textile workers in Passaic, New Jersey, I prepared and saw through publication a sensational brochure of pictures which I called *Hell in New Jersey*. If I recall correctly, about one hundred and fifty thousand copies were sold. I took part in the preliminary organization meetings that led to the launching of the *New Masses*, contributed random pieces to many of the Left magazines, and for some months conducted a tri-weekly column of comment and satire in the *Daily Worker*.

That my political orthodoxy left much to be desired may be surmised from my experiences with the last-named enterprise. Since I rarely went to the editorial offices, merely sending my contributions by mail or messenger, I did not realize that my column had brewed a tempest in the teapot there. I tried in the column to provide a leaven of humor and light-hearted irony for the dough of class-war news and "theses" in the *Daily Worker*. I packed my space with frivolous jingles, skits on people and events, now and then more serious divertissement—but often on subjects remotely if at all related to the revolution. Just where and how I offended the communist proprieties, I was never to discover. But I did discover that my column was being furiously attacked and defended. It threatened schism in the editorial ranks. In the interests of unity and peace, I promptly quit my short-lived role as columnist.

3

By 1926, the repercussions of the Communist Party struggle in Russia, with Stalin and Trotsky as the principal adversaries, were being felt in America. Many of the Russians arriving in the United States on commercial and other missions, it became evident, were thus being shunted from the Soviet arena by Stalin's party machine under guise of important foreign assignments. Our Tass dispatches were being minutely scrutinized on the other side for symptoms of partisanship. In the ranks of American communism, too, leaders and would-be leaders were choosing sides.

On the whole sentiment among American communists, as among communists everywhere outside the Soviet Union, was preponderantly for Trotsky, Zinoviev, Preobrazhensky and the rest of the "Old Guard." The romantic period of the Russian revolution may have become a faint memory at home, where the strident prose of practical problems and sacrifices drowned out the poetry of revolt. Abroad, the romantic period persisted, though in a twilight haze—in a sense it is still alive—and the great names of 1917 and 1918 were still magical. The name of Trotsky, in particular, still connoted all the thrill and throb of the revolutionary honeymoon. Many of the Americans now in the camp of Stalin jeered at him as long as Trotsky and Zinoviev still seemed to have a chance of winning out. Their present ardor is part of the penance for having bet on the wrong horse at that time.

The will to power is sometimes incredible and a little ludicrous to people who do not possess it to any marked degree. It creates dynastic struggles for the leadership of lodge Number 2387 in some absurd fraternal order or for the chairmanship of some women's club. The nail-and-claw struggles for leadership and influence in the American communist movement, as I watched them here and later from Moscow, seemed to me to be touched with the spirit of *opéra bouffe*. The movement which these people sought to dominate was so small, persecuted, impotent as yet that leadership offered at best larger opportunities for abuse and imprisonment. The spoils of victory were so meager in proportion to the bitterness and vigor of the struggle. Yet men and women, impelled to the radical way of life by their thirst for justice, suspended ideals, and elementary decencies, in an unprincipled scramble for control of the party machinery. They played low politics. They flattered those who were on top. They lied to themselves, to their followers, and particularly to the arbiters of their party destinies in Moscow, in a frantic determination to win at any price.

There is always, of course, an element of economic necessity in such a struggle. Shriveled and juiceless as its plums may be, political victory does mean a place on the payroll as editors, lecturers, officials, writers for people who have perhaps sacrificed their possibilities of earning a living in the capitalist set-up. It may mean jobs at Moscow headquarters of the Comintern or the Profintern.

The so-called "professional revolutionist" has been glorified by Lenin, who considered the overturn of an established order a full-time job and career enough for any one lifetime. Perhaps he was right. His view is shared, curiously, by the most conservative labor spokesmen who favor "professional trade-union leaders," and in both cases the counsel may be that of practical necessity. Certain it is that the professional revolutionist is in a most ambiguous position psychologically when an internal fight develops in his particular party. However earnest and high-minded he may be in his stand on the principles and policies at issue, his livelihood, too, is at stake. Such practical compulsions were operative at the heart of the American extension of the Trotsky-Stalin fight, unavoidably, and were surely influential in driving many leaders into the camp of Stalin as his triumph over Trotsky became more assured.

But overshadowing such personal motives was the genuine anxiety to keep the revolutionary regime in Russia and the international communist movement intact. The rank-and-file members, especially, watched in mounting panic a clash which threatened to pull down the whole Soviet structure. To prevent that disaster they rallied to Stalin as they would have rallied to anyone who retained control of the Kremlin, the party machinery, the functioning state. Right or wrong, Trotsky meant schism, a communist movement minus the first communist state.

Even we who worked by his side in the same narrow offices—by this time under the roof of the Associated Press—could not guess where Durant's personal sympathies lay in the fight. Perhaps he had none, because his basic loyalties were to the Soviet system of power as such, regardless who might seize control of its instrumentalities. The fact that Jacob Doletzky, the Tass chief in Moscow, was a Stalinist machine politician very early tinged our work with a faint anti-Trotskyist color.* The further fact that the American communists were so strongly Trotskyist tended, if anything, to deepen that tinge—between our office and the American

* In 1937, strangely enough, Doletzky was arrested as an alleged Trotskyist, and attempted suicide.

communists there was always a tension at times amounting to a feud.

When the die was cast, however, and the Trotsky group indubitably defeated, our office instantly became a Stalinist fortress. Durant's flare for smelling out heresy had new scope. Not only renegades in relation to Russia as a whole, but deviationists from Stalin's "line" now engaged his talents. He scrutinized dispatches from Moscow for traces of pro-Trotsky bias and called such horrors to the attention of the American editorial headquarters involved. Anyone who spared a counter-revolutionary sigh over the fallen leaders, or suggested that the victors' tactics were in any wise questionable, instantly became an enemy to be crushed.

In the atmosphere of the Tass office, I sided automatically with the victorious faction. I could not in my heart, however, think of Trotsky, Zinoviev, Radek and others who had been glamorous symbols of a new world in my most impressionable years, as enemies of the revolution. The secret margin of sorrow over their fate gave me a gnawing sensation of sinfulness in the presence of Kenneth's cold, implacable orthodoxy. Nor was I alone in my clandestine grief. Others around me carried a hidden hurt while we denounced the fallen idols in the name of discipline and unity.

4

In August, 1927, it was my professional duty to report in cable dispatches the tragic climax of the Sacco-Vanzetti case. Russia followed the details of the impending executions more anxiously than any other nation and we were under instructions to report every move. There was the tense night of August 10th, when the doomed men were prepared for death, while the rotund, smiling Governor Fuller of Massachusetts considered the plea for a reprieve. Hour after hour I hovered over the Associated Press wires. By eleven p.m.—one hour before the scheduled electrocutions—he was still withholding his decision; he was squeezing the last drop of sadistic relish out of his cat-and-mouse game while the whole world looked on in horror.

In a daze I typed out two messages ready for "flashing" to Moscow: "SACCO DEAD"—"VANZETTI DEAD." These were not names in the headlines; in a deep sense they were members of my family, but close as few blood relations can be. At 11:24—thirty-six minutes before the hour set for the official killings—Fuller announced a twelve days' reprieve.

Then came the day and the night of August 22. In my memory they have a nightmare quality. My role was so gruesomely routine—the preparation of "flash" cables, the vigil at the A.P. wires, the filling in of the exact minute of Sacco's death, then of Vanzetti's death—all so businesslike. . . . The case which was integrated with my own existence, intimate as few things in life ever become intimate, was over, finished. Nothing to do but go home to bed . . . I remember wondering why I could not weep and shriek with the hurt of it, just as I was to wonder seven years later at my father's coffin.

A few weeks later I shut myself into a room at Kenneth Durant's home for privacy, day after day for over two weeks, and wrote the story of two simple peasant boys, born in Italy to die in America in full view of all the nations on the globe. Or rather, the book wrote itself. Leafing through *The Life and Death of Sacco and Vanzetti*, I am astonished to find passages so eloquent in their passionate restraint that they seem to have been written by another person. At points in the terse narrative I find a poetic vein that transcends my normal literary powers. It was the alchemy of feelings too deep for tears precipitating a style of their own. Except for minor editorial revisions, my first draft, copied by Margaret Larkin, went to the printers. The book was subsequently translated into German, Italian, Russian and Yiddish and widely read in those languages. Two Russian editions, published while I was in Moscow, sold some 130,000 copies. Only the original English version never reached more than a few thousand readers. In 1933, the Nazis paid the book the compliment of immolation on their funeral pyre to German culture. It burned in as fine a literary company as was ever assembled outside a library.

5

I had met a number of United Press officials while Tass operated from their headquarters on Park Row. The President of the United Press, Karl A. Bickel, was on the friendliest terms with Durant and greatly impressed with his political perspicacity and journalistic talents. In anything touching Russia, Bickel usually consulted Durant. In 1926 the post of Moscow correspondent fell vacant. Aware of my fervent hope of getting to the Soviet land, Durant suggested my name among others. The suggestion, I was chagrined to learn after the event, had been seriously considered but ultimately discarded.

When the post was again available, more than a year later, Bickel revived the suggestion. Before offering me the job, however, he consulted Durant, who not only agreed but supported the appointment in the warmest terms. He merely asked that I remain with Tass until he returned from a trip to Russia for the celebration of the tenth anniversary of the revolution. Bickel acquiesced though it meant that his Moscow Bureau would remain with only a Russian woman secretary, a Miss Jmudskaya, in charge.

Durant was away several months, during which I conducted the American work of the Tass service, with Joe Freeman assisting. Thousands of foreign sympathizers had gathered in Moscow and Leningrad for the decennial festivities. Lenin had been overjoyed when the Soviet regime lasted beyond the seventy-day record of the only other proletarian government in history, the Paris Commune. And now the revolution had endured an entire decade! The thrill of that achievement—of mere survival!—could be felt right around the world. Even embittered foes of the Soviet idea felt the importance of the historic moment. Though a large section of that decade had been wasted on costly civil warfare and in fighting off interventionists and economic strangle holds, and in convalescing from a debilitating famine, the young state had a great deal to show. The record of economic and cultural reconstruction before 1928, exhibited with the Russian genius for stage-setting in the celebration of November, 1927, made a most impressive total.

In spirit we participated in the celebration. The press accounts of the demonstrations and congresses and speeches and military displays may have been merely picturesque to other Americans. To those of us who regarded the Soviet land as our spiritual home, these were things that lifted us to a rarefied altitude of joy. Only the futile attempt of Trotsky and his followers to speak to the Soviet masses above the heads of the victorious Stalinists marred the festivities. In the elation of the soaring moment it was easier to brush such annoyances aside than to think them through.

The knowledge that in a few months I should be there, not merely looking on but reporting what I saw to an audience of a hundred million readers, colored this period of impatient waiting with all the tints of impending excitement.

Durant's eye-witness report on his return heightened my expectancy. He had been not only in the capital and in Leningrad but in Soviet Karelia. Everywhere he found the reigning proletariat joyous, enthusiastic, perhaps a little bewildered by its unaccustomed glory and freedom, but adjusting itself to its new dignity. I recall his description of the anniversary demonstration on Red Square as Ernestine Evans, Billy, and several others of us drank Chianti at a little Italian restaurant in Greenwich Village. Through his eyes we saw the Caucasian horsemen dashing across the square, the massed banners, the flood of exultant workers, and our own romantic and too willing imaginations added high colors to the recital. He told a few touching homely anecdotes of lowly peasants and workmen whose eyes were still blinded by the incandescence of the revolution.

"God! Those are the things I want to write when I get there!" I exclaimed. "How do the other correspondents fail to report such things? They're worth tons of statistics!"

If anyone ever went to the Soviet realm with a deep and earnest determination to understand the revolution, to slough off petty detail and dig down to the hard, enduring core of a great event in human history, it was the newly appointed United Press correspondent. My problem, I felt, would be to tone down the rhapsody to the humdrum level of American journalism. I was not deserting the direct service of the cause for the fleshpots of capitalism. (The United Press, as a matter of fact, was paying me only a few dollars more than Tass.) I was accepting, rather, a post of immense strategic importance in the further service of that cause, and doing so with the whole-hearted agreement and understanding of my chiefs in Tass and therefore, presumably, of the Soviet Foreign Office.

If I was aware of a congenital ineptitude for fanaticism, it was a secret and guilty awareness. I reckoned it a serious flaw in my nature, a lurking enemy who must be shown no indulgences.

Mine are the faults, I explained to myself, of a too idealistic radical education, an abstract idealism too frail for the storms of a real revolution.

"I shall not pander to these weaknesses! Truth," I told myself, "does not consist of so-called facts. A picture may be 'true' in detail yet compose into a nightmare lie in its totality. My task is to devote myself to the underlying truths rather than the surface facts. *Mine must be the larger objectivity of history in the making.*"

The farewell party arranged by my friends included the cream of the communist intelligentsia, with not a deviationist in the company. They were sending off one of their very own, proudly aware of his determination to use the opportunity for spreading the gospel whose fountainhead was in the Kremlin.

The following evening, December 31, 1927, on New Year's Eve, I sailed with Billy and our five-year-old daughter, Eugenie, for the land of our dreams.

Mine are the faults, I explained to myself, of a too idealistic radical education, an abstract idealism unfit for the storms of a real revolution.

"I shall not pander to these weaknesses," I told myself, "does not consist of so-called facts. A picture may be true in detail yet [illegible] task is to devote myself [illegible] the significant facts [illegible] in the making."

The [illegible] of the [illegible] company. [illegible] aware of [illegible] the [illegible]

The [illegible] Lve, I [illegible] for the [illegible]

BOOK 2

HALLELUJAH!

I. Moscow and Muscovites

THE red stars, with their insignia of crossed hammer and sickle, brought poignant confirmation that we were at last and indubitably in the land of proletarian dictatorship. They seemed to glow on the peaked caps of the Red soldiers with an inner light of their own, in the deepening twilight of our railroad coach. They shed an aura of intimacy and authenticated, in the mysterious language of symbols, the revolution and everything it stood for in our minds. After a life-time in which established authority is synonymous with reaction and exploitation, the flesh-and-blood vision of a communist soldier or a communist policeman verges on the miraculous.

The train had paused under a wooden arch inscribed "Workers of the World, Unite!" precisely as in the photographs I had once published in *Soviet Russia Pictorial*. The Polish officers in their comic-opera uniforms and dragging swords and provincial foppishness had stepped off, and the Red soldiers boarded. They wore greatcoats that reached the floor, snow-flakes clung to their homey peasant faces, and the red stars, perhaps reflecting our ardor, shed an effulgence over their features. We tried our first words of Russian as we handed over our passports. "Good evening, *tovarishchi*," we said, relishing the word—"comrades"—and the familiarity it implied.

The soldiers saluted and smiled faintly. They met the faithful arriving tremulously day after day and were possibly a bit bored with the performance.

As we chugged into the frontier station, Negoreloye, night fell suddenly, like the angry closing of shutters overhead. Sullen-looking porters, grimy burlap aprons over their padded coats, took our baggage to the customs house. We followed into the snow and the cold. The customs house at that time was a dingy, dimly-lit barn of a place, the more cheerless in contrast with the clean concrete structure we had left a little earlier at Stolpce, on the Polish side.

Neither a forlorn-looking station nor cold nor darkness could douse our high mood of expectation. More than the returning Russians, apparently, we felt this moment as a homecoming. Elsewhere dinginess might be depressing. Here it seemed to us romantically proletarian, without stupid bourgeois frills and pretensions, in the revolutionary tradition of gloom and starkness. The sound of Russian spoken around us seemed in itself worth the journey. The presence of Lenin, Stalin, Rykov,* and Kalinin in framed lithographs on the walls made this melancholy place one in spirit with all the radical headquarters and meeting halls in my memory.

The thrill of finding one's private, esoteric symbols installed in the role of authority!

On the train next morning I was up and dressed soon after dawn, impatient to see the Russian land jog by. I was fearful of missing something, anxious to soak up impressions, to absorb a new world. Peering through the swirling curtains of snow, I saw only a montonously flat white landscape, occasional huts half buried in snow, now and then a huddled peasant driving a sleigh. At stations, gray, grotesquely bundled figures moved about, exhaling great clouds of visible breath, stopping to wipe icicles from bearded faces with their coat sleeves. Slovenly women in patched coats, felt boots and thick head-shawls offered roasted chicken, hard-boiled eggs, and pickled cucumbers with filthy fingers. Third-class passengers filled their tea-kettles with boiling water from the station samovars and rushed back to their cars, pursued by the biting winds. Our porter served us tea in glasses and zwieback. He shrugged his shoulders helplessly when I tested a few phrases from my Russian primer on him. Either the primer or I were mistaken, and in either case the illusion that I had made considerable progress in the language since leaving New York was punctured.

Toward noon, on February 8, 1928, we reached Moscow.

There is no human creature more helpless than a foreigner arriving in the Soviet capital for the first time. But Louis Fischer

* Imprisoned in 1937.

and my Russian secretary, Miss Jmudskaya, met us at Alexandrovsky Station and took control of our destinies. They packed the Lyons family and its baggage and themselves into a dilapidated Ford, which burrowed its way noisily through the snow and deposited us at the door of the Grand Hotel—the not-so-Grand Hotel I was to re-christen it privately soon.

My cramped position in the car had shut out the view of the streets and I felt cheated of the first glimpse of the city to which I was entitled. The next few weeks, indeed, were filled with snowstorms and intense cold and disturbing incidents that hid the city from my sight and deepened a curious and almost panicky sense of bafflement that I did not quite shake off for months. "Bewilderment" was the word that I used most often in my first letters home.

Not until we were settled in a large room on the fifth floor of the hotel, eating sturgeon and black bread and receiving lackadaisical answers from Miss Jmudskaya to our fumbling questions, did I realize the peculiar difficulties of my situation. Here I was in a strange land, with scarcely a word of its language, with the care of a wife and five-year-old child on my conscience, not a penny in the bank, and full responsibility for the news of a vast, mysterious country on my shoulders. The mood of romantic anticipation resolved for the moment into a thousand formidable immediate problems, ranging from milk for Genie to news sources for the United Press. The bill for our modest repast when it arrived, did little to brighten the picture.

"There must be some mistake," I insisted.

She studied the reckoning through her pince-nez.

"No, it's right, quite right. Prices are high here and going higher every day. . . ."

"But a full meal and champagne at the Ritz-Carlton would have cost me less!"

Miss Jmudskaya shrugged her shoulders. She had been through the civil wars as a young girl. She had shifted for herself all these years, despite her near-sighted, school-teacherish appearance. She had searched for her mother for six or seven years, then run into her accidentally on a Leningrad street one day when the search had been abandoned as hopeless. Neither now nor ever after could my worries or excitements perturb her.

"At this rate," I said, "my salary won't half cover the cost of eats alone."

"You don't have to eat at the hotel," she consoled me. "I'll show Mrs. Lyons where to shop—things are much cheaper in the markets. I suppose you brought an electric cook-stove and utensils? . . . Well, you will borrow one from some of the Americans. Of course, it's against the rules to cook in the hotel rooms, but that's all right."

Miss Jmudskaya's nasal voice was as monotonous as a high-pitched buzz-saw. In the two years that she worked with me, I never once heard that voice touched with enthusiasm or even bitterness. I was to meet hundreds like her, in whom suffering seemed to have burned out all emotion. Only the charred husks of their character remained.

2

She steered me a little later through the blinding snows along zigzagging streets to the Foreign Office building on Vorovsky Square. I waited while she negotiated a permit—a *propusk:* the word that looms gigantic on Russia's horizon. It allowed me to enter the musty old building, to follow my secretary through a maze of dark corridors, and finally to meet the censors. These corridors and the censors themselves were to remain among the focal points of my existence for six years. I came to know their idiosyncrasies and sharp windings as an Indian runner knows his trails.

A podgy little intellectual, bearded and shrill and full of words, was the head of the Press Department: Theodore Rothstein. He was genial and clearly desirous of setting me at ease. I would soon learn the ropes, he assured me, and his department existed only to assist the correspondents in everything. It censored dispatches only *pro forma* and largely to safeguard us against falsehoods and malicious rumors. My fame had preceded me, I gathered, and as a "sympathetic" and "friendly" correspondent I was counted upon to hew close to the line of official information, avoiding the temptation to sensationalize or to believe malign libels.

That suited me perfectly. Indeed, I was impatient to begin to serve. When, for instance, could I see President Kalinin? There was so much fantastic exaggeration about peasant recalcitrance in the foreign press these days. I meant to counteract it, and an interview with the homespun peasant President should do the trick effectively.

Mr. Rothstein, however, was shocked. He shook his beard reproachfully and marveled at the temerity of Americans.

"Mr. Lyons," he asked in a hurt voice, "would a foreign correspondent arriving in Washington, let us say, have the nerve to ask to see President Coolidge? Yet as soon as you fellows arrive in Moscow—"

"But, Comrade Rothstein, a correspondent in Washington would see the President as a matter of course at press conferences twice a week and would be allowed to ask questions. What's more, he would see the Secretary of State usually every day, and other Cabinet members almost as often as he wished."

The little man's astonishment was boundless. Though he had lived a large part of his life in England, officialdom remained for him, as for all Russians, a race apart behind the barbed-wire of inaccessibility. The Asiatic ritual of mystification around high personages, inherited from tsardom, was complicated by a strange touchiness. The newly powerful, like the newly rich, are on the alert against any slight to their dignity.

Mr. Rothstein's first assistant was no less cordial. Jacob Podolsky, his head as bald as an egg and his chin decorated with a square black beard, looked a little like an Assyrian priest come to life; he was full of good-natured cynicisms and laughed easily, though most non-committally. My eagerness to do justice to the Soviet Union—the facts that I meant to collate and the people whom I meant to interview and the American misconceptions about the revolution that I meant to dissipate—either amused or embarrassed him, I am not sure which. It surely amused Mironov, a sour, phlegmatic man whose large hooked nose all but met his chin when he frowned—and even his smile was a frown. His sarcastic expression, as nearly as I could decipher it, said, "Huh . . . another ignorant American on my poor head . . . and the difficult kind at that—an idealist!"

The head of the censorship division was replaced several times during my Moscow years, but Podolsky and Mironov were to remain there always, like fixed stars in our professional firmament.

The years did nothing to alter the non-committal laughter of the one and the sarcastic frown of the other. The stirring or tragic events that passed in review under their official blue pencils rarely fluttered their resigned boredom.

Returning from the Foreign Office, I stopped to lace my shoe just as we were passing a large, square, rococo building. Instantly two soldiers with fixed bayonets rushed at me. Miss Jmudskaya's hurried explanation saved me from being gored. It appeared that I had picked the G.P.U. headquarters, of all places, to pause at, and that such a procedure was fraught with danger. Later I found that many Muscovites made a detour to avoid passing that segment of innocent-looking sidewalk.

In the evening I trudged through the snowstorm from the hotel uphill on Tverskaya, in the company of a gifted American cartoonist, William Gropper. The cobbled street and broken sidewalks were treacherous under tight-packed snow. Ghostly frost-covered trolley cars crawled close to the curb. At every step we were accosted by women, in high felt boots, their heads wrapped in thick shawls, their faces glowing with the cold, cigarettes smoldering between painted lips. Several of them pulled our coat-tails and tried a few words of pidgin English on us. A few well-stocked shop windows seemed ill at ease in their embarrassing prosperity among the dusty windows filled with debris and emptiness. The strumming of a guitar reached us from some basement restaurant. The sing-song of a persistent beggar clung to our heels. Bundled-up droshky drivers, their beards streaked with frost and icicles clinging to their nostrils, sat in front of miniature sleds. One or two of them whipped disconsolate horses into action and followed us half-heartedly. . . .

That first day in Moscow remains with me in minutest detail, something mounted and fixed like a scaled model, which I can draw out and study at will. A special permit to enter a public building, alarmed soldiers if you paused at the wrong spot on a city sidewalk: the sense of being in a city besieged and closely guarded, which was to recur to me throughout my long residence in Russia, was born on this day.

Prostitutes, beggars, food difficulties: I had known these things existed and was prepared to confront them. I was fully aware that Russia in 1928 was far from socialism and that it contended with many of the evils of other lands and some of its own. In my romantic heart, however, I had not quite credited this knowledge. The tangible evidences had to be assimilated.

3

The physical Moscow began to fall into focus. After the first confusion, the pattern of the city emerges: the walled-in Kremlin on whose eastern flank is the spacious Red Square; a second crenelated old wall enclosing Kitai Gorod, the so-called Chinese City in which there are no Chinese; beyond that two concentric rings of wide boulevards, A and B; and outside the B ring, the spreading city encroaching far into the farm and forest lands.

Broad avenues radiate spokewise from the center and form important squares where they cut across the boulevards. Theoretically straight, these avenues have a wayward manner of changing course unexpectedly or narrowing sharply for no reason, as though tired of the outlandish efficiency. Within the neat design of avenues and boulevards is the maze of side-streets, narrow, tortuous, often turning snakelike on themselves, and a mystery even to old Muscovites. The serpentine Moscow River, always intruding where it is least expected, adds to the tangle.

Russians used to call Moscow the largest village in their land. Despite several "skyscrapers," the tallest of them twelve stories, it was still a straggling, meandering place, and its utterly Eastern character rather astonished me. Moscow is Asiatic in its sprawling chaos, its squat houses, its quaint old churches, and profusion of colored cupolas. The strongly Mongoloid faces everywhere, the fantastic rags of the beggars, and the makeshift garments of the majority of the population underlined this un-European appearance. Gliding along at night noiselessly in a diminutive sleigh through the labyrinth of alleys, every turn of the street revealing a new roof-line like quaint Arabic script against the sky, I often had a powerful sense of nearness to the Orient.

Winter is the most difficult time for a newcomer to adjust himself to the Soviet capital. The intense cold, frequent blizzards and snowstorms, and the night that comes so soon after noon make it an aloof and forbidding place. For me, plunged at once into the exacting business of gathering news, having it censored, and filing it at the telegraph office, the adjustment was that much more difficult.

And yet, I am pleased that I came upon Moscow in its winter character, because that, I was to realize, it its true inner nature, dark, huddled, blanketed in snow, its nose stuck into a voluminous sheepskin coat against the crisp cold. A city accustomed through all its centuries to the inclemency of nature, the mystery of brief days and interminable night. A city, above all, with an eerie beauty of ghostlike houses, skeleton trees and hushed, hurrying people, hidden deep within their patched and padded garments. Foreign tourists who visit Moscow only in its brief dusty summer incarnation never come near the essence of the place.

We were taken to the Dom Gertzena (Herzen House), a club for writers, where carefree and high-pitched literary bohemianism was making its last stand. Soon enough this bohemianism was to be wiped out by the new policies of an embattled Kremlin intent on industrializing and socializing the country, wiped out along with the cafés, the dance halls, gypsy music, jazz, fun-for-fun's-sake, and all other forms of "bourgeois decadence." Already fingers of gloom touched the life of Dom Gertzena—the Nep holiday was nearly over. A fierce proletarian Puritanism was in the offing.

But the irrepressible Pava was still there, darkly handsome, banging the piano, hammering with fists in sheer overflow of spirits and singing lustily. We got to know her and love her in the years that followed. Long-haired writers of an older vintage were there, and young poets swaggering in the *apache* proletarian manner of Mayakovsky, Russian newspapermen escorting ballet girls, and lordly G.P.U. officers. Food was still plentiful, though costly, and the feasting did not reach its height until after midnight. Billy, contributing an American song occasionally to the festivities, instantly became a favorite in those precincts. Some of the writers, journalists, and actors took us in on a comradely basis as few other foreign correspondents, probably, had been accepted before.

Russians are a gregarious folk. Until food stringency and growing political fears put a damper on such things, Moscow was a city of endless parties. We were fortunate in reaching the country just before this intense social life was snuffed out. There was scarcely a week in the early months of 1928 when we did not participate in a few house parties in the one- or two-room "apartments" of Soviet writers, technicians, officials, workers.

The procedure was always in the routine of Russian tradition. The guests sat close-packed around a large table, literally for hours, consuming vodka and *zakusky*, drinking toasts to the host, the hostess, the hostess's blue eyes, the guests *en masse* and one by one, everyone getting a little more flushed and a lot louder as we proceeded. Then, if the home boasted an old horned gramophone and a few cracked records, a space was cleared for dancing. If there was a piano, it became the center of a spontaneous choir, singing old folk songs and the brave new hymns and marching songs of the revolution; or, most frequently, the old tunes with Soviet words. Occasionally someone brought a seven-stringed guitar or an accordion to enliven the gathering, and Billy's "uke" was in great demand.

I accepted more such invitations, no doubt, than were strictly good for me, in an insatiable thirst for meeting more and still more Russians, identifying myself a little more closely if possible with their ways and their problems. I prowled in their common kitchens, peeped shamelessly into neighboring "apartments" in the common corridor, and tried to steep myself in the Russian atmosphere.

Sometimes a group of us capped a night's festivities with a visit to some beer hall on the Arbat, a gypsy restaurant on the Tverskaya, Dom Gertzena, the Artists' Club or a coöperative café. Whatever the hour, we found these resorts crowded and filled with noise and smoke. I instigated these excursions light-mindedly. I did not as yet realize that I was compromising those Russians whom I inveigled into appearing in public in a foreigner's company.

At our first Foreign Office reception for the correspondents' corps, we became acquainted with the Soviet newspaper fraternity. A few of these men we came to value in the following years. I remember the gathering particularly because there was a camaraderie between the native and foreign newspapermen never again repeated.

At the home of Comrade Yonov,* head of a publishing trust

* Arrested and exiled in 1936.

and brother-in-law to Zinoviev, we met a few Kremlin officials, painters and authors, several of whom remained our friends, within the narrow limits of discretion in the suspicious years to follow. Yonov, whom we had met in New York, was a bibliophile and a man of cultivated taste generally. He exhibited rare first editions and spoke fervently of the fine printing his organization was doing. To his typographical tastes the Soviet Union owes those lovely *Academia* editions of the Arabian Nights and other classics known to book collectors the world over.

In the "salon" of Rachelle Ossipovna, we found a congregation of artists and near-artists, opera and ballet hopefuls, and the slim young men for whom the hostess had a sweet-tooth. Elsewhere I met the irrepressible Sergei Trivas,* whose job it was to entertain visiting Americans and Englishmen. He headed the Anglo-American Department of Voks (the Society for Cultural Relations with Foreign Countries). He made no secret of his service in the G.P.U. But if he started to cultivate me in the line of duty, he came in time, I like to believe, to relish that duty, if only because he found me a sympathetic listener to whom he could safely confide his hopes and boast of his amorous escapades.

And thus, through a hundred different contacts and accidental meetings, we added to our acquaintances minor officials, simple factory workers, office clerks, students, and particularly, as was only natural, intellectuals of both the pre-revolutionary and the new generation. We learned to drain wine glasses while someone sang a *charochka* and the company clapped hands and chanted, "*Pyei do dna, pyei do dna!*" ("Drink to the bottom") at the top of its lusty voice. We learned to join in the choruses of all the songs. We acquired a few words of mispronounced Russian. Above all, we learned not to talk politics, domestic or international, but to stick close to safe subjects like the theater, the new ballerina, the weather, and the relative virtues of the Caucasus and the Crimea as vacation resorts. On days when some startling decree or other news sensation filled the press and without doubt filled everyone's mind as well, no one referred to it at social occasions. Discretion had been hammered home by experience.

Our presence both attracted other guests and made them a little

* Executed in 1930.

jumpy—the blend of fear and fascination, traditional hospitality and distrust of a stranger which made up the ordinary Russian's attitude to a foreigner. We discovered that Americans, in particular, were infinitely fascinating to Russians. For the older generation nurtured on democratic hopes, America was the land of vast freedoms and individual opportunities. For the younger people, thrilling to the vision of an industrialized future, it was the land of marvelous technique.

"Fordization" was a magic word just then in Russia, seeing mirages of mass production in its desert of goods shortages. How amazed the Sage of Dearborn would be, I often thought, to realize that he occupied a prominent niche in every young communist's private pantheon. An American intellectual, distrusting the belt system of production as a new species of exploitation, did not always find it easy to share Soviet enthusiasm for miracle-working Fordization.

America to the ordinary Russian meant roughly anything west of the Atlantic. More than once someone said hopefully, "Oh, you're from America! Maybe you know my brother in Rio de Janeiro!"

4

I took in the Russian theater, ballet and opera in great draughts. Ardently if illogically, I gave the revolution credit for everything cultural that it had inherited from the tsarist era. A hundred years of classical ballet, the meticulous art of Stanislavsky's theaters, the piled-up treasures of Russian music and stagecraft were for me, as for all foreign worshippers, subtle confirmation of Karl Marx's theories. Tchaikovsky and Mussorgsky, Moskvin and Madame Geltzer have made more converts to Sovietism among visiting outsiders than the marvels of the Five Year Plan or the adroitness of the guides.

The comparative tolerance of the "Nep" period had invigorated the Soviet theater. With few exceptions the finest things in post-revolutionary Russian drama, cinema and dance belonged to that time: Eisenstein's and Pudovkin's best motion pictures, Bulgakov's and Olesha's best plays, the ballet *Red Poppy*, the superb stylized productions by Granovsky in the Jewish Kamerny Theatre, the sensational innovations of Vsevelod Meierhold and a hundred other achievements. It is largely upon these that the new Russia's glamorous reputation in the theater and cinema still rests. Some of them were robust enough to weather the stormy years that followed.

In the theater, the people on my side of the footlights interested me even more than those on the stage. Russian dramatic art is old; even Meierhold did most of his pioneering before the revolution. The audiences were new. Those citadels of snobbery in all lands, ballet and opera, had fallen to the masses. Working men and women thronged not only the music halls and moving picture houses, but the finest dramatic theaters. High admission prices (even with the reductions to trade-union members) still barred the lowest categories of labor from some of the theaters. Nevertheless, the greater part of these audiences would have gone through life without seeing a first-rate play, let alone a ballet or opera, had it not been for the revolution. The description of a working woman in head-kerchief, perhaps a servant or sewing-machine worker, sitting at ease in the Imperial Box at the Bolshoi Theater has become a cliché of Soviet travel books. There was nothing stereotyped, though, in the emotional lift I got out of such sights.

Whether in the theater or out of it, these audiences and their life provided me with continuous stimulation. Their existence seemed to me pitched on a higher plane of intensity, in which joys and sorrows alike were sharper and more meaningful. Elsewhere poverty and wealth, hope and despair, were the commonplaces of old social systems and of direct interest only to the individuals affected. Here, where the revolution had destroyed old relations and established a new set of social values the lot of the individual, whether pleasant or horrible, seemed novel, transitional and historically important. Or so it seemed to me, studying Russians avidly in the light of my socialist convictions.

Elsewhere men, women and children had private existences distinct from their social status. Here they epitomized for me classes and groups: Soviet Youth, Backward Peasants, Bourgeois Intellectuals, Class-Conscious Workers, Bureaucrats, and so on. They were thus capitalized in my eyes as I watched them on the streets, at social gatherings, in restaurants, offices, factories. It was largely my own mind which gave them this rich social coloring.

It turned all of Russia for me—throughout my six years, because the novelty never wore off entirely—into a moving spectacle.

A prying curiosity took me to churches, markets, homes, nearby villages, theater rehearsals—wherever, off the beaten tourist track of factories and museums, I could see the people of the new Russia at their private preoccupations.

II. The Kremlin's Guests and Poor Relations

WE SOON met most of the Americans with whom we were to be in contact in the ensuing years. The attitude of the seasoned Moscow reporters ranged from frank pity for my innocence and ignorance to no less frank disdain for my imported enthusiasms. I was pulled up short by the discovery that journalists who sounded so cocksure in their published eulogies of the Bolshevik world were less certain and less eulogistic in their unpublished views.

Those Soviet developments which loomed largest in their minds and conversation at this juncture, I realized immediately, were not mentioned in their dispatches or at most conveyed in hints. The important things in Moscow are so often the intangibles—atmospheric pressures, as it were—which cannot be captured in news accounts. At the moment members of the press corps at all sensitive to changes in political weather were aware of gathering electrical storms—a tightening of the ranks of the ruling minority, a tremor of apprehension in the mass of the population. Casual table talk among the newspapermen treated as matters of common knowledge facts which I had vehemently denied for so many years—facts for which I had helped consign friends to the garbage-heap of "renegacy."

The veteran Chicago *Daily News* man, Junius B. Wood, lived at our hotel; a growling, sharp-toothed bear of a man, whose redoubtable reputation and gruff ways rather intimidated a fledgling correspondent. Only our daughter was not fooled by his growl. He might be composing another biting commentary on Soviet news when Genie strode in (Junius looked upon the "Kremlin gang" as just another set of politicians and treated their works and professions as unceremoniously as though they were Tammany stalwarts), but whatever devastating piece of realism he might be inditing, it waited while he entertained the young lady by playing the piano as she sat on the lid, her little legs dangling.

The American colony in Russia was destined to expand under the first Five Year Plan into a heterogeneous mass of technicians, skilled workers, salesmen, job-hunters, political quacks, amateur journalists. At its peak it was to provide fascinated Russians with a goodly cross-section of America's Main Street. At this point, though, it was still a select company of accredited newspapermen, pioneer businessmen, and a few concessionaires.

Among the newspapermen, Walter Duranty, a little Englishman who had been in the New York *Times* service since the war, reigned supreme. Urbane, clever to a fault, a scintillating talker, he remained, after all his years in Russia, detached from its life and fate, curiously contemptuous of Russians. He spoke of Soviet triumphs and travail much as he might of a murder mystery he had read, but with not half the passion or sense of personal involvement. His spoken views of the Russian scene, when the mood was upon him, would have shocked New York radicals who mistook him for a Soviet enthusiast, even as they shocked me.

Among the concessionaires, the Hammer family, father, mother, and sons, held first place. Drawn to Russia from New York by their genuine interest in the revolution, the Hammers had found it a fertile field for their commercial talents; they risked their modest capital in the new Russia long before others ventured it. First as foreign trade intermediaries, then as pencil manufacturers on a concession basis, they mixed the business of helping themselves with the pleasure of helping Russia. In a great house on Sadovaya Kudrinskaya they dispensed hospitality with a baronial hand.

A contingent of foreigners which had for me, as for all of Moscow, a particular fascination was concentrated chiefly in the Metropole Hotel. It consisted of refugees from the Chinese counter-revolution. One of the most attractive of these refugees, an American girl named Rayna Prohme, had died suddenly in Moscow a few months earlier and the legend of her remarkable personality and tragic end was still fresh when I arrived. Vincent Sheean's *Personal History* stands as an inspired tribute to this red-headed girl.

The soaring revolutionary hopes in China, fed by Kuomintang victories under Soviet Russian guidance, had collapsed in gory tragedy. Sheean and others have given us vivid pictures of both the victory and the defeat. Every radical and liberal had in some measure lived and suffered that drama in his own heart. The small company of refugees was therefore haloed by our mixed feelings of pride and pathos.

There was Madam Sun Yat Sen, the widow of the revered leader of modern China. She was a fragile, bird-like creature; exquisite in her native costume, its flowers touched by the sunlight streaming into the hotel room, a little tremulous in her shyness, she seemed a lovely animated Chinese figure. She rarely ventured out of the hotel and saw few people outside of those who had worked with her in China. But I met her several times. It seemed a little unreal and even disconcerting to find this delicate little woman possessed of a sharp mind and robust character.

And there was Eugene Chen, who had been Foreign Minister when the Chinese revolution was at its glowing apex. In his case, too, a small physique somehow set off his vigorous mind dramatically. He had been born in Trinidad, in the West Indies, with a considerable admixture of Negro in his blood. He had married a handsome Negro woman—the children showed me photographs of her—and she bore him two boys and two girls. They owned land, were thoroughly British in their education, and might easily have remained in Trinidad as typical humdrum natives of mixed blood. But the Chinese heritage asserted itself. Chen traveled to the land of his forebears and, without knowing its language, became a leader in the revolutionary upsurge. His official notes and manifestos as Foreign Minister were the delight of the radical world. I found that he spoke as he wrote, with a diplomat's care for the meaning and an artist's sensitiveness for the proper word.

Both Madam Sun and Mr. Chen soon left Moscow—she for Shanghai, he for Paris. The four Chen children remained in Russia, learned Russian and made themselves part of the new surroundings. We came to know them intimately and to admire them for their charms and their talents. All four ultimately married Russians. The historical fate which linked China and Russia for a few years and may again link them in the future is curiously personified in these four born in Trinidad, educated in England, touched in China by a new faith that came to flower in Russia.

2

Then, as now, there were two foreign colonies in Russia and they rarely met. One was "bourgeois," and its center was in the expensive hotels, the embassies and legations, and relatively comfortable private apartments. The other was communist, and its center was at the Lux Hotel set aside for the use of foreign Bolsheviks, at the offices of various Red Internationals, and in the communist schools. Both colonies were suspect, for to the Soviet mind an outsider, whatever his politics, is an alien creature of curious habits and unstable faith. The bourgeois group was openly under surveillance. The visiting brethren of the faith were watched less candidly but more minutely. I know no American who has succeeded in making himself a part of both those colonies.

My natural impulse was toward the communist colony, of course. I knew most of the permanent American representatives in the Communist International, the Red Trade Union International, and other organizations. A few of them had been friends and frequently guests at my home in Sunnyside, Long Island. I had expected confidently that my Moscow friends and political guidance would come from that direction. If I experienced any sense of intrusion or self-consciousness over a false position, it was, rather, in the company of the capitalist newspapermen and other denizens of the bourgeois American camp.

Until we were politely but unequivocally excluded from its sourish precincts, Billy and I were therefore constant visitors at the Lux Hotel, on the Tverskaya, in the crowded room of one or another American communist. A few Russian functionaries, in need of "living space" and influential enough to wangle this privilege, had also obtained temporary quarters in the Lux. Among them was Constantine Umansky, for many years my long-distance co-worker in Tass. We called on him, too, when in the building.

How were we to guess that in crossing the Soviet frontier, even before I had written a single heretical line or voiced a single unorthodox sentiment, we had been turned mysteriously into untouchables? How were we to surmise that in visiting old friends we were exposing them to capitalist contagions and, what is more to the point, endangering the most valuable asset in their political climbing—their spotless orthodoxy? All unaware of our new dignity as capitalist plague-bearers, Billy and I trudged through the snows to the Lux, at least once and sometimes several times a day. I shudder to think what havoc we wrought among the more eager careerists of our acquaintance.

It was, and presumably still is, an extraordinary place, the Lux Hotel. Physically it had the character of an overcrowded tenement, an overflow of untidy perambulators in the lobby, pervasive and peculiarly unpleasant food smells, slatternly housewives, cooing and quarreling audible in the corridors. The elaborate precautions in guarding the inmates added a prison aura to the cabbage odors. The population of the hotel consisted of men and women, boys and girls, of all nations, colors and tongues, few of them able to understand one another, all of them awed by the grandeur and the might of the enthroned revolution. Various as they were in race and language, their creed was one. In a curious way, too, their looks were one. If there is such a thing as an international communist type, it was to be met in the Lux realm—if not the same features, at least the same negligent dress, unkempt hair, and the same expression of anxious devotion.

Ostensibly agents or employees of an international organization, these people had no doubt of their real status. They were the guests of a successful government, the Kremlin's poor relations, eating its food, protected by its police, shadowed by its spies, their tenure of employment and sojourn in the final instance dependent on how they measured up in the graces of their hosts. The poor-relation humility was unmistakable in the shrill pride with which they boasted of Uncle Kremlin's importance and strength, and particularly in the anxiety with which they catered to his every whim. He was a frowning, cantankerous uncle just then, suspicious that his foreign nephews and nieces might forget themselves and play with those horrid Trotsky brats.

Most of them, fresh from cities where they were despised and persecuted, had never been so close to the honeypots of power and found the taste heady. Not, mind you, the make-believe power of leadership in an oppressed or underground revolutionary party, but the power that is spelled in armies, airplanes, police, unquestioning obedience from underlings, and a vision of ultimate world dominion. Relieved from the risks and responsibilities under which they labored at home, their yearning for position, career and privilege in many cases took on a jungle luxuriance.

Never before had I witnessed so much naked, unashamed sycophancy and career-building concentrated under one roof. Who stood well with whom was the theme song of most conversation. Breathlessly Comrade X, almost within earshot of her meek spectacled husband, boasted that she had slept with Comrade Y, "a terribly important communist, you know . . . close to Stalin!" She was helping her husband get places. The arrival of a communist dignitary from Germany or France, a visit in some room by a third secretary to Stalin's secretary, the rumor that the Hungarian comrade, the lucky girl, was having an affair with that influential Chinese comrade—these were the raw stuff of gossip, speculation, and envies. I saw the "professional revolutionist" theory reduced to obnoxious absurdity.

With few exceptions, the Lux inmates knew no Russian and were cut off from such realistic guidance as they might have received from the local press. They met few, if any, Russians other than those told off as liaison officers for the foreign communist elements. A special news bulletin was prepared for them, in which Soviet developments were perfumed for their orthodox nostrils. Several of the bolder Americans in Moscow surreptitiously dropped into my office at intervals for years to find out what was happening in Russia by reading my files of American papers!

The guests of the revolution lived a narrow, ingrown life, stewing in their own juices, shuttling between the bureaucratic offices of the various international headquarters. The Americans among them might just as well have remained near Union Square, New York, instead of Red Square, Moscow, for all that they learned of Soviet realities. Their ignorance of Russia remained correctly official, stereotyped, and self-righteous.

3

Almost every evening there was a gay party in some Lux comrade's room, in which vodka and dance music flowed freely. We always met approximately the same people, and it was normally the same routine of *zakusky*, liquor, flirting and dancing, aimless talk in English, German, French, with a rare word of Russian.

One such gathering was in the room of Kostia Umansky. It was predominantly German in character, Umansky's wife being a German. A child prodigy of the German communist movement, Heinz Neumann, was the pampered guest; a few years later this boy was to become virtual dictator of the movement in Germany as Stalin's most trusted lieutenant. We sat on the floor of the stuffy room, drank, played jazz, and had a gay time of it. Returning to the hotel towards dawn, Billy and I decided that having accepted so much hospitality, the least we could do was to throw a party in return.

The result of that counsel of conscience was a gathering about a week later in room 441 of the Grand Hotel. (We had quickly relinquished the elegance of our first suite, with its bath and running water, for this cheaper room.) The party was in every respect a carbon copy of the other—the same people, the same food and drinks, even the same gramophone and records—except that it was in the Grand instead of the Lux and that I paid the bills. Umansky was having a pleasant time along with the others, the only fly in the ointment being the protests of neighbors. But evidently his official conscience was bothering him. He drew me aside.

"You know, Gene," he confided, his face suddenly glum and official—he was putting me in my place—"this is quite a condescension on our part."

"I don't understand. What are you condescending about and to whom?"

"I mean our attending a *bourgeois party,*" he smiled his smile full of gold teeth.

"A bourgeois party! But, Kostia, these are the same people, the same everything as in your room the other night. . . ."

"No matter!" he laid down the law, this commissar-to-be. "This is the Grand Hotel and this is the room of a bourgeois correspondent."

I retorted much too politely, but with sufficient vigor to leave no doubt that such sectarian and formalistic "revolutionism" seemed to me merely ludicrous. The tension of mutual dislike between us, I suppose, was born at that moment.

This was the first of a series of hints which slowly penetrated my self-assurance. But for more than a month I continued to contaminate the sacred purlieus of the Lux with my heathen presence. At the end of that time one of my more intimate acquaintances in that establishment took the matter into his own hands, or perhaps he had been commissioned to speak to me.

"It's rather embarrassing," he stammered, "to have a bourgeois journalist calling on us. Of course, we all know you and like you and that sort of thing. But this isn't New York. It's Moscow and one must watch his step. The slightest suspicion of any of us and we go out on our backsides. I'm sure you understand. . . ."

I tried to make the onerous errand easy for him.

"Is it that they mistrust *me* or mistrust *you?*" I asked.

"God knows! Everybody distrusts everybody and everything here, and the only safe way is to keep your mouth buttoned up and stick to your job and avoid seeing anyone or anything that's not strictly *kosher.*"

"But after all," I was thinking aloud rather than arguing, "I worked for Tass for four years. They're preparing to publish my book on the Sacco-Vanzetti case. In fact, I only accepted the Moscow assignment from the United Press with Moscow's explicit permission. It was understood that I would use my strategic position for the cause."

My informant shrugged his shoulders, sadly.

Had I been less than snow-white in my revolutionary conscience I suppose I would have required fewer hints. A number of extraordinary incidents would have served as danger signals and kept me from intruding my brand-new capitalist personality where it was not wanted.

There was the episode with Comrade Foushman for a starter. That began in New York. One evening, at the home of an acquaintance, we met two Soviet visitors. One, a short, compact little man with a warm smile, was Serebriakov,* a Bolshevik of considerable importance, at one time a secretary of the Communist Party, whose political ups and downs are no part of this tale. The other was Comrade Foushman, who was in the United States for the Soviet textile industry in connection with Soviet cotton purchases. He was thick-set, red-headed, ebulliently friendly. We all played poker, and relished the anticipation of our interesting comradeship in Moscow.

* Executed in January, 1937.

By the time we parted at a taxi door in the rain after midnight, Foushman and the Lyons family had plighted friendship in the way that people who like each other spontaneously will do. He insisted that we take a Soviet silver ruble from him by way of pledge of the new entente and over and over again he made us repeat the promise.

"Just as soon as you get to the frontier," he rehearsed the arrangements, "you telegraph me to the address I gave you. I'll meet you at the station and put you up at my house. . . ."

At Negoreloye we debated whether to telegraph him and decided not to take advantage of his good nature. But our first evening in Moscow, Miss Jmudskaya got him on the telephone for me. He sounded genuinely hurt at our failure to notify him earlier of the momentous event of our arrival, but in the end forgave us.

"What room are you in? I'll be right over to see you," he said.

I saw him about four years later.

That first evening we waited and waited in vain. I wondered vaguely whether in his rush to see us he might have been run over. For several days I tried to reach him by telephone, but he was never available. About four years later my New York editor asked for information on some matter pertaining to Soviet-American trade and my secretary arranged with the Commissariat for Foreign Trade for an interview. I arrived at the appointed place and hour, having paid no attention to the identity of the official who would receive me. And suddenly I was face to face with Comrade Foushman! He, too, apparently had not expected his old poker partner. Both of us pretended blushingly that we had never met before, and few interviews in my experience were so strained and unsatisfactory. At its conclusion, however, he detained me a moment as my secretary walked out. In a thin, apologetic voice he asked:

"How are you? And how is Billy?"

And he sighed, much as to say, "By this time you understand how it is. . . . I'm really not to blame. . . ."

In those first weeks the strange disappearance of Comrade Foushman was one more element in the cumulative bewilderment. When I told Louis Fischer, the communist publicist, about the man's curious behavior, he smiled knowingly. "Don't you understand? He doesn't dare come over. . . . The Grand Hotel, you know, and a foreign correspondent. . . . Foushman is under suspicion of Trotskyist leanings and can't take any chances." I wondered whether Fischer knew that he was himself under that dread suspicion. A Soviet journalist in Berlin had taken particular pains to warn me against associating too closely with him on that ground.

Another rebuff that should have enlightened me, but alas! did not, was my meeting with my recent absentee boss, Jacob Doletzky, the director-general of Tass. I had counted heavily on his friendly advice in my new job. For four years we had corresponded and he was privy to all my hopes for utilizing my new position in the interests of the revolution. It took me more than a week of continuous and in the end slightly panicky insistence to receive the favor of an interview. Finally I found myself in his outer office. After I had been kept waiting for half an hour, the doors were thrown open and I was in the blessed presence.

At the far end of a long room stood a vast and shiny desk covered with many telephones and push buttons, and behind its imposing expanse sat a bearded, obese little man, blinking behind thick glasses. Mussolini, too, makes his visitors walk the length of a great chamber before he recognizes their petty existence. I was fated to become excessively familiar with the species of ex-revolutionary known as a bureaucrat—people who once risked their lives for a cause but now trembled at the thought of risking their job by a bold word or gesture.

"So," he greeted me sarcastically, "you have gone over to the enemy?"

I staggered under the unexpected blow.

"But, Comrade Doletzky, you yourself agreed that I should accept Bickel's offer. Don't you recall—I was to learn Russian and get closer to things, then return to Tass? I—"

"Oh, well, now you're a bourgeois correspondent all the same."

And he changed the subject. We talked polite formalities and he made it clear that I was not to presume on my record of service in the Soviet employ to expect special consideration from Tass. His organization was in contractual relations with my opposition, the Associated Press, and Tass would therefore regard me of necessity as a competitor. In conclusion, by way of social salve, he promised to call me soon and take me and Mrs. Lyons to the theater. By the time we left his country, six years later, he had not yet gotten around to keeping his promise.

One of the few Luxites who remained until the end uninhibited in his friendliness was Big Bill Haywood, former generalissimo of the I.W.W.'s. Unluckily his end came too soon. He died three months after we reached Moscow. In the broken, abnormally corpulent, homesick man with whom we played checkers at the Lux, there was scarcely a trace of the dynamic Haywood who had made labor history in America. A little of the old fire came into his one eye as we recalled episodes and mutual acquaintances in the I.W.W. movement. Then he relapsed into a tragic and hopeless boastfulness. The bust a Moscow sculptor was making of him, a diploma of some sort which he had been presented. . . . He reached avidly for American cigarettes and waxed lyrical over the memory of American grub.

Though stupidly regarded by so many as "un-American," Haywood's every nerve and muscle was rooted in the American soil, and the movement which he started and led—a movement of hoboes, drifters, unskilled workers, lumberjacks and miners—was likewise authentically American in a sense that made it incomprehensible to foreign students. He had fled to Russia with other I.W.W. men while out on bail and was therefore forever cut off from his native land. This robust, two-fisted American, essentially democratic and idealistic in his instincts, found the Bolshevik system of impersonal brutality hateful and fumed inwardly because he could say and do nothing about it. After a lifetime of fighting what he considered the delusions of political action, he could not swallow a super-state, whatever slogans it might profess. He was suddenly an impotent alien, dependent on the bounty of a dictatorial state, and unable to return home. Out of one prison he had escaped into another. He was a pathetic ruin.

The solace of his last years was a Russian wife much younger than himself, who nursed him and coddled him with great devotion. It was her firm hand which kept him from drink and imposed absolute rest and thus prolonged his life. The one time that he overrode her insistence ended him. He heard about a party for the Lyonses at Fellow-worker McLeod's—another I.W.W exile—on the other side of the Moscow River. "Mammy," a Negress who had lived in Russia thirty-five or forty years, would be there to prepare American food. Billy would be bringing an American ukulele. For the first time in more than a year, therefore, Bill Haywood left the Lux, trailed by his protesting wife. The party, unfortunately, grew much too hilarious and Big Bill was caught up in it. Recklessly he drank vodka and ate "Mammy's" waffles and joined in I.W.W. songs to a ukulele accompaniment.

Only his wife knew how seriously ill he was and pleaded with him to desist, but he kissed her gaily and tried to reassure her. After the party he took to bed and two weeks later died in the Kremlin hospital. It was on May 18, the same day the Shakhty sabotage trial began. In cabling his death I "scooped" the other American reporters by many hours—the first of these petty successes and a victory that was all sorrow. Haywood's ashes were buried in the communist cemetery on the outskirts of the city.

4

We were first led to the "salon" of Rachelle Ossipovna by several of the Negro comrades studying at the Lenin Institute and other communist institutions. A few of these black Americans were fully aware of the risks and rewards of the communist career they were embracing. Others saw in communism only a short-cut to racial equality, ultimately for all their people, but immediately —and that was far more important—for themselves. They were not only accepted as equals by the comrades but given a privileged role by virtue of the bourgeois slavery their color symbolized.

A good many of these Negro recruits, however, had stumbled into the communist career ignorantly. The most pathetic in this group was a thin, sad-eyed little girl from Chicago, flat-nosed, thick-lipped and black as India ink. She told us her story:

She had never graduated from elementary school and dreamed of an education while washing dishes in a Chicago restaurant. She confided her burning hope for learning to her friends. Then one of them brought her amazing news. Some organization was offering free scholarships to several young Negroes for an education in a Moscow university. She had never heard of communism or world revolution. She had at most a faint notion that there was a country called Russia somewhere in the far far-away. But the tidings of the scholarship fired her imagination—not merely an education but a "university" and travel!

"Well," she said, "I sure applied but didn't have no hopes no-how that I'd be chosen but I prayed hard to the Lawd even while I washed the dishes. I didn't know then why they chose me and I don't know yet, because I sure ain't fit for it. But they looked me over, they did, and said I'd make 'good material.'

"When I told the folks at home I was going to Moscow my mammy cried and my old man threatened to thrash me, but I explained that I was gonna get an education in a university and wouldn't have to wash no more dishes, then I would come back and get myself a good job teaching or office work or something. Anyhow, about a year and a half ago I got to Moscow. . . .

"Then the trouble began. Instead of teaching me writing and figuring and such things, why, they began to lecture me about Marxism and dialectic materialism and the Party line and the class war, which sure ain't gonna help me get no better job back home, is it now?"

To make things worse, the barracks in which she was housed was less attractive than the slum she had left behind in Chicago, and the monthly stipend was not enough to live on. By the time it penetrated her bewildered and unlettered mind that she was being trained to lead revolution, a year had passed. It would be hard to face her family without the education she had promised them and it was difficult to extract return fare from the committee at the Lenin Institute. So she decided she might as well finish the three-year course. . . .

At least she was a great social success, invited out every night to some Russian home. Negroes are such a rarity in Russia that people stop to stare at them in the streets. They are sought after as exotic additions to any party. Among the male Negroes was one who subsequently ran for Vice-President of the United States on the communist ticket. They were the most popular men in the Soviet capital. To the fillip of their astonishing color they added the tang of their status as symbols of the oppressed nationalities of the world in revolt.

"Yes," one of the Negro boys said, "we're hauled out everywhere, at meetings and clubs as samples of the oppressed races, and we make speeches which nobody understands, but everybody applauds and cheers anyhow. That's not so bad. It's the womenfolks drive me crazy, always telephoning and wanting to be loved. You know there's a limit to a man's time." He laughed lustily.

One Saturday night this man had swallowed a few more vodkas than his quota in the Grand Hotel ballroom. I was present when he staggered out and addressed the droshky driver.

"How much you gonna charge me from here to Lenox Avenue and 135th Street, boss?" he asked in English.

The cabbie was taking no chances, even if he didn't understand the foreign gibberish. "*Pyat rublei*," he said.

"Five rubles to Lenox Avenue," the customer laughed, "too much, boss, too much," and staggered away on foot.

Well, it was through the good offices of the budding Negro revolutionaries that we met Rachelle. She and her husband (who was a supernumerary in that household) were relatively well fixed. For themselves, several sons and a servant girl, they had two good-sized rooms, and were therefore the envy of four or five neighbors in what was formerly one apartment. In the pre-revolutionary days Rachelle had run a real literary and artistic salon in Petrograd. Persons of consequence had been among her guests. Now, reduced to two rooms, into which she had crowded an immense amount of furniture and other debris of her former affluence, the urge to hunt artistic lions was still strong upon her. The animals she snared, alas! were not very leonine: a few ballerinas, American Negroes, a number of opera hopefuls, and a miscellany of people who enjoyed her food. But her anxious imagination turned them quickly into lions all the same. She introduced them to one another and to outsiders as great dancers, opera stars, literary luminaries, important foreigners, etc. She was herself the only one who believed it.

Under her eccentricities and innocent pretensions, Rachelle Ossipovna had a lively mind and a heart of pure gold. From the first she developed a soaring admiration for Billy, and showed her a thousand signs of unselfish devotion. In those first difficult months, when the people on whose friendship we had counted began to ostracize us in the interest of their political careers, Rachelle's friendship was one of the few things we could count on implicitly.

There was a dark moment when our daughter suddenly fell ill

at the hotel. Finding doctors and medicines at unusual hours with only a few words of Russian to help us and a most inadequate purse was no simple matter. We felt ourselves indescribably alone. Several people who would have helped were frankly afraid to come to the hotel. It was unsafe even then for a Soviet citizen to visit foreigners under such public auspices. Rachelle, however, rushed over immediately and remained for some forty-eight hours, until Genie was out of danger.

Despite restrictions, our circle of acquaintanceship grew. Russians in political positions and communists with ambitions to nurse, naturally steered clear of foreigners—unless they were specifically "assigned" to encourage such intercourse. Those who remained, in the long-run, were the lowly and the average, run-of-the-mill actors, singers, writers, sometimes brave in the absolute purity of their conscience, other times too naive to understand the risks they were running. Like all sensible foreigners, we learned to curb our social instincts and waited always for Russians to make the first gesture toward continued relations, to spare everyone concerned possible embarrassment. As it became increasingly risky for them to associate with a foreign journalist, we received fewer invitations, entertained less, and were driven increasingly into the foreign colony for sheer human warmth, but on the whole we continued to have more day-to-day contacts with all sorts of Russians, as far as I am aware, than any other non-communist correspondent in the country.

III. Nep: Burlesque on Capitalism

I CAUGHT Moscow in a critical moment of transition. Within less than a year it would have a totally new character. I did not realize it at the time. Only in retrospect the significance of that point in Soviet history became clear to me.

Trotsky was an exile in Alma-Ata, Turkestan, and his name was being expunged from Soviet text-books, records, and history. His more prominent supporters were scattered in concentration camps, prisons and places of exile in Siberia, the Far North or Central Asia. All of them had completed the tragic cycle: from exile through revolution to exile. The remnants of Trotsky's sympathizers in the ranks of the ruling Communist Party were being mopped up with small consideration for fairness and none for sentiment. In my first fortnight in Moscow, I read the letters of a young workman, the brother of an American I.W.W., whisked from his factory bench and hurled into Siberia for expressing regrets over Trotsky's defeat too loudly. I heard stories of idealistic young communists who committed suicide in despair over what they considered the collapse of the revolution, though I could not check the truth of such stories.

"Nep," the New Economic Policy of socialist-capitalist compromise introduced by Lenin in 1921, was in process of "liquidation." Without actually decreeing the end of that period, the Kremlin was effectively choking it to death. Confiscatory "tax arrears" were imposed which automatically wiped out one private enterprise after another. The Nepmen, the private traders of this compromise period, were arrested for real or imaginary infractions of real or imaginary laws and hustled to Siberia or the North. The tolerance under which the more industrious or shrewder peasants expanded their holdings in land, livestock and other property was abruptly reversed.

There were intervals of doubt this year, in which there seemed a possibility that the attack might be restrained. Its wishful-thinking victims believed at moments that the worst was over; but they were dismally wrong. A new epoch had begun: what was in effect a die-hard drive for full socialization.

Had I arrived ten or twelve months later, so rapid was the process, I would have missed the momentous change. As it was, I had a fleeting but unforgettable glimpse of the Russia which the newly entrenched leader, Joseph Stalin, had doomed. Despite the ruthless proofs that their day was over, many of those who had thrived under Nep dosed themselves with deceptive hope. How could the government shut down all private trade, they asked, when it had no economic machinery for the effective distribution of goods ready to take its place? How could it crush the small enterprises and artisan establishments manufacturing everyday necessities for the population when it was unable to manufacture those things itself?

"Nonsense," the proprietor of a private seed shop around the corner from the Grand Hotel argued with me, "they can't do it. Already the *muzhiks* are hiding their grain or refusing to sow more than enough for themselves because they can't get manufactured goods or seed. The Kremlin will not be insane enough to make this situation worse by closing shops like mine and cutting off the supplies provided by handicraft workers."

A few weeks later this same seed merchant, however, came to me in a condition of utter panic. The financial inspectors had piled ruinous retroactive taxes on him, knowing full well that he could not pay them. His career as a trader was ended.

"For God's sake," he pleaded, "let me work for you. Anything —I'll run your errands, or make your stove—anything so I can claim that I am gainfully employed. Maybe I will then be allowed to join a trade union after a while. If not, it's expulsion from my apartment, maybe Siberia."

A few of the more perspicacious foreign observers were aware of the implications of this process of "liquidating Nep." I recall that Paul Scheffer of the *Berliner Tageblatt* was the first to write boldly that Nep was ended, and that Duranty, who was his disciple and wisely so, followed his lead in this regard, though more guardedly as was his way. Most of the others recorded the individual episodes in the process without venturing to make clear-cut deductions. As for the Russians, they were instinctively apprehensive and excited by the tension of impending change. But no one, perhaps not even the responsible leaders in the Kremlin, guessed how quickly and how thoroughly Nep would be swept out, to give way to the slogans and sacrifices and inspired cruelties of the Five Year Plan.

The Tverskaya, Moscow's, and therefore Russia's, "Main Street," of that time, remains in my mind as almost a symbolic representation of the transitional moment. It was, or seems to me in retrospect, a microcosm of the half-socialist, half-capitalist Russia which was expiring. Along its length were private stores, state shops, private restaurants, gypsy cellars, the government-operated gambling Casino, private peddlers, beggars and prostitutes, the offices of state trusts and the headquarters of the leading newspapers.

The street runs from the fringe of Red Square northward to the Triumphal Arch commemorating the Muscovite victory over Napoleon, past the Alexandrovsky station, and on to the city of Tver (from which it takes its name) and beyond that to Leningrad. It is the first street traversed by tourists arriving from the West, since it connects the railroad station with the hotel district. It is the street with which they are likely to become most familiar in the ensuing days, because it holds such standard tourist fare as the Anti-Religious Museum, the Museum of the Revolution, the Lenin Institute, the Moscow Soviet and the new Telegraph Building. The first impressions of Moscow are thus the gift of the Tverskaya.

The blood of Russian history has flowed through this artery as through no other. The pulse of the Tverskaya is the pulse of Russia. On holidays, now as for centuries, it is the most lavishly decorated and illuminated, the most crowded and most sensitive to popular feeling. Until 1917, imperial parades, religious pageants flowed through it; and since then, the floods of singing, cheering humanity under a froth of red banners. It was here, in the palace of the Governor-General that is now the home of the Moscow Soviet, that the Bolshevik staff had its headquarters in the crucial days of November, 1917. It was here, from the corner balcony of the National Hotel, a few blocks farther down, that Leon Trotsky made his last dramatic appearance in Moscow in November ten years later, and was howled down and yanked away by G.P.U. men. The melodrama of Russian history, the colossal ironies of its last great change, seem more sharply reflected on the Tverskaya than elsewhere. The very buildings on both sides of the street, the names and monuments, attest the revolution. Yet they retain a brooding sense of something ageless and unchanging.

On a pedestal opposite the Strasnoi Monastery (now the Anti-Religious Museum) Russia's great national poet, Alexander Pushkin, has stood since 1880, watching the ebb and flow of the Tverskaya's human tides, mulling over the rotation of chronological and political seasons. Nothing can surprise him any longer. Once there were self-important officers with their shoulders squared off by heavy epaulets, uniformed civil servants, ragged peasants; now the officers were no longer epauleted, the civil servants carried brief cases, the peasants were still ragged. Always there were children racing and shrieking their delight around the base of his pedestal; always the lovelorn passed him without recognition, absorbed in one another and quoting his lines without knowing it; always the aged, the beggared, the heartsore. And they must seem to Pushkin the same people, the same loves and despairs that he found on the day he mounted his pedestal.

2

At the time of my arrival I did not quite grasp the meaning of Moscow's "Main Street," where Nep was having its last hysterical fling. The Nep period was an armed truce at best. The resumption of hostilities was inevitable. But the truce had lasted seven years and the nation had come to regard it as more or less permanent.

A new middle class of Nepmen—private merchants, artisans, small-scale manufacturers, professional men, bureaucrats in comfortable berths, more prosperous peasants, the criminal elements which are the excrescence of private initiative—had come into being. Some of them were resuscitated middle-class people of the pre-revolutionary era, others were tasting affluence and the sweets of privilege for the first time.

No more extraordinary class has ever been called into being and blown into oblivion in the memory of humankind. Because it was young, born in chaos and in some measure outside the law, because it was at bottom uncertain of its tenure and therefore desperately eager to make the most of its advantages immediately, it was exceptionally vulgar, profiteering, crude, and noisy. Under capitalism the bourgeoisie has the poise and self-assurance that come with power. It has a culture of its own and an ideology of self-justification. In Nep Russia, for the first time, there was the anomaly of a large bourgeoisie without political power, without culture, without respect for its own class.

It was a class existing by sufferance, despised and insulted by the population and oppressed by the government. It became a curious burlesque on capitalism, self-conscious, shifty, intimidated, and ludicrous. It had money, comforts and other physical advantages, yet remained a pariah element, the butt of popular humor and the target of official discrimination.

And the stamp of this strange middle class was everywhere on Moscow. Its fitting sign, it seemed, was the prostitution that thrived on the sidewalks of the Tverskaya and in front of the leading public baths. Its desperation was mirrored in the Casino, a gambling hell run by the government. Every night until late dawn the Casino was filled with the newly rich, embezzling officials, underworld characters, and foreigners with money to throw away. The Soviet regime took a heavy rake-off on roulette, chemin-de-fer and other games, the G.P.U. marked off its future victims by watching who had more money than he could comfortably explain, and everyone suspected that the games were not quite on the level. But that did not affect attendance.

About one-quarter of the shops in Moscow were still privately conducted and carried the names of their owners. The rapidity with which such personal names retreated before the synthetic official titles was one of the symptoms of the new revolution ushered in by Stalin's era of industrialization. Soon there was not a single private name inscribed on any shop. Ivanovs and Abramoviches gave way to "Mosselproms" and "Mostorgs."

The private shops were higher-priced than their government competitors next door—they had to be to meet the staggering taxes. But they had more and better merchandise, and exerted themselves to please the customers. By contrast the official stores were pitifully poor, crude, and unprofitable. In the production and marketing of articles of general use, the Nep sector of the nation's economy clearly had the edge on the government, despite official discrimination, punitive impositions, and frank persecution.

For the first time in history, individual and government industry were pitted against one another throughout a great nation, their wares displayed in adjoining stalls, as it were, in open and ruthless competition. "Unfair" and "unethical" are mild bourgeois words for the competitive methods used by the state, but it was being badly worsted notwithstanding—so badly worsted that it inevitably invoked its sovereign right to exterminate its competitors altogether.

But meantime, as a matter of common convenience, we met in private cafés and ice-cream parlors. We ate in private restaurants, of which there were a dozen along Tverskaya. We shopped in private stores, called in private physicians and used the services of private photographers, dentists, and other professional people. Everyone else, from commissars down, did likewise. By the end of the year most of this private traffic was ended.

Since we could not afford to eat in the hotel—except for the extravagance of an occasional breakfast—Billy learned to cook on a single-heater electric stove, despite regular warnings from the hotel management that it was strictly prohibited. She accepted the hardships smilingly. Considering her theatrical background and Broadway tastes, I had feared Billy would find Moscow intolerable. But she proved more resilient than I did. With only a few words of "kitchen Russian" at her disposal, she bargained with the peasants on Hunters' Row, returning to the hotel triumphantly with chicken, vegetables, meat, dairy products and fruit in tow. There were still numerous markets where such foodstuffs, not to mention clothes and the products of home industry, could be bought at prices which seemed to us steep, but in a few months were to seem, in retrospect, incredibly cheap. Later we were to hear Russians sigh over "the good old days," referring to the Nep days rather than the tsarist times. Having tasted a little of the vanishing plenitude in the twilight hours of Nep, we could understand their nostalgia. Private kiosks sold candy, flowers, sausages. Sidewalk hucksters offered home-made brassières, toothpicks, wooden toys, aprons, frozen apples.

The figure of one of these hucksters, around the corner from our hotel, sticks in my mind: a sad-eyed fellow who announced the wares on his improvised push-cart and their prices in the sing-song of synagogue chants, more engrossed in the sacred melodies than the profane words.

A number of narrow shops, mere crevices between buildings, specialized in domestic and imported sausage for which the Russians have an inordinate fondness. The succulent garlicky aromas were more effective advertising than the most spacious show window would have been. One of these crevices, by some accident, survived for years after all other private trade was extinct. There is in Russia always at least one startling exception to prove even the most rigid rule, as though tolerated for purposes of dramatic contrast, or by way of museum exhibit.

3

Our chief personal problem, as that of every other permanent resident, was housing. A city with accommodations, at most, for a million, already had a population of over three million. Tens of thousands more poured into Moscow every day: clerks in the unwieldy bureaucratic apparatus, peasants anxious to become proletarians, youth seeking an education or a new start. Flats that formerly housed one family now contained half a dozen, with an overflow of "house workers" (servants) sleeping on boxes in the corridor, on the kitchen floor, on the common oven.

On most apartment doors there was a card listing the inmates, with complicated instructions for ringing:

Alexandrov	ring 1
Stepanov	ring 2
Lazarovsky	ring 2 short, 1 long
Kagan	ring 4 short, 3 long; etc.

At the first stir of the bell people in their crowded cubicles automatically paused in their work or play, quarrels or love-making, to count the rings. Little things in a new environment have a way of impressing themselves on the newcomer's mind out of proportion to their importance. A curious awareness of the intimate life of Moscow being suspended for a moment over and over again

—like a motion picture that suddenly stops moving—became part of my private sense of the Soviet capital.

No one who has not lived through a space shortage in a great city can imagine the terrors of the situation. It cannot be apprehended at second-hand. People married and divorced, lied and denounced their neighbors, for a little space. The law courts were jammed with cases growing out of disputes over living quarters.

In the midst of this hideous overcrowding, however, many privileged officials, police officers, and particularly Nepmen had managed to acquire the luxury of entire apartments of two or more rooms. Space was the measure of affluence, as a bank balance might be in America. Many Nepmen who had read the handwriting on the wall were at the moment trying to dispose profitably of their apartments and were especially anxious to lay their hands on foreign currency. In the following years we blamed ourselves for stupidity in not snatching up such a bargain. But the prices seemed exorbitant to us, fresh as we were from New York. We felt certain that the housing situation would improve—it would have been disloyal to think otherwise—and that such an expenditure, even if we could borrow the money, was inadvisable. One such apartment remained as a glamorous memory to taunt us: half of an eight-room lay-out, with a tiled bathroom and other alluring conveniences, which was offered to us for a mere three thousand dollars down and a rental thereafter.

Had we accepted it, we would have missed the nightmare years on Chistiye Prudy (Clean Ponds) Boulevard, as occupants of one half of a former stable. We paid fifteen hundred dollars for the privilege of entering the place, the United Press having come to our rescue with a loan deducted from my wages. Further payments agreed upon, fortunately, went by default, because the Nepman who had remodeled the stable was sent to a concentration camp in the nick of time.

The other half of the glorified stable was occupied by a Soviet bookkeeper, his fat and slovenly wife and a brood of snot-nosed children. We shared a kitchen and an improvised bathroom between us, and a corridor in which their servant girl slept on boxes. Our servant girl slept more comfortably in the parlor. Human labor was the only commodity cheap and plentiful in Moscow, so that even an underpaid bookkeeper could afford a servant; indeed, every family needed an extra person to stand in lines and to explore distant markets in the perpetual search for food.

Our share consisted of three narrow rooms, the abnormally high ceilings turning them even narrower and giving them an exotic look. We carpeted the floor and disguised the stable with the camouflage of wall hangings, pictures, maps, lamps, until it took on the character of a queer but colorful bohemianism.

Our chief afflictions on Chistiye Prudy Boulevard were moist walls and unpleasant neighbors. The house was without a foundation, and as the winter thawed into spring, the walls began to sweat. Great leprous patches along the floor line and on the ceiling spread slowly but surely. Consultation with engineers hatched the device of a secondary set of walls of building board, with a few inches of air between. When the board was found and the inner shell built, with much tribulation and expense, and all of it painted jet black, our apartment looked quite "Greenwich Villagey." The wetness was for the most part foiled, though it made repeated and sometimes successful forays.

The neighbors, however, could not be foiled. Although their half was exactly the same size and shape as ours, they lacked our skill in camouflage. Their rooms were crowded, filthy, and emanated obnoxious odors. We painted our doorways and thresholds with chemicals intended to bar the vermin that luxuriated unnoticed and uncontrolled on their side. Often enough I was tempted to administer the chemical to Sashka, whose continuous whining—a peculiar off-key soprano with tremolos, trills, quavers and consecutive fifths—embittered my existence. The entire family took a reactionary view of the machine age and refused adamantly to use a toilet bowl as modern science intended, preferring to squat on it in traditional Asiatic fashion. The bathtub we had finally found and installed seemed to them the most natural place for the disposal of garbage.

Because our half of the stable was colorful and perversely clean, we became in the eyes of our neighbors horrible exemplars of the capitalism which they actually envied and therefore thought that they hated. The two "apartments" branching off from a common corridor did, indeed, provide a symbolic model of two worlds. On one side, cleanliness and relative comfort; on the other, dirt, noise and poverty at ease in its own offal.

The entrance to the place was through a common yard, around which several score other families lived in verminous ant-heaps. Though we deliberately tried to dress Genie in clothes bought in Moscow, so that she might be less conspicuous among the other children, her neatness and foreign manner set her apart. She learned to speak Russian almost immediately and played with the Russian children, but she remained an *Amerikanka* and a *boorzhooika* in their young ideological eyes. Our better food, our American clothes, our well-dressed visitors, the fact that we possessed a telephone and a gramophone, made us conspicuous. We were closely observed and openly envied. Under the surface politeness, there was a resentment of our advantages which we could understand and forgive.

As in all Moscow courtyards, the iron gates were closed in the evening. By midnight the *dvornik,* or concierge, a limping, bearded old man straight out of Chekhov, was invariably drunk and dead to the world. No amount of ringing could arouse him. Billy and I learned to scale the gate, though it was fifteen feet high, and in time were so adept at this exercise that we no longer ripped our clothes on the spikes. We always felt like thieves in the night while clambering over the grilled barrier and expected to be arrested for house-breaking. Once a militiaman did question the procedure and only our lack of Russian saved us from a trip to the police station.

Casual visitors at our Chistiye Prudy palace could not guess at the moisture, the persecution by envious neighbors, and a thousand other discomforts. They exclaimed over the charm of the "artistic" black walls and the knick-knacks with which we sought to make the place tolerable as a permanent abode. A near-communist from New York, in the exaltation of her tourist sojourn in the communist Mecca, found our quarters distressingly "bourgeois." Evidently, she had counted on me to demonstrate the sincerity of my radicalism by wearing a Russian blouse and giving right of way to the neighbor's bedbugs. Returning to her spacious and elegantly furnished apartment on Madison Avenue, she reported to mutual friends that Gene Lyons was living in Moscow like a *bourzhooy*.

It was the beginning of a legend in New York revolutionary

circles—the legend that I had suddenly and inexplicably gone capitalist.

Moscow abounds with Americans who demonstrate the ardor of their faith by wearing Russian shirts, shaving their heads, defiling their vocabulary, and snubbing everyone who fails in these externals of the ritual. Long after the Russian communists had stuck their shirt-tails into their trousers and blossomed out in gaudy neckties, these outsiders persevered in their romantic nonsense.

There was the heart-rending plight of a young lady who struggled bravely to survive on a Soviet ruble salary. She dressed and lived like a Soviet worker, would not supplement her rations with foreign-currency purchases and hinted darkly at the sacrifices she was making for the cause. Her father was a Mid-Western millionaire.

Another couple, man and wife, likewise kept themselves to the discipline of living like Russians. They disdained the bourgeois comforts of the better hotels and the solace of dollar-shop food supplies, boarding instead with Soviet citizens and keeping within a modest budget no larger than a well-paid Russian's income. Only the fact that everyone knew them to be wealthy as well as socially prominent in America spoiled the sympathy which they merited.

A former American concessionaire had lived in Russia for many years in ample style. He professed to be a communist at heart. The discrepancy between his manner of living and his professions bothered him and in the end he decided upon reform. He would live like a Russian! He therefore summoned his servant, that is to say, house worker, and announced the new regime. The house worker was a hunch-backed old woman.

"The old life is over," he told her. "Hereafter we will live like Russians. We will not buy in the foreign shops any more. Beginning tomorrow you will buy in the markets and *you will stand in line like other house workers.*"

Unluckily, I lacked the talents for these surface conformities. When I wore a *rubashka* it was for the un-ideological reason that it seemed more comfortable at the moment. When I shaved my head it was in the un-Marxian hope of arresting baldness. We did not conceal the fact that an American wage and the privileges extended to foreign correspondents made existence easier for us.

Neither did we scruple to be seen in public in the company of other foreigners or to dance occasionally at the Grand Hotel.

These were serious and costly errors of judgment. Not that Russians objected. On the contrary, they were often offended by foreigners who "dressed down" to them. They ridiculed the mock-revolutionism of certain foreigners. But every detail of my bourgeois indulgences, from the hangings on the wallboard to the fox-trots in the hotel, were duly reported to my friends in New York, with fine embellishments. And thus they knew that I was on the highroad to capitalist perdition.

IV. Hallelujah!

IF LOVE is blind, faith is both deaf and blind. These blessed imperfections of deeply rooted belief, which are also its strength, help explain the perennial mystery about Russia.

That mystery is why two foreigners, equally honest and intelligent, having passed through the same routine of sight-seeing and interviews, emerge with diametrically opposite impressions of the Soviet land. What is to one a "gray, unsmiling population" is for the other the inspiring spectacle of a "grimly determined population." One speaks of "magnificent industrial discipline," the other of "factory serfs." One declaims about the tyranny of fashion having ended—"an uninhibited, unpretentious and truly democratic attitude towards clothes," as the new U.P. correspondent put it early in 1928. The other dismisses this achievement of the revolution in some such phrase as "ragged, pathetically patched people."

The contrast goes much farther than different interpretations of the same physical facts. The facts themselves sometimes fade from the mental retina of the faithful, or by the same token, are vastly enlarged in the mind of the unbeliever.

It is no special perspicacity that enabled me to recognize and forgive blind spots as large as all of Russia in the anxious tourists who came to me, as to all other permanent residents, with letters of introduction. It merely happens that my inner experience compassed almost the whole range of reactions between a purblind enthusiasm that shouted down its doubts and an aching disillusionment that sometimes did less than justice to the Bolsheviks.

I have watched an American communist leader in the Soviet Union, a young man of genuinely idealistic instincts, wash out all disturbing sights and sounds with vodka, filling the interstices of sobriety with erotic excitements, so that he might bring back his faith to New York intact. I saw a soft-hearted Seattle clergyman take to bed to avoid seeing too much that hurt him. His daughter, who writes many books about the glories of the new Russia, cautioned me to say nothing to the old man that might distress him, and I agreed to the conspiracy. Another clerical gentleman sat in my office bewailing the fact that the age-old motives of greed and self-seeking were still rampant in Russia. Indeed, I consoled him with the hope that young people at least were developing new, more socially-minded goads to action. He left Russia to compose, in all sincerity I am sure, a book to prove that brand-new motivations guided conduct under the Soviets.

Such crude self-deceptions, however, are the exception rather than the rule. Faith needs little conscious assistance. It brews its own deceptions far below the surface.

I recall a scene in the hotel room of another correspondent. A well-known British journalist, Ashmead Bartlett, was attacking everything Soviet in bitterly sarcastic detail. A half-hearted and unconvincing defense was being put up by a Soviet functionary, Sergei Trivas. Trivas himself felt constrained to admit certain facts which shocked my sensibilities. I listened in mounting anger, then turned furiously on them both. They were maligning the revolution! Nobody here was lining his own pockets as in England or America! In the face of the greatest event in all human history they were bickering about mistakes in policy. And to think of a Soviet official admitting such libels on the revolution! Trivas quickly retreated and left the field of battle to Anglo-American journalism. The dispute became more heated and finally was halted on the sheer brink of a fist fight.

Yet Bartlett, Trivas, and the others in the room had only taken for granted commonplaces evident to the naked eye and the naked intelligence—facts which I too was to accept as a matter of course a few months later. (That clash with Bartlett, incidentally, was duly reported to the G.P.U. and raised my stock considerably in those mysterious quarters, I was to learn later.)

I needed no help in retouching everything I saw to match my expectations. No one who has not been close to the revolutionary movement in his own country can quite understand the palpitant anxiety with which a foreign radical approaches the realities of an established and functioning proletarian regime. Or the exaltation with which he finally confronts the signs and symbols of that regime. It is a species of self-fulfillment, a thrilling identification with Power. Phrases and pictures and colors, tunes and turns of thought connected in my mind with years of ardent desire and even a measure of sacrifice were now in evidence all around in the places of honor, dominance, unlimited power!

A strong sympathizer with the communist point of view, arriving in Russia, is in a curiously hectic state psychologically and emotionally. A member of a small and maligned sect, he finds himself magically in a place where his sect holds complete sway. All his life, perhaps, the massive head of Karl Marx was associated in his consciousness with a fervent mission. Now he finds that symbol in every office, every railroad station, on postage stamps, in ten thousand store windows, on pedestals in the public squares! The word "comrade" was the password of a small and ridiculed minority. Suddenly it is a title of nobility and a talisman of power! The revolutionary jargon, until yesterday known only to a few initiates, today is the official and dominant tongue over a sixth part of the globe's surface. The brawny, flame-eyed proletarians of the revolutionary posters, once symbols of revolt, are suddenly become symbols of dominion!

Consider the emotional force of the song *International* for such a visitor. At home it was played and sung, perhaps, in secret. At best it was surrounded with an aura of social rebellion, dangers of arrest, economic hazard, the risk of deportation. Suddenly that song is blared forth mightily by a dozen combined military bands on Red Square, its pulse is carried to millions of workers deployed in the streets of Moscow, challenging and threatening and exulting. Diplomats representing the whole world meekly bare their heads in token of respect to its rhythm. It is no longer a marching song, but a triumphal hymn, backed up by a government and armies and air forces and secret police.

Small wonder that this visitor is in no condition to grasp or hold lowly facts. His world is in the soaring clouds. Whether it will take him a year or ten years to descend again to earth depends on his own make-up. It is presumptuous to expect foreign communists to see the Soviet social landscape except through the prism of their own feelings and convictions. Their minds become finely adjusted instruments for selecting impressions in harmony with their exalted state. The validity of their life's work, their sufferings, and their sacrifices is at stake. Who can estimate the pain and frustration that have gone into those books of communists who came to their Russian utopias and found them unacceptable! Their minds and hearts are a shambles of bleeding illusions, and the insults from their former comrades are salt on their open wounds. Such men and women are scarcely to be blamed if they shrink from the realities and seek sanctuary in desperate rationalizations.

It was through an emotional haze that I viewed the new Bolshevik world around me. My early dispatches out of Moscow were laudatory, though toned down to conceal my bias. Each of them sheathed a poison dart aimed at the heart of the capitalist system. Every fact which might be misunderstood by a world of infidels was carefully explained and turned by implication into one more proof of revolutionary wisdom or courage.

I often read the messages of my colleagues in comparing notes on how we covered some event or decree. Junius Wood of the Chicago *Daily News* had a talent for piling up indisputable detail which somehow added up to ridicule. Duranty juggled his phrases, and even in his ostensible eulogies left a fuzzy margin of uncertainty. Edward Deuss of the International News Service wrote with a bread-and-butter realism that ignored the "deeper meanings" of the revolution. William Henry Chamberlin of the *Christian Science Monitor* was always exact and scholarly and passionless.

But all of them seemed to me so exasperatingly calm and composed in the midst of high historical drama. I resented their boredom. I was continuously astonished how many unsavory stories they found right in the Soviet newspapers which somehow escaped my attention.

My dispatches in these months, as I say, were consistently and ardently partisan. It was a fight to the death between capitalist and socialist elements, in which those in the capitalist trenches deserved and received no quarter from my typewriter.

The necessity to report individual episodes under the limitations of cable economy was a distressing factor. Excerpted from their context of larger purposes, the isolated news events—the slaughter of grain collectors here, the execution of alleged kulaks elsewhere, the arrest of a few hundred more "speculators"—seemed too harsh. I envied the special correspondents of individual newspapers who could cable lengthy explanations. But I deluged my editors with "think pieces" interpreting these events, every interpretation an undisguised justification echoing the official press. Mine was the satisfaction of being at once on the side of the authorities and on the side of the righteous. It is a comfortable and heart-warming position that encourages observers anywhere to give those in power the benefit of every doubt.

2

That first winter was an exceptionally bitter one, even by Moscow weather standards. Waiting on queues for bread and other necessities was that much more agonizing. Everywhere these ragged lines, chiefly of women, stretched from shop doors, under clouds of visible breath; patient, bovine, scarcely grumbling. Private trade channels were being rapidly shut off, before the government was able to replace them with official channels. Manufactured goods of the type that flowed from artisan families fell to a dribble and soon dried up entirely. New pressures were being applied to the more industrious, more unscrupulous, and more prosperous peasants, and the flow of meat, fowl and other foodstuffs from the surrounding countryside slowed down perceptibly with every passing day.

The authorities did not hide their deep concern over the hostility of peasants to the official plans for "collecting" grain—that is, for purchasing it at government prices, regarded by the villages as outright confiscation. The disparity between the prices of farm products and manufactured goods, the so-called "scissors," had long been a deterrent to peasant production. If they could not exchange their rubles for boots, matches, salt, textiles, kerosene, the peasants had small incentive to grow more grain than they needed for themselves and their animals. As the capitalistic outlets were blocked and compulsion increasingly used to extract grain from the growers at official prices, the peasants simply restricted sowings and concealed the size of their crops.

Bread, which constitutes the larger half of the ordinary Russian's diet, became a "deficit product." This, in turn, obliged the desperate authorities to exercise more force on the peasants. The vicious circle was a tightening noose around the government's throat.

The outside world had accepted Stalin's victory over Trotsky as marking a swing to the Right. It was Trotsky who had warned against the emergence of a new capitalist class in the villages and demanded that the extra-legal repressions used against Nepmen, the urban bourgeoisie, be extended to richer, so-called kulak elements in the country; he who had demanded a speedy, planned industrialization of the country. The world was wrong. No sooner had the success of the Stalin machine—what Trotsky called the "dictatorship of the secretariat"—been completed, than the Kremlin stole Trotsky's thunder by turning on the kulaks.

Russians were as surprised by this turn of affairs as the outside world. Having been happily freed of the bugaboo, Trotsky, they were confronted with much worse: his policies being put into effect by a more centralized and more ruthless dictatorship under Stalin.

The most astonished and chagrined of all in this about-face were those Bolshevik leaders who were not content to be rid of Trotsky, but honestly opposed his Leftist notions. Men like Alexis Rykov, the head of the government, and Mikhail Tomsky,* the head of the trade unions, and Nikolai Bukharin,† the outstanding theorist in the Party line-up, suddenly found their leader, Stalin, in some of the very political positions from which Trotsky had been forcibly ejected. In a sense they remained true Stalinists when Stalin himself veered suddenly to the Left. In remaining faithful to Stalin's earlier views, they were to become, by the end of 1928, a new anti-Stalin faction, the so-called Right Opposition.

When the Kremlin carried its new socialist offensive into the villages, the peasantry fought back with the only weapon at its disposal. It refused to feed the pampered cities and armies. In 1919-21 its tactics of non-coöperation had forced Lenin to abandon military communism in favor of the New Economic Policy. These tactics were now revived, and the country, in the midst of its growing food shortage, watched uneasily the gigantic tussle between an organized state and some hundred million of its citizens. Government grain collections (the pretense of voluntary sales to the official collectors was belied by the very use of this

* Committed suicide in August, 1936.

† Arrested in 1937.

word) fell off alarmingly. The exportable surplus disappeared—the name "Bread Export Trust" on a building across the street from the Grand Hotel became the target of half-illicit political gibes. And the bread lines grew longer, drearier, more sullen throughout the land.

The government retaliated with a series of what it called euphemistically "extraordinary measures." They amounted to confiscation of grain supplies in many instances reminiscent of the methods of military communism. Red troops were sent into the more intractable villages to halt leakage of grain through private channels. Bread "bazaars" that had operated legally in the towns were closed down. The state's agents were instructed to meet their quotas of grain collections by any means, and dozens of them paid with their lives for the attempt.

The political legend then started and since raised to the dignity of official history is of a peasantry divided, with the government championing the poor peasants against their exploiting kulak neighbors. The simple fact is that the countryside, except for an inconsequential group of *batraks*, or landless peasants, was a solid phalanx in opposing the government. Under Nep, for the first time almost in Russian history, the vast majority acquired land that it could call its own and had not the slightest inclination to relinquish it.

For some time the press veiled the intensity of the conflict with generalizations about "kulak resistance" and the need for "Bolshevik vigilance." Moscow buzzed with rumors of localized rebellion in the Kuban, Ukraine, and other sections; of workers goaded by food shortage into striking—and strikes under Soviet conditions are equivalent to rebellion. When the press was permitted to speak more openly, many of the rumors appeared to be true. From all sections of the country came reports of local communists, visiting grain agents, and tax collectors assaulted and murdered. One official estimate, I recall, placed the murdered communists at more than five hundred. Batches of kulaks and "kulak agents" were summarily executed for counter-revolution.

Though few of us realized it, we were witness to the opening battle in a war that, with brief armistices, was to culminate in the famine of 1932-33.

That Stalin and his advisers took an earnest view of the dangerous conflict may be surmised from the fact that by July the Kremlin formally admitted that its extra-legal methods had been a serious "error." It pledged solemnly that the error would not be repeated. Outwardly, peasant non-coöperation seemed to have scored another victory—the last in its tragic history. For a few months it looked as if Right sentiment might prevail, after all.

This agrarian struggle provided the melancholy background for everything else that transpired in the country. It was the dismal setting for the first sensational sabotage trial which began in May, for the relentless campaign against critics of Stalin in the ranks of the Party, for the intensified persecution of Nepmen. The kulak opposition, dramatized in assassinations on one side and mass executions on the other, provided a plausible popular explanation for bread and other food shortage. The bugaboo of industrial sabotage was its counterpart in explaining shortage of manufactured goods. In both instances the struggle was reported in terms of bloody warfare and with small regard for facts. Every official news item was a communique from the war fronts and its purpose was to maintain fighting morale.

I had certainly reached the new Russia at a critical stage in its career.

3

Spring turned the snows to mud and stripped housefronts, cobblestones and cluttered back-yards of their merciful winter swathings to reveal the drabness underneath. The miniature sleighs disappeared overnight to be replaced by decrepit, knock-kneed droshkies. Days grew longer and nights more limpid. Shawls gave way to red and white flowered handkerchiefs; misshapen padded coats and sheepskins were shed for less grotesque if no less patched garments. The girls outside the "family baths" and on the Tverskaya smoked their cigarettes and paced their beats less morosely. On clear evenings the strains of accordions floated over the boulevards and couples promenaded slowly, silently, hands interlaced in front of them and heads touching.

As May Day approached, innumerable pictures and busts of Stalin, Lenin, Karl Marx, Voroshilov and other leaders, living and dead, suddenly filled the shop windows; gigantic wood and cardboard representations of workers, peasants, and soldiers and models of machines and factories blossomed at the main intersections. Creepers of red bunting proliferated across the houses, inscribed with boasts and threats and promises.

American tourists, the first swallows as harbingers of the holiday season, alighted in the hotel lobbies, twittering excitedly of crèches and museums and factories. They called one another and every Russian in their vicinity "comrade" with such deep childlike relish and looked at everything around them with the hypnotized eyes of lovers. Though the *International* was in their souls, they listened to the Grand Hotel band play *Hallelujah* raucously and interminably.

This American jazz song for some unaccountable reason captured and held the Russian fancy for years after it had been forgotten in America; it was literally inescapable, being played earnestly for entertainment and ironically as symbol of bourgeois decadence.

In 1928 the American tourists were almost entirely Russian Jews returning for a glimpse of their native land and communists on pilgrimage to Mecca. The more lucrative invasion by the middle classes and the rich did not get well started until two years later, when the depression made them more susceptible to Soviet preachings. But already there were anxiously heretical professors, atheists in search of a religion, old maids in search of revolutionary compensations, radicals in search of reënforcement for a wavering faith: the types that were to grow so boringly familiar to me in the next years.

The last evenings of April the skies over Moscow were incarnadined with the reflection of thousands of red lights illuminating streets and show-windows, framing huge portraits of the leaders, spelling out defiance of Austen Chamberlain and other enemies. Extra food supplies had been concentrated in the coöperative stores. The press was loud with optimism. Radio horns blared martial music on the public squares. The streets echoed to the tread of throngs in a holiday mood—a mood expertly evoked by all the tricks of ballyhoo and patriotism. Billy and I mixed in the crowds and beat time mentally to the marching songs.

Earlier that month we had made a round of the churches on Easter Eve. We had seen the believers march, chanting, behind bearded long-haired priests in their magnificent vestments, behind acolytes in shimmering white; each of them shielded a lighted taper against the wind. We had watched them intoning fervently "Christ is risen!" and kissing their neighbors. They were not molested, but everywhere there were knots of unfriendly, sneering onlookers. By contrast with May Day Eve, the Easter ceremonies were pallid. Insofar as the Orthodox faith was a pageant, it could not long compete against the official pageantry.

On May Day, the tourists were deployed on both sides of Lenin's tomb. They thrilled to the massive display of military strength, the rumbling tanks, the armored cars, the machineguns and searchlights, the airplanes buzzing overhead. They cheered the horsemen galloping across the square in mass formations at a furious pace, shouting hurrahs that plucked echoes from the clouds, the horses' hooves striking sparks from the cobblestones. Then they saw the armed workers, the Red Cross divisions, and the hours-long flood of humanity under banners and floats, cheering and singing and cheering again. Stalin and his principal lieutenants stood on the wooden ramparts of the Lenin Mausoleum, smiling, saluting, chatting. The slogans and floats this May Day attacked Austen Chamberlain, kulaks and saboteurs—the enemies abroad and the enemies at home.

There was little in this standardized scene to give strangers an inkling of the volcanic forces under the surface, and of the impending struggles. If there were hints of the strained situation in agriculture and industry, outsiders were neither equipped nor in a state of mind to read them. The tourists and labor delegations returned home to spill their superlatives in newspaper interviews or at dinner tables, smugly ignorant of what was going on behind the scenes of the greatest show on earth.

I was caught up by the sweep and magnitude of May Day—of revolutionary Moscow in its holiday character, loud, brightly lit, defiant, in military formation. Immense quadrangles of Red soldiers taking the oath of fealty. The Kremlin cannon firing salutes. Hurrahs that rolled through Red Square like waves. Above all, the masses marching across the enclosed space, their eyes and minds fixed on Stalin. Newsreels have made this scene familiar to the whole world, but they can only echo faintly the thunder of released emotion that shakes a sympathetic newcomer plunged into the scene for the first time.

Not until the Nazis in Germany took over the mass demonstration technique and carried it even further was there anything in the world to compare with Soviet parades. They have been mistakenly described as exhibitions of loyalty and popular enthusiasm, as though they were merely like conventional parades in other countries, but on an immensely larger scale. Nothing can be farther from the truth.

These Soviet parades are rather demonstrations of the government's organized and disciplined strength. I saw New York go wild with fervor in welcoming the armistice, and then in welcoming Lindbergh home after his flight to Paris. Those were great tides of emotion, unorganized and unrestrained, dissipating their strength as they pounded against the city's skyscrapers. What makes a Moscow demonstration more imposing and more ominous by contrast is its complete organization: the tides are on leash and the leash is in the grip of a small group on Red Square. A million roaring men and women uncontrolled is one thing. The same million in battalions under banners, meekly waiting their turn for hours for the privilege and duty of crossing one square, passing one spot, glimpsing one leader—that is quite another thing.

Moscow demonstrations are infinitely more than parades—and a good deal less. They are reviews of fighting forces, a counting of heads. The slogans are in no sense a spontaneous expression of public opinion. They have been carefully selected and announced by the ruling group in formal edicts. Not simply the subject matter, but the precise wording has been officially prescribed. The synthetic enthusiasms and hatreds have been meticulously apportioned among the objects of approval or abomination at home and abroad. Whether the inscription on a strip of bunting means anything to the men who hold it aloft is never certain, since they did not themselves choose it. The only certainty is that they are sufficiently disciplined to hold it aloft.

Journalists who find a reflection of popular attitudes in banners and red bunting and cardboard insults to the Kremlin's enemies are either fooling themselves or their readers. What they see reflects only the attitudes of the governing minority. How far the prescribed emotions correspond with the real emotions of the marching masses—and whether it makes any difference as long as they do march—it is for every observer to calculate as best he can.

In my first parade, of course, I did not raise such quibbles. As far as I was concerned every slogan came straight from the hearts of those who carried it across Red Square before Stalin's reviewing stand. Around me in the section immediately to the right of the Lenin Mausoleum were the foreign diplomats and newspapermen. But I felt myself a stranger among them. I belonged with the radical delegations in other and more crowded sections and in my heart echoed their every hallelujah.

V. Censorship

MY WORKING day began usually with the reading of the morning papers, which in this topsy-turvy land appear in the morning.

The Soviet press is officially owned and more rigidly controlled than any other of the state properties. It is frankly and proudly a kept press—kept by the government, the Communist Party, the trade-unions, which are but different names for the same centralized power. The very memory of an "independent" newspaper, in serious disagreement with the government, has faded out.

Every sentence in every paper has been censored. Not merely what it actually says but the inflections and overtones of its dreaded voice are political weather-vanes to the initiate. Its very silences are portentous. An editorial is the equivalent of an official pronunciamento. The faint hint of a new attitude toward some sector of the population in a random article may foreshadow destiny for millions. The kind of news published, the stress placed on an occurrence, the failure to mention certain events at home or abroad, all have an importance they do not possess where the press is relatively free.

The whole ethical baggage of journalism in democratic countries has been thrown overboard by the Bolsheviks. No claim is made for "unbiased" or "objective" reporting. No pretense is made of newspaper independence and no reference is ever made to the freedom or dignity of the Fourth Estate. All this baggage, in fact, the communists regard as a piece of bourgeois hypocrisy. The press is not primarily a conveyor of news at all. It is first of all an agency of the Soviet regime in accomplishing its political and economic objectives. Its full force is always focused upon the achievement of specific practical results.

In the editorial offices on the top floor of the slate-gray five-story *Izvestia* building, a prominent Russian newspaperman was explaining this to me one evening.

"But how about truth and facts?" I prodded him. "Here am I, a stranger in your midst. What you print is my chief source of information. Can I believe it?"

"If it's printed, it's truth for us. We don't know and don't care about bourgeois notions of facts. We Soviet journalists are not just reporters. We don't boast of standing above the turmoil like recording angels. On the contrary, we are in the thick of the fight, pioneers in the job of changing our country. If certain information retards this work, we would be crazy to print it. As far as we are concerned, it is then neither news nor truth. It becomes plain counter-revolution."

"Well," I smiled, "maybe that explains the first political anecdote I heard in your country. I understand that it's your oldest and best-known popular Soviet joke. I refer—"

He laughed.

"I know, I know. There is no truth in the *News* (*Izvestia*) and no news in the *Truth* (*Pravda*)."

The surface of the Soviet press is painfully drab and monotonous. When news and views are prescribed from a central source there is small margin for originality of style or content. The stilted repetitious language of the Party "theses" prevails throughout, since safety for the news writer and commentator lies in conformity. Originality, even as to the phrasing of a thought, is dangerously on the borderline of heresy. Why risk a startling metaphor or an individual turn of thought when the orthodox formulation of every current theme, from the campaign to raise more potatoes to the drive to liquidate a million kulak families, is at hand?

But once you learn to break through the dull surface, the press becomes a mine of surprises and excitements. In some casual phrase you may discover a clew to a puzzling chain of events. A minor item out of Kuban or Georgia or Turkestan may prove a peep-hole through which a whole region and its struggles are visible. The tone of an editorial comment or the fact that someone's name is mentioned again after a long silence, the routine announcement of the removal of one official or the appointment of another, imply, for those who know the code, thrilling news affecting the lives of the entire population.

The perusal of the day's sheaf of newspapers and the analysis of the news grist that it yields were therefore a challenge to my intuition about news and a constant test of my comprehension of the Soviet scene. My first duty to my job, I soon realized, was to learn to decipher the newspapers, to recognize the solid facts behind official euphemisms, the accent of an article as something distinct from its ostensible contents.

In the first months I was almost wholly dependent upon my interpreter and secretary, the phlegmatic Miss Jmudskaya. But gradually I learned to read Russian and, more important, to read between the lines. The press in a dictated country, whatever the high professions of the dictators, is a thick curtain to obscure the facts, but it always has fissures and accidental peep-holes for the practiced reader. The Russian people themselves had become sensitive to the overtones of their press. They fed their hopes and their fears on published hints and innuendoes, discounting the surface of statistics and formulas.

The foreign correspondent of the legend is a virile swashbuckling fellow who obtains sensational news by the exercise of daring and dexterity in the whispering galleries of diplomacy, occasionally in scented boudoirs, and always at great risk to his neck. That glamorous legend sheds its rays even on the humblest in my trade. The unromantic fact, however, is that the average correspondent cribs three-quarters of his news from the local newspapers. The fourth quarter he draws from official handouts, the mendacities of paid tipsters, and his own fertile imagination.

It is his skill in recognizing the significant item or his deftness in making it sound significant to a distant audience that chiefly distinguishes the superior foreign reporter from his plodding uninspired colleagues. There may be correspondents who wind up their particular capitals before going to bed to keep them running and who tell premiers where they get off, but I have yet to meet them outside of novels. Those whom I have met and watched at work are much too busy deciphering papers and chasing hot tips and doing other low-down chores to spare the time and energy to run the local governments.

Any attempt to throw an aura of romance around the correspondents for press agencies (as distinguished from those representing individual newspapers) is especially thankless. To fictioneers seeking a foreign correspondent for the role of hero, I recommend earnestly that they avoid the press agency man like the plague. The poor fellow is much too hard-worked and under too heavy a nervous strain for heroic nonsense. He is eternally racing against the clock; every split second counts heavily in the relentless competition among the news wholesalers. The special writer, being a retailer, gathers his facts and weaves them quietly into a connected story; he may even add a little fancy embroidery of his own guess-work. But the agency man can hold no scrap of information for later use. It must be flashed forthwith. The scraps are assembled hastily by the home editor and the finished story reflects neither the sender's thought nor manner.

2

I can testify that the press agency correspondent is the slavey of the profession, perpetually tethered to the sending end of the cable, fighting against time. In the sense that I never dared to be out of touch with my home, which was also my office, I worked twenty-fours hours a day. There was no "deadline" after which I could relax—every minute is the deadline for a United Press client somewhere on the globe. I filed news directly to New York, London, Berlin and Tokyo each of which in turn distributed it to its area of operation.

A thousand times in these years I abandoned an opera or a party or a poker game, always at the most exciting point, of course, in response to a summons from the Foreign Office Press Department. I found a dozen other correspondents similarly torn away from their various sacred or profane activities. After long waiting we were rewarded, as likely as not, with a dull communiqué about President Kalinin's reception to the new Afghan plenipotentiary, the lack of progress in Kamchatka fishery negotiations, or some other item unlikely to excite my readers.

Merely by way of filling the cup of our travail to overflowing the communiqués were often issued to us at the home of one or another of the censors, rather than at the Foreign Office. Under Moscow housing conditions these functionaries were scarcely at fault if they lived in distant and inaccessible corners of the city. But it meant that the representatives of the press of the entire civilized world must leave bar or bed to foregather in an outlying part of the capital in the tiny flat of a censor for the boon of a mimeographed, half-legible document that sometimes made history but most times did not even make sense.

One such scene remains etched on my memory. The whole world was waiting anxiously for an expression of Soviet sentiment on a matter of foreign affairs of major international import. For days we had begged and clamored for it in vain. Finally it came through, in the form of an *Izvestia* editorial. In consideration of its critical significance, the editorial was made available to us the night before it reached the news-stands. Hundreds of millions of readers in a score of nations, perusing the solemn dispatches soon thereafter would have been shocked if they could see the setting in which the Soviet Union transmitted its message to the world. Two dozen correspondents of many nationalities and their secretaries, equipped with portable typewriters and none too amiable after the midnight trek to a faraway alley, were jammed into the tiny rooms of one of the censors. The censor, symbol at the moment of a great nation's might, was in bathrobe and slippers; on the other side of a partition one of his children was crying plaintively; every so often his wife, sleepy-eyed and in a frayed negligee, plopped by on her way to or from the kitchen. The promised editorial was two hours late in arriving. The world press camped there amidst the censor's domestic intimacies until it did arrive.

It was as a physical nuisance that the correspondents resented the censorship, even more than as a professional barrier. A dispatch required the signature and official seal of the Press Department before it would be accepted at the central telegraph office. We thought with deep envy of cities where one wrote out his dispatch, pressed a button, and the process was completed. In Moscow, every message must first be carried to the Foreign Office. There one waited until the censor, who was usually importantly in conference, was good and ready to read the projected dispatch. Its precise wording having been bargained over, passages deleted, and compromise formulas found for telling the news while blurring its meaning, it must be carried to the one window in the one telegraph office authorized to accept press dispatches for transmission.

Should it become necessary to send a news story during the hours when the censors were off duty or retired for the night, they must be trailed to their hiding places or routed out of bed for the indispensable signature and seal. These harassed officials, stalked and badgered by the foreign reporters, may easily be forgiven if they were less than hospitable at our intrusions.

Except for the attendant physical annoyances, the censorship did not seem to me at all stringent. Most of my dispatches passed muster so easily that I could only wonder why certain of my colleagues fussed and fumed at the restraint. The editorial changes suggested by Rothstein, Podolsky, or another of the censors, were usually, I thought, reasonable and often positively helpful. Sometimes I felt that they had saved me from cabling implied criticisms of the Soviet regime into which I had been betrayed by an extravagant adjective or a too literal reading of the news.

No censorship anywhere seems harsh to a reporter who agrees enthusiastically with the viewpoint of the censors. That was approximately my situation. I collaborated readily with the Press Department in rewording a piece of news so as to take the sting out of it: the department had developed a genius for bland equivocation in any of the world's major languages. I wrote a number of feature stories, in fact, on the mildness of the Soviet censorship as compared to the stringency of those in Italy and other countries.

A basic rule-of-thumb in the Press Department was that we could cable anything which was published in the Soviet press because it had already passed internal censorships. Since I accepted this published material without much question, my messages met little opposition.

Correspondents were grouped in official eyes into "friendly" and "unfriendly," rather than truthful and lying. Not their veracity but their attitude toward the Soviet government was the measure of their character. I was distinctly and proudly "friendly" and more than willing to go out of my way to prove my title to the classification. My quarrels with the censors were largely on matters of rhetoric. The dictates of cable economy forced me to condense events so closely that they sounded starker, more brutal than I intended. I sighed for the freedom of the special correspondents who could write around an unpleasant new decree, instead of blurting it out in one blunt sentence so easily misunderstood by the hostile capitalist environment. How I envied the New York *Times* man in particular! There was no rigid cable quota to cramp his style and he had no economic or other inhibitions in displaying his erudition and conversational charms at fifteen cents a word. The same decree padded in classical allusions, reminiscences of the World War, and references to the French Revolution did not strike the New York readers quite so hard.

A batch of my articles on American themes were published by Soviet magazines. The foremost literary publication, *Krasnaya Nov'*, gave some twenty of its earnest, closely printed pages to my description of periodical literature in America. It was a whimsical piece, satirizing the "true story" magazines which had given me a living for a period, the pseudo-intellectual monthlies rummaging timidly in the capitalist chaos, the million-circulation magazines that filled the interstices between soap advertisements with gooey romance. The *Journal of Foreign Literature*, then edited by Sergei Dinamov, ran several of my articles on American literature. Others used vignettes of the American scene.

For four years I had seen my dispatches from New York in the Soviet newspapers, but always under the imprimature of Tass. It was thrilling now to see articles in influential Russian publications under my own signature, and my name listed casually, as of right, in the tables of contents among Soviet authors. The thrill derived, no doubt, from this proof in black-and-white that I still "belonged" in the Russian revolution. The rebuffs from communists had wounded me more deeply than I cared to admit to myself. With my name cheek-by-jowl with Gorky's or Koltzov's or Dinamov's, I was not wholly outcast despite my equivocal position as capitalist reporter.

Sergei Dinamov, one of the editors with whom I dealt, was a young man of considerable personal charm. His friendship was a pleasant element in our first Moscow year. He was lanky, spectacled, studious and soft-spoken, cut out by nature to be a provincial pedagogue. Though I liked him for other qualities, I was not impressed with his cultural or mental equipment for the calling of literary critic. This needs mentioning because in due time he achieved editorship of the politically dominant art publication, the *Literaturnaya Gazetta.* His rise among the literary dictators seemed to me in time an indictment of that period.

My Sacco-Vanzetti biography was published twice in Russia, under different titles and under circumstances that were embarrassing to the author. The first publication, in an edition of ten thousand copies, was by the Moscow publishing trust, *Zemlya i Fabrika* (Land and Factory), arrangements having been made by Yonov, the director of the trust. The book was warmly commended in the press and the edition was exhausted in a few days.

Soon thereafter I was visited by two excited representatives of a Leningrad publishing organization, *Krasnaya Gazetta.* They informed me that they were in a distressing situation. Without realizing either that the author was in their midst or that *Zemlya i Fabrika* was publishing it, their trust had translated my book from its German version.

"In fact, we have printed 120,000 copies," they told me. "It's all ready, needing only to be bound. Suddenly we discover that Yonov has published another edition, and that you are in Russia. Well, now we cannot proceed without your explicit permission. If you don't give it to us, comrade, we will be in trouble, lots of trouble!"

"I have no objections," I assured them. "On the contrary. But will *Zemlya i Fabrika* have anything against it?"

"No, no," one of them laughed at such an absurd notion, "they and we—all part of the same governmental enterprise. This isn't New York or Paris, you know. There's no capitalist competition."

Though I did not doubt them, I tried to reach Yonov. Unfortunately he had gone off to the Caucasus on vacation—Russians always do at critical moments. Under renewed pressure and reassurances that the procedure was entirely ethical, I finally gave the Leningrad men a written authorization. When Yonov returned, the storm broke over my head. He charged that the Leningrad emissaries had lied, that I had betrayed him in allowing them to issue my book, etc.

"There's a strong demand for your book," he taunted me, "but I shall not allow any more editions to be printed!"

It was my first discovery that competition between two organizations within the Soviet structure could become almost as bitter and ruthless as under capitalism.

My career as a Russian author foundered, like so many things in Russia, on the rock of fear—in this case the Russians' fear of contact with a foreigner. A magazine editor telephoned to inquire whether a promised article was ready.

"Yes, I am just finishing it," I told him. "If you come right over, I'll have it waiting for you."

He fumbled and stammered and finally decided on honesty as the best policy.

"Well, you understand, I would gladly come," he said, "in fact, I should enjoy coming over and chatting with you. *No nye udobno*—but it is not convenient."

I was becoming thoroughly familiar with that phrase. It meant that for political reasons it was not quite safe for him, a Soviet editor, to be seen entering or leaving the home of a foreign correspondent. *Nye udobno!* My temper got the better of my sympathy.

"It's all right to publish my writing, but it's inconvenient to be seen in my company, is that it? My thoughts are acceptable, but my person is contagious. Well, you can go plumb to hell!"

I wrote no more articles for the Soviet press.

VI. Demonstration Trial

THE morning of May 18, 1928, was the color of lead. The gloomy weather did not dampen the circus spirit of the crowds milling around the squat, neo-classic structure once called the Nobles Club and now called the House of Trade Unions. A spirit of festival touched with hysteria—a crowd come to see a righteous hanging. Fifty Russian and three German technicians and engineers from the coal industry were to be tried publicly on charges of counter-revolutionary sabotage and espionage.

Militiamen labored to keep people in line and forced a passage for those of us lucky enough to hold special passes. In the spacious Hall of Columns, there was an atmosphere of carnival. Crowds poured in noisily and jockeyed for advantageous seats. The boxes gradually filled with diplomats, influential officials and other privileged spectators—much bowing and hand-shaking. Sputtering Jupiter lights played on the scene, photographers and cinema cameramen maneuvered their equipment into position, nearly a hundred foreign and Soviet reporters settled down at the foot of the high rostrum. Only a row of trimly uniformed G.P.U. soldiers, at rigid attention in front of the prisoners' box, their fixed bayonets glinting in the floodlights, added a note of grimness to the carnival.

The gleaming white marble columns had sprouted ugly clusters of loud-speakers. Immense crystal chandeliers shimmered in the shifting lights. But the dominant note was a blatant red—red cloths on the tables on the platform, red inscriptions on the walls.

The Shakhty sabotage trial was about to begin: the first of the melodramatic "demonstration trials" which year after year were to bewilder the world with their spectacle of men confessing incredible crimes and embracing death with grandiloquent gestures.

For over two months the Soviet press, radio, official speeches had built up towards the climax of this show. Dark hints of enemies within conniving with enemies abroad, villainy that cut production and took food out of the mouths of hungering masses, treachery that threatened the socialist fatherland—all brought to a sharp focus at last in this case. In recent months there had been many laconic announcements of executions for economic counter-revolution—here at last was a public demonstration of the reasons for such extreme measures. The Shakhty men were pilloried not merely for their own misdeeds, but for the crimes of the whole embittered, rebellious intelligentsia.

The tightening pinch of goods and food shortage was making people grumble with pain. The ruthless extermination of Trotskyism and other communist deviations was eating into the faith of more conscious workers. The Shakhty trial offered a tangible object for the hatreds smoldering in the heart of Russia. That morning's newspapers in every city and town shrieked curses upon the bourgeois plotters and their bloodthirsty foreign confederates. Week after week the press, radio, schools, newsreels, billboards had waved the promise of traitors' deaths aloft like crimson flags. They had treated every accusation and every far-fetched implication as established facts.

This was no spick-and-span trial on the democratic model, with its hypocritical blindfolded Justice dangling a silly pair of scales. This was Revolutionary Justice, its flaming eyes wide open, its flaming sword poised to strike. It was the same Revolutionary Justice that had presided over the guillotine in the French Terror, that had ruled men's minds whenever tyranny was overthrown. Its voice was not the whining of "fairness" but the thunder of vengeance. The charges would not be proved—the "preliminary investigations" behind closed doors presumably had done that. There was a sheaf of full or partial confessions that fitted neatly one into the other. No, the charges would merely be "demonstrated" before the whole country and the whole world, as theatrically as a powerful government with all the whips of mass indignation in its clenched fist could manage.

The accused men were coming into court pre-judged. Many of them had made fulsome confessions. And yet, there was surely a wide margin of the unpredictable. When half a hundred men are coralled for an ordeal of death in the sight of the entire world, the best-planned melodrama may go askew. Even Russians might refuse to die meekly, minds might crack, neat patterns might crumble, unsuspected peaks of courage or abysses of cowardice might be uncovered. Who knows what might happen! The crowds therefore pushed and clamored for a glimpse of the proceedings. It was the first large-scale public trial in some years and stirred the embers of the sacrificial romantic moods of the earliest years of the revolution.

Nikolai Krylenko, the prosecutor, was the first to stride to the platform. He took in the spectators, the foreign reporters, the cinema paraphernalia, and radio microphones with a slow, defiant scowl. This was to be his show. A small, tightly knit athletic figure, only a few inches over five feet, with a large shaven head and a flat face, he saw himself and made others see him as revolutionary vengeance incarnate. Throughout the six crowded weeks of the trial he wore sports clothes—riding breeches, puttees, a hunting jacket. We called it a hunting outfit and its fitness for his role added to the drama of the proceedings. Krylenko, the man-hunter.

Then came Professor A. Y. Vishinsky, the blond, spectacled presiding judge. He sat behind a microphone on a raised dais, with two associate judges on either side of him. The defense lawyers, older men with something tentative and apologetic in their manners, took seats and fussed with brief cases and papers to cover their embarrassment. Their faces have faded out of my memory; they were timid supernumeraries, an empty concession to appearances. Then the accused men filed in and took seats in the fenced-off space: a motley collection of old men and young, gray, unsmiling. Ten or twelve of them were to emerge in the following weeks as distinct personalities, but the rest remained a blur of names and faces.

The Jupiter lights snarled and flashed as they were turned full on the judges, the defendants, the audience. Their glare and sputter rarely ceased. It was the raucous, distracting element in which the entire trial was immersed.

The names of the accused men were read off by the clerk and acknowledged from the prisoners' box. Every session began with this ceremony of roll-call. Suddenly there was a hitch. Prisoner Nekrasoff did not answer. There were only fifty-two men instead of fifty-three. His counsel explained that Nekrasoff, unfortunately, was suffering hallucinations and had been placed in a padded cell, where he screamed about rifles pointed at his heart and suffered paroxysms.

The vision of Nekrasoff howling in his padded cell was a sinister element that deepened with every passing day. Every so often, in the routine of questions and answers and quibbles, some casual statement or incident would thus light up the depths. Sometimes these flashes left us limp with the impact of horrors half-glimpsed. What had driven the man to madness? What had transpired in the G.P.U. dungeons and interrogation chambers in the months since the men were rounded up? How did men like Krylenko, who sneered and snarled while the world looked on, behave when there were no witnesses and no public records? Whenever the proceedings yielded a flitting glimpse of that mysterious background, the spectators were electrified, the judges leaned forward, the prisoners fidgeted, Krylenko tensed for a spring. . . .

The long Act of Accusation was read. It had been published in full, a quarter of a million words, in the leading newspapers and was familiar to us. But in the courtroom, within the shadow of death, it sounded infinitely more ominous. It described an organized network of sabotage and espionage, with centers in Moscow and Kharkov, Warsaw, Berlin and Paris; emissaries carrying instructions and money from expropriated mine owners abroad to Russian engineers in the Donetz Basin coal area where Shakhty was located; technicians spoiling machinery, undermining the revolution's fuel supplies, inveigling the Soviet government into wasteful expenditures; preparations to destroy the coal industry as soon as war or intervention started; German firms palming off defective machinery with the connivance of bribed engineers.

Here was international plotting on the grand scale: revolutionary Russia pitted against a hostile world, intriguing capitalists and nefarious émigrés and desperate agents gnawing at the economic vitality of the land. The clichés of political rhetoric—the "hostile capitalist environment," the "class enemy in our midst," the "dastardly saboteurs, plotters, spies"—were bodied forth in a superb drama, bolstered by confessions and documents. Ten of the accused men had confessed and implicated the others. Six others had made important admissions. The rest, including all three Germans, pleaded innocence. All the information had been dredged from their minds in secret "preliminary investigations," the very thought of which—such was the sinister reputation of the G.P.U. —made Russians shudder.

It was an awesome picture that emerged from the Act of Accusation. In its general charges and larger contours it was strangely convincing, particularly in this setting of radio microphones, red drapery, bayonets, livid lights and newspaper hysteria. Only when the document moved closer and focused on details did the picture seem to blur. The citations of specific words and acts were curiously trifling, petty, inconsequential in relation to the grandiose world-wide plots involving governments, gigantic private corporations, and a supposedly organized, heavily financed movement. A turbine that went wrong. A mechanized mine which in someone's opinion should not have been mechanized. A raincoat sent from Germany as a "signal" for sabotage. A servant girl whom someone else had supposedly denounced to the Whites. Where were the magnificent deeds of desperation called for by the big pattern? Throughout the long exhausting weeks we fluctuated thus between vast accusations and the closer scrutiny under which they dissolved into conjectures and hearsay.

We waited in vain for a genuine piece of impersonal and unimpeachable testimony—an intercepted letter perhaps, a statement or document that did not carry the suspicion of G.P.U. extortion. The "far-reaching international intrigue" never did emerge. There was ample evidence of individual chicanery and occasional collaboration, but hardly any conclusive proof of the organized, centrally-directed conspiracy charged by the prosecution and assumed to be a fact by the press.

2

I despair of summarizing the weeks of trial. It was a strain on one's nerves and credulity, watching men writhe under Krylenko's whip, watching them go one after another through their roles like puppets while cameras were grinding and the Jupiters hissed. Most fearful was the macabre miracle of puppets unexpectedly coming to life, struggling to escape their nooses, protesting, accusing, pleading, while the prosecutor pulled the rope tighter.

The traditional Russian court procedure is far more casual and informal than in the West and therefore provides more scope for dramatic surprises. Long speeches are in order, witnesses confront and harangue one another, lawyers are unlimited in their wiles in leading or misleading those whom they question. The defendant is not guided and guarded by expert lawyers and protected by rules of procedure or an Anglo-Saxon assumption of innocence. He is left to flail in a panic like a drowning man, or to save himself cleverly, depending on his own abilities and nervous make-up.

Each prisoner began with a statement of his career. A few of them talked for more than an hour, tracing their life's course from birth to the impending death. Often they achieved real eloquence, and even the most inarticulate among them occasionally found words that lit up the vistas of his ordeal. I doubt if half a hundred men from the same social layers in any other race could have done so well as these Russians. Certainly no other race would have offered so much natural histrionics. Those who confessed and willingly played Krylenko's game, tended to overplay their roles. With an artist's instinct for emphasis they built themselves into arch-traitors, into personifications of the bourgeois intellectual and everything communists despise. The Slavic talent for hyperbole was among the things most fully demonstrated in this demonstration trial.

Having told his whole story unimpeded, the prisoner was then questioned by Krylenko, by his defense counsel, and brought face to face with his accusers and with witnesses. He interrogated these people himself and called upon others in the prisoners' box for corroboration. Often four or five defendants were grouped around the microphone questioning one another, bickering over disputed points and shouting "Liar!" while Krylenko and Vishinsky prodded them expertly to involve one another. Often these men who had spent their lives in equipping and operating coal mines grew more excited in defending some technical point of minerology than in defending their lives.

We saw the color ebbing from men's faces, we saw horrified disbelief staring from their eyes, as too-willing fellow-prisoners calmly dragged them into their elaborate confessions. A web of mutual hatreds and suspicions was woven under our eyes among the fifty-two prisoners, none of whom cared to die alone. We watched the skill with which Krylenko, narrowing his eyes and twisting his lips into a sneer, inflamed these hatreds, setting man against man and sowing insinuations.

My job was to dash off bits of information that make headlines in the American papers. A piece of extempore drama that would provide a good feature somewhere among the department store ads. A startling hint of foreign intervention plotted in a Berlin café. The exciting confrontation of two prisoners, brothers or life-long friends, that would make good human-interest stories. Somehow I must wring more and better stories out of this performance than my competitors.

But the dispatches did not begin to reflect the reality of that tangle of passions, fears, suspicions and desperations. When I saw my reports in type they seemed to me only vaguely related to the Roman circus that I was witnessing. An American or English reader must see the exotic spectacle through the lenses of his own knowledge and experience, and these did not touch at many points the emotions and overtones of the Soviet political trial.

Nor did the published dispatches so much as hint at my own inner reactions or the disturbances set up in the deeper recesses of my mind. I readily accepted the great trial for what it was: a revolutionary gesture in which the concept of justice did not even enter. It was a court-martial in the midst of a strenuous social war, where ordinary notions of fairness must be suspended. We wrote of evidence and witnesses and judicial rulings, fortifying the illusion that this was, in a rough and strange way, a tribunal of justice. All the time I knew, as those around me knew, that the innocence or guilt of these individuals was of no importance. It was the indubitable guilt of their class that was being demonstrated. What were the lives and the liberty of a few dozen men against the interests of the revolution? They were merely a batch of exhibits, the best that could be gathered at the moment, to impress the populace with the fact that the revolution was still honeycombed with enemies.

I accepted this version, as I say, as a working hypothesis and did nothing consciously to throw doubts on the essential justice of the thing in my readers' minds. If their narrow, individualistic code of justice was violated at every point, that larger justice which is Historical Necessity was being served. Not one of the American correspondents was naive enough to regard the performance as in the literal sense a trial to assay men's guilt. Not one of them was so insensitive to the by-plays and under-currents as not to be aware of the "defense" as a cruel farce, of threads leading into mysterious Secret Service realms, and of purposes so far beyond the fate of the men in the prisoners' box that they might have been straw dummies instead of flesh and blood. If they described the proceedings as though it were a genuine judicial tribunal, it was because of the censorship, the necessity of living on terms of friendship with the rulers of the capital where they worked, the difficulty of making outsiders see the thing in any other light—or a combination of these reasons.

As for myself, I counted it my specific duty to strengthen the illusion abroad that this was, indeed, a court of justice in the ordinary meaning of that phrase.

But I could not bring myself to hate the fifty-two men who symbolized the capitalist enemy. My mind had been too deeply conditioned by the years when I fought for justice to political prisoners in America, by the reams of indignant words I had written for I.W.W. prisoners, anarchist deportees, Charles Krieger in Tulsa, Sacco and Vanzetti in Boston. Despite myself I came increasingly, as the trial continued, to see the accused men as creatures baited, badgered, insulted and denied a sporting chance. I came increasingly to feel the demonstration trial as a hoax—not merely on the outside world which received it naively as a species of justice, but a hoax on the Russian masses themselves who were being offered a lightning rod to divert their resentments.

3

Six of the men ultimately sentenced to die were reprieved as reward for "services in elucidating the facts"—that is, for turning state's evidence. It was principally through their enthusiastic, well-rehearsed stories that the others were adjudged guilty. The first prisoner to tell his story in the prescribed opening statements, on the initial day of the trial, was of this company.

It was Berezovsky, a middle-aged engineer, tall and spare, speaking calmly and with mounting emphasis. A full hour he talked into the microphone and his words echoed a careful, organized mind. He was extricating himself from death, with the same skill and cold-blooded precision he might apply to solving an engineering problem.

He was evidently put first on the list by Krylenko to serve as arch-type and perfect specimen of the "bourgeois intellectual." Knowing or sensing this, Berezovsky tried to measure up to specifications. From earliest childhood, he recounted, success measured in money and acquisitions was the ideal implanted in his soul. That was the swamp in which were bred all his later crimes against his country. The revolution had interrupted his steady rise in the coal industry and was therefore his enemy. As a matter of course he sided with the mine owners against the insurgent workers, with the Whites against the Reds, and finally with the émigrés against the Soviets.

It was not himself alone that Berezovsky was describing, but an entire class; not his personal tragedy, but a revolutionary epoch that swept a nation's life from its moorings. Without effort this engineer managed to depict what all great art strives to convey: a great slice of humankind through the delineation of one character, a whole period through the experiences of one victim.

Samoilov, Kazarinov, Matov, others, elaborated this picture. They watched for Krylenko's every hint in rounding out the design, accenting what needed reënforcement and binding the unwilling prisoners more securely into the plot. They deserved their reprieve. A few emphasized their proletarian or peasant origins in a call upon the judges' sympathy. If only they were allowed to live, they promised to repay the revolution for its generosity by working always and only for the common good. Such pleas of a miraculous reform under G.P.U. auspices and the threat of shooting drew smiles and laughter from the crowded audiences in the stuffy Hall of Columns.

It was a new audience every session: deserving factory workers, school children, out-of-town delegations, visiting peasant groups, vouchsafed a peep at the spectacle. More than a hundred thousand, it was estimated, in this way saw a tiny segment of the proceedings. The luckier among them witnessed some episode of high tragedy, some stirring passage-at-arms between a prisoner and his accuser. The trial, of course, was not all melodrama. There were long arid stretches of technical bickerings, dull repetition, and sensations which did not come off sensationally. Some days, indeed, the Soviet press did not find it easy to maintain the atmosphere of epic villainy unmasked and its reports sagged to anticlimax. But for the spectators inside the courtroom, even the dullest sessions were not without dramatic highlights.

The few who insisted upon their innocence—Imineetov, Kuzma, Andrei Kolodoob, Eliadze and the rest—provided the biggest thrills for spectators. To see them at bay, their backs arched, panic in their voices, turning from a stinging question by the prosecutor to ward off a statement by a fellow-prisoner, swinging around to meet a judge's admonition—spinning, flailing, stumbling over their own words—finally standing still, exhausted and terror-stricken, staring into the auditorium as though aware of spectators for the first time, was indeed keen sport: lucky shock-brigadiers who drew such a session!

Or one of the days in which prisoners tried to withdraw their confessions. Perhaps they were frightened by the doom that crept closer, or given new courage, after their prison isolation, by the incredible sight of so many free people in one room. In any case, they tried desperately to pull themselves free of their signed statements and often tangled themselves more deeply in the effort, like insects caught on flypaper. There was Bebenko, for instance. He had been arrested the previous summer and had therefore been in the hands of the G.P.U. without trial nearly a year. He admitted having signed a "confession" but now wished to renounce it as a pack of lies.

"I scarcely knew what I signed," he said, while the audience tensed with new interest, the prosecutor and defense attorneys drew nearer. "I was driven to distraction by threats, threats, so I signed. . . . I tried to withdraw it before the trial, but . . . but . . ."

He looked at Krylenko and could not finish his sentence. Whatever the power that drove him to distraction, he was still under its spell. He realized that his words were ominous, evoking visions of G.P.U. torture chambers and third-degree horrors in the popular imagination. And these were the very things which Krylenko must obliterate from the view of the foreign reporters at the foot of the rostrum. He looked at the prisoner at bay. His voice was dangerously soft and concise.

"Do you want to say that you were intimidated, threatened?" he asked.

Bebenko hesitated, dropped his eyes. He was defeated.

"No," he whispered.

We who sat through the trial ten and twelve hours a day, who had worked our emotions and vocabularies to the point of prostration, needed spicier meat to stir our interest than the one-session visitors. We waited for days such as the elderly Skorutto or the Kolodoob brothers provided.

One evening Skorutto was reported too ill to attend. The next morning, however, he was the first to be called. It was an ash-gray, trembling figure which staggered to the mahogany pillar on which the microphone was perched. There was that in his demeanor, and in the alertness of Krylenko, which galvanized the courtroom into expectancy. Even the businesslike cameramen and lighting technicians were nervously attentive. And the atmosphere of impending thrill was more than justified.

Skorutto was one of those who had denied any complicity in the sabotage. In his examination he stuck valiantly by this denial, in the face of pressure from half a dozen of the prisoners who labored to implicate him. He had been abroad in connection with some purchases in America when the round-up of Shakhty engineers was begun. In Berlin he had read of the arrest of many of those who worked close to him, and could expect nothing less than his own arrest. Nevertheless, he had returned to his native land and his Soviet job. Was it a token of clean conscience? Or perhaps supreme gall? Or maybe, as the more romantic reporters preferred to write, an expression of Slav "fatalism"? And now this man, a shattered replica of the one who entered the courtroom at the opening, stood tremulously before the microphone and informed the court that he had an important declaration to make.

"Last night," he said in effect, "I wrote out and signed a statement confessing my own guilt, as well as the guilt of Rabinovich, Imineetov and others. . . ."

The words had barely registered on our minds when the courtroom was electrified by an unearthly shriek from the box where the relatives of the prisoners sat; the piercing notes wrenched from the throat of a wounded animal. It was a woman's voice.

"Kolya," the woman cried, "Kolya darling, don't lie! Don't! You know you're innocent!"

The prisoner collapsed into a chair as though the cry had been a hammer-blow on his head, weeping aloud, beating his breast, and writhing in that utter agony without shame. A shudder passed like a wind through the tight-packed auditorium. . . . Hurriedly Vishinsky adjourned the session for ten minutes.

The audience, released, exploded into animated talk, out-shouting one another. It is Skorutto's wife, the news flashed through the crowd. The prisoner was led away, still wailing his despair.

When the session was reopened and calm restored, he came once more to the microphone.

"Yes, I wrote a confession last night. That was at nine o'clock. But I could not go to sleep. For eight hours I struggled with my conscience. At five in the morning I wrote another statement in which I withdrew the first one. I could not betray my friends. I am innocent."

Krylenko was once more master of himself—cool, relentless, at his most sarcastic. It was not the guilt of this one prisoner that he must establish, but the name of the G.P.U. that he must protect. One dread thought hammered at everyone's mind: what were the pressures which had driven this Skorutto, while allegedly too ill to attend the trial, to indite a confession only to withdraw it eight tortured hours later?

Did anyone force him to confess, Krylenko wanted to know. The inflection of his voice was ominous. Was he threatened?

Skorutto was like a man who had lost his mind. He wrung his hands and wandered about the platform. No, nobody had forced him, he finally said.

"These men had lied about me," he tried to explain, "my own friends and they lied about me! So I lied about them. . . . It has been agony! Can't you understand? My God, can no one understand? Eight nights I have not slept. I took drugs, but I could not sleep, and finally I decided to confess. . . ."

He staggered from one corner of the rostrum to the other, like one caged. Then he stopped at the microphone.

"I never did these things of which they accuse me. Never! *Though I knew what waited for me. . . .*"

The sentence remained unfinished. Again the shadow of the unspoken things behind the curtains of the public trial. Again Krylenko and the judge putting questions to erase that shadow. Why had he confessed, Vishinsky pinioned the distracted Skorutto with the spear-point of his anger.

"I had hoped that this court would be more lenient with me if I pleaded guilty and accused the others," Skorutto blurted out.

And if the day needed one more sensation to make it memorable, a ghost stalked across the stage. Casually, in the course of someone's interrogation, the name of Gavruchenko was mentioned. And suddenly we became aware that Gavruchenko should have been in the prisoners' dock, but he had committed suicide before the indictment was published. . . . Had he? How and why? The questions remained unanswered. We knew only that a prisoner was dead and that under the G.P.U. system of justice not even his wife and his children would ever know precisely how it happened. They did not even see the body, there being no *habeas cadaver,* let alone *habeas corpus,* in revolutionary Russia.

The following morning Skorutto once more stepped into the limelight. He spoke in a monotone, like a dead man from the grave. The confession was true, he now declared, and its retraction a lie. It was the agonized cry of his wife which yesterday had broken his determination to attest his guilt—and the guilt of those whom he had implicated.

4

Another day's audience, jammed into the columned hall for the grab-bag of thrills, drew a Cain-and-Abel scene such as remains eternally exciting to the sons of Adam. They watched Emilian Kolodoob sweating and puffing as he labored to turn his own brother, Andrei Kolodoob, into a traitor. Emilian had confessed sabotage, while Andrei denied it. Now, with very little encouragement from the prosecutor, Emilian looked unflinchingly at his brother and insisted that they had both plotted, both received émigré money, both lied to the Soviet state for which they worked.

Was I reading my own distaste into the quieter, tenser mood of the spectators, or were they really embarrassed by this unnatural exhibition? The revolution and its chaotic aftermath had loosened the bonds of family loyalties, yet even to Russians there must have been something obscene in the performance. The obscenity was raised to a pitch of horror when, immediately after being betrayed by a brother, Andrei Kolodoob heard his own son demanding his death. A letter from the twelve- or thirteen-year-old Kyril, published in that morning's *Pravda*, was read into the record.

> I denounce my father as a whole-hearted traitor and an enemy of the working class. I demand for him the severest penalty. I reject him and the name he bears. Hereafter, I shall no longer call myself Kolodoob but Shakhtin.

In later years the Kremlin came to alter its view on family relations. It was to preach once more the importance of blood ties and the beauty of domestic loyalties. When I read the news in New York, the memory of Kyril Kolodoob flashed through my mind and how, all his life, he must carry the name Shakhtin like the mark of Cain to remind him and all men of what he did to his father. I thought of other sons in other Soviet exhibition trials who had similarly urged death for their fathers, for this piece of theater became a routine procedure in sabotage trials.

Engineer Bratanovsky, tall and well-groomed, provided us with further opportunities to discuss Slav fatalism and Russian psychology, and draw the stale analogies with Dostoievsky characters. He, too, had been abroad when the arrests of Shakhty engineers began. He had not the slightest doubt that he would be arrested, yet he did not remain abroad. As though there was nothing remarkable in walking open-eyed toward the certainty of imprisonment and shooting, Bratanovsky told of his return in the matter-of-fact tone of a well-bred person at a dinner table.

One after another the puppets and the men stalked across the red-draped stage, some cringing, others weeping, most of them composed in the calm of ultimate despair. The last of the fifty-two to tell his story was perhaps the most impressive and certainly the one most eagerly awaited. We had become familiar with the seventy-year-old Rabinovich in the weeks before his turn came. Again and again he had been yanked into the recitals of other men. The rest were small fry compared to this stocky, gray-haired, earnest old man. In 1920 Lenin himself had summoned Rabinovich and invited his coöperation, as the foremost coal-mining engineer in Russia. In the following seven years, until the day of his arrest, he was virtual coal dictator. Often he had taken part in meetings of the Council of People's Commissars when technical questions were on the agenda. His presence among the accused engineers was the most fantastic touch of all.

During Kuzma's interrogation, Rabinovich had risen in his seat and asked to be heard. He stepped forward to defend the younger man—the only defendant in the whole trial to come unasked to another prisoner's defense! There was a dignity and self-assurance in his bearing, an authority in his voice, which set him apart from the rest.

Rabinovich spoke now for over an hour, tracing his career from its dimmest beginnings sixty years ago. Starting at the bottom, he had attained first place in the coal industry before the revolution. He had become rich. His personal interests were on the side of the capitalists and, naturally, he could have no love for a revolution that took away his mines and banished his associates. But he loved his work more than his wealth, and when Lenin honored him with his confidence he was determined to merit that trust. Others had talked about sleepless nights and harrowing thoughts and nightmares.

"As for me," Rabinovich said, "I sleep as soundly in prison as in my own bed. I have a clear conscience and I have nothing to fear."

A man by the name of Mookin was brought into the courtroom by G.P.U. guards, direct from a prison cell to testify against Rabinovich. He was pallid, scared, bewildered by the lights and people. Parrot-like he spoke a piece accusing Rabinovich of plotting sabotage. Every so often his voice broke and he asked for a drink of water. His hands trembled, so that the glass rattled on his teeth. When he had finished his testimony, Rabinovich moved forward so that the witness must look into his face.

"Is it me that you are talking about, or someone else? Look at me and answer!"

Mookin staggered under the question and like a man blinded, groped once more for the water glass. Finally, he wrenched the word from his gullet. "You," he said.

Stammering, drinking, fidgeting, he repeated his accusations under Krylenko's prompting and bulldozing. But as a state witness the man was doubly a failure. The trial's impresario had committed his greatest blunder in dragging this harried creature from the gloom of his cell into the floodlights of public attention. In the first place, Mookin was too clearly intimidated and anguished. In the second place, he stood as living proof that others—God knows how many scores or hundreds—were in the custody of the G.P.U. on similar charges, though they were not in the prisoners' dock. Krylenko had blundered. It was one thing to know, as we all did, that only a handful had been winnowed for public trial: only enough to give verisimilitude to the pattern of an international plot and an organized gang of saboteurs. The rest languished in prison or faced the firing squad without benefit of publicity. It was quite another thing to see a specimen of those who had not been chosen for demonstration purposes—and a pitiful, broken specimen at that. Another lightning flash disclosing a little of the background which, more than the trial itself, held men's thoughts.

Krylenko's closing address lasted six hours. He justified once again his fame as an orator. How his eloquence swept uncertain regiments into the ranks of the Soviets was part of the legendary of the revolution in its earliest days. That eloquence now lashed the fifty-two men and many of them cringed, as though his words were physical blows. He stirred the auditorium into a frenzy of hatred, so that they applauded wildly the demands for "the highest measure of social defense"—"*Rasstrel!*"—"shooting." The word exploded in his speech over and over again like a pistol shot. He asked death for twenty-two of the prisoners. Only when he reached Rabinovich did he falter. It was painful to him to ask for it, he said, knowing the old man's past services, but—"*Rasstrel!*"

The defense speeches were faint and tremulous and apologetic. These lawyers selected for the dangerous task of pretending a defense were in a most uncomfortable position. Men whose reputations dated back to tsarist days and tsarist courts, they belonged to the same social group as the men whom they ostensibly defended and knew well enough that the blood thirst in the eloquence of Krylenko and the applause of the crowd included them no less than the accused technicians. Meticulously they avoided any suggestion of doubt as to the genuineness of the confessions, or anything which might reflect on the G.P.U. Each of them had a specific group of prisoners as his special charges, and therefore felt free to attack the rest of them as furiously as Krylenko himself. The total effect of their speeches, therefore, was to reinforce the state's case!

Then several so-called prosecutors for the people took the radio "mike." The formal fiction was that they represented the public and, having sat through the entire trial, now gave their views. Each of them added his quota of abuse and ended with an impassioned demand for death sentences. Among them, it happened, was a large, bearded, impressive-looking man representing the engineering societies. Several years later he was to appear on the same platform in the same setting of lights and ballyhoo, but in another role. He was himself arrested for economic sabotage.

The final ceremony, in accordance with ancient Russian usage, was a "last word" by each of the prisoners. It turned into a fantastic and incredible parade of naked passions. There were those who begged for mercy and those who spoke words of defiance. They cringed and snarled and begged and blundered. Fifty-two men stampeded by the fear of death. Only a very few, among them the two aged Jews, Rabinovich and Imineetov, retained their self-respect intact. Imineetov said, "One day another Zola will arise and will write another *J'Accuse* to restore our names to honor." A tall man, when his name was called, staggered to the microphone and shouted, "I don't want to die! I don't want to die!" Another walked forward calmly and in the most urbane manner said, "I am guilty. I do not deny it. That is all."

On the whole they made a sorry picture. Only by a violent stretch of the imagination could one cast these groveling men in heroic roles, either as martyrs or as great conspirators. Guilty or innocent, they were men defeated, impotent, without a deep faith or hope for the future to sustain them. Not one of them had advanced any more exalted motive for spoiling machines or opposing the revolution than his own desire for more wealth. Not one of them had even tried to raise his behavior to the level of a social cause or the defense of a principle—any principle, the right to private initiative, or democracy. . . .

In other Soviet trials of which I had read—of churchmen or

Social Revolutionaries—some of the accused men and women had held their heads high: they had plotted and connived for God, for fatherland, for a new revolution. There was no trace of such idealism to dignify the Shakhty trial, in which those who admitted guilt were by their own description small, self-seeking, uninspired persons, filled with chagrin over their private losses and never once thinking beyond their own bellies and purses. A few among them showed that they possessed a certain human dignity. But the group as a whole seemed to me a sad exhibition of what the age-old system of private greed does to its most devoted servants.

The verdict was announced for four in the afternoon, but the public was not admitted until eight. An hour later the prisoners filed in and took their seats. But the judges did not emerge until midnight. Ancient custom required that the presiding judge write out the verdict in his own handwriting and it was a lengthy document. There was an ironic touch in such preservation of an inherited form of justice when so much of its substance had been deliberately violated. The long waiting added to the tension. Everyone remained standing (another inherited formality) while Vishinsky, for a full hour, read the verdict.

Eleven were sentenced to death, six of them with recommendations for reprieve in consideration of their helpfulness. Thirty-eight other Russians were sentenced to prison terms ranging from one to ten years. Rabinovich was given six years. One of the Germans was acquitted and the other two received suspended sentences, which amounted to the same thing. The show was over, except for a formal announcement three days later of five executions.

5

The next days were a sort of convalescence for me after the fever and strain of the long trial. Even physically it had been exhausting; besides reporting the proceedings in the former Nobles Club, I had to keep abreast of all other news developments throughout the Soviet Union. Far more exhausting, however, were the currents of self-searching generated by the trial. I had proceeded on the assumption that the revolution can do no wrong, since even its crimes are justified by its mystical mandate from

History. Something in the weeks of trial, I could not place my finger on it yet, challenged that mystical assumption. Whatever the infinite purposes of History, whatever the compulsions upon its finite human instruments, did it relieve them and me of all responsibility?

Turning my impressions over and over in my mind, discarding the ranting of politicians and sifting, as best I could, the palpable lies from what rang true, I felt certain of only these things:

First, that most, if not all, of the accused men were guilty either of actual sabotage against the Soviet regime, or of such utter apathy toward their work that the results amounted to sabotage. Men of their sort were, at best, prisoners of the revolution, obeying its orders and dreaming of escape.

Second, that the melodramatic international plot projected by the Soviet rulers to impress their people and the outside world was largely a figment of their own stagecraft.

Third, that behind the trial was a story of mass arrests, forced confessions, unprincipled and inhuman third-degree methods that broke the body and the spirit of its victims. I sensed horrors touched by sadism, though I could not prove it and tried hard to wipe my mind clean of their shadows.

Fourth, that the trial was in a peculiar way a form of exhibitionism: a group intoxicated by untrammeled power showed off its new strength. It renounced the hamperments of principles and decencies and respect for human life to give its fresh energies the widest play.

I do not say that these were the facts. I record only that those were my inner conclusions—conclusions some of which I buried far out of sight, because they would have inhibited me in serving the revolution.

I shouted down similar conclusions when they were voiced by Russian or non-Russian acquaintances. In the courtroom, watching the spectacle and reading closely the newspaper accounts, I came to believe that the whole Soviet population was accepting without serious question the official version of the trial. But outside, in day-to-day contact with Russians of all types, that belief was quickly shattered. I discovered that the government's victory was far from complete. In a guarded phrase or a politically off-color joke or in tense silences, people betrayed their doubts and cynicisms. Whatever they might say aloud, few in their hearts doubted that the confessions had been extorted by threats or actual torture, and that the sabotage and apathy of the technicians had been blown up to the size of an international plot for obvious political reasons.

The fact that production troubles kept increasing despite the "liquidation" of such conspiracies fed the cynicism. In the very heart of the Shakhty coal area output declined in the next months and accidents increased—as was only natural with the technical directors either arrested or paralyzed by fear.

The effect upon the pre-revolutionary intelligentsia, upon whom, however little they relished it, the Bolsheviks had to depend for technical leadership in old and new industries, was disastrous. While the Shakhty exhibition may have led some to desist from overt acts, it drove all the rest to the most costly and overt of all acts—inactivity. They avoided responsibility as though it were a plague. Why undertake anything if failure might be construed as sabotage? They had seen men treated as traitors because the mines they had mechanized at great cost proved unprofitable. They had seen others accused of issuing sabotage "instructions" in telling technicians that turbines would be spoiled if handled in a particular way. The only safety was in doing nothing, in "passing the buck" of important decisions to someone else.

During the greater part of the Five Year Plan period the strength of the technical intelligentsia was crippled. It worked in fear and trepidation, aware that it was a pariah class, distrusted, easy game for petty tyrants, and convenient scapegoats for the mistakes and ignorance and mismanagement of others. The Shakhty trial and the persecution of the intelligentsia which it initiated and symbolized seemed to me, with every passing year, as much a blunder as a tragedy. For me, as for others, it remained a glaring proof of the dangers of immense unrestrained power with its inevitable temptation to use unstinting force where force was least effective.

VII. Journey Through Russia

IN THE summer there is traditionally a wholesale exodus from the cities to the country in Russia. Long before the advent of Moscow's brief and dusty summer, people talked of nothing but *dachas* (country houses). When the snows were still on the ground, more prudent Muscovites traveled into the villages nearby and rented rooms or cottages from the peasants. By June, wagons loaded with household goods began to rumble towards the country districts. Peasant householders in pleasant locations earned more by renting to summer tenants than they did by plowing the soil. They moved to shanties or crowded their families into a windowless garret to make room for the profitable visitors.

For anyone accustomed to summers in New York, the season should hold no terrors even on the equator. The Russian summer, we were to discover in time, was merciful by comparison. The general and frenzied preparations for the annual evacuation, however, alarmed us into a frantic search for a *dacha*. Billy explored the suburbs, returning with sad tales of failure. Befouled, ill-smelling cottages shared by the peasants and their cattle could be rented only for sums beyond our bank account—probably the prices were stepped up as a subtle compliment to the supposed affluence of all foreigners. Livable quarters had already been preëmpted by bureaucrats, embezzlers, G.P.U. officials, and others who could stand the tariff. In the end, Billy and Genie joined the families of two Foreign Office employees who were going to the Baltic seashore near Riga for the summer, while I faced the terrors of the summer alone.

It turned out far from terrible. The annual exodus, in fact, proved as much a social convention as a necessity. I visited at the *dachas* of Russian and foreign friends, learned to play *gorodki* (a Russian variant of skittles), and bathed nude in the Moscow River beyond the city limits and in the lakes and brooks where the summer colonies were clustered. I discovered the charms of the countryside of the region: forests of slender silver birch or darkling pine, rolling meadows of tenderest green, and sudden brooks where men and women bathed and soaped themselves with only an imaginary boundary line between them. I picked huckleberries and blackberries in woods carpeted with pine needles, woods as dim and hushed as Gothic cathedrals.

To the peasants whom I met, a foreigner was a minor miracle and an object of endless curiosity. They plied me with questions about American peasants and American skyscrapers—in part, I am sure, for the sly fun of hearing my stumbling Russian. My shoes, my trousers, my horn-rimmed glasses, everything foreign set them clucking with admiration. Even to peasants on the periphery of Russia's metropolis, the outside world was a fairyland on the other side of the moon.

Whether in town or country, the summer nights were magical interludes of only two or three hours at most between the late sunset and the early sunrise. Coming out of a party at a hotel or a home at one or two in the morning, I would find the deserted city silhouetted delicately against a violet dawn in the east, while the western sky was still a bluish gray studded with expiring stars. The violet turned to rose as I took the longest route home and watched the sun's first rays edging pastel-colored church cupolas with gold. These early dawns in Moscow have for me a quality of enchantment that, in retrospect, seems a dream half-remembered. Perhaps it was the contrast with the noisy, crowded day filled with problems and slogans that made these intervals so fancifully precious. Moscow seemed a place bewitched, its everyday life suspended as the tints of morning filtered through the sieve of night.

In the matter of news, too, that summer provided a lull—the calm, had we known it, before the storm that was to break before long and uproot millions of families and plunge the country into a panic of ruthless speed. The Kremlin's fervid promises to desist from further violence against the peasantry had brought a new spurt of energy to farming and the press reports of crop progress were for the most part optimistic. All important officials were vacationing on the fringes of the Black Sea or spending most of their time at their *dachas;* a number of the finest old estates and the most attractive summering sites were reserved for G.P.U.

leaders and the more privileged communists. The lull enabled me to enjoy the country and occasional excursions to more distant spots celebrated for their palaces, ancient churches or scenery.

I flew to Riga for a few days to visit my family and found them and their Moscow companions thoroughly disillusioned with the "Baltic riviera" of which Russians speak so glowingly. The clear warm days were so rare that one could easily keep count of them. And the bathing was regulated with a prudishness that seemed fantastic to the more natural Russians. Riga itself, almost Dutch in its freshly-swept look, its shops running over with food delicacies the memory of which had begun to fade in my mind, was a healing respite from the intensity of Moscow. We took in an American movie, the captions of which were flashed in three languages—Latvian, German and Russian—and shopped for the sheer thrill of shopping. Like Russians themselves when they confront capitalist abundance for the first time, we simply wallowed in the plenitude. Six unbroken months in the Soviet Union with its new standards are enough to make the old bourgeois world incredible. Foreigners deeply immersed in the new Russian life must rediscover capitalist civilization when they emerge.

2

The one piece of sensational news centered in Moscow that summer of 1928 was in itself a comforting vacation from the Shakhty trial, food queues, chastisement of heretical communists, peasant terror and other news staples of the preceding months. I refer to the ice-breaker *Krassin's* rescue, in July, of survivors of an Italian dirigible expedition to the North Pole. Though the melodramatic events occurred in the extreme North, the information reached the world in large measure through Moscow, which made it our story. And how we gloried in it! A towering human-interest yarn at last, in which we could let ourselves go without fear of offending sensitive officials or drawing down Bolshevik lightning on our heads!

Literal Marxists think bougeois reporters in the U.S.S.R. lie in wait with mouths dripping saliva for Soviet horrors and disasters to pounce upon. They would be cured of this dismal vision had they seen the eager relish with which we pounced on the heroic exploits of the ice-breaker *Krassin,* its crew and its aviators. Out of the grudging formal communiqués we fashioned a saga of Soviet daring which will forever embellish the records of Arctic exploration. We did this despite the bureaucratic attitude of a censorship apparatus so rigidly geared for suppression of facts that it automatically hampered the transmission of a story more favorable to its reputation among the peoples of the globe than anything that had happened in years. The actual events were sufficiently stirring, but the correspondents—in a sort of holiday of the spirit after the oppressive Shakhty proceedings—spread wide the wings of their fancy in blowing up Samoilovich, Chukhnovsky, and the other heroes to almost mythological dimensions. The ice-breaker itself, blunt-nosed, powerful, imperturbable, turned under our typewriter keys into a symbol of Soviet strength rescuing the world.

That those to whom the Red Samaritans brought succor were Black Fascists enhanced that symbolism. The irony of Soviet Russia bringing life to stranded Italians and putting Mussolini's realm in their debt was not lost on the world. For nearly six weeks the whole world had watched in fascinated horror the desperate and seemingly hopeless attempts to find survivors of the dirigible *Italia* somewhere on the floating ice masses off North East Land. It saw one rescue party after another wrecked or returning empty-handed. One of these parties, led by Roald Amundsen, never returned and the details of its fate remain a mystery to this day. Meanwhile Soviet ice-breakers carrying seaplanes and several of the country's ace fliers were slowly nosing their way through the ice floes toward the scene of the tragedy. Their laborious climb northward was scarcely noticed. But as they neared the scene, the civilized world became abruptly aware of their persistent struggle and watched excitedly as the *Krassin* and the *Malygin* elbowed their way through crashing ice masses.

On July 11, Boris Chukhnovsky flew from the *Krassin* and reported by radio that he had located three men on an ice-floe, two of them standing up and waving frantically to him, the third apparently lying down. He had circled over them as signal that they were seen. In attempting to get back to his base he made a forced landing. Apparently he urged the ship to go pick up the castaways before bothering about him.

"Never mind me, save the others!" we reported him as saying, and the phrase became famous—a theme made to order for editorials and sermons. Blushingly I record that the phrase was invented in the little room near the censor's office where we worked. But if he didn't say it, he easily might have—and, no doubt, said words no less stirring.

Thirty-six hours later the *Krassin* reached the stranded group; there were only two instead of the three Chukhnovsky thought he had seen. The same day the ice-breaker also picked up five other survivors, while the press in all countries cheered itself hoarse. It was seeing those sinister Bolsheviks in a brand-new role.

The scanty details of the exploit were reported by the ship's officials and several Russian newspapermen on board directly to Moscow. We were driven to the raw edge of apoplexy by the battle to wrest this information from its official keepers—all of it was treated as a state secret, when elementary good sense should have led the government to help us smear the yarn as thick as strawberry jam on bread.

Chukhnovsky's report of sighting three men stirred up unsavory and slightly macabre controversy. It had been instantly assumed that the three were Captain Filippo Zappi, the dirigible's navigator, Captain Alberto Mariano, pilot, and the young Swedish meteorologist, Dr. Finn Malmgren, who had started off together after the crash on the chance of bringing aid. The *Krassin* found only Zappi and Mariano. They explained that Dr. Malmgren had died a month ago, and that what Chukhnovsky mistook for a third figure was a shadow or a roll of blankets. But there were those, especially in Dr. Malmgren's native land, who refused to believe their story, charging that the Italians had abandoned the young Swede and taken his clothes and supplies. There were even gruesome hints of cannibalism and some writers made much of the report that the Italians were wearing some of Dr. Malmgren's clothes. Ultimately, experts came to believe the two survivors' account. But while the mystery lasted it gave Moscow, where every grain of information was fought over, something to chew on.

In the general anxiety to do the story up brown, the Associated Press correspondent pulled a "boner" which embarrassed that great agency for some time. The communiqué reporting that

Mariano and Zappi were taken aboard the ice-breaker and that Dr. Malmgren was dead was so crudely worded that we all believed Dr. Malmgren's body, too, had been retrieved. My colleague thereupon wrote a colorful and most sentimental account of the scientist's "funeral." He had touching speeches, weather-beaten old Russian tars weeping over the corpse, bowed heads and the rest of the effects appropriate to such an occasion. The imaginary funeral, worse luck, carried the date-line, "On Board the *Krassin*," instead of Moscow, to give it an authentic eye-witness flavor. The lugubrious tale was published in the United States and I was duly reprimanded for my failure to "cover" the funeral before it became known that Dr. Malmgren's body had been neither recovered nor wept over.

The Arctic drama had been spread in the Soviet newspapers as in the rest of the world, and a wave of national pride rolled over the population. Books, articles, lectures, and motion pictures converted the tale of individual courage and skill into another proof of triumphant socialism. Chukhnovsky's expert flying, Professor Samoilovich's knowledge of polar conditions, the captain's fine seamanship seemed convincing, if illogical, testimony of the rightness of Marx and his victorious disciple, Stalin.

National patriotism in the Western sense is something relatively new to Russia. Before the revolution it was propagated largely by the new intelligentsia, and even with them it was mystically racial more than nationalistic. Patriotism presupposes an awareness of the surrounding world in which one's nation is a distinct unit—an awareness of boundaries. Primitive peoples reserve their patriotic sentiments for their immediate village or region, everything else being an infinite and mysterious cloud. To a peasant in Kostroma or Viatka, Russia was too vague and limitless a concept to stir a profound loyalty. It has been one of the curious functions of the revolution, in ironical disregard of its internationalist dogmas, to stir national consciousness in Russia. The mere emphasis on the hostile capitalist encirclement has tended to mark off the frontiers of their country in the minds of millions. The dramatization of heroic episodes like the *Krassin* story, sensational air flights or industrial achievements has fed the nascent patriotism.

3

I made my first long journey through Russia in the early autumn, visiting Kiev, Odessa, the Crimea and the Caucasus, Rostov, and other sections. I visited these places many times in subsequent years and it is not easy to disentangle my first impressions from the cumulative memory. I kept no notebook (a stupidity for which I cannot forgive myself), and my articles on the trip, like nearly everything I wrote in this period, are far from a literal record of my reactions. Deliberately and with a clear conscience I wrote for effect. My duty as I saw it was to strengthen the faith of the world's workers in the first socialist land, and I did not permit myself knowingly to cast doubt on the perfection of the Soviet scenery, let alone its economic system and leadership.

I brought back from the tour a heavy heart; the routine miseries of the period were more apparent in the provinces than in the capital. But I wrote pieces which could, with only slight emendations, have been published in one of the Soviet propaganda magazines in America. Having mentioned that I had met "persons of the most diverse temperaments and social interests," I added:

> Almost without exception these people reflected a warm conviction that just ahead of them lies a bright future, for their cities, for their country as a whole. They talked with enthusiasm of the new factories, the new power stations, the rows of bright new workers' homes, the grain elevators that were going up in places where they live and work. They talked of these things, moreover, as though they were personal possessions.

I met, indeed, people who talked in the strain of a *Pravda* editorial, especially officials whom I cornered and plied with questions. But they were the exception. Casual acquaintances made on trains, in hotels and restaurants, were more likely to complain about food shortage, overbearing bureaucrats, and other troubles. My American clothes, a glimpse of my wrist-watch or fountain pen or razor blades, were enough to pluck complaints about hardships and the barrenness of their lives from envious Russians. I found myself repeatedly trying to convince them that their fate was not as bleak as it seemed. The gew-gaws of capitalist production, I assured them, were small compensation for a system of bourgeois exploitation and slavery.

Leaving Moscow, I shared the bare wooden shelf in the "hard" or third-class carriage with a tall, clean-cut fellow in a semi-military overcoat and good boots. He might easily have posed for the portrait of a Stalwart Workingman. In removing overcoat and jacket and making himself comfortable for the long journey to his home, Odessa, he left his revolver in full view. The dumb-show was intended too obviously to impress everyone and the foreigner in particular with the fact that he was "somebody." Then he became a little ashamed of this childish show-off. He put away the revolver and blushed like a schoolboy. He transferred his boastfulness from a personal to a national level, and for an hour or two enlarged on the achievements and "perspectives" of the Soviet regime and the genius of Stalin.

But gradually it dawned on him that this emissary from the capitalist world was already sufficiently convinced. Abruptly he changed his tune and long before we reached Kiev we had exchanged roles. I was reduced to convincing him that things were not nearly as bad as he thought and the difficulties which distressed him only temporary sacrifices on the road to socialism.

"Ekh, brother," he interjected ever so often, "it is easy for you to speak. You have an American passport and can thumb your nose at us if you like and go back to America. You would talk differently if you were caught here like the Russians."

I felt that his complaints were no deeper than his boasts; he was caught and confused between his theoretical convictions and his practical discomforts. We parted at Kiev. A week later I looked him up at his home in Odessa and he showed me through the city, again vacillating between pride in the future and disgust with the present. Only when he pointed out the sites of civil war battles and recounted the terrible but romantic events of those stirring days, with particular reference to his own role, did he achieve unequivocal enthusiasm.

My traveling companion was an American I.W.W. of Russian extraction who had returned to his native land after the revolution, by name Belinkes. Awkward, kind-hearted but not overly intelligent, he did yeoman service as interpreter when my pidgin Russian failed me, and worked veritable miracles in obtaining tickets at railroad stations where others had been waiting days and weeks for accommodations. Unfortunately, he considered it his patriotic function to act as guide and political mentor, tasks for which he was peculiarly unfitted. Somewhere, perhaps in the American movies, he had developed a fixed idea that the principal object of travel was to see monuments and could never quite grasp why I preferred to see people, cafés, theaters, smelly side-streets. All of these, he felt, no doubt, were amply available in Moscow and therefore did not justify the cost of travel.

We traveled "hard," sleeping on the bare worn shelves when we were lucky enough to stretch out at all. The idea was to get closer to the Russian people. It was a sacrifice on the altar of professional duty which I did not willingly make again. Open windows are, as everyone in Russia knows, unhealthy; besides, they encourage the "wild boys" who still infested the stations to reach in and help themselves to everything that can be grabbed by ingenious and well-trained little thieves. Spitting and more distressing types of bodily relief were unrestrained. ("City folks are strange people," a peasant once told me, "they carry their sputum in little pieces of cloth, instead of spitting it out on the ground like decent folk.") A crowded, air-tight carriage, after its inmates have drawn off their boots and made themselves at home, is scarcely a sweet-smelling place.

The warm friendliness of fellow-passengers, however, was some compensation for the discomforts. Most of them felt it their duty to assist a foreigner. They brought me hot water at stations and were always ready to share their bread and sausage. Or they guarded my belongings while I stepped out for air and to buy food; the station lunch-counters at this stage were still fairly well stocked, and at most stations local peasants sold food at steep prices. At night we put our coats and shoes under our heads both as cushions and by way of guarding against theft, and we tied the baggage to our wrists or ankles with ropes so that we would be wakened if anyone made a foray.

I found the cities without exception shabby. "The new Russia," I wrote to console myself and reassure my readers, "is busy with innumerable more pressing affairs, and its towns will remain sadly out of repair for a few years longer. To the stranger the first impression is still an unpleasant one. It takes a lively imagination, and a background of appreciation of what the country has been through, to overcome it." My imagination was not always equal to the task, though not for lack of trying. The beauty was there. Looked at through half-closed eyes, or in the kindly dusk of sundown, it could be discerned—in a thousand fine old buildings, in sweeping panoramas, in breath-taking skylines. But it was a beauty hidden for the time being under layers of dirt, rust, discoloration.

Kiev, sprawled on hillsides, with the Dnieper threading through it, had a magical quality when seen in perspective. At close range this quality evaporated: streets, old churches, magnificent palaces looked dilapidated and forlorn. Sebastopol, approached from the Black Sea, was a truly beautiful sight: a steep hillside thickly sown with white houses that splintered the sunshine. It has the character of some of the Italian hill towns. But once in the town, climbing its old stairways, I was more conscious of neglect than of beauty. Even Yalta, once the show-place of Crimea, I found down-at-the-heel and no match for its fabulous reputation. Shop windows in all the cities were desolate holes, where rags and tag-ends of goods seemed to have been thrown in at random. In the larger cities the hotels were tolerable, and their food not too bad, but even in Odessa and Rostov we fought a losing battle with vermin.

Psychologically, the atmosphere mellowed the farther south we penetrated. In Moscow, the austerities of the communist faith seemed to throw a shadow over the city, but the gloom lifted gradually until it almost faded out in the Caucasus. In Batum, people sat at little tables on the sidewalks or on the cobbled streets outside of cafés, indulging in Turkish coffee, conversation, and backgammon. In Tiflis, we visited several of the numberless *dukhans*, little restaurants, where every client is a connoisseur of wines and food. In the best of them there were splendid displays of appetizing fish and meats in endless variations. The Caucasians wear daggers embellished in silver and semi-precious stones even over their most ragged clothes, which is proof enough that they take life with grand gestures.

In most of the cities south of Moscow there was a general exodus of people from their homes after sundown, a heightening of the romantic temper. There is no street in Moscow to match the Ulitsa Vorovskovo in Kiev or Ulitsa Lasalya and Feldmann Boulevard in Odessa for movement and humming life in the evenings. The Feldmann (formerly Nikolayevsky) Boulevard, on the steep ledge of land overlooking the Odessa harbor, presents a scene at night without parallel in Russia. It is thronged with people, young and old, by twos and threes and entire families, strolling endlessly in the subdued light. The crackle of sunflower seeds is in the air, and a web of flirtations lies over the promenaders like a tangible and mildly stimulating presence.

Though new friends in the city complained that it was melancholy compared to its old self, Odessa was by all odds the pleasantest spot I had as yet found within the Soviet frontiers. Its large cafés still had the warmth one associates with Vienna cafés. Before the war it considered itself the Paris of the Black Sea. It even had bad men to match the Paris *apaches*. Many of them, I was told, used their courage and their proficiency with weapons to more useful purposes in the civil war in punishing pogroms and repulsing invaders. The legend of Mishka Yaponyets, a Jewish gangster whom the revolution turned into a hero, was still fresh in the city. His exploits have been celebrated by the gifted Soviet writer, Babel, and others. Mishka organized and led Red volunteers, many of them drawn from the criminal elements, to defend Jews against massacres by the Whites, and he died fighting the White foe.

Along the waterfront, at the foot of the ledge on which the city is propped, were the haunts of the bad men and their thorny lady loves, as wicked and colorful as the dives of Marseilles. Some of these haunts still exist, but an industrious excursion convinced me that the color has run out of them.

I received a flaming reception when I returned to Moscow. Literally. As I stepped into the backyard I saw flame and smoke pouring from the door and windows of my apartment. Our servant girl lay stretched on the ground, bleeding, while neighbors shouted and wrung their hands in helpless excitement. There was no sign of my family. I rushed into the house and plunged flailing through the thick smoke, calling the names of Billy and Genie. Then I realized that the flames were confined to the kitchen and the rest of the house was filled with smoke, but otherwise untouched. A defective kerosene stove had started the fire almost at the moment of my arrival and was extinguished in a few minutes. The servant had dived through the closed kitchen window, though the door was wide open. Her lacerated arms and my singed eyebrows were the only casualties. Billy and Genie had gone to meet my train and missed me, and the fire was over when they reached home.

Fifteen minutes behind them came the firemen, bustling and self-important. Despite the evidences of a *bona fide* fire, they were offended that we had sent a "false alarm" and threatened to fine me for having put out the fire without benefit of their nice new hatchets and fire-hose. I promised, however, that next time I would not be so rash, but would keep the fire going for them, and everything was forgiven.

The journey through the hinterland gave me a new appreciation for Moscow. If the city had seemed to me, coming from the West, bleak and impoverished, it impressed me as a veritable metropolis after Kiev, Novorossiisk, Batum and the thousand towns and villages which I had glimpsed in passing. The shops now seemed opulent and the people well dressed. Above all, the vital cultural life of theater, music, radio and newspapers, and the sense of proximity to the political dynamos of the land, made Moscow wonderfully full and alive. I could understand how a native of Kazan or Minsk—even of Rostov or Odessa—might feel himself transported to a wonderland of civilization on confronting Moscow for the first time.

It was a pity, almost, to destroy this illusion by a vacation in Berlin. At the Adlon Bar on Unter-den-Linden I met correspondents stationed in Germany or passing through on their way to assignments. They had been nearly everywhere and seen nearly everything. Yet Russia was a magnetic land of mystery even to them. They questioned me eagerly about the Shakhty trial, peasant disorders, food queues, the new political lines, and particularly about the redoubtable, inaccessible and rather ominous Stalin.

More than the filing of stories and the sight of my "by-line" in newspapers, this fraternization with well-known international reporters made me feel authentically a correspondent. I liked the shop-talk that embraced the whole globe, the offhand way in which great names and great events were tossed into the conversation. Outwardly, the talk was casual and touched with languor—cynical boredom is a convention of the trade. But under it these men and women who were the eyes and the ears of America in the outside world were conscious of their privileged vantage point and moved by a keen interest—sometimes no more than a sporting interest, it is true, though none the less real—in the revolutions and counter-revolutions and political jockeying of pre-depression Europe.

VIII. Iron Monolith

THE period of the Five Year Plan has been christened Russia's "Iron Age" by the best-informed and least sensational of my American colleagues in Moscow, William Henry Chamberlin. I can think of no more apt description. Iron symbolizes industrial construction and mechanization. Iron symbolizes no less the ruthlessness of the process, the bayonets, prison bars, rigid discipline and unstinting force, the unyielding and unfeeling determination of those who directed the period. Russia was transformed into a crucible in which men and metals were melted down and reshaped in a cruel heat, with small regard for the human slag.

It was a period that unrolled tumultuously, in a tempest of brutality. The Five Year Plan was publicized inside and outside Russia as no other economic project in modern history. Which makes it the more extraordinary that its birth was unknown and unnoticed.

The Plan sneaked up on the world so silently that its advent was not discovered for some months. On the momentous October first of 1928, the initial day of the Five Year Plan, we read the papers, fretted over the lack of news and played bridge or poker as though nothing exceptional was occurring. It was the beginning of a new fiscal year, precisely like the October firsts preceding it. The "control figures" or plan for the ensuing twelve months were rather more ambitious, with new emphasis on socialization of farming through state-owned "grain factories" and voluntary collectives of small holdings. But they were not sufficiently different from other years to arrest the attention of competent observers.

The fact is that the Kremlin itself was far from certain that a new era had been launched. It had not yet charted a course. Or rather, it had charted alternative courses and hesitated in which direction to move. Not until Stalin and his closest associates see fit to reveal what happened in the crucial months of that autumn will we know how close the Soviet regime came to choosing a course which would have altered the whole history of Russia and therefore of the present world.

There was nothing in the figures for the fiscal year of 1929 that committed the ruling Party to a Five Year Plan of the scope eventually announced. But a feeling of tense expectancy now stretched the country's nerves taut. A sharp turn of the wheel to one side or the other was inevitable, and the population squared for the shock. Economic difficulties were piling up dangerously and the Kremlin could not steer a middle course much longer. Food lines were growing longer and more restive. The producers of food had tested their strength and tasted a measure of victory; they rebelled more boldly against feeding the urban population and the armies for rubles which could buy nothing. Millions of grumbling mouths had to be either filled with food or shut by force.

A partial crop failure in southern Russia aggravated the situation. Grain collections were not going well and, as always happened under these circumstances, the collectors began to resort to strong-arm tactics. Arson and assassination flared up once more in the villages, and Red troops were said to be "pacifying" the most unruly districts with lead. Schools, clubs, government buildings, and other institutions typifying the Soviet power were burned down in dozens of places. The published details of the peasant revenge were sufficiently harrowing, and what the press reported, we all assumed, was no more than a fraction of the picture. Death penalties, with and without trials, were the government's automatic answer. But they did not suffice. Something decisive had to be done that would either placate the peasants or end their insubordination.

For a while the hope of drawing in foreign capital postponed a decision. If enough goods could be produced to meet the food growers' demand for a fair return on their labor, the problem would be more than half solved. A decree invited the capitalists of the world to come in and develop Russia's resources practically on capitalist terms.

Had the outside world, especially the United States before whose eyes the temptation was dangled most frankly, accepted the offer, there would perhaps have been no Five Year Plan, no liquidation of kulaks, no "Iron Age." The Great Depression might, indeed, have been less acute had world capital found a profitable outlet in the development of Russia's natural resources. But the bourgeois world still regarded Russia as an "economic vacuum." The phrase is Herbert Hoover's, whose knack for finding the right word for the wrong idea amounted to genius.

In the light of future developments, it is curious to remember that Hoover's election to the Presidency in November created a considerable flurry of optimism in Moscow. The Russians knew his hatred of Reds and had at various times excoriated his alleged role in overthrowing Bela Kun's Soviet government in Hungary. But Moscow had a fixation on engineering; the engineer is to the communist faith what the prophet has been to older faiths. With all his faults, Hoover was in Bolshevik eyes an engineer. How, then, could his judgment of economic possibilities be warped by personal feelings? "Hoover is a realist," was the burden of Soviet comment, "he must see that his country stands to gain by encouraging trade and investments here." The optimism, of course, was short-lived.

The failure of the capitalist world to accept the invitation determined, as much as any other single consideration, the turning of the wheel to the Left.

Reports of serious disagreement among the Kremlin leaders as to the next step echoed through Moscow. Stalin formally denied that there was any dissension or "petit bourgeois heresy" in the Politburo—which was accepted as proof that the reports were well-founded. Kalinin, generally regarded as spokesman for the peasants, was said to favor placating them. Klementi Voroshilov, War Commissar, whose Red Army was preponderantly a peasant army, likewise counseled moderation on the agrarian front. Nikolai Bukharin, editor of *Pravda* and foremost theoretician in Stalin's entourage, had published an article decrying undue pressure on the villages as "feudal exploitation" of the peasantry.

While counsel of moderation of this type was tolerated, and the path to such policy left wide open, the drift to the Left was not halted. Private traders and artisans employing labor—the urban kulaks—continued to be "liquidated" without let-up. "Speculators," which is Soviet for private merchants, were arrested by the hundred and the thousand, their property confiscated and themselves banished.

The final decision was Stalin's. Whether he had hesitated in deference to the prevailing Right sentiment or because of his own doubts will probably never be known. The Stalin legend is one that cannot countenance the admission of even a temporary uncertainty. His choice showed an amazing daring and an awareness of absolute power. The moment may well be accepted as marking the final emergence of Stalin, the Party secretary, as Stalin, the dictator. He had bided his time with Asiatic patience. An inconspicuous commissar and Party functionary under Lenin, then an equal member of a triumvirate with Zinoviev and Kamenev, now indisputably the uncrowned monarch.

No doubt he derived intellectual self-confidence in his choice from the humbled but still Leftist supporters of Trotsky who, one after another, had crawled back on bleeding knees, ready to serve him. Stalin was more at ease maneuvering men than maneuvering ideas. Chastened Trotskyists like Piatakov,* Radek, and Preobrazhensky were invaluable intellectual reinforcements. Stalin's espousal of policies close to Trotsky's provided the returned Trotskyists with a perfect justification for seeming betrayal of their whilom leader. It took the sting from humiliation and spread balm on a sore conscience.

But while this accession of brains may have given a fillip to Stalin's assurance, it does not detract from the audacity. His decision ran counter to the sentiment not alone of the population, but of the rank and file of the Communist Party. Supporters of Trotsky like to believe that "pressure by the masses" forced Stalin to throw his Right allies overboard and steer reluctantly to the Left. Doubtless there was a portion of the more revolutionary workers, especially among the younger people, bitterly opposed to any compromise with the "bourgeois elements" in the country. But the pressures, it was evident to anyone in Moscow at the time, were overwhelmingly in the other direction.

2

The defeat of Trotsky was complicated by personal antagonisms, theoretical disputes, and a struggle for sheer power. In essence, however, it was a repudiation of Leftism. The Russian people,

* Executed in January, 1937.

including the communists, were in a mood for truce. The failure of revolutionary efforts in Germany, Hungary, and China had bankrupted the hope for world revolution and foreign allies. Millionfold classes, not the least of them being the vast bureaucratic apparatus and entrenched police machine, had developed a sizable stake in the *status quo* of Nep. The existing system, like any system ever devised, had developed a robust will to survive—to make a permanent abode of the historical half-way house. In attacking the talk about "permanent revolution" and more vigorous struggle against Nep, Stalin had voiced the weariness and the despair of a people surfeited with struggle and sacrifice.

The Party membership itself was in the main content to let things be. It had been considerably watered in the last years by the admission of hundreds of thousands of new members without personal memory or intimate relation to the old revolutionary struggle. The admixture was largely from the factories. The diluted Party may have become much more "proletarian," but its cultural average was lowered and its contempt for intellectuals raised. Never much enamored of democratic rights, unable indeed to grasp the meaning of such rights, the newcomers were not impressed with efforts to safeguard the relative internal Party democracy that had existed under Lenin. The strong-arm methods of less finicky men were closer to their inherited tastes. As long as they held their jobs and their privileged status, they were content to shift the responsibility of thinking upon "practical," down-to-earth professional leaders.

Stripped of all secondary factors, the defeat of Trotsky expressed a genuine and growing annoyance with intellectuals and idealistic "dreamers," with world revolution and with new revolutions at home. It reflected a natural yearning to settle down and bite into the fruits of the revolution.

It was a reaction, when all is said and done, against internationalists and Westernizers (a large portion of them Jews, it happened) and a straining back to folk ways and national self-sufficiency. Though not consciously anti-Semitic, the movement had distinct anti-Semitic undercurrents, in that it reacted against the Jewish type of mind: idealistic, missionary, and without tough roots in the Russian soil. To the extent that the reaction turned inward along national lines, threw off its "duty to the world revolution," repudiated intellectualism and handed over all power to divinely inspired leaders, it was distinctly "fascist."

Stalin's rough ways may have aroused misgivings in the heart of the dying Lenin; they aroused a comforting confidence in the people trained by a thousand years of history to expect and respect naked power, a people distrustful of democratic gadgets. Stalin might be a swarthy Georgian, but his methods—cunning, patient, brutal—were Russian compared with the loose idealistic talk of Westernized alien-minded Lefts.

In adopting the main features of Trotsky's program, except for its international implications, Stalin was therefore thumbing his Caucasian nose at the tides on which he had ridden to the dictatorial apex. Confident that his political machine was now invulnerable, he pitted his will against his closest advisers, against the mass of the population, and against the majority of his Party.

No estimate of popular sentiment, naturally, can ever be made. I can only record my own certainty at the time that the country and the Party were overwhelmingly Right and accepted Stalin's unexpected course in a sullen and frightened spirit. Every time the Kremlin in a speech or decree hinted a let-up in socialization, greater leeway for the abler peasants, more immediate comforts for the workers, wider private trade—in short, a tendency toward the Right—the feeling of relief in Moscow was unmistakable.

On the eleventh birthday of the revolution, November 7, 1928, the course was still uncertain. The Congress of the Comintern (Communist International) which had ended the month before had been violent in its language but vague in its practical commitments to action; there was little enough clew to future policy in its fulminations. After the November holidays, however, things moved swiftly. The Right point of view, until then tolerated, suddenly blossomed into the blackest of heresies. It became, in the official jargon, the "chief danger."

Stalin achieved a bloodless victory. Never again was his decision on any matter, large or small, to be questioned. The "monolithic" Party, a Soviet equivalent for the "totalitarian" parties in fascist countries, was in absolute control. The Russia which it created in the next few years was as different from the one bequeathed by Lenin as it was from the tsarist Russia.

3

The face of world communism was to change no less completely. It takes its coloring always from the domestic Russian situation and is adjusted to suit the needs of the Soviet state. The Comintern Congress, the first to be held in four years, met for six weeks, from July 17 to September 1. Its reverberant generalities thus came before Stalin's decisive swing Leftward, but they served as a foundation for the new world policies of communism elaborated in the following year.

In the early summer months, foreign communists had begun to drift into Moscow for the impending Congress. Some of them, coming from countries where the communist movement is illegal and therefore "underground," arrived under strange pseudonyms on bogus passports. Even certain American representatives, for reasons that I could not quite figure out, traveled on synthetic passports. In a few instances documentary materials for these delegates were sent from the United States in my name, presumably to foil American officials who might be tracing the whereabouts of these delegates. The owners of each shipment knew of its safe arrival in Moscow even before the postman delivered it to me: the contents of my mail were clearly no secret to the postal authorities.

The political complexion of the foreign delegations was distinctly Right. The American group was captained by Jay Lovestone, Bertram Wolfe, and others expelled in the following year for Rightist heresies. In the other national groups were men like Brandler, Sellier, Kilboor, Roy, Jilek, whose elimination was likewise in the cards.

The most curious aspect of this conclave of world revolutionists, indeed, was its apparent domination by men who were soon thereafter discarded. As a test of the real authority of the Congress and the world-wide movement it ostensibly represented, the fate of its supposed leaders is enlightening. There was not another Congress in seven years, until 1935. The policies and activities of the organization were to undergo profound changes in this period. But the people who thought they were directing the 1928 gathering, who fought over programs and bargained for advantage, were for the most part expelled and branded as agents of the bourgeoisie in less than a year. The real power, it is all too evident, rested safely elsewhere and was exercised independently of the dictates of what was supposedly its highest governing body.

The Comintern is the organization that gives all honest and not-so-honest capitalist householders nightmares. It may be some slight consolation to them that it spoils the sleep of Kremlin leaders as well, though for other reasons. The Soviet regime is in the uncomfortable position of running a great nation pledged to keep hands off other nations and simultaneously an international revolutionary movement pledged to the exact opposite purposes. It takes consummate jugglery to achieve this with a measure of grace. The artificial separation of the mutually exclusive functions may do for diplomatic camouflage. It helps not a bit in solving practical clashes of interest.

Shall the immense power of the one communist government be used to promote or at least support communist revolutions elsewhere? Or shall the influence and sheer nuisance values of the international communist forces, on the contrary, be used to promote the interests of the Soviet government as such? How shall the day-to-day collisions between the immediate needs of the U.S.S.R. and the immediate needs of world revolution be adjusted? The answers to these questions are obviously loaded with the dynamite of schism for the Comintern and dangers for the Soviet Union's foreign relations. In theory, formulas to conceal this contradiction have been found. In practice, communists are continually torn between their loyalties to the first and only communist state and to their native revolutionary movement.

The delegates were far too absorbed in their criss-cross of political squabbles and the desperate defense of their own titles to leadership to pay much attention to the Russia of bread lines, sabotage trials, and political prisoners. The formal reports on the state of the Soviet Union gave them as much as they needed for their parochial purposes, so why bother looking out of the windows? Any extensive organization, be it a church, a peace union, or an international Rotary, develops an internal life of its own that blots out the rest of existence. Who should be expelled, who allowed to run the Communist Party of Ecuador or the United States, how the trade-union policy would be phrased—such matters occupied the delegates more than conditions in the Soviet Union, about which they could learn by turning to the proper page. American, English, and German delegates with whom I talked after they had been in Moscow for months showed small knowledge, let alone understanding, of elementary physical facts in Russia.

The non-communist press was excluded from the Comintern deliberations, but the principal speeches were published. Finally a "manifesto" was launched to the workers of the world and a program of policies and action was adopted. Precisely because the complexion of the Congress was Right, its verbal thunder out-lefted the Lefts. But foreign communists, no matter how meek, are not as easily managed as Russian communists; the threat of expulsion is not nearly as potent as the threat of concentration camp. Behind the façade of unanimous resolutions there was considerable acrid bickering. The manifesto blustered:

> This is not a document of timid groveling before the bourgeoisie, nor of a cringing peace with it. This is not a rotten pharisaic and contemptible declaration of unity with the bourgeoisie, a unity which signifies nothing else but treacherous flight into the camp of the class enemy, desertion, faithlessness, treason. It is rather a guide in the struggle of millions of the oppressed against their oppressors, in the struggle of the proletarian masses, in the struggle of the toilers, white, yellow, black, in the tropics and in the farthermost outposts of the globe, in factories and on plantations, in mines and on railroads, in forests and deserted steppes—wherever the class war rages. It is the program of the unity of the working class and of its mortal struggle against the bourgeoisie. It is the program of the inevitable world dictatorship of the proletariat.

There is healment for the spirit in a good round bout of cussing and self-assurance of this sort. After you have suffered humiliation in China, have sent Lenin's comrades to Siberia, and been taught to heed the whip yourself, a spirited manifesto does wonders. Because the world revolution had been set back in a dozen places, it is the more "inevitable"! A long array of enemies was chastised with words of flame. The League of Nations—"that child of Versailles, the most predatory treaty of recent decades"—came in for sizzling vituperation. Lying "pacifists" received their quota of abuse. Renegades, that is to say communists who differed on dogma, were anathematized in Biblical periods.

But the hottest coals were reserved for the socialists and "reformists." The "Social-Democratic parties have sided with the oppressors, with the imperialists, the predatory imperialistic governments and their agents" in the colonial question. They have been no less infamous, the manifesto insisted, on every other issue. In the preceding years Moscow had flirted with reformists and half-way revolutionists and been led into futile, costly and undignified adventures in the process. It had joined the Anglo-Russian Committee, the LaFollette progressive movement, the Kuomintang in China. Those who denounced such collaboration with the enemy had been thrown out of the communist fraternity for their pains. Now the Congress adopted these denunciations as its very own.

Out of this reversal grew the theory of "social fascism," according to which socialists were really fascist wolves in Marxist clothing. What the Congress began, the permanent leadership in Moscow was to develop in the next months to a point where the disease of collaboration seemed mild by comparison with the cure of non-coöperation. It was the policy which prevented the democratic forces anywhere in the world from combining to fight fascism, which thus received a clear right of way. More than any other single factor it helped to boost Hitler to dictatorial heights, to destroy socialism in Austria, and to give fascism a head-start elsewhere.

The Congress adjourned and its participants scattered to their respective countries, many of them to be duly expelled as "agents of the bourgeosie." Stalin's success in purging the ranks of the international movement of Trotskyists and near-Trotskyists had finished what there was of self-government within the movement. Thereafter expulsions of dissidents by one and by thousands became commonplace. Whatever doubt there may have been as to which was the kite and which the tail was ended.

Internationally, even as inside Russia, the "monolithic" Party—a Party run entirely from headquarters in Moscow—was an established fact.

IX. Savor of Life

IN ONE respect, at least, Moscow is exactly like every other place I have ever visited. Its weather, in view of natives, is "unusual." Thus my first autumn under the hammer and sickle was protracted and slushy as never before—a circumstance that held true every subsequent autumn. You wore galoshes, which placards commanded you to remove in the vestibule wherever you went. You spent half your time, or so it seemed, standing on line to deposit them and the other half to retrieve them. At crowded house parties someone always walked off in all innocence with your new pair and left leaky ones in their stead; sometimes they were both for the right foot, perhaps as a subtle political insult. The rarest thing in Moscow was a trouser cuff without mud on it.

It is comforting to record that even in the arena of an epochal revolution the vagaries of the weather provide the staples of conversation. Only the subject of food received more social attention. The extraterritorial privileges for foreigners in the matter of food were not yet organized. It took practically all the time of one person to round up provisions for a family. People looked back regretfully to the ample days of six months ago, when the private market at Hunters Row flourished. You discussed the new "Party line" and the bread line or kerosene line with equal intensity: they were not entirely unrelated.

The one crop that never fails in the new Russia is the crop of politically off-color jokes. These stories spring from the soil of immediate conditions and preoccupations and are therefore significant. Many of them are so intimately related to the news of the day that they make no sense out of that context. They are parables that circulate with lightning speed, sharpened and given new twists as they spread. A large collection of this acid humor arranged chronologically would constitute a history of the revolution—caricatured, it is true, but easily recognizable. Much later I toyed with the idea of such a *tour de force*. I jotted down hundreds of stories, but my patience gave out. Current jokes were not only available, but unavoidable. The "latest" was whispered in your ear a dozen times a day. But the older ones were not easily garnered. People who had written them down were afraid to admit it. The G.P.U. has a special division to gather and conserve this bitter-sweet humor. One of these days the archive will be opened to historians who will write serious tomes tracing the social conditions which gave rise to new cycles of anecdotes.

The bumper harvest of such stifled and unhappy merriment was to spring in the near future from the food shortage. Already the early pre-ration food jokes were being spread. You asked someone, "How are you getting on?" and he replied, "*Lootche tchem zahvtra*—better than tomorrow." Or he said, "Oh, like Lenin in his mausoleum." "How do you mean that?" you inquired, knowing that a joke impended. "Because they neither feed us nor bury us," was the answer.

But the Stalin-Trotsky battle was still the major target of the underground humorists. One of them represented Stalin, after having banished Trotsky, summoning to the Kremlin a rabbi famed for his learning and wisdom. "My rival is out of the way, and I am committed to building socialism in one country," Stalin told the sage, "and yet I am not certain that it can be done. You are a wise man. I command you to tell me truly, without fear, whether it is possible to build socialism in one country." The rabbi replied that he could not answer such a difficult question without consulting the sacred books and pondering deeply. He was given three days to ponder. At the end of that time he returned.

"Well," Stalin asked eagerly, "have you the answer?"

"I have," the rabbi said. "I have consulted the holy texts and thought a great deal."

"What is it? What is it?"

"Well, I can assure you that it is altogether possible to build socialism in one country. But to live in that country—that's impossible."

Though grave decisions were being made within the Kremlin walls and the whole nation was in a state of nervous uncertainty, individual men and women were of necessity riveted to their commonplaces of work, pleasure, and petty worries. Political and economic facts were the raw stuff of a correspondent's day-to-day job, but his life was not lived on an austere level of political analysis. Trifles loomed enormous on the horizon of their own day—particularly the morsels of "spot news" and the details of their transmission.

My chief competitor was the plenipotentiary of the Associated Press. The A.P. had an exclusive contract for the exchange of news with the one and only Soviet agency, Tass, which was the chief and frequently sole repository of information in the Soviet Union. This meant that the rest of us had to connive and sweat. There were "leaks" and one learned tricks for circumventing the opposition's advantages. The home office, moreover, was well aware of the handicap and pardoned inevitable beatings; the situation even gave one a perfect alibi on beatings that were by no means inevitable. Yet I carried perpetually the feeling that something important was happening. Not merely without my knowledge, which was bad enough, but with the knowledge of the Associated Press, which was a lot worse. That feeling was a constant in six years when everything else kept changing.

There was no lack of diversions. In Moscow the correspondents were lumped with the diplomatic corps for formal social purposes. Soviet receptions to the diplomats automatically included us; and diplomatic functions in any of the old merchants' palaces now used as Embassy residences similarly brought us invitations. I met diplomats and their ladies whom I continued to greet warmly for six years without quite learning their names or quite remembering their countries. The diplomatic type, especially in the lower registers, is fairly standardized. How was I to distinguish between a Scandinavian and a Greek Third Secretary when they made the same vapid remarks and smiled the same non-committal smile and were as uncertain of my identity as I was of theirs? Since I did not play bridge and could not distinguish one champagne from another, I remained always on the periphery of diplomatic circles.

National holidays of the various countries, royal birthdays and the like meant diplomatic parties. You went for the food, the helpful rumors, and because everybody else went. You always found the same Russians. The fact that they were in dress clothes, their wives in evening gowns and jewels, soothed your radical conscience. But always there was an undertow of guilt, to be wearing a starched shirt and stretching your equator with sturgeon, caviar, imported fruits, and a dozen kinds of meats and cheeses while around the corner long queues waited all night for a little bread or herring. The Foreign Office crowd was there; sometimes the censors; always General Budenny of cavalry fame, with his brand-new, curly-headed peasant wife; young and buxom Madame Lunacharsky in foreign finery; the diminutive and thoroughly urbane Comrade Baron Steiger;* the red-faced *Chef de Protocol* Florinsky,† the large, handsome Red Army Commander Tukhachevsky,‡ and a few others. You came to expect a lavish table at the Polish and Oriental receptions and more abstemious fare in certain other embassies.

For amplitude of provisions, music and entertainment, however, the Soviet Union's own receptions had no rival. On the evening of November 7th the government, in the person of President Kalinin, was host to the foreign colony. Half a dozen commissars, including War Lord Voroshilov, were in evidence, as well as a handful of the more famous Russian literary men. Only Kalinin was in workaday clothes, everyone else being correctly decked in formal black or uniforms. Coming on the heels of the great mass demonstration on Red Square, in a city ablaze with red lights and bunting, the party was not without its obvious ironies. I shall never forget the bafflement and anger of the correspondent of the New York Jewish *Freiheit*, a communist paper, when he was excluded from such a reception because he lacked a dinner jacket. That blow to his proletarian pride, I would wager, was not confided to his readers. In later years the formalities were relaxed on the revolutionary anniversary, apparently as a result of the gibes which correspondents could not resist.

2

Two "cultural" anniversaries in this season were to remain in Moscow's memory as a reminder of the more tolerant atmosphere on the eve of the Five Year Plan era. They were the cele-

* Reported mysteriously "missing" in 1937.

† Exiled from Moscow about 1934.

‡ Executed, along with seven other Army chiefs, in June, 1937.

brations of the centennary of Tolstoy's birth and the thirtieth birthday of the Moscow Art Theatre, respectively. Both Tolstoy and the Moscow Art Theatre are far from the Bolshevik regime in spirit, but the Kremlin did itself proud on these occasions, notwithstanding. That inveterate and eloquent speechmaker, Anatole Lunacharsky, then Commissar of Education, orated for two hours at each celebration. The story was told in Russia of a fire that was blazing while a crowd looked on. The fire brigades were there and the roof was falling in, but they did nothing to arrest the conflagration. They could not get started—because Lunacharsky had not yet arrived to make the opening address. . . .

As a Christian anarchist, pacifist, humanitarian, and mystic, Count Tolstoy, had he been alive, could scarcely have supported the Bolshevik cause. Scores of Tolstoyans were even then in prison and exile for their anti-Soviet attitudes. For those acquainted with these facts the festivities were both cynical and tragic. But for Stefan Zweig and other foreign guests who traveled to Yasnaya Polyana, the great writer's estate, the proceedings were presumably grave enough and impressive. Lunacharsky's impassioned eulogy conveniently avoided discussion of Tolstoy's beliefs insofar as they ran counter to Soviet ideology. The aged Alexandra Lvovna, daughter of Tolstoy, faithful to her father's ideas, had driven a sharp bargain with the new masters for countenancing the celebration. She obtained the virtual lifting in Polyana of Soviet laws that violated her father's philosophy. For a while, therefore, the Tolstoy school on her old estate was the only one in all of Russia that did not teach atheism or militarism. After escaping from Russia several years later, Alexandra Lvovna wrote a moving and bitter book accusing the Soviet government of arresting and betraying herself and other Tolstoyans.

The Moscow Art Theatre anniversary celebration, in the spacious and ornate Big Theatre, was an extraordinary scene. Its aroma does not easily fade from memory, for it was the aroma of camphor. Furs, silks, laces, brocades, and black broadcloth packed away since 1917 were drawn out once more by surviving members of the suppressed classes. Whatever remained of the bourgeois intelligentsia ventured timidly from its crevices and corners to pay homage to Vladimir Stanislavsky and the intellectual tradition that his theater represented. Sartorially it was a revival almost of the styles of 1900-1917, with only the foreigners in full dress and the Soviet officials in Soviet clothes to mar the period. Though Stalin and other leaders were present and the whole ceremony a gesture of respect for Russia's cultural heritage, the *Workers Gazette* was goaded by the scene into making the bold remark that "all ranks of the proletarian state were invited to celebrate the anniversary except the workers."

An additional impetus to my natural interest in the amusement arts was given by an invitation to "cover" the Soviet domain for *Variety*, the most influential American trade journal in the theatrical and related fields. It was an excellent discipline, forcing me to follow this phase of Russian life a lot more closely than other correspondents needed to. Quite aside from the pleasure I got out of it, the attention was not without value in the way of political guidance. The stage and even more so the screen are highly sensitive barometers of pressure under a regime of complete artistic censorship.

Variety is written in a hard-boiled and picturesque jargon all its own. Only seasoned readers can really interpret all its verbal short-cuts and Broadway allusions. For nearly five years everything that appeared in its pages out of Russia, whether signed or not, was mine. The authentic *Variety* slang was above my acrobatic skill. But it was fun trying, a little like learning a new language. Eventually a sentence of mine received the accolade of public recognition as genuinely in the *Variety* manner: proof that my devotion was not altogether wasted. In an erudite article on the remarkable style of this journal, Gilbert Seldes quoted a sentence in which I reported that the only "love interest" in Eisenstein's film *The New and the Old* was provided by the mating of a bull and a cow.

A Russian-American tenor of great personal charm and talent, Sergei Radamsky, and his lovely blonde wife, Marie Williams, gave a series of concerts that autumn. The Russian public took with great enthusiasm to their Negro spirituals. Something primitive and intense in these songs touched the Russian heart; perhaps their blend of joy and sorrow so familiar to Russians in their own folk plaints. Soviet audiences, however, were not aware of the religious implications of the spirituals. Musical programs, like everything else, must pass a censorship. Had the Radamskys' repertory been Russian instead of English, the Negro hymns would never have passed muster. As it is there were awkward moments. One evening, at the Moscow Conservatory, Sergei had rendered *All God's Chillun Got Shoes.* It evoked great applause and a clamor for its repetition. After he had acceded and again been rewarded with an ovation, someone sent up a note.

"Will Citizen Radamsky please explain to us what the song is about," the note suggested.

For a moment the tenor looked non-plussed—and tenors, as everyone knows, do not easily non-plus. Then he remembered that deception is the best policy. He explained:

"You see, comrades, it is about poor black slaves who live in misery. They have no shoes, no robes—only work and sorrow. But they dream of the beautiful future, after the revolution has freed them, when they will all have shoes, robes and the things their hearts desire."

A satire put on by Tairov's Kamerny Theatre and quickly squelched was the most memorable theatrical event of the season. It was by Michael Bulgakov, the author of *Days of the Turbins,* and showed his remarkable versatility. It was called *The Purple Island.* As devastating a take-off on stupid censorship as ever was written, its dynamite was so neatly concealed that it actually reached the public and survived a few performances. The action is set in a provincial theater with a play in rehearsal. It is a vapid melodrama with music. As the rehearsals proceed, the self-important provincial censors—blood brothers of their Moscow betters—discover ideological flaws. One questions the "class line" and the accommodating director instantly turns the rollicking sailors into class-conscious proletarians. Another finds fault with the attitude toward colonial and semi-colonial peoples, a third protests that the campaign for potato culture has not been given its due. The play is revised on the spot and emerges in the final act as a hilarious burlesque on inept propaganda drama.

Many a pompous policeman of the arts in that first-night audience must have squirmed in his seat. The banning of the play, the second of Bulgakov's to win that compliment in one year, was sufficient proof that the farce had not exaggerated. Bulgakov was barred from the theater for a period, then allowed to return as a director of other people's works for the Moscow Art. His subtle revenge was the play *Molière*, in rehearsal when I left Russia. Ostensibly an anti-religious drama, showing a French playwright of old persecuted by Jesuits, the parallel with his own hounding by Bolshevik Jesuits is perfectly evident.

In the beauty of the Soviet theater, ballet, and opera—in the deep charm of the Russians as a people—in the sheer excitement of absorbing a new world—I found ample compensations for disappointments and intruding doubts. As mirrored in my writing the new Utopia was still nearly perfect.

3

At last the city was matted with snow. Melancholy twilights came once more soon after noon to erase brief overcast days. Something unreal and subdued, like the tinkle and glitter of Northern fairy tales, filled the air. The darkness was studded with tiny nails of light; detached church domes and towers seemed to float overhead. Once more diminutive sleighs glided by noiselessly, the double-decker windows were puttied for the winter, people were bizarrely padded and swathed in heavy scarfs. Moscow settled back into the long nights when it is most like itself, somber, mysterious, and timeless.

Cutting winds raced through the walled-in silences of the Kremlin, where about a thousand visitors from all parts of the vast Soviet empire were gathered for the world's strangest "parliament," the *Tzik* or Central Executive Committee of the nation. About half of them were delegates elected by the last All-Union Congress of Soviets; the rest were invited spectators. The function of both groups was about the same: to listen, applaud, and return home with tidings of the Soviet government's strength and wisdom. The "legislative" powers of the *Tzik*, except on paper, were limited to raising hands for unanimous approval of whatever was submitted by the government.

Under the turrets from which tsars watched their enemies slain by the executioners in Red Square, these parliamentarians wandered through the ancient Kremlin, stopping to gaze at the Byzantine contortions of centuries-old churches, touching the cannons captured from the first Napoleon. Most of them simple workers and peasants and provincial communist officials, their mere presence within the Kremlin walls must have seemed to them a thing for endless wonderment. Their additional dignity as "legislators," however empty of real meaning, must have raised the wonderment to a sort of miracle.

They were the strangest agglomeration, these new rulers in whose name laws were promulgated and plans were launched and a nation's life turned upside down. Close-packed on straight wooden benches in the Great Kremlin Palace, they presented an amazing patchwork of races and cultures. Though it was eleven years after the revolution, they looked a little like intruders obviously overawed by the marble and crystal and magnificence of the setting. Many of them, perhaps, had only learned to read and write in the last year or two. Neither slogans nor Marxist formulas could express the marvel of their waking dream.

Perhaps I was reading more into their earnest demeanor than was really there. This was only my second view of the Soviet "parliament" in session, and I was almost as impressed and excited as the delegates themselves. I called to mind the dignity of an American Senate, a German Reichstag, the House of Commons—the atmosphere of pompous worldly success, social eminence, sartorial respectability, and the buzz of connivings in a bourgeois legislative chamber. Not eleven years, but eleven centuries separated that memory from the huddled mass of Soviet legislators before me. Rough-hewn faces of men and women from the mills and fields. Faces ingrained with soot and grime. Stolid expressionless faces of old men from Siberia. Be-turbaned, gray-bearded faces from the Asiatic deserts. Youthful, eager faces from Moscow and Leningrad and Kharkov factories. Few had troubled to shave for the occasion and men rubbed the thick stubble meditatively as Kalinin called the session to order. It seemed to me not a parliament but a new world in solemn session. Why cavil about their powers or legal status? If only as a pageant of the emerging new order their role seemed to me to transcend that of legislators in any other land.

In the Hall of St. Andrew where the sessions are held, huge square pillars, thickly crusted with gold embellishments, grow into a richly inlaid vaulted ceiling. Immense clusters of crystal lights set all the ornaments of the former ballroom ablaze. But from each of the pillars grew two large black radio horns—the new grafted upon the old, the utilitarian imposed upon the merely magnificent. A steep rostrum was built across the front end of the great chamber, where once stood a monarch's throne. A red-draped table ran the length of this rostrum and behind it sat leaders of the Soviet dictatorship. Stalin, too, was among them, but sitting a little farther back, chatting now with one, now with another of the men on the platform. He was there as a guest merely, not being a member of this august assemblage. Over the rostrum the portrait of Lenin smiled down on the gathering and on the opposite wall was the severe face of Karl Marx.

I sat among the correspondents in the press box. In an adjoining box were the diplomats of all nations. For all of us this "parliament" was unique, strange. But for me, perhaps for one or two others, it was stirring beyond the compass of such hackneyed words.

I watched a peasant woman, dull-eyed and rather scared, trying to follow Rykov's exposition of the grandiose plans for industrializing her country. She represented, perhaps, a quarter of a million peasants like herself. Rykov spoke simply, forcibly, despite the impediment of a stammer. (His successor as Premier, Molotov, also suffered from the same impediment, though not quite so markedly.) Rykov was reputed to be a heavy drinker—vodka was called "rykovka" in some quarters. But his long, deeply-lined face, with its straggly beard, under a shock of unkempt hair, seemed ascetic: the type, I thought, of the pre-revolutionary idealist. The effort of following his exposition was too much for the peasant woman and she gave up: her interest lagged and died and her strained expression relaxed. She took out a pen-knife and pared her nails, smiling at her own thoughts, as the Premier unrolled a few more billions' worth of plans.

Two young legislators, a boy and a girl, thinking themselves unobserved, held hands and looked into one another's eyes, as though in a movie theater, as the intricacies of the agrarian policies were expounded to them.

Individuals here and there may have amused me. The pretense that they legislate for a sixth part of the globe may be for gullible children. But the gathering in its entirety was a match for my expectations; it was a conclave inconceivable under any other regime. The last were indeed first.

For some ten days, the *Tzik* met in the gold-and-white splendors of the Great Palace, listened to hours-long speeches bristling with millions and billions. One evening Litvinov spoke to them of great world affairs, of his proposals for total disarmament and partial disarmament and the refusal of the capitalist world to act. That was something to carry back to a town or village in the heart of the Urals or Siberia!

After each of the major speeches, individual *Tzik* members took the floor and discussed the subject from the angle of their own localities. They never disagreed with the main speakers—such an audacity would never even occur to them. But they elaborated on the points he raised, citing examples from the local experience and pointing to problems that the government in its infinite wisdom might deign to consider. There might be little they could add to Litvinov's report on international relations or Kuibishev's on the basic plans for industrialization. But they were eloquent in denouncing the local bureaucrats who prevented the completion of a road in their township or some other such detail. To the shrewd leaders of men on the platform these hints and suggestions and meek complaints were valuable indices to the conditions and the state of mind of the country.

On the face of it the government was reporting to its parliament. In fact it was the parliament reporting to and petitioning its government.

Stalin's decision to steer the nation far to the Left had already been made. The *Tzik* resolutions neither added nor subtracted anything, but merely embodied his decision in legal forms. They were adopted unanimously. No dissenting voice, to my knowledge, has ever shocked this legislature. The thought of a lone delegate voting against a proposal from high places is so inconceivable that it seems a grotesquerie. The *Tzik* was not a law-making body in the Western sense. At most it was another technique of propaganda: a method for giving the population a sense of participation in big affairs, and a channel for conveying the wishes, the threats, and the promises of the dictatorship to the masses.

A five-year plan of agrarian socialization was voted, and a five-year plan of industrialization. The contours were left sufficiently vague to permit the planning authorities to work them out in detail. The Five Year Plan which the world was to exclaim over was not formulated and made public until some months later. No shadow of doubt, however, was left that Stalin had signaled full speed ahead towards the ultimate eradication of private ownership in both farming and industry. Every *Tzik* member must have departed with a distinct premonition, at once exalting and frightening, of immense purposes to be carried through at immense cost.

I shared that premonition. And I was content that I had reached the one proletarian country on the edge of a new epoch.

There was plenty for our forebodings to feed upon. Counsel of desperation prevailed in the Kremlin in its treatment of the peasantry. The methods used were described by the correspondents, with much exaggeration but much justice as well, as a "revival of militant communism against the peasants." It was a violation of the Kremlin's solemn promises of a few months before; the peasant population came to regard the government's word as so much empty sound. In the cities the ultimate fear—fear of the disappearance of bread—led to panicky hoarding. Men and women waited throughout the night in sub-zero weather to buy a little more bread in the morning. In the factories and mines and on construction jobs, the engineers and technicians, tarred with the brush of counter-revolution by the Shakhty trial, became hunted creatures, presumed to be guilty of treachery and sabotage by the mere fact that they were "bourgeois intellectuals," educated people of the pre-revolutionary days.

In this atmosphere of strain 1928 ended. The foreigners celebrated New Year's Eve at the hotels in counterfeit gaiety. Russians met the New Year in lively but surreptitious parties. It was not quite respectable to recognize the Christian calendar in this fashion, but habit prevailed. At the party which I attended there were communists as hilarious under the influence of vodka and gramophone music as anyone else. Christmas trees had been bootlegged in the capital despite the official ban on this remnant of ancient superstition. One of them stood in the corner in full view of the sardonic plaster Lenin looking down from the mantelpiece.

The year that began with the exile of Trotsky ended with the adoption of the major planks of his program. The year that opened with the crushing of the Left Opposition ended with a heresy hunt against the Right Opposition. It had taken Stalin six years to destroy the first; less than six months would suffice to destroy the second. While fighting Trotsky, the new leader had perfected the mechanism of his power. It was now a flawless machine, the most potent, considering the scope of its dominion, ever built in all history.

X. Life is Rationed

IF HELL is efficiently departmentalized, the large section reserved for foreign correspondents will have a special torture to dispense. It will provide its guests with juicy and exciting morsels of news but cut off all channels of communication with their newspapers.

We had a foretaste of that agony at the end of January, 1929. Most, if not all, of us knew that Leon Trotsky and members of his family had been withdrawn from their place of exile in Alma-Ata and were being zigzagged across the U.S.S.R. on their way to Turkey. Each of us carried the scorching hot news carefully under his coat, praying that other correspondents did not have it and would not have it until we had succeeded in transmitting it. But there was the rub. The censors would not let us send anything; they pretended to know nothing about it.

International telephone connections, which in later years enabled us to beat the censorship when the news deserved the risk, had not yet been opened. We could, and ultimately did, use the mails, especially the diplomatic pouches of friendly legations. But a resident newspaperman thinks long and earnestly before circumventing the censors on a story which they have specifically forbidden. The longer we carried the news the more painfully it burned into our professional flesh.

Negley Farson had replaced Junius Wood for the Chicago *Daily News* and we teamed up for mutual assistance; these alliances are not unusual in places like Moscow, where information is scarce and vague. When he phoned excitedly and talked of a big story, I linked it immediately to rumors I had picked up in other quarters. We met to compare notes.

"But it sounds cuckoo," Negley said. "Why should Stalin let his Number One Enemy out of his personal control and send him where he can shoot his mouth off? Maybe our story is cockeyed after all."

"It does seem incredible," I agreed, "but Trotsky has been pretty sick, I hear, and it may be Stalin doesn't want him to die on his hands. Just imagine what a stink it would raise if Trotsky did die suddenly. Everybody would say that he was done to death."

For days we hugged the knowledge to our breasts, convinced that we had a "world scoop" but almost powerless to make use of it. Not until later did we realize that nearly every one of our competitors held the same mistaken conviction. I experimented with different ways of hinting the news to the home office, but could get none of it beyond the censors' blue pencil.

The censorship that had seemed to me mild suddenly became harsh, insuperable. Censorships are always liberal—until they have something to conceal.

Negley's courage exceeded my own. He sent the news in the diplomatic dispatch bag to a neighboring capital, whence it was flashed to Chicago. But I succeeded in getting it to the United Press the same day. Sergei Trivas, of Voks and the G.P.U., arrived for one of his frequent social visits. He broached the subject without prodding.

"Have you heard about Leon Davidovich?" he asked. Davidovich is Trotsky's patronymic.

"Of course I have."

"Well, why don't you send it?"

"The censors turn thumbs down on any reference to the subject," I sighed.

"I don't have to tell you how to get around that, do I?" Sergei smiled.

About this time it dawned on me that he was speaking under instructions. While the Foreign Office was formally denying the whole thing with its usual vehemence, the G.P.U. was not averse to having the news leak out indirectly and a little incorrectly.

"Well, I could send it as a private message to Billy in New York," I ventured. (My family had returned to America for several months.) "Do you suppose it will go through—and that I'll be hauled over the coals here when it does?"

"Just send it," he now winked. "I assure you it is all right. Just say that L.D. is going to Turkey of his own free will."

Eventually it appeared that Trotsky was expelled from his

native land by sheer force, protesting every inch of the way. Trivas had probably been mobilized to inspire my breach of censorship with a view to spreading a contrary impression. In any case Billy received my mysterious message, a code word being used in place of Trotsky's name, and telephoned it to the United Press. The dispatch was published under a London dateline for my protection. Whether it was the first authentic news of the fallen War Lord's deportation to be published was a disputed point for months, as if it mattered to anyone but ourselves.

Fully a week after the whole world had displayed the news on its front pages, the Moscow correspondents were permitted by the Foreign Office to hint at it in their censored cables. For the Russian population it remained a vague and dangerous rumor, until it was confirmed in a few lines among the trivial "miscellaneous news" on inside pages.

To Stalin, no doubt, it seemed shrewd to push Trotsky beyond the Soviet boundaries. For a brief period the expulsion shocked and titillated world opinion. Then it was forgotten. Trotsky in banishment in Central Asia, the caged lion with Stalin as keeper, was a more dramatic and touching figure than Trotsky in Turkey. In Asiatic exile his voice had a resonance it lacked outside. A short message smuggled out by Stalin's prisoner had more effect than a long article by Trotsky, the deportee. With the leader gone, moreover, the Left Opposition inside the U.S.S.R. lost its sense of cohesion.

Trotsky's deportation was preceded by a series of exciting events. Wild rumors of another sweeping round-up of his suspected followers over a period of weeks were finally confirmed in an official announcement that one hundred and fifty Trotskyists had been arrested, tried in secret, and condemned to long terms of "rigorous isolation." Among them were men and women well-known in political, scientific and literary circles.

The announcement was backed up by accusations more startling than any laid at the door of the Trotsky faction before. The G.P.U. had uncovered the underground press which was flooding Moscow and Leningrad with leaflets. It had disrupted an "underground railroad," so-called, whereby exiles communicated with one another and with friends abroad. Tricks perfected in the revolutionary movement under tsarism, brushed off and used once more in the same Siberia, the same cellars and garrets, with the same fervor and at infinitely greater hazard! But the present rulers had themselves been on the subversive side of the struggle in the old days. They knew and called every trick.

2

The renewed warfare on the Left Opposition, coupled with furious attacks on "Right deviators," raised a miasma of fears over life in Moscow. The crushing sense of terror was strongest in the ruling Party itself; summary arrests and imprisonments of communists with long revolutionary records were an everyday occurrence. As for the small fry in the Party, an unguarded word or a malicious anonymous denunciation meant a search of their homes, exile, or worse. Men in positions of authority one day were mysteriously missing the next day and you never saw them again. Something furtive and hunted came into the manner of minor officials in Soviet offices that remained throughout the next period. It became almost the mark of their calling.

People shied away more nervously than ever from conversation that might be misconstrued as remotely political. They went carefully through their address books and private papers and destroyed traces of anyone who might be in the bad graces of the government. Those whose homes were searched or whose relatives were under arrest, became instantly contagious creatures to be shunned by their fellow-men. The most pestilential breed of all, of course, were foreigners. Only the more daring or more foolhardy Russians ventured within their infected orbit.

The groundswell of distrust of pre-revolutionary intellectuals—engineers, technicians, scientists and other specialized workers—started by the Shakhty trial, inundated factories and institutions throughout the country. Suspicion of the so-called "technical intelligentsia" quickly expanded to the proportions of a national phobia.

A *chistka* or cleansing of the ranks was carried through in the Communist Party and in the Comsomol (Communist Youth) League, tens of thousands being expelled for small reason or none. A new Puritanism was setting in which regarded amusement and laughter as politically immoral. Dancing and card-playing and gypsy music and vaudeville without a political lesson had flourished under Nep. Therefore these things now became symbols of "bourgeois degeneracy." Communists found themselves deprived of their membership in the ruling order because they lived too expansively, drank too much, or were in some other way unworthy examples for the proletariat. But above all they were expelled for heretical thoughts. The cleansing was retroactive; hundreds in every city and town were punished for views they had expressed in former years, when open internal controversy was still permitted.

Another and more far-reaching *chistka* was launched in offices, banks, museums, the thousand and one government institutions. Its purpose was to ferret out and expel "class enemy elements" who might be "hiding" in respectable positions. Hundreds of thousands of "former" people, the remnants of the pre-revolutionary upper classes, merchants, priests, socialists, Tolstoyans, had in fact adjusted themselves to the new system and were working as unobtrusively as possible in government service. Twelve years after the revolution, most of those of the "declassed" people who survived were of necessity earning their livings in some corner of the great government machine. For years they had been unmolested. They thought themselves safely forgotten in their crevices. Now they were pried out into the open and stepped on without pity. The liquidation of Nepmen, in addition, had in the last year or two driven them for sanctuary into official enterprises, especially in the distribution end of Soviet economy. They, too, were ordered out. No one in the ruling circles even raised the question as to how these outlawed masses would live now that they were deprived of a chance to labor. To hint any concern in that direction was "bourgeois sentimentality."

A thousand incidents crowd to my mind. A meek old man who had been bookkeeper in a government office for many years now cast out as a class enemy. A young teacher dismissed because her father had been a shopkeeper. A student in the technical school thrown out for "concealing his social origin" by claiming descent from a poor peasant when, as a matter of fact, his father had owned four cows. "Nests of former people" uncovered in museums, libraries, or research institutions: broken-down middle-aged and elderly people suddenly hounded from their jobs solely because of their "social origin."

A sharp increase in street beggary marked these initial months of 1929. The whining professional mendicants who followed one for blocks if they were not bought off with a few coins were familiar enough. So were the peasant families in fantastic rags huddled in a heap on the sidewalk looking with pleading eyes at every passer-by until a militiaman came to drive them away. But now there were new types on the Tverskaya, Dmitrovka, Petrovka and Kuznetsky Most. Old men and women, with something of dignity in their bearing despite threadbare clothes and heads bowed in shame, stood against walls with hands timidly outstretched for alms. I recall a blond consumptive-looking man, still young and aristocratic in his bearing but incredibly ragged, whom I passed every day on my way to and from the censorship office; he held out his hand silently and pretended not to notice when coins were dropped into it.

Another sign of the renewed pressure on the *byvshiye*—"former people"—was the sudden opulence of the "commission shops." These emporia, several on every main street, either bought goods outright from individuals and resold them for several times as much, or accepted articles for sale on a percentage basis. They now began to fill up with antiques, silver, furs, old furniture, rare ceramics, paintings, miniatures, jewelry, rugs. The remnants of pre-revolutionary wealth, salvaged somehow through twelve years of revolution and confiscation, were drawn out of their hiding places and turned into cash. Foreigners were the most avid buyers, though Russians in the higher income brackets bought heavily too.

Most fearful of all for its victims was the process of disfranchisement then under way. The right to vote was cherished not for itself, since it is an empty gesture, but because to be deprived of it was equivalent to being branded as an enemy of the revolution. In connection with elections to the Soviets, special commissions everywhere were drawing up lists of those entitled to vote and stringently excluding the better-to-do peasants, those in any wise tarred with the pitch of Nep trade, anyone whose social origin was unsatisfactory, people who for a thousand reasons had incurred the displeasure of the Soviet regime.

These became *lishentsi*, disfranchised people, without any rights or legal standing. To be among the *lishentsi* was to be an outcast. They could not work in government enterprises, except in the lowest categories of "black" or unskilled labor. Their children were the last to be admitted into elementary or higher schools, which under conditions of overcrowded schooling meant that they were not admitted at all. When food rationing was introduced, from the end of March forward, they were denied rations. When revisions of the rights to occupy "living space" were undertaken, the *lishentsi* were the first to be ejected from their homes.

In their totality the number of these pariahs (even babies were not spared) came to millions. Those in the villages survived until the "liquidation of kulaks as a class" the following year, when they were driven from their homes into inhospitable regions to live or to die. How did the others, in the cities, manage to live, denied work or food rations, harried from their living quarters, burdened with taxes and subjected to refined cruelties? I asked this question of officials, communist friends, ordinary Russians in the following years, because it was a fascinating mystery. None of them could give me a satisfactory answer, except the amazing tenacity of the human animal in clinging somehow to life.

Part of the answer of course is that a large proportion of them did not survive. Suicide and death from the diseases of undernourishment decimated their ranks. The rest hung on to existence somehow with bleeding fingers, doing odd jobs, teaching, begging, "smuggling" themselves into jobs by lying about their status only to be exposed and driven out again before long. Only Hitler's treatment of the Jews in Germany a few years later gave the world anything resembling this systematic persecution of a large class of the population.

Partly because of fear and even more so because of the food difficulties, Russians gradually ceased to entertain. Social life was muted. Those with the money or political influence to obtain enough food for a party, now conducted it in a kind of secrecy. It suddenly became both disgraceful and dangerous to eat better, dress better, or enjoy life more fully, than those around one. There was a renewal of the asceticism that characterized the first years of the revolution, only more of it now was protective coloration, hypocrisy rather than necessity or conviction. The chief

cattle; bread at official prices was cheaper than fodder at market prices. First in one city, then another, and soon throughout the U.S.S.R., the synthetic wish for rations was met. Every manual worker under the new dispensation was entitled to two pounds of bread daily; white collar or brain workers to one pound. Relatively low prices were fixed for these rationed quantities, and prices twice and later four or five times as high for bread bought without ration coupons. In effect it was a method of supplying workers at comparatively low prices. The *lishentsi* and those not belonging to the trade unions for any other reason were not entitled to rations.

A shudder of apprehension passed down the country's spine. Rationing had ugly connotations in the Russian mind. It recalled the most tragic days of the war and the civil wars. In the twelfth year of the revolutionary era, in the midst of the new boastful slogans being raised by the Stalin regime, it seemed a depressing omen. Young people who had grown to maturity in these twelve years were reminded that the revolution was not something in history text-books, but terribly immediate.

From that moment until the autumn of 1933 nearly five years later, the food situation grew steadily worse. Difficult as 1929 may have been, it was to seem from the vantage point of 1932 or 1933 a time of plenty. As in a city besieged food becomes the one absorbing subject, dominating all thought and all conversation, even so in the Soviet Union of the Five Year Plan the search for food, the struggle for sheer physical subsistence monopolized men's minds and drained their energies. National events and foreign affairs had a meaning for the mass of Russians only to the extent that they might affect the food supplies: all things unrelated to the stomach, the one gnawing reality, seemed of no consequence except for the professional politicians. Men changed their trades, their creeds, their friends in the hope of a little more sunflower seed oil or tea or bread.

The outer world was made to see Russia as a beehive of enthusiastic activity, where men labored and sacrificed in a spirit of fanatic self-abnegation. I did more than my share in building up that idyllic picture. Yet I know that the "average Russian," if there is such a thing, was less interested in the billions and trillions of the plans than in his hope of finding another herring, another pound of potatoes. I watched men and women map out intricate campaigns of flattery and wire-pulling to obtain a little more milk or a pat of butter for their infants. I saw them risk their careers or put themselves in danger of exile to a concentration camp for an extra ration.

The enthusiasm, or the ruthless will to achieve, was at the top. Below was naked want and desperation. A population meek by nature was made meeker by undernourishment, and therefore more amenable to manipulation by its rulers. People who spend every free moment looking for food have no time to mutiny or even to ask questions. It is not true that people revolt when they are hungry: revolt needs more strength than hungry men can muster. The fear of hunger or the memory of it is a more effective spur to protest than the debilitating fact itself. At any rate, I know that the grumbling in Russia was bolder at moments when the food situation eased up a bit.

Foreigners, too, were given the privilege of rations. The inflation of the Soviet currency, however, made them all affluent, so that they could afford to feed themselves at non-ration prices. The physical hardships involved in standing in line to buy—and the total absence of some products—were their principal problems. Later the government solved these in part by organizing for foreigners special shops where they could purchase within liberal limits whatever the government had to sell, which was frequently less than enough for a balanced diet. We had to hire another "house worker," the lanky, aging Vera Ivanovna, to give all her time to corralling food supplies and helping Billy prepare meals. In the old days this Vera Ivanovna had been cook in a well-to-do family, with maids and scullions at her elbow, and she resented her decline more bitterly than any multimillionaire reduced to penury. Her temperamental fits were worthy of a prima donna.

The food shortage was seriously aggravated by the Kremlin's decision to meet foreign trade obligations with food exports. As conditions became steadily worse, the knowledge that their government was exporting food became perhaps the deepest of the silent grievances of the Soviet people.

It was with rationing that the lush verdure of half-illicit humor on the theme of food sprang up everywhere. I could fill a thick volume with the tragic "jokes" that multiplied and spread; new ones and variations on old ones arose nearly every day and swept the country. "Why is ours the most cultured country in the world?" a popular riddle asked, to which the proper answer was: "Because nearly everybody has at least one book and treasures it —the food book." "Why has Trotsky been sent abroad?" another asked. "Because we export all our most necessary products." "Papa," a little boy was represented as asking, "why don't Jews eat ham?" At which father turned angrily on his son. "And we Russians," he said bitterly, "do *we* eat ham?" Another anecdote told of a conference which discussed ways and means of fighting prostitution. The question arose as to which of the government departments should be entrusted with the task. Some favored the Commissariat of Health, others the Commissariat of Education. But the wisest among them said: "And I, comrades, suggest that we entrust prostitution to the Commissariat of Trade. Then it is sure to disappear. That's what has happened to everything else it manages—bread, sugar, tea, milk. . . ." A former Nepman is asked how he feels. "Oh, just like a moth," he sighs, and explains that he has already eaten his wife's coat (by selling it through a commission shop, of course) and is now eating his own fur collar. Endlessly these "anecdotes" were hatched and elaborated.

It was no laughing matter. None of the subjects of political humor are in themselves funny. It is the humor begotten of pain. I saw the tremulous excitement that touched a Russian family when some member of it brought home a decaying herring or a verminous bit of meat. A reputable Russian actor came to me shamefacedly, with tears in his eyes, to beg a little cereal and a bit of sugar for his sick baby. Women offered their bodies in the hope of a real meal. A woman visiting the home of a General Electric engineer saw white bread, touched it incredulously, and burst into hysterical weeping. I telephoned half a dozen legations to find a lemon for a Russian friend whose dying wife needed it. The advantages of foreigners, with their greater opportunities for buying edibles and their right to import some, made them a class apart, as far above the mass of their neighbors as J. P. Morgan might be above a workman on relief. Conversation in Russia might begin anywhere, in the clouds of philosophy or art, but it spiraled down always and inevitably to food. I saw all work in offices paralyzed when someone mentioned that an article of food could be bought at a certain market or coöperative store.

There was enough to eat in the better hotels, it is true, but at prices far beyond the reach of any but a few privileged officials or successful embezzlers. A meal at the Grand Hotel might cost the equivalent of a factory worker's income for a week. Tourists and visiting delegations, unless they were uncommonly stupid, could not be totally unaware of the food shortages. There were the queues, the empty shelves in shops, the haggard faces. But they ate amply themselves and saw workers and officials eating in the favored factories. There were also individuals, thousands of them, who did not know deprivation personally, either because they were earning large amounts or had enough political pull to obtain necessities denied to others. For the masses these lucky exceptions only underlined their routine miseries.

Americans who had worked with the American Relief Administration in the Volga famine areas have told me how guilty and bestial they sometimes felt to be hiccupping with satiety when they knew that people were dying of hunger beyond their doors. In the midst of a robust mouthful, a woman told me, she suddenly recalled the starved little faces and swollen bellies of children she had seen half an hour before, and it made her sick with nausea.

A little of this ordeal was ours, the shame of filling one's belly three times a day when all around was shortage. Not famine, but the shortage that causes men's bodies and minds and spirits to sag—the shortage that makes the stomach the core of existence, the center of every waking and dreaming thought—the shortage that makes all other human values, art, beauty, ideals, philosophies, an empty mockery.

XI. Social Slag

WITH open, wakeful, horrified eyes I saw a nightmare. Five floors crowded with human wreckage: an unholy offal heap of some seventeen hundred cripples, beggars, old prostitutes, thieves and cutthroats, drug addicts, sex perverts—men, women and children in the lowermost depths of poverty. For months the loathsome memory haunted me and colored my thoughts. When I described my visit in a restrained dispatch, I inserted and underscored these sentences:

> The house is a heritage of the days of tsardom, and must not be held against the Soviet regime. The derelicts to whose use it is dedicated are of the type whom no change in government or in economic structure can possibly help—the dregs of the teeming city population.

This was reassurance not so much for the readers as for myself. In the twelfth year of the Soviet revolution I had found the "night's lodging" depicted by Maxim Gorky in his *Lower Depths* not merely intact but more terrible in its reality than any stage director had managed to make it. As with everything else that distressed me, I discounted it as a left-over from the past, thus exonerating the revolution.

Under the surface of every great city there is another submerged city, a life far out of sight which few natives and no strangers can even guess at. The nightmare that I stumbled across was a microcosm of that slimy nether life. Through the accident of a casual acquaintance I was led to the *Dom Nochlyega:* the "House for a Night's Lodging," still known to the denizens of Moscow's lowest strata as the "Yermakovka," after the millionaire Yermakov who built it long before the revolution. There were six such institutions at this time in Moscow, together accommodating about four thousand lodgers. This acquaintance, who had traveled much in his day through Europe and the Americas, was singing the praises of Western culture and civilization.

"Culture, civilization," I bristled. "What about the misery and poverty and crime that it breeds? Do you know the East Side of New York or London's Whitechapel, the slums and hell-holes of that civilization? You judge by the suave surfaces."

"And here, under the Soviets?" he smiled.

"I admit the surfaces here are far from pretty. But that's because the veneer has been ripped off, and we are seeing things as they really are. Here there is no pretense and no concealment. The sores are visible to the naked eye and they will be cured."

"So you think it's all on the surface, do you? You think you have seen the worst of it? Well, my young friend, maybe I can show you that even what you see here is only a veneer. Down below life is putrescent, worse than anything London or Paris or New York conceals."

How he managed it I do not know, but several nights later he led me to the Yermakovka. No other foreigners, as far as I know, had been there and certainly no American correspondent until then had been through it. I knew flop-houses on the Bowery, wretched tenements, and steerage holes. I started for the Yermakovka expecting misery but convinced that it would be only a Russian variation on the ancient world-wide theme. What I found, however, was so much more loathsome than anything I had ever seen with my own eyes that it seemed of a wholly different order of horror.

We went through chamber after chamber and floor after floor, accompanied by armed guards, to look at a lengthening exhibition of broken and degraded humanity. These "night's lodgings" are the refuge of the homeless, the helpless, and the criminal who can beg or steal the fifteen kopeks to pay for a bed. It is the last refuge, too, of those who shun the law and their fellow-men. It is the one place where they need not show documents or even give their names.

The corridors were wet and slippery with grime and filled with an awful stench. Everywhere were diseased and perverted faces or blank faces emptied of all human meaning and feeling. In the women's section I saw haggard creatures in rags sprawled half nude on their cots, too hopeless and apathetic to notice our intrusion; and younger women, with sick and leering faces, who threw obscene words at us. There were some 350 women in the house that night, about a dozen of them with infants at their breasts or crawling among the rags. In the men's section there were special rooms to which were assigned cripples, criminals, drug fiends, and so on. While no questions were asked, the administration was familiar with the types and separated as far as it could those driven to the lodging by poverty from those who made up the diseased and criminal elements.

The large barracks set aside for the deformed was something out of a Dantesque imagination. A huge roomful of men without arms, without legs, paralytics, blind men, hunchbacks lying on hard beds in the grotesque postures necessitated by their deformities, many of them groaning and writhing. A roomful of distorted bodies, faces and minds. In the wing for criminal elements our arrival was resented and foul names were yelled in our direction. In one room the guard drew his revolver to silence the growling. Hundreds of the inmates seemed mere boys.

Back in the office of the administration I asked an official who these creatures were, whence they came, and where they would end. His answers were far from explicit. Every evening beginning at six the line of applicants for a night's lodging formed in the yard of the Yermakovka and until midnight the city's homeless kept coming. Often they failed to get admission after hours of waiting.

"There has been such an influx of peasants fleeing their villages," he said, "that every night now we turn away from three to five hundred. It's sad but it can't be helped. We can only guess who these people are. Some are beggars: you see them on the Moscow streets. Some are whores too old or ugly to find customers. Others are hiding from the police. But a large number are just poverty-stricken people without a roof over their heads. We have many here who come with recommendations from their trade unions. We let them stay for two weeks or even more. All the rest are turned out every morning. We can't guarantee that they will find their bed when they return at night—after all, this isn't a hotel!"

"They say," another official volunteered, "that members of the old aristocracy have been reduced to living in the Yermakovka, but we have no way of telling. There's a very old woman in one of the rooms tonight—she comes here often—who is said to have owned a great estate in the Crimea, but I accept these stories with a grain of salt."

New lodging houses were being built, they said, and in the next year or two these plague spots would perhaps be eliminated. Meanwhile even a bed in the Yermakovka is better than none, comrade, isn't it?

"We try to clean the place, but what's the use? It's a foul stable again as soon as the mob comes at night. But we have instituted a medical department in the basement. While we don't force anybody to get treatment, we let them know that they can get it. Mostly mothers and babies use the clinic."

I inspected the clinic, then fled from the place. I could not contain myself and mentioned the visit to a communist acquaintance.

"The dregs of the capitalist civilization that we're eradicating," he said, untouched. "It's just a lot of nonsense putting them up in night's lodgings of any kind. They should be drowned and forgotten. We are starting from scratch and don't have to drag along the past."

2

When I cabled detailed accounts of the trial of anti-Semites from Minsk, my London editor, Webb Miller, unkindly but not untruthfully described them as "alibi" for the expense account. The trial was, in fact, an excuse for a close-up of this town. My curiosity had deep roots. For some centuries before its transfer to America, my family had lived in that region, and members of it in Minsk proper. The town is the first railroad station beyond the frontier point when one enters Russia through Poland, and I had promised myself a more detailed view. Like all things heard or glimpsed in early childhood, the name had overtones of glamor for me, however commonplace it might sound to others.

I use the past tense advisedly: one good look at the bedraggled capital of White Russia wiped out forever the faintest suggestion of glamor. Poverty and ignorance, both ancient and deeply incrusted, were written indelibly on the old town and its environs. Streets and houses were more woebegone, droshkies more rickety and direputable-looking, even the horses seemed hungrier and wearier than in any other city I had as yet seen. The pulse of new construction that disturbed the sluggishness of other Soviet towns seemed absent in Minsk, a slow-moving, and seemingly hopeless place. Its major industry, from the looks of it, was photography—probably explained by the fact that nearly everybody in the former Jewish "pale" has relatives in America who must be reminded with portraits of folks in the old country. The principal streets were overrun with holes-in-the-wall calling themselves modestly Rembrandt, Rubens, Michelangelo, or Repine photograph studios. Shop windows specialized in fly-specks and portraits of the Soviet deities. The ill-smelling side-streets lined with decrepit houses were so reminiscent of scenes remembered from the tales by Sholom Aleichim and Mendele Maikhar Sforim that they surely could not have changed much in the intervening generations. A scant twenty-five miles from the Polish border and therefore destined to be among the first victims in the event of war, Minsk suffers neglect. Moscow's sensible policy is to concentrate new industries in less vulnerable geographical areas.

The city having been viewed and discounted in short order, the trial became the sole local interest for me after all. Three young rowdies were accused of anti-Semitic outrages against a twenty-year-old Jewish girl, Druzye Barshai, in the glass factory where they all worked; another woman worker, a factory official and two policemen were brought to trial with these three for their failure to protect the girl. Neither the stupid pranks nor the victim in themselves merited national attention, but the episode was singled out for the limelight because of its very pettiness. It served as a sample of routine, habitual Jew-baiting in the government's unending fight against Russia's heritage of racial hatreds.

The Minsk exhibition trial took place in the auditorium of the Railroad Workers Club, decorated with posters, pictures, and red bunting, and crowded to suffocation by a local population whose life is not often enlivened by events of national importance. About half the inhabitants of Minsk are Jews, the rest being White Russians, Poles and Great Russians. The life of the city—its Soviets, police stations, courts, street signs and even lavatory signs—is conducted in four languages: a disconcertingly literal application of the principle of racial equality.

The trial, however, was not attuned to local needs. The "Barshai affair" became a kind of banner in the campaign against anti-Semitism. What would normally have amounted to a police court case of hooliganism was converted into a charge of counter-revolution, for which the extreme penalty is death. No one seriously expected this penalty to be invoked, but its mere shadow threw the proceedings into sharper relief. Leading journalists from all over the country attended the trial and my own presence as the only foreign representative (aside from correspondents for American Jewish publications) was played up by the Soviet press as proof of international interest.

Despite earnest efforts to eradicate it, anti-Semitism still flourished in Russia. Traditionally the scapegoats for hardship and disaster, the Jews were blamed by the more ignorant sectors of the population for the deeds of the Soviet regime and the misdeeds of anti-Soviet elements; they were hated as Nepmen and as the liquidators of Nepmen. Prejudice has no need for logic. On food queues I heard the Jews cursed by simple suffering people, though the Jews were on the queues with them. Even within the Communist Party the disease was prevalent: a party of millions inevitably reflects the superstitions and prejudices of the population from which it is drawn. The great number of communists expelled from membership for anti-Semitism is sufficient indication of its spread in the ruling minority; the dilution of the Party in recent years by drawing in hordes of factory workers had operated to deepen its anti-Jewish streak.

To the most ignorant layers of the Soviet population, Lenin is still a Jew and his regime is still a Jewish regime. Occasionally one hears Russians assert, without realizing the irony of their remark, that they *approve* of the Jewish government. The Kremlin is keenly aware that anti-Semitism is frequently an indirect expression of anti-communism and must be combated as such.

The triviality of the actual incidents involved and the unprepossessing personality of Druzye Barshai took the edge off the exhibition. The girl was a creature of stunted mind and body, illiterate and uncommonly ugly, the sort of unfortunate doomed to be the victim of backward ruffians whatever her race might be. The young hooligans had tripped her up, played obscene tricks on her, and in general made her bleak life more miserable. They were now completely bewildered that their "fun" should have become an affair of world-wide importance dignified by the charge of counter-revolution.

They blinked stupidly in the flaring arclights and even in the improvised courtroom kept referring to Jews in insulting words —the only names for Jews that they knew. Though they were pitifully contrite and insisted that they really had nothing against the *zhidy* (the traditional foul designation for the race by Jew-baiters in Russia), it was evident that they were unconvinced that their behavior was criminal.

The factory heads and the policemen, among them communists, who had not moved a finger to help the Barshai girl and had chuckled at the obscenities of her tormentors, were the real culprits. The prosecution directed its fire against them even more than against the illiterate rowdies. Sentences ranging from six months to three years were imposed on all the accused. The factory officials no doubt paid for their complacency by the loss of their posts and their Party membership.

3

At the Amo automobile works on the outskirts of Moscow, several hundred men and women were gathered in a large room, listening to a long and tedious speech. Their boredom was too evident. Hungry glances were cast at a counter against one wall heavily laden with sandwiches: red caviar, cheese, and other rare delicacies. When I entered and took a seat in the rear, the speaker was discussing Geneva, disarmament and imperialism. From world politics he descended by stages to national affairs and finally to the Amo plant and its duty to produce more and better motor cars.

"It is Comrade So-and-So, of the Moscow Committee of the Party, an important communist," my companion whispered.

He was followed by other speakers, evidently communists working in the plant. All of them lectured the audience like school teachers lecturing a class of retarded pupils who needed the same thought repeated endlessly. The classroom effect was given additional color by an "examination" which one of the speakers conducted.

"Let us see whether our department has learned its political A B C," he said. "In the great task of building socialism, all workers must be politically conscious, vigilantly on guard against enemies at home and abroad. Why is Right opportunism the greatest danger at this stage of the revolution?"

Silence greeted the question.

"Don't be bashful, citizens and comrades," the speaker urged. "Who can answer the question?"

Another silence, more urging by "teacher," then a bright pupil ventured an answer, and after him half a dozen others stood up and stammered things half-remembered from recent speeches and editorials. One of them got his answer sadly garbled, so that it ended in gibberish and evoked laughter. The men at the red-draped table in front held a whispered consultation, and the speaker resumed:

"The correct answer, citizens, is the one given by Comrade Ivanov. Yes, Right opportunism is the chief danger because it is the ideology of kulaks, Nepmen, and disguised Trotskyists. Comrade Ivanov receives this prize for his answer."

A framed lithograph portrait of Stalin was passed overhead to Ivanov, and everybody applauded.

Other questions and answers followed, with books, pictures, a plaster bust of Lenin awarded to the best parrots. Then there was an adjournment while sandwiches were distributed. Refreshed, the meeting was resumed.

It was an "election" to the district Soviet by the workers of one department of the factory. "One hundred percent of the voters took part," the press would announce the next day.

A list of names was read by the presiding functionary. It was the "ticket" drawn up by the communist nucleus in the department, and it contained many names of non-communists. The discussion was brief and almost entirely laudatory. Two or three workers expressed their hope that the Soviet delegates would do something about improving the service in the factory buffet. Finally those in favor of the list were asked to raise their hands. Nobody was opposed.

It was my first view of an "election." The following day I saw another, in a workers' club. Miscellaneous citizens not attached to large factories or institutions, among them servant girls, free-lance writers, janitors, were electing their delegates. I heard approximately the same speeches and even more perfunctory discussions of the candidates.

I attended dozens of these meetings that year and in subsequent years. Sometimes the discussions were more spirited. Several objections were raised to candidates on the ground that they drank too much or did not devote enough time to social activities. But not once did anyone even by implication raise a fundamental question of larger policy. No one pretended that the electors were deciding anything; at best they were selecting the instruments for putting into effect decisions already made in mysterious upper regions. Whatever these election meetings might be worth as a school for drumming in the ideas of the Kremlin, they were empty farce considered from any other point of view.

4

Any number of Russians might bite any number of Russian dogs—perhaps they do—without winning a line in the Soviet papers. Unless their carnivorous tastes carried some political implications they would not be news to a Soviet editor. Events without a social purpose, the thousand and one hilarious and calamitous accidents that befall mortal man, rarely if ever find space in the Russian press. Ordinary crime, low-down homicide or robbery without social pretensions—crime for crime's sake, as it were—is simply snubbed. The rare exception to this rule, such as the reports of the "Volga pirates," therefore made a large impression on the public mind.

Not that the Soviet press did the story justice, journalistically speaking. As the scanty and colorless news dispatches trickled through the more obscure columns of Moscow's newspapers I could not help thinking:

"What a holiday this tale of lusty butchery and blood-soaked bravado would have provided for the American tabloids! A million stenographers would have lost their hearts instantly to the swaggering Kuznetsov reciting the details of his murders and plundering with professional pride. How they would have envied his beautiful mistress!—well, she would have been beautiful in the tabloids."

The girl was only twenty-three, her name was Voronina, which is Russian for "carrion crow," and she was the only female in a bandit trust of over thirty strong. In prison she sang and danced to keep up the spirits of her paramour and maybe her own. The gang had terrorized the Volga region for years, preying on individuals, banks, shops, and evading the G.P.U. until early in 1929. Kuznetsov himself may have been boasting when he counted his killings by the dozen, but fifteen of them at least he described in convincing style, among them the murders of his own wife and child and an uncle. He believed that murder begins at home. He led piratical raids on Volga steamers.

"I never robbed the poor," Kuznetsov explained. On the contrary, he helped the widows and orphans, including those whom he personally turned into widows and orphans. The proletarian preachments had not been wholly lost on him. He told many stories of his gallantry and essential kind-heartedness. One of these sticks in my memory:

He held up a droshky and robbed the passenger of a cash payroll for his factory just drawn from the bank. The cab driver, scared out of his wits, drove off in a panic, but Kuznetsov sent the gang after him. When the trembling cabman was brought back, the robber chieftain read him a lecture on fairness and considerate conduct.

"You should be ashamed of yourself, running off in this cowardly fashion," he chided the man. "Why, you're the only witness of this robbery. Without you, how will this poor fellow prove that he was really robbed? He would be accused of having disposed of the money himself. You have to stick by your fellowmen, and we'll see to it that you do."

Paper and pencil were found and the minutes of the robbery were written out. The cabman signed it as witness and the document was presented to the victim as a receipt for his payroll.

These humane gestures did not save Kuznetsov from the firing squad. Ten years of imprisonment is the highest punishment under Soviet law for any crime except counter-revolution. That simplifies matters. Whenever the government prefers to dispose of a bad customer it calls his crime counter-revolutionary; organized brigandage usually comes under that head. A batch of his underlings died with Kuznetsov and the girl friend received a long prison sentence.

The kind of crime that did figure frequently in the press was distinctly political in character, chiefly corruption in office. Scarcely a week passed without a major scandal in some part of the country: diversion of official funds for private orgies, the abuse of bureaucratic power to terrorize entire towns, the entrenchment of criminal elements in control of the Party apparatus in various cities and provinces. The misuse of their official authority to force women employees into concubinage—often "mass rape" of women in a spirit of degenerate fun—was especially in vogue.

The foremost leaders in Moscow itself were rarely touched by the breath of scandal,* but elsewhere depravity in high places was all too common. The honey-pots of power draw insects under any system. The vast number of these parasites exposed by the central authorities, and duly reported in the press, left no doubt that many more were still undisclosed. As long as "elections" are an empty formality and secret arrests, exiles and shootings leave the individual citizen subject to intimidation, the temptation to misuse power remains almost insuperable.

"Bureaucratism" is the name given by the Bolsheviks themselves to the system which breeds such corruption. They are incessantly announcing campaigns to wipe out the evil. It flourishes notwithstanding. The campaigns against bureaucratism themselves assume a bureaucratic character, tangled in red tape, favoritism, espionage, fears, and grudges.

Shocking details of demoralization in the higher reaches of Moscow trade-unions—in the shadow of the Kremlin itself!—were published in January, 1929. Leading officials of the Moscow section of the Trade Union of Construction Workers had formed a fraternity calling itself "Kabuki." Its object was debauchery in the grand manner, using union funds, and intimidated women employees for the purpose. Drunkenness, embezzlement, sale of favors were among the numerous charges made against the "Kabuki" bravos by the Control Commission of the Party. The details of the Saturnalias were too foul for publication; the Russian imagination is fertile.

In the important proletarian region of Smolensk and its environs, the party earlier had uncovered rottenness that makes

* In 1937 Henry Yagoda, after his dismissal as head of the G.P.U., was accused of having embezzled state funds; if the charges were true, it means that the corruption described here had spread to the very top in the next few years.

Tammany Hall seem puerile by comparison. The communist heads of the local Central Executive Committee of the Soviets and of the Smolensk Party Committee were busy with orgiastic parties while the local police fraternized and shared loot with the local bandits; while factory directors exacted payment *in natura* from women workers under threat of dismissal from their jobs; while tax collectors and financial chiefs feathered their own nests with public funds. I take the word of *Pravda* for these facts. The central government did a thorough job of house-cleaning once it became aware of the situation; a number of the communists paid with their lives; but that neither explained nor destroyed the swamps that breed such corruption.

Then there was the astounding tale of Veli Ibrahimov, chairman of the Central Executive Committee of the Soviets of the Tartar region in Crimea. An old-fashioned brigand chieftain, he lorded it over his domain in the name of Marx until detected by Moscow and liquidated. The list of crimes for which he and his band, "communists" all, were shot included cold-blooded murder of political enemies.

Analogous decay was uncovered in Irkutsk, in Artemovsk, in dozens of cities. Of communist leaders arrested in Sochi, a lovely garden spot on the Caucasian riviera, *Pravda* was able to write: "Their orgies usually ended in the mass rape of a woman. The girls of the Communist Youth organization were commanded to come at night to the secretary of the district committee of the Party. If anyone of them refused, she lost her job." The Soviet journalist Mikhail Koltzov was able to report out of Syr Darya in Turkestan, following the clean-up of a corrupt Party leadership:

> In general it became clear that the local committees, the Soviet authorities and the Party cells of this region contained a large number of sneaks, authentic thugs, genuine thieves, and highway robbers, and that the Party was obliged to prepare for the Soviet elections with the help of such human material.

I know that these perversions—and I could cite dozens more from the official press accounts—were in no sense typical of Soviet political life. They were merely extreme symptoms of the disease of bureaucratism. The average Soviet official, I am still convinced, is more virtuous and conscientious than the average capitalist official. But there are millions more of them in a "monolithic" state. The departures from the average—absolutely, not relatively—are therefore more numerous. Milder manifestations of the disease were visible in every office, factory and institution.

The Soviet regime has never minimized the extent and seriousness of bureaucratic depredations. But the Kremlin stops short at that point. It cannot follow the diagnosis to its ultimate implications, because the root of the disease is in the prevalent hierarchy of power. Absolutism at the top implies hundreds of thousands, even millions, of large and small autocrats in a state that monopolizes all means of life and expression, work and pleasure, rewards and punishments. A centralized autocratic rule must function through a human machine of delegated authority, a pyramid of graded officialdom, each layer subservient to those above and overbearing to those below. Unless there are brakes of genuinely democratic control and the corrective of a hard-and-fast legality to which everyone, even the anointed of the Lord, are subjected, the machine of power becomes an engine of oppression. Where there is only one employer, namely, the state, meekness is the first law of economic survival. Where the same group of officials wields the terrible powers of secret arrests and punishments, disfranchisement, hiring and firing, assignment of ration categories and living space—only an imbecile or someone with a perverted taste for martyrdom will fail to kow-tow to them.

When dishonesty assumes the proportions of a pervasive national phenomenon it is sheer nonsense to set it down to "ill will" or "hostility of class enemies" or some other catch-phrase. There were men of ill will and there were hostile class enemies, but the conditions which put them in positions of leadership were not of their making. Those conditions were the direct result of the suppression of every vestige of democratic expression in the Party organizations, in the factories, and in Soviet life generally.

These, however, were conclusions taking shape, as yet, in the remoter regions of my mind. Not only in my dispatches but in my conscious views I discounted the engulfing corruption—drove it out of my range of vision where possible—to safeguard my vision of the socialist Fatherland.

XII. The Great "Break"

THE mass of the population was caught between its fear and its despair, bodied forth in food queues, rations, repeated cleansings, waves of arrests, new hordes of disfranchised, coercive loans, new restrictions on religious organization, more stringent requisitioning of farm products.

But a minority was galvanized into a fierce enthusiasm: fanatic, self-sacrificial and pitiless, magnificent in its sheer will to carry on. It was the inspired minority, with the whole arsenal of a nation's means of propaganda and instruments of terror at its disposal, that spoke and acted for the whole country. The only voice that could be raised above a whisper or a smothered groan was the voice of this minority. It now filled the Russian land and echoed through the nations of the world, until it seemed even to the Kremlin's enemies the authentic voice of the whole country.

That enthusiasm was deep and genuine; only the pretense that it represented the Soviet masses, or even the Soviet proletarians, was false. The voice was authentic, but it was magnified through the loud-speakers of the Kremlin's propaganda. Whatever doubts there may be about the measure of fulfillment of the *Piatiletka* (Five Year Plan), there are none about the overwhelming success of the world-wide ballyhoo around it. High-minded capitalist investigators viewed the Soviet economic landscape through veils of shimmering statistics and pronounced it perfect. Even breeders of journalistic *canards* about the Soviet Union in neighboring capitals came to accept as literal truths the high-flown metaphors about crowding a century of progress into five short years, new industries blossoming on the Russian steppes, an epochal experiment, etc.

I did more than my share in fortifying those metaphors in the world's imagination. Few foreigners in Moscow outdid the United Press man in the glorification of the new socialist objectives. "How the government proposes in the short space of five years to drag a backward agrarian country into the front ranks of industrialized European nations" was the theme song of my daily dispatches.

I viewed successes in all their splendid immediacy, but regarded attendant confusions and brutalities through half-closed eyes from the vantage point of future history. It's a neat and solacing trick of perspective, practiced expertly on every page of the books singing hymns to Soviet industrialization. You look at the new factories, the collectivized acreage, the figures for tractor building in close-up in the here and now. Then you step back a few generations or centuries and look at the human costs of these achievements through the telescope of posterity; naturally they seem small and unimportant at that distance.

I was intimately aware of the sullen indifference and stifled resentments of the mass, but I yielded my emotions to the enthusiastic minority. Hardships and routine cruelties became "sacrifices" and "casualties" in a war for socialism. Every present-tense difficulty that I was obliged to report I proceeded to dwarf by posing it against a great future-tense vision. As soon as any vast undertaking can be translated into a "campaign" with fighting "fronts" and "battles" and "shock troops" and "enemies," its generals are relieved of every obligation of restraint and humaneness: whether it be a campaign for the supremacy of the Aryan race or the establishment of collectivization. A mistake costing a million lives and subjecting a nation to untold miseries becomes a "tactical error" to be disposed of in a neat war communiqué. Garden variety tyranny is rationalized as "military discipline" and the obscenest perversions of justice pass muster as "courts-martial."

It was in an exalted mood, in any case, that I accepted the new period in its first stages. Socialism in one mad leap! I saw its daring but disregarded the madness. Hundreds of thousands of Russians similarly found the new spirit of military regimentation, the focusing of the nation's energy on clear-cut goals, the "scientific" generalship that reckoned not costs, acceptable. Their flagging faith in socialism in their own time was revived. The idealism of youth and its hunger for adventurous action found an outlet.

To comprehend this new epoch, the "Iron Age," one must take cognizance of both the inert, sullen millions and the exalted, driving thousands. A charge of dynamite may be negligible in size by contrast with the mountainside into which it is injected, but it explodes that mass. The history of the next five years is gibberish without an understanding of the explosive energy in the minority and the flaming faith in an all-socialist future that touched off the fuse.

Young communists who had reached maturity in the last eight years and knew the glorious legends of the civil war period largely from hearsay now thrilled at the new opportunity for deeds of daring. Many heartsore old Bolsheviks sadly resigned to the defeat of their earlier hopes, and grieving over the humiliation of Lenin's old comrades, suddenly awoke to a new zest in revolution. What matter who led the revolutionary armies now that the fortresses of hated capitalism were being stormed! The few communists isolated in hostile villages and the poorest peasants, having watched their despised neighbors prosper, recognized an outlet at last for their smoldering hatreds.

Thus a mobilization of revolutionary sentiment was effected. Its banner was the Five Year Plan of National Reconstruction. Its rallying cries were "socialism in one country," "storming the citadels of the bourgeoisie," "to catch up with and outdistance capitalist economy." The natural human instinct to make a virtue of necessity had its place in this mobilization. The politically more conscious sector of the industrial proletariat gratefully rationalized its burdens as temporary war measures. Communists who may have been irked by the increasing centralization of their Party and the snuffing out of internal rank-and-file democracy, now could yield themselves in an ecstasy of supreme duty to an unavoidable "military discipline." Former Oppositionists could capitulate without losing face. The time for discussion was over. It was a time for action. A "monolithic," totalitarian Party was now a necessity.

2

In April, a conference of Communist Party officials gave formal sanction to Stalin's ascendancy and Stalin's decision for a furious drive to the Left. Two versions of the Five Year Plan had been worked out by Gosplan (the State Planning Commission), a "basic" normal plan and a more ambitious "optimal" plan. There was a difference of about 20% in the total production and construction envisaged by these variants.

The optimal plan was foreseen by its authors as possible only under the most favorable conditions. They even specified four of those unlikely conditions: the absence of any serious crop failures, broader commercial ties with the rest of the world, a sharp improvement in the "qualitative indices" of Soviet industrial and farming output, and relatively smaller expenditures for national defense. Riding high on a wave of enthusiasm, the conference disregarded these cautions and announced the more ambitious version as its official goal.

In point of fact not one of those favorable conditions was to eventualize. There were crop failures, serious war scares, failure to raise quality, and staggering blows to foreign trade as a consequence of the world depression. In the intoxication of optimism whipped up by unrestrained propaganda, however, the plans in the first year were revised upward, as we shall see, beyond all logic instead of being switched back to the basic figures. A few whose sense of proportion exceeded their sense of self-preservation warned against such extravagance and found themselves condemned and punished as "Rights," "defeatists," and "capitalist restorationists."

The program of agrarian socialization was presented to the conference by President Kalinin. In the light of what was to happen at the end of the year, it is important to note that this program, though it seemed extreme at the time, called for only 20% of the peasantry to be socialized in the whole five-year period. In twelve years of revolution, despite continuous propaganda for collectives and all sorts of government subsidies, less than 2% of the peasantry had been collectivized. To induce 20% to join up in five years seemed a sufficiently daring goal.

The Plan did not limit itself to industry and agriculture. It embraced every department of the nation's and the individual's life. Meticulously Gosplan detailed the great improvements in education, housing, and feeding that would be brought to the masses. It went to the length (later a pesky embarrassment) of charting the higher standard of living. Because wages in terms of money would be rapidly increased through higher productivity of mechanized industry, and the purchasing power of the Soviet currency would appreciate 20%, the workers' "real wages," the Plan promised, would rise by 66%, and their cost of living would be lowered by 14%. They would eat 27.7% more meat, 72% more eggs, 55.6% more dairy products. The promises to the peasantry in this respect were more moderate but large enough to evoke a vision of plenitude in the mind of an underfed poor peasant.

This phase of the Plan was lost and forgotten in the shuffle of later boasts. But for the average Russian worker and peasant it was this phase that counted most. They would have been less than human had they not reacted in some measure to the flood of promissory propaganda. I talked to dozens of factory and office workers. Their immediate difficulties became a sort of investment for the future. They would work hard, deny themselves everything for a few years, then enter upon that ampler socialized life projected in the *Piatiletka.* The five years were a prison sentence or a term of compulsory military service beyond which lay freedom and comfort.

Party orators and press panegyrists, radio, theater, and cinema forgot all caution in their optimistic encouragement of this naive dream, this mirage in the desert of present hardships. The inauspicious beginnings, in rations and official pressures, became for many of the sufferers a curious portent of glories to come, even as his mundane travail is accepted by the religious martyr as a guarantee of celestial bliss to come. Perhaps the Kremlin would have been wiser to restrain its hosanna-singers who were sharpening the cutting edge of disillusionment.

The Trotskyist Opposition press abroad claimed the Five Year Plan as theirs in inspiration—the fruit of their long agitation—though it condemned the extravagance and lack of proportion in the Plan. Stalin's retort was that the gigantic enterprise which he sponsored in 1928-29 would have been premature and disastrous in 1927. However that may be, national planning was not a stroke of Stalinesque genius. It is inherent in the very theory of Marxist socialism. Stalin's role was the launching of a plan at the time he did, and carrying it through with a ruthlessness, a defiance of caution and logic, that turned the period into an "Iron Age."

Nor is the industrialization of Russia as such a purely communist inspiration to be credited to Stalin's genius. One need only look at the rest of the backward, semi-colonial East—Turkey, Persia, China—to recognize the same urge to "Westernize," mechanize, industrialize. Kemal Pasha uses almost the same language as Stalin in mobilizing his new Turkey for its industrialized future through a ten-year plan. When I interviewed the self-made Shah of Persia some years later, he did not boast of the art treasures of his nation but of the railroads and cement factories under construction. In Russia that urge dates back to Peter the Great, whose spirit and methods of catching up with the West were strikingly prophetic of the Bolshevik effort. The fact is that industrial growth in Russia just before the war compares favorably with the Five Year Plan. In 1913 production amounted to 7,357,800,000 rubles as against 6,177,900,000 rubles the year before—an increase of over 19% and therefore close to the average increase under the Five Year Plan. Indeed, if one remembers that the rubles were stable, the quality of the output vastly better, the over-advertised triumphs of the Five Year Plan, considered merely as to quantity and quality, lose some of their effulgence.

The real difference, of course, is in the social institutions which emerged in the process rather than in industrialization itself. The real yardstick of success for the Five Year Plan is therefore not at all statistical. It is human. I tended to analyze the Plan in terms of the bodies and minds of men, women and children, rather than kilowatt-hours and acreage.

3

Stalin later described 1929 as the year of *perelom*, the "break" —the year of the great break with the past. His description seems in retrospect even more true than it did at the time. Policies foreshadowed in the preceding year took concrete shape. What happened in the following years was but an extension and intensification of the attitudes fixed in 1929. The year stands as a sharp frontier in time: a challenge to the past and a bid for the future. The "line" of the ruling group acquired a disciplined hardness such as it had not possessed before.

Isolated incidents in this rapid hardening of purpose and method do not tell the whole story. In reading through my own and other people's running press reports for that year I find small evidence of the *perelom*, except by implication. The introduction of rations, the announcement of a definitive Plan, the purgings in many branches of government economy and everyday life, the new drive for collectivization, the bitter attacks on socialists and other moderate labor elements abroad, were in themselves news events of colossal importance. But individual episodes, each affecting life in one or another department, obscured for the moment the spirit that ran through them all. Only by tracing the common ingredient of these and a hundred other events to its source do we come to the core of the period, the iron heart that pumped a new spirit into everything with mechanical precision and a mechanical disdain for logic or conscience. That spirit was intolerant, cocksure, cruel—the ultimate cruelty of gods or demons loosing deluges that cleanse and deluges that drown.

In its first years the revolution had been warmly human even in its most brutal moments; I mean that it had been deeply and consciously *idealistic*, aware of suffering and sensitive to mass emotion. Now it became strangely impersonal and machine-like, important in its effects but as empty of real human content as a thunderstorm or a flood. It was something decreed from above and therefore inescapable but largely unrelated to the wishes or wills of the people upon whom it operated for good or for ill. Small groups helped the process along with a bigoted fury; other groups fought against it with suicidal fury; the population as a whole simply accepted it helplessly as a natural calamity.

The marvels of achievements against great odds and the horrors of human wreckage and degradation alike were products of this new impersonal spirit. I do not pretend to the Olympian aloofness that measures the relative values of the achievements and the horrors: I have found no common denominator to which they can be reduced for such super-accountancy.

I know men and women without the ability to keep their own household accounts in order who have no hesitancy in tackling the godlike bookkeeping of human destiny that balances results against costs. They assert that the price paid was quite reasonable or dirt cheap or exorbitant, as the case may be. Their yardstick of measurement is History. But it is a yardstick made of rubber, since everything depends on whether they regard history as a span of ten years or ten thousand.

The questions that pounded ever more insistently on the doors of my conscience and my mind (no one knows where thought ends and feeling begins) were of a different order. Dare any group of human beings, however wise and good they may count themselves, arrogate to itself the divine role of meting out death and suffering to the rest of mankind? The Biblical legend, crystallizing countless ages of mortal suffering through mysterious agencies beyond their control, tells of the divine anger that flooded a world with death, sparing only Noah and the creatures in his magic ark. It tells of Sodom and Gomorrah wiped out by divine wrath. Most tribes and religions have similar fables. What I saw was a handful of men in the Kremlin translating those fables into fact, assuming for themselves the supernatural prerogative.

Without hesitation, they doomed millions to extinction and tens of millions to inhuman wretchedness in the mystical delusion of their divine mission. (They called it "historical" instead of "divine.") Could one grant them this prerogative, even in principle, without justifying every self-righteous maniacal minority that decides to enforce its visions on humanity by wars, inquisitions, and dictatorships? Anyone who decided to torture and kill one man or woman for the good of the victim's unborn great-grandchildren would be adjudged insane. Is he any less insane when he decides to torture and exterminate millions of men and women for the good of their unborn posterity? Have only the unborn generations a right to happiness, so that the anguish of the living generation is a trifling investment for its great-grandchildren?

The logic of that "investment" turns mankind into a donkey following the carrot hung before its nose but always out of reach. The carrot of happiness for future generations is no more real than the carrot of bliss in paradise dangled by religion; both of them may serve as justification for flogging the donkey. A thousand things may snatch the theoretical happiness from the coming generation; it may even have a different concept of happiness than the group now brandishing "the sword of history." Only the anguish of the living generation is real and indubitable.

Sentimentality? All life is sentimental, if it is worth bothering about at all. If human life has no intrinsic value, then revolutions are senseless, ideals a mirage. Surely it is as sentimental to grow excited over the bliss in store for unborn millions as over the misery of existing millions.

If it is permissible to exterminate a sector of humanity for the sake of History, then there is no sensible reason for drawing the line at five million or five hundred million. Drown them all, comrades, leaving only a he-Stalin and a she-Stalin in their monolithic ark to start things over again from scratch!

I did not raise such issues in my cabled reports of the Soviet scene, published in some twelve hundred newspapers the world over. Imagine the consternation of an editor in Kalamazoo or Bangkok if he were to find my speculations on life, death, and history tacked on to a routine dispatch about "twenty-eight more kulaks and speculators executed this week, bringing the known total for the month to one hundred and fourteen." Philosophical doubts are not precisely spot news. The conventions of news reporting call for sharp-edged facts.

Behind the neat matter-of-fact dispatches, as cold as a coroner's report, were my private perplexities—so far behind that only a few of my more perspicacious friends at home detected them.

The lineaments of the *perelom* were outlined for me gradually in its cumulative works. They will grow clearer as this narrative proceeds. At this point it is necessary to summarize a few of its more decisive principles of action, all of them related expressions of the new dehumanized spirit that turned words like "idealism," "compassion," "love" into insulting epithets. Those principles, implicit or openly expressed, were:

First: The Communist Party became sacrosanct, its shifting policies—the "Party line"—invested with a mystical validity beyond logic. This was a far throw from the earlier conception of Party discipline. That discipline had been utilitarian, intended to assure unity of action after a question had been discussed and decided. Mental reservations, as long as they were not translated into action, were not in themselves treacherous. Communists were expected to sink their differences of opinion but not necessarily to *believe* differently overnight. Now there were no longer differences of view: there were only heresies. Decisions molded through discussion gave way to inspired pronouncements from on high. Reason gave way to faith.

Second: Stalin became the personification of that sanctity, the inspired oracle and the repository of all wisdom. The word *vozhd* —meaning not merely leader but *the* leader, with all the implications of the title *duce* in Italy or later *Fuehrer* in Germany—was applied more frequently to Stalin. Soon "our *vozhd*" acquired all the overtones of heavenly inspiration in the Soviet land that *il duce* has in the fascist land. In the deification of Stalin the logic of dictatorship was carried to its final level.

Third: The conviction that human life as such is valueless, merely the raw stuff of history, took a firmer hold on the ruling group. Larger purposes seemed to them to transcend mere flesh and blood, so that any number of people might be sacrificed on the altar of the true faith. A strange pride in the capacity to kill for the cause developed and it called itself "Bolshevik ruthlessness" or "Leninist firmness."

Fourth: "Social origin," proper proletarian or poor-peasant parentage, became the measure of personal value. A fierce pride in respectable family descent, a fiercer persecution of "enemy" blood grew into phobias. The same government that boasted of its crèches and kindergartens doomed hundreds of thousands of children born under the hammer-and-sickle to misery and death because of their hereditary taint, barred them from schools, sent them into exile with their parents. The sins of the fathers were visited upon Soviet children and the stain of "original sin" was declared ineradicable.

Fifth: Class war was proclaimed as the supreme method of social advance, being artificially stimulated where it did not exist. The Marxian analysis of society recognized class struggle as a social fact arising because of inherent conflicts of economic interests. The Kremlin went a lot further. It proceeded to nurture hothouse class struggles, as it were, if necessary inventing antagonisms and enemies where there were none.

Sixth: In the non-Soviet world, revolutionary individuals or organizations which did not accept Moscow's leadership were thereafter to be considered "social fascists" and more poisonous even than the capitalists. In practice, this involved continuous warfare against Social Democrats, moderate labor organizations, communists of other than the Stalinist denominations—a warfare which shattered the strength of labor and gave fascism unobstructed right of way.

I do not mean that these principles were formulated anywhere in this fashion, though they each found expression at one time or another in language more vigorous than I have used. They were various aspects of the temper of the new period—irreconcilable, hard-boiled, relentless, without a doubt or a regret to relieve the harshness. The revolution once had warm blood in its veins; it now preferred molten iron.

4

The great shaggy head of Karl Marx receded in the May Day decorations in 1929, leaving Lenin and Stalin dominant. Russia is a nation of icon-worshippers. Symbols have a potency beyond anything in the West. The prominence given to different saints and miracle-workers, living and dead, corresponds with mathematical exactitude to their current influence. This May Day saw Stalin lifted to a place of equality with Lenin in the outward symbolism of the faith. On Red Square, on the buildings opposite the Kremlin walls, huge faces of Lenin and Stalin were displayed. Their gigantic full-length portraits were mounted on scaffolding on Theatre Square, looming high above the Metropole Hotel on one side and the Grand Hotel on the other. In the mass demonstration, effigies of Stalin inscribed with his quotations and thick flattery outnumbered all the other floats and placards.

Stalin—and industrialization. These were the two ideas from this time forward. They were blended. They became interchangeable. Stalin's dark, fleshy visage came to mean smokestacks, oil derricks, scaffolding, tractors, and each of these things came to mean Stalin. The man Stalin who quarreled with enemies and connived with allies, human and fallible, was swallowed by the idea Stalin, at once fearsome and benevolent. Twelve years after the dethronement of Nicholas the Last, Holy Russia had a Little Father once more—too distant for personal love or hate, an invisible force to be flattered and propitiated. The very memory of the man's former insignificance now seemed too bizarre to be credible. It was fitting that history should be frantically rewritten to magnify his importance. One day he emerged as the real giant of the civil war period, the next as the real force by Lenin's side in the tense "October days." Others were pushed aside unceremoniously to make room for Stalin in the revised legend.

The focusing of all wisdom and all authority in one man at

the top was reflected in every department of Soviet life. More dictatorial power was extended to individual directors in factories and institutions. Even the pretense of rank-and-file control of the ruling Party was forgotten. Everywhere respect for mass opinion and notions of popular participation in factory management were thrown overboard.

The process went under the brave label of "tightening discipline" for the sake of efficiency—the standard excuse for dictatorship and authoritarian methods in all countries where democratic notions are outlawed. Even as in Italy, foreign correspondents whose personal liberties and privileges were left intact, exclaimed over the "splendid discipline." They wrote home about the "amazing concentration of national energies," and marveled at the "fine faith that accepts without murmur decisions which mean new sacrifices and further tightening of the belt." I was among those correspondents. Only this I can say in extenuation: that in my case these phrases were not cynical formulas of friendship for those in power, dashed off between cocktails and dinner and forgotten. They were earnest attempts to explain to myself more than to others. I had need at least to conciliate my radical conscience.

Each day the screws were turned a little more tightly on the intellectuals. Members of the Academy of Science, though their special fields were as far from socioligy as medicine or botany, had to prove their fealty to Marxism if they were to survive not merely as academicians but as functioning scientists. Writers, composers, painters, actors were given to understand unequivocally that they could not remain above the Five Year Plan battle: neutrality was tantamount to treachery and punished as such. The homes of technicians and "intellectuals" were searched, they were hauled to the G.P.U. for questioning on the slightest suspicion or none.

Not only the declassed millions, but millions of fully enfranchised citizens, because they did not labor with their hands, were thus treated as prisoners of war. And the soldiers themselves, the workers at the benches, were submitted to a new and ever more constricting "discipline." By the end of May, the former head of the trade-unions, Mikhail Tomsky, had "resigned." Actually his functions had been taken over by Shvernik, a Stalin underling, months before, and his expulsion in itself made little difference. But it put a period on the old type of trade-unionism.

The unions became mere bureaus for registering and regimenting the workers for the state, another whip in the hands of the rulers. They became in effect "company unions," whose primary job was to help the "bosses," in this case the state. A strike (and desperate, underfed and overworked proletarians occasionally resorted to strikes despite all the risks) must now be directed against the trade union no less than the administration.

I watched the tightening control from above with growing misgivings. Whatever the formal justification, it removed the workers a few steps more from the dictatorship exercised in their name and stripped them more thoroughly of the last possibility of defending their personal rights as workers against the larger rights of the organized and omnipotent state. The last pretense that the workers owned the state was dropped—the state frankly owned the workers.

New techniques for raising the productivity of the workers were developed. "Shock brigades," or pace-setters, were organized in every factory and office, every mine and construction job. The brigadiers, or *udarniki*, worked harder, wasted less time and set an example for their more indolent or less interested fellow-workers. Patriotic devotion to the national cause was a large element in this brigadiering, which enlisted the communists and the more socially conscious workers.

But the motives were not unmixed. *Udarniki* became a class apart on any job, compensated for their brigadiering by extra rations, priority in the distribution of deficit goods, first claim on new housing space, and other privileges. Their children were the first to receive milk or places in the schools. The best vacation resorts were set aside for their use. Shops on Moscow's principal streets began to display luxuries like boots and textiles with placards announcing "For sale to *udarniki* only!" They became a sort of aristocracy within labor.

Like so much else which happened in Russia, brigadiering has been romanticized by superficial enthusiasts as a spontaneous expression of popular fervor. It was that in part. In even larger part the *udarniki* themselves preferred to believe that duty rather than the extra rations or pair of boots turned them into brigadiers. But the official approval was not often shared by the workers outside the brigades. For the run-of-the-mill proletarian the *udarnik* was frequently someone who curried favor with the administration and forced down wages per unit of production by setting new standards of speed.

I recall a conversation with our friend H——, a young woman working at a sewing machine in a Moscow clothing factory.

"Well," I asked her, "have you joined a brigade?"

"No, not me."

"Why not?"

"Oh, I work hard enough as it is for my bread and water. Besides all the toe-lickers are becoming *udarniki*. I've got too much pride to join."

It took a few months of increasing food shortage and clothes shortage to humble her pride. She finally became an *udarnik*. She had a new dress and a pair of *valinki*, felt boots, to show for it.

"Some of the people in my department pretend that it's for the Five Year Plan that they're in the brigade. But they're in it for the *valinki* like myself."

H—— may have underestimated the idealism of her fellow-*udarniki*. Unquestionably the immense propaganda for industrialization was having its effect in tapping deposits of unselfish social emotion. That it did not suffice to stimulate the best efforts of the workers may be judged from the fact that ultimately the Kremlin had to appeal more directly to the motives of self-aggrandizement through old-fashioned goads to personal initiative like piece work, bonuses for better work and "docking" for inferior work.

Another of the techniques for stimulating production introduced at this time was "socialist competition." Factories in the same industry, departments in a single factory, sometimes entire industries, challenged one another to contests in fulfilling production plans. The press and factory bulletin boards gave the progress of such contests as much prominence as American papers give baseball scores. The winning side received banners and loving cups and had to maintain its records or lose the trophy. Even poets undertook "socialist competition" in producing verses to inspire the *udarniki.* Novels and plays appeared in which shock-brigadiers were the heroes and socialist production contests, the plot and counter-plot.

This intensification of labor, whatever its motives or its methods, had a magnificent sweep. The sheer magnitude of the effort was imposing. It was like a mobilization of an entire nation for war. More so. War ordinarily leaves a large portion of the population unaffected, carrying on its accustomed life of work and pleasure in the old way. This Soviet mobilization left no one undisturbed. Whether in terms of new tasks of labor, new persecutions, new deprivations, life was altered fundamentally for everybody.

The calendar itself was wrenched out of its ancient moorings. We reported it to the outside world melodramatically as "the nationalization of Sunday," and the atheists were indeed well pleased with the innovation. By turning the Sabbath into a humdrum working day it made church going possible only by absenting oneself from work, and abstention without good reasons acceptable to the administration could mean discharge from one's job. But the Godless victory was a mere by-product of the reform. Actually it amounted to the nationalization of all seven days of the week for the Five Year Plan. The traditional pause, when an entire nation simultaneously rests from its labors, was abolished. The "uninterrupted work week" was introduced into one industry after another, and finally into all Soviet undertakings. Every fifth day was a "free day" for one-fifth of the employees only. The day of rest was thus staggered, so that the wheels of labor never stopped turning.

The change affected the quality of life under the hammer-and-sickle more deeply than a mere statement of the fact indicates. Mankind is habituated to dividing time, with a Sabbath to mark the break. The day of repose, not for one man but for all, provides a goal toward which the days of work can march, a counterpoint of holiday in the symphony of labor. All that was sacrificed for the Plan and efficiency. Every day became like every other day, with only three national holidays when the sense of total rest could be recaptured. The individual had his "free day," but it was like laying off for twenty-four hours on a week-day, with none of the heightened value that a general cessation brings. It did not correspond, except accidentally, with the "free days" of his friends or even his family. The color of life, already monotonous gray, was made flatter. The psychology of embattled desperation fostered by the new Kremlin policies seemed to reach its logical conclusion in this merging of time into a treadmill of uninterrupted work. There are no holidays in the trenches.

XIII. Accent of Moscow

AT THE other end of Clean Ponds Boulevard there was a Red Army barracks. Going to and from their weekly baths the soldiers marched, singing, under our windows. Sometimes in the dawn hours we heard their voices dimly far off, then louder and closer and suddenly thundering in our ears, the cobbled street a drumhead for their heavy boots. Little Genie was soon singing all the marching songs, though she understood scarcely a word of them (which was just as well, the words are often ribald enough). We could tell by the pace of their music whether the warriors were going to or coming from their ablutions. Going, their songs were slow and touched with melancholy. Returning, they sang briskly, and their young voices glowed like their steamed and parboiled faces. Billy learned to give a musical imitation of the Red Army before and after steaming which remains a hilarious family classic.

I have read tourist gurglings in which the singing of Soviet soldiers was cited as proof of the happy mood of the Red Army. Russian soldiers sang lustily, of course, long before the revolution. Most of the tunes are still the same, though the words have been brought into line ideologically. "Ekh, Dunya, my little Communist Girl!" the chorus of one such song now exults. The adventures of red-kerchiefed Dunya are earthy and well-spiced, for she is the rhymed favorite of soldiers, sailors, commissars. She goes through a gate and the whole army follows. She twists her thick braids and there is a stampede of sailors. The rhymed couplets beloved of the Russians now deal with Soviet themes as well as the ancient plaints:

> By radio we met and by radio we wed,
> And by radio we got—a little baby Red.

Or:

> I have no mom, I have no pop,
> I was born in the gutter—a hen brought me up.

The chorus for these rhymes, flung to the Moscow skies by a marching Red division, sounds like a challenge to capitalism in the ears of keyed-up tourists. But the words are far from Marx, being approximately:

> Tea she drank and the samovar she lit;
> The dishes she smashed and the cook threw a fit.

A soldiers' ditty that I liked especially recounts in marching measures a peasant mother's farewell to her gawky son departing for army service. The chorus ends on a note of affectionate maternal irony:

> *Without you the Bolsheviki would be lost . . .*

There were also songs never before intoned by Russian soldiery. Workers' revolutionary marches from 1905. Rough and pungent melodies born, no one knows how, in the guerilla fighting of Siberia and the Far East. The inspiring hymn of Budenny's Cavalry, surely among the greatest marching tunes in the world. I have seen General Budenny's huge mustaches stand at proud attention, pointing upward like bayonets, when this march was played in his honor at the races or during some demonstration. The sight and the sound of the singing Red soldiers, swinging along through the principal streets, became pleasantly intimate. Years later, far from the place, a snatch of the familiar music, echoing in memory, evoked for me the magnetic Moscow that I love above all other cities I have known.

My memory, I think, is strongly aural: distinctive sounds remain in my mind long after other circumstances have faded and they stir nostalgic emotional depths. My first years in Moscow are suffused with the soldiers' singing and the insistent church bells. The bells would start sonorously somewhere in the city and wake answering chimes on all sides in a thousand different keys and measures until the world seemed brimful of living, cavorting notes, chattering, scolding, exulting. Later the ringing was prohibited as a public nuisance and the bells themselves were hauled down and melted for their metals. But somewhere a few timid bells had been overlooked in the sweep, and occasionally they tinkled forlornly in the twilight.

Woven into the sound-memory is also the hoarse caw-caw of the black crows swarming over the city and the cries of bearded

Tartars in our back yard: "*Staryo pokupayem!*" (We buy old things.) The old-clothes men were silenced about the same time as the bells. Only the crows could not be liquidated: they continued to rise like clouds of cinders when the Kremlin cannons boomed a salute. The American jazz melody *Hallelujah*, strangely Russianized, pulses through the memory too, something desperately secretive about its forced gaiety; it was played at half-illicit house parties and in bourgeois hotels, so that it came to have a counterpoint of yearning for the forbidden fleshpots of the capitalist world. And the *International*, whose powerful challenging voice was something deeply personal for me, speaking of mornings on East Broadway in the Socialist Sunday School. On Red Square, in the opera house, wherever it was played, my mind followed it automatically with the words I had learned as a school boy:

Arise, ye prisoners of starvation,
Arise, ye wretched of the earth,
For justice thunders condemnation,
A better world's in birth!
No more tradition's chains shall bind us,
Arise, ye slaves, no more in thrall;
The earth shall rise on new foundation,
We have been naught—we shall be all!
'Tis the final conflict,
Let each stand in his place!
The International Party
Shall be the human race!

The obbligato to my sound-memory, however, was the off-key whining of little Sashka next door. We became accustomed to it in the way one becomes accustomed to a chronic neuralgia. His voice was a needle that threaded our home life with its zigzag of fine wire.

Moscow was becoming more crowded every day and the job of getting around the city more disagreeable. Eventually it forced the correspondents to import automobiles, but at this point the New York *Times* correspondent was the only one in the American corps thus provided. After a day of struggle on Soviet streetcars, the loss of a leg in France seemed a small price to pay for a motor car in Moscow; we almost envied Duranty his misfortune. He had a neat trick of quoting "conversations in the street-car" in his dispatches in gauging public sentiment on current problems, as though to rub in the fact that he was the only one who didn't travel on street cars. The street-car conversations that I recall were more concerned with the ethics of stepping on other people's toes and digging elbows into the abdomens of pregnant women than with public affairs. In a New York subway quarrels are left to their protagonists; in a Moscow street-car nearly everyone immediately takes sides and the argument becomes general, continuing long after the offending party has been disgorged or has retreated into guilty silence.

In the face of inhuman crowding and accumulating shortages, the press and Soviet leaders talked of subways, new communal housing, and plans to make the city the world's most beautiful capital. They boasted of their plans as though they were already accomplishments. In life, as in my dispatches, every present-tense discomfort was matched with a future-tense promise. The mass of the population may have ignored these promises, but the smaller group of communists, enthusiasts, "activists" found life more tolerable because they attuned it to the projected future. This capacity to accept the plan for the reality occasionally led to disastrous futility—too many planners felt that the job was completed once they had perfected an impressive blueprint and framed it for their office walls. But it also enabled them to relish in anticipation things which were years off.

2

Except for desultory self-instruction in brief bursts of industry, I did not study Russian. Yet words and entire sentences did begin, amazingly, to emerge from the blur of gutturals. Immigrant variations on English are so common in America that we ignore them or make sport of them. Russians, on the contrary, feel subtly flattered that any glamorous foreigner should make the effort to learn their humble folk speech. It seems curious to them, too, that anyone able to speak mysterious foreign languages should find difficulty with the ordinary Russian that their children and the village idiot speak so easily. They involved me in small talk often, I am sure, merely for the joy of watching me butcher the tongue of Pushkin and Tolstoy. If I failed to understand them, they shouted louder and still louder, as though the fault were with my hearing.

When they wished to know how I liked the Russian language I assured them that "it's not a language, it's a torture." There was, in fact, no point of contact with English on which one could take his stance in attacking the speech. Its very philosophy seemed to me different from English—at once more complicated and more naive, richer in colloquialisms and nuances, its meaning somehow fuzzier and its accents more dramatic than in English. After a while I gave up trying to juggle the grammatical endings. I picked up the first one that came to hand, which was invariably the wrong one. Billy and I were constantly asked about our relative progress, and time reduced the reply to a formula: "Gene speaks *better* but Billy speaks *more*."

The semi-haze of language that separated me from Russians lifted, and I felt less of a stranger among them. The arguments in trolley cars and the grumblings on food lines, the casual remarks overheard on streets and the floods of amiable cabmen's obscenity began to make sense. The language in newspapers and on the radio, being strongly political, seemed to me different enough from everyday speech to constitute a new tongue. Russians told me that for them, too, it was almost a foreign language, it was so clean-cut in its meanings, lacking in the baby-talk diminutives, and so full of Russianized Latin—*mashinizatsiya, industrializatsiya, electrichesky, dialectichesky*, etc. There is a historical moral in the fact that there are no Russian words for the new life of industrialization and socialism; practically its whole vocabulary is imported.

My secretary-interpreter, Miss Jmudskaya, went through the newspapers mechanically and made appointments for me with officials and searched for facts that could never be found. Her boredom was undisguised. My eagerness to dig under the surface of official news seemed to her, I am sure, a little ill-mannered. Here I was receiving first-category rations, practically immune against the G.P.U., allowed to go abroad whenever I wished, but instead of being grateful I insisted ungraciously on prying into the Kremlin's private affairs. . . .

Besides the economic and political news which were the staples of my daily work, I enjoyed seeking out and transmitting "human interest" material that seemed to me authentically Russian, the very stuff of Chekhov and Gogol and Dostoievsky. Among the carbon copies of stories which survived somehow from those first years (if only I had had the sense to save them all!) there are a great many which begin: "Like an episode out of the most morbid pages in Dostoievsky . . ." or words to that effect. Little did Dostoievsky dream that one day he would be the mainstay of foreign writers unable to understand or explain events in Bolshevik Russia!

One such story recounted the suicide of a former general in the tsar's army, the fifty-year-old Georgi N. Khvostchinsky. He wrote a rambling ten-page letter to his Soviet employers in the Leather Trust and shot himself through the brain. There is a tale by Chekhov in which a petty *chinovnik*, or functionary, sneezes in the theater and sprays a shining bald head in front of him. He is shocked to discover when the man turns around that the head belongs to the pompous director of his bureau, who frowns, wipes his pate, and forgets about it. The *chinovnik* apologizes profusely, passionately, he can think of nothing else and no longer follows what is going on behind the footlights. Then he returns home to brood on the enormity of what he did and in the end, of course, kills himself. Citizen Khvostchinsky's story is proof that Chekhov did not exaggerate. At a conference of officials of his trust, the ex-general suddenly remembered that he had failed to carry out instructions transmitted to him months before. He had placed the letter in his pocket and did not think of it again until this conference. No one had noticed the mistake and there had been no harm done. But the general, now a *chinovnik*, was completely shaken up. Three days he tortured himself with thoughts of his unworthiness and the losses which *might* have accrued. Then he wrote the ten-page letter "confessing his crime" and blew out his brains. A career begun amidst the brilliant trappings of the old regime thus ended ridiculously in the littered offices of a Soviet bureau.

Other episodes were equally fascinating for the very opposite reason, because of their close relation to the revolutionary upheaval. A political assassination which did not receive nearly the attention it deserved sticks in my mind. It was a perfect parallel, in many ways, to the shooting of Hetman Petliura several months earlier in Paris by a young Jewish watchmaker named Schwartzbard. Early in 1929, the press recorded briefly the shooting of Jacob Slashchev, Red Army commander, in his own apartment in Moscow. A few days later it was disclosed that a twenty-four-year-old Jew named Kolenberg was under arrest for the murder. Beyond that the affair was veiled from public view by the strictest official silence. But in time I managed to piece together the ironical story.

In the civil war days, Slashchev had been General Slashchev and had fought against the Reds under Denikin and under Wrangel. He won a reputation as a man without mercy and was credited with the summary executions of thousands of communists and with instigating endless pogroms on the Jews. About 1922, however, he changed sides, and the Bolsheviks, sadly in need of trained military men, gladly accepted his services. He taught in their military academy and won himself a place of honor and respect in the Red Army. The Soviet government had forgiven him—but the surviving victims of his earlier cruelties had not. In one of General Slashchev's pogroms the father and one son in a wealthy Jewish family near Kherson had been murdered. Another son, then fifteen, had escaped. For nine long years he nursed passionately the dream of vengeance. The boy's name was Kolenberg and his dream came true when he shot the White—now Red—general in Moscow.

These were the things that gave news in Moscow their special quality of the bizarre and their atmosphere of significance. Everything that occurred had its specific "Soviet angle." There was the strange funeral on Red Square of Captain Paxton Hibben, whom I had known in New York. Born in Indianapolis, a relative of President Hibben of Princeton, a former American diplomat at the tsar's court, he was interred as a Red hero in the New Virgins' Monastery on the fringe of Moscow near the graves of many Romanovs. He died in New York but it was his last wish that he be buried in the Russia he loved.

There was the endless piquancy of the aged Professor Pavlov, the great physiologist, incessantly defying the new masters, flaunting his faith in God under the noses of the Godless, openly scolding the proletarian government which supported his work and took pride in his achievements. The Kremlin had begun to liquidate the bourgeois character of the Academy of Sciences by expelling some of the academicians and diluting the membership with Bolshevik additions. Professor Pavlov raised no objections to Bukharin, Pokrovsky, and Ryazanov, but he denounced other candidates as ignoramuses whose admission would disgrace the Academy founded by Peter the Great. The liquidation went on despite his thunders; within a year or two the Academy was as meekly obedient as any communist cell. But the spectacle of one man who was permitted to speak his mind among one hundred and sixty million was sufficiently exciting.

Most exciting of all, however, were the things that did not make "stories" for the press—the impact of daily life, daily discomforts, widening human contacts. I visited dozens of Soviet offices in the course of routine work, until their noise, tea-drinking, shabby signs and posters, amateur "wall papers," and their litter of cigarette stubs and mislaid papers, their hopeless slowness and confusion, no longer seemed strange or exasperating. I became familiar with the aroma and the beat of museums, coöperative shops and department stores, factories, movie houses, and tourist show-places like nurseries and model prisons. The sense of strangeness never quite wore off. Moscow can never become completely intimate to a foreigner as Paris, London or Vienna might. The margin of bafflement and paradox may be narrowed but it can never be quite erased. Each time I returned from a vacation, I confronted the capital's heaped-up desperations and magnificence with new wonderment and a revived hunger to absorb it somehow with mind and senses.

But mine was no longer that hectic, flushed reaction of the first arrival: no longer the bewildered anxiety that I saw driving tourists to test, argue, or explain away everything they met. Even the symbols of the revolution with familiarity lost their edge of the miraculous. The existences of individual men and women, somehow overlooked in the obsession of sociological research and the to-do about historical novelties, began to register on my mind. So gradually that I was not aware of it, I began to see the physical and social landscape through Russian eyes. The people you met took the revolution for granted, and its evolution mattered only to the extent that it affected their own jobs, food supplies, housing, and safety.

You might discuss the news of the day—the latest bend in the Party line or the arrival of the British businessmen's delegation—with Soviet journalists, officials, communists. But you avoided such things in conversation with Gisa, who worked in a clothing factory, or Nick, who was a rising cameraman in a movie trust, or the novelist Zamyatin, whose political standing was too unsteady to be tampered with. Everyone carried his private load of troubles, love tangles, ambitions and frustrations and took no more interest in larger national policies than the average New Yorker.

But national policies here affected the individual's life more quickly and more directly than in most other countries—the dependence of ordinary people upon the moods and methods of the Kremlin was greater and more obvious. Whatever we talked about, whatever we did together, therefore had for me deeper significance. The kind of shows we saw, our skiing excursions, the clothes Gisa wore, the picture Nick was doing, the story Zamyatin had succeeded in passing through the censorship, had for me social implications of which they were not themselves conscious.

3

There is much to be said for round-world flights, no doubt, as sport and as science. But no Moscow correspondent can reasonably be expected to say it. The things we did say are not fit to print. Russia sprawls across half of Europe and all of Asia—some seven thousand miles and each of those miles an acute headache for American reporters in the Soviet capital. It was our business to report the whereabouts of fliers from the moment they crossed into Russia until they left a few days later, or were properly smashed up. Nobody along the route was especially interested in keeping the world advised of these specks in the Russian skies. Besides, in Russia stretches of country as wide as a few World Powers are unpopulated wildernesses.

In the early '30's the circumglobular headaches became chronic. We became familiar with the sleepless nights, the feverish searching, and the frantic inquiries from the home office. But in August,

1929, the thing was still a novelty. All I was expected to do, sitting in my remodeled stable on Clean Ponds Boulevard, was to follow and report accurately the course of the Graf Zeppelin on the Russian leg of its first world-circling flight, from the time the dirigible sailed across the Latvian frontier until it touched the brink of the Pacific.

My principal competitors in this matter were the other two American press agency men, and both of them had handicaps on me. International News Service representatives were on board the Zeppelin and would report directly by short-wave radio. The Associated Press, because of its contractual relations with the Soviet news agency, Tass, would have a monopoly of such information as the Soviet press obtained. The United Press had nothing but succinct and emphatic instructions to offer me, the gist of which was that I must cover the flight in detail, faster and more accurately than anyone else.

The Zeppelin's path across the Russian continents had been announced in advance. It was to follow the main highway to Moscow, and then the Trans-Siberian railroad tracks to Manchuria and Tokyo. All I needed to do, obviously, was to station a relay of scouts along the whole route to wire the news to me as soon as they sighted the German giant. That being impossible, I did the next best thing. I wrote to the editor of the local newspaper in the larger cities along the route. I told him that one of these days or nights the famous Zeppelin would be flying over his district. It was his manifest duty as a public-spirited citizen and builder of socialism in one country, I explained in effect, to inform the world instantly when the Zeppelin comes in view, and the only way to do that was to flash the fact to the United Press reporter in Moscow. I addressed him as "dear colleague"—as one newspaperman to another—and made him realize that in helping me he was breaking the narrow walls of provincial journalism and entering the wide open spaces of international news.

Rather to my astonishment, most of them agreed. Unbeknown to my competitors I therefore had volunteer correspondents stationed all along the Zeppelin's charted path. Each of them had telegraph forms addressed to myself ready to send, with a space in which to write in the exact time of the sighting.

The indifferent Miss Jmudskaya being rather helpless in such subtle maneuvering, I hired the services of an aggressive Russian boy named Grisha Gruzd. Grisha was twenty-two or -three and had lived in Chicago several years; he boasted a go-getting streak rare in Russians. Grisha interviewed the officials of the Soviet society of amateur radio short-wave enthusiasts and induced them to instruct members throughout the country to eavesdrop on the Zeppelin and report what they could learn of its whereabouts to Moscow headquarters. He established friendly relations, too, with the aviation department in the Comsomol organization. Then we sat back and waited; nervously, but not without confidence. The United Press never cries "uncle."

On August 7, the dirigible took off from Lakehurst, N. J. On August 14, it took off from Friedrichshafen, Germany, headed for Moscow. I wired my volunteer brigade that their big moment was at hand. The next day the ship crossed the Latvian border and was, so to speak, in my lap.

And then my plans were sent flying higher than a dirigible. The Zeppelin blithely broke its promise and took a course a mere hundred miles or so to the north of its projected line and, what is more to the point, north of my line of volunteers. It was a good plan—I am still proud of it—but it didn't work. Two dozen provincial editors lost their one chance to contribute to world journalism gratis. Because of weather conditions, Commander Eckener steered some thirty miles north of Moscow and maintained that bias along a route that took him over uninhabited Siberian tundra instead of the railroad line. He saved a few hundred miles' distance and no one was the worse but a distraught reporter on Clean Ponds Boulevard.

Grisha was even more distressed than his chief. His blond hair stood on end and the sweat of honest chagrin ran down his collar.

"At least," he consoled me, "we still have the amateur shortwavers to fall back on. That arrangement is air-tight!"

I agreed that hope lay in that direction, and thither Grisha rushed. But short-wave headquarters had closed for the day! Our brilliant arrangements remained a theoretical triumph. We caught the Comsomol aviation enthusiasts about to shut down their offices as well, and induced them to remain open beyond their usual hours. With their assistance we did obtain a few "sightings." Meanwhile I opened long-distance parleys with newspapers this side of the Urals in cities along the new course and was fortunate enough to run across another sighting or two, enough to save my editors in New York, London, Berlin, and Tokyo from apoplexy. The telephoning had to be done at the main Telegraph Building; no long-distance connections could be obtained at that time at any other place.

The Zeppelin sailed on majestically while the reporters phoned and fretted and guessed at its location. Sverdlovsk was then the most easterly point within telephone reach. According to my vague calculations the dirigible should be passing that city sometime after midnight. But the Sverdlovsk paper could not be reached by telephone. Comsomol headquarters were shutting down. There seemed not the slightest chance of news till next morning, and eight hours without news—particularly when my opposition might be well supplied with it—was a serious matter.

"The fellow at the Comsomol office," Grisha said, "suggested that if you couldn't get the Sverdlovsk paper you might try the military *kommandant* there."

I clutched at this straw. Grisha asked to be connected with the garrison at Sverdlovsk. When the connection was made, he asked for the commander. I told him what to say.

"I am calling you," he said under my instructions, "at the suggestion of the Comsomol organization here in Moscow. I am speaking for a foreign correspondent. The Zeppelin should be passing Sverdlovsk. Is there any sign of it? The Zeppelin! A German dirigible. You never heard of it? Well, you're hearing of it now. We'll be obliged if you watch for it and we'll call you back."

The garrison head had seemed terribly impressed by the long-distance call, and upset because he knew nothing of the Zeppelin that was coming toward his post.

About an hour later we called once more. Again Grisha merely acted as my mouthpiece. I emphasize this for reasons that will soon become clear.

"Has the dirigible passed yet?" he asked. "What! A battalion? My God!"

He dropped the receiver. He was pale and he trembled.

"What is it? Take a hold of yourself!" I pleaded.

Grisha stammered:

"The commander said . . . the Zeppelin hasn't come yet . . . but . . . well, *he has a battalion in the field waiting for it!*"

"He has!" It was my turn to grow excited. "Here's where the round-world flight ends on the fields of Sverdlovsk, like the last of the Romanovs."

We stood there in the Telegraph Building staring at a vision of the unsuspecting Zeppelin being riddled by rifle fire. It was evident that the *kommandant* was under the mistaken impression that he was in contact with Comsomol headquarters. And why should he order out a battalion except to bring down the German invader?

Our first instinct was to flee from the scene. There seemed small hope of getting the long-distance connection in time to avoid a catastrophe—that a catastrophe was in the making seemed certain to our over-wrought, fatigued minds. Then I decided to try it anyhow. It took an hour to get Sverdlovsk again and it felt like a week. Finally the commander was at the other end. It was now about 3 A.M.

"The dirigible passed here a minute ago," he reported cheerfully.

Our fears had been unwarranted. The intentions of the battalion had been friendly from the first. Yet we felt as though a disaster had been narrowly averted. I flashed the Sverdlovsk sighting and it proved a "scoop" over the opposition correspondents by several hours.

Beyond the Urals it was impossible to trace the Zeppelin. I sent such scraps of information as I could beg or steal from the editorial rooms of the Moscow newspapers. All of us were still looking for the ship somewhere over Lake Baikal when it landed safely in Tokyo.

I paid Grisha off and thanked him for his help. He seemed in a nervous state over the night we had spent in the Telegraph Building. Contact with military garrisons, even in as innocent a matter as a world flight, and merely in the role of intermediary, was not to the taste of Soviet citizens.

His apprehensions were well grounded. Early one morning a few days after he left my employ, Grisha's wife came to me in tears. The G.P.U. wagon had come that night and taken him away. I called at the Foreign Office instantly to lodge a protest. Whatever the boy had done, it had been as my mouthpiece, and if anyone was to be punished it was I, I insisted. Besides, we had done nothing remotely wrong. At most we were guilty of excessive zeal in obtaining information on a matter that surely was not secret.

"The arrest of Citizen Gruzd," I was told suavely, "has nothing whatsoever to do with his work for you, Mr. Lyons."

I knew that this was untrue, but there was no way I could prove it. Day after day I fumed at the Foreign Office and elicited the same smiling assurance that Grisha's crimes were in no way related to his brief employment with the United Press.

Through sources which I dare not disclose here, however, I learned definitely that the phone calls to Sverdlovsk were responsible for Grisha's exile to a Northern concentration camp for three years. I did not hear from him again directly. Indirectly I learned that he had been given an office job at Kim, outpost of the forced-labor lumber regions, and was therefore in a better position than other prisoners. In reading Professor Tchernavin's book *I Speak for the Silent* six years later I found Grisha's name mentioned casually among the people whom the author had met.

When Grisha returned to Moscow in 1932, he very carefully avoided meeting any foreigners. He had burned his fingers. That go-getting streak acquired in Chicago would not get him into any more trouble if he could help it.

XIV. Picnicking in a Graveyard

ADVANCE divisions of the Great Tourist Invasion reached Moscow during this summer of 1929. The main body of amateur sociologists, bubbly school teachers, liberal ministers, earnest probers, socialite thrill hunters, and miscellaneous neurotics did not take posssesion until the following years.

They were predominantly Americans, these tourist hordes. And they were a new breed of the Baedeker animal. Not scenery but statistics, not the exotic but the economic, mattered to them. Every alimony widow killing time by travel turned political economist on crossing the Soviet frontier. Every undergraduate and tractor salesman hatched the original notion of telling "the whole truth" at last about Russia in books and articles. These new-style tourists had a hectic mental complexion: they were flushed with special fervors and intent upon proving something to themselves or to others.

So they bustled from museum to crèche to factory dining hall, from theater to workers' club to ballet, taking notes, snapping pictures, and gushing with enthusiasm. Their theme song was "Ah! and Oh!" Nice girl guides answered their embarrassing questions with pat phrases and were set right by the interrogators themselves if the answers deviated from the standard formulas. They interviewed minor officials whom they mistook for real "commissars." In other countries they had been left to shift for themselves. Here they were herded and guided and stuffed with information. There were organizations devoted to their enlightenment on all matters Soviet.

It all made them feel important and their visits seemed somehow significant. The most modest of them began to feel a little like a "delegation;" two or more foreigners arriving anywhere in Russia, even at a lavatory, were a *delegatsiya* in Russian eyes. Most of the Soviet solicitousness, it is true, was pretty messy and there was plenty of squawking among the visitors. They threatened to write to Stalin, and a few of them did, to complain about the way the faucet leaked. Even the privilege of protesting self-importantly about the inefficiency and confusion, however, was a unique experience in self-assertion for tourists, normally the meekest of mortals.

To the Russians these foreigners were an endless source of wonder. From their places on the block-long food queues Muscovites stared at these creatures from another planet, so sleek, so brisk, so free, in their strange plus-fours and glamorous store gowns and stout walking shoes and tortoise-shell spectacles. Tourists could not guess that behind the seemingly vacant eyes and expressionless faces anger flared at the sight of these satisfied strangers. They could not guess that the muttered remarks of Russians who gazed after them were far from complimentary.

Once I was with a group of Americans who stopped to talk to a Russian woman outside a bakery; one of those things that would enable them to write, "I talked personally with ordinary Russians and despite the barrier of language I sensed their devotion to the Five Year Plan." It fell to me to interpret. The woman answered our questions evasively, trying to say the "proper" thing and embarrassed by the attention. As she talked she fingered the stuff of an American dress and studied the women's hats and shoes. Then, timidly, she inquired about the cost of various items of our clothing and whether they were difficult to get. Finally she said in a deprecating voice in which there was an undertone of cautious irony:

"Ask them how they like our life here."

I translated the consensus of group opinion:

"They think your life is very difficult just now, but most interesting!"

"Interesting!" The woman made a wry face; the word cracked her discretion. "Interesting! Sure, it's interesting to watch a house on fire. But we're *in* it! Tell them that, citizen!" And she turned away angrily.

That resentment was not exceptional. Even functionaries whose business it was to propagandize the tourists privately despised them for their complacent gullibility. Americans and Englishmen and Germans who raised a row because there was no toilet paper in their rooms were eloquent in justifying hardships for Russians.

They were prepared to see the Five Year Plan through to the bitter end if it killed every last Russian in the land.

Between mouthfuls of chicken *à la Kievsky* they said, "What if it does mean the sacrifice of a generation, or two generations, if it helps the construction of socialism!" Loudly and lustily they exercised their precious freedom of speech to prove that it was all right to muzzle Russians.

To me there was from the first something obscene in the invasion of smug foreigners in this time of national distress. Often I liked them individually. They brought a welcome whiff of home. Entertaining visiting firemen was one of Billy's and my own chief occupations during tourist seasons and we enjoyed most of it thoroughly; some of those who came to us with letters of introduction we now count among our dearest friends. All the same there seemed to me a scavenger element in the business of prying into a nation's open wounds and exclaiming over the lovely Russian sacrifices. I had been in the country long enough, apparently, to see through Russian eyes.

If only these tourists showed some sympathy and humility in the face of a nation's travail! Their gushing enthusiasm seemed to me an insult to those who suffered, and I knew many men and women who smarted under that insult. Rare, indeed, was the tourist with enough sense of humor to recognize the absurdity of the whole procedure. Rarer yet was the tourist with enough humanity to feel decently apologetic to the Russians before whom he paraded his well-fed, well-dressed body. For the most part the attitude of tourists implied that the current miseries were a divertissement staged for their edification.

They guarded their foreign passports like the apple of their eye while sizzling with enthusiasm over this "new Soviet civilization." They gave their cast-off store clothes to guides and other deserving natives while packing away statistics of Soviet production marvels. It was all most cozy, combining the joy of travel with the pleasures of social research. Too few of them realized that they were picnicking in a graveyard.

"They should be sent in batches to Solovky and Narym in cattle cars—that might knock the smugness out of our fellow countrymen," an incisive American engineer said, and I agreed warmly.

The most insufferable of the breed were the twittering American intellectuals of the Left. At the drop of a hat they were ready to argue solid facts out of existence. They asked questions, and if the answer was out of line with their convictions, they proceeded gently to set you straight. Condescendingly they explained that the talk of food stringency and concentration camps was "exaggerated, you know." They were even astounded to find "Riga inventions" credited by Moscow correspondents and put it all down to a "bourgeois mentality." Their smiling denials of things recorded and admitted by the Soviet government itself sometimes goaded me into telling them more of the facts than I intended. I was furious with them and with myself for being driven into disclosing more than I did in my published dispatches.

2

The most redoubtable contingent in this summer's invasion consisted of ninety-odd American politicians, journalists, educators, salesmen, and assorted big-thrill hunters calling themselves for some mysterious reason a "businessmen's delegation." Its outstanding figure was Albert Ottinger, a former Attorney-General of New York State, then considered gubernatorial timber. A loud, bustling, thick-set little man of the back-slapping school, he provided the window dressing for the supposed delegation. The contingent was honeycombed with professional friends of the new Russia who had made a business of being go-betweens for the Soviets—men who were used by the Kremlin but distrusted.

It was the largest organized group of Americans that had ever arrived on the Soviet scene, and the government went the limit in entertaining them. They visited all the standard show places, trooped through factories, tanked up on statistics, and took a long trip through the country. On their return to Moscow the authorities tendered them a banquet which was to remain an indelible memory in the American colony. Billy helped the Grand Hotel dance orchestra to learn the *Star-spangled Banner* for the occasion—for all her efforts, it sounded like a Russian folk song in syncopated rhythm when the great moment arrived. Important Soviet trade and cultural bureaucrats were present. A meal in grand-ducal style was served. Then there were speeches, mutual eulogies, and fervent promises that the two greatest "republics" on earth would get together.

The main speech, of course, was Mr. Ottinger's. This well-meaning gentleman had been a politician too long to change his spots, and he orated for all the world as if he were seeking the Soviet nomination for governor. His peroration is memorable. Having enlarged on the wonders he had witnessed in the U.S.S.R. he raised his arm, turned his eyes heavenward, and exclaimed:

"And I trust, my friends, that *with God's help* you will carry your wonderful Five Year Plan to a great success!"

I don't know how God felt about this invocation, but the Godless Bolshevik officials were most embarrassed.

I knew a great many members of this delegation, having worked with some of them in the American radical and liberal movements. Through them I learned with a shock that hurt more than I cared to acknowledge, that I had already been ostracized by my former comrades in New York.

The Press Department in Moscow, it is true, reckoned me among the most "friendly" correspondents, despite occasional clashes. But pro-Soviet circles in New York had cast me off. My writing evidently conveyed more than I was myself aware. The doubts and questioning that were under the surface of my mind showed up in an ironic phrase, a cynical turn of thought, a stress on the untidy side of Soviet life which had passed not only the official censors, but the far more rigorous censorship I was applying to myself.

The instinct of my former friends was correct. They had smelled out the waning of my imported beliefs. So they disowned me in a panic before the friendship might disturb their own comfortable faith.

Loyalty to my own years as Soviet propagandist was at the bottom of my efforts to clean up the Soviet picture for foreign perusal. Consistency is an overrated virtue. I needed many years to recognize that intellectual integrity must take precedence over surface consistencies. But the anxiety to retain my standing among my radical friends, too, was a strong element in my attitude. I recalled the unreasoned hatreds that had flared in my own heart against those who dared to question the sublime wisdom and untarnished idealism of the Kremlin. The fear that such hatreds might now be directed against me was most unpleasant.

The need to satisfy my former comrades as to my basic loyalty to the revolution was always with me. Kenneth Durant, in particular, was looking over my shoulder as I typed my stories—bitter, biting, intolerant—and I knew that I could count on neither understanding nor forgiveness. The circumstance that he was still writing me in the old affectionate, comradely manner seemed to me a solacing proof that I was not the political renegade others made me out.

Then I learned the truth from one of the delegates. Durant's friendly correspondence was a "blind," while privately he spread tales about my apostasy. The news was like a physical blow. I wrote him a long letter in which I tried to explain my sentiments and asked whether it was true that he was attacking me. I knew his dyspeptic bitterness too intimately to doubt that what I heard was the truth, yet I hoped illogically that he would deny or explain it away. It was easier, I tried to make him see, to remain unmoved by colossal miseries from a point five thousand miles off than when they are under your eyes. If my reactions to the Russian realities were not to his taste, did he not know me well enough to grant at least that I was acting honestly within my own lights?

The answer was prompt and incisive. It was one of those masterpieces of satirical invective I had watched him indite against many another man during the four years we worked together. The gist of it was that I was an "ingrate"—as though he expected me to suppress what I saw and felt, out of gratitude to him!

Thus I knew that forever after I would be among the private demons to whose extermination Durant's inverted Quakerism was dedicated. The friendly correspondence had been a machiavellian trick. For months the shock of this break in a long friendship was with me. It rankled. It was not the loss of one man's good opinion that bothered me, but the proof that I had cut the bridges between myself and the communist milieu in America. At the moment it was depressing: I had lost the comfortable feeling of belonging to a group. Excommunication from a church is a painful matter even if the communicant's faith has faltered. But in the long-run it proved a wholesome purge. The lacings of the straitjacket of conformity on my mind and conscience were loosened. Durant's inquisitorial eyes no longer peered over my shoulder as I wrote my stories.

3

The Journalists' Club, an organization of Soviet newspaper writers, presented a hilarious skit to an invited audience. It showed a Soviet citizen abroad trying to study the life of foreigners but everywhere meeting only more Russians. Every time he thinks he has cornered a genuine specimen of the genus foreigner, it turns out to be another Russian on some economic or scientific mission. In the final scene the traveler returns to Moscow and announces that the only place to study the life of foreigners is among the American correspondents and engineers in the U.S.S.R.

The allusion was twofold, to the growing number of Russians sent to foreign lands to buy machinery or study technique, and to the greater number of foreign specialists drawn into Russia.

There is a magic word in the new Russia: *komandirovka.* It is a shiny business-like word with a foreign look to it and has a fascination for modern Russians among their new technical toys. It may be roughly translated as "assignment" though it carries overtones of self-importance and military precision to the Russian ear. The simplest errand from one town to another becomes a *komandirovka* and transforms the errand boy into an official. At any given moment a hundred thousand Russian functionaries are on trains and ships, rushing slowly from one city to another on urgent *komandirovkas,* drawing the additional pay allowed while traveling and indulging the sense of expanded prestige that comes with an urgent mission. Elsewhere most such missions are accomplished by letters or telephone calls. But the method of *komandirovka,* or face-to-face negotiation, flatters the Russian weakness for dramatizing commonplaces and turning the simplest matters into "problems." The word has cost the Soviet regime millions of rubles, but it has given a hundred thousand portfolio-bearing citizens the illusion of accomplishing things. They shuttle back and forth between Moscow and Leningrad, Moscow and Vladivostok, carrying little pieces of paper with big seals and flowing signatures on them. Their assignments are always urgent or super-urgent and a lot of poor devils are forced off trains to make room for them.

The most sought-after assignment, naturally, was the foreign *komandirovka*. The needs of the Plan opened enormous opportunities for visits beyond the Soviet frontiers. Thousands of big and little officials who had for years been dreaming of capitalist fleshpots now schemed for a foreign assignment: to investigate German or American practice in some industry, to inspect a machinery purchase, to engage foreign specialists in some line, etc. Hundreds of them succeeded in going abroad. The rigorous prohibition of foreign travel gave the outside world a dizzy allure. The Soviet press might describe the bourgeois countries as swamps of poverty, iniquity and exploitation; the Soviet theater and cinema might paint the capitalist world as a madhouse of jazz, courtesans, and bourgeois degeneracy. This propaganda only sharpened the Russian appetite for foreign countries: those supposed treasure-houses of victuals, soft textiles, limousines, and uninhibited fun.

There was endless talk among Russians in the first flush of the Plan about these foreign visits. *Za-granitsei*, literally "beyond-the-frontiers," loomed large on the horizons of hope. Those chosen seemed to their fellows the favorites of fate, like winners in the sweepstakes. They returned self-conscious in new clothes, wearing collars and neckties, and bringing foreign five-and-ten-cent luxuries to amaze their friends. At public meetings in clubs and factories they talked of the misery and exploitation out there, giving "abroad" credit only for its high industrial skill. In private they glowed with the excitement of remembering well-stocked stores and movie palaces, night clubs and fashionable clothes.

But a large proportion of them did not return at all. The lure of the unaccustomed plenitude, the sudden release from the pressures of discipline and fear, went to their heads. They became émigrés, cut off forever from their families and friends in the Soviet Union. Desertions became so extensive that the Kremlin tightened the selective process. Only the more trustworthy were chosen for foreign *komandirovkas*. If there was a shadow of doubt, their wives were not allowed to accompany them, serving as hostages for the speedy return of their husbands. Many a wife, however, was sacrificed by officials who could not face Soviet life again after the intoxication of a lop-sided but relatively free world. In the end the government prescribed *death* as the punishment for officials who did not return in time, should the deserters return to their native soil. Thereafter an emissary outstaying his leave unduly knew that he must remain an émigré forever.

The American colony took on mushroom luxuriance as the Plan got well under way. Notwithstanding the absence of diplomatic relations, the juiciest plums in the way of "technical aid" contracts went to American firms. By the end of the first year of the Plan, our specialists were at work on the whole "industrialization front," directing construction projects, installing machinery, teaching Russians to run American machines, acting as foremen, or negotiating new contracts. Scores of skilled workers were imported as foremen, teachers, rationalizers. A fairly good foreign mechanic could pass muster as an engineer, at the least a "technician," with the emoluments in cash and prestige that the title carried.

A year earlier, we knew every American in Moscow. The arrival of another compatriot was an event. But now their number was too large for such close contact. They filled the best hotels, special apartment houses were told off for their use, or they shared quarters with Russians in houses belonging to their production trust. Construction experts, road builders, steel specialists, textile technicians—by twos and by the dozen they flocked to the land of the hammer and sickle: most of them hard-headed, open-eyed men who knew their jobs inside out but neither knew nor cared two cents about economic theories and social ideals.

This political naivete or indifference proved to be their strongest card in the difficult game of working with Russian bureaucrats and adjusting themselves to the peculiar living conditions in the new land. The Kremlin leaders came to value the single-track minds of these strange apolitical Americans who were neither for nor against Bolshevism but merely doing a technical job well. In the various sabotage trials involving suspicion of foreign collusion, Americans were never even mentioned. The phlegmatic, cigar-smoking American, honest, efficient but politically illiterate, became a standardized type in the Soviet theater and screen plays of the Five Year Plan era.

Doing business with a bureaucratic government was not always easy and a great deal of friction inevitably developed. Soviet agencies made serious blunders in hiring men and were constantly chagrined because square pegs would not fit into round holes. At other times foreigners pretended to technical qualifications they did not possess and covered their ignorance with bluster and protest. Russian representatives abroad too frequently made promises in the matter of living and working conditions which the home office in Moscow or the Urals was unable to keep.

But principally the trouble grew out of psychological incompatibility. It took an exceptionally adaptable man to work in the atmosphere of confusion, the clutter of red tape, and the pervasive helplessness of an average Soviet factory or construction job. Scores of American specialists poured the tales of woe into my ears. Their complaints added up to an indictment of the Russian character complicated by bureaucratic fear of responsibility. The Damocles sword of a sabotage charge hung over every Russian administrator's and engineer's head, making him jumpy, over-cautious, or nervously over-bold, and above all anxious to foist the onus of a definite decision on someone else. Americans felt themselves tangled in office intrigues they could not possibly understand. The largest single item of complaint was the pigeon-holing of plans and suggestions. Any number of my closer friends among the technicians spent most of their time and energy in forcing action —a clear-cut acceptance, rejection or criticism—on the ideas which they were engaged and well paid to work out.

There is the story, now a classic, of the American executive brought to Moscow to help rationalize the railroad system. The commissariat had moved heaven and earth to lure him into its service and was paying him a fabulous fee. But having arrived at the capital, he was obliged to hang around the Metropole Hotel for days, then weeks, before he could so much as meet the appropriate officials, meanwhile drawing his big salary. There was the highly qualified engineer imported from New Jersey to help organize production in a ball-bearing factory only to find that the factory had not yet been built; his contract was up about the time the plant was completed. I remember the distress of a well-known technical expert held in such high regard that the government put a special car at his disposal from the frontier to the capital. Once in the capital, however, he could not find a place to sleep and spent the first night on a cot in a common bathroom at the Grand Hotel.

Despite the mountainous muddle and wastage of technical talent, however, there is no question that foreign technical brains made a tremendous contribution to Russia's headlong industrialization. Russia was able to buy experience that other nations had attained in slow and costly experimentation. Those who make glib comparisons between the percentual growth of industry in Russia and that in other capitalist countries fail to discount this factor. They speak as though the Soviet regime were starting from scratch, as the bourgeois world had started with the industrial revolution, instead of starting with a century of cumulative progress.

Each time Moscow imported a new machine it was taking a short-cut over a road other nations took decades to prepare. It transported bodily plants and processes from Detroit, Gary, Manchester, Lyons, and Munich that had cost other countries generations of experiment. Russia does not represent a new industrialization so much as an extension of Western industry. It is in the new social institutions, the new relations between man and machine, that Russia differs and it is on those things rather than on industrialization *per se* that the world's judgment of the Soviet regime must rest.

4

Counting over in my mind the American and other foreign specialists whom I knew most intimately, I find that they fall into two distinct categories. Those who belonged emphatically to one or the other class succeeded in their dealings with the Soviet machine; the rest merely muddled through and went back home soured.

Jack Calder of Detroit will serve as the type of one category. Jack was a tall, lean, staccato person, pipe-smoking and hard-boiled. Enough of a diplomat to avoid offending his Soviet employers, he nevertheless talked sharply to those in power and used the big stick against those under his direction. His was the self-confidence of precise knowledge and executive ability; he worked hard and drove astonished Russians to follow his pace and ignored politics. He considered himself a hired expert paid to do specific jobs and limited his Russian interests to those practical tasks. Though

plexes. The hotels for foreigners were haunted by lovely women all too willing to be seduced by a foreigner, almost any foreigner. It was an open secret that most if not all these women worked for the G.P.U. The rare exception was promptly drawn into the secret service as soon as she formed a liaison. It was part of the price she paid for the silk stockings, the three full meals a day, the comfortable home that a foreigner could give her. Most of these girls were the daughters of "former" people and therefore outlaws. They could not or would not accept the rigors of the new existence and thirsted for the counterfeit capitalist atmosphere in which foreigners lived. At the core of their life was the glowing dream of escape abroad. Sooner or later some foreigner—if not her present bed-mate, then the next or the one after—would marry her and transport her to the wonder world beyond the barred doors of the Soviet Union.

For a few of them the dream came true. I was to run into them sometimes in New York in subsequent years, a little wistful over their lost fatherland and usually disappointed in the bourgeois dreamland; those American husbands who seemed rich and unique in Moscow proved very small and drab fry in their native settings.

These liaisons were not without their deep pathos. I knew many a woman who had started an affair blithely at the behest of the Foreign Department of the G.P.U. who came to admire or even to love the man and suffered at the need to spy on her lover. There were the times when wives arrived for a visit to their husbands in Moscow and the traces of the Russian substitute had to be hurriedly removed, the interrupted household resuming its course when the wives had departed. A good many of these temporary partnerships assumed a deceptively stable look. Friends who were with the American Army of Occupation in Germany tell me of the tragic separations from German girls which the end of the occupation occasioned. Much of the same tragedy was enacted as members of the foreign army of technical experts in Russia ended their service.

XV. Two Plus Two Equals Five

INDUSTRIALIZATION went forward with a great roar and frenzied war whoops. Reports of building, factory output, new collectives and state farms elbowed all other news off the front pages. There was a constant beating of alarm drums: a breach on one or another economic front, cries of sabotage, sudden arrests and shooting of engineers and administrators. Notwithstanding, plans were everywhere being fulfilled and even surpassed. New energies and enthusiasms, new threats as well, were having their effect. Food shortage was not yet at its acutest and the sapping of physical strength and working morale through undernourishment had not yet set in fully.

Optimism ran amuck. Every new statistical success gave another justification for the coercive policies by which it was achieved. Every setback was another stimulus to the same policies. The slogan "The Five Year Plan in Four Years" was advanced, and the magic symbols "5-in-4" and "$2 + 2 = 5$" were posted and shouted throughout the land.

The formula $2 + 2 = 5$ instantly riveted my attention. It seemed to me at once bold and preposterous—the daring and the paradox and the tragic absurdity of the Soviet scene, its mystical simplicity, its defiance of logic, all reduced to nose-thumbing arithmetic. . . . $2 + 2 = 5$: in electric lights on Moscow housefronts, in foot-high letters on billboards, spelled planned error, hyperbole, perverse optimism; something childishly headstrong and stirringly imaginative. . . . $2 + 2 = 5$: a slogan born in premature success, tobogganing toward horror and destined to end up, lamely, as $2 + 2\frac{1}{4} = 5$. . . .

The preliminary triumphs which evoked the slogan $2 + 2 = 5$ were in many ways disastrous. They corroborated the taskmasters' inherited conviction that any miracles could be worked through the sorcery of naked force. At the same time the first triumphs encouraged a costly revision of plans upward beyond the range of reason. Under their pseudo-scientific exterior of charts and blueprints the planners were religious mystics in a trance of ardor. Their optimism was hyperbolic. The maximal version of the Plan, for instance, called for 10 million tons of pig iron in the fifth year. They boosted it arbitrarily to 17 million. How far out of line this was may be judged from the fact that actual production in the final year was just over 6 million and that the goal for the end of the *Second* Five Year Plan was to be only 16 million. The coal schedule they boosted by fiat from the original 75 million tons to 90 million—only 64 million were obtained. Right down the line analogous increases were ordered, to be wiped out a little sheepishly when the intoxication of the first victories wore off.

On the agrarian side the same excess of zeal prevailed. The hope for the collectivization of one-tenth, then one-fifth, of the peasantry by 1933 had seemed over-ambitious when announced earlier in the year. Now it was ordained that fully one-half the peasantry must be herded in collectives by 1932. With class war as the persuasive weapon, wielded by the G.P.U. and the Red Army where necessary, great peasant masses did rush blindly for shelter under the collective roofs. From every village in the nation came boastful accounts of peasants erasing the boundary lines between their private strips of land, pooling their animals and their implements for joint cultivation. Always the boasts concluded with grim references to kulaks and "kulak agents" who blocked collectivization and must therefore be destroyed.

In great glee I cabled the statistical triumphs to the outside world. The derision of capitalist economists when the "astronomical figures" were first announced could now be thrown in their teeth. Their own deepening economic crisis made these bourgeois experts so much more vulnerable. Their self-esteem was at low ebb.

But under the roar of industrialization life was increasingly muted. The modest indulgences of the year before seemed long, long ago and rather incredible. A full meal became life's central preoccupation for the mass of the population. Overhead the heavy artillery thundered and spat fire; in the trenches of everyday existence people stepped cautiously, doused their lights and spoke in whispers. The laconic announcements of executions lost their power to interest, let alone move people. On a day when I had counted over forty executions in the morning papers—"speculators," saboteurs, opponents of collectivization, counter-revolutionary priests—I asked a Russian acquaintance who was reading the same papers:

"Well, anything exciting in the news?"

He glanced through his *Pravda* again conscientiously and decided, "No, nothing important."

"Nothing important? Just count up the death sentences at Novorossiisk, Krasnodar, Rostov—"

"Oh, that!" and he smiled wryly.

Executions were no longer news. In 1928, a report of five or ten kulaks put to death deserved a line or two in the day's dispatches. From 1929 forward, we totaled the deaths during a week or two weeks. The censorship permitted us to send whatever was published but we could not hint that the published items were a negligible part of the total. How many deaths we mentioned in our cables depended largely on how many papers we read and how carefully we counted them. Only the more important cases were mentioned in the central press: hundreds of official shootings were recorded in the provincial press or did not get published at all.

A methodical German correspondent subscribed to several score of local newspapers and employed several extra secretaries to read them for interesting items. In weeks when our totals of executions, based on Moscow's press, came to a mere twenty or thirty, our German colleague tallied a hundred or more. He was proud of his advantage.

It was inevitable that the "war on superstition" should be intensified at the same time, particularly in the villages where religion and the priesthood retained considerable influence. The Godless Society had been lying low during Nep. It now roused itself to the greatest campaign of its career. The drive for collectivization became strongly anti-religious in character, since the priest, deacons, and church-goers in most villages corresponded roughly to the older, more conservative portion of the population. In thousands of villages, local communists and Comsomols called meetings which voted over the heads of the congregations to demolish churches, melt down the bells for scrap metal or turn church buildings into granaries, lunchrooms, nurseries, libraries. A semblance of popular consent was thus obtained. When brigades arrived to remove the bells and the icons, they sometimes found believers armed with sticks and pitchforks ready to defend their church. The Red Army and G.P.U. troops in many instances were summoned to crush these riots and the ring-leaders found themselves quickly enough in prison or before the firing squad. In the environs of Moscow I saw bearded peasants and their women-folk on their knees, wailing, crossing themselves and beating their foreheads on the ground as bells were being yanked down; younger people jeered at them and mimicked their laments.

Anti-religious parades were organized throughout the country for Easter Eve. Edward and Harriet Deuss, of the International News Service, Billy and I tramped the muddy streets, from crowded church to crowded church. Tens of thousands of young and older people marched everywhere under flares and banners, laughing, singing, cheering. As the parades passed a church, voices rose to a shout, flares were brandished aloft, and the blasphemous anti-religious tunes blanketed the sonorous chanting of the priests and acolytes. The believers, walking round and round the church in the traditional fashion, shielded their tapers a little more intently, huddled closer to one another and pretended not to notice. They did not look up to see the grotesque floats and cardboard effigies of priests, deities, and kulaks in ludicrous postures.

At the Cathedral of Christ the Saviour, toward which the parades converged, an open-air motion picture screen was erected at the very entrance. Anti-religious films were being shown on one side of the door while thousands chanted "Christ has risen!" on the other side. Many a young person hesitated uncertainly between the free show outside and the solemn proceedings within.

Early in the morning of July 30, 1929, I was wakened by the telephone. An American friend at the Grand Hotel informed me in an excited voice that the celebrated Shrine of the Iberian Virgin, visible from the hotel windows, had been demolished during the night.

"I got up early," he said, "and looked out of the window. I saw a few old women weeping and wringing their hands. Then I noticed that the gate to Red Square looked different. There was a gaping hole where the Iberian Shrine had been."

I dressed and rushed over to the scene. A few dozen people stood around and stared in consternation at the spot where the blue-roofed shrine, studded with silver stars, and the miracle-working painting of the Madonna had been, as if its disappearance, too, were a species of miracle. I don't know what they expected would happen. It was the most famous and the holiest shrine in all of Russia. For twelve years the government had hesitated to touch it, though it stood like a taunt and a challenge in the very path of proletarian demonstrations, on the very threshold of Red Square. The Godless had contented themselves with a tablet on a nearby wall, within view of those who made pilgrimages to the shrine, reading: "Religion is the opiate of the people." Now, without warning, the Iberian Virgin had been removed and thrown into the storehouse of a small church in another district, and her shrine destroyed. The Godless, keyed up by this supreme gesture of their defiance, were a little startled by their own audacity.

For three or four days Moscow buzzed with talk of the shrine. Legends about it coursed through all of Russia. Then it was forgotten. No clearer demonstration of the general indifference to religion and the helplessness of the dwindling number of believers could have been given. Russians were infinitely more concerned with the loss of their strips of private land and other economic possessions than the demolition of their icons.

The renewed drive against religion drew more attention abroad than any other phase of Stalin's great offensive. Inside Russia it was a very minor note in the picture, the business of a handful of fanatic Godless and a small sector of the believers.

2

My Russian friends and closer acquaintances were most of them writers, actors, dancers, technicians. I saw a good deal of the impact of the mounting difficulties of living through their effect on these people. The promises of higher living standards meticulously outlined in the original plan were never so much as mentioned now. Human destiny seemed reduced to impersonal figures and skeleton percentages. Amusement and the simple amenities of life were politically immoral. The theater and literature took on a more somber, desperate tinge—became, in fact, as coldly abstract as the graphs and percentages on the front pages. Plays carried over from the Nep period, if they emphasized private instead of social emotion, were for the most part stamped out. The new plays were machine-made rites of machine worship. The plaintive and mischievous folk music smacked too much of the introspective, soul-searching past and the new era would have none of it. It became practically counter-revolutionary to sing it or to play it on the accordion. The vigorous, self-confident revolutionary tunes had right of way; if the population thirsted for its ancient melodies, so much the worse for their backward gullets! Even Tchaikovsky was kicked out as too "sentimental."

The depredations of know-nothing fanaticism in the domains of culture occupied a large place in my personal view of the Soviet landscape. My own interests and contacts were disproportionately in those areas of Russian life. The increase of literacy among the Uzbeks or Samoyeds was automatically bracketed in my mind with the rapid deterioration of literary and journalistic standards; reading was not an abstract value but related to the books and papers available to the newly literate. I could not help viewing those figures on enlarged cinema and theatrical facilities for remoter towns in direct relation to the type of pictures and plays permitted by the censors.

But the afflictions in the cultural domains ran truly parallel with conditions in most other departments of life. Under the dictatorship of the proletariat, existence is so integrated that close observation of one sector gives an accurate clew to all the rest, just as the pulse may be taken on any vein as an index to the condition of the whole body.

The novelist, Boris Pilnyak, was singled out for an organized attack on the literary front. He had been overtaken by the worst disaster that can befall a Soviet writer: he was being praised by the wrong people abroad. Accidentally the manuscript of his story *Mahogany* had gotten to Berlin and been published there before it was issued in Moscow. It was a too realistic description of the difficulties and desperations of life in a Soviet provincial town, and the Russian émigré press was moved to say nice things about it. No sooner had one Soviet paper given the signal, therefore, than the entire press and the whole writing fraternity converged on Pilnyak in a yelping pack.

The politicians of literature, organized in RAPP (Association of Proletarian Writers) led the onslaught. Every writer with an active will to survive was obliged in self-defense to spit at Pilnyak. All but a few did and the conspicuous abstension of the intrepid few marked them as "class enemies." Neither the content nor the quality of the story in question mattered. Few of those who barked angrily had even read it; their synthetic indignation was distinctly second-hand. Ultimately the self-same story, only slightly medicated, was woven into the novel *The Volga Flows to the Caspian Sea* and was praised by the very critics who now snarled at the author.

RAPP (in English the name is singularly appropriate) had set out to achieve "the seizure of power in literature." The narrow orthodoxy of this period made that objective all too easy. According to its catechism it was not enough for an artist to approve and celebrate the communist goal; he must devote himself to the prescribed details of the immediate economic and political methods for reaching that goal. Indeed, emphasis on the freedom and beauty to come was in RAPP's opinion a waste of artistic energy that should be invested in practical tasks. "Enough of the sky and the strangeness of things! Give us more plain nails!" the RAPP poet Bezimensky shrieked. The artist who dared to look at the sky and betrayed an awareness of the strangeness of things, who could not conceal his intuitive sense of life and human destiny as larger than the plain nails, was a cultural kulak. It did not suffice that he admitted the importance of plain nails if he dared hint that the sky was studded with stars.

At the head of RAPP, and by that token the Stalin of Soviet culture, was a certain Leopold Auerbach,* whose literary style, according to Max Eastman, "has that rare and generous quality that you sometimes find in a business-college sophomore studying to become a publicity writer for a scenic railway." That good-natured pedestrian pedant, Sergei Dinamov, was raised to editorship of the all-powerful *Literary Gazette*. Third-rate journalists with a talent for toe-licking and a good memory for the latest official "theses" became the tsars in every branch of creative art.

I met Pilnyak about this time. A big, blond, unwieldy fellow, with a huge smile and a huge appetite for wine, women, and life.

* Arrested for "counterrevolution" and embezzlement in 1937.

Though he had Volga German blood in his veins, he was Russian in a salty elemental way—one of those who could scarcely breathe, let alone write, except on and about his native soil. I came to know many others of this stamp, whom neither changing governments nor social systems could alienate from Russia, who preferred servitude in Siberia to freedom in a foreign land. Pilnyak, talented and naive, with a zest for living joined to a disdain for life, seemed to me a personification of Russia. It may explain why he was kept hopping by the powers-that-be between extravagant adulation and no less extravagant denunciation, sometimes the two simultaneously.

The attack on Pilnyak was a warning that the time for half-loyalties was over. Novelists, poets, playwrights, even musicians and painters, must devote themselves specifically to the advancement of the Five Year Plan or be branded outlaws. A few preferred to stop writing, painting and composing; the rest rushed for the proletarian bandwagon.

The last spark of Moscow's literary bohemianism expired. Dom Gertsena, the Artists' Club, and other gathering places of the creative intelligentsia turned into drab, hushed restaurants. The spirited Pava no longer pounded the piano, except in private under safe auspices. She taught Billy her favorite songs, and her vibrant voice echoed through our remodeled stable.

Stories or poems which did not raucously celebrate the glories of industrialization, iron discipline, death to class enemies, could no longer find publication. The *agitka,* or crude propaganda work, until then recognized as a useful form but treated a little condescendingly, now became the prescribed and exclusive literary fare. Those who could not or would not manage it might as well throw away their pens.

Vladimir Mayakovsky, a burly bellowing fellow who had traveled all the way from his pre-war futuristic poetry to the blood-and-iron of proletarian poetry, popularized the phrase a "social order" for his fellow-writers. He laughed at "inspiration" and "moods" and introspection. A "social order" from the Communist Party was all the inspiration that a Soviet poet required. There was no place for dreamers and spinners of images, he insisted, poetry must be pounded out with sledge-hammers and ironed into shape with tractors. Mayakovsky dressed and swaggered like a class-conscious *apache;* he wrote magnificent lines in praise of the death-dealing G.P.U. and did not cavil about applying his talent to celebrate Soviet mineral water or Soviet loans. But the swagger and the noise were a pathetic attempt to shout down his genuine poetic instinct.

"Social orders" sent bewildered authors scurrying to electric stations, factories, collective farms, scientific expeditions, tasting the new Soviet life like literary adolescents. They exchanged their inspirations for notebooks and painfully concocted dull books and plays ordered by trusts and commissions. Pilnyak himself went off to Central Asia to retrieve political respectability by writing about the Five Year Plan in that part of the country. Literary mediocrity had never in human history touched such heights of power or such depths of drabness.

It was at this time that the more fanatical notions of "collective authorship" were put forward. Any collective of workers, the theory ran, could turn out a literary masterpiece if it made the effort. A miner could do a masterpiece about mining, a collective farmer about farm life. Genius and natural talents were outmoded inventions of individualist bourgeois exploiters. Down with the pretensions of artists! The purpose of evoking latent talent in simple workers and peasants was sound enough, but it was vitiated by a disdain for talent as such and a tendency to eulogize trashy manuscripts if they were grubby with proletarian fingerprints and boldly ungrammatical. The theory did not go much farther than stupid fulmination. But it was indicative of the revolt against culture and intelligence: part of the same hatred of the better-educated and more sensitive human beings which was manifest in the persecution of engineers, arrests of professors and scientists, baiting of aged Academicians.

There arose a vogue for simon-pure collectivism in the more idealistic and optimistic strata of the population. Real communism was presumably around the corner. Groups of workers in factories and students in their barracks anticipated its arrival by forming voluntary collectives. They pooled their earnings and drew from the common fund according to their needs. Entire factories in some instances decided to merge their incomes and equalize wages. In the plans for new housing certain ideologically correct architects disdained the old-fashioned individual kitchen, bathroom, or nursery: eating, hygiene, and the rearing of children would be a communal matter. Proposals for new cities in which children would be brought up by the community were made in all seriousness and discussions unfolded as to the extent parents might safely be permitted to maintain contact with their offspring.

Few of these things went beyond the theoretical stage or touched more than a fevered few in the population. These ideas, however, are clews to the illusions of the moment. The communist millennium seemed to a few faithful just over the horizon—but they were the few who wielded the power of the state and could enforce their distortions upon a sixth part of the globe. It was a mood which stopped at nothing to attain its objectives. Something of religious hysteria—the hysteria of a Mohammedan army fighting infidels—was in it.

The news of the Wall Street crash and the capitalist Depression that it ushered in came as confirmation of the communist prognosis. The capitalist structure was tottering. Against the background of mounting unemployment, crashing banks, riots and doles, the Soviet effort gained dramatic significance. The press did not conceal its glee. It jeered at the famous American prosperity and the vaunted capitalist "stabilization." It ridiculed those communists who had doubted that world revolution was "the order of the day."

Practically, the depression hit Russia as hard as the rest of the world. Its foreign trade, an important element in the Five Year Plan, was undermined. The prices of machinery it imported went down, but the prices on its exports sank much faster. Lack of "valuta," foreign capital, became the greatest stumbling block on the road to industrialization and internal inflation assumed disastrous proportions. But psychologically and politically, the depression had its uses. It gave the Kremlin new confidence. It evoked a cocky, boastful, derisive attitude toward the outside world which made Russia impervious to foreign criticism and more smugly self-righteous than ever in its ruthlessness.

XVI. The War Nobody Knew

DURING most of that year of 1929, the Red Army fought a war against the Chinese in Manchuria in defense of the Soviet Union's half-interest in the Chinese-Eastern Railway. The provocations on both sides were more than ample, and the fighting was real enough, but the hostilities were never dignified by the official designation of war. Like the Japanese invasion of Manchuria several years later, and the Italian attack on Ethiopia later still, the Soviet punitive operations in China were conducted without a formal declaration of war.

It began early in spring with Chinese charges that Russia was using the railroad personnel and railroad funds for communist propaganda in Manchuria. Toward the end of May, the Manchurians raided the Soviet consulate at Harbin in search of documentary proof of what everyone in Moscow assumed to be true: that an insurrectionary movement under Feng Hu-Siang, the so-called "Christian General," had Soviet encouragement. Soviet officials and citizens were arrested. In a few thrusts in the following months the Chinese ousted Russians from the railroad and other strategic economic positions, arresting thousands in the process.

Red Army units were mobilized; one after another classes of reserves were called to the colors; and a Special Far Eastern Army was created. That army remained on a permanent footing, vastly strengthened with every year and perhaps destined ultimately to test Soviet strength against Japan. General Bluecher, the tall, soldierly fighter whose prowess was a by-word in his country, was placed in command. Several years before, the same Bluecher, under the *nom de guerre* of General Galen, had been the mysterious Russian genius behind the victorious northward march of the Kuomintang revolutionary armies in China. He had guided the hand of a young half-literate peasant soldier who was now virtual dictator of Nationalist China, the same Chiang Kai-shek who now protested to the world against Soviet entry into

Manchuria. General Bluecher-Galen's place at the head of the invading Red troops was a startling measure of the changes wrought by a few years. The Chinese had a healthy respect for this Russian's skill and strength when he started. That respect was deepened by the end of the year.

At first the Soviet citizenry was kept apprised of developments and in a state of half-hearted resentement against "Chinese and White Russian bandits." Then the war was all but forgotten, both in Russia and in the rest of the world. Serious enough in terms of casualties and political consequences, it remains to this day the war nobody knew.

In July, Moscow sent an ultimatum to China. Millions of Russians responded quickly and noisily to the Party's order for mass demonstrations against the violation of Soviet rights in China. In Moscow at least half a million men and women paraded past the Chinese Legation building, shouting insults against the Chinese bandits and their White Russian hirelings. After the parades the public all but forgot the whole business. By the time the war was actually under way, only faint echoes reached the people, busy with more pressing matters like shock brigading, rations, and class war in the peasant regions.

On the night when China's answer to the ultimatum was due, at the end of July, a great many of Moscow's resident Americans, including all the correspondents, were at a gay party in the palatial home of the Hammers in honor of some members of the delegation of so-called American business-men. The house was loud and gay this night, a long table sagged under its weight of rich foods, and the vodka flowed generously.

But through the noise the correspondents listened for the ring of the telephone that would call us to the Press Department for news of China's answer. We did not get it until 2:30 A.M. and learned to our distress that Tass, the official news agency, had transmitted the Chinese reply to the whole world by wire three hours before it was released to us in Moscow. The chain of agencies allied with Tass—the Associated Press in America, Wolff in Germany, Reuters in England, etc.—were well content with their scoop, but the rest of the foreign press corps were indignant. To make things worse for myself and others who were "beaten," Negley Farson wrote for his paper a fulsome description of the

Hammer party which we attended. Unintentionally he created the false impression that we had neglected our duty in order to attend this lively gathering. I heard from my home office on the matter, as did others.

I obtained the first and only interview on the Manchurian situation with the Assistant Commissar of Foreign Affairs, Karakhan,* by way of smoothing my own ruffled feathers. But the bureaucratic news policy dominated by Tass remained unaltered. A hundred times I tried to make the Press Department officials see the wisdom of establishing a second news channel through which those correspondents not in the ring of the world's official agencies might get their information. Tass would thereby carry out its contractual obligations to its official news allies, while the rest of us competed on equal terms. The Press Department agreed, talked of the reforms to come, but, Russian-fashion, nothing happened.

The Chinese-Eastern matter had earlier precipitated me into an acrimonious passage at arms with the censors. I had received an urgent inquiry from New York about the Soviet "reaction" to the raid of its Harbin consulate. It was the first I had heard about the event: news is too closely guarded in the U.S.S.R. I wrote a dispatch indicating that the affair was still unknown to Moscow outside of official circles. I took it to the Foreign Office for the needed censor's signature. Arriving at the Press Department, however, I was informed that Mr. Rothstein, the only censor on hand, was "in conference." I waited. Waiting in the outer room of the censorship division was the correspondents' principal and most exasperating job in Moscow. We resented the lackadaisical disregard of time and general inefficiency of the process even more than the censorship itself. A hundred times I heard American, French, German newspapermen with world-wide reputations threaten that they won't stand being kept waiting like office boys while the censors finished their tea-drinking. But they continued to stand it; there was nothing intentional about the insulting procedure, just routine procrastination. In any case, there I was waiting for Mr. Rothstein while the world waited for some word on the Harbin developments out of Russia.

At quarter-hour intervals I tried to break into Mr. Rothstein's

* Reported arrested as Trotskyist "counterrevolutionary" at the end of 1936.

sanctum, to be informed with a shrug that he was still in conference. At the end of an hour I wrote out a cable reading approximately as follows (I quote from memory):

> An embargo on all outgoing news was instituted in Russia today. Correspondents arriving at the Press Department of the Foreign Office found that the censorship facilities, without which news cannot possibly be sent, were mysteriously shut down. There was no indication whether or when the embargo might be lifted, as no official comment on the sensational action could be obtained. Well-informed quarters assume that only some internal or foreign crisis of great seriousness could have prompted the Foreign Office to isolate the nation in this fashion without warning.

I took the dispatch—which I had no intention of sending, of course—to the secretary outside Mr. Rothstein's door.

"Please place this message before Mr. Rothstein, conference or no conference," I said grimly.

"But—"

"There are no buts. This is most urgent, just do what you're told."

Fifteen seconds later I was in Mr. Rothstein's office. He had apparently been conferring with himself. No one else was present or had come out of his office. His temper, having read my make-believe message, was a match for my own. The first hostilities in the Sino-Russian war occurred there and then. My relations with the Press Department were strained for a while—every correspondent went through these "mad" spells periodically, then submitted helplessly to the pervading inefficiency and delay which neither his indignation nor anything else could change in the slightest.

Diplomatic relations with China were broken. By September, large Red forces, supported by war planes and tanks, were pushing into Manchuria. By the end of November, the Chinese had been completely routed, many Manchurian towns were demolished and Russia was in control of northern Manchuria. Just when the Chinese capitulated and the fighting ceased, Secretary of State Stimson in Washington decided to invoke the Kellogg Pact to prevent the war that had already been fought to a finish. This fiasco in itself indicated how little the world knew about what was happening in Manchuria. The Soviet press jeered at "Stimson's belated and uncalled-for intervention." Litvinov sent a stinging reply which American public opinion considered insulting and there was a general feeling even among communists that Litvinov's genius for offensive satire for once had outweighed his diplomatic shrewdness. What might have been an opening wedge for Soviet-American understanding, Litvinov angrily converted into another barrier.

Suddenly the world was excited by the war it had ignored. The Moscow reporters were driven to the edge of apoplexy by the futile effort to obtain news of the peace negotiations started in Khabarovsk. Secrecy bred sensational rumors. Refusal to disclose the extent or cost of operations or the terms of settlement kept us hopping. But little as we knew, the general public knew less. The peace, like the war, did not touch a population on the eve of a much greater and more terrible war: the policy of "liquidation of the kulaks as a class" had just been promulgated by Stalin.

"The masses and the communist rank and file have been kept in far greater ignorance than even the foreign press," a New York *Times* dispatch out of Moscow declared. Then the correspondent added: "Yet there was no grumbling or demands for news. Well may the communists boast of the discipline which stood such a test."

Since that correspondent is not wholly naive, it may be assumed that he had his tongue in his cheek in putting this curious interpretation upon the apathy and meekness of the communists and the masses. No one boasted of this discipline except the New York *Times*. Silent acceptance of accomplished facts without "grumbling or demands for news" by this time seemed to me no longer novel enough to be worth cabling as news.

2

We shared a *dacha* that summer with Rachelle Ossipovna and her family at Silver Forests, at the northernmost end of the Moscow street car system. The gleaming birch woods of this popular suburb are thickly sown with summer cottages owned by city people. In addition, local peasants let their dilapidated huts, trimmed with wood embroidery, at a price that enabled them to live through the winter. Only those in the higher brackets of earning power could afford the traditional summer transfer to a *dacha,* so that our neighbors were the more privileged officials, better-paid technicians, writers and the like. Rachelle's entourage of obscure celebrities from the theaters and concert halls enlivened the summer months of 1929.

The presence of an American family in their midst was slightly disconcerting to the middle-class Soviet denizens of Silver Forests. Frequently they saw tourist automobiles struggle through the narrow lanes to our door, bringing American friends in their dazzling elegance of sport clothes, cameras, and new embroidered Russian blouses. Our guests deepened that dangerous but fascinating bourgeois atmosphere which surrounded foreigners. But curiosity sometimes conquered discretion and a good many of the *dacha* boarders ventured into our more carefree and better-supplied circle.

Rachelle's hospitable samovar always sang a welcome and her desperate yearning for the vanished glamor of her Petrograd past drew the gayer young dancers and poets and opera hopefuls to our lawn. Her bald-headed, near-sighted husband wandered in meek embarrassment among the young people, cornering me every so often to tell the latest political joke for a third time that day or to beat me again at chess. There were soft evenings when Billy paid for the Russians' folk songs with the *St. Louis Blues* or Negro spirituals or I.W.W hymns. There were boisterous afternoons of swimming and leap-frog in the Moscow River. The conventions required that we dress and undress in full view of everyone on the crowded beach: walking from the house to the river in a bathing suit or even a bathrobe was shockingly indecent. Like the Russians we soaped ourselves and scrubbed one another's back on the river's edge.

Endlessly we were questioned about American skyscrapers, cowboys and Indians, J. P. Morgan and Rockefeller. The American tourists whom we invited to the *dacha* became the focal points of local interest, their clothes and private biographies frankly investigated and commented upon. It was the nearest most of those visitors came to real Russians out of earshot of their guides. The softer country atmosphere melted away a little of the fear that crusted Russian minds and we came closer to our neighbors than we could in the city.

When we left for a European vacation at the end of the summer we carried long lists of commissions from Russian friends and resident Americans. These included medicines, corsets, leberwurst, garters, caps, eye-glasses, dance records, nails, violin strings, the thousand and one things for which Russia yearned. Like all foreigners we went with empty suitcases to return with full ones, ready to do battle with the customs officials in defense of the miscellany of gifts.

Throughout our stay in Berlin or Paris or Vienna the thought of those commissions was a dead weight on our conscience. Somehow the bothersome purchases were always postponed to tomorrow in the thrill of tasting capitalist excitements after a six months' absence. That meant frenzied shopping at the last moment and the guilty fear that we had overlooked someone's dramatic plea for hairpins and someone else's meek hope of a recent fashion magazine. Usually we forgot who asked for what. Now what was it Anna Pavlovna was so intent on having, silk stockings or castor oil? No, the stockings are for Lyev Borisovich—probably for that new ballerina of his—and the castor oil is for the director of the building coöperative. What could it have been we promised poor Anna Pavlovna? The Americans' requests for breakfast foods, ketchup, lemons or pancake flour were particularly annoying.

Back in Moscow, the problem of distributing the gifts involved a month's travail. The films for a *Pravda* reporter proved to be the wrong size and the leberwurst got badly tangled with the nails. Lyev Borisovich had in the meantime been arrested and we dared not guess whether he had intended the lipstick for his wife or his girl friends. Lida had suddenly become frightened of her bourgeois contacts and failed to claim that ten-cent bracelet; but just after we had presented it to someone else, she arrived surreptitiously to collect it. That American engineer was deeply offended because we had forgotten the chocolate bars.

In the autumn the problem of Genie's schooling became more pressing. The ordinary kindergartens and schools were badly overcrowded. In the previous year, we were aware, they had been closed down nearly half the time because of epidemic illnesses. Nevertheless we visited a few. If we could find one general school with a clean toilet, we would chance sending her there. We could not find it. The only hope was to have her admitted to one of the special kindergartens organized by the more important institutions for the children of their own employees. The Foreign Office had one of the best, and there we applied. The application created a serious diplomatic situation. Through friends we discovered the turmoil we had started. It was slightly inconvenient to refuse a simple favor to an American correspondent, a "friendly" one at that. On the other hand, could the dictatorship of the proletariat risk the presence of a "bourgeois element" in its undefiled school?

For about a week Mr. Rothstein stalled and cleared his throat. Finally he informed us regretfully that while the Foreign Office would be delighted to give a proletarian education to my daughter, it was unfortunately overcrowded, etc., etc. In franker quarters I was informed that Genie was considered undesirable as a "bourgeois element"—at the age of six and a half! A few weeks later, despite the overcrowding, the two children of Louis Fischer were admitted to this school. Sins of the fathers! In the end we found a disfranchised pre-revolutionary teacher who gratefully accepted the tutelage of Genie and the children of a Soviet physician as a private kindergarten group.

3

Moscow was brightened for us for a week in November by the arrival of the little Napoleon of American journalism, Roy W. Howard. The Press Department officials who were with me to meet him, awed by his reputation, stared in consternation at the small, chirping newspaper magnate in his natty clothes and loud shirt: like a bright Christmas package from another world as he stepped off the Trans-Siberian. It was my function as one of his minions to act as guide and mentor on matters Soviet. His intelligent curiosity and bubbling sense of fun turned the chore into a holiday.

The highly optimistic views of Russian affairs which he brought back to America were a fairly accurate measure of my own attitudes at the time. If visiting communists carried back wry reports of my bourgeois defections, visiting capitalists were fortified in their suspicion that the United Press was represented by an emphatic admirer of the Soviets.

Frazier Hunt—"Spike" after the first fifteen minutes—happened to be in Moscow at the same time as Howard on an assignment for the Hearst organization. They were both at the Hotel Savoy. I phoned down and told Spike what the Trans-Siberian had brought out of Japan. In a few minutes he came crashing through like a playful tornado, over six feet of ebullient vitality, swept Howard into his long arms and swung him around the room over the publisher's contralto protests. It was a loud and memorable reunion. George Slocombe has described Spike as the only American correspondent who is not cynical; he combines, indeed, the technique of a veteran with the wide-eyed romantics of a cub reporter on his first big fire.

Billy's talents as a cook shone with a special incandescence in the land of rations. Russia's past reputation for good cooking rested largely on the French chefs employed in the best homes and hotels. The Lyons table achieved a wide if unideological fame. Sojourners of the extreme Left, having enjoyed thoroughly one of Billy's meals, were convinced that anyone who fed his guests so well must be lacking in his political morals—revolution like good medicine should be hard to swallow.

Except for the lack of fresh vegetables and fruits, the foreigners' food problem was not a serious one. Technically our purchases in the diplomats' shop were limited to definite though generous amounts, to prevent us from feeding needy Russian friends. In practice these limits were often stretched. There was not one foreigner in Moscow who did not help a few of his Russian acquaintances with an occasional pound of sugar, butter, potatoes, or a package of cigarettes. The cigarette shortage hit the country almost as hard as the lack of bread and meat. Russians are inveterate smokers. People stopped strangers on the street to beg a puff or two. Ragged boys hawked a few dirty cigarettes, probably stolen somewhere, at fancy prices.

For all its inconveniences, life was full to overflowing for a correspondent in intimate touch with the news. The tension of existence invested the simplest routine of daily affairs with new emotional dimensions. The country lived on the brink of novelty, in a state of nervous expectancy: a new decree, a new intonation in Stalin's latest speech, might alter the quality of life for a hundred million people. Elsewhere in the world there was an intrinsic and discernible logic in events. Changes flowed from conditions, major social calamities grew out of causes that had ripened slowly. In the Russia of this epoch the relationship between cause and effect seemed to have been suspended, since everything except the weather depended on the arbitrary will of the rulers.

Whatever this may have meant in terms of fear, hope and uncertainty to the Soviet masses, it provided an extraordinary spectacle for an outsider whose duty it was to observe the process; not always a pleasant spectacle, but always epic in scope. The sheer scale of Russian events stirred the imagination. Where death sentences were spoken of in dozens elsewhere, they were reckoned in hundreds here. Where political prisoners and exiles in Italy or France or Rumania were reckoned by the hundred, they must be counted here by the hundred thousand. In estimating the immediate effects of new policies or procedures, the normal unit of calculation was a million families.

And I never ceased to marvel at the direct and instantaneous impact of the governing will upon individuals. An unwonted warmth would come into people's voices, a fresh springiness to their step, and I knew that the change was derived from a more liberal decree published that very day. Or a deeper tone of gloom and worry clouded people's expression, and I knew as surely as if it had been written in words on their foreheads that another purge of offices and apartment houses had been ordered. The arrival of a shipment of herrings or potatoes, the opening of a few new shops, affected the temper of the Soviet capital as only the declaration or ending of wars affected other capitals.

Sometimes I visualized the Russian population as a huge anthill, with Stalin poking a stick into its center. Every casual prodding destroyed the contours of life for a few more million of the insects. Perhaps I came to see the process from the ant's lowly vantage point rather than Stalin's. It was about this time that in a letter to an American friend I coined an aphorism which explained my state of mind even if it explained nothing about Russia.

"It is not pleasant," I wrote, "to watch men driven like sheep, even if they're being driven to heaven."

The initial two years of my assignment in Utopia had taken the starch out of my Soviet enthusiasms. I still retained most of them, but they were wilted and drooping. I was essentially unhappy and uncomfortable in the realization that, for all I could do to drive them back to their subterranean lairs, fundamental doubts were rising to the surface of my consciousness.

BOOK 3

DOUBT

I. Stalin Launches a Slogan

THE gnawing ambition of every correspondent, the far-off beacon of hope by which he steered his life, professionally speaking, was an interview with Joseph Stalin. Few had troubled to press him for this boon in the first years of the Soviet universe, when he moved vaguely in the haze around major planets like Lenin, Trotsky, Zinoviev, and Dzherzhinsky. After Lenin's death, Stalin's star rose quickly in the political heavens, but he was still, in foreign eyes at least, one of many. During this period a Japanese correspondent succeeded in interviewing him. Stalin said to him —and the saying has become celebrated—"I, too, am an Asiatic." By 1929, he was dictator in all but name, the sun around which the Soviet universe revolved, and the most coveted object of interviewers among the great of this earth.

The more stubbornly he denied himself, the more desirable he seemed. Journalists and publishers of world repute knocked at the Kremlin gates until their knuckles bled but they could not reach him. This inaccessibility passed the comprehension of American editors. At regular intervals I received instructions to obtain "Stalin's reaction" to some national or international event. All other American correspondents received analogous orders. We learned to ignore them. We stopped trying to convince our distant editors that Stalin was the one exception. He could be snared by neither flattery nor threats, neither favors nor trickery.

I decided one evening to try oblique insult.

At the moment it seemed pure inspiration. In sober fact my impertinence grew unconsciously out of a conversation with a Soviet official weeks before. He had known Stalin before his ascent to glory, both before and after the revolution. The audacity that resides in a flagon of vodka where lemon peel shavings drift like seaweed enabled him to utter the ineffable name.

"Stalin " he said meditatively, "has one weakness. His Achilles' heel. That's his vanity. He may pretend to be annoyed with the hallelujahs of praise, but he does nothing to stop them. He allows himself to be convinced too readily that the genuflecting is politically useful. He reacts to the mildest slight on his dignity as though it were an electric shock."

Some part of my mind must have caught the seed of an idea in that estimate. Insult is the antithesis of flattery and therefore "dialectically" its consort. Of flattery Stalin had an abundance beyond my strength to add, so why not its Hegelian mate? Thus the seed sprouted and the fruit it bore was a letter in which I hinted very broadly at the popular view of Stalin as a crafty, merciless recluse, peremptory and sour, awful in his boundless will to power. Maybe in my subconscious mind, where everyday things throw their grotesque shadows, I really gave some credence to this picture of him as the ogre-like dictator of folk-lore. In any event, I wrote him in part:

> An enormous amount of nonsense about you has been spread throughout the world. Some through ill will, others through ignorance, have depicted you as a taciturn recluse hiding behind the Kremlin walls, unapproachable and scarcely human. Indeed, I saw one item in the press insisting that you did not exist at all, that you were a mere figment of Bolshevik imagination.

My letter implied that there might be some truth in these insinuations. The only sure way to disprove and dissipate such notions, I urged him, was to break his silence by receiving the United Press correspondent. Having dispatched this bit of lopsided logic, I waited for the thunder and the lightning of divine wrath. Several days later a messenger came to Clean Ponds Boulevard bearing a large envelope decorated with a great wax seal. Inside were a few typewritten lines in Russian on a half-sheet of white paper, without so much as a letterhead, signed in red ink in the small neat handwriting of the dictator. The letter read:

> I am sorry that I cannot at the present time grant your request for an interview. Motives: (a) interviews do not destroy legends but rather create an unhealthy atmosphere for new sensations and legends; (b) I have not at the moment free time for an interview.

I ask your pardon for the delay of the answer. There is a lot of work and the matter lay awaiting an opportunity for answering.

Respectfully yours,

J. Stalin.

My first impulse was to publish the letter and the reply. Any direct word from Stalin was a "story" well worth the cable tolls. His opinion of interviews as a class was news. Stalin's lieutenants, I learned subsequently, were astonished that I did not exploit this correspondence. I was astonished myself, if the truth be told. Such restraint is not in my journalistic nature. But I told neither my editors nor my friends about the exchange of amenities.

Instead, I ignored section (a) of his "motives" as a philosophical generalization and accepted section (b) as a concrete undertaking to receive me when he could spare the time. Since pressure of other business prevented him from giving me an interview "at the moment," I wrote in thanking him for the prompt reply, I would wait patiently until the pressure eased. A month later I sent another letter referring to his "promise" and expressing the hope that he would soon find the time to keep it. Periodically I plagued him thus with a gentle reminder of this tangential "promise" I had read into his refusal.

The figure of Stalin expanded on the nation's mind. It grew Gargantuan and more than a little sphinx-like, a symbol more than a man. The ether trembled at the mention of his name and it seemed overwhelmingly strange that the exalted essence should have not only a face but a distinct mustache.

Twice each year, on May 1 and November 7, the Moscow masses saw him flittingly through a blur of excitement as they swung past Lenin's tomb: a robust, large-featured, typically Caucasian person in a military great-coat, a flat-visored military hat, a certain sculptured stolidity in his calm pose. There was something monumental in the very drape of Stalin's clothes. But he never spoke in public except behind the barred doors of special Party and technical conferences. Not once had his voice, tinged with the familiar Georgian accent, been heard over the radio. Only very infrequently did he show up in the news-reels. Even his photographs were few and standardized.

The rarity of his public statements weighted his every carefully edited word with a power such as Napoleon's or Lenin's or Mussolini's never carried. Lenin's pronouncements had been the basis for discussion. Stalin's were the basis for obedience. Coincident with the November holidays, he released a signed article entitled "The Year of the Great Break." It both reflected and deepened the somber tone of the national life. Its every sentence became a war cry. Sycophants and bigots read into it a wisdom beyond the compass of a merely mortal mind.

Six weeks later came a nation-wide display of worship for Stalin such as no tsar or emperor had ever been vouchsafed. The *vozhd* was fifty years old on December 21, 1929, and the birthday was made the occasion for a demonstration of servility, flattery, and a sort of religious propitiation. Russians excel in the arts of enthusiastic self-abasement. There was the flavor of the *Arabian Nights* in the flummery that inundated the land. To an alien ear it sounded fantastic. The reams of "greetings" dripped with honeyed panegyric in the extravagant style of courtiers in bad novels. Every politician and *litterateur* whose name meant anything to the public—including yesterday's Oppositionist exiles—rummaged in his memory for stories to set off the courage, infallible sagacity, and leadership of Stalin.

There was little of simple affection in the demonstration, almost nothing to hint that the distant object of adulation was of flesh and blood. Though they called him Comrade, this Stalin was as far-off and unimaginably mysterious to the simple Russians as the tsars before him had been. The tsars, too, were called "little father." Deity is ever extolled in the familiar "thou." In the birthday greetings there was that folk quality of awesome intimacy which merely makes its object seem unreal.

The sticky adulation made me squirm. It seemed to me an imbecile anti-climax of the dream of erect men that the first socialist people should prostrate itself before a leader. When I hinted at a deep betrayal of the spirit of the revolution I was called romantic and sentimental. It was of small use to insist that there was nothing more romantic and sentimental than the theory of Stalin's infallibility or the changing of a man into a god.

For several days the flood of eulogy covered the land. Then Stalin graciously responded in a few lines remarkable, I thought, for their Biblical flavor. Until the age of eighteen the future Stalin, then Joseph Dzugashvili, studied in a Greek Orthodox seminary in Tiflis, and the imprint of those years remained on his mind. It is said that to her dying day his pious mother nursed her disappointment that "Soso" did not become a priest. If she were less literal she might understand that her ambition has been fully gratified: her son is chief of a militant faith consistently ecclesiastical. His acknowledgment of the mountain of invocations was printed in big letters on every front page in the U.S.S.R.:

> Your congratulations and greetings I credit to the account of the great party of the working class which gave me birth and raised me in its own image. You must not doubt, comrades, that I am ready in the future, as in the past, to give to the task of the working class, to the task of proletarian revolution and world communism, all my strength, all my abilities, and if necessary all my blood, drop by drop.

2

Most of the waiters at the Grand Hotel, like the great chandeliers and the gigantic potted palms and the blue-and-gold crockery and the napkins with grand-ducal coats-of-arms in the corner, were left-overs from the old regime. The blend of subserviency and camaraderie of their earlier training was overlaid with a new slovenliness, like a fine antique covered with fresh dust. Two or three of the older men, in particular, made no secret of their disdain for their latterday clients. All too rarely there were diplomats in dinner coats and their ladies in evening gowns to recall the ancient grandeur. For the rest, the dance nights drew a miscellany of commonplace foreigners hardly worthy of the Alexander II dishes. Callous-handed technicians and correspondents and vulgar salesmen ate caviar out of deep bowls and washed it down with vodka and Caucasian wines and Armenian brandy, indulging themselves on the thinnish fat of the land by virtue of inflated rubles. The Russian customers were always fewer, more apologetic and self-effacing.

The only genuine proletarians in the place were probably the puffing musicians in the lofty gallery between the two marble-walled ballrooms. Heroically they strained to imitate the syncopated groaning and shouting and caterwauling they heard on American jazz records; they even sang an occasional chorus in what they and other Russians imagined was the English language. For all their honest sweat, the result was as Russian as *blini*.

A permanent expression of astonishment was on their faces as they looked down between dance numbers into the muted gaiety of the ballrooms, where people seemed to take miracles like sizzling *shashlik* and almost-white bread and steaming *gurevietsky kasha* as a matter of course. Perhaps they could see from their perch more clearly than others the paradox of this tiny islet of satiety and safety in the oceans of the country's deprivations. There were some among the foreigners themselves, I know, who could not shake off a consciousness of the contrast.

The invisible wall that always separated foreigners from Russians grew thicker as living conditions in the country deteriorated and police pressures increased. Their more ample life and greater freedom isolated foreigners, so that they looked upon the sufferings beyond their narrow inclosure as if from a great distance. They came to accept the poverty and drabness and chronic uncertainties of the great masses as normal and divinely ordained, even as white men all through Asia accept the wretchedness of the natives; came to accept it so completely that they no longer noticed it at all. The advantages of their foreign money in the midst of inflation, above all the sanctuary of their miraculous foreign passports, gave the humblest among them a sense of superiority, as though nature had fashioned them of more delicate materials.

To complain of the deepening miseries of the Soviet population seemed to most of those complacent foreigners a little quixotic, as though one were to complain of the low living standards of cattle. "But they are Russians, my dear man, and they've never known any better . . ." A good deal that passed abroad as liberal tolerance and understanding of the Kremlin's policies, much that seemed to readers in New York or London a "friendly attitude" toward the revolution, amounted to little more than this smug condescension. Implicit in the lop-sided approval was the patronizing satisfaction that the Great Experiment was being tried out in the Great Social Laboratory so safely far away from home: upon the teeming Russian coolies instead of the sentient citizens of the West.

The headlong inflation of the Soviet currency helped to widen the distance between foreigners and natives. As in the Germany of the post-war inflation period, though within mucn narrower bounds, foreigners possessing a little foreign money suddenly were transformed into persons of wealth. They tasted the lordly feeling that nothing which money could buy was beyond them. True, Russia had little to offer at the moment. But that little meant much because it was denied to others and because it frequently had the flavor of forbidden fruit. Machinists and reporters who had never known the thrill of ordering in a restaurant without even glancing at the right-hand side of the menu, now called for all the delicacies that were available without a second thought of cost. Rubles could buy gew-gaws in the commission shops, sometimes a jewel or picture drawn from its twelve-year-old hiding place by a hard-pressed "former" person; rubles could buy the company of the luscious girls who hovered around the foreign colony.

Foreigners knew the lift of safe extravagance. The process of exchanging foreign money for the inflated rubles involved a faint sense of guilt, but familiarity erased that in time. Strictly considered, it was illegal to exchange money anywhere but in the state banks, where the fictitious official rate of two rubles to the dollar prevailed. But the foreigner who actually brought his dollars, pounds, or marks to a bank and returned with rubles was a rare apparition. There were a few, fearful of a blemish on their ideological record, who attempted to get along without recourse to inflated rubles, by earning enough Soviet currency locally to meet their needs. But there was not one resident foreigner—and I am mindful of the Americans who acted as spokesmen for the Kremlin—who regularly gave up his good dollars for bad paper rubles. One who now makes a particular point of emphasizing his purity in this regard, was the first to induct me in the procedure.

The whole business was a good deal like drinking during the prohibition era in America, technically *verboten* but so universally practiced that it carried no consciousness of law-breaking. Yet it was lined with a false and futile embarrassment, evidenced in silence and evasion by people who wrote on Soviet affairs. Those who had a professional interest in remaining in the good graces of the authorities simply did not touch this tender spot in the economic anatomy of their hosts. Among themselves, they discussed the situation openly, if only to ascertain whether they were being "gypped" on the rate. In print, they preferred to avoid the subject.

Several of the correspondents with strong embassy connections depended on the diplomatic pouch for their supplies of inflated rubles. Abroad the rate was often twice as high as in Moscow. One of them used to phone regularly to a friend in Warsaw asking for a few "bowls of cherries"—cherries being the code-word for *chervontzi*, or Soviet banknotes. The rest of us depended on local contacts. No foreigner was ever molested in this connection, and in time the intermediaries were mostly G.P.U. men, sensibly gathering in the valuta directly, instead of extracting it afterwards from Russians. The authorities recognized that any effort to force foreign guests to live on the make-believe official standard would result in a wholesale exodus. Such conformity would have been a strain on the resources of a millionaire, let alone a hard-working foreign salesman or reporter.

Once upon a time—the story has acquired a legendary ring—the cantankerous correspondent of an American newspaper, out of sheer cussedness, insisted on taking the financial fiction of "stable" money at face value. With tongue in cheek, he announced that he would obey the law to the letter. This was before the government had simplified matters for us by accepting foreign currency for payment at hotels, restaurants, and certain shops. Buying every ruble at the bank, his costs soared to alarming heights. His room-rent came to thirty dollars a day, every droshky ride cost him ten or twenty dollars, every meal fifteen or twenty dollars. Russian news at that price seemed unreasonable to his newspaper and he was quickly transferred to another country, as he had expected. His successor was advised formally by the Press Department, on arrival, not to engage in such quixotic leg-pulling, but to do as all his colleagues did.

The loose talk about "speculating in rubles," directed by communists abroad against writers whose Russian views they did not approve, is malevolent nonsense. Despite the sinister sound of the word speculation, the talk merely referred to the fact, known to every child in Moscow, that all foreigners of necessity obtained currency for their everyday needs—rent and food and services—on the unofficial inflated exchange basis.

The resident foreigners worked out a conclusive test of idiocy as applied to exuberant innocents from abroad. Anyone who emerged from a Soviet visit of more than two days without realizing that the national money was vastly inflated had passed the test. A few economists of worldwide reputation passed with flying colors. It did not prevent them from writing weighty tomes on Soviet economy.

The more pious foreigners of the Bolshevik persuasion might hold out for a while against the monetary pressures. But the Marxian laws of economic determinism did not exempt them and in the end they were forced to resort to the universal and recognized practice. Witness the plight of a young American near-communist whom we may call Miss Brown because that is not her name. She was holding a Soviet job and subsisting on a ruble income. One afternoon she arrived at the home of the dean of American correspondents. After fidgeting a bit she blurted it out. . . . She was in trouble.

"I want your help," she stammered, "for—for—well, an illegal operation."

The correspondent was shocked only because Miss Brown, so plain and earnest behind her spectacles, was not one whom he would normally suspect of romantic blundering and its dire consequences.

"Why, of course, I'll do all I can," he reassured her. "Just don't worry. These things are easily arranged here in Moscow."

"You see," Miss Brown explained, "it's not just for myself. It's also for my sister Kate."

"Well, I'll be hanged! Two illegal operations!" the correspondent exclaimed. He had not suspected Kate either of an amorous temperament.

"No, just one operation for the two of us," Miss Brown corrected him.

The biological puzzle at that point became too complicated for one mind. But Miss Brown made herself clear. It was a foreign exchange operation she had in view.

"About fifty dollars' worth of rubles will see us through," she told him.

3

A German princess who became autocrat of all the Russians, Catherine the Great, extended the hospitality of her adopted empire to groups of Germans, chiefly Mennonites, seeking refuge from religious persecution. About two and a half centuries later, in the autumn and early winter months of 1929, ten thousand descendants of those exiles tried to escape Russia to some refuge from what they considered economic persecution. Their frustrated attempt was one of the most pitiful and dramatic episodes in the titanic tragedy of the Soviet peasants.

The Germans had settled on the lower Volga in the vicinity of Saratov, in what is now the Volga German Republic; they also established colonies in Siberia, Crimea, and the Caucasus. Through all the generations they have retained their racial and religious identity. They differed from the Russian peasants largely in this: that they were less meek and more energetic. Had the Kremlin faced a population of their kind, not all the Red Army and G.P.U. could have tamed them. The despairing Russian peasant waylays and murders a few local officials, sets fire to a few government houses, then waits for the worst to happen. But the German peasant on the Volga, in Siberia, in Crimea, began to scheme escape. In Canada, in the United States, in South America, there are large Mennonite settlements. The dream of migration spread through all the German farming communities in Russia. Did "counterrevolutionary elements" propagate the wild idea, as Moscow officials subsequently charged? Or did the despair of those peasants conjure the mirage of a new life in the Western hemisphere?

Suddenly all the trains from the east and the south began to bring these Germans to the capital. Before the authorities quite realized what was happening, six or seven thousand had converged upon Moscow—men, women, and children, lugging their bedding and other household effects. The G.P.U. hastily cut off the sale of railroad tickets in the German districts. Police agents went through trains and forced hundreds to return to their abandoned homes. Had the exodus not been halted, the streams of Germans pouring into Moscow would have reached twenty or thirty thousands in a few weeks.

Normally, this mass movement would have been crushed by the government as quickly and ruthlessly as it was crushing other forms of "recalcitrance" among its hundred and twenty million peasant subjects. But two circumstances pulled the Kremlin up short. In the first place, the German Embassy, on instructions from Berlin, manifested a deep interest. In the second place, the world press had become aware of the drama and was watching developments with an attention that inhibited the Soviet authorities.

In the bleak, muddy suburbs of Moscow I found and talked to these Germans. Having sold their homes, livestock, and other property that could not be dragged along, they had all started with a little money. They paid Moscow peasants well for the privilege of crowding several families into a narrow hut. In one foul cottage, I saw more than twenty Germans jammed on the floor among their bundles and wailing children. Others erected makeshift tents. They were not entitled to rations, and even money could not buy sufficient food. The diseases of undernourishment, typhus, and scurvy were spreading among them and infecting the local population.

At the time the outside world became aware of their plight, most of them had been camping on the outskirts of the capital for weeks, a few of them for months. Their delegates besieged the German Embassy, clamoring for help. The Soviet Foreign Office, seeking to avoid an international scandal, agreed to issue passports, exacting the exorbitant fee of 220 rubles, more than most of them could afford. But it made the issuance contingent upon visas from Germany. Germany in turn hesitated to promise visas until the Canadian government had agreed to admit them; it did not relish the responsibility of thousands of pauperized Russian-Germans at a time of growing unemployment. While the complicated negotiations were under way, the funds of the refugees dwindled, their courage waned, and disease made deeper inroads upon them.

I saw among them pathetic scenes and anguished faces that will never fade from my memory. A group of us went from house to house, talking to wretched men and women, sick, hungry, bewildered. Everywhere it was the same story. They could not leave the country—and they had nothing to go back to.

"The G.P.U. is packing us into cattle cars and sending us back home. Home!" The woman smiled bitterly through her tears, "but we have no home. We sold everything for kopeks—practically gave it away."

While negotiations for their emigration dragged, the G.P.U. came each day to drive hundreds more into stinking box cars for the long journey back to the demolished homes. The new contingents who were evading the embargo on travel and arriving in Moscow were not allowed to alight. About one thousand, it was said, did obtain passports and visas and went on to Canada. The rest were hustled unceremoniously to the places of their origin. Rumor had it that many of the cattle cars packed with Germans were diverted to the far Northern forests and dumped where the government needed labor. How many of the ten thousand survived and how they rebuilt their shattered lives, we could not ascertain. In the greater calamity of the next months ten thousand more or less became utterly negligible in the total of millions.

This German episode shook many foreign observers out of their complacency. It gave them a glimpse of the terror that had already gripped the nation's peasantry. We had become inured to newspaper and private accounts of murder, arson, mass arrests, and indiscriminate executions that year. Sheer repetition took the edge off the whole business, just as in time of war casualty lists tend to lose their human content and turn into monotonous rows of dull figures.

As pressure in the villages increased, tens of thousands flocked to the cities. The garbled stories of the German exodus spread by word of mouth put the idea of escape into Russian heads as well. Moscow railroad stations began to look like encampments. Additional border guards and bloodhounds were placed along the western frontier to stop the wild scramble of frightened peasants from Russia into Rumania, Poland, and the Baltic countries. Finland protested against the influx of peasant refugees from Soviet Karelia. Stringent orders were issued to local Soviets and railroad functionaries to prevent the flight of peasants. Those without formal permits to travel were put off the trains. Despite these measures, thousands more arrived in Moscow and other large cities every day, to lie around helplessly, waiting for a miracle.

My dispatches during these months spoke of the remarkable "success" of the collectivization policies. In the Ukraine, for instance, 1,400,000 hectares were already "socialized" although it had been planned to socialize no more than 1,300,000 hectares in five years! In the country as a whole about 10% of the peasantry was already in collectives as against the 4% scheduled for that year.

It was an open secret that these "successes" were based on naked force. Repeatedly, the same weapon had been used against the peasants. Each time the government had been obliged to retreat, but the Kremlin's patience proved greater than the peasants' resistance. This time there would be no retreat.

The official villain in the concentrated attack was the kulak, though precisely who he was no one knew for sure. Before the revolution, the kulak had been a fairly well-defined category in the social structure of the countryside. He was the peasant whose energy, shrewdness, and lack of scruples combined to lodge economic power in his hands. He was a money lender, perhaps owned a mill where he exacted ungodly toll from his neighbors, leased other people's land on one-sided terms. Through hard work, usury, and exploitation he often gathered the lives of the less capable peasants in his fist—the word *kulak* means "fist." Tsarist statesmen, such as Stolypin, recognized the kulak's role as the rural capitalist and encouraged him to wax fat. He was ardently despised, and no less ardently envied, by the mass of poor peasants.

Foreigners writing about the agrarian phase of the Soviet revolution too often have accepted the term kulak in this pre-revolutionary sense, sometimes in ignorance, more often with deliberate cynicism. That made it easier to represent what happened from 1929 forward as an indignant revolt of the masses against a small and hateful group of parasites. Soviet propaganda standardized the kulak as a fat-bellied, blood-sucking monster, a sort of human spider luring innocent peasants into his web. This over-simplification soothes the consciences of those writers or their readers. It has little bearing on the truth.

After the revolution, the opprobious label of kulak was stretched to cover any peasant who employed labor or who owned a little more property than the rest. By 1929, it was converted into a generic term of abuse, with only a tenuous reference to economic possessions. Whoever failed conspicuously to fall into line with the Soviet policies was thereby marked as a kulak. If his poverty was such as to make the title preposterous he was called a "kulak agent" and treated as one anyhow. In the old days, there might have been one or two or a dozen kulaks in a village. Under the new dispensation, their number rose into the hundreds. Any peasant who was too outspoken in the general dislike of collectivization, taxes, grain deliveries, became a kulak. In the tragic months of forcible collectivization, there were scores of villages without a single kulak, in the economic sense, which "liquidated" 4 or 5% of their inhabitants as kulaks and kulak agents all the same.

On December 27, the press published the text of an address made by Stalin two days earlier to a group of agrarian officials, in which he raised the slogan of "liquidation of the kulaks as a class." It was the signal for the most startling piece of brutality, considering its dimensions, in the annals of revolution. Stalin neither defined a kulak nor cautioned against excesses. Meek Russian historians and their complacent foreign parrots have carefully revised the record of this time to shift the responsibility for the horrors from Stalin to his supposedly "over-zealous" local agents.

No one who was there on December 27 and the months that followed had the slightest doubt who issued the order or what the order was. What Stalin said and the deliberate vagueness and ambiguity of his use of the word kulak were an unequivocal invitation—more, an imperious command—to smash and disperse between five and ten million peasant men, women, and children as quickly and rapaciously as possible.

4

The celebration of the bourgeois New Year was forbidden. Dire penalties, the press hinted, awaited those who absented themselves from work because 1929 turned into 1930. Since the date had neither religious nor economic connotations, the Marxian logic of the taboo was somewhat blurred. In subsequent years, the date was restored to respectability. But the mood of the Kremlin at this juncture had no need for logic. The non-stop year must not be interrupted by astronomy or calendars. Anyone who was caught wishing anyone else a Happy New York, rumor had it, would be punished by the G.P.U. The rumor was unfounded of course, but it reflects the temper of the moment.

New Year's Eve was celebrated all the same. There were staggering drunks in all the streets of Moscow to attest the fact, and whispered invitations to New Year's parties behind locked doors. Indeed, the tang of danger seemed to sharpen the edge of the festivities. Billy and I visited several of the gatherings in Russian homes, and we ended the night at the Grand Hotel.

We found as loud and gay a gathering as Berlin or Paris could boast that night. Every inch of space was crowded. Champagne bottles lounged nonchalantly in their silver buckets. Pretty girls hawked balloons and dolls at shameless prices, the air was a wilderness of paper streamers, and we walked ankle-deep in confetti. The raucous near-jazz from the lofty gallery struggled to make itself heard above the laughter and the shouting. The mildewed waiters were for once in their ancient element: this was the extravagance, the rowdy gaiety, the holiday spirit that they remembered from the past. They picked their way through the crowd in a glow of excitement, carrying heavy-laden trays. It was a New Year's Party in high gear, hitting on all cylinders, with slightly inebriated drivers at the wheel.

Most of the guests were foreigners, but the Russian representation was larger than usual. All those who had the means and dared to be happy in public—writers, actors, a few G.P.U. agents, etc.—were at the hotel. Balloons popped. In one corner a woman laughed hysterically. An American engineer staggered and flailed his long arms among the dancers, but no one minded him. Somewhere a discordant chorus sang, "For he's a jolly good fellow." Somewhere a drunken voice brawled, "Now you lay off my girl or I'll knock your goddam head off." Glasses clinked and an exuberant member of the Maly Theatre smashed a glass on the floor. *Vashe sdoroviye! Skol! Prosit! A votre santé! Salute! Mud in your eye, you old son-of-a-gun!* The orchestra again, for the tenth time that night, played *Hallelujah!* Hour after hour, the party gained momentum.

Beyond the marble walls of the Grand Hotel, women were already on line waiting for the stores to open hours later. Murder and arson, arrests and exiles by the tens of thousand, were under way in the villages. The masses of *lishentzi,* disfranchised people, counted their crumbs of bread and waited to be expelled from their apartments. The dread slogan of "liquidation of the kulaks as a class" had just been uttered by Stalin.

No, this party was unlike anything in Montmartre or on the Kurfuerstendamm, despite the balloons and dolls and confetti. It was touched with hysteria. Even the foreigners, though safe themselves, could not be wholly unaware of the ground that trembled under them as they danced, that would explode soon in a fearful orgy of violence and brutality. There was a macabre zest to this New Year's Eve celebration. It was a party on a battlefield, in a besieged city, on the edge of a volcano belching death.

II. The Peasants Are Conquered

SIXTY-FIVE days elapsed between Stalin's launching, on December 27, of the slogan "liquidation of the kulaks as a class," and his order, on March 2, calling a halt to the lawlessness that ensued. For sheer volume of piled-up cruelties there are few comparable spans of time in all human history. The ruthless crushing of more than a million better-to-do or less tractable families—five or six million people—had begun before the fateful slogan was announced. It continued spasmodically after the Kremlin had called off the orgy of violence. But the process reached its fevered heights in these tumultuous days.

The casual, half-illicit brutalities tacitly encouraged by Moscow all through 1929 were now sanctified by Stalin's explicit prescription.

The restraint of the original figures calling for 20% socialization of agriculture in five years was forgotten. It was now ordained that the most important grain-growing regions, such as the Lower and Middle Volga basins and North Caucasus, must be completely collectivized that very year, that the rest of the country's grain area must be completely collectivized in the following year, and that "kulak farms" must be wholly eliminated.

The strategy of the campaign was plain enough. Obliteration of the allegedly kulak elements was not only an end in itself, but a means for stampeding the rest of the population into submission to collectivization. Whatever hocus-pocus of village meetings of the poor might be invoked to select the quota of victims, the palpable objective was to scare the poor and middling peasants themselves into merging their land, livestock, and implements. Indeed, the only sure way to prove that they were not kulaks was to apply and be accepted as collective members. The fearful kulak doom was a weapon for terrorizing the rest of the peasantry. The true measure of the terror, therefore, is not alone in the millions who were despoiled and deported from their native soil, but the sixty million peasants who rushed madly for the shelter of hastily organized *kolkhozes,* collective farms. In a few months about 50% of the peasants suddenly discovered the virtues of socialization; all of them would have made the discovery if the process had not been abruptly curbed.

Hell broke loose in seventy thousand Russian villages. The pent-up jealousies of a generation, the sadistic instincts of self-important little officials, the inflamed zeal of local communists, were unleashed and whipped into fury. The haphazard persecutions of the preceding months were systematized and legalized and invested with a high crusading fervor. Seventy thousand localized Red Terrors, with the G.P.U. troops and the Red Army to make them effective. Though no one knew precisely what a kulak was, there was no dearth of them anywhere. Sometimes mass meetings of the village poor, under the steamrollers of local or visiting officials, confirmed the choice of victims; frequently this empty mummery was dispensed with. As many as 15 or 20% of the peasants were "liquidated" in some villages.

A population as large as all of Switzerland's or Denmark's was stripped clean of all their belongings—not alone their land and homes and cattle and tools, but often their last clothes and food and household utensils—and driven out of their villages. They were herded with bayonets at railroad stations, packed indiscriminately into cattle cars and freight cars, and dumped weeks later in the lumber regions of the frozen North, the deserts of Central Asia, wherever labor was needed, there to live or die. Some of this human wreckage was merely flung beyond the limits of their former villages, without shelter or food in those winter months, to start life anew if they could, on land too barren to have been cultivated in the past.

No dependable computation of the number liquidated has ever been made, and in any case there is no arithmetic to estimate human suffering. The total was beyond reckoning. Forcible migration of millions could not be organized or provisioned, but must proceed in fearful confusion.

Tens of thousands died of exposure, starvation, and epidemic diseases while being transported, and no one dared guess at the death rate in the wilderness where the liquidated population was dispersed.

Locomotives dragged their loads of agony from every part of the nation under armed guards and when the human debris had been emptied in some forest or desert, jogged back for more.

Thousands of bewildered refugees, panic fear in their eyes, flocked to the cities, where they were once more corralled, stuffed into disease-ridden cars, and hauled away to the dumps.

The plague of *bezprizorny*, homeless waifs, from the civil war and famine years had almost been cured; now new thousands of boys and girls, mere infants some of them seemed, roamed through the land. They were the children of kulak parents who had died or who preferred to leave their children to shift for themselves rather than to drag them into exile.

I saw batches of the victims at provincial railroad points, under G.P.U. guards, like bewildered animals, staring vacantly into space. These meek, bedraggled, work-worn creatures were scarcely the kulaks of the propaganda posters. The spectacle of peasants being led by soldiers with drawn revolvers through the streets even of Moscow was too commonplace to win more than a casual glance from the crowds on the sidewalks. I talked to refugees who came to our doors to beg a few crumbs of bread, to officials who had taken part in the liquidation in Ukrainian villages, to Soviet reporters assigned to describe the great Stalinist "successes." No man can see with his own eyes a social upheaval of such scope. But from isolated tales of terror, from the scenes I happened to witness, from the hints and tell-tale circumlocutions in the press, I came to know and to feel some part at least of the unfolding nightmare.

At the moment it was distinctly "unfriendly" on a correspondent's part to describe these events in detail. Those who wished to remain in the good graces of the Kremlin regime had to limit themselves to the spurious formulas used by the press and the statistical boasts about collectivization victories: to reduce a major human catastrophe to meaningless impersonal percentages. For a few correspondents it provided a useful opportunity to demonstrate their "friendship" and "loyalty" for the Soviet regime by explaining away ugly facts, wrapping them in the cellophane of Marxist verbiage, slurring over them with cynical allusions to broken eggs for Soviet omelettes. Others were curbed by the censorship, and grateful enough on occasion for this convenient alibi for silence.

The occasional dispatch that betrayed the horror felt by even the most cynical among us seemed "sensational" to readers abroad, against the consistent evasions of the general run of press reports. And thus it happened that the world at large was scarcely aware of what was occurring in Russia. The world was aroused, instead, on issues that were secondary. The capitalist press became alarmed at the statistical triumphs of Soviet industrialization and raised the ludicrous cry of "dumping." Accepting at face value the boasts of Soviet propaganda, exaggerating Russian industrial expansion in the pessimistic mood induced by the world-wide depressions, bourgeois opinion actually imagined that the world would be drowned tomorrow morning in a deluge of cheap Soviet-made goods. The noisy and far-fetched "anti-dumping" campaign attested how thoroughly Soviet propaganda had concealed the mounting hardships of its industrialization efforts, the deplorable quality of its output, the staggering economic cost of its production, the collapse of its currency. Whatever they may have said publicly, Bolshevik leaders were not half as optimistic about their Five Year Plan as the editorial writers in capitalist lands.

At the same time, the Pope initiated, early in February, a holy crusade against the Soviet Union for its persecution of religion. He designated March 19 as a day of prayer for the cessation of Soviet anti-religious terror. Other religious elements, Protestants, Jews, Mohammedans, joined the crusade. Moscow's offensive against religion was no more than a subsidiary maneuver in the larger strategy against Nepmen, private farmers, pre-revolutionary intellectuals—of relatively minor interest both to the Russian government and the Russian people.

But that was the only aspect of the Russian situation which touched the conscience of mankind. The more basic human tragedy under the matter-of-fact phrase "liquidation of the kulaks" was ignored.

2

Stalin's claim to statesmanship of a high order must rest in large degree upon his formula of "liquidation of the kulaks as a class." He provided a convenient name for the technique of terror that had been gathering momentum for months. His formula gave the whole process new dimensions of revolutionary self-righteousness, and almost "scientific" justification. Haphazard persecutions were turned overnight into a high-minded campaign.

There was a certain genius in the choice of the magic phrase. The words "liquidation of the kulaks" carry few implications of human agony. It seems a formula of social engineering and has an impersonal and metallic ring. But for those who saw the process at close range the phrase is freighted with horror. In my own mind it evokes that sharpening sense of multitudinous miseries, of catastrophe overwhelming a huge population like some sudden flood or earthquake, which came to me vividly at that time. Running through that sense, giving it the special macabre quality in memory, was the awareness that the destruction and suffering, which seemed a natural calamity, were in fact man-made, artificially whipped up—that they could be stopped by a word of command from one man, as indeed they were stopped, too late.

It was as if, in the midst of a terrible volcanic eruption, one were to catch sight of someone turning a crank that kept the hot lava pouring over men and towns. The fine motives of those who turned the crank made the image no less gruesome.

There are smug economists and sociologists who inform us that all great social changes take a heavy toll in human life. They take many pages to prove that certain changes in land tenure and industrial processes in England, between 1700 and 1850, caused widespread suffering commensurate in volume with that caused by the "liquidation of the kulaks." That sophistry fails to distinguish between a natural evolutionary economic process developing inevitably through decades and centuries, and an arbitrary decision by a handful of men, compressed into a few months of terror.

Let those "scientific" historians recall that what Anna Louise Strong calls "the most spectacular act of ruthlessness which occurred in those years" was a decision calmly made by a political machine, in defiance of the majority opinion in its own ranks and in defiance of the people in whose name—for whose "own good" —it was made. There were few in Moscow who doubted that rank-and-file opinion in the Communist Party was opposed to such drastic and costly methods. The self-appointed apologists among foreigners not only admitted this, but pointed to it proudly as another proof of Stalin's daring leadership. Theirs was the perverted logic which holds that if it takes courage to inflict pain on one, that courage is magnified a millionfold if it inflicts pain on a million. "*Strong must have been the faith,*" the saintly Fabians, Beatrice and Sidney Webb, were to write of this episode years later in their comfortable library, "*and resolute the will of the men who, in the interest of what seemed to them the public good, could take so momentous a decision.*" No doubt just such self-satisfied Fabians must have commended the strong faith and resolute will that enabled other men in other times to order holy inquisitions and St. Bartholomew's Day massacres.

Men have ever rationalized their deeds in terms of some inspired goal, and self-righteous bigots have done more blood-letting than criminals and fiends. The capacity to kill and torture, whether wholesale or retail, is equally pathological whatever its motives, and surely more dangerous when those motives are ostensibly idealistic. The more fundamental problem is whether any group of mortal men, however sincere their faith or their phobia, may arrogate to themselves the prerogatives of dispensing death and misery to millions of their fellowmen; whether humankind dare entrust its destiny to men who regard themselves as History incarnate, mad Jehovahs loosing the floods of their fury to cleanse a wicked world.

The cleavage in the upper reaches of the ruling minority became sharpest at this time. The policy of liquidating the kulaks and coercing the peasants into improvised collectives, the most drastic enterprise in the whole course of the revolution, was acting as a touchstone of men's essential character. Outwardly, there were differences in theory and political principle and much bandying of sacred texts from Marx and Lenin. But these were no more than crude rationalizations of deeper differences, of the heart rather than the mind. Night after night I discussed the conflict with communists; what was true of them was true of those near the apex of power.

The real division was between those who could go through with a terrifying piece of brutality and those who could not; those who, whether they formulated it in such wise or not, regarded human life as in itself valid beyond sanctified words or pseudo-scientific theories, and the others to whom human life was so much worthless raw stuff for their laboratories; between the despised and soft-hearted "idealists" and the hard-boiled "realists."

It is no accident that those contaminated with Western influences found themselves inevitably in opposition. The new leadership, profoundly disdainful of life and indifferent to individual suffering, ready to mortify the nation's flesh for the sake of its immortal soul, stemmed from Russia's entire past. The decision was not made just by Stalin and his lieutenants, but by Peter the Great and Ivan the Terrible. It was preordained by a thousand years of consistent history, whose symbols are the torture chambers under the Kremlin and the ancient execution block still standing outside its walls.

What occurred in these sixty-five days has been described as a "second agrarian revolution," in many ways greater than the first. I have myself played variations on this theme. And the description is true enough if any violent change affecting a large sector of mankind is a "revolution." But revolution in its idealistic sense, in the sense that social rebels and prophets even unto Lenin have accepted it, implies a spontaneous and instinctive human explosion. It implies masses goaded beyond endurance revolting at last against injustice and oppression.

And in that sense what we witnessed was certainly not a revolution. It was not an eruption from below, but an organized imposition from above. Forcible collectivization was no more a "revolution" than the seizure of India by Englishmen or Abyssinia by Italians, than the expulsion of the Jews from Spain in 1492 or the subjugation of red men by whites in the Americas. In the first agrarian revolution, in 1917, a pent-up fury and hunger broke through the dams of an established order—peasant masses "liquidated" the landlords and seized their lands and a government rode to power on the crest of their revolt. But in 1930 a powerful dictatorship used its armies and its legalized local officials and social machinery to "liquidate" a portion of the peasantry and to intimidate the rest.

No, it was no revolution but *a conquest of the peasantry*. To argue that it may have been necessary or that it will ultimately benefit the people whom it affected, or that it had support in some sections of the invaded area, makes it no less a conquest; those are precisely the justifications advanced for every conquest from time immemorial.

The ground was prepared in the skirmishing of 1929. The conquest was carried through in the first months of 1930. What followed in the next few years, when the liquidation of kulaks was completed and collectivization firmly established at an enormous cost in human life, was the "pacification" of the vanquished, which always follows the conquest of a people stubbornly opposed to compulsory blessings.

3

The fevered atmosphere of forcible agrarian collectivization was spread far beyond the villages. It raised the revolutionary temperature everywhere to delirious levels. "Dizziness from success" was the phrase later minted by Stalin for the overstrained condition. City Soviets would not remain behindhand as against their country colleagues and sought to match liquidation of the kulaks with a no less hasty liquidation of the miserable remnants of private trade. There were days in which tens of thousands of "speculators" were arrested, imprisoned or driven from the cities: harried creatures, denied respectable employment by law, who sold toothpicks, home-made garments, second-hand boots, stale hunks of bread, matches, a little sunflower seed oil, in the private markets. Further revisions of living space were ordered in Moscow and elsewhere, so that former Nepmen and other class enemies, whether eight years old or eighty, might be expelled from their cramped quarters.

The underlying assumption of the period was that anything might be achieved by stalwart Leninists with knout in hand.

The wholesale closure of prayer houses and harassment of believers gained impetus. Christmas celebrations early in January (because of the Greek Orthodox calendar) were marked by noisy anti-religious parades and insulting demonstrations outside church doors. Batches of priests and rabbis were rounded up and imprisoned, their fate hardly noticed in the Russian turmoil but evoking shrieks of protest from co-religionists abroad. Solemnly the Godless Society aped the State Planning Commission by announcing a "five-year plan for the liquidation of religion." For the first time since the early outbursts just after the revolution, public bonfires were made of icons.

In the domain of industry and construction, things seemed to stall momentarily, adding to the general chaos of exhortations and threats. The capitalist depression forced down world market prices, so that Russia was obliged to ship out even more of its food to pay for the same machines. Rations inevitably grew shorter and the value of the ruble dwindled. Not only must a people accustomed through all its history to dawdle be sweated, but sweated under conditions of chronic undernourishment.

Small wonder that more than half the output of important factories was spoiled beyond use. Bitter wags whispered that the plan for *brak*, meaning defective goods, had been "overfulfilled," and grudging official statements gave point to the witticism. A mere 15 or 20% of spoilage was considered "normal" by factory managers. Small wonder, too, that workers would not stay put at their jobs, but moved restlessly from city to city, from construction site to construction site, searching for the non-existent place where food supplies and living conditions were more tolerable. In certain plants, the press complained, the turnover of labor was 100% a month! The wanderings of a dissatisfied proletariat assumed the proportions of a confused zigzagging mass migration, parallel with the forced migration from the villages.

For foreigners, life went on without much change. The Grand Hotel orchestra still perspired over *Hallelujah*. In palaces built by merchant princes foreign diplomats gave lavish receptions, where opera stars warbled and ladies in décolleté thrilled over new ballerinas and American correspondents gloriously forgot their manners. Cynicism being the convention of our trade, we mixed current atrocity stories with champagne and retailed "Radek's latest joke," which probably was not Radek's at all. One such anecdote had it that the denizens of the Kremlin, from Stalin down, were suddenly infested with body lice like unto an Egyptian plague. Science could do nothing to eradicate it and finally Stalin sent for Radek. "The solution is simple," Radek supposedly said, "just collectivize the lice, then half of them will die and the other half will run away." Few of the facts of desperation and disaster which filled our conversation showed up in our dispatches. The taboos of a powerful government in an angry know-nothing mood are not broken lightly by resident newspapermen who have jobs to protect and families to feed.

By the middle of February, the government could claim that

50% of the peasant households were collectivized. In important grain regions the percentage was close to one hundred. By the end of February the general percentage of socialization had risen to sixty. The conquest was thorough.

But the body social, like the human body, can stand so much pain and no more. Every good surgeon know this, and now the social surgeons in the Kremlin were to learn it, though they forgot the lesson too soon. The country reacted to the pressure in an unexpected and calamitous manner. Before capitulating to compulsory collectivization, the peasants took the precaution of slaughtering their livestock. Even before the order to liquidate the kulaks as a class was decreed, the peasants had begun to kill their cattle and sheep and pigs for meat and hides, rather than merge them in socialized herds. Now this practice became epidemic. In some places more than half the livestock was destroyed, and in the country as a whole the depletion was alarming, the losses being in direct proportion to the coercion used to achieve socialization.

The Kremlin prescribed heavy imprisonments and other punishments for the slaughter of cattle. Then it decreed *the death penalty for killing livestock*—an extraordinary measure even for an extraordinary time. But the animals continued to be destroyed by the hundred thousand all the same. It was this frightful slaughter —a sort of convulsive reaction to pain—which, more than any other single factor, recalled the Kremlin to its senses. The government might not be alarmed by the human slaughter, by the death of tens of thousands of kulak infants, it might ignore the meek plea of Lenin's widow for mercy, but it could not ignore the destruction of the nation's horses and cattle. That represented working power and food and raw materials, whether socialized or privately owned. It meant the impoverishment of the agrarian resources they wished to socialize.

The economic losses entailed by the sixty-five days of ferocious compulsion were almost incalculable. The most efficient farmers were put to cutting timber, digging canals, or just killed off. More animal power had been destroyed by far than could be replaced for many years by mechanical power. At one blow, the Stalin regime, for all its undaunted "realism" and hard-boiled practicality, had handicapped the revolution by a catastrophic sacrifice of meat, dairy products, wool, leather, and other animal products.

A large measure of the food and goods shortages of the following years may be attributed directly to the extermination of animals by desperate peasants as their automatic reaction to forcible collectivization. In 1929, Russia had replenished the losses of the civil war period and the famine; it had more domestic animals than in 1916. But by the end of the Five Year Plan it had lost half of its cattle and horses, two-thirds of its sheep and goats, two-fifths of its pigs. The greater part of these staggering losses occurred in the months of which we are now speaking, the rest when similar methods of coercion were revived later. Bolshevik leaders admitted that it would take a decade under the most propitious conditions to restore livestock to the 1929 level.

The ludicrous "idealists," those who hesitated to inflict too much pain on the population, may have been nearer right, even in practical economic terms, than the thick-skinned heritors of Ivan the Terrible and Peter the Great.

4

On March 2, Stalin peremptorily called off the terror. In an article entitled "Dizziness from Success," he blamed the misguided zeal of local officials for the "excesses." He jeered at "r-r-revolutionaries" who "think they can start a collective by pulling down church bells" or socialize unsuitable regions by "military force." Had those imbeciles forgotten that collectivization must be "voluntary"? How dared they force collectivization on Central Asiatic nomads or far Northern primitive tribes! Why must the idiots push collectivization immediately to the extreme of socializing pigs and chickens!

In short, the ruling group in the Kremlin, though it had not uttered a word of caution while the delirium gained sway, now sanctimoniously disavowed responsibility and championed the persecuted peasantry. In a sense, it turned the bewildered local officials over to the wrath and sometimes to the furious vengeance of their village neighbors. The country was asked to believe that Stalin and his associates had remained ignorant of the atrocities and the "military force" which were familiar to every child in Moscow—even to foreign reporters. Having discovered the sad facts belatedly—after millions of obdurate peasants had been torn by the roots from their native soil, and the country had lost a substantial part of its animal wealth—Stalin now acted bravely to stop the outrages.

The lie was transparent. But the sense of relief was so overpowering that nobody could think of blaming Stalin. On the contrary, he was praised jubilantly for his merciful sagacity. There was something that partook of the supernatural in the power of the man's word. One day, a great nation was steeped in gloom, huddling in stupefied fear under black clouds amidst darting lightning. Next day, the skies were clear and the nation breathed more freely. And all because one man had caused a short article to be published.

"Its statesmanship," the New York *Times* correspondent cabled enthusiastically, "appears to put Stalin on a level with Lenin himself." The peasants, like the correspondent, were too joyful for logic. They forgot that Stalin had given the signal for the terror which he now magnanimously halted, that he had kept it going in the face of "excesses" too much on the surface to be missed. The very fact that a word of his sufficed to stop the horror made him clearly responsible for the failure to speak it in time; this, too, they ignored. Instead, they kneeled before their icons to praise his kind heart and measureless mercy. Distorted echoes of the Pope's campaign had reached the villages and many peasants praised the Pope as well as Stalin for saving them from the rapacity of their local communists and "activists." The notion that Stalin and the Pope jointly had intervened in this hour of adversity spread far and wide.

Nearly two-thirds of the paper collectives collapsed. The 63% of collectivized farms fell quickly to 22%. Many of the peasants remained in the collectives simply because, having killed off their draft animals, they had nothing with which to resume individual farming.

The Soviet newspapers suddenly recognized "great mistakes." If, until March 2, it had been the mark of a counter-revolutionary to believe the terror stories from the villages, now it became creditable "self-criticism" to tell those stories in gruesome detail. Pagefuls of atrocity tales were published by way of exemplifying the "r-r-revolutionary" stupidities now graciously outlawed by the Communist Party. Those correspondents who had taken it upon themselves to "deny" the "absurd" reports about mass terror were left in a somewhat uncomfortable posture.

The pressure was turned off by Stalin just as a few months earlier it had been turned on: a faucet opened and closed at will. None of this, however, could restore the dead and patch together the millions of shattered homes. The forests were populated with degraded liquidated kulaks, their wives, and their children. Hordes of the unfortunates were put to work on bread-and-water rations to cut logs and dig canals and build roads. An employer with a big job to do—a collective employer, the state—now had a vast supply of cheap, half-starved, frightened and helpless workers to draw upon.

It was on the basis of the new, ever-growing mass of so-called kulaks in exile that the system of forced labor was to grow apace. Before long, Dnieperstroi, Magnitostroi, every important construction job, had its crowded barracks for the deported kulaks, virtual prisoners of the state, as well as for the actual convicted prisoners who were locked in at the end of the working day. Conveniently enough, the supply of kulaks and convicts increased as the need for cheap labor increased.

The concentrated terror of the sixty-five days marked a frontier in my thinking and feeling. For two years I had been building an intricate structure of justifications for the Soviet regime. Now, without my willing it, the structure began to disintegrate around me. The color and the strength seemed to have run out of the symbols of the faith for me; the socialist slogans and songs, the brave revolutionary promises, the parades and invocations for a better world, now seemed to me touched with mockery.

It was at this time, too, that I faced more consciously the problem with which I was to wrestle for many years: *to tell or not to tell.* As vividly as though it were yesterday I recalled my private pledge never to attack the Soviet regime, but I was no longer so certain that a recital of Soviet actualities constituted attack on the proletarian revolution. What if the revolution at this stage needed the defense of exposure to world opinion? What if the concentration of autocratic power in the fists of a few leaders needed the corrective of public responsibility for their deeds?

It was not a problem unique to myself. Communists and Soviet sympathizers the world over were trying to solve it to save their intellectual integrity. Some of them had decided that the Stalin regime was not necessarily synonymous with communism and revolution, any more than the Christian Church is always synonymous with the ideals of Christianity. A few went further and insisted that the world revolution must not be burdened with the mistakes and failures of the Soviet Union, but must dig the grain of socialism out of the Soviet soil and renounce the dirt and dross. The rest held steadfastly to the theory that it was all a family affair, to be hidden from strangers and hidden especially from the working classes: that victories must be exaggerated, failures denied, and the vision of a socialist fatherland nurtured at all costs.

Though I was increasingly outspoken in my reports of the Soviet scene, I still held in the main to the last alternative.

III. We Move to a Mansion

WHILE graver issues were being decided on a hundred fronts of the *Piatiletka* (Five Year Plan), I became embroiled in a minor war of my own making. The straw that broke the back of my patience was so light that I no longer recall what it was. But I fired the secretary-interpreter whom I had inherited from a chain of U.P. predecessors.

Since I had not hired her, the chances are that I exceeded my authority in firing her. In any case, in a few days an order came through from President Bickel to "put Jmudskaya back on the payroll." I obeyed. I informed her that she was again on the payroll but warned her not to show up to work because she was still fired. The argument by cable grew acrid and I was reconciled to dismissal in defense of my divine right to choose my own secretary.

And at this point the Soviet government, whose benevolence, like God's mercy, embraces small things as well as large, took a hand in the matter. Apparently it had no wish to lose my services; for all my recent skittishness I was still very much in the harness of a "friendly" correspondent. As usual, Trivas was the liaison officer.

"That's quite a row you're having over Jmudskaya," he smiled.

"Yes, how do you know?"

"Oh, we have ways of knowing," he winked. "And that female is saying God-awful things about you in letters to Bickel and Keen. The girl has imagination."

"How would you know what she writes to them?"

For answer Trivas drew out a notebook and read me excerpts from Miss Jmudskaya's rather hysterical complaints to the head offices.

"You mean that you are reading her letters?"

"Not me, of course. But they're being read, and headquarters thought you ought to know what she is saying. You see, we should be very much distressed if the United Press recalled you."

I confess that I relished the amusing situation: knowing the contents of the embattled enemy's postal onslaughts long before the letters reached their destination. My protests against the official snooping at the post office were possibly less vigorous than they might have been. It was the revolution's way of helping my cause.

Then Ed Keen, head of the U.P. in Europe, was rushed to Moscow to adjust the quarrel. He found me stubbornly deaf to pleas for compromise and all but packed to go home. Acting as guide to Keen was Miss Jmudskaya's last service to the United Press.

Keen had come equipped as for a siege in the Arctic, but perversely the winter turned mild and mushy. The political situation on the contrary was lustily inclement, and his veteran reportorial instincts told him that even the Lyons-Jmudskaya conflict was minor compared with the class conflict in the villages. If he failed to placate his correspondent, he succeeded in interviewing Premier Rykov. All the resident correspondents had been clamoring for such an interview. As usual the plum fell into the lap of a visiting journalist, much to the chagrin of the permanent press corps.

Rykov pooh-poohed the idea that his regime was persecuting religion. The "successes on the anti-religious front," the bearded Premier informed Keen, must be credited to voluntary citizens' organizations like the Godless Society. The government was neutral. Incidentally, this was Rykov's last interview as Premier; soon thereafter he was replaced by Molotov.

I took Keen to see how the sovereign people was tearing down the ancient Simionovsky Monastery. The initial dynamiting of the building, heard everywhere in the capital, was turned into an anti-religious holiday. Thereafter volunteer brigades of factory workers, communist youths, and children from the Red Pioneer organizations helped to finish the job. As we picked our way through the rubble I kicked a round dirt-crusted object aside. It rolled slowly in front of me and I stared into the empty sockets and fleshless grin of a skull; there had been burial vaults on the monastery grounds.

We attended Sunday services in the Cathedral on the Moscow River and Godless meetings, ate in "factory kitchens," and photographed the block-long queues outside food coöperatives. Like all calm observers, uninvolved emotionally in the revolutionary effort, Keen was thoroughly impressed with the teeming contrasts of enlightened social experiment in a milieu of barbarous cruelty: children cared for in crèches and children turned into homeless savages by the liquidation of their parents; people taught to read and write while scientists and professors were sent to Siberia for failure to toe the Marxist line in biology or mathematics; new workers' clubs and new prisons under construction at the same time. He wrote a series of articles which showed a deep sympathy for the sufferings of the Russian people and an appreciation of the courageous economic tasks undertaken by the Soviet regime. No matter how perspicacious short-term visitors to the U.S.S.R. may be, their reactions usually reflect the monitorship under which they studied the scene.

Miss Jmudskaya stayed fired and I experimented with a succession of temporary secretaries. There was the handsome Countess Tolstoy, a niece of the great novelist. And Varvara Ivanovna Briusilova, daughter-in-law of General Briusilov, now living with a new husband in what was formerly the bathroom of the General's town house. Deeply religious, she remained cheerfully hopeful for her own and Russia's future, despite a personal ordeal Job-like in its complicated miseries. Her life since 1917 had been little more than a series of imprisonments. Once she had been under sentence of death for her part in opposing the government's seizure of church treasures during the famine year. But her spirit was unbroken; she continued active in ecclesiastical circles and outspoken in her detestation of the anti-religious campaign. About 1932, she was sent to the Solevietsky Islands, the dreaded Arctic prison, for a ten-year term.

In the end, I engaged a girl recommended by Percy Chen. Nathalie Petrovna Shirokikh was the daughter of an English mother and a Russian father. Her mother had come to Russia as governess to a wealthy family, married a Russian engineer, and never returned to her native land. After some thirty years, she was still thoroughly English, spoke Russian with great difficulty, and felt herself a stranger in the land of revolution. Nathalie, whose father died early in the revolution, was now the sole support of the family—a tall, good-looking, life-loving girl unscarred by the hardships of the years. She developed into one of the most efficient secretary-interpreters in the American colony and remains with the United Press bureau to this day.

2

An ill wind that stripped foreign concessionaires of their holdings suddenly blew the Lyons family into undreamed-of comforts. When the government liquidated the Hammer pencil concession, it left a residential mansion in Dr. Hammer's possession. His wife and sons having returned to America, he decided to rent part of this space. With a foreign correspondent installed on the premises, he realized, there was less likelihood that the government would attempt to take the building over for its own uses. When he proposed that we move in, we naturally grabbed at the chance, pleased enough to pay any rental for the new amplitude.

Thus, with the advent of spring, we found ourselves settled in the magnificent Hammer place at Petrovsky Pereulok 8, across the street from the squat, carrot-red Korsh theater. Moscow's charitable winter mantle of snow was turning ragged. Already the town showed discolored roof-tops and gaping wounds in the pavements where only a few weeks ago it sparkled with silver. The diminutive sleds which glided silently through snow-muffled streets were put away and moth-eaten landaus driven by moth-eaten cabmen rattled along in their stead.

The winter magic was melting away, but magic enough to be free at last, after two years, of Sashka's whining and the flat-footed *plop-plop* of our next-door neighbor, free of the gregarious bedbugs across the corridor and the dripping walls and the need to climb over a spiked gate at nights. It was good-by to Clean Ponds Boulevard. For nearly three years—until the English-language *Moscow Daily News* under Michael Borodin invaded the place and crowded us into a corner—we were to live spaciously in almost embarrassing comfort.

The house was excessively ornate within and without, its doors reinforced with elaborate grillwork, its stone façade tortured with sculptured decoration, and a broad inner stairway of gleaming marble spiralling majestically to the upper story. The place was filled with rococo statuary and paintings, and reindeer heads looked down in astonishment from the vestibule walls. The generous proportions of all the rooms, especially the immense high-ceilinged ballroom, represented heady freedom after our cramped years in a remodeled stable. A former cloakroom off the vestibule was large enough to serve as my office; a former bedroom, delightfully irregular in shape, was transformed by Billy's talent for home-making into a colorful living-room. The vast kitchen, with its oven as broad as a field, was upstairs and we shared a paneled dining hall with Dr. Hammer.

Until the revolution, the house had belonged to a Swedish merchant. His aged Russian widow still lived the life of a recluse in a wing somewhere on the other side of our wall. Except for an occasional angry banging when a late party in the ballroom grew too noisy, we were unaware of this woman's mysterious existence; I did not see her once in all our four years on Petrovsky Pereulok—a ghost of the dead past who banged on the wall from time to time.

In a great many of the old palaces some human fragment of the former occupants clung to a forgotten room or crevice, sometimes a bewildered old retainer of the family that had fled, sometimes a member of the family itself. On Ulitza Vorovskovo, once the street of opulent merchants and now lined with embassy residences, there is a palace occupied by a German diplomat and his family. Around the ceiling line of its main ballroom is a lovely frieze of sculptured cherubs, their laughing faces as fresh as life. In the basement of the palace lived an old, broken-down woman; she was there when the Embassy took over the building and they let her stay on. Every now and then the woman came timidly from her basement and asked permission to remain awhile in the ballroom. For many long minutes she stared at the cherub faces. She was the former owner of the palace and the cherubs had been modeled from her own children by a fashionable sculptor forty or fifty years ago.

Our luck in entering the Petrovsky Pereulok mansion made us the envy of the whole press corps. As the largest American home in Moscow it automatically became a sort of center of social life in the colony. The *pereulok* runs between two of the principal avenues in the center of the city, the Petrovka and the Dmitrovka. The food shop for diplomats and correspondents was just around the corner on the Dmitrovka, the hotels and the telegraph buildings within a few minutes' walk. Our lives were suddenly ample beyond our hopes.

Visiting Americans carried back tall tales of the splendors and comforts in which we luxuriated. Since it all coincided with a gloomier tinge in my dispatches, the legend of my "going bourgeois" was now complete.

3

Billy did a few roles in Soviet films. Having had a brief experience in Hollywood, both the similarities and the contrasts fascinated her. The "star" system was frowned upon at this time; the real "prima donnas" in the movie "factory" were the directors: Eisenstein, Pudovkin, Preobrezhenskaya, and the rest. A picture which Hollywood might have pushed through in two or three months, Moscow worked over for a year or more. The fantastic salaries and sunken bathtubs and million-dollar spectacles of Hollywood were unknown, but the glamor of the silver screen was almost as strong upon Russians as upon Americans. Ambitious boys and girls thronged the studios, struggling newspapermen dreamed of escape by writing scenarios, third assistant directors and cameramen were sought after by the girls eager to break into the movies.

Our contacts in the literary world of Moscow were constantly extended. Pilnyak, Zamyatin,* Nikulin, Lidin, Katayev, his brother, Petrov, and Petrov's inseparable collaborator, Ilya Ilf,* and a number of others were strongly enough entrenched politically to risk friendship with foreigners.

My reports to *Variety* fitted into an unfolding interest in America in Russian films. The exaggerated esteem which American opinion developed for Soviet movies rested largely on pictures made before the Stalin era had become deeply entrenched, pictures like *Potiomkin, Last Days of St. Petersburg,* Gorki's *Mother, Storm Over Asia, October,* etc. New York received only the cream of the film crop from the U.S.S.R.; it could not suspect how dully uninspired, how dismally boring, the average Russian film could be. On the screen, as on the stage and in literature, didactic propaganda with tractors and factories as heroes and the Five

* Died in 1937.

Year Plan as the only legitimate passion, had become obligatory. The George M. Cohan formula of "Mother, me, and the flag" was, in terms of the *Piatiletka,* Stalin, and the flag, the only respectable theme.

Always an incredibly heroic communist was thwarted by an incredibly villainous counterrevolutionary who was defeated in the final act while the red sun of revolution rose—rose in literal pasteboard—in the background and the red flag was unfurled triumphantly by the victorious shock brigade. Once upon a time, nine out of ten Russian tales ended with a suicide; having maneuvered his people into a hopeless tangle, the author needed merely to choose among various methods of self-annihilation to bring down his curtain. Now Russia was as solidly committed to the politico-economic happy ending as the *Saturday Evening Post* is to the romantic happy ending. Stalin's Russia was "down" on anything mystic, cloudy, soft, or morbid. It affected to be through with Slav fatalism, the "Russian soul," sentimental moonshine about loves and doves.

When love figured at all, it was edged with ludicrous or outright villainous implications. As soon as a suave factory director or engineer on stage or screen began to sidle up to somebody else's wife, or used honeyed words to the pretty machinist, the Soviet audience knew that he was cast for the villain's portion.

There was a picture called, most inappropriately, *Real Life,* made by the White Russian Kino Trust. The heroine was a Comsomol girl devoted to the "Five Year Plan in Four Years." Every time the percentage of widgets turned out by her factory rose, her features shone with pride. Came the serpent in the alluring guise of the journalist Sasha and he proffered the apple of love and Eve-Sonya was tempted and by guile and gallantry did he lure the working girl to a life of shameful domestic bliss. Eve-Sonya's place at the machine was vacant while she cooked *kasha* for Sasha. The details of her fall from grace are too sad to relate. Suffice that the newlyweds sank ever deeper into the slough of happy comfort, while the percentage of widgets dropped and the "Five Year Plan in Four Years" trembled in all its figures. No telling where the tragedy might have ended, if not for the timely intercession of the scenario writer and the censor. On the brink of complacent bourgeois marriage, Sonya realizes the error of her ways. Red bunting blooms on every wall when she returns to her machine amidst the hosannas of her fellow-workers and the enthusiastic discords of the cinema pianist, and the widget total shoots up like Jack's beanstalk.

> You can tempt the upper classes
> With your villainous demi-tasses
> But censors will protect the working girl.

What happened to Sasha I do not recall, but it was something drastic enough, I am sure, to cure him of any predilection for misleading honest working girls into ruinous domesticity.

To demonstrate its ideological loyalty, the Moscow Art Theatre put on a collectivization drama, *Bread*, by Vladimir Kirshon.* It was a *Pravda* editorial in dramatic form, but such is the skill of Stanislavsky's theater that it made a stirring play despite its machine-made characters. As usual, the stage communist got the short end in affairs of the heart. The straitlaced communist, Mikhailov, loses his wife to the unworthy communist, Rayevsky, but the audience is assured that it isn't much of a loss. Rayevsky, just back from Berlin with creased pants and a shiny suitcase, gives the flighty Olga what she has been thirsting for: gallantries, kisses, playboy stuff. But those Don Juanesque triumphs are for Trotskyists like Rayevsky and other decayed remnants of the old order, while strong, unbending builders of the new world like Mikhailov proceed to rout the dastardly kulaks and the collective marches forward to the tune of the *International*. Duty always triumphed over romantic yearnings, over everything in the Soviet "moralities" that now displaced all other entertainment.

Every now and then even a "morality" turned into an exciting picture or play or novel. But on the whole the tractors proved as dully monotonous as brillantined Hollywood Adonises. The Soviet audiences were sick unto nausea of machine worship. There was a wild rush for American or German pictures, though they were flickery thrillers or comics of an early vintage. The only popular revolt I ever saw in Russia was in a movie house. The night's program began with a news-reel showing factories and electric stations

* Included in *Six Soviet Plays*, edited by Eugene Lyons, an English anthology of Soviet drama. Even Kirshon, the type of the conformist literary man, came under attack as a "Trotskyist bandit" by the end of 1936.

and shock brigades. Then came a picture named *Spring*. The title held the promise of a human story, perhaps a spring of romance. The audience settled back hopefully. But there were no real human beings in it at all. The spring of the title was a season for the opening of new factories and the organization of new collectives: a delirium of pistons, wheels, hammers, factory belts, photographically admirable but humanly blank. Half the audience left in loud disgust. The other half remained to hiss and whistle and catcall.

4

The tragedy of that stifled, gritty period in Soviet art was underlined, for me at any rate, by the suicide of the poet Vladimir Mayakovsky.

Mayakovsky had begun his literary life under tsarism as an imagist. He welcomed the revolution as unshackling creative energies and giving a right of way to literary experiment. But he accepted also its profounder purposes as social change. Unlike a good many other poets, he harnessed his Muse to the needs of the new era not only willingly but with loud hurrahs of enthusiasm.

If Sergei Yessenin, the lyric playboy of the emotions, represented the "pure" poet, free and singing, Mayakovsky made of himself the disciplined poet, who had tamed his talents and used them like domestic animals to do the work of the revolution. Yessenin wrote a farewell note in his own blood and hung himself in 1925. Mayakovsky wept over that death but castigated that futile gesture. "In this life it is easy to die," he wrote, "—to build life is hard."

Mayakovsky lived, lived lustily and fully, in the day-to-day tasks of the harsh years. He jeered at the "Russian soul" and romantic private emotions. He hammered out hymns to ruthlessness, to machinery, to the G.P.U. that was his country's new Fate, and he bellowed his disdain for the romanticists and esthetes. His poems were staccato and shrill, he shrank from no vulgarity, he dragged the moon and the stars down to earth as raw stuff for the Five Year Plan.

A tall, broad-shouldered fellow who dressed like an *apache*, Mayakovsky gloried in tough-guy gestures and wore the adjective "proletarian" like a challenge to the world. But there was too much bluster in his attitude to be wholly convincing. In an occasional nostalgic line of rare beauty, in a casual sigh in the very midst of some blood-and-thunder invocation to duty, he betrayed the suppressed lyricist and romanticist.

Some of his readers lacked the sharpness of ear to detect the weeping under his Homeric laughter; others pretended not to hear. He was accepted as the hard-boiled voice of a hard-boiled epoch.

And suddenly in April, 1930, the news was out that Mayakovsky had killed himself; more shocking than that, killed himself because of a silly love affair with a married actress. He left a shamefacedly flippant note to his comrades on RAPP, indicating that his "love-boat" had foundered on the shoals of reality. The man who had made of himself a symbol of impersonal, collectivized emotion, whose derision of bourgeois parlor-and-bedroom dramas still echoed all around him, died like a Dostoievsky character. "I know this is not the way out," he apologized, "I recommend it to no one—but I have no other course."

Curiously enough, no one thought it strange. In its subconscious mind, the Russian people had never really believed his bluster. The denial of the importance of individual happiness or individual pain enforced by the Kremlin was only on the surface. The petty literary dictators pretended to regard the suicide as a sort of fit of insanity unrelated to the real Mayakovsky; they scolded him for his despair. Yet they knew what the Russian people felt instinctively: that Mayakovsky's suicide was the answer to the dehumanized brutalities which he had himself celebrated.

The poet's body lay in state at the Writers' Club and hundreds of thousands of Muscovites came to pay him honor. His was the most solemn funeral since Lenin's; it was not a demonstration by official edict but a spontaneous outpouring of emotion. The press might assume that the people were moved by the memory of his stirring hymns to the G.P.U. and the Five Year Plan. The very journalists who wrote those assumptions knew better; the people were moved by that act of desperation which brought Mayakovsky down from the commanding heights of the ruling supermen to their own human level of private sorrows. In his death he was flesh of their flesh.

Some months before he died, he published his last poem, a curious self-appraisal called *With a Full Voice.* At the time, its overtones of despair were lost in the bluster, but now the bluster fell away and only the overtones could be heard. The poem was read again as an epitaph, as perhaps he intended it to be read:

". . . I am the scavenger and water-carrier, mobilized and called by the revolution. . . . The *agit-prop* [agitation propaganda work] stuck in my teeth and it would have been more profitable and beautiful for me to scribble romances for you. But I humbled myself, stepping on the throat of my own song. . . ."

It was the Mayakovsky who wept for his suppressed song whom the populace followed in reverent affection.

I wrote a piece in which I tried to convey this fact and it was published in the *New Republic.* The poet's suicide, I intimated, kicked the props from under the new cocksure intelligentsia which renounces individual feelings "as though communism were somehow incompatible with the timeless ingredients of life." Soviet writers, even those among them who passed as model proletarian writers, read it and agreed. One of them said it was true, but "this is too soon to admit it." But poseurs in the brand-new "proletarian" literary circles in New York were scandalized. They preferred to believe that the suicide was an accident rather than face the fact that political labels do not alter the human heart. My article concluded with these words:

Mayakovsky is dead by his own hand. It is not enough to say, as already the politicians of literature are saying, that he was too weak for the fray; that he carried over bourgeois tendencies from his past. It is too easy to patch bewilderment with the ready-made labels of the *agit-prop.* It would be better, far better, to admit the full tragedy of this poet's inward struggle, to admit the reality and potency of intimate individual feelings. It would be better, far better, to do so before the present attitude, the attitude forced upon the new Russia by war and revolution, hardens into a new insensate skin.

IV. Locomotives Come to Central Asia

AN ODDLY assorted trainload of people it was that pulled out of the Moscow station one day for far-off Central Asia, where the Turksib—the Turkestan-Siberian Railroad—was about to be opened officially. There were the two major divisions, Soviet citizens and foreigners, and distinct gradations within each division. The foreigners were meticulously separated into communists and infidels. Among the Russians, there were the horny-handed and stubble-cheeked "shock troopers," some self-important officials with brief-cases as the insignia of their position, and a contingent of the conforming intelligentsia: newspaper reporters, novelists, playwrights.

It was a microcosm, come to think of it, of the Soviet world and its capitalist encirclement. The range may be indicated symbolically, at the one end, by the venerable Japanese communist exile, Katayama, with something of the Oriental priest about his intense serenity; and at the other end, in our bourgeois wing, by the sartorially correct little Japanese diplomat, so polite and affable, lugging binoculars and a camera nearly as large as himself. An elegantly accoutered and generously stocked dining car served the pampered capitalist guests, while a simpler diner and more Spartan fare served the proletarian hosts.

The two camps rarely mixed, though there were both Russians and foreigners caught embarrassingly between them. Hard, indeed, was the plight of certain Soviet writers whose effete tastes in food, conversation, and women drew them irresistibly to the bourgeois purlieus of that world on wheels, though their political allegiance lay with the shock troopers. Nor was the fate of certain loudly left-wing foreign writers more kindly, to have their corporeal selves caught in the cloying comforts of our side while their ideological souls were four or five cars behind, with the proletarian heroes. There were even sad episodes of political miscegenation.

For over three weeks, these people slept and ate, drank deep of political controversy and headier beverages, flirted and fumed, within the confines of this special train, closed off from the rest of the world like a ship at sea. Now and then they flocked to shore at land-ports like Alma-Ata and Tashkent, Samarkand and Bokhara, and a score of lesser stations. But always they returned to the train and its complicated social structure. The class struggle and the "contradictions" within each class—in living replica like a traveling exhibit!

A team of Soviet humorists, Eugene Petrov and Ilya Ilf, turned that journey into chapters of hilarious satire in their novel, *The Little Golden Calf*. The materials were ready to their hand. The American newspapermen forever foraging for "stories" and interviews. Boris Smolar of the Jewish Telegraphic Agency forever foraging for Jews—and always finding them, whether in Alma-Ata or Bokhara or a desert settlement. The battles of gallantry for the attentions of unattached American females. The factory workers watching with fascination the antics of strange poker-playing, beer-drinking, snapshotting outsiders in golf togs. A copy of *Lady Chatterley's Lover* happened to be on board, new at the start but frayed and dog-eared by the end of the trip, and it added an amorous aura in the cars where it circulated.

The several married couples had coupés to themselves. Billy's charm and seven-stringed guitar, enhanced by a larder of smoked ham and canned luxuries, made our own compartment at the extreme end of the correspondents' car a social center second only to the dining car itself. Many of the Soviet journalists were lured into fraternizing with us and the fighting morale of the class war was badly damaged. The less discreet of the Soviet literary men, too, took an ideological holiday and spent most of their time in the bourgeois dining car, in the Lyons den, and in paying court to good-looking class enemies.

Retribution overtook them before long. The proletarian wing, of course, had its "wall paper": a sort of bulletin devoted to the affairs of the train. Soon it bristled with insinuations pointed at the wandering literati. "Working class company is not good enough, it seems, for certain 'great' writers in our midst," the wall paper said in effect. "They prefer the *rostbif* and perfumed ladies in the foreign cars. But we shall fulfill the *Piatiletka* in four years despite them. Long live Turksib! Long live Stalin!"

And the great writers sobered instantly; they knew their masters' voice. Hurriedly, they organized literary evenings in the proletarian diner and read excerpts from their books to the shock troopers and pretended to admire the jejune compositions of young factory hands with literary ambitions and contributed good-natured satirical squibs about the foreign correspondents to the wall paper. For the rest of the journey, they lost no chance to demonstrate their subservience to our proletarian traveling companions in the third-class wars.

Several of the left-wing foreigners spent a large part of their time similarly currying favor with the shock troopers. Social climbing may take different forms in different societies, but remains equally humorous to an unambitious observer in the sidelines. The buxom American lady who had just attended a party in the third-class carriages returned aglow with excitement, like Mrs. Jones returning from a dinner at the Astorbilts; she had been "accepted," thank God!

Before the church domes of Orenburg, that last outpost of Europe, had quite faded from the western sky, Asia, the ancient and enigmatic, asserted itself. On either side of our train, the parched steppes of Kazakstan unrolled to horizons as round as an ocean. Ragged camels lumbered wearily under heavy loads. Sometimes a string of them crawled on the hairline horizon, silhouetted against the sky. A lonely yurt—the circular, felt-covered tent of the Central Asiatic nomads—came into view, or a small colony of them, like a cluster of mushrooms in the distance. Sometimes a horseman shaded his eyes under a peaked fur cap and watched us without curiosity and without answering our greetings.

These seared plains, larger than half of Europe, sparsely covered with a stubble of sagebrush, support a thin population, less than two to the square mile. Their camels and hardy ponies graze on the desert weeds and provide them with the *kumis* (mare's milk), horse flesh, and camel flesh that are their nourishment.

At the forlorn-looking and widely-separated wayside stations, unsmiling faces presided over trays of dried fish or withered vegetables; swarthy Kazaks squatted Buddhalike and immobile against walls and railings—flat-faced, slit-eyed, passive creatures.

A Mongol world of heat and dust and timeless droning on desert wilderness. Our trainload of Europeans and Americans, eagerly curious, restless, were the West; and these quiescent, sunbaked people, slow-moving and indifferent, were the East. We were in a Mongol world, intruders. Even the lazy flies seemed contemplative and Asiatic, astonished by our impatience.

Nearly two days, we jogged along at about twenty miles an hour across the arid plains from which the heat rose in shimmering waves. Rarely the country burst into the green of an oasis, more often it fell off to the yellow of total desert. A day out of Orenburg, we had a glimpse of the phosphorescent Aral Sea, its banks for miles inland streaked with salt. The next day, at the station of Arys, to the north of Tashkent, the East was upon us in all its dusty, ill-smelling drabness and nostalgic appeal. This railroad junction has a mixed population of Russians and natives—Kazaks, Uzbeks, Kirghiz—and all of these milled in the crowd which awaited our flag-decked train. But the Russians were blotted out for us by the picturesque Asians. Their swarthy faces under fur hats or turbans, their long robes of bright hue or tight-waisted Kazak coats, evoked echoes of the Bible and the *Arabian Nights;* these were Noahs and Abrahams and young Aladdins out of childhood picture books.

Their immediate concerns, however, were a lot more up-to-date. They talked of collectivization: how cruel local tyrants, Russian and native, had been forcing them into socialized farms; of the terrible shortage of food. The rumor had spread through all their world that "the government" was coming from Moscow and these people had awaited our arrival for days, brimming over with questions and complaints and elaborate petitions for Stalin and Kalinin. A delegation clamored for an immediate conference with Lenin and Trotsky. Deep was their chagrin and their doubt when informed that this was not "the government" at all but an assortment of people from many lands come to see a new railroad riveted upon an ancient land.

At other stopping places these scenes were repeated. Central Asia, allowed by the tsar to go on its own primitive way, was being vigorously shaken up by Bolshevik innovations. Women were being taught to make bonfires of their veils and Comsomol children to flout the traditions of their fathers. Worse than that, their herds and their lands were being seized and men turned into laborers on the land they once owned. It was here that "military force," according to Stalin himself, had been used to make collectives, here that officials had denied the precious irrigation water to individual farmers.

The country turned greener as we proceeded northward, and on either hand mountains soon lifted silver peaks against deep blue skies.

2

The final meeting of the northern and southern sections of the Turkestan-Siberian Railroad, on April 28, 1930, will never be forgotten by those who witnessed it. The hackneyed contrast of East and West, of primitive life and modern science, was no longer hackneyed but a pageant epic in extent and in depth.

The spot called Aina-Bulak was no more than a name in the void, without so much as a railroad station as yet to mark it. When the work was begun in 1927 from opposite directions, no one could have foretold precisely where the rails would meet. But a more effective theater for that event could scarcely have been selected by a great stage director. Mountains on all sides formed a natural amphitheater. A huge grandstand had been erected on one side of the rails and it was crowded with delegations from all corners of the Soviet land; streamers of bunting all around the stand shouted the coming of the new life to Central Asia. On the other side of the rails, massed on sloping ground, were Kazak horsemen by the thousand; men with inscrutable expressions, immobile on their mounts as though man and horse were one; their padded coats flaring from tight waistlines to show colored robes and pantaloons underneath. Hundreds of Kazak women were there, too, most of them with infants slung on their backs; they gazed shyly from under foot-high turbans.

Early that morning, a silver spike was driven into the tie which completed the railroad. Russian, Kazak, and foreign representatives added hammer blows to that ceremony, and then a locomotive plastered with slogans and alive with flags puffed slowly over the stretch of rail that included the juncture.

A meeting followed. For five hours, thousands sat on hard benches and on horseback while government and Party spokesmen in many tongues eulogized the railroad and the power of the Soviets. Loud-speakers carried their voices to the outermost fringe of the crowd. An airplane circled overhead. The sun rose higher in the sky and beat down fiercely, but no one stirred except to cheer the speeches and the men who were decorated with the Red Banner of Labor for their share in building the Turksib.

Even to us, for whom locomotives and loud-speakers and airplanes were commonplaces, the spectacle was exciting. How much more so to these Kazaks from the hillsides and the desert places! A few of them came timidly to our diner later and grew as excited as children when they saw their own faces in a mirror. Locomotives and airplanes for people who had never seen a mirror!

Of the mammoth enterprises of the Five Year Plan the Turksib was the first to be finished. The work was rushed so that the ceremonial might coincide with the May Day holidays and the reports of this "victory on the front of industrialization" might be spread before the nation as it turned out for the spring demonstrations. Though this priority was accidental, it had its symbolic implications. In its great effort to industrialize, Russia was drawing upon the technique of the West, but its face was turned to the East. The course of its empire, in terms of ultimate export markets for the products of its new machines and ultimate influence for the ideas of its new social system, flowed in that direction. The great struggle for the pocket-books and the minds of Asia's millions will unquestionably shape world history in the next few generations, and in Turksib the Soviet land had fashioned a powerful new instrument for that tussle. Missionary zeal and economic self-interest have ever gone hand in hand.

The hero of this fervid but uncomfortably hot pageant was Vladimir Sergeyevich Shatoff, known to his myriad American friends as "Bill" Shatoff. His personality, indeed, was one of the most memorable things we met in this wilderness of hill and plain. The Order pinned on his shirt was a trivial thing compared with the childlike adulation with which he seemed to be regarded throughout Kazakstan.

Bill Shatoff was twenty when he went to the United States in 1907. He worked as printer, tinsmith, common laborer. He rode freight-cars with other migratory workers and became active in the I.W.W. organization. He led strikes and made speeches and fought American capitalism in the front trenches of the class struggle. But at the same time he learned the lessons that American capitalism could teach him. When he returned to his native land in 1917 to help along the revolution, he was saturated with that peculiarly American driving force and constructive energy. At first he commanded armies of volunteers and brought order out of chaos as police chief of Petrograd. Then, with the end of the civil wars, he turned his dynamic Americanism to the peacetime tasks of industrial life. A stout, chunky man, breezy and good-natured, he was adopted by the American correspondents as their very own. His English brimmed over with juicy Americanisms ten or fifteen years out of date.

At Shatoff's temporary home in Alma-Ata, I found an American oasis in that Asiatic desert: a shelf of American books, a pile of recent American jazz records. But most characteristic of all were the framed aphorisms on his walls: American verses which would have gone straight to the heart of any Rotarian in Kalamazoo or Los Angeles: verses celebrating "stick-to-it-iveness," punctuality, hard work. The I.W.W. agitator turned builder, bringing the slogans of an American "boom" to arid Asia. Already he was impatient to begin a new job of industrial conquest somewhere.

His American years were fresh in his mind. He questioned me about Gurley Flynn, Carlo Tresca, "the Saint" (Vincent St. John), and others of his old friends and comrades-in-arms. His face lighted up in remembrance of daring deeds and futile gestures in the brave "Wobbly days." Billy led in the singing of Wobbly songs: *Hallelujah, I'm a Bum*, and *Hold the Fort for We Are Coming* and *Oh, Mr. Block, You Were Born by Mistake*. In the radical atmosphere evoked at this party in the Shatoff home, it was a little shocking to realize that some of the guests, formerly influential communists, were here in Kazakstan as exiles because of their political views—"on vacation," as one of them explained in a low voice, not without bitterness.

After the ceremonial meeting, a great feast was spread in the open air, in which some five thousand took part. The Europeans sat at long rough tables, and the natives sat cross-legged on the ground and on immense wooden platforms. Billy and I and a few other Americans joined the squatters and took snapshots to record the meal. Rice and dried fruit, mutton and *kumis,* were plentiful this day.

Then the horsemen worked off their accumulated excitement in mass races and fierce contests of agility and endurance, with gaily colored calico and tea as the prizes. Their shrieks filled the air. We watched thousands of them racing enormous distances, or fighting cruelly with blood-curdling yowls in what seemed to us more like a primitive free-for-all than a game. This was the species of men who seven hundred years ago had dominated an empire larger than Rome's.

It required an effort to place this horde back into the contemporary picture—Soviet citizens to be regimented into the ranks of proletarians and proletarianized farmers, to be drawn without interlude or transition into the pattern of an industrialized socialist state. At least, as one of the communist officials in our party put it, "they have nothing to unlearn." There was a deep truth in that observation. Here there were no capitalist classes to clear away, no capitalist habits of thought to dislodge. The struggle for sheer existence has been so bitter, the standard of living so desperately low, that the gifts of socialist industry will seem attractive, no matter how meager they may appear in European eyes. Also, arbitrary rule by outsiders has been their lot so long that they accept it meekly, almost as a divine visitation.

To speak of a "proletarian dictatorship" from within Central Asia is the rankest nonsense, since the revolution found no proletarians to act as dictators. The dictatorship is from without, a civilizing agency from the industrialized West, imposing an alien economic set-up and alien ideas upon backward, bewildered, and frequently reluctant peoples. This agency is creating a local proletariat and educating it to the communist viewpoints as a native support for the dictatorship. The U.S.S.R. needs the cotton, the rubber, the other products, that Central Asia, properly reorganized, may provide in abundance.

Reports of the Aina-Bulak celebration, the marvels of the "black iron horse," the great feast spread for multitudes, were carried back by the horsemen to the yurtas scattered over Central Asia. Heroic legends will flourish around the names of Lenin and Stalin and Shatoff, no less stirring than those recounted century after century about the great Timur and Genghis Khan. Perhaps Bill

Shatoff, who rode the rods in America, will rank in the Kirghiz fables by the side of Tamerlane. Who can guess which of these heroes, the old warriors or the new builders, will affect Central Asia more?

3

Alma-Ata, where we saw the May Day demonstration, already showed the effects of this boom in the desert. Two years earlier, it seemed a suitable place of exile for a man like Trotsky, remote from civilization, inaccessible. Now, it was on a main highroad to Siberia and to Europe, its population of eighty thousand nearly double what it had been during Trotsky's enforced sojourn.

Certainly Trotsky's residence made small impression upon Alma-Ata. Scarcely anyone knew where he had lived. Soviet officials gave us no encouragement in hunting down this "story," although they put no obstacles in our way and allowed our cables on the subject to pass unaltered. The address, Krassin Street 75, was whispered from ear to ear like the address of a speakeasy, and the foreign correspondents, singly and in groups, stole to the place, a little furtively, to talk to neighbors and photograph the house.

We found that even the working-class families now living in the six-roomed, two-storyed house where Trotsky spent a year, were not thrilled by the distinction. Lev Davidovich and his family had been and were gone, so what of it? Neighbors remembered him as a pleasant, affectionate man engrossed in his writing, who went often into the hills to hunt. They recalled that in the last months of his stay he seemed morose and complained more often against his unbearable inactivity. But they did not realize the excitement that his comings and goings caused throughout the world and wondered why thirty correspondents, from distant America and England and Germany, should want to see the white-washed rooms where Trotsky had lived.

The wide poplar-shaded streets of the New City, or Russian section of Tashkent, are no longer bright with gold-braided and epauleted emissaries from St. Petersburg. They are brisk with portfolio-bearing functionaries, as in any other Soviet town, but a good many of them are dark-skinned Uzbeks, their flapping native robes replaced by ill-fitting factory-made coats and trousers.

The meek horses dragging bizarre carts of the region—enormous wheels eight feet high, the drivers crouched on the horse rather than the cart—are getting used to the speeding horseless monsters.

Deep and far-reaching as this intrusion of the West may be—and it is an intrusion that was well under way long before the revolution—it has left the surface of the Old City, the real Tashkent, overwhelmingly Oriental. You glance down a muddy alley between the blind walls of its windowless homes and you might easily be gazing at a street in Jerusalem two thousand years ago. A veiled woman comes toward you, covered from the crown of her head to the ground by a shapeless gray *paranja*, a black impenetrable horsehair veil over her face, like a hideous walking pillar, scarcely human. Huge men jog along on donkeys half their own size, their thick calves contrasting with the spindly legs of the animal. A bearded Uzbek strides toward you, his gaily striped robe flapping in the mud.

Curiously enough, the most Soviet things in the Old City were the straggly queues stretching from government bakeries and cooperative food shops; women, veiled and unveiled, clutching their ration books exactly as in Moscow or Kiev.

A concert at the Radio Center deepened our sense of the new life seeping into the substance of the old. Folk songs played on the long native flutes gave way to something which, with an effort, we recognized as the *International*. Uzbek children, with the red kerchief of the Pioneers around their necks, sang ancient tunes with new words that scorned the ways of their backward parents. Two girls, their pitch-black hair twisted patiently into a hundred thin braids, danced the slow coquettish Uzbek dances, eyes flashing, limbs winking, like little Salomes, but as they danced they fitted new songs about freedom to the old erotic rhythms. Not for them marriage by barter, the harem, and the imprisonment of a *paranja*.

Some years before the revolution, another such girl had been sold at twelve into marriage to a man five times her age. From the primitive Moslem home of a poor peasant she entered the well-stocked harem as fourth wife. Instead of settling down to long-suffering wifehood, she listened to the undefined stirrings in her young mind, even as a million other girls sold into polygamous households and shut from the world must have listened.

For two years this child endured her prison. Then she ran away to Tashkent. It was no mere school-girl escapade. A brutal death at the hands of her husband and his relatives must be her portion if she were caught; such insult can be wiped out only in blood. But the urge of a freedom-loving mind was stronger than the fear of death. For several years she shifted for herself in the Old City of Tashkent, outcast, homeless, on the thin edge of starvation, but learning somehow to read and to write and saturating herself with a great ambition for her bonded sisters.

Then came the revolution. Her passion flowered into a gift of oratory. Her knock-about life had hardened her courage and practical abilities. She was active in establishing the Soviet power and was soon as idolized by the new Uzbek women as she was detested by the mullahs and land-owning beys. Her hair clipped in mannish style, a cigarette defiantly between her full lips, a military coat over her trim figure, she became the symbol incarnate of the emancipated woman, in a world where women were chattels of their male owners.

And now—in her early thirties, good-looking, the flame of her personality burning high—she was Vice-President of the Soviet Republic of Uzbekistan, of which ancient Samarkand is the new capital. Comrade Abidova! It was she who greeted our special train when we reached Samarkand. The suffragette and women's rights movements of the West are amusing parlor games compared with the grim struggle carried on by these Central Asiatic women. Death and torture, at the hands of those whose religious fanaticism or class honor is inflamed by the new propaganda, are so frequent that they are no longer news. One such woman who went into dark villages to preach emancipation was returned to the city cut to pieces in a sack on which was the inscription: "There's your women's freedom."

Comrade Abidova was frankly scornful of our eagerness to see the remnants of the old civilization, when we could look at a new irrigation system, hospitals and clubs, silk mills and day nurseries. What cared bob-haired Abidova for the last resting place of the adored Bibi or the sky-blue old *medreshes?* She seemed nonplused by our infidel indifference to the new shrines and *medreshes* of industrialization. We managed, however, to see both the old and the new, and each gained in vividness because of the other.

Samarkand had been the goal of conquerors, of whom Alexander the Great is the first known to history. After him came the Tadjiks, who left their language and much of their culture; next the Arabs, to be followed by the Turks. Then all of them were covered by the flood-tide out of Mongolia, under Genghis Khan, and under Tamerlane two centuries later. With the disintegration of Mongolian rule, the city was governed by local Emirs until conquered by Russia in the 1870's.

Of them all, the imprint of Tamerlane is strongest. He loved his Samarkand and lavished upon it his choicest spoils. He brought the most skilled artisans of Asia, and even Europe, to build its mosques and tombs and religious schools. The ruins of those monuments to his fame and his expansive taste still dominate old Samarkand, which, like old Tashkent, seems unrelated to the new Russian city.

We walked through the old city like people inspecting a half-remembered dream. This East, crowded, odoriferous, colorful, is a common memory for all of us: the source of our religion, our folk-lore, our deepest nostalgia. We went through the winding bazaar; through the street of the cap-makers, ablaze with gold and silver and purple skull-caps; the street of the silversmiths, filled with gorgeous confections of semi-precious stones set in silver; the streets of coppersmiths, silk dealers, and cobblers. The narrow alleys were thick with buyers and sellers. Tall Uzbek lads balanced on their heads trays piled high with small, flat bread loaves. Water carriers threaded through the crowds. The long multi-colored robes, the turbans and skull-caps, even the somber triangles of horsehair veils contributed to a scene that remains electric in memory.

A short dozen years ago, the eight miles of earthen wall running around Bokhara inclosed the quintessence of the East. Barbarous splendor and fearful dirt flourished undisturbed. The tsar's benevolent supervision left the reigning Emir, whose son I had met in Moscow, an absolute monarch in all local matters; an obese, bearded, splendiferous person amidst his fabulous wealth, his vast harem, and his boy concubines. Merchant princes lived in a style reminiscent of the *Arabian Nights*. Jews wore signs of their degradation and dared not ride while Moslem walked, but many of them were enormously rich and their girdles of servitude were spun of fine gold. Next to Mecca, this was the holiest city, its Oriental face unblemished by a single modernism; its first factory was not built until 1928.

And Bokhara was still exotic enough to thrill a Westerner to the quick. The miles of intertwined alleys, some of them covered, here and there knotted under old arches; the tangle of traffic on donkeys, horses, camels, high-wheeled carts; the stagnant water reservoirs; the long rows of box-like shops; the tangle of hammering and shouting: something desperately ancient, grown in upon itself. There was as yet no New City, though hundreds of Russian families had come to live within the sacred walls.

The Emir's palace itself, a large earthen fortress enclosing many ugly and pretentious buildings, is now the seat of the regional executive committee of the government. But the harem grounds and palaces were being used as a sanatorium for mentally defective women—an Oriental insult, perhaps, to the liquidated past. Once the fat Emir watched his concubines disport themselves in the pool. Now the pool was a dry basin, empty except for dust and debris.

At night, the charm of Bokhara was deepened by a sense of mystery and danger. We ignored the queues waiting for bread and the few new buildings and were aware only of the brooding East. As we lost ourselves in the winding alleys, we stopped before *chai-khannas* and listened to the melancholy tunes plucked from curious stringed instruments; even the beggars displaying their loathsome wounds fitted into the picture. Then we wandered accidentally into a hall where several hundred Russians and Uzbeks were discussing heatedly the problems of the local coöperative shops.

The picturesqueness of Bokhara is crumbling. It is doomed. The medieval life nurtured on rich trade is no more and there seems no good reason for its survival. The rich brocades, silks, copperware, rugs, and jewels remaining from the old days are being confiscated or bought up by government agents for export to Fifth Avenue and Rue de la Paix and the Strand. The thirty correspondents and other foreigners helped the process immensely by stocking up on embroidered robes, wall hangings, and bits of jewelry. As regional center, with a few factories, it will retain some population no doubt. But Bokhara—"high, holy, divinely descended Bokhara"—will dwindle to a drab provincial town.

4

The taste of Central Asia was strong on my mind's palate when I returned to Moscow. I had seen a proletarian revolution under way in a vast territory without a proletariat: whose first task, in fact, is to create a working class in the Marxist sense. Exceptional as its forms may be, it was the modern West of machines and literacy and women's rights roughly elbowing aside the East; even as Western civilization is blotting out the East elsewhere in Asia.

There were lusty debates in the bourgeois cars on the return trip as to whether what we had witnessed was a sort of "Soviet imperialism." A British writer argued that the differences between Moscow's role in Bokhara and London's role in Bagdad were more of seeming than of essence.

"These people may accept Soviet industrial blessings and new ideas," he argued. "I have seen thousands of Indians who accept the British blessings and ways of life quite as enthusiastically. But in both cases it is change imposed by a foreign conqueror, not change springing from the heart of the old civilization."

"Except that the natives will get the benefit of all that is being done," someone objected, "instead of filling the pockets of foreign capitalists."

"What you mean," the Englishman smiled, "is that Soviet Russian rule is good for these backward people, and I agree with you. In fact, that's exactly what a British imperialist says of *his* particular method of bringing civilization to the uncivilized. As for the lining of foreign pockets, let's be realistic like good Bolsheviks. European Russia needs its Asiatic colonies quite as much as England needs Egypt or India, for its own economic interests. Central Asia must supply Russia with cotton above all other things, to make it independent of American and British cotton. All those plans they told us about in the interviews amount to exactly that."

"But Central Asia has local self-government. The heads of the government are natives. Remember Comrade Abidova."

"Sure, but that's old stuff," the Englishman persisted. "We Britishers are past masters in the local self-government stuff. All we need is a line of carefully located army garrisons, and you've noticed that the Red Army garrisons are pretty much in evidence too."

The argument remained unsettled.

At a small station somewhere on the Asiatic side of Orenburg, we noticed a long train of freight cars on a siding, G.P.U. soldiers with fixed bayonets standing guard near it. The word spread through our own cars that a trainload of liquidated kulaks was there, as if for our inspection. Neither the soldiers nor the officials in our midst could very well prevent us from approaching the human freight. Small apertures high up at one end of the cars were the only source of air and light for the hundreds of men, women, and children jammed into the prison cars. These apertures were now crowded with peasant faces, craning for a view of the station full of foreigners: weary, hopeless faces deeply ingrained with dirt.

"Where are you going?" I addressed myself to a batch of the prisoners.

"We don't know," one of them replied.

"They say," another added, "that we're being taken to Turkestan —to the canals."

The same irrigation canals of which Abidova and other officials were so proud! This was the other side of the medal. Whatever Stalin's article on "dizziness from success" may have done to protect the poorest peasants against excessive force, the liquidation of kulaks was still going on—it would go on for two more years.

"But why are you being taken there?" I asked.

"Because we're kulaks," an emaciated-looking woman replied.

No one among her fellow-prisoners contradicted her. These creatures did not even dispute the right of the government to deprive them of everything, pack them into cars, and haul them into Central Asia to dig canals. Government was something too far away, too omnipotent to be questioned; its decrees were like the decrees of nature, part of a harsh destiny. This acceptance of their fate in a sort of bovine stupor seemed more horrible than liquidation itself; it explained why the Kremlin could carry out policies which elsewhere would have stirred irrepressible mutiny.

The impress of this accidental confrontation with a contingent of exiles was as sharp as anything that we had seen in the crowded, exciting journey. I have found its traces since then in the books and articles written by many of the foreigners in our cars.

The relations between Russians and non-Russians on our train became tenser, more inhibited, the closer we came to Moscow. Fraternization became more risky, political barriers more intimidating. Friendships had developed among many of us, but we all knew that they could not be continued in the capital; it was too dangerous for the Russians.

A few days after we abandoned the train, all the Russian journalists and literary men who had been with us gathered in the ballroom of our house on Petrovsky Pereulok. The Russians consented to have present only one foreigner aside from Billy and myself, and that at our insistence. It was a gay, noisy, friendly party which did not break up until far beyond dawn.

At the door, as he gripped my hand in saying good night, a young communist newspaperman said quietly:

"What a pity that we cannot continue these friendships. Maybe, some day, it will be possible. . . ."

V. Search for the "Real Russia"

THE Moscow River broke through its straitjacket of ice and hurled sparkling boulders on the banks. Hundreds of people leaned over the balustrades and lingered on the bridges watching the ice crash and tangle as it moved down the river. Behind them the gold and blue and orange cupolas and towers of the Kremlin splintered the sunshine. The skeleton trees on the boulevards suddenly burst into tender green buds. Winter was turning into summer without the formality of a real spring.

Padded coats and felt boots were abandoned for *tolstovkas* and patched leather boots, cotton *sarafans* and canvas shoes. Peasant nursemaids pushed home-made perambulators—egg-boxes on wheels—along the broad paths of Alexandrovsky Park under the crenelated north wall of the Kremlin, and before long they had an escort of laughing Red soldiers. On the Tverskoi Boulevard, between the statues of Pushkin and Gogol, an ancient and faded carrousel was turned by hand to cracked music-box tunes, while its tiny passengers shrieked their delight. Other children were taking rides in the roomy saddle-pockets on either side of a weary camel. Blushing couples were being photographed against crudely drawn backgrounds of waterfalls or pillared palaces.

I lost myself in the turgid, tangled currents of pedestrians, most of whom carried parcels in dirty newspapers or clutched brief-cases. Despite the disguise of a Russian blouse, the beggars spotted me as a foreigner and wailed aloud, "Little uncle, give me bread!" I entered shops where crowds milled around in dizzy futility near vacant counters under vacant shelves. In the large department stores, bold signs announced the goods that were not there; only the corners given over to busts and tinted lithographs of Lenin, Stalin, and Marx were always well stocked. Outside the windows of the special "closed" shops and restaurants reserved for favored categories of citizens, little knots of people watched silently as the fortunate ones came and went. Everywhere the crowds overflowed the sidewalks and shiny automobiles plowed through them like speedboats cutting water.

At night, the Hermitage and Aquarium, amusement parks, were filled with promenading people, young and old; girls in starched shirtwaists, red kerchiefs or berets; young men with scrubbed faces and oiled boots. I paid the admission price and sat over stale weak beer at little tables covered with grimy cloths and smiled back at coquettish girls. A rumble of applause came from behind the high canvas wall where an open-air vaudeville show was going on. Between the acts of *Rose Marie* people streamed out of the theater and joined the concentric circles of promenaders, moving in opposite directions for easier mutual inspection.

Though all other squares and boulevards were jammed and noisy, Red Square was always deserted at night. Pedestrians walked through briskly and *izvozchiki* whipped up their horses; no one loitered except occasionally foreigners from the hotels nearby. It seemed detached from the city's life, hushed under the stars like an autumnal field. St. Basil's Cathedral, a cluster of queer mushrooms, loomed against the night sky, unrelated to the Kremlin walls on one side, the severely angular tomb of Lenin under it, and the squat elongated building on the other side. Soldiers stood immobile with fixed bayonets at the tomb and at little booths near the two arched gates to the Kremlin. Every fifteen minutes the clock tower overlooking the execution block chimed the time. On the Kremlin wall just beyond the mausoleum, a red flag flapping in the breeze was lit up from below. It seemed the only live thing on the Square: a red tongue of fire hissing defiance at the dead gold eagles immolated on high at both ends of the walls, a red tongue mocking the stillness below and above. At midnight the clock tower chimed the *International* and the notes were carried through the ether to radio loud speakers throughout Moscow.

2

Izvozchiki, the drivers of dilapidated sleds and carriages, had practically disappeared from the streets of the nation during the fierce attack on kulaks and "kulak agents." Their reappearance helped the back-to-normalcy atmosphere which prevailed briefly in the capital. After Stalin's "dizziness" article, those who had not killed or sold their horses ventured from their hiding places.

With that easy optimism which is an aspect of ultimate despair, remnants of the private traders dared come again into the city's markets. Doctors and dentists became less fearful of private practice. Pre-revolutionary educated people lifted their heads a little more hopefully.

Peasants deserted the collectives as rapidly and more joyously than they had entered them. In Moscow province, for instance, of 75% of the peasantry collectivized only 25% remained; this according to *Pravda*. In thousands of villages, indeed, there was no need for de-collectivization; the socialization was only on paper anyhow. The Easter services, crowded as usual, were subdued, but there were no hostile demonstrations like the year before. The Godless Society contented itself with free theatrical performances, movies, lectures, and even dances, to divert the youth from church attendance.

The gods, it seemed, as well as the godless, had relented. Our cables reflected the more cheerful mood. But the optimism was short-lived. The Kremlin had no intention of being robbed of its victories on the agrarian front. Having deflated paper collectives and warned against a few of the grosser excesses, it renewed the campaign. For about six months, until the new harvest was in, a measure of discretion was desirable; local "hotheads" must be kept in check. Then they would be given free rein once more. The "artel" type of collective—in which the peasant retained his home, a garden plot, a cow, and smaller domestic animals—was now made standard, rather than the fully communized type. Liquidation did not cease. Cargoes of kulaks continued to be unloaded wherever labor was most needed. It was a neat arrangement: free land, horses, and tools for the collectives at one end, free labor for the lumber industry and construction jobs at the other end.

The entire process of rural socialization by this time had a different physiognomy than envisioned by the Kremlin a year or two earlier. Then the collectives were pictured as islands of prosperity in the oceanic expanse of agrarian misery. The government would see to it that the *kolkhozes* prospered. The whole weight of bank credits, tractors, selected seeds would be on their side, plus the property seized from the class enemies. Manufactured goods, schools, libraries, radio, motion picture theaters would bring the benefits of urban culture to the peasants who relinquished their individualistic prejudices. These idyllic promises filled the press and the speeches. Private farmers would watch their thriving socialized neighbors grow fat. Soon enough they would beg for the privilege of admission.

The very success of the pressure, however, killed the idyl. With four or five times as many collectives on its hands as originally planned, the government was swamped; it could not help them to prosper. There were not enough competent directors, machinery, seeds, or culture to go around. The wholesale destruction of draft animals sharpened these shortages, and the apathy of peasants who felt themselves coerced or tricked into collectivization did the rest to make the *kolkhoz* member for the time being a poorer, more wretched mortal than his impoverished private neighbors. The natural extension of the movement which was to have come by dint of example was now out of question; force—now more, now less, but naked force—remained the chief and often sole technique of agricultural socialization.

Abroad, and among the more naively rapturous foreigners in Moscow, the *kolkhoz* was regarded as a glorified coöperative. However exorbitant the cost, it was assumed, at least a beginning had been made in socialism on the land. Nothing can be farther from the truth. In essence, the *kolkhoz* is no more socialistic than farms cultivated for the church or the crown in other countries, paying their farmhands on the basis of the crops produced: share cropping for the government. Every detail of management—the acreage and crops to be sown, the disposal of the crops, payment to the peasant workers, etc.—was decided at central headquarters, in Moscow, Kharkov, and Rostov, often stupidly and uneconomically. The directors were sent by headquarters and were not responsible to anyone else. The *kolkhoz* was denied the right to own tractors and other machinery. Everything was concentrated in Machine Tractor Stations and rented to the collective in return for 20 to 30% of its total crops. The peasant was a collective owner largely in the sense that a hired laborer on government land anywhere is theoretically a part owner of that land.

"In the old days we worked for landlords," peasants put it

bluntly, "now we work for the government. What's the difference?"

Whatever collectivization might promise theoretically for the future, in the here and now it amounted, in the view of the ordinary peasant, to a restoration of the serfdom abolished seventy years before by Alexander II. It is essential to understand this if the turbulent war between the collectivized peasants and its omnipotent absentee landlord, the state, in the next few years, costing millions of lives, is to make sense.

3

Conscientious foreign observers considered it their duty to make contacts with Workers and Peasants and Real Communists. They went to endless trouble to meet exemplars of these capitalized classes socially, paying court to genuine factory workers or collectivized farmers who happened on their path.

"The trouble," they were always being told, "is that you don't know the real Russia, but just a lot of left-overs from the past." The rebuke bored deep into their conscience. They searched for that mysterious "real Russia."

Of course, there were the proletarians one saw in the streets and on queues, on trams and in busses; the crippled *dvornik* who came sleepily to open the gate at night; the peasants who hauled your load of firewood from the lumber yard. There were the communists with whom you dealt in offices in the regular course of business or met at official Soviet functions. But somehow they did not measure up to the "real thing;" they belonged to the gray, drab, unsmiling mass on sidewalks and street cars, rather than the brave new breed in *Izvestia* editorials, Meierhold plays, and Eisenstein movies.

I lost no opportunity for meeting the "real thing." If callous-handed citizens showed an inclination to associate with a humble *boorzhooy*, they met an eager welcome. Usually they proved disappointing: the kind of people who, if put into a proletarian novel, would bar it from publication.

Consider the case of Piotr, a carpenter in burlap apron, who came into our lives briefly to build bookshelves in my office on his free days and evenings; a regulation shock brigadier if ever there was one, newly literate, a candidate for Party membership. At first he was cagey and correct in his political opinions, but quickly enough drifted into a vein of bitter complaint against nearly everything. He had a way of referring to "*nashy noviye bary*"—"our new overlords"—which disqualified him for Eisenstein and Meierhold. When I pressed him for the source of his wood, a deficit product, he admitted with a wink that he helped himself at the warehouse of the *noviye bary:* G.P.U. officials for whom he was doing some carpentering.

Or consider the still more distressing case of plump Irina, from the Tri-Ugolny Textile factory. A New York communist brought her to the house one day by way of exhibiting the genuine article in the line of proletarian youth. She returned again and again, enchanted with Billy's rendition of Russian folk songs and Russian meat cakes. Here at last was a factory "activist," a Comsomolka raised under the hammer and sickle, suckled by the revolution, her portrait once in *Ogoniok* as an outstanding pace-setter. But she showed an eager and unorthodox interest in jazz dancing, European clothes, and off-color ditties not prescribed in the Comsomol catechism.

The fourteen-carat Proletarian had a curious way of disclosing wide brass streaks on closer assay; of turning, in short, into a normal workman who feared his director, resented speed-up tricks, and was more interested in pig than in pig-iron. Like workers the world over, and this was always disconcerting, he dreamed that his sons at least would escape the fate of proletarians by becoming policemen or communist officials. If his boy was an active Comsomol, he mentioned it proudly as a matter of career rather than revolutionary ideals, much as an American father might boast that his son was getting on in the world as a stock salesman or political henchman.

The "real thing" was always one step removed from the workers and peasants one actually came to know. The exceptionally enthusiastic worker at a factory bench or on a farm developed, on closer acquaintance, to be simply more ambitious than his fellow-workers. The "activist" attending all the meetings, whooping it up for the new government loan, proposing higher labor quotas, and organizing volunteer groups to go weeding on some *kolkhoz* or to help demolish a monastery was curiously like the pep-it-up-team-work-factory-spirit fellows I knew at home, and equally detested by his clock-watching fellow-workers.

The fact, of course, is that the simon-pure Proletarian was a figment of the propagandist imagination: a projection of the ideal worker-to-be in an ideal society-to-be. The hero of half the plays and pictures and novels was as synthetic a creature as the heroes of wishful-thinking literature under any system. He was significant as a rough sketch of the Proletarian of the hoped-for future, a clew to the virtues and standards being held up before the population by its Bolshevik regime, but only vaguely related to the living men and women behind the machines and the plows.

The recognition of this fact enabled me to solve (or so I thought) the most disturbing of the paradoxes of Soviet power: the deification of the Proletariat in the abstract—on posters and postage stamps, in official theses and official literature—while the flesh-and-blood working masses were treated most cavalierly. The communist functionary who worships the Proletariat as a class and spits on the self-seeking, wretched specimens of the class whom he handles in everyday life is not necessarily a fraud. On the contrary, his contempt for Ivan Ivanovich may be a measure of his respect for the Ivan Ivanovich-to-be. The selfish, stubbornly unappreciative people whom he must whip into the shape of his vision seem to him an affront to the idealized Proletarian for whom he went to tsarist prisons, for whom he fought civil wars. Workers who achieve power cannot be expected to idealize other workers as romantic upper-class people do; they know the creatures too intimately.

Perhaps there is no contradiction at all in the inspired ruthlessness with which men, cherishing the vision of a "New Peasant," exterminate the old, earthy, uncouth and self-centered peasants who now usurp his place. Does this sound fanciful? Turn to the Webbs, Sidney and Beatrice, and taste their frank abhorrence of the Russian peasants, with their "characteristic peasant vices of greed and cunning, varied by outbursts of drunkenness and recurrent periods of sloth," these "stubborn" peasants "formerly servile" now "becoming rebellious." (Have the Webbs never heard of other rebellious Russian peasants, in the days of Bulatov, Stenka

Razin, and Pugachev?) With that attitude of loathing established in Volume I, they need not be blood-thirsty to accept complacently the horrors of forcible collectivization in Volume II. Turn, if you prefer, to the Hebrew Prophets cursing their people with sadistic curses because they do not accept the ways of the Lord of Hosts. It is the divine mission of prophets to despise and castigate the Chosen People or the Chosen Classes.

VI. Bargains in Ideals and Omelettes

THE Soviet capital was fast becoming a paradise for mediocrities and misfits from other countries. Anything from the mysterious and glamorous "abroad" was a magnet to draw Russians, who had been cut off for nearly a generation from the main currents of the world's culture and were famished for warmth and beauty free of shoddy propaganda. Frequently a first-rate European or American artist came to Moscow, content to perform for worthless rubles in return for the thrill of seeing the land of the Five Year Plan. But mostly those who came to show their derelict vaudeville acts in the Music Hall, to exhibit their sculpture and painting, to sing or play at the Conservatory Hall, were has-beens or never-beens, unknown or forgotten in their home lands. They expanded under the unaccustomed appreciation, and lived pinched lives on the rubles they earned. They said the proper things to interviewers in Moscow and to interviewers at home—if they rated press attention—to keep the gates of the U.S.S.R. open, and in time many of them came to believe the things they said by dint of repetition.

Contraltos or 'cellists known only to Friends of the Soviet Union audiences in their own countries made nationwide tours here. They wrote pieces for the Soviet magazines on the degradation of bourgeois culture. Painters and sculptors whose art never went beyond independent shows and arty cafés at home, gushed about the great progress of the Dictatorship of the Proletariat and saw their work installed in Moscow's leading museums. Third-rate writers with aching inferiority complexes promised to shed their last drop of blood in defense of the U.S.S.R. and received bundles of torn rubles as an advance on the translations of their works, which were never published. Skilled mechanics thrown out of work at home blossomed into engineers here, with the coveted admission cards to the "foreign stores."

From this time forward the Soviet Union was a colossal department store of ideas and opportunities for the modest price of a first, second, or third category tour. Thrills and easement of spirit at bargain prices. Everything from nude bathing to billion-dollar dams, from free love to concentration camps. A new up-to-the-minute social faith, fashionable in the nicest circles since the depression, with one shot in the arm. The most ingratiating floor walkers from Intourist and Voks and the Foreign Office; commissars in person and little intimate receptions in the former palaces of merchant princes for special customers.

Everyone found what he wanted most, and a sense of superiority into the bargain. It was easy to feel superior to the rabble who stood on lines, who were shooed off trains to make way for the cash customers, who regarded a tweed skirt or a fountain-pen as a miracle, who were rationed and liquidated and mobilized for parades. The only place in the world where you could stand at the apex with dictators and merge ecstatically with the masses simultaneously: a synthesis of absolute power and absolute humility heretofore vouchsafed only to rare mystics and martyrs. One could become not only a proletarian but a proletarian dictator for the price of a third-category tour.

Hard-boiled capitalists found the spectacle to their taste: no strikes, no lip, hard work on a bread-and-water diet; and one good look at a Soviet factory cured them of the fear of Russian competition. Soft-boiled idealists found familiar slogans, day nurseries, model prisons, bigger and better uplift. Pale advocates of juiceless causes—birth control, Esperanto, new calendars, sex equality, prison reform, big families, futurist dancing, modern education—found surcease from contempt. Everyone outside the Soviet Union who accounted himself enlightened and advanced veered toward Intourist under the pleasant illusion that Bolshevism was a new, more gloriously intransigent bohemianism.

The obliging floor-walkers always found something in the department store to match the crankiest of tastes. I saw Voks sell the glories of mass production to a couple of California back-to-nature, hand-loom faddists. Vegetarians fleeing bourgeois standards swooned in an ecstasy of admiration for Soviet slaughter-houses equipped with American machinery.

Virginal school teachers and sex-starved wives came close to the masses, especially the male classes, and some of them were so deeply impressed with the potency of Bolshevik ideas that they extended their visas again and again. A few of them emerged to write shrill books extolling the Soviet Union's "new unshackled attitudes," the equality of the sexes, abortion clinics. One such volume—which I described uncharitably as "a horizontal view of Russia"—saw the glorious new morality chiefly through the eyes of a stalwart Red Sailor.

British and American ladies with triple chins and overwhelming bosoms, having tried and discarded other spiritual diversions, now "found" Bolshevism. One of them was moved to verse in the best Sunday-school manner:

"Oh! Why are words so poor and weak?
Hopeless to write and hard to speak,
To tell of all that you have done
Since your great Victory was won.

Your children are a happy band,
Knowledge and Freedom hand in hand.
War, Crime, Disease will disappear
For perfect Love can cast out Fear!"

Unappreciative Britishers and Americans residing in Moscow suggested that Perfect Love casting out Fear would make an ideal slogan for the liquidation of kulaks. It should be inscribed, we said, over every concentration camp. But the Kremlin never took up the suggestion.

The antics of these foreigners were an endless source of amusement to us. Earnest seekers after "the truth at last about Russia," new philosophies in sugar-coated pill form, confirmation of their private phobias, revenge on the world. Job-seekers prepared to devote their lives to the Soviet Cause at a decent salary and a "foreign store" ration book. They gamboled merrily among the queues and liquidations and found oily dialectical salves for their various frustrations. The humor of eminent foreign economists, educators, sociologists being flattered and gulled—of simpler folks gulling themselves and doing the flattering—was shot through with pathos.

We saw rapturous visitors, beginning with approval of cigar-box architecture, conductorless orchestras, the Dalton system, or free abortions, extend it to include approval of Russia's age-old methods of policing its meek subjects and Petrine tactics in forcing chunks of Westernism down recalcitrant Asiatic gullets. They joined the Friends of the Soviet Union and felt themselves bold iconoclasts participating in the rebirth of the world. When the Kremlin ultimately outlawed the cigar-box architecture, prohibited abortions, adopted Baptist codes of morals and Victorian standards of art, these people must have felt themselves betrayed.

I think back to Jane, a thin, high-strung New York liberal who quivered visibly at the sight of a new man. In Bolshevism she found not only a job but escape from the restraints of an unsatisfactory husband and the supervision of a middle-class family. Sitting on an unmade bed in her hotel room she could talk for hours about freedom for women under the Red flag. "Starvation, forced labor, the extermination of the intelligentsia," she said, "bah! It's worth it, it's worth it, I tell you, because Russia has liquidated sex bugaboos. Equality of men and women, the single standard. . . . It's worth it!"

Or the spinsterish Sarah, a Los Angeles intellectual whose inhibitions fell away like a moth-eaten garment as soon as she crossed the Soviet frontier. Stored-up passion gave her every article in the *Moscow Daily News* a peculiarly high-pitched school-girl quality. Or the Mid-Western professor with the soft, clammy hands who pinched the rosy cheeks of boy interpreters and gushed indiscriminately over every Soviet theatrical performance.

The English-language paper founded at this time for the edification of the growing American and British population provided a sanctuary for as bizarre a collection of incompetents and twisted personalities as was ever gathered under one roof. Michael Borodin was put in charge of an army of amateur journalists. Once he led a Chinese revolution; now he quarreled with office boys—an embittered and broken giant. The paper at first was published as a "five day weekly," *Moscow News;* then it was turned into a daily. An immense staff turned out a four-page sheet, chiefly warmed over from yesterday's Russian-language papers. Every obscure celebrity from the U.S.A. or England was quoted as a matter of course by this paper as thrilled by the wonderful progress that he saw immediately on reaching Moscow and determined to expose the bourgeois lies about food shortage and terror as soon as he returned home.

Sometimes, on returning home, these people instead confirmed the lies. The *Moscow Daily News* thereupon produced a sheaf of statements and confessions to prove that the ingrate had been drunk, incompetent, a speculator, and a rapist while in the U.S.S.R.

2

The apex of absurdity, a sort of summation of all this foreign lunacy, seemed to me the international congress of proletarian and near-proletarian writers in Kharkov. RAPP, which Stalin himself two years later kicked into the ash-can and which ranks high among the acknowledged "mistakes" of this period, was in command of the gathering, as it was of all cultural life in the country. Soviet writers were living in a state of terror under the whip of half-literate dictators of literature like Comrade Auerbach. Men of genuine talent had committed suicide, or ceased to write, or manufactured proletarian pot-boilers for which they hated themselves. Literary criticism had become a function of the Secret Service. That Soviet literature at this time had touched incredible depths of mediocrity is no longer disputed even by hundred-percenters.

Against this background, several score pamphleteers and politicians from a dozen countries gathered to formulate tactics for spreading the blessings of RAPP to the rest of the world. Each of them pretended to represent the "advanced sector" of literature in his own country. They brought "fervent greetings" from the cultural front of their respective nations. They boasted of the horrors in their homes—the political prisoners, the suppression of revolutionary writers, the decaying democracy—like barkers outside side-shows. And they pointed with pride to Soviet achievements on the literary front. The Alice-in-Wonderland innocence of these men, in even daring to mention here subjects like political prisoners and suppression of revolutionary thought! In eulogizing a literature they could not read and a system whose jesuitical intricacies were beyond their simple minds!

The proceedings of the congress read like a much madder Mad

Hatter's party. I was close enough to the literary inquisition to savor the epic insanity to the last "Hail Auerbach! Hail Stalin!" To amplify the spurious importance of the conclave, Dinamov's inquisitorial *Literary Gazette* inflated every foreign delegate into an "outstanding writer" in his country, citing as proof his stereotyped undertaking to defend the U.S.S.R.

The "outstanding writer" from the United States was one Gold, a slightly hysterical little man in baggy clothes, with inflamed eyes in a sallow, dissipated-looking face. Gold thought bitterly of American writers who lived in penthouses and delivered himself of impassioned "Hails!" He left no doubt at all that an American RAPP was needed and must come quickly to liquidate Heywood Broun, H. L. Mencken, and others who poked fun at Gold; to liquidate, particularly, those swinish writers and publishers who had never even heard of him.

The panegyrics by educators, Professor Dewey and Professor Counts and a bevy of sub-Deweys and sub-Counts, were of particular interest to those of us who had the problem of educating children in Moscow to solve. Most of these theoreticians of pedagogy recognized instantly that the Soviet planners had cribbed some of their favorite ideas, which put them in a highly amenable frame of mind. On paper the Soviet educational plans and curricula combined the best features of Dewey, Dalton, Montessori, *et al.* A few model schools made a brave and usually futile effort to live up to the plans, within the limits of the shortages of paper, pencils, teachers, and hygienic facilities. I do not know what methods the specialists from abroad used to investigate Soviet education. Presumably, they stocked up on theoretical official plans and brochures and had a glimpse of the model schools, just as famous economists tanked up on blueprints, official statistics, and naive premises.

Each time I read another hyperbolic report by another well-meaning modern educator, I hastened hopefully to the schools he mentioned or inferred. I discovered that somehow he had failed to look at the toilet; missed the fact that the school had been closed half of the term because of epidemic diseases; forgotten to note that one teacher, badly in need of schooling herself, must supervise sixty or seventy undernourished and excessively mischievous little pupils. The enthusiasm of these educators attested their kind hearts and modernist daring, but their judgments belonged with the effusions of the ever-lengthening line of self-deluded outsiders.

Fortified with an introduction from the Foreign Office, Billy went to interview an Assistant Commissar of Education. The need to put Genie into a school became more insistent; perhaps somewhere in Moscow and its environs there was in fact a school worthy of the foreign educators' more sober lines. The Assistant Commissar was most affable. He listed the very best of the schools, the models among the models, and explained the special virtues of each.

"Go and look at them—well, look at them again," he said. "I shall give you a letter. Whichever you decide upon, your child will be admitted instantly. You have my word on that."

She thanked him, put away the letter, and departed. Just outside the door she felt a detaining hand on her shoulder. It was the Assistant Commissar. He was slightly embarrassed.

"Mrs. Lyons, I wanted to say something more," he said. "In there I talked to you as an official of the Commissariat. Here I can talk to you as a father. I have children too. Tell me, is there any reason why you *must* keep your daughter in Moscow?"

"Why, no," Billy said. "It's simply that we would like to have her with us."

"You mean you have the possibility of sending her to study abroad?"

"Of course. We know some excellent schools in Berlin and Geneva and—"

"Then why do you hesitate!" The Assistant Commissar's tone was an amalgam of astonishment and envy.

We put Genie into the Berthold Otto Schule, at Lichterfelde, Berlin. She remained there until Hitler came to power.

"There you are! Afraid that their kid will be infected with communism in a Soviet school!" Our friend X, whose Soviet orthodoxy was his stock-in-trade in a hard world, shook his head sadly. But just three months behind Genie, the children of Comrade X, too, came to Berlin for their schooling and they, too, remained until Hitler came to power.

3

The big house on the Spirodonovka where the Foreign Office entertained was an adolescent dream of grandeur come true; opulence as envisioned by a provincial storekeeper. Suits of armor, complete with lances, posed in hollow dignity by the shallow steps leading from the vestibule to a great foyer paneled in mahogany; in the background, for no reason at all, a gigantic Chinese vase covered with the writhings of bronze serpents held the eye. The gold and ivory ballroom was vaguely Japanese in intention. Gold *fleur-de-lis* provided the *motif* in a medieval French chamber hung with Gobelins; a cabinet filled with the original owner's porcelain figures remained intact here, even unto a piece of erotica pointed out to newcomers when the ladies were not looking.

But the crowd converged on the immense, neatly rustic hunting room, where the long table loaded with food was located. Leaning against the capacious fireplace, the U.P. and I.N.S. correspondents agreed ruefully, between mouthfuls of roast duck washed down with Naperouly, that these "press teas" were not what they used to be. Constrained and a little awkward.

"The trouble," said I.N.S., "is that in the old days, two or three years ago, they used to invite low-down newspapermen who had nothing to hide. Now we get only big shots, editors and *feuilleton* writers, and you can't talk to them about what really interests you. Looks too much like digging for secrets!"

"Sure," U.P. grouched, "mustn't ask them questions because they might know the answers. It's a silly business anyhow. What's the use of meeting them, when they don't dare come near you between parties?"

From the corner of an eye, they watched the New York *Times* in lively conference with Karl Radek and wondered whether he was getting some valuable inside dope on the forthcoming Party Congress. Radek's face, framed in a fringe of straggly brown hair sailor fashion, seemed out of focus, as though seen in a crooked mirror; his smile uncovered decayed teeth and implied that he knew something nobody else even suspected.

Arens,* who had succeeded Rothstein as head of the Press De-

* Later Soviet Consul-General in New York.

partment, was concentrating on a bearded and spatted gentleman from England. The fresh arrival always gets most attention, U.P. thought; late bird gets the worm, the matter phrased itself in his mind. Arens was more shifty than his predecessor, but more energetic; there was a distinct aura of secret service about his personality and many rumors afloat to confirm it.

"We don't hide our difficulties and mistakes," Arens smiled, and the Englishman smiled back. When the censor's throaty voice emerged again it was pooh-poohing the censorship: "Our function is merely to help the correspondents, to prevent them from making mistakes. No trouble sending facts and figures, but we must draw the line on lies and exaggerations." The Englishman nodded his beard; he understood.

I.N.S. nudged U.P. and indicated with his head toward the farther corner, where censor Podolsky was signing a dispatch for A.P. Now *that* was really disquieting. Lucky dog, getting all the Tass stuff exclusively. A.P. sauntered by, shying away from the accusing eyes of his competitors.

"Something hot?" I.N.S. called after him.

"Oh, no, just routine," A.P. said, with a wink.

They didn't like his manner; cat that ate the canary. Their evening was definitely spoiled. What if it *were* a really important story—somebody dead, or something with an American angle? Separately they cornered the censors and tried to pry a hint out of their bored smiles. Well, maybe there would be a communiqué tonight, Arens admitted. Small consolation that, with A.P. already filed and finished.

U.P. was joined by the sole Austrian correspondent, who whispered that he had something interesting to confide. The Austrian liked to catch the Soviet statisticians in lies, and, though scared to death of expulsion, could not resist the temptation of reporting it. He was always on the verge of being thrown out of Russia but managed to retract the offending article in the nick of time.*

Meanwhile, I.N.S. approached the German contingent. Their embassy was well informed; one might pick up a scrap of news. At the moment, however, they were only rehashing the old scandal of Paul Scheffer's expulsion. For many years the *Berliner*

* Finally it happened—Nicholas Basseches, of the Vienna *Neue Freie Presse*, was expelled in June, 1937.

Tageblatt correspondent had been Moscow's favorite: a man who could take the "long view." But with the advent of the Stalin era his view had become much too long and the last time he was out for a vacation he was refused a re-entry visit.

"Your American colleague!" *Lokal Anzeiger* twitted I.N.S. "In all the years Herr Scheffer was here he swore by him—now that he's been kicked out, he swears *at* him."

A group of Soviet novelists, invited to give the party tone and body, was devoting itself industriously to the carafes of vodka and brandy. They enjoyed the eats and drinks, but were aware of the insult implied in the invitation; honest-to-God proletarian novelists and poets were not invited for these impious contacts with infidels.

In the French room, Anna Louise Strong and Maurice Hindus were comparing notes on their most recent visits to *kolkhozes*. Hindus, as usual, had dug deep into the muds of his native village. A batch of relative newcomers was listening in, tingling with the virtuous consciousness of gathering first-hand impressions from experts. One of them was making notes unashamedly. "Do you mind repeating that?" he said every now and then. They didn't mind. "Yes," the note-maker murmured, underlining venomously, "I suspected the talk about terror in the villages was a lie; what a comfort to *know* that it's a lie."

There was something beautifully big-hearted about the way experts were willing to forgive and forget the "occasional excesses by hot-heads" before Stalin's "dizziness" article. They nursed no petty grudges.

By common impulse everybody suddenly began to depart, like children released from classroom. The faces of I.N.S. and U.P. were furrowed with worry. They had failed to find the trail of the A.P. story.

4

At eleven that night, the Foreign Office summoned them. Accompanied by interpreters and carrying portable typewriters, correspondents gathered in the narrow ante-chambers of the censors' offices, and after half an hour's waiting received smudged mimeographed sheets. It turned out to be only a speech by Mikhail

Tomsky, the former head of the trade unions, delivered last week in Tiflis in praise of the "monolithic Party" under the genius of Stalin's leadership.

U.P. and I.N.S. were disgusted. Seven hours of waiting and worry—for that! The story had its points, if one were permitted to write a long "think piece" about it. The speech meant that Tomsky, a Right Oppositionist, was giving up the fight, recognizing Stalin's overlordship. It meant that the forthcoming Congress, the first since the one in 1927 which expelled Trotsky, Zinoviev, Kamenev, and their followers, would be a cut-and-dried affair. But who in America understood or cared? The paragraph of news that might be pressed out of it had already been pre-empted by A.P.

Nevertheless U.P. typed wearily:

tomsky oppositionist leader again recanted political errors speech tiflis yesterweek publicked today wellinformeds consider significant marking collapse antistalin opposition reliquidation kulaks tomsky said quote monolithic party under leadership genius stalin best disciple lenin always right stop right opposition left deviationists tools kulaks kulak agents unquote

He glanced toward New York *Times*. "No quota," he thought enviously, "always writing reams of stuff. How can one compete with that? I suppose he's doing another editorial on collectivization."

As a matter of fact New York *Times* at this moment was on his second page:

. . . And so again Stalin is getting away with it, because when all is said and done he represents the ruthless Asiatic spirit so suitable to this backward population accustomed to Asiatic autocracy stop as your correspondent clearly foresaw and reported fortnight ago right opposition is knuckling under which cinches scheduled communist congress for stalin stop mind you your correspondent holds no brief for shall we say unusual methods used to liquidate betteroff peasant but like stalin he recognizes this is war dash class war stop your correspondent has been convinced by ten years intimate study of soviet situation that you cant make omelettes without breaking eggs.

The egg-and-omelette theory, dashed off nonchalantly one midnight, was destined to achieve a sort of immortality. It told exactly nothing about Russia, since eggs were being smashed for omelettes in a lot of other countries. But it told a lot, apparently, about a type of reporting. At any rate, whenever anyone thereafter wished to imply a tongue-in-cheek reporter playing the game of those in power, he referred to the immortal omelette. Sinclair Lewis in *It Can't Happen Here* has a complacent foreign correspondent who takes the long view on an egg-and-omelette basis. Malcolm Muggeridge, a vitriolic English journalist, wrote a book called *Winter in Moscow* in which he pinned down a lot of Soviet specimens with cruel accuracy. The egg-and-omelette line was the identifying tag on the correspondent whom he called Jefferson.

His puny dispatch signed and sealed, U.P. carried it to the Telegraph Building, a good mile's walk. I.N.S. and a few others had gotten there first—every minute counts—and their messages lay neatly piled up. The U.P. dispatch, being the last to arrive, was on top of the pile and would therefore be cabled first when the clerks got around to it.

He went to sleep in a sour mood. In his dreams he saw a huge bowl; Arens and Stalin and the bearded Englishman in spats shoveling in kulaks, Tomskys, foreign reporters; all of them working on power from Dnieprostroi; great yellow omelettes, each signed and sealed by the censors, were coming off a belt and a lot of Americans with the New York *Times* tucked under their chins were eating greedily.

An insistent bell roused him out of his sleep. It was a messenger with a cable from London: "ASSPRESS REPORTS TOMSKY SURRENDERED HOW." By this time London had his dispatch—no need answering. Damn Tass! And damn the telegraph service here! He worked off a little of his temper in a sarcastic note to the Commissariat of Posts and Telegraphs. "It takes ten minutes," he wrote in part, "for a cable to reach from London to Moscow, and then ten hours for it to travel the two blocks from the Telegraph Building to Petrovsky Pereulok. Now I ask you, comrades, is that the way to overtake and outdistance capitalism?" He had written such notes before.

Several weeks later, a letter came from the Commissariat of Posts and Telegraphs:

Citizen: Your complaint has been investigated by a Special Voluntary Brigade for the Investigation of Complaints and the messenger responsible for the delay of your message number 7846-a has been reprimanded and removed from his post.

U.P. sighed and reproached himself. Now I, too, he thought, have broken an egg for the *Times* omelette. The cables, of course, continued to be delivered from ten to twenty hours late.

VII. Revolt Against Intelligence

PEOPLE under dictatorships, it has been well said, are condemned to a lifetime of enthusiasm. It is a wearing sentence. Gladly they would burrow into the heart of their misery and lick their wounds in private. But they dare not; sulking is next-door to treason. Like soldiers weary unto death after a long march, they must line up smartly for parade.

Obediently, Moscow's working population turned out once again in mass demonstration, a million strong, converging upon the Big Theater from factories and offices throughout the city. The occasion was the opening of the Sixteenth Congress of the Communist Party, in the summer of 1930. The demonstration was not for the Congress but for the demonstrators. It was a disciplinary ritual. Workers who trudged five or ten miles under the weight of a banner must be deeply impressed with the might and significance of the gathering in whose name it was ordered.

In the months preceding the Congress, foreign reporters had inflated its importance in order to create news. We blew our own speculations into the empty bladder of another commandeered meeting of meek bureaucrats until it bellied with synthetic significance. Formally this was the highest organ of authority in the ruling Party and all previous meetings had been tense with genuine controversy. Here Lenin had frequently fought for his policies; here Trotsky had gone down fighting furiously at the last gathering three years ago. Would Stalin's audacious course in agriculture and in industry be criticized? Would the grousing leaders of the Right—Rykov, Tomsky, Bukharin,* Uglanov,* Lenin's widow—lash out at last as Trotsky had lashed out at the 1927 Congress?

Earnest discussion of such questions made "copy" in a dull season. With the mien of sideshow fortune-tellers, we read the politi-

* Imprisoned in 1937.

cal horoscope and prophesied victory for Stalin. It was a safe prophecy. Even the possibility of criticism directed against him was by this time unthinkable. In the past, there had been real discussion in communist cells before a Congress; now there was only desperate competition in panegyrics for Stalin and his appointed lieutenants, congealed in boring resolutions of fealty. A wayward thought, though whispered in private, reached the sharp ears of the police and meant expulsion from membership or worse. The G.P.U. had become custodian of the Party's mind and conscience.

And the Congress unwound according to schedule: fighting unity, forged in the white heat of honest controversy, had been replaced by petrified unanimity. On the opening day, the stolid Caucasian visage of Stalin covered almost the entire front page of *Pravda*, with a tiny insert of Lenin in the corner to attest the direct succession. Monotonous praise rattled in the editorial columns, on the radio, in machine-made resolutions; no one ventured to deviate from the set phraseology of self-abasement, the orthodox litany of "Hail Stalins" prescribed for the faithful. Delegations from factories, institutions, army sectors, foreign communist organizations, passed one after the other across the floodlit stage of the opera-house, stammered their greetings and disappeared.

Stalin spoke for seven hours, a record even in Russia. The speech was published in full and we studied it painstakingly for pegs on which to hang dispatches. Whatever I may have thought about the cumulative cruelties of his regime, I could not but feel an awed respect for the sharp, single-minded, unfeeling certainty of this man's attitude. Nowhere in it was there so much as a tremor of fellow-feeling for the millions uprooted and dispersed, for the battalions in forced labor camps, for a population staggering under burdens and weakened by deprivations. Not even glowing hatreds. Stalin was a calm engineer building a new world within the frame of the old, diverting great rivers of national history, blasting out millionfold classes, bridging centuries of backwardness, leveling mountains of opposition. Listening to his formulas and statistics, I had the sense that he was working with earth, stone, and water rather than flesh and blood; describing the tensile strengths of steel, the resistance of granite rather than the tensions of human hearts and the stubbornness of human minds.

Nothing his enemies can say of Stalin—not even the toadying of his petty worshippers—can detract from the essential greatness of the man. He belongs in the succession of monstrous genius with Caesar and Hernando Cortes, Peter the Great and Napoleon, the genius that is too often an affliction upon mankind.

The shattered lives implicit in his statistics were so much debris which, like a good engineer, he was using to fill swamps and fortify weak spots in the structure. Stalin felt no need to explain or apologize. The expansion of the lumber industry in the Northern forests, the emergence of new industries in waste-lands based on kulak and other involuntary labor, were justification enough. When he finished his seven-hour report, nothing remained for the rest to do, except shout "Amen!"

Only when he paused to attack the weak-kneed humanists and deviators, the creatures tangled in mortal hesitancies and squeamishness, did Stalin break through his calm. But he would not pay them the compliment of flaming anger, covering them instead with derision and humiliation. He reduced all their principles and decencies to the muddy level of cowardice. He jeered at them:

> Should the slightest hardship appear, they are already worried that something may happen. Let a cockroach stir somewhere, even before it has managed to crawl out of its hole, and already they rush back, become frightened and begin to yell about a catastrophe, about the destruction of the Soviet power. (General laughter.) We quiet them and try to convince them that there is nothing menacing, that it is only a cockroach, which they need not fear. But nothing doing! They yell their "Who says cockroach? It is not a cockroach but a thousand wild animals. It is not a cockroach but destruction of the Soviets."

The Congress rocked with laughter. The waves of hilarity washed Rykov and Tomsky onto the rostrum. (Bukharin was saved from appearing by a merciful illness.) Rykov, short, stocky, with the smoldering eyes and ascetic face of a fanatic, had succeeded Lenin as chairman of the Council of People's Commissars. All his life he had fought for the Bolshevik cause, but never before had he been called a coward scared by cockroaches. For a moment, perhaps, he considered the need to strike back, to die defending himself. Then he looked into the sea of taunting faces, felt the sting of the laughter, and gave up. Meekly, he recited his rehearsed speech of contrition. He was not an enemy of the revolution, he pleaded weakly, but had allowed himself blindly to become the mouthpiece and instrument of enemies. The audience jeered; not enough! The penitence did not ring true! The old warrior lifted his shaggy head for once with a defiant gesture.

"It is not an easy thing," he threw at them, "to make a speech such as I am making!"

Then his defiance fizzled. He gave the delegates a full measure of his humiliation.

He was followed by Mikhail Tomsky, whose principal fault was that he had sought to make the trade unions a genuine bulwark against impersonal exploitation by the state; he was a small, hunched man, intense, the type almost of the underground revolutionary. He, too, went through the gestures of recantation.

Their only consolation was that no one in his senses believed their penitence. Like the demonstration and the resolutions and the laughter, it was a ritual prescribed by the priesthood: a sacrament of public confession.

A high point in the proceedings was provided by the arrival and presentation of a shiny new tractor, the gift of the recently completed Stalingrad Tractor Plant. It was described as "the first tractor to come off the belt." Everyone knew that the belt was not yet moving, would not move for weeks, and that this gift had been carefully hand-tooled under American technical supervision. But that, too, did not matter—another act in the ceremonial. A cockroach as symbol of the opposition, a tractor as symbol of Stalin.

2

Rykov for the time being was allowed to remain in the Politburo. Tomsky and Bukharin were removed. Three new members were designated: Kaganovich, Kirov,* and Kossior. The Politburo was further purged of its Leninist heritage. Tough-skinned, ruthless drill-sergeants from the ranks of the proletariat had displaced the argumentative intellectuals.

It was no accident that all three of the new members were self-taught, men who had never been abroad or tasted Western civilization. Even Lazar Kaganovich, now the only Jew in the

* Assassinated in 1934.

Politburo, the only orator in the uppermost circle of leaders and the only one with a genuine flair for theoretical polemics, despised intellectuals. Unlike Trotsky, Kamenev, Zinoviev, Radek, Litvinov, and other Jews among revolutionary leaders, he knew nothing of the émigré revolutionist's romantic career, and had never received a formal education. He had risen from the dregs of the poverty-stricken Jewish community in Gomel, fashioned his hatreds into a stout ladder for his ambitions, and now stood firmly planted at the right hand of Stalin. Kossior and Kirov were blunt, hard-working, disciplined officers in a machine of power, lesser Stalins in their respective principalities: Kossior in the Ukraine, Kirov in the Leningrad area. They cared nothing for speech-making and nothing for argument. Their strength lay in obedient action, decrees, midnight arrests.

To understand the new Russia, Stalin's Russia, one must gauge the immense differences between the Politburo headed by Lenin and the one into which Kaganovich, Kossior and Kirov were inducted. Only Stalin and Kalinin remained as links between the General Staffs of 1920 and 1930: the two men who had seemed most out of place in the scintillating company around Lenin. Kalinin's was a peasant shrewdness that had nothing in common with the intellectuality of a Zinoviev or a Lunacharsky. Stalin's taciturn, patient efficiency had nothing in common with the brilliant inspirations of a Trotsky or Lenin.

By education, experience, and interests the group around Lenin had been cosmopolitan and internationalist; it was brilliant and cultured, at home in Europe and European languages; and it was middle-class in its origins. Stalin's Politburo, though it contained two Georgians, a Lett, and a Jew, was earthy, Russian through and through, aware of the West only as something hostile and treacherous. Only one of its members (Molotov, who soon took Rykov's place) was not clearly proletarian by birth and upbringing.

Whatever hopes and slogans of internationalism it may have inherited, the Stalin regime was profoundly nationalistic. The internationalism to which it aspired was a world state under Russian dominion, which is something totally different from the super-nation which Lenin and Trotsky envisioned. Stalin's world would always have the Moscow Kremlin as its center, even as

Paris was Napoleon's center; but Lenin's might just as easily have been London or Shanghai.

I do not mean that Stalin's regime was as yet consciously nationalistic, as Mussolini's or Pilsudski's were. It was utterly Russian, rather, in the very fiber of its psychological make-up, its thinking, and its acting, its natural renunciation of the standards and prejudices of Europe. Stalin's was the Russia under the thin veneer of Westernism deposited by the centuries since Peter first brought in Dutchmen to build ships for him. It was, indeed, most Russian where it pretended to be European and American, in the adaptation of socialism imported from Germany and France, in the adaptation of industrialism imported from England and America.

3

Vladimir Khenkin, a popular comic actor, had a sure-fire "gag." It meant nothing to the uninitiated, but it convulsed Russian audiences with laughter. There were those in the audiences who winced and only pretended to laugh.

"One night," he said with a straight face, in the course of his famous monologue, "I heard a vigorous knock at my door. *So I took my little suitcase and went to open the door.*"

He paused for the guffaws and they always came. The reference was to the simple fact (incredible to anyone outside of Russia) that professional men, engineers, technicians, and other pre-revolutionary intellectuals usually had a few things packed in readiness for the emergency of a sudden arrest. Any night "the wagon" might arrive, and it was the part of foresight to have an extra change of underwear, a little dried bread, a few other things that might lighten the burden of imprisonment, always on hand. The possession of such a suitcase was certainly not a token of guilty conscience, except the guilt of being alive, prematurely literate, and belonging to the wrong category of human beings.

Most of the educated classes were guilty, indeed, of a deep and incurable crime, namely, skepticism. For the most part, they regarded the Kremlin's efforts as fantastic, its "tempos" of industrialization foolhardy and doomed to failure, the human cost of the whole enterprise barbarous. The vague charge of "sabotage" under which so many thousands of them were rounded up, tortured, exiled, and executed amounted, when sifted down to essentials, to just that ingrained doubt complicated by discontent over physical privations and mental reservations.

One need not be guilty of an overt act to have his house searched, himself stuck away in a foul cell, his family terrorized. An anonymous denunciation by someone who coveted his room or his job might do it, or the fact that he had been seen playing chess with someone else who was denounced. Perhaps his name was listed in the address book of a suspected person, or a second cousin by marriage, in the course of interrogation, had mentioned the relationship. Worst of all, the German machines he had helped buy or install, after being manhandled by peasants accustomed only to managing wooden plows, had broken down mysteriously.

Those who remember the war-time atmosphere, in which everyone detected spies in his neighbors and the intelligence divisions in all countries were deluged with denunciations, can appreciate the ordeal of the technical and managerial forces in the Russia of the *Piatiletka*. The engineer or administrator was the obvious scapegoat for promises that could not be kept, for plans that went askew. He was punished for "underestimating (or overestimating) the possibilities" of his particular enterprise, for risking (or shirking) a crucial technical decision.

The G.P.U. agent, reckoning his usefulness by the number of "confessions" he extracted, was hardly fitted to trace the tenuous borderline where inefficiency or sheer carelessness ended and sabotage began. The arrested intellectual himself was no longer able to locate that border-line after being held incommunicado for months, aware that his relatives were in danger, confronted with "confessions" by colleagues implicating him, and conscious also of his deeper inner disapproval of the Bolshevik ideology. One can understand how men signed "confessions" filled with impossible detail. The hysteria sucked accusers and accused alike into the maelstrom of its lunacy.

I knew dozens of men and women who lived in a state of chronic terror, their little suitcases always packed, though they worked diligently and avoided even facial expressions which might cast doubt on their loyalty. To awaken in their own beds in the morning was a daily miracle for such people. The sound of a doorbell at an unusual hour left them limp and trembling.

The roster of scientists, historians, Academicians, famous engineers, technical administrators, statisticians arrested at this time reads like an encyclopaedia of contemporary Russian culture. Many of them were held for months, for years, without so much as discovering the mysterious crimes charged against them. In addition to almost unlimited raw labor, the G.P.U. now had an unlimited supply of technical brains at its disposal.

The revolt against intelligence, signalized in the new personnel of the Politburo, held true in the whole life of the U.S.S.R. Distrust of the educated man or woman was magnified endlessly by the disappointments, the despairs, the bitterness of a hundred and sixty million individuals.

VIII. Forty-eight Ghosts

IN SEPTEMBER the government, through Intourist, took thirty-odd foreign journalists on a grand swing of European Russia: by train to Nijni-Novgorod, down the Volga by boat as far as Stalingrad, then on land again through the Rostov area, the Caucasus and Crimea; or rather, this being the Soviet Union in the throes of socialization, a tour of factories, construction sites, state farms, sanatoria, and other social-economic scenery disposed on that route.

It was an investment in international good will. Rivers of favorable publicity for Russia as a tourist paradise were to flow from this journey. That summer's tourist flood, the largest as yet in Soviet history, had left a considerable sediment of glittering *valuta* —the possibilities of cashing in on world-wide curiosity suddenly bulked large in the Soviet imagination.

An Intourist official of important rank, a Comrade Kutuzov, was in command of the expedition. Subsequently, he went the way of most Intourist functionaries: to prison and exile. A job with that organization, if not a certain, was by all odds the swiftest road to counterrevolutionary perdition. Since it involved daily contact with foreigners, European clothes and ideas, foreign currency, Intourist bristled with temptations and crawled with bourgeois contagions—only the purest of heart and most adroit of mind survived that test. But that was in the darkling future; for the present Comrade Kutuzov and his pretty blonde wife were in charge and enjoying the responsibility. We had our very own commissary chief, a charming Georgian whose long name was boiled down to "Gogo"; he not merely fed us in the weeks of this tour but stuffed us unmercifully.

Besides resident correspondents, our company counted a most cosmopolitan assortment of writers come especially for this trip. The Italians, being a melodramatic folk, came dressed like mountain climbers and laden with cameras, binoculars, first-aid kits, and other paraphernalia—just fascist distrust of dictatorships, I suppose. The most earnest member of our party was an undersized and taciturn Frenchman who was forever taking notes; once I found him gazing at the scenery and jotting things down, apparently interviewing the clouds. Germany's contribution was a blond, lusty, good-looking fellow who did more than Intourist to make the junket memorable for the ladies in our company.

As always, the American delegation was largest. A red-headed and bellicose young man, Bob Allen, short and compact, brightened the journey for us; Bob was still with the *Christian Science Monitor,* which was to fire him next year for his share in a most unmannerly book called *Washington Merry-Go-Round.* Albert Rhys Williams was along; one of the small band of Americans which witnessed the Bolshevik revolution and championed it ardently in its first romantic years, he now sought, with a determined and melancholy mien, for traces of the dream and blew conscientiously upon the embers of his ardor. And Charles Malamuth, a large, near-sighted young man with a gaudy taste in socks and shirts to balance his academic mind and training.

Charlie had been a thorn in the side of the Slavic Department of the University of California because of his outspoken Soviet sympathies, and now, after a month or so on Soviet soil, was in a panic of bewilderment as his communist preconceptions fell to pieces in the harsh contact with reality. He was a good deal like a man who has hoarded a fortune in banknotes, defended it with his life, and suddenly learns that the banknotes are mostly counterfeit.

Despite a few congenital skeptics and disillusioned communists, however, the tour seemed a sensible publicity investment for Intourist. The majority of the journalists were seeing the interior of Russia for the first time. Their notebooks soon brimmed with fine statistics. The Russians in the party were decent likeable people, whose warm hospitality should be repaid in the coin of enthusiastic travel stories.

That the investment in the end went wrong, that the propaganda purposes of the whole tour were knocked into a cocked hat, was no fault of Comrade Kutuzov or "Gogo" or Intourist. Larger forces were at work, unaware of the thirty-odd junketeers making notes on the Volga and interviewing the clouds, but destined to wrench their tour out of its nicely-greased groove and scatter the statistics like so much chaff in the wind.

2

Nijni-Novgorod, older than Moscow and once more coveted, seemed to have slumped to a drab provincial city of ragged crowds, muddy streets, crumbling houses and impoverished or boarded-up shop windows. We stood on the city's Kremlin hill, looking down on a panorama spread below us like a relief map. In the foreground the Kremlin wall underscored with zigzag strokes a portion of the crowded lower city. From the huddled rooftops rose a cluster of pear-shaped blue domes; a ribbon of roadway showed here and there: all of it like the engravings one runs across in old Russian books. Beyond that, a flat country, with the Volga (at this point just a timid stream) winding through it, and branching from the Volga, the river Oka. Leaden clouds pressed down on the distant horizons.

The young communist newspaperman who volunteered to show me his city saw neither the fifteenth century engravings nor the flatness beyond. For him it was only the physical foundation for the city-to-be. He knew by rote the budget figures for industrial projects under way which must make Nijni-Novgorod, he assured me, a great metropolis—the prosperous northern terminal of the 13,000-kilometer Volga.

In the center of the ancient Kremlin, a new House of Soviets was going up: an angular, barrack-like structure, more like a warehouse than a municipal palace. It seemed a blasphemy upon the time-soaked Kremlin walls and I hinted as much to my enthusiastic guide.

"We are tired of picturesque backwardness," he said without smiling. "We want comfortable standardized prosperity, just like you Americans have. Over there, where the Oka and the Volga meet, we shall have our Russian Detroit."

The *Karl Liebknecht*, which started its career on the Volga as the *King Albert*, was a broad-beamed comfortable ship. As it slid smoothly down the glassy surface of the river, from Kazan toward Samara, we listened to a concert recruited from the local populations for our entertainment. More convincingly than any map or statistical chart, that concert epitomized for us the astonishing diversity of races settled in this region, and the persistence with which they cling to their racial intonations.

Nearly four centuries have elapsed since Ivan the Terrible conquered the heart of Tartary, yet the music we heard from the lips of a lovely young singer from the Kazan opera-house had not a suggestion of Russian in it. The same was true of the other folk music. A dark-haired Bashkir boy, with such old, old eyes, blew through a home-made reed instrument mournful tunes which had more in them of Mongolia than anything this side of the Urals. A Chuvash girl sang shrill songs careering through two full octaves, with something in them of the cries of untamed desert animals. Then a Tartar peasant accompanied himself on an accordion in songs which reminded us how recent after all is the release of these people from chattel slavery; it helped one comprehend the fierce opposition to giving up their new-found dignity as private owners of a strip of land, no matter how narrow and barren.

In this region we felt how un-Russian is much of Russia. Kazan is the capital of Red Tartary, the Tartar Soviet Socialist Republic, checkered with the autonomous territories of other racial groups. An area about as large as Germany, which in Russia is only a crumb of land, contains half a dozen racial areas, sundered not alone from the Russians but from one another: Tartars, Chuvashes, Cheremissians, Votiaks, etc. Broaden the limits somewhat and they take in the Volga Germans around Samara, the dispersed Mordvians, the Kalmuks near the mouth of the Volga, as well as colonies of Jews, Ukrainians, the first outposts of the Central Asiatic peoples.

A representative of the Kazan University, Professor Nossa-Baer Verslin, talked to us of the past and particularly the projected glories of Red Tartary. His university numbers among its alumni Lenin, Lenin's brother Alexander, Rykov, Count Leo Tolstoy, and is proud of its traditions. That pride was in Professor Verslin's voice as he boasted of what "we Tartars" have done and what "we Tartars" planned to do. Through a window, while he unfolded his vision of an industrialized Tartary, I watched a batch of men straining against the ropes which harnessed them to a heavily-laden barge. They threw their weight forward until they were nearly level with the mud, tugging, tugging, like overworked mules. These were the men who inspired the Volga Boatman's Song made famous throughout the world by Chaliapin; but they were not singing, only tugging, straining. . . . This glimpse of the present injected a curiously dramatic counterpoint into the professor's recital of the mechanized future.

When Professor Verslin concluded, Charlie Malamuth and I cornered him for a private question. The Hebraic Nossa-Baer of his name coupled with the emphasis on "we Tartars" had intrigued our interest.

"What sort of a Tartar are you?" we asked him.

"I?" he laughed, "why, I am a Tartar from Dvinsk, in the former Jewish pale."

Jews were formerly barred from Kazan University; now its official representative was a Jew.

In the office of the Stalingrad Construction Trust, a mild-mannered, bespectacled young man named Midson S. Khvesin told us in the most matter-of-fact fashion that he was directing the investment of some 900 million rubles to build up the city and its environs. In the capitalist world he would be classed as a captain of industry. Khvesin was a barber by profession, he told us when we pressed him for personal information. In the civil wars, he had won the Order of the Red Flag which he wore on his semi-military olive-drab jacket, and now he was in the front trenches of the industrial battle—it was as simple as that.

"But the civil war," he smiled, "was easy compared to what we are up against now. All we had to do then was to fight and die."

The dream which was framed in blueprints and architectural sketches on his office walls and which he explained so patiently seemed the more startling when we were back on the rutted weary streets, so hot and dusty and torpid, amidst decayed houses; then out in the barren, uninviting suburbs, where everything looked and smelled stagnant. Eighteen kilometers out, at the famous tractor plant built under Jack Calder's direction, the dream seemed less impossible. There was, indeed, a piece of Detroit, like some monstrous accident, strayed to the frontiers of Asia.

From the large contingent of American engineers and technicians still at work in this plant we heard the usual tales of insufficient food, over-crowded housing, and Russian ineptness with machinery. But for all the difficulties, the plant was getting into stride and the workers, though fresh from the farms, were learning their jobs. Most of these were young people, mere boys and girls; they seemed to us alert, good-humored, and curiously conscious of their role as industrial pioneers.

National fame had come to a clapboard wayside railroad station, oddly named Verblyud—Russian for camel—to which we traveled from Stalingrad. It was the center of an immense state farm (*sovkhoz*), or government "bread factory," as the communists liked to call it.

There were no humps on this Camel. Its nearly 300,000 flat acres rolled to the horizons all around and the impatient eye detected mirages on the edges of this monotonous disk. Its directors used airplanes to get around the place. But one of the seeming mirages revealed itself as an administrative center; a collection of two- and three-story houses, set in correct rows like an American real estate development. Though not the largest of the "bread factories"—the neighboring "Gigant" was more than twice as large—the Camel had become the showplace of Soviet agriculture, trudged over by an endless stream of native and foreign tourists.

The chief reason for this was the energetic, thirty-five-year-old Comrade L. S. Margolin, slight in build, his thin features lit up by a boyish smile that was almost shy. Comrade Margolin answered our eager questions about yield per acre, wages, living conditions.

Around the bend of a fine new road came a cart drawn by oxen, a family of peasants lounging on dirty straw. They stared open-mouthed at the strange array of monsters on the field: the tractors, drillers, combines which had arrived to disturb their thousand-year-old sleep.

We arrived at Rostov, capital of North Caucasus, in the haze of evening when outlines are charitably blurred. Viewed from the balcony of Grand Hotel, the main street might have been in some well-kept German city rather than the heart of the Don district. But the unkind light of the next day ripped the veil from the face of Rostov to show the pockmarks of poverty. Reputed to have been among the finest cities in the Russian empire, it was now tragically out of repair, its windows dusty and neglected, house fronts crumbling, a sadly derelict look about the crowds and the queues.

That morning we walked many weary miles over the grounds of the newly-built "Selmashstroi," probably the world's largest plant making farm implements. And in the afternoon we sat around a red-draped conference table with the Presidium of the Central Executive Committee of Northern Caucasus: sharp-edged, determined men, with heaps of official papers in front of them. Concisely, without beating around the bush, they replied to questions, countering every reference to immediate shortages and hardship with a citation of accomplishments and plans. Their businesslike certainties left no room for sentiment or doubt. They were a military general staff engaged in a major maneuver and had already discounted the cost in men.

Towards twilight, Albert Rhys Williams, Bob Allen, and I were strolling through side-streets, and suddenly the chiming of church bells came through the haze; the first church bells that I had heard for a year. We followed the sound to the beautiful Rostov Cathedral whose great thistle-like blue domes dominate Rostov's skyline. This happened to be a holy day dear to the Orthodox believers, the Elevation of the Cross, celebrated by one of the most impressive of the Orthodox services. The gold and purple vestments, the full-voiced choir, thousands of lighted tapers, the long-haired priests moving majestically amidst the sacred trappings, some three thousand men, women, and children crowding the cathedral to its doors—an extraordinary contrast it was to Selmashstroi and the embattled Presidium, remnants of an old world surviving, pretending to be still alive, within the new.

Even the faces of the worshippers seemed different from those we had seen in factories, offices, on the state farm. They were amazingly like characters out of old plays on the stage of the Moscow Art Theater, or out of those paintings of pre-war life one sees in the museums. In the vestibule, we observed a line of old monks, white-haired, patriarchal figures all of them, their black cowls ragged and their faces touched with pain. They held wicker baskets into which worshippers placed eggs, pieces of bread, other gifts.

On inquiring, we were told that these monks had just been dispossessed from their monastery and had been allowed to live in the cathedral, subsisting on charity.

Rhys Williams was deeply touched by their plight. His earnest face furrowed with sorrow and he stooped a little more than usual, as though feeling the yoke of these ancient men's fate. I recalled that he had once been a minister. Inside, the entry of the foreigners caused a slight localized flurry of interest. "You see," a man whispered in my ear, "we still pray to the Lord despite *them!*"

An old woman was selling tapers. Bob nudged me as Williams —the left wing of our company, as it were—walked over to the woman and paid a ruble for a taper; we were prepared to josh him about helping the religious counterrevolution, but there was a solemnity in his face that warned us against levity. But Rhys Williams, who had known Lenin and Trotsky and still likes to think himself a Bolshevik, was aware of our amusement. As we left the cathedral, he turned to me sharply.

"Gene," he said, "your heart is touched by the miseries of the intelligentsia, but it remains unmoved by the persecution of these monks and priests and honest believers. You're as narrow in your prejudices as any Bolshevik, only they're different prejudices. I'm not ashamed to admit that I feel the sorrows of these men of religious faith who are going through as terrible an ordeal as the intelligentsia, maybe worse."

It was somewhere between Rostov and the Caucasian mountains that those larger forces, working inscrutably behind the back of Intourist, overtook our foreign sightseers and destroyed the patterns we had been building in our minds and note-books. Everything we had seen and thought and decided suddenly lost its validity, everything had to be reconsidered in a new light. The neat little piles of figures garnered as we went along were scattered, the notes contributed by Comrades Verslin and Khvesin and Margolin were canceled and their professions must be re-appraised.

What happened was that forty-eight corpses, not invited by Intourist, joined our tour. They remained with us and their shadow is on the books and the articles that came of this journey. In every factory and sanatorium we visited, the ghostly forty-eight were by our side, insisting on being heard; and behind them were thousands of other ghosts conjured from the void by the shock of a wholesale official murder.

On September 22, the press announced that the G.P.U. had uncovered a "counter-revolutionary society" headed by Professor Alexander Riazantsev of the meat industry, to undermine the country's food supply. Forty-eight professors, agronomists, and administrators in the food trusts were under arrest charged with sabotage.

The next day the press was noisy with editorials and resolutions "demanding" the highest measure of social defense, death by shooting, for the villains. These synthetic demands had only the unsupported word of the G.P.U. to go upon, except the towering fact that the nation's food supplies were indeed depleted, rotted, hopelessly inadequate, and confused.

And on September 24, two days after the "plot" had been announced, the forty-eight were shot. Their names were neatly listed in the newspapers, many of them names familiar to readers of Russian scientific and technical publications.

This mass execution, though unscheduled, became the chief event of the grand tour. The rest of the journey unrolled under a cloud, the Russians self-consciously aloof from the arguments that now swept through the company, the "lefts" among the foreigners a little hysterical in defending the slaughter. Everyone was upset—half-apprehended terrors and despairs were suddenly focused in the killing of the forty-eight, as in a sacrificial rite. The rivers of publicity that must flow from the Intourist investment in international good-will would, unavoidably, be tinged with blood.

The government now published excerpts from the alleged confessions of the forty-eight: confessions extracted during months of secret interrogation followed by a secret trial and secret shootings, published after the professors and administrators were dead and buried. Buried? Years later, though there had been many other mass executions, the ghosts of these forty-eight still haunted the nation.

3

The tour to that point had drawn me back into an older, more comfortable attitude. I was leaning back once again on the price-paid-for-the-future theory of suffering and terror, in a desperate attempt to adjust my old faith to the new experiences. At every important stop on the route, I had dashed off an article and sent it on to Nathalie, my secretary, in Moscow for transmission abroad. Those articles adhered to the placating arithmetical formula—distress on one side of the ledger and the planned future on the other, with the balance in the Kremlin's favor. Against the muddy squalor of Nijni-Novgorod, the "Ford" factory; against the barren despair of Stalingrad, the tractor factory; against the liquidation of the kulaks, the triumphs of Comrade Margolin's state farm. These articles, practically unedited, were published as a series in the *Moscow News*, which is proof enough that they were a successful effort to whip my conscience into line.

With the shooting of the forty-eight, I was hurled back abruptly to the point where the horrors of liquidation at the beginning of the year had left me. I felt again that something barbarous, ugly, and inhuman had been mixed into the socialist dream.

"Now the Kremlin," I said in the course of an argument, "has acted to solve the meat shortage by slaughtering forty-eight professors."

This gory saying was duly reported and deposited against me in my *dossier*. It became the keynote of some of the travel stories written by the government's guests. Forty-eight deaths more or less were in themselves of small consequence: that the socialist hope was in the keeping of people capable of inflicting those deaths, boasting of them as a proof of their "Leninist firmness," surrounding the blood sacrifice with a hocus-pocus of jejune lies, posthumous confessions, and elaborate stupidities, seemed to me the crux of the tragedy.

We went to one of the meetings (hundreds of them were reported in the papers day after day) in which "the proletariat fervently thanked the glorious G.P.U., the unsheathed sword of the revolution, for its splendid work in liquidating this dastardly plot." We saw no fervor, but only lukewarm routine applause for lukewarm routine speeches and routine acceptance of another resolution prepared in advance by the steering committee. No one, least of all the speakers, believed that this audience approved the wholesale killings. Even Russians, inured to such things, shuddered at this deed.

Only one correspondent among all those who reported Soviet news regularly for the outside world took the executions nonchalantly in his stride. "To your correspondent," the New York *Times* man wrote, "the most surprising thing is that the punishment was so long delayed. . . . With due allowance for the ignorance and inefficiency and for the difficulty of organizing state or municipal distribution in a backward country, it is hard to believe there was no sinister intent behind such appalling waste. Anyway, the Soviet public believed there was and clamored for stern justice."

That clamor was only in his imagination, of course, and a clamor for stern justice for dead men based on posthumous statements—statements, moreover, which sounded strangely alike, as though dictated by one mind—is in itself fantastic enough. The "sinister intent" must have continued after the minds where it existed had been consigned to the worms, because the "appalling waste" grew ever more appalling.

There was a saying in the old days which ran, "Russia is big and the tsar is far away." That saying was paraphrased for me in Tiflis, the lively Caucasian capital, when I commented on the softer, less hysterical mood in the city: "The U.S.S.R. is big and Stalin is far away." The fact that Stalin is himself a Georgian surrounded by other Georgians only added spice to the remark.

The woes that afflicted the rest of the country were sufficiently in evidence here too, but Tiflis would not let itself be depressed by lack of food and goods and personal safety. The difference is really one of climate and scenery. Here we were in the South, in a South made wondrous by the Caucasian mountains and valleys and the pounding Black Sea. Soviet Georgia is a Switzerland and Italy rolled into one, a Switzerland on the Mediterranean as it were.

The city fathers of Tiflis greeted the group of visiting journalists with a party such as would be almost impossible in Moscow. Hospitality is a virtue of which the Georgians are especially proud. The hosts set a pace in drinking which even parched Americans found it hard to follow. Dignified officials threw themselves into wild Caucasian dances, and they even aided and abetted the foreigners in dancing the infidel fox-trots.

An American journalist rose to express the appreciation of our group. I confess that I framed it for him to be called upon because he was so far gone in his cups. But he rallied nobly to the call. Rising slowly to his feet and balancing himself carefully, he looked around at the friendly, smiling faces, and he was sure that he was no longer in Russia.

"We're very grateful," said he, "very grateful, and damn glad to be here. You know we had to get through Russia to get here and we're damn glad to be in a place again where people can smile and be happy. Yes, sir, damn glad!" And he collapsed.

Our communist hosts applauded and drank another toast to America. Of course, they did not understand a word he was saying, and the volunteer interpreter did not tell them.

The Caucasian and Crimean riviera provides symbols of the changes wrought by the revolution in such dramatic sharpness that one suspects a master stage director behind the scenes. Bearded peasants, the primordial loam still clotted in their pores and hair, lounge in the spacious pavilions of Livadia, the summer residence of Nicholas the Last. Dressed cleanly in the gray sanatorium nuiforms, they wander uneasily amidst the trappings of their late "Little Father." The scene seems to have been made to order—probably it was. In turning over the tsar's favorite palace to the simplest moujiks as a vacation resort, the Bolsheviks must have had an eye to the theatrical effects of their act.

Everywhere along the great stretch of natural playground, the palaces of grand dukes and millionaire merchants were being used by workers and peasants. Sallow-skinned factory girls strolled along the cypress-lined paths through gardens originally laid out for grand-ducal mistresses. They were installed (as was our party of journalists) in a gorgeous chalet brought piecemeal from Switzerland to Gagri's mountain flank by a Russian nobleman. It all begins to unfold as a grand pageant; no Stanislavsky or Reinhardt could have done anything better to summarize the fundamental fact of the revolution.

In isolated spots, we found dim reflections of past elegance. There were several vacation places reserved for the G.P.U. and higher officials: quieter, less crowded, with an air of superiority setting them off from the popular resorts. And there were the few hotels and sanatoria still open to individual visitors at relatively exorbitant prices. Here the wives of professional men, well-paid actors, and writers made a pathetic attempt to ape the French riviera. There was an element of the comic, too, in their efforts to dress up and to revive a little of the glitter associated with superior seaside vacationing.

In Yalta—where I abandoned the company for pressing work in Moscow—we lived in a meandering old hotel overlooking the harbor. Several foreign freighters were in port. Gay sun-tanned groups from the surrounding sanatoria enlivened the main streets. The echoes of accordions and laughter came to us through the balmy night air. For a moment, we seemed to be far from the privations and fears of which we had seen so much in those weeks.

Then we turned down a side-street. It was after midnight. A block or two and we came upon a straggly line stretching from a closed, dark shop. Some fifty men and women sat on boxes or on the sidewalks, several were stretched out asleep in the queue. Only the hour made this scene unusual.

"What are you waiting for?" we asked one of the women.

"How do I know?" she answered. "Maybe a herring, a bit of meat if we're lucky."

"Most likely nothing," a man near her said.

"But the shop is closed—"

"It will open at eight in the morning," the man explained. "I've been waiting since eleven tonight."

"Don't you have to work tomorrow?" I asked.

"No, it's my free day. Other nights my wife waits on line. Unless one waits all night there is not a chance of getting anything."

Not in itself a startling piece of information. But somehow the joy was no longer in the echoes of laughter and accordions. The forty-eight ghosts accompanied us to the hotel.

IX. *Rasstrel!*

OF ALL the enormities contrived in the haloed name of socialism, the most singular, perhaps, was a decree offering generous cash rewards to patriots who informed on relatives, friends, and neighbors. Nothing niggardly about the offer; 25%, a full quarter share, of all money, valuables, and other property seized by the government would go to the informer. The despised profit motive invoked for a fittingly despicable purpose! Somewhere in the Elysian fields, the shades of Marx and Lenin (if they are on speaking terms after all that has happened) had a delicate problem of dialectics to argue over.

Whether the patriot, having collected his 25% of the booty and been thereby enriched perhaps beyond the bounds of proletarian decency, was thereafter a proper subject for profitable denunciation in turn by his best friend or favorite child was not made entirely clear in the decree.

But whatever the wording of the law, it may be assumed that the government in one way or another got that quarter back. For the government was in need of capital, desperately in need, especially the kind acceptable to capitalists abroad. Even in lesser matters it had long ago thrown off the encumbrance of principles and ethical prejudices; small reason why it should not go the limit when the urgency referred to capital, money, the very protoplasmic stuff of its new economic religion.

Denunciation, night raids, searchings, hostages. The victims were chiefly disfranchised people, intellectual trash, those receiving money from relatives abroad: people, in short, upon whom neither sympathy nor bothersome legalities need be wasted. The formal pretext for seizing the remnants and scourings of wealth from the Nep period or the pre-deluge epoch was "re-taxation" on past earnings. Fearful that the culprits might hide some of their belongings, they were not notified in advance. First, the G.P.U.

swooped down on them at night and made a thorough inventory of what they owned, tearing up floor boards and rafters, ripping open pillows and mattresses in search of concealed money or jewels. Then the assessors had something to go by; the "tax" was usually a safe distance above 100% of the inventoried property. If the victim and his family were allowed to remain in their "living space," or even in the city, despite their failure to pay the full tax, they had ample cause to bless their luck.

It was an arduous undertaking, and volunteer brigades of workers demonstrated their devotion to the Five Year Plan in Four Years by assisting in the searchings. Informing on one's neighbors has ever been a source of human pleasure, and now it was also a well-paying business, almost the only enterprise for private profit countenanced by the enthroned revolution. The nightly chores of raids, searchings, and arrests grew larger all the time and the G.P.U. had need of volunteers: "light cavalry" is one of the proud names applied to the brigades by a grateful press.

Where the taxation comedy could not for some reason be played, a "voluntary contribution to the *Piatiletka*" was extracted, duly attested by a signed statement to that effect. Future research in the archives of the early 1930's will disclose stacks of these statements, a very epidemic of patriotic philanthropy, the more remarkable because the givers usually had small reason to love the government upon whom they lavished this charity. Such was the magic of the revolution, historians will find, that even its natural enemies were moved to benefactions in its favor.

The outward sign of the state hunger for capital was in inflation of the Soviet currency. Between May and October of 1930, the rubles in circulation increased by 35%. Russians referred to the paper as *sovznaki*—"Soviet signs"—to distinguish it from real values such as gold or foreign money. When cabmen demanded a *grivenyik,* literally ten kopeks, to take one from the station to the hotel, they meant ten rubles, one kopek being their contemptuous valuation of the ruble. People asked: "Which is the jolliest currency for traveling with abroad?" and the answer was: "The ruble—everybody laughs at it." Officially valued at fifty-one cents, the ruble in truth had a purchasing value of three or four cents provided there was something to purchase; but the shortage of some goods and the complete absence of others often turned the ruble into an empty symbol.

The collapse of popular faith in the currency led to an extraordinary episode late in 1930. The Soviet Union awoke one morning to find itself mysteriously short of small change; copper and silver coins were annoyingly few and in several days disappeared altogether. A little thing, it would seem, but the machinery of everyday life, already complicated and burdensome enough, was put further out of joint. Clerks in shops, conductors on street-cars, peddlers in the markets could not make change. The banks and post-offices rapidly ran dry of all coins. Beggars stood with empty cups, since no one had coins to spare. The telephone pay-stations, normally overcrowded, now stood idle.

The mystery was not mysterious after all. Millions of peasants throughout the country had decided by a common impulse—one of those inexplicable brain waves sweeping with the speed of light across seven thousand miles—to hoard silver and copper. Suddenly and almost simultaneously throughout the vast nation, the peasants lost the last shred of respect for the national currency and held on to coins for their intrinsic worth as metals. Rapidly, the whole supply was drained off into their coffers.

Municipal authorities hurriedly issued "scrip" in denominations from one to ten kopeks. Stores gave credit slips instead of cash for change. A week or two and the crisis was over.

Is it a curious intuition or a telepathic flash that moves millions of simple people continents apart to some common action, though they have no leadership, no contacts, no press? Again and again I have seen them act—or rather, react—with amazing unanimity. Thus it was in the previous winter, when peasants separated by a thousand miles met forcible collectivization in exactly the same way, by slaughtering their cows, as consistently as though they had conspired in advance. But the hoarding of coins, less important in itself, was the clearest indication of this almost psychic mass consciousness.

Police-minded officials instantly shrieked "Plot!"—a kulak plot or Trotskyist plot to destroy the Five Year Plan. Foreign reporters echoed "Plot!" because the word fits nicely into headlines and because the newspaper mind, like the police mind, thrives on melodrama. A few of us hinted darkly at "sinister" influences, precisely as one of us had done in smoothing over the forty-eight-fold execution.

Like those doctors who prescribe the same medicine for all ailments, the Kremlin was prescribing the death penalty to cure its social ailments. *Rasstrel!* How many times the word—"shooting"—crashed like thunder in open court! How many more times behind the sealed doors of military and G.P.U. courts!

Railroad accidents were growing at an alarming rate, owing primarily to the excessive load thrown on a disorganized system and inferior rolling stock; these physical faults would be corrected in the course of time, no doubt, but meanwhile—the death penalty for careless railroad workers.

More and more Soviet commercial and diplomatic agents in foreign countries hesitated to obey orders to return home, chiefly because they were afraid of the G.P.U. The result: the death penalty *in absentia* for such hesitancy.

Outlawed intellectuals, persecuted peasants, rejected communists, discontented workers in droves tried to steal across the frontier despite the heavy guards and bloodhounds. The result: the death penalty for those caught in the act.

And so the hoarding of coins, too, was now made a capital crime. A few of the guilty peasants were actually condemned to death and the verdict ostentatiously published. It is unlikely that the enforcement went much beyond that: to shoot all who were guilty of hoarding would have cost the government more metal in bullets than it could collect in coin. But the decree stood, presumably stands yet. In any event, the coins were back in circulation. Soon, the government decided that if there was to be any hoarding it would do the job itself. It withdrew all the silver coinage from circulation, putting a cheap nickel alloy in its place.

The same urgency in the matter of capital forced the Kremlin to dispose of its products in foreign markets in as large quantities as possible, often at ridiculously low prices. Soviet wheat, butter, fish, eggs, petroleum, pulpwood—most of them sorely needed at home—were poured upon the world in alarming volume. This time, it was the turn of frightened capitalist competitors in those markets to cry frantic "Plot!" and discern sinister motives. The U.S.S.R., they howled, was "dumping" goods below cost of manufacture in order to undermine capitalism and stimulate world revolution. Many governments placed hinderments to the flow of Soviet products, several announced total embargoes. Cloaking their economic fears with a belated and lop-sided humanitarianism, they now raised the issue of "forced labor." The fact that the charge was in many instances correct is neither here nor there: capitalists were no more concerned with the horrors in Soviet labor camps than with slavery in Abyssinia or chain gangs in Mississippi.

Technically, "dumping" means the sale of goods below cost of manufacture. But how could anyone figure those costs, when all labor and all products were the property of the same state which did the exporting? What was the cost of producing lumber, when the forests and the supply of exile and outright convict labor alike were almost inexhaustible? The truth is that all labor based on rations, inflated money and endless compulsions is an approximation of prison labor. There are no unemployed slaves.

The Soviet government's denials of forced labor put the finishing touches on the diverting Olympiad of hypocrisy involved in the "anti-dumping" campaign. "Prisoners everywhere work, why should not ours?" the Kremlin asked indignantly, thus evading the issue, which was why the U.S.S.R. possessed so many hundreds of thousands of prisoners. It did not explain whether a million or so men and women transported forcibly to places where there was only one job and one employer and then given a free choice of employment were "forced labor" or not.

For the special purpose of appeasing American public opinion, an American "commission" was dispatched to the lumber area and in due time it attested truthfully that it had not *seen* forced labor. No one in the foreign colony was more amused by this clowning than the "commissioners" themselves. They were: a salesman of American machinery, long resident in Moscow and dependent on official good-will for his business; a young American reporter without a steady job and therefore in the U.S.S.R. by sufferance of the government; and the resident secretary of the American-Russian Chamber of Commerce, a paid employee of the organization whose usefulness depended on maintaining cordial relations with the Soviet authorities.

I knew all three men intimately, and it is betraying no secret to record that each of them was as thoroughly convinced of the widespread employment of forced labor in the lumber industry as Hamilton Fish or Mr. Deterding. They went to the North for the ride, or because it was difficult to refuse, and they placated their conscience by merely asserting ambiguously that they personally had seen no signs of forced labor; they did not indicate that they made no genuine effort to find it and that their official guides steered the "investigation."

Their findings, published with all solemnity and transmitted obediently by the American correspondents to the United States, were a good deal along the line of a later "commission" in search of forced labor in the Don Basin coal area. One of the "commissioners," the famous American photographer with the more famous three children of *Around the World in Eleven Years*, Jimmy Abbé, put it to me this way:

"Sure, we saw no forced labor. When we approached anything that looked like it, we all closed our eyes tight and kept them closed. We weren't going to lie about it."

2

The second year of the Plan provided victories enough and to spare for propaganda purposes: the press in October was able to list hundreds of enterprises brought into operation that year. But the hallelujahs were neither as loud nor as jubilant as the year before. The margins of failure to achieve the over-ambitious "control figures" for the fiscal year were especially wide in heavy metals, transportation, coal and factory construction; in the essentials, that is to say, of an industrialized society.

Each of these failures, moreover, affected the others, for an integrated industrial system like a chain is no stronger than its weakest link; a steel mill without coal is completed only in the statistical sense, since it will not produce steel; and coal production without adequate transportation to move it is likewise a statistical triumph only. Transportation troubles were especially harassing. Besides, the planned increase in productivity of labor was far in arrears and the quality indices were in many cases falling instead of rising.

The Plan had taken curious turns, its outstanding achievements and outstanding difficulties alike being largely unexpected and certainly unplanned. The plan for agrarian collectivization stood formally accomplished in less than two years, seemingly the greatest success of all. But it was surely not an unmixed blessing, considering the disastrous loss of livestock, the terrible shortage of foodstuffs, and the problem of peasant opposition still to be solved. Catastrophic inflation was under way where a strengthening of the currency had been planned. Living standards and "real wages" were depressed where percentages of improvement has been meticulously planned. Thinly veiled types of conscript labor and extensive concentration camps, neither of them listed in the detailed volumes of the published Plan, had become essential features of it.

A number of the most advertised victories, in addition, were of dubious character. The boast that millions more workers had been drawn into industry than originally planned was a most illusory triumph, though many self-styled economists abroad accepted it innocently as such. If those economists had planned to build an outhouse with two laborers, but had been obliged to use four laborers, they would scarcely have boasted of "100% over-fulfillment of the plan." Yet they accepted just that boast on a national scale from Soviet sources uncritically.

The vaunted "liquidation of unemployment" was in large measure due to the low productivity of labor per unit. Two men had to be put to work where it was hoped one would suffice. Women had to be torn away from their home duties or their leisure and put to hauling logs, running machines, acting as hod-carriers and street cleaners. That might be naively glorified as equality of the sexes but it represented a most unsavory "overfulfillment" of the unemployment plans.

Not only did the Five Year Plan job take a lot more labor than planned, but it cost a lot more money than planned. That, too, was shouted to the skies as a glorious overfulfillment! And professional economists, among them some who hated Bolshevism but seemingly hated thinking more, applauded. Not only did it take four workers to build their outhouse instead of the two planned, but the job cost twice as much as they had expected—hooray! $2 + 2 = 5$. . . .

These optical illusions kept the hosanna-singers at home and abroad happily thrilled; they were ignored or accepted with ill-concealed sarcasm by the mass of Russians; but they worried the leaders. Shrill optimism covered a deep and pervasive discomfiture. The hunt for scapegoats grew more spirited. New attacks on Rykov, Bukharin, and other alleged Rights filled the press—by the end of the year, Rykov was pushed out of the post formerly held by Lenin, the chairmanship of the Council of People's Commissars, and the colorless, uninspired Molotov was put in his place. Prominent economists and administrators, among them men in key positions not only in industry but in the central planning institutions, were arrested charged with sabotage, espionage, counter-revolution: the agricultural expert, Professor Kondratiev, the leading statistician, Professor Groman, the greatest Russian authority on thermodynamics, Professor Leonid Ramzin, hundreds of their kind, thousands of less important personalities.

The time was ripe for another of those pyrotechnical demonstration trials to serve as circus for lack of bread, to dramatize the idea of a nation besieged by enemies within and without. The trial was already in the making—thousands were being sifted for those few who would tell a convincing story willingly and impressively.

Eight were finally selected, with Professor Ramzin heading the list. There could just as easily have been eighty or eight hundred; the government revealed that at least two thousand were in prison as directly implicated in the same alleged conspiracy. But the stage directors had decided on a small cast.

X. "Death to Wreckers!"

PLANNED hysteria reached its highest pitch in the Ramzin affair. Few things in Soviet history can compare for the size of the audience and the calculated melodrama of the proceedings. In my mind it figures as the classic example of the demonstration trial—those attributes which set the show trial off from ordinary trials seem to me to have been most sharply delineated in this instance.

In subsequent years there would be trials more significant historically, particularly those that ended with the annihilation of Old Bolsheviks like Zinoviev, Kamenev, Smirnov, Piatakov, Serebriakov, and military heroes of the revolution like Marshal Tukhachevsky and General Yakir. But not one of them was to approach the Ramzin show for scientifically inflated sensationalism and for the transparency of its make-believe.

Consider the dimensions of the conspiracy, as outlined in the indictment published on November 11, 1930, and developed at the trial that began two weeks later. An underground "Industrial Party" comprising thousands of Russian engineers and official planners allegedly worked for years with the connivance of the General Staffs of a dozen nations. Its activities supposedly involved such names as Raymond Poincaré, Aristide Briand, Colonel T. E. Lawrence of Arabia and Sir Henry Deterding abroad, and men in key positions in the Five Year Plan at home. By undermining Soviet industry the ground was to be prepared for a sudden and concerted foreign attack. Even the slate of the new government to take control after the rout of the Soviets was supposedly drawn up. Counter-revolution on an all-European scale: as startling a picture as was ever unveiled by any regime.

Consider the audience. All the gadgets of ballyhoo were used to bring the fears and angers of a nation to a boil; and several dozen representatives of the world press were on hand to report the hysteria for other nations. The exaggerated frights and enthusiasms evoked by events in Russia in a world suffering economic jitters helped to draw all eyes to the improvised courtroom in the faded magnificence of the former Nobles' Club.

And consider, what was of the most immediate significance, the background of embattled desperation within the Soviet frontiers. A ruthless straining of energies under conditions of semi-starvation; political pressures without precedent even in Russia; the unfoldment of a system of involuntary labor for millions of prisoners and economic conscripts—any spectacle to explain and justify this background had need for melodrama of the most pyrotechnic kind.

And it is as a spectacle that unavoidably I must think of the trial. I find it hard to discuss it seriously as a *judicial* procedure. The guilt of the accused had been fixed and accepted as beyond doubt in advance; the object of the trial was simply to *demonstrate* that guilt as effectively as possible, for purposes not even remotely related to justice in the legal sense. The flood of carbon-copy resolutions urging the death penalty (one of them by the Academy of Science!) took such guilt for granted. There could be no flaws in procedure, no miscarriage of justice; an inept scene would merely be a blunder in technique. It is in terms of drama—of a political morality play—that this, and all other demonstration trials, must be judged. How else, when the defendants, their "defense counsel," prosecution, and judges all work together to prove a plot? When, indeed, the accused often outdo their accusers in their eagerness to make the official story stick?

The demonstration trial is the unique Bolshevik contribution to the art of propaganda. Though couched in the verbiage and set in the general pattern of formal justice, with judges and lawyers and witnesses, the resemblance ends there. Nothing is allowed to occur, except by sheer accident, that is not prescribed in the indictment-libretto. Every actor, from the judges down to the "extras," knows his assigned role and dovetails it nicely with every other role. Should he stumble, or begin to improvise, everyone is embarrassed and moves quickly to bring the action back to the script.

Like all other correspondents, I was instructed to spare no efforts or cost in reporting the Ramzin proceedings. For once there would be no counting of words, no "downhold" orders or stinting.

I did not miss a single session. I became as familiar with the court and its people, with the routine of the whole business, as a soldier with his trench. And when it was ended I emerged a little dazed, like one returning from a long and unpleasant journey who must slowly re-establish contact with a humdrum existence. The experience remains with me as an organized and clean-edged memory.

More than half a million workers from the factories and offices of Moscow marched through the snows in the grayish dusk on November 25. They marched under banners inscribed, "Death to the agents of imperialism!", "Kill the wreckers!", "No mercy to these class enemies!" Hour after hour as night engulfed the city the gigantic parade rolled past the Nobles' Club and its shouts of "Death! death! death!" could be heard in the columned ballroom where the trial was under way since three in the afternoon.

The eight scholarly men in the prisoners' box heard the baying outside; the several thousand privileged spectators jammed into the chamber as for a circus, under fifty-six blazing chandeliers, heard it; and some seventy-five Russian and foreign reporters at the foot of the platform. In thousands of towns and cities other such parades were taking place at the same time, and these, too, we could hear across the vast distances. The same tom-tom of "Death! death!" pulsed through endless editorials, speeches, resolutions, radio exhortations, cartoons, billboard signs.

It was a synthetic delirium, its very phrases prescribed; a litany of blood-thirst. At the proper moment it would be shut off as artificially as it had been loosed upon the country. Only the bitterness and hatred were real, because they sprang from real pain and anger.

The courtroom scene was a repetition of the Shakhty trial, except that its temper was heightened and its mechanics more practiced. Prosecutor Krylenko's bullet-head shone in the arc-lights, his flat Scythian features tensed in his cruel sneer. With the judges on the raised dais sat a factory worker from Leningrad, one Peter Ivanov, the inert symbol of the proletariat in whose name the show was unwound. Several loges were crowded by members of the diplomatic corps, many of whose governments were involved in the charges. The prisoners' dock, draped in gray cloth, was a speck of alien color in the pervading red.

Photographers, reporters, electricians worked in a panic of hurry; they crawled through the solemnities intent on their own business like scene-shifters in a Chinese play. The paraphernalia of publicity—microphones, klieg lights, cameras, rows of typewriters in the corridor section fenced off for the correspondents—held first place; the eight defendants seemed supernumeraries. The paraphernalia of propaganda and the cries of "Death!" rolling in from all sides and pounding against the outer walls. . . . The opening day in particular had a touch of shrill holiday about it.

Next to Krylenko stood a fat black beetle of a man, with a Mephistophelian beard, waxing red and choleric and spluttering from time to time, but mostly silent and glowering. That was Krylenko's assistant; throughout the trial, behind the refined stiletto-cruelty of the prosecutor the crude sledgehammer cruelty of this assistant.

The defendants were the least villainous looking of mortals, several of them wearing neat professional beards and spectacles. They shuffled papers and made copious notes, as though awaiting their turn to speak at a scientific conference. They seemed a meek, harmless and unimpressive group to have roused such a storm.

After the published indictment had been read, each of the eight in turn stood up and pleaded guilty. Only two of them, Sergei Kuprianov and Xenephon Sitnin, accepted defense lawyers, the others waiving this dubious privilege. Sitnin, fat-faced and oily, was the one whose young son had demanded his death before the trial. This was by now a standardized piece of business in important show trials. "My father is to me a class enemy, nothing more," young Sitnin told the press and his words were published as an example to Soviet youth.

For three hours Ramzin on the opening day told the story of his political sins. A small, clean-shaven man in his early forties, with a square white face and drawn features, his forehead high and pale under a mop of light-brown hair, he spoke in the calm, precise tones of a trained lecturer. It was almost impersonal. The Industrial Party, he said, had been born in 1925 and by 1929 it had more than two thousand members. Its leaders, going abroad frequently on technical missions, were able to make contacts with the French General Staff, Balkan military men and rich émigrés. Contacts were also made through Monsieur "A" and Monsieur "K," foreign consuls in Moscow—they figured as initials throughout, though they sat in the diplomatic box and we all knew who they were.

Ramzin's recital, as monotonous as a technical classroom lecture, sounded abstract and academic. It was clear on the larger objectives but fuzzily obscure on details. Like so much of the economic planning of which he spoke, the counterrevolutionary planning seemed grandiose in blueprint but unrealized in practical application. Krylenko would have a job of it, we all felt, to fill in the outline with convincing detail. The kind of regime projected by the Industrial Party, according to Ramzin, was one dominated by engineering minds: an interesting anticipation of the technocracy ideas which soon thereafter swept America.

Day after day the eight men took turns, singly and in batches of two and three, in front of the microphone that carried their voices to millions, while cameramen ground away, reporters rushed back and forth importantly, and giant arc-lights flared and sizzled. At first, the older men shaded their eyes against the criss-crossed streams of hot light but in time they gave up and bore the drenching without a struggle. Day after day, they asserted their guilt and accented their humiliation, while the khaki-clad Krylenko and his black beetle grimaced and glowered.

There was a monumental irony in the vast precautions taken to safeguard the court against mythical dangers of assault, as the conspirators competed in belly-crawling confessionals. Subtly the idea was conveyed that bands of desperate saboteurs might try to pull off a daring rescue, or that any minute the corpulent Poincaré might come dashing at the head of an army of invaders. The ballyhoo created a sense of imminent danger of foreign attack. The aging Maxim Gorky addressed an eloquent appeal to the workers and peasants and intellectuals of the world to act quickly to stop intervention. The incongruity between these assumptions of imminent counter-revolution and invasion and the meekness of those contrite and ineffectual professors attested that human credulity is indeed inexhaustible.

Even as in the Shakhty trial, the attempt to provide concrete detail for the generalized structure of international plotting fizzled. Gloatingly Krylenko drew out specific samples of sabotage and spying—but they seemed petty in relation to the sweeping charges. The amounts mentioned as bribes over a period of many years came to ludicrously small sums for the world-shaking job allegedly performed. The supposed connivings with premiers and military commanders and millionaire plotters, when the matter came down to cases, proved curiously indirect and inferential at best. It was all done, if done it was, through intermediaries thrice removed.

And not once in all the eleven days was any impersonal, documentary evidence introduced. The thousands of plotters must have been models of circumspection and the secret service exceedingly stupid, for there was not a scrap of paper, not a receipt or an intercepted letter to bolster the state's case. Nor was there a single witness not himself a prisoner and therefore fighting to save his own life. The trial ended as it began—with confessions made while under G.P.U. control and mutual accusations by men in the shadow of death. Watching through news columns darkly, the outside world saw the mountain of propaganda in labor giving birth to an anemic mouse of a plot.

Eleven days of trial, stretching deep into the night hours, left small doubt that these men and hundreds like them despised the Soviet regime, dreamed of its overthrow, and were ready to deliver it to enemies abroad or at home. Several of them were former members of liberal political groupings (the Kadets, for instance) and despite themselves betrayed that they still mourned the perished dream of a democratic Russia on the French or American model. No doubt these men had talked counterrevolution among themselves and with friends out of their pre-revolutionary past in Europe. They clearly had encouraged émigré delusions about the speedy "liberation" of Russia. They had been apathetic toward the industrial tasks entrusted to them, and often had thrown monkey-wrenches into the economic machinery.

More than enough, in short, to make them traitors in Bolshevik eyes and deserving of traitors' deaths. But on these truths the state had elaborated a top-heavy superstructure of imaginative falsehood and exaggeration to explain current hardships and to justify current brutalities. The eight men in the court may have been counterrevolutionary scoundrels, but the great international plot seemed to me, and to most of the foreign observers, "sewn with white thread," as the Russian phrase has it.

A few of the stitches were pretty raw and obvious. Any tyro of a defense attorney in a free court would have pulled out those white threads and watched the case fall apart. For instance, the slate of the new government to displace the Bolsheviks after a successful counterrevolution, embodied in the confessions, contained the names of two men who had long been dead at the time the slate was supposedly drawn up. One of these dead men, Riabushinsky, was scheduled for the premiership, no less. Another instance: at the time Ramzin is supposed to have talked with Colonel Lawrence of Arabian fame in London, the Colonel was not even in England.

Such tell-tale blunders in the structure of confessions the trial took blithely in its stride. Defendants and defense lawyers alike pretended not to notice the blunders, the Soviet press kept mum, the foreign press was fed phony explanations, and the demonstration trial went on without a hitch. The defense was indistinguishable from the prosecution.

And all the time the thunder of vengeance rolled through the land in still more editorial attacks, stereotyped resolutions, mass meetings. That had no direct reference to the mumbo-jumbo of examination and testimony in the courtroom.

2

The most weird hours, in this as in former trials, were provided by witnesses dragged from the darkness of their G.P.U. cells into the circus brilliance of this ballroom. They spoke their lines hurriedly, in confusion, and were dragged off again to the darkness where they had languished for months. To what fate? we could not help wondering. The awareness of thousands of others corralled in G.P.U. prisons—droves of professors and technicians and officials under lock and key, of whom we were allowed to see only a few samples—came to overshadow everything else in the exhibition.

By what logic were the eight selected out of the mass? The answer was not far to seek. The defendants in a show trial are chosen because of their special fitness for their parts. Sometimes willingly, more often unwillingly, they are *cast* for their roles in the limelight. Not the degree of their guilt, but their social backgrounds, their physical and psychological make-up—frequently their capacity for self-abasement—are the primary considerations. The government intended to paint a specific picture in the public mind at home and abroad; these eight sufficed for the purpose. We would know, in a general way, what happened to Ramzin and the other seven; we would never know what happened to the thousands presumably tried and condemned behind closed doors.

One day the witness was Professor Osadchi, until his arrest Vice-President of Gosplan and therefore one of the chief authors of the Five Year Plan. Osadchi had been on this rostrum before. In the Shakhty trial in 1928 he was one of the "people's prosecutors." Now it appeared that he had been play-acting: at that time he was already a member of the counterrevolutionary group. Instinctively we looked at the present "people's prosecutors," and wondered whether they, too, would have their turn.

Osadchi was a large, pompous-looking old man, round-faced, white-bearded, and spectacled, with a heavy rounded paunch. For a full minute he stared into the audience, confused by the lights and gadgets. Then he began to speak in harsh self-accusation. And suddenly he began to sob aloud. "Let me live," he begged the audience, "let me live and my whole life will be devoted to the proletariat and its Soviet power." He was on the stage only a few minutes, then was hustled off again.

On December 4, Krylenko made his closing address. He spoke for four hours. Not so much the guilt of the accused men, but the guilt of their kind of people at home and abroad was his theme. He was underscoring the moral of the play. He read selected translations from Paris papers describing a gathering of Russian exiles—grand-dukes, bishops, merchants—which had protested against the Ramzin trial. The description drew guffaws of laughter from the Moscow audience. Everything that had been outlawed and crushed by the revolution was on trial, and the eight defendants were little more than a few minor, unimportant proofs of it all. Again and again he was interrupted by listeners with cries of "Death to the wreckers."

Two days later the eight men made their final pleas, one or two in tears, the others with pedagogical calm. "This is my last public lecture in fifteen years," Ramzin smiled sadly. "Perhaps the case is not quite as simple as the comrade prosecutor says. Man does not risk his life for money alone. Two paths were open to us after the revolution—one that led to the Kremlin, the other to Paris. We chose Paris and this is where it led us. . . ." And in ending he said, "We came to court not to defend ourselves but to capitulate. I am happy I confessed. My soul is quieter."

"I have only a few more years to live," said Alexander Fedotov. "I am an old man. But I don't want to die a traitor's death. Give me a chance to expiate my sins." He was a tall, heavy, dignified old man. He wore a black cutaway of ancient vintage and a stiff collar and looked like an after-dinner speaker. Once or twice during the trial his sense of grievance had broken through his caution —he had defended his past as a liberal democrat. And as always on those rare occasions when a prisoner showed a sign of self-respect, the audience had been shocked into attention.

Victor Larichev, Nikolai Charnovsky, Ivan Kalinikov—all begged and promised. A few tried flattery. The great and wise and mighty proletariat, they said, surely would not be moved by vengeance and could afford to be generous with broken-down, unworthy creatures like themselves.

Larichev had been a member of the Gosplan. A wisp of a goatee made his thin, sallow face more ineffectual and a little comic. "A handful of intellectuals trying to overthrow the mighty proletariat," he had ridiculed himself and his comrades during the trial. Charnovsky seemed the type of the pre-revolutionary *barin:* a stolid, conservative landowner out of the pages of Turgenyev or Tolstoy. The sixty-five-year-old Kalinikov, with his white hair, his precise Van Dyke beard, and carefully pointed mustaches, had also been in the Gosplan. "A man raised like myself," he had explained to the court, as though demonstrating a technical problem, "could never understand why the lowly workers should rule. . . . I was simply unfit to submit to the proletariat."

And now, as we listened to the eight lacerating themselves, swinging between an eagerness for the death that expiates and tearful pleas for pity, pausing in the most subjective moments to deliver generalizations on life and destiny, we knew that Dostoievsky had not exaggerated his Russians.

Five of the men were condemned to death. The verdict brought a storm of applause and cheers which the presiding judge could not stop. Two days later these death sentences were commuted to ten years of imprisonment. This unexpected act of mercy shocked Russia more deeply than the verdict. Almost as suddenly as the hysteria had been launched, it was now ended. The show was over. Before long we heard that Ramzin and others were back at work, talking to technical classes. The closing words in the Nobles' Club were not their last lectures after all.

But for a few years—until Hitler came to power in Germany—France remained "the spearhead of intervention" in the official propaganda. Poincaré ("Poincaré-War" he had been nicknamed) displaced Austen Chamberlain as the chief devil in Soviet demonology.

A second trial, closely linked with the Ramzin affair, took place several months later. A group of prominent Mensheviks was charged with conspiracy to overthrow the government—the charge resolved, in the final analysis, into one of harboring Marxist views unlike the official Kremlin version. The trial had more dignity than the Ramzin affair. A few of the prisoners made a meek defense of their faith, a feeble and tangential defense but sufficiently impressive in a court-room ill-smelling with human degradation.

I was vacationing in America when this second trial took place. I followed the proceedings through the press reports. And I realized how utterly impossible it was for the outside world to understand the demonstration trial. No matter how often the point was made that this was not ordinary justice, but staged, flood-lighted revolutionary symbolism, the reader accepted it as a real trial to ascertain guilt or innocence. He read of witnesses and evidence and confessions, judges and verdicts, and translated those words in the language of his own experience with ordinary judicial procedures. He waited for the *verdict,* as though it had not been prescribed in advance. Even I who had sat through such trials, caught myself reading the dispatches about testimony and cross-questioning as though it were all real.

An ironical fate pursues the Soviet show trials. Always some magnificent lie throws its shadow on the whole texture of eager confessions. In the Ramzin exhibition it was a "conspirator" who had been dead for years before the conspiracy was hatched. In this Menshevik trial the revealing lie was even more startling. One of the leaders of the Second International, Rafael Abramovich, was supposed to have made a secret visit to Russia on specified dates in the summer of 1928; the whole Menshevik plot centered around that visit, and the defendants "confessed" meetings and discussions in detail. Unfortunately for the G.P.U. stage directors, Abramovich was attending an International Socialist Congress in Brussels at that very time. Photographs of the delegates made at the very moment he was supposedly plotting in Moscow showed Abramovich in Brussels.

That, too, the demonstration trial took in its stride. To this day the Russian people are unaware of the cynical hoax, since the press passed over it in silence.

XI. An Interview with Stalin

THE image of Stalin, immense, vague, sinister, had been expanding rapidly upon men's minds in the years since I came to Moscow. More than ever an interview with him was the world's most coveted and apparently most hopeless newspaper prize. For the fifth or sixth time I ventured to remind him of his "promise" to receive me.

The provocation this time was more than ample. Giddy headlines throughout the world were announcing Stalin's assassination. Rumors from Riga and Bucharest were re-enforced by rumors from Helsingfors and Kaunas and confirmed by Warsaw and Berlin. I asked for no more than a minute or two in his presence, just time enough to obtain his personal denial and to attest that he was indubitably alive.

Every other correspondent in Moscow saw and seized the same opportunity, so that Stalin's secretariat was besieged by reporters of many nations, but most insistently by the go-getting Americans. Letters, telephone calls, cablegrams from the home offices of newspapers and agencies poured in upon Stalin's staff urging that it was his duty—nay, his great opportunity—to emerge at last from behind the barriers and smite the rumor-mongers.

The "assassination" had come as the inevitable climax to a flood of sensations out of neighboring capitals which none of our denials could stem. It was the Soviet Union's periodical dividend on censorship, but a lot more gory and circumstantial than usual. The mere existence of the censorship gave news sources on the capitalist side of the Russian frontiers a specious authority, and it must be admitted that on occasion Riga was able to report significant Soviet events more quickly, and surely less inhibitedly, than we in Moscow. Its batting average was not very high, but every so often it hit a home run.

But that the border countries would know of major developments even unto bloodshed and rebellion in Moscow itself, without the resident newspapermen being aware of it, was fantastic. The Soviet capital is a huge whispering gallery: scandal and sensation echo throughout the city like the rumble of thunder. And there was probably no Moscow correspondent, however "friendly" and "loyal," who would have hesitated to flash news of the sort now spread by Riga and other capitals, especially the alleged murder of Stalin. The means for circumventing the censorship are always at hand, provided the reporter is willing to risk official reprimand or expulsion. The death of Stalin would have been a news story worth the risk.

Not since the balmy days when Lenin and Trotsky were shooting and stabbing each other regularly in Riga and Warsaw dispatches, did imaginative journalism about mysterious shut-in Russia run so loose and wild. Starting with a few trenchant truths about widespread arrests and disaffections (truths which the Moscow correspondents did not exactly conceal but certainly soft-pedaled) exaggeration and gullibility did the rest. Soon the Red Army was exploding with mutiny, War Lord Voroshilov was defying Stalin, the streets of Moscow were running with blood, Red Square was strewn with corpses, and the government was huddled in the center of the Kremlin waiting for the skies to crash. An English traveler even gave the press his personal "eye-witness" account of the blood and the cadavers.

We insisted that the first snows of the season showed no traces of blood. In the center of the Kremlin, I advised my readers, I found only an exclamatory band of tourists making its rounds of palaces and churches under bored guides. As for Red Square, I admitted that it did have one corpse: the embalmed body of Lenin in its new mausoleum, with several hundred citizens queued up for a glimpse of the father of Bolshevism. But rumor thrived on denials. The defiant answer to our joint obduracy was the "assassination" of Stalin.

Each flourishing a sheaf of messages from home editors recounting the exciting news, the correspondents pleaded for an interview: the one thing that would smother rumor-mongering and restore law and order in the U.S.S.R. for a doubting world. We pleaded, but without real hope of success.

On the afternoon of November 23, my telephone rang. A man's voice in good English said:

"Mr. Lyons? This is Comrade Stalin's office."

A frayed old gag—I was equal to the occasion. "You don't say! How very interesting! Give him my kindest regards, and Mrs. Stalin too."

"But this *is* Comrade Stalin's secretary." The voice was embarrassed. "Comrade Stalin has received your letter and wished me to tell you that he will be glad to talk to you in an hour, at five o'clock that is, in his offices at the Central Committee of the Party."

"Thank you, I shall be there."

No tocsins were sounded, no flags were hoisted, no skies crashed, but the impossible had come to pass! A simple telephone call —and the unthinkable was suddenly as matter-of-fact as a cocktail party or train schedule. Stalin was about to give the first interview since he had achieved his pinnacle of power.

Every minute brought the appointment nearer, nearer, like an approaching locomotive, and suddenly it was right upon me, huge, loud, puffing and formidable. I was in the ante-room to Stalin's office on Staraya Ploshchad (Old Square), with Charles Malamuth of California University's Slavonic Department; he was with me when the thrilling telephone summons came through and I mobilized him as emergency interpreter.

The headquarters of the Central Committee were just inside the ancient Chinese Wall, a six-story building, plain and businesslike. The G.P.U. guards at the door were expecting me and passed us through immediately; another guard led us to the ante-chamber of the most powerful, most feared, least known human being on the face of the globe. An amiable woman secretary asked us to wait; Comrade Stalin would be free in a few minutes.

The building and this office were as unlike the usual, littered, chaotic Soviet institution as possible: quiet, orderly, unhurried but efficient. It was, above all, stamped with an unmistakable simplicity: the hall-mark, I was to learn in the next hour or two, of Stalin himself. I had a sense of concentrated authority, the more impressive because it was devoid of the trappings of power, curiously austere and self-assured, without elegance of gold braid or shrieking symbols: power naked, clean, and serene in its strength.

Half a dozen or so people were waiting in this room, some for Stalin, some for other leaders with offices on the same floor. A tall, unshaven fellow, with matted black hair and dirty boots. An elderly woman in a leather jacket, red kerchief on her head.

"Provincial Party secretaries, come to report or complain," Charlie guessed.

"Probably," I said. "Imagine what the ante-chambers of the former rulers were like, the pomp and grandeur, the courtiers and generals, and look how simple all of this is! Stalin may be inaccessible to reporters and diplomats, but I should judge from these folks that he is accessible enough to his own Party people."

We could not pursue this line of thought. The woman secretary said Comrade Stalin was waiting, and an office boy led the way.

2

One cannot live in the shadow of Stalin's legend without coming under its spell. My pulse, I am sure, was high. No sooner, however, had I stepped across the threshold than diffidence and nervousness fell away. Stalin met me at the door and shook hands, smiling. There was a certain shyness in his smile, and the handshake was not perfunctory. He was remarkably unlike the scowling, self-important dictator of popular imagination. His every gesture was a rebuke to the thousand little bureaucrats who had inflicted their puny greatness upon me in these Russian years.

We followed him to the extreme end of a long conference table, where he motioned us affably to chairs and sat down himself. His personal interpreter, a young man with bushy black hair, was there. Stalin pushed over a box of cigarettes, took one himself, and we all lighted up. The standardized photographs of Stalin show him smoking a pipe and I had a feeling of faint disappointment that he was not measuring up to the clichés, even in this regard.

In my letter the previous day, I had specifically asked for "only two minutes" and I had assumed that the interview was to be no more than a brief formality to enable at least one reporter to testify that Stalin was still fully alive. But I saw him stretch out his feet and lean back in leisurely fashion as though we had hours ahead of us. With that natural gesture of relaxing in his chair, Stalin turned a straitjacketed interview into an unhurried social call. I realized that there would be no time limitations.

And here was I, unprepared for this generosity, with only one question ready—the superfluous question whether he was alive or not! I cursed myself inwardly for a bungler not to have mapped out an organized campaign of interrogation that would probe to the very center of the Soviet situation.

"Tell Mr. Lyons," Stalin addressed his interpreter, "that I am sorry I could not receive him before. I saw his letters, but I cannot easily find the opportunity for interviews."

There was no need for translation. My Russian would probably be adequate to the occasion, I smiled, and if I got stuck, these gentlemen would come to my rescue. Several times in the next hour Stalin harked back to my letters. To this day I do not know precisely why, among the score of permanent correspondents in his capital—many of them less outspoken in their criticism of the regime and more amenable to the discipline of the Press Department—he had selected me for this first interview since his rise to supreme power. Any one of a dozen other correspondents would have served Moscow's purpose just as well. But unquestionably my letters over more than a year played a part in the selection.

"Comrade Stalin," I began the interview, "may I quote you to the effect that you have not been assassinated?"

He laughed. At such close range, there was not a trace of the Napoleonic quality one sees in his self-conscious camera or oil portraits. The shaggy mustache, framing a sensual mouth and a smile nearly as full of teeth as Teddy Roosevelt's, gave his swarthy face a friendly, almost benignant look.

"Yes, you may," he said, "except that I hate to take the bread out of the mouths of the Riga correspondents."

The room in which we sat was large, high-ceilinged, and furnished simply almost to bareness. Its only decorations were framed pictures of Karl Marx, Lenin, and Engels—there was no portrait of Stalin: probably the only office in all his empire without one. Stalin wore the familiar olive-drab jacket with stand-up collar, belted at the waist, and his trousers were tucked into high black boots. The negligent austerity of his attire was of a piece with that room. Though of vigorous physique, he seemed to me older than his fifty-one years; his face was large-featured and fleshy, darker in tinge than I had expected and faintly pockmarked, his shock of black hair thick, unruly, and touched with gray.

For over an hour I asked questions and answered them. Again and again the talk debouched into argument; I was aware afterwards, though not at the time, that I did not hesitate to interrupt him: another proof of the essential simplicity of a powerful ruler who could put a reporter so completely at his ease. The "ethics of bourgeois journalism" came in for considerable discussion; though at the moment he had sufficient cause to be indignant with that journalism, there was no bitterness in Stalin's comments.

I asked him about Soviet-American relations, about the chances for world revolution, the progress of the *Piatiletka*, and such other obvious matters as came to my mind. He listened without the slightest sign of impatience to my labored Russian and repeated sentences slowly when he thought I might not have grasped the meaning. Often I reached a linguistic impasse from which Charlie and the other interpreter retrieved me. Stalin never once spoke impetuously, never once resorted to mere cleverness or evasion. Sometimes he thought for many seconds before he replied, his forehead furrowed in lines of concentration, and the answers came in strangely schematized array: "firstly, secondly . . . and finally. . . ." I recalled that note he had sent me the previous year with its "Motives: (a) . . . and (b) . . ." There had been no affectation in it: that was how his mind worked. It had been conditioned, perhaps, by long years devoted to driving elementary predigested ideas into simple minds, in simple a-and-b formulations.

"It seems to me," I said at one point in the rambling conversation, "that the American press has been making a more determined effort to obtain fair, objective news about the Soviet Union than any other country. We have the largest group of correspondents here and all of them, I think, trying to tell the truth as they see it."

"That's right," Stalin agreed thoughtfully. "Economic classes in the United States are not yet quite as rigidly differentiated as in Europe—you have no deeply rooted landed aristocracy."

The economic interpretation of journalism! To Stalin, as to all Bolsheviks, there are no "good" men and "bad" men, but only men reacting to their social environment and economic compulsions.

In the midst of the interview, someone opened the door and, noting that Stalin was occupied, was about to withdraw. It was Klementi Voroshilov, the Commissar of War!

"Oh, I'm sorry," he smiled apologetically.

"No, no, do come in and join us, Comrade Voroshilov," I said boldly. As though cornering Stalin were not triumph enough for one day, my luck was corralling the War Lord for me as well.

Stalin smiled his assent and Voroshilov, having shaken hands with Charlie and myself, joined the group at the table. Later I wondered whether his arrival was quite as accidental as it seemed. The sensational reports abroad had been full of supposed trouble between Stalin and his military chief. But Voroshilov himself, having heard of my doubts, declared that his intrusion had indeed been entirely fortuitous; a piece of luck which heightened greatly the dramatic value of the interview.

Voroshilov plunged warmly into the conversation. He was brimming with questions and opinions, slapped his thigh vigorously to express satisfaction. His is a warm, high-mettled nature with something impetuously boyish about it, a startling contrast to the deliberate, methodical, very earnest Stalin. Voroshilov's vitality seemed effervescent against the immense, highly disciplined power in reserve which characterized Stalin. Once or twice, I thought I detected a shadow of annoyance on Stalin's face at Voroshilov's ebullience, but I may have been mistaken.

I felt that I was taking more of Stalin's time than I had any right to do, and that the talk would go on and on interminably if I did not call it off myself. Outside this office the tides of revolution rose and fell, hammered at people's lives and shivered the certainties of the world. But here, with Stalin, there was no suggestion of this violence and hectic urgency: he was enveloped in his own atmosphere of calm assurance.

"Comrade Stalin, the press of the world is by this time in the habit of calling you dictator," I said. "Are you a dictator?"

I could see that Voroshilov waited with interest for the answer. Stalin smiled:

"No, I am no dictator. Those who use the word do not understand the Soviet system of government and the methods of the Communist Party. No one man or group of men can dictate. Decisions are made by the Party and acted upon by its chosen organs, the Central Committee and the Politburo."

"And now," I said, my embarrassment all too evident, "may I ask you some personal questions? Not that I myself care to pry into your private life, but the American press happens to be interested."

"All right," Stalin consented. His tone implied amused astonishment, as though the curiosity of bourgeois barbarians were beyond communist comprehension.

Voroshilov chuckled, like a little boy at a circus. "Sure, that's what the world wants to know!" he said.

Under my questioning, Stalin thereupon admitted that he had one wife, three children—one of them working, the other two youngsters still in school. Voroshilov was not concealing his enjoyment of the situation. When Stalin reached his five-year-old daughter, his War Lord added in mock earnest: "And she has as yet no well-defined political program." And then: Didn't I also have a young daughter? he wanted to know. I told them that she was in school in Berlin.

And thus it was, of all things, on an intimate domestic note that the party broke up.

"I don't want in any way to interfere with what you may write," Stalin said, "but I would be interested to see what you make of this interview."

"On the contrary," I said, "I am anxious that you read my dispatch before I send it. Above all things I should hate to misrepresent anything you have said. The only trouble is that this is Saturday night and the Sunday papers go to press early. Getting the story to you and back again may make me miss the early editions."

"Well, then, never mind." He waved the matter aside.

I thought quickly.

"But if I could get a Latin-script typewriter," I said, "I could write my story right here and now and show it to you immediately."

Stalin thought that was a good idea. With Charlie and myself at his heels, he walked into the adjoining room, where several secretaries were standing around chatting and asked whether they couldn't dig up a Latin typewriter. The relation between Stalin and his immediate employees was entirely human, without so much as a touch of restraint. To them, obviously, he was not the formidable dictator of one-sixth of the earth's surface but a friendly, comradely boss. They were deferential without being obsequious.

The typewriter was found and I was installed in a small room to do my stuff. I could hear Stalin suggesting that they send in tea and sandwiches as he returned to the conference room. I was nearly an hour in writing the dispatch. Several times Stalin peeked in, and inquired whether we were comfortable and had everything we needed.

I interrupted myself only once, to telephone Billy.

"Where are you, dear?" she asked. "Have you forgotten that we have a party tonight? The whole gang will be here."

"I hope you will forgive me," I teased her. "You see, I am very busy at the moment, and may be tied up another hour or two."

"But where are you?"

"Oh, in Stalin's office . . . just had a chat with him and with Voroshilov."

"Stop your kidding! Where are you?"

"No joke, in Stalin's office. All right, you don't have to believe it. Tell you all about it when I get home."

Voroshilov was still with Stalin when I took in the typewritten sheets. Both leaders smiled as the dispatch was translated, particularly at my detailed description of Stalin's looks and manner, Voroshilov's boyish exuberance and the references to Stalin's family. Four or five times Stalin interjected minor corrections and suggestions, none of them of a political character. That finished, I said:

"Would you be good enough to sign this copy for me? It may simplify matters in getting the story by the censors. You know, there is a censorship on news here."

He wrote: "*More or less correct, J. Stalin.*" That autographed copy is still in my possession.

Then I wrote a few words of thanks for his patience on one of the carbon copies, signed it, and left it with him.

3

The unthinkable interview was over. The two minutes had stretched to nearly two hours. As we left the building and hailed a droshky, I said to Charlie:

"I like that man!"

Charlie agreed, but in a lower emotional key. A little more analytical than I, and less involved in the sheer thrill of the newspaper scoop, he discounted much of Stalin's personal charm. Warm hospitality is a racial characteristic of the Georgians. Perhaps he could recognize more of the hardness under the charm than I did, in my mood of gratitude for this gift of the first interview.

But in the years that followed, with ample time to reassay my impressions, I did not change my mind about my essential reaction to Stalin's personality. Even at moments when the behavior of his regime seemed to me most hateful, I retained that liking for Stalin as a human being. I could understand thereafter the devotion to the man held by certain writers of my acquaintance who had come to know him personally. There was little in common between the infallible deified Stalin fostered as a political myth and the Stalin I had met. In the simplicity which impressed me more than any other element in his make-up, there was nothing of make-believe, nowhere a note of falseness or affectation. His friendliness was not the back-slapping good-fellow type of the politician, but something innate, something that rang true. In his unpretentiousness there was nothing pretentious.

Subsequently another American correspondent was received by Stalin. We compared notes, and it was as if we had met totally different men, our impressions were so completely at variance. He carried away the imprint of a ruthless, steel-armored personality, with few of those human attributes which I had seen to relieve its harshness: a picture more consistent with Stalin's public character. For years I wondered which of us was closer to the truth, or whether there were two truths. Then I read the autobiography of H. G. Wells, where he gives a vivid word picture of his interview with Stalin. His reactions to the man were so close to my own that he used almost the same words to convey his impression of Stalin's essential humanness and simplicity. It was reassuring to know that if I was wrong, I had eminent company in my error.

I sought out the censor, Podolsky, in his home and handed him the dispatch. He collapsed into a chair, literally, with the Russian equivalent of "I'll be damned!"

When I reached home, the party guests had arrived, practically all the American correspondents among them.

"Well, a nice host you are!" one of them exclaimed. "Inviting a lot of people and then walking out on them."

"Yes, where have you been?" another said. "Scooping us all, I suppose."

"Well, where do you suppose I've been?" I answered, as nonchalantly as I could manage. "With Comrade Stalin, of course!"

That didn't even evoke a laugh. The joke was worn too thin to be funny. No one guessed that I was telling them a literal truth. But I was too full of the excitement to bottle it up indefinitely. Before the evening was over, I convinced them that it was no wisecrack, and the congratulations were tinged with chagrin.

The interview was "kept on the ice" by the New York office for Monday morning, when it would get a better break, journalistically speaking. It was front-paged throughout the world, quoted, editorialized, put on the radio by the "March of Time" as one of the ranking "scoops" in recent newspaper history. My description of Stalin as a likeable human being seemed to touch the world's imagination. "Congratulations to the United Press," said an editorial in the New York *Daily News*, "on the most distinguished piece of reporting of this year, if not of the last four or five years."

The flood of rumor from neighboring capitals was stemmed. An amusing commentary on the Riga news mentality came to my knowledge. Donald Day, one of the Riga veterans, in a letter to Junius B. Wood of the Chicago *Daily News*, inquired confidentially whether Gene Lyons had really obtained that personal interview or had it all been imaginary!

In the next days I was deluged with congratulatory telegrams from all over the world—from editors, foreign correspondents, acquaintances. Outwardly I preened myself on the achievement (though 95% of it was luck) and took all the laurels without demur. But only Billy, Charlie, and one or two other intimates knew that inwardly I was far from exultant.

I thought of all the searching questions which I might have asked but had been too idiotic and too timid and too grateful to ask and I was overwhelmed with a conviction of failure. I had failed to confront Stalin with the problems which were by this time weighing on my own conscience—the use of terror as a technique of government, the suppression and punishment of heretical opinion within the ranks of devoted communists, the persecution of scientists and scholars, the distortion of history to fit new policies, systematic forced labor, the virtual enslavement of workers and peasants in the name of the socialism which was to emancipate them. In my purely professional thrill of a Stalin interview, I had been content to remain politely on the lacquered statistical surface of the Soviet scene. I had accepted the glib assumptions of the monolithic Party as the unquestioned basis for an interview.

It would have been not merely more enterprising but more honest to probe deeper, to question less politely. I must have left an impression with both Stalin and Voroshilov that I was closer to them in my views of Soviet life than I was in actuality. For this I was to reproach myself often in years to come.

Amidst the telegrams and letters and the jubilation of my employers, I was depressed by the feeling of a magnificent opportunity frittered away.

XII. American Interlude

WE WENT to America, on vacation, by way of Berlin and Rome: Berlin to say good-by to Genie, who was remaining at school, and Rome in the hope of interviewing *Il Duce*. The Italian dictator, it is true, was being scalped by newspaper braves too often to count as in itself an achievement, but Mussolini's scalp, by the side of Stalin's, would have made a unique display for any warrior.

I was fairly familiar with Berlin, having visited it two or three times a year, and was trying to keep myself posted on the crucial struggle for survival being made by the Republic against the combined assaults of Nazis and communists. Our arrival at the Adlon bar, unofficial headquarters of the American press corps, had become a sort of homecoming. Even little Genie climbed the high stool for a lemonade and potato chips, and was greeted by Fred, the bartender, like an old and highly valued customer. Her command of the German language in those few months made her parents feel like the hen in the fable as the duckling paddled off on the lake. We had arranged for her to spend week-ends with a Soviet family in Berlin to keep up her Russian as well.

A batch of correspondents was usually on hand at the Adlon, exchanging casual bits of information about world events while rolling the poker dice with toothpicks for chips. I had been there during Christmas week two months earlier, feeling less of an outsider than usual because of the trailing clouds of glory from the Stalin scoop. Moscow was, after all, my first foreign assignment and in the midst of these veterans of a dozen news centers I was conscious of being a mere tyro.

Before the war foreign news had been largely a matter of personalities and spectacles: the rise and fall of politicians and rulers, the doings—and even more so the misdoings—of royal personages, etc. Since the war foreign news had become an ever more intricate business calling for some understanding of history and economic forces; classes had in large measure taken the place of individuals as protagonists in the great show. While not essential for holding an important post and even for acquiring an international reputation, brains no longer in themselves disqualified a man for a correspondent's job.

"Are you a correspondent?" we liked to say to newcomers; "well, I'm a prostitute too." We made it a point to be casual and nonchalant about kings and dictators and premiers. But our nonchalance was only skin-deep. Underneath it we were thoroughly impressed with the importance of our calling and our privileged vantage point on History in the Making. The bibulous school of foreign journalism was already in decline—even old-timers recognized grudgingly that a teetotaler might make a pretty good correspondent notwithstanding. Foregathering at bars was largely a salute to tradition.

The tragic events which were soon to overwhelm Germany gave special depth to a conversation with a German communist in Berlin. I had met him long before, in New York. I knew that he had been in Moscow several times in recent years.

"Yes, I've been to Moscow," he said, a little apologetically. "I didn't look you up. . . . You know how these things are. . . . It's all a mess, Gene. I can't face the German workers any longer and tell them that everything is lovely in the socialist fatherland. Too many of them know the truth and think me a liar."

He had not yet brought himself to the point of speaking out, except as now in private. Some months later he did—or perhaps his private views were carried to headquarters—and he was duly expelled from the Party.

"But look at the tremendous vote the Party rolled up in the German election," I consoled him.

"It's meaningless. The Hitler movement is growing just as fast, and the strategic advantages are all on their side. The worst of it is that every communist vote is also a potential Nazi vote, because we have failed to attack fascist methods and the fascist mentality. And we can't do that without coming out at the same time against similar methods and a similar mentality in Moscow. We're just a sect, with our faces to Mecca in the Kremlin. Either they don't understand it in Moscow or don't care; the effects are the same in any case. Anyone who tries to tell them is kicked out of the Party. Our German leadership has become a stupid megaphone for Moscow, more interested in remaining in the good graces of Stalin than in steering away from disaster at home."

"Yet, you have the *Rot Front* and a fighting spirit. Every intellectual one meets here seems to be a communist or almost a communist."

"I'm not minimizing our strength," he said, "but the real danger is in over-estimating it. Too much of that fighting spirit is directed against the wrong people. The moment is critical but we are spending most of our energy hammering down the Republic for our enemies. Many of these intellectuals you talk about are fascists at heart. They'll step over the line at a moment's notice. They hate this blundering Republic and we are giving them a 'decent' and high-minded excuse for hating democracy."

The so-called "united front from below," that is to say, over the heads of more conservative leaders and organizations, had by that time created in Germany, as elsewhere, the soporific illusion of communist strength. There were innumerable societies and leagues and unions presumably of a popular kind—but all of them different names for the self-same coterie of sectarian leaders. It made a fine show in reports to Moscow headquarters and a loud noise in the communist press but it was (as events demonstrated) a childish delusion.

From Berlin we went to Rome. Italian friends made in San Remo the previous summer and Italian newspapermen whom we had met in Moscow conducted us through nurseries, museums, model tenements. They assured us that the people were accepting enthusiastically the immediate sacrifices and ruthless disciplines for the sake of the glorious future, that Italy was a backward peasant country in hostile surroundings, and that great national revolutions like theirs could not be made with silk gloves. It was all so familiar, the litany of monolithic dictatorship. I talked with certain American correspondents dear to Mussolini's heart: "friendly" and "loyal" correspondents who were appreciative of Latin hospitality and broad-mindedly accepted hardships and terror for other people in the name of the long view; after all, they said, trains were running on schedule and the Italians were really unfit to govern themselves.

At the Press Department, an Italian version of Mr. Arens, with the same secret-service aroma about him, explained that the fascist regime did not censor the foreign reporters. His department was there "to help the correspondents and to shield them against the falsehoods spread by counterrevolutionary elements." But look how some of them paid with insult for all this solicitude! And he complained against some statements made by Webb Miller, another U.P. man.

Nevertheless, he would inquire about my interview with *Il Duce*. Having small hope that the inquiry would do any good, I booked passage on the *Augustus*, sailing from Naples in a few days. Then, to my surprise, I was notified that Mussolini would be away from Rome for a week or ten days in connection with some international conference, but would probably agree to receive me on his return. The probability, however, did not seem strong enough to be worth weeks of waiting and I decided to sail.

Beneath the professional excuse for the Rome visit was my long-cherished personal hope of showing the city to Billy. Ever since the gloomy day exactly ten years earlier, when a paternal *commissario* had quoted his Sicilian adage and advised me to come back with the girl whose picture he found in my pocket, I had played with that idea. Now I took Billy to the spots where Norman Matson and I had dreamed and schemed and exulted over the bright new world being born in Russia. I showed her the Danish *pension* where we had lived and the cafés where we had loitered. One golden afternoon we drove out in a hansom cab to the catacombs; stopping at a roadside *trattoria* for lunch, we were served by the *padrone* and his family with a two-hour meal and special vintages and flowers—one of those meals that stand out like monuments in one's gastronomic history.

Naples, for all its exotic flavor, was a disappointment. It did not measure up to my ten-year-old memory; the very burros and streets of flowers and ragged street boys had lost their grand-opera color and swagger. The change, alas, was not in Naples but in me; I had been only twenty-two then and about to become the John Reed of the Italian Revolution. . . .

2

My head was still haloed in the radiance of that Stalin interview when I reached New York in March, 1931. A fast-fading radiance and a tarnished halo, but United Press publicity burnished my reputation with vigorous strokes for display purposes. It was as good as new by the time the ships news reporters boarded the *Augustus* off quarantine in New York harbor. What small hope I nurtured of going into cozy vacation privacy somewhere, to assess what I had experienced in three full years under the Soviets —or at least to avoid the need for making such an assessment in public—was shattered by young Manley, secretary to President Bickel. He came aboard with the reporters and informed me casually that I was booked for radio talks, dinner speeches, interviews, and a lecture tour.

My repolished fame, such as it was, was catapulting me into the public light, and a consistent attitude to the Russian revolution, a working hypothesis, was essential. I needed urgently a fairly rigid framework of assumptions and principles within which I could organize the multitudinous facts and impressions, otherwise they would be as hopeless a jumble of contradictions as life itself. The reporter or the historian, however sincerely he may pride himself on his cold objectivity, is in the final analysis a creative artist, sorting, rejecting, arranging the data of his experience into a sensible pattern. The whole experience of one man in one day cannot be condensed into one large volume, as James Joyce has demonstrated in *Ulysses;* how then condense the experience of a great nation over a period of years?

Reporting is a highly selective process, usually carried on far below the surface of the conscious mind, by a man's deepest instincts, his faith and prejudices and eager hopes. Only those who are most completely subject to this law deny its existence; their inner censors are so well concealed, their prejudices so well oiled, that the process seems automatic and their creative, purposeful shaping of the stuff of life into a public image of their private soul seems a triumph of "objectivity." It is when the inner censors, sifting the daily grist of experience, begin to quarrel among themselves that the trouble begins.

In the first year or so of my Russian sojourn, my imported convictions were a sieve that sifted events for me; reporting was no more than a physical job of finding and transmitting "desirable" information; I needed only a little dexterity in wishing away or explaining away the rejected materials. Later, when doubts obtruded themselves and my instincts were more and more hurt, the sifting became a conscious mental effort, paid for in self-reproach. The anxiety to "belong" in the dominant social circles in Bolshevik Moscow, the fear of being rejected by the only circles that mattered to me at home, played their roles in keeping me "friendly." But beyond that, far more effective, were the bugaboos of loyalty and consistency, the need to safeguard my faith: a frantic desire to save my investment of hope and enthusiasm in the Russian revolution.

All the way across Europe and the Atlantic, I wrestled with the problem of how much of what I had seen and what I had thought I should tell. Before leaving Moscow I wrote a series of articles summarizing my three Russian years. I found, on returning, that it had been played up wherever the United Press had clients, which means every city and town of any consequence in the country, with the usual ballyhoo. *The Truth About Russia* in foot-high letters on newspaper delivery trucks (I saw photographs of them) made me feel like an impostor. The "truth" indeed, when I was so far from having evolved a workable truth for myself, let alone others. The "truth" indeed, when I knew every paragraph to be a labored formula of compromise between looming doubts and waning loyalties, complicated (even if I did not admit this to myself) by the wish to hold my job and return to Moscow on the comfortable old footing of a "friendly" correspondent.

One visit to my old office, the Tass bureau, wiped out any lingering misapprehensions as to the attitude of former comrades; the atmosphere was wintry and the Tass employees pitifully embarrassed—even poor Bessie, the office stenographer, could not make up her mind whether shaking hands with me was sinful, and stood poised uncertainly as though waiting for a Party decision on the problem. But it no longer seemed so important to me whether I would be labeled as a renegade by former comrades. Against what I had witnessed in Russia that consideration seemed fantastically petty.

In the end, my old inhibitions, the inner compulsion to save face for the revolution, won out in my mind. In private conversation I let off plenty of steam, especially when I was talking to near-communists. Most of Russia's worst troubles, I said, could be traced directly to its frantic misuse of the weapon of terror. But in public, on the lecture platform or before the radio "mike," I uttered none of these things.

I had returned to an America of depression and millions of unemployed, in which the ruling classes still boasted of their rugged individualism. For millions, the epic of Russia, where unemployment had been liquidated, spelled hope. Russia's slogans of national planning were penetrating even to capitalist economists. I took the easiest, the pleasantest, and, it seemed to me, also the most "decent" and "loyal" course of sustaining those hopes. The general public, where it knew me at all, regarded me as a supporter of the Soviets. A super-patriotic society with headquarters in Chicago sent advance notices to the communities where I was to appear, warning them that I was a Bolshevik propagandist in respectable reporter's clothing.

My audiences were for the most part businessmen, in their luncheon clubs, Chambers of Commerce, and Rotary Clubs. This simplified matters for me. This was only 1931 and the depression had not yet erased the smugness from their expressions. In the official economic weather forecasts, prosperity was still around the corner. Looking into their self-satisfied faces, I could forget my doubts. I wanted only to make these men squirm, to pay them off for the unemployment and the distress they were accepting so placidly, to throw a monkey-wrench into the machinery of their automatic thinking.

"You gentlemen," I liked to say, looking some especially overstuffed specimen in the eye, "are men of influence in your community by virtue of your business and your money. But if you were to arrive in the Soviet Union, you would realize quickly enough that you had better not boast about your possessions.

"Your money would make you an outcast, little better than a criminal. Only your American passports would save you from being liquidated as social leeches. Any schoolboy would explain that you acquired your wealth by robbing and exploiting your fellow-men. He would tell you that you are a parasite living on the sweat of the workers and that a concentration camp was too good for such a public enemy."

If the overstuffed gentleman thus pinned down began to squirm and grow purple under the gills, I would blandly add:

"I am merely trying to explain to you the Bolshevik point of view, for which, of course, I am not personally responsible."

My lectures took me through about twenty cities in the northeastern section of the country. The first of them, in Youngstown, Ohio, was the most difficult. Instead of an intimate luncheon group such as I had visualized, I found myself on a vast throne-chair on a vaster stage in the largest auditorium in the city crowded to capacity. The local communists had turned out in full force as well as the city officials and Chamber of Commerce elements. I felt small, helpless, trapped, as I stared from the edge of my throne-chair into the crowded gallery and the field of faces stretching (or so it seemed to me) to a far horizon. It was a cold, rainy Sunday afternoon, but sweat crawled down my collar.

But after a few blundering minutes, the fear fell away miraculously, and I was spinning along with a fluency which the audience accepted as a matter of course, but which astonished the lecturer. I lost my place in the prepared notes and never found it again, but I had no need of guidance. I was speaking to the simple, hopeful men and women in that audience rather than the city fathers and big businessmen. I spoke of the hardships and sacrifices imposed by the Five Year Plan and the rigid discipline enforced upon the whole population, but I made these things look small in comparison with the great achievements and the greater promises. Sometimes I touched upon sore points in my own mind, such as the hounding of intellectuals and the liquidation of kulaks, and the hidden resentments came to the surface. I drove them back to their subterranean lairs. The vociferous applause of the Left Wing in the audience (massed for organized heckling should the need arise) continually interrupted my talk and indicates sufficiently the drift of my story.

My abandoned notes, had they guessed it, did not merit communist applause. I had intended to paint a much more realistic picture. But the simple believing people, their eyes pleading for reassurance like the eyes of famished creatures begging for food, could not be denied. And always, in this tour, I spoke more enthusiastically than I felt.

At a luncheon meeting of the Women's Press Club, in Washington, I discovered that I was ensconced in the very midst of an array of officers of the D.A.R. The organization, it happened, was holding its annual convention and the club invited the officers to be present. They were precisely the sort of women, so safe and snug in their congealed heritage, who set my mental teeth on edge. My talk, in consequence, took a more militantly pro-Soviet line than ever. For too many of these women the American Revolution was a fossilized thing in their private little museum. I knew that often an illiterate immigrant, come here to seek freedom, possessed more of the American Revolution than many a sanctified Son and Daughter. In the question period, one of the D.A.R. ladies asked about the attitude of Russian women.

"A hundred and fifty years from now," I said, "there will probably be an organization known as the Daughters of the Russian Revolution who, despite their name, will be reactionary and intolerant. But as yet the revolutionary women of Russia are truly revolutionists," and on in this vein.

This, my first speaking tour, left as residue in my mind a conviction of the futility of lecturing. In all, perhaps ten thousand people gave up two hours of their time for "the truth at last about Russia" in pill form. They heard a nervous young man boil down three years of intense mental and emotional adventure into a fistful of rough-grained facts only vaguely related to his larger experience. Because they wanted to know only whether it was "good" or "bad," a "success" or a "failure"—large, meaningless words unrelated to the essence of the revolution—he assured them that it was good and successful.

3

I found in the radical *milieu* of New York the self-same delusion of communist strength as in Berlin. Though on a smaller scale than in Germany, its make-believe was more intensive. American communists were lost in a maze of self-deception. In Europe, where communism was a mass movement, the self-styled "united front" organizations at least had working men and women in their membership. In the United States, it all seemed to me a house of sand, built by middle-class intellectuals whom the depression had driven out of their accustomed burrows. Well-meaning clergymen, social workers, writers, dentists, pacifists, Negro religious maniacs lured into Leagues-for-This and Bureaus-for-That: an elaborate false front and respectable window dressing for a structure that did not exist.

Communist majorities in America had been expelled at Moscow's behest, so that the minorities became majorities until the next split; thinking had been replaced by slogans changed, on occasion, overnight; and a new jargon for initiates was evolved, full of deviations, plenums, theses, social fascists, fronts, and orders. A talent for machiavellian intrigue and foul language had become the mark of the "Third Period" mock-revolutionary, and a horde of middle-class ladies and gentlemen with a taste for the bogus melodrama of revolution were amusing themselves with passwords, countersigns, cells, Party lines, ideological hair-splitting, and proletarian pig-Latin.

America was fertile ground for such extravagant self-deception. The depression had transposed to a sociological key the same jejune thrills they or their fathers had formerly found in the Fraternal Order of Sanctified Buffaloes, or its equivalent, the same soul-warming discipline of obedience to orders ("Party directives" they were now called) from the Sacred Fount of the Omnipotent Poo-Bah, now in Moscow instead of Baltimore or Cincinnati. This proletarian Mumbo-Jumbo—the psychological equivalent of the Ku Klux Klan in its blind obedience, its enthusiastic renunciation of logic, its rites and fetishes—did not extend far beyond limited circles in New York, Chicago, and a few other cities. But there it was fast becoming fashionable: already the proletarian brotherhood counted a good many millionaires' sons, professors, successful authors, and influential critics.

The writers and critics in particular, since the whole movement was on an imaginative level divorced from low-down realities, were succeeding in setting the tone for the more advanced intellectual circles; whilom liberal magazines put on nice new totalitarian blinkers; literary columnists wrote with one eye on Mrs. Reid or Mr. Ochs and the other on the *New Masses*. "Innocents'

Clubs"—different names for the same group of communists, but trimmed with "respectables" from churches, colleges, social settlements, etc.—grew apace and on special occasions, such as May Day, forged united fronts with themselves.

Such was the communist movement in America in 1931: a middle-class sect of heresy-hunters encased in a fungus growth of proletarian voodoo. No more than a mild beginning, it was, of the luxuriant lunacies still to come, as the deepening economic depression made believing more attractive than thinking.

4

My friend Boris Pilnyak, the novelist, had preceded me to the United States by a few days. Ray Long, editor of *Cosmopolitan Magazine*, had arranged a reception banquet for him at the Metropolitan Club and had radioed me to get off and push the S.S. *Augustus* because he had already postponed the reception once to enable me to share the honors. I pushed and we landed just in time.

The post-prandial amenities of that banquet were interrupted by the slap heard round the world, with Sinclair Lewis at the receiving end and Theodore Dreiser administering. Hostilities were opened in the after-dinner speeches, when "Red" Lewis balanced his warm welcome to a fellow-novelist from the Soviet land with an even warmer insult to a fellow-novelist in his own land. Whatever the newly-crowned Nobel Prize winner may have thought of communism in general, he made it clear that he objected to literary expropriation before the revolution. The company included the cream of American popular literature and a nice pink sauce of Soviet sympathizers. The atmosphere was electric, and Ray Long, being a Bismarck among toastmasters, immediately called on Irvin Cobb to divert the lightning. The humorist faced the Soviet guest and spoke in the following sense:

"Mr. Pilnyak, all of us here can welcome you with a most genuine cordiality, for the simple reason that few of us know you. As soon as America recognizes your talents and you become a real competitor, the cordiality will ebb and you, too, will be subject to attack. One of the risks of the trade, you know."

The lightning was stayed. But later, when most of the guests had gone, Lewis and Dreiser in their social peregrinations met in one of the smaller rooms off the dining room, and a few hot words on Lewis' part drew the celebrated slap. I was told of it the next morning, with the injunction to keep the matter quiet; all those who were eyewitnesses to the affair had agreed to squelch the trivial incident in silence. But there is always one leak in every conspiracy, otherwise newspapers would close down shop. The whole story was on the front page of the New York *Post* by noon and girdling the globe a few minutes later.

Thus a slap overshadowed what was in itself a noteworthy gathering. The consummate showmanship of Ray Long was the chief explanation for the fact that about a score of leading literary men in America turned out to greet a Soviet writer. The eminent authors and editors, with few if any exceptions, knew exactly nothing about post-revolutionary Russian letters, and Boris Pilnyak was just so many outlandish syllables to them. But for Americans anything from the U.S.S.R. was now charged with curiosity and a good deal of awe as well. What was ostensibly a testimonial to Soviet literature was in reality a testimonial to the Five Year Plan.

Ray Long had visited Russia early in November to "buy up" literary material for his magazine and for the Hearst book publishing organization. Few men in the history of American publishing had a keener nose for the trail of literary merchandise or greater persistence in stalking their quarry; with Hearst money for ammunition, the hunt in Europe was not too difficult. But he found quickly enough that the Soviet Union was a new kind of hunting ground and Soviet authors a new kind of animal. After two weeks of negotiations with VOKS, RAPP, and other alphabetical mysteries, he was so completely lost in the jungles of official red tape that he was ready to give up the chase.

Being somewhat more familiar with that jungle, I was able to come to his aid. One by one, I invited those writers whose stories might conceivably fit into his plans to my office and direct arrangements were made for about half a dozen Soviet short stories to go into *Cosmopolitan* and several books to be published, Charles Malamuth doing the translating. The first Soviet fiction to appear in any popular national magazine in America can thus be traced to Petrovsky Pereulok, as well as books like Pilnyak's *The Volga*

Flows into the Caspian Sea, Valentine Katayev's *Time Forward*, and *Little Golden Calf* by Ilf and Petrov. (The publication of the remarkable melodrama, *Chocolate*, by Tarasov-Rodionov,* I arranged with Doubleday-Doran while I was in America.)

Billy and I had accompanied Long to Leningrad, ostensibly to meet certain writers in that city, but actually because the editor was eager to meet the eighty-five-year-old mother of his friend the portrait painter, Leon Gordon. Among those who came to the Hotel Europe was Alexei Tolstoy. Tentative terms were discussed for the publication of his works. Everything having been agreed upon, Tolstoy pulled a solemn face.

"Only one other condition I must make," he said, "without which our entire negotiations will collapse."

"What is it?" Long asked, alarmed.

"You must agree to send me a pound or two of good European or American tobacco for my pipe."

Long kept that part of the bargain, although the books were never published.

More memorable by far than the literary conferences was the meeting between the aged Mrs. Gordon and the American editor. Watching the scene, Billy and I could understand what had made him so successful in the popular magazine field. The sentimentality of the fiction on which he built the immense circulation of *Cosmopolitan* was no accident or affectation; it was in the editor's own heart. No old-mother scene in the pages of his magazine could match the one we witnessed in that overcrowded Leningrad flat. Without a word in common in any language, Long and Mrs. Gordon understood one another instantly, expressing their affection in embraces and tears. For Long she was not only the beautiful gray-haired mother of his gifted friend Leon—she was all the mothers in the world, all the mothers who had wept and suffered for the edification of *Cosmopolitan's* millionfold public, rolled into one. Leon's brother, Hilary Gordon, a Soviet engineer, celebrated the occasion in true Russian style by challenging his American guest to a contest in vodka drinking. It may be recorded for the glory of the Red, White and Blue that America won out in this contest, but not without casualties. At the ballet that evening—

* Arrested in 1936.

Swan Lake, with the great Semionova dancing—Ray insisted aloud that "these are not swans but girls and no one can tell me different; if those lovely legs are swans' legs, I'm an Indian." In which his neighbors in a radius ten rows around would unquestionably have concurred had they understood English; as it was, we had to leave the theater all too suddenly.

And so Ray Long, of all the unlikely people imaginable, now stood sponsor for Soviet letters in the United States. Here he was, Pilnyak to the right and a Moscow correspondent to the left, launching Bolshevik literature on this side of the Atlantic with champagne and beer in the presence of the shock troopers of American literature. The occasion ranks in my mind with Mr. Ottinger's invocation to God to help carry through the Five Year Plan for atheist Russia as an example of American naivete in relation to all things Soviet.

5

With this literary banquet as a starter, my education in the new American attitudes toward the Great Experiment in Russia proceeded apace. A day or two later, as though for my particular edification, an excellent display of middle-class pro-Soviet enthusiasts was gathered at Town Hall. The exhibit styled itself a "We-Have-Been-to-the-U.S.S.R. Dinner" and contained first-rate specimens of practically every variety of eulogist, from the simple third-category tourist through the high-powered salesman with a fat Soviet contract in view. The pep-it-up booster spirit, that moves mountains and sells real estate, prevailed, and indiscriminate enthusiasm for everything Soviet gushed and popped and crackled.

"Down with us!" would have been the appropriate slogan for the dinner, since a large majority of the guests, had they been Russians, would have been crushed long ago in one or another purge. Liberal intellectuals with kind hearts and fuzzy minds: exactly the breed which was just then being liquidated wholesale in their "spiritual fatherland." A few of those at the speakers' table, indeed, would have been liquidated on their looks alone, they were such clear-cut bourgeois types.

Several score ladies and gentlemen who had made the pilgrimage, most of them as ordinary customers of Intourist but some as members of formal delegations, fortified themselves with a large dinner, and proceeded to pile up superlatives. Could it be the same Russia which I left a few weeks earlier that they were exclaiming over in such childish delight? Did this gray-haired little lady from some college really approve the works of Comrades Menzhinsky and Yagoda of the G.P.U.? Did this cheerful Rotarian defender of civil liberties actually believe that Russia was the "freest country in the world" and the home of "*real* democracy"? And the bald-headed little clergyman with spectacles on the tip of his nose, why was he of all people so thrilled with the Five Year Plan for the Liquidation of God?

Had the fabled visitor from Mars stumbled upon this little party, he would have carried back an account of a curious country called the U.S.S.R., devoted largely to lovely day nurseries, free abortions, new architecture, and teaching peasants to read; a country in which everyone at last was free and equal and supremely happy; a country in which men and women danced at their work. The Soviet officials present must have blushed for the monumental simplicity of these Americans. These, mind you, were not ruthless Bolsheviks wielding their "sword of history," let the heads fall where they may, but effervescent outsiders who mistook the heads for croquet balls. The hardships and sacrifices which they mentioned in passing seemed, in their speeches, merely to add a fillip of excitement to the thrilling Russian game.

A gathering of class-conscious *boorzhooys* was a relief after Town Hall. About fifty important industrialists and editors congregated around a banquet board at the Lotos Club as guests of the United Press, with myself and the Rome correspondent, Tom Morgan, as the attractions. They, too, were untouched by the woes of the Russian population, but for the logical reason that they really did not care. The indifference of the Lotos Club was not, as in Town Hall, obscene.

A microphone was brought to the table and for fifteen minutes I read into it on a coast-to-coast broadcast. The subject I had chosen was Stalin. My pleasant impression of the man in personal contact was still fresh in my mind and the talk was consequently in a key of appreciative analysis of his character. The Lotos Club setting underlined my perverse impulse to shock the capitalists and millionaires around me, and the consciousness of a nation-wide audience underscored my decision to save face for the revolution. In my peroration, therefore, I drew a parallel between Stalin and Abraham Lincoln—the same humble origin, the same readiness to make costly decisions in the interest of their social faith, etc. The comparison was far-fetched and I am not too proud of it. A number of professional patriots were scandalized, perhaps not unjustly, and protested against the blasphemy in vigorous language in the course of the next few days. Certain communists, on the other hand, professed to be no less scandalized. "Why must you drag Stalin down to Lincoln's level?" one of them complained.

It was the first broadcasting experience in my life and I was running with the sweat of honest stage-fright when it was over, though Mr. Aylesworth, then President of N.B.C., who was among the guests, was generous enough to compliment me on the delivery when we met socially in the lavatory later that evening.

After the lecture tour, I went to Washington to meet Mr. Stimson, the Secretary of State. President Bickel sat in on the interview. I found the Secretary an extremely likeable and genial person, but I emerged from the half hour's conference without having said very much, good or ill, about the Soviet Union. Ostensibly, I was in the capital to give Mr. Stimson the benefit of my Russian experience, but he was so brimful of opinions on Russia and communism that I could scarcely get a sentence in edgewise.

The American people, he told me in effect, are individualists, every one of them. There is not the slightest chance, therefore, of socialistic notions being accepted or tolerated here. We have been raised and prospered as a nation upon free competition and any political philosophy which means regimentation has no chance here. And more in this strain.

Senator Borah, when I dropped in on him in the company of red-headed Bob Allen, was sitting at his ease, feet on desk, reading a booklet. It was a reprint of my own series of articles—so perhaps my arrival was not as unexpected as it seemed. In any case, the Senator was good enough to tell me a great deal about Russia without urging. In fact, wherever I went people were ready to give me the low-down on Russia. It was the one subject on which everyone had definite and usually exclamatory views, ranging from pop-eyed detestation of the whole business to pop-eyed admiration. Usually, it was hated and admired for the wrong things.

This intense, passionate interest in Russia, strange and ludicrous as its manifestations may have been on occasion, was the most significant single impression I carried back to Moscow from my American visit. The Soviet experiment at this stage, coinciding with the economic depression in the non-Soviet world, was a challenge to all the old certainties. Whatever the ultimate fate of communist ideas in Russia itself, they were entering the stream of human thought, a yeast and a ferment.

Back in Berlin, I was kept waiting nearly a week for a Soviet visa, though normally I received it within an hour or two. For all my restraint in public speeches and interviews, reports of heretical statements on my part must have been relayed to Moscow; very likely my less guarded remarks in private conversation had been reported. When the visa was finally issued, no explanation of the delay was provided. But some months later, War Commissar Voroshilov told me smilingly that there had been distressing reports to the effect that I had "scolded" them, reports which on investigation proved exaggerated.

BOOK 4

DISILLUSIONMENT

I. "Socialism" Revised

THE Five Year Plan in Four Years—2 + 2 = 5. On Soviet Square a huge map rashed with dots, stars, crosses, to mark projected industrial developments. A giant scoreboard: *Over There:* unemployment, strikes, fascism, etc., and *Over Here:* new factories, shock brigades, unemployment liquidated, Dnieprostroi, etc. On billboards, livid zigzag lightning (G.P.U.) strikes gorilla-like villain head—"Death to Wreckers!". In a filthy restaurant, paper flowers in flowerpots are thick with dust, on plates the legend, "Through public feeding to socialism," and prices for playwrights and embezzlers only. On billboards, also, rabbits now multiply: through rabbit cutlets to socialism: 2 + 2 = 5. On every street, kerosene queues and bread queues and tramcar queues. Viscuous ooze of swarming dung-colored people, not ugly but incredibly soiled, patched, drab; the odor and color of ingrained poverty, fetid bundles, stale clothes. Spring mud squelches slippery underfoot. Tramcars tight-packed with humanity, squirting heads, legs, arms. The familiar stink in vestibules where your documents are inspected and grimy men issue *propusks*—permits. At the doors of public and near-public buildings, mills, bakeries, everywhere—soldiers with fixed bayonets. At every pile of brick or rubble, a decrepit old watchman in sheepskin or cast-off military greatcoat, armed with a decrepit old rifle—futile symbol of protection. Private doors are completely locked and barred; they open suspiciously only after complicated bell signals. The poverty everywhere carefully protected against marauders; a desperate emphasis on private possessions that flows from poverty, every scrap and tag-end in the garbage heap anxiously guarded amidst the socialized slogans.

A few "commercial" shops have appeared on the main streets, resplendent with ivory pillars of butter, festive chains of sausage, pyramids of sugar and cigarette boxes. The doors are open to all comers, but the prices—ten or twenty times higher than on the same goods rationed—are barriers; otherwise the shops would be picked clean in a few seconds. People come in to look (secretly they call the new emporia "Stalin museums"); a few buy minute amounts and run off excitedly with the tiny treasures. These shops give a new popular measure for earnings—the average national weekly wage is half a pound of commercial butter, or ten packs of commercial cigarettes, or a pound of sausage. Acidulous anecdote runs: "Have you seen the atheist shops?" "Why atheist?" "The prices are ungodly." The ordinary coöperative stores are more drab by contrast.

New stories are being added to old buildings on nearly every street, with small respect for the original architecture: raw patchwork effects. Ostensibly built for the "workers" in various enterprises, they are in fact occupied by factory directors, trade union functionaries, communists with a pull. But the ancient skylines of dome and cupola and tender tracings on gray cloud masses are as yet unchanged; at twilight, the flat silhouettes seem cut from cardboard to illustrate tales from the *Arabian Nights*. The hushed, mysterious Muscovite night is crumbling at both edges: soon it will be a mere sliver of darkness.

Four months' absence suffices to overlay Moscow with strangeness. Not the tinsel-strangeness, this time, of the first arrival, but a half-angry astonishment that the memories you edited out are true after all. Away from Russia, your mind imposed its own favorite designs upon the Soviet contradictions, choosing, discarding, arranging, hastily repairing the damage wrought by three years of immersion. Whatever your American lectures may have done to the listeners, they almost convinced the lecturer. By compromising with your experiences you nearly sneaked back into the comfortable groove of uncritical faith. Against the uncertainties of depression America you raised the future-tense certainties of Russia. You slid into the soporific illogic of *status quo:* the dead are dead and the maimed are dying, and what if another million dung-colored Russians are driven into the marshes and forests and deserts, if the great idea marches forward toward a painted rising sun on a painted horizon and our side wins; meanwhile, you relish a private vengeance against the soup lines on Times Square.

Had I remained in America permanently I might have evolved a new, if badly scarred and patched, enthusiasm. In the following years I was to think occasionally, with a sense of having escaped something vaguely shameful, that if I had not returned to Russia in 1931, I might have ended by contributing high-minded lies to the *New Masses* and slept happily ever after.

I made a quick survey of my Russian acquaintances for casualties. As always, a few had disappeared mysteriously; one had been executed; a few had returned from exile, but were still exiled for us since they dared not nod recognition. Others formerly under a political cloud were back in the sunlight of divine grace, one of them so cocksure that he came boldly to our door. A more tolerant attitude toward intellectuals and technical specialists was impending; already the tone of the press was somewhat milder towards them. A number of acquaintances from the halcyon days of 1928 therefore timidly revived our friendship, as though emerging from some long illness; apologetic about the yearslong absences: "you know how it is. . . ."

But the waves of arrests had not subsided; that "little suitcase" was not unpacked. The complicated fears were as oppressive as ever. The center of attack might be shifted from one social element to another, but the total pressure was, if anything, enlarged. A slight lifting of the weight from the educated classes was more than balanced by renewed terror applied to former "Nepmen," to Jews with relatives abroad, and to others who might be made to bleed gold. And behind these urban activities of the G.P.U. was its steady, plodding, monotonous punishment of "recalcitrant" peasants: those kulaks and "kulak agents" and poor peasants with "kulak mentalities," who multiplied paradoxically in precisely those areas where they had been officially "liquidated 100%."

"Valuta arrests," of which I had heard vaguely before departure, had in the interim become epidemic: anyone suspected of possessing foreign currency or gold was liable to sudden arrest. Even servant girls denounced as owning a tsarist gold coin were hauled in and given the works. Had I heard how a blundering militiaman picked up the wrong Petrov and he turned out to be a friend of Stalin's but he had four days of the *parilka* (torture by heat) before the mistake was found out?

The newspapers were filled with the same braggadocio and threats. Victories, successes, triumphs, but the plan for spring sowing far behind; three shot for sabotaging the rabbit-breeding plans;

engineman and signalmen shot for counter-revolutionary negligence in connection with a disaster on the Kursk line; eighty-four arrested for forging bread ration cards. Another internal loan was being oversubscribed—"voluntary" contributions of a month's wages or two months' wages. Another blast-furnace started in Magnitogorsk. Poincaré-War and agents of imperialism and dastardly kulaks and Left-Right and Right-Left deviators and secret Trotskyists and heil Stalin and 2 + 2 = 5. A sixteen-column speech by Lazar Kaganovich flaying the deviators and the kulaks who'd smuggled themselves into the collectives and hail Stalin, our dear beloved, the genius of the revolution. Kaganovich quoting Stalin's quotation of Lenin's quotation of Marx's quotation, the editorials quoting Kaganovich, and all the frightened moles with dispatch-cases under their wings quoting the editorials to play safe.

No, says Nathalie, my secretary, no cable news today. Sorry.

A reporter returning to Moscow after a few months' absence cannot take up his work where he left off, as he might in another capital. He must peel off the strangeness and re-focus eyes and mind to the scene. He must refresh his understanding of the euphemistic code in which events are recorded for the masses and sharpen his perceptions of the overtones of the news.

2

Feeling my way through dim stale corridors to the censors' office for a frigidly cordial reception. We all know I'd been kept waiting in Berlin for a visa this time as a disciplinary measure . . . a hint to the wise, you know. But we say nothing about it. For all my caution I had evidently said too much in America; I would have to exert myself mightily to reconquer my status of "friendly" correspondent. . . .

Kostya Umansky, the new censor, smiled through his gold teeth and blinked through his thick glasses and asked pompous questions about American recognition. Yes, he knew I had seen Secretary of State Stimson. Oh, we know everything, everything, Gene. There was the unspoken feud between us begun three years ago at my party in the Grand Hotel. Our conversation was on a high level of international affairs, but under it I read in his golden smile, "You dislike me because I'm an egocentric Soviet go-getter, but watch me rise to commissar. . . ." And he must have read in my smile, "The pompous little careerist, beneficiary of the revolution. He hates me because he knows I see through him. A little storekeeper with a corner on revolution: ladies and gents, the genuine article in proletarian dictatorship!" In this suavely scheming Comrade Umansky, clever with the devious shrewdness of a clothing salesman, ironical to underlings and toadying to higher-ups, discreetly indulging a sybaritic streak, I was coming to see (perhaps unfairly, but despite myself) the quintessence of revolutionary technique.*

The Hammer mansion on Petrovsky Pereulok, where we lived, with its marble staircase and vast ballroom, its immense pseudo-artistic nudes, its kitchen as large as a field and Shura cooking barley-and-mushroom soup for the American prodigals, was some more $2 + 2 = 5$. Around the courtyard, in what were formerly stables and servants' quarters, more than a dozen families were squeezed together. The sight of the foreigners' spacious life, the sound of their American gramophones, the odors of their daily meat must have been a constant taunt. The children stood on tiptoe and looked into the wonder-windows. Dr. Hammer's big untamed wolfhound was chained all day in the corridor leading to the kitchen, and at night was unchained to guard the "black," or servants', entrance against intruders. I must get used once more to the indecency of living safely and comfortably in the encircling dreads and shortages.

Not that the comforts were idyllic. The bathtub, it is true, was tremendously large; but when the heating device, after hours of fussing, yielded only a few gallons of hot water, the size of the bathtub was less a blessing than a jeer. While I was in America my extension of Hammer's telephone had been cut off without explanation. Covering the news without a phone being impossible, I plunged into a two months' battle against bureaucratic procrastination in which I enlisted the Foreign Office and the G.P.U. for ultimate victory. The roominess of the mansion made it a natural gathering place for celebration occasions in the American colony, which was pleasant enough but a heavy drain on the exchequer.

* Umansky came to Washington in 1936 as Counselor of the Soviet Embassy.

Charles Malamuth occupied our space while we were away and upheld its record for hospitality. His wife, Joan London (daughter of Jack London), had joined him in Moscow. Later E. E. Cummings, American poet, moved in for a while. Other Americans, among them the Gene Tunneys, had been entertained in the style which a foreign food shop and Shura's cookery made possible. Shura and her glowering ways were attaining international fame of a sort. Her clumsy peasant figure, the flashes of earthly shrewdness and peasant greed out of the depths of her tight-lipped reticence, impressed foreigners as enigmatic. Shura figured in Cummings' book about his Russian sojourn as "ogress"; Dr. Hammer appears as "Chinesey," Charlie as "Turk" or "Assyrian," Joan as "Turkess" or "Harem." Incidentally, what I understood of that book, *Eimi,* was so good, so penetrating, that I still wish he had not written it in puzzlewords.

Though Joan's father is one of the most widely read foreign authors, ranking with Russia's greatest story-tellers in popular favor, her presence was adamantly, and a bit ostentatiously, ignored by the press and in literary circles. Her husband's outspoken dislike for the more brutal aspects of the Bolshevism for which he gave up his college career may have had something to do with the snub. Joan had inherited much of her father's passion for social justice, which is the worst possible equipment for an appreciation of the U.S.S.R. Her abstract admirations had disintegrated almost instantly into seething angers and ironies between the time I had seen her in New York and this reunion in Moscow. Such speedy disillusionments annoyed me unreasonably—mine had taken three years—and I found myself reproving her for the intensity of her objections to the Soviet atmosphere and policies.

With every week after my return I came to feel more ashamed of my mealy-mouthed caution while at home. Deep under those excuses I had made for myself, I now was forced to admit, had been the subconscious desire to remain *persona grata* with the masters, to retain my job. I was protecting my status as a "friendly" correspondent. And at that I had just about crawled under the line. . . .

I watched the men and women in queues, in fetid street cars, in fear-soaked offices and felt as though I had played them false. In the first half of my Soviet sojourn, I had felt guilty *toward the revolution* every time the exigencies of my trade obliged me to report facts that sounded discreditable to the U.S.S.R. In the second half, I was to feel constantly more guilty *toward the Russian people* whenever the exigencies of my trade obliged me to keep mum about some unpleasant truths. It was this gradual and inexorable shift of vantage point that sums up the transformation in me. The change may have been accomplished before I left, but it was upon my return—in the gnawing suspicion that I had somehow betrayed the Russian people by minimizing and concealing their sufferings—that I came consciously to recognize my new viewpoint.

3

Where the basic conditions of existence for a hundred million people may be altered with one brief and arbitrary *ukase,* history becomes curiously telescoped and foreshortened, like those motion pictures where you see the growth of a plant from seed to full flower in a few seconds. Processes that elsewhere mature slowly, in a totalitarian state sometimes come to fruition in a week or a day. In going off on a vacation you may miss the turning point of another "epoch."

Though the implications of the break were not at once apparent, I did recognize that I had missed such a turning point. Charlie, who had held down my job creditably during these months, brought me up to date on the outward signs of the change. The piece-work system of payment for labor, against which trade unions all over the world have carried on a relentless war, was introduced throughout Soviet industry, and even on collective farms. A complicated system of prizes, bonuses, and other cash rewards for better work was instituted. Shock-brigadiering or pace-setting on the job had been from the beginning stimulated by tangible privileges, but painstakingly draped in pretenses of undiluted patriotism; much of the pretense was now dropped and the emphasis placed more frankly on the material rewards.

The common denominator of these and related changes was the abandonment of "equality"—in income, living standards, social privileges, etc.—as a socialist objective. It had never existed, of course, as a practical reality, but had been accepted as a motivating ideal, as one of those patterns of perfection which all societies set up. Even during the Nep period, when disequality had been as wide as in any capitalist land, and a lot more vulgar, the central star of socialist idealism—"from each according to his capacity, to each according to his need"—had been undimmed. The few isolated "communes" in various parts of the Soviet Union, where all were expected to give their best work and then drew from the common wealth according to their needs, had been the pride of the Soviet leaders, the ultimate hope in functioning in miniature.

With the end of Nep, that hope had been intensified. The impetus behind the Five Year Plan and the ruthless drive for agrarian socialization had been collectivist. Among the members of the Communist Party themselves the ideal ever since Lenin's days was symbolized in the "party maximum"—a ceiling on income reminiscent of the Christian vow of poverty in certain monastic orders.

Early in 1931, this ideal was thrown overboard. These anticipations of collectivism were not merely liquidated but drenched with ridicule. Marx and other socialist prophets were re-interpreted; the "party maximum" was raised and ultimately abolished; wage differentiation was not only recognized but made obligatory. Plays and novels which celebrated equality were suddenly out of date and even "reactionary." Those foreign books which stressed the theoretical economic equality of commissars and ditch-diggers became obsolete and rather preposterous.

It was, of course, the practical needs of industrialization which caused the revision of fundamental faith. To make the newly created industries more productive, to reduce spoilage, to extract more labor from its people, the Kremlin had decided to bring back the driving force of personal gain. To make the Communist Party members more ambitious, the limitations on incomes were removed and membership converted from a semi-religious vocation into a profession, like politics in other countries.

I am running considerably ahead of the story. Though achieved by fiat, the change, amounting to a reversal of philosophy, took years to deepen and harden and to systematize its justifications in brand-new theories of socialism. Higher productivity of labor, more "profitable" conduct of state trusts—in short, efficiency—could not be raised above the older and traditional socialist ideals overnight. Factory output could not supersede the well-being of the workers as the primary socialist goal without a term of violent mental adjustment. Thousands would be punished as "Left deviationists" and "petty bourgeois romanticists," before the new pattern of perfection would be fixed upon the nation's mind and spirit. Vestiges of mankind's ancient dream of equality—that dream running through all religions from Christianity to essential communism which, for all its "impractical" and "utopian" character, has molded mankind's history—would have to be stamped out.

It required a year or two of ideological jugglery before the absence of equality, once an evil to be faced and mitigated, was turned into a positive Bolshevik virtue. It was Stalin who made the word *uravnilovka*—the equalizing of economic returns—a term of contempt and one of the major Soviet sins from this time forward. It was Stalin, too, who in February, 1934, would characterize equality as "a piece of petty bourgeois stupidity, worthy of a primitive sect of ascetics, but not of socialist society organized on Marxian lines."

On June 23, 1931, Stalin made a speech at a closed conference. Early in July it was published. We transmitted it to the world as marking a new turn in Soviet policy almost as sharp as Lenin's announcement of the New Economic Policy just a decade before. But most of us failed to see, and all of us failed to report, two significant differences.

In the first place, Lenin's turn had been preceded by an intense open discussion within the ruling Party and to some extent outside its ranks; whereas Stalin consulted neither the people nor his Party. He consulted only his immediate advisers, and the about-face took the communists as much by surprise as the general public.

In the second place, Lenin's move had been frankly a compromise with realities, admittedly a step backward, and made without scrapping the fundamental socialist dream. Stalin's "new economic policy," on the contrary, was represented as a step forward. In reducing the worker more effectively to an inert cog in the productive machine, in strengthening the foundations for new classes and castes in the population, there was no hint of strategic retreat.

This was no temporary compromise but a permanent acceptance of the totalitarian principle of unstinting exploitation of workers for the impersonal profit of the corporate state-employer (as against the capitalist principle of personal profit for a private corporation-employer).

Stalin promulgated a six-point program for raising productivity and reducing waste in Soviet economic life. Considered purely from the standpoint of production, the program was sane enough. It called for more rigid cost-accounting. It eliminated the last trace of "interference" by workers with the operation of any plant, prescribing centralized and personal responsibility, with the management accountable only to the directors of the trust. It made piece-work and other familiar efficiency devices universal and obligatory. It called a halt to indiscriminate persecution of technical specialists, asserting that the opposition of this class had now been broken.

Though cushioned in standardized banalities about victories and proletarian enthusiasm, Stalin's speech was a more devastating indictment of Stalin's economic regime than any of his enemies had made. In the majority of Soviet enterprises, he revealed, the turnover of labor forces was "at least from 30 to 40% . . . during half a year or even a quarter of a year." The vast majority of workers were deserting their jobs "to go elsewhere, to a different place, to seek fortune." "Rationalization of industry," he said, had "long ago gone out of style." Soviet enterprises had "long ago ceased to count, to calculate, to make up actual balances of incomes and expenditures." Many of the plans presumably fulfilled, or even overfulfilled, were just "on paper." The non-stop work-week, foisted on the population in the most callous disregard of its own comfort or wishes, Stalin now admitted to be uneconomic, harmful, merely "an uninterrupted week on paper."

In short, near the end of the third year of the Five Year Plan, at a time when officially the U.S.S.R. had entered the stage of "real socialism," millions of workers were in perpetual migration "to seek fortune"—to seek, that is, tolerable living conditions. In the fantastic eagerness to set records of speed, to crowd five years into four, to provide boastful statistics at any cost in human suffering, industry has been thrown tragically out of balance—some branches growing by 40%, others (among them basic branches like the coal industry and heavy metallurgy) by only 6 to 10%; and much of this growth chiefly "on paper." "Nobody is accountable for anything," Stalin complained. Worse than that, the leaders of industry understand all that, but—I quote Stalin's words again —"they hold their tongues. Why? From all evidence, because they are afraid of the truth." He did not, however, explain *why* these leaders are afraid of the truth. That would involve public admission that the truth is dangerous, that those who dare to protest end up in concentration camps, that an economic system under the knout of the G.P.U. makes blind obedience the only guarantee of safety.

Stalin's speech was greeted by his own press, and by the parrot communist and near-communist press abroad, as another manifestation of his genius. Under any system of life which holds leaders responsible for their blunders, particularly when those blunders mean privation and death for great masses of people, a speech such as this would automatically have eliminated Stalin and his associates from public life. Under dictatorship, however, the recognition of disaster three years too late, after exiling and imprisoning and executing those who dared warn or oppose the blundering regime, becomes a superior sort of wisdom. Stalin was praised rhapsodically for his long blindness—just as he was glorified the year before for recognizing too late his own mistakes in the precipitate liquidation of the kulaks.

Dialectic materialism, whatever else it may be, is the smuggest and most convenient philosophy ever adapted by a ruling caste to its political needs. It finds a bogus consistency in the most startling inconsistencies. There is something monstrous in a dialectic materialism which exploits in order to end exploitation, which flouts elementary human values in the name of humanity, which fortifies new classes to achieve a classless society; which, in brief, presumes to be as heartless as history, instead of opposing its dreams and its hopes to history's heartlessness.

4

Out of the Russian Revolution has grown a lush literature of apologetics, nurtured by faith, fertilized by professional self-interest, feeding upon the ardent hopes of mankind for a juster world. That literature sounds the whole register of motivation, from principled jesuitism to unprincipled cynicism, from frantic self-deception to calculated deception of others. It has been particularly prolific in the United States, if only because geographical and cultural distance from Russia and political naivete make Americans especially credulous.

Having some acquaintance both with the authors and their subject matter, I have found that literature fascinating, a little like watching jugglers and conjurors at work. An intelligent and talented American woman long resident in Russia, for instance, used to visit us frequently and often bared her aching doubts; her Puritan conscience was wounded by the sight of useless brutalities, her mind lacerated by organized suppression of thought. But I studied her books and found in them no trace of her wounds and doubts, and I marvel at the mental and emotional sleight-of-hand that pulls such pretty rabbits out of the Soviet hat. A free-lance American journalist vehemently denied the stories of valuta tortures; then I learned that he was trying to rescue his own Russian relatives from the torture chambers!

Charitably, I had preferred to believe that these people were lying for the cause, sacrificing the lesser truths for those they considered greater. But ever so often I was confronted with a statement so cynical that I could not bring myself to believe its piety, an insult to the readers' sanity so pointed that charitable interpretation could not compass it.

A book by Louis Fischer, having eulogized the G.P.U. forced labor battalions as a "cure by labor," and having indicated casually that this "cure" has been "administered to untold myriads in all parts of the country," said:

> The G.P.U. is not merely an intelligence service and a militia. It is a vast industrial organization and a big educational institution.

Thus virtual slavery for "untold myriads in all parts of the country" is disposed of in one sentence. The system of large-scale forced labor, with a hundred thousand concentrated in a single penal camp and scores of such camps festering everywhere in the land, summarized in one precious euphemism!

A visit to Bolshevo, a boys' reformatory run by the G.P.U. near Moscow, was Fischer's immediate occasion for the extraordinary generalization. Bolshevo is one of the standard tourist show-places, and deservedly that: an enlightened colony for criminals in line with modern prison reform ideas. It is no more typical of the G.P.U. concentration camps than a model prison in New York is of chain-gangs in the South. For every thief or rowdy in places like Bolshevo, there were a thousand political offenders, "recalcitrant" peasants, non-conforming professors and engineers, deviating communists, living and working and dying like flies in forced-labor camps. The myriads to whom Fischer refers were filling swamplands, chopping timber, mining metals and chemicals, cutting canals, building railroads under police lash, in conditions so vile that the few straight-forward accounts which have been written (in books like the Tchernavins' and George Kitchin's) make Dante's Inferno look like a vacation resort. For every model prison, there were dozens of foul holes brimming with horror; for every Bolshevo, half a hundred Butirkas.

No tourist parties were taken to visit those places. The few foreign correspondents who attempted to visit them were always prevented. A Canadian newspaperwoman who succeeded by wile in entering a concentration camp and dared to write about it was quickly expelled from the country. Though even an accredited Kremlin press agent occasionally refers to "myriads" taking the forcible "cure by labor," the government concealed the extent of forced labor. However, from the isolated official admissions by the government (at least 200,000 prisoners engaged on the Baltic-White Sea Canal, several hundred thousand in double-tracking the Trans-Siberian Railroad, etc.) a conservative estimate of the total at the time when Fischer's "vast industrial organization" was at its vastest would be two millions. If we add the exiled peasants transported to areas under G.P.U. supervision—technically free but as helplessly the creatures of the G.P.U. as any prisoner—the total would at least be tripled.

Those who shouted hallelujahs to the Five Year Plan either were ignorant or pretended ignorance of the fact that the most extensive and most effective taskmaster and employer of labor was the police apparatus of the government. Its concentration camp near Moscow alone—one of several along the trek of the Moskva-Volga Canal under construction—contained more prisoners than all of Hitler's concentration camps put together. It contributed large contingents of forced labor to Magnitostroi, Dnieprostroi, and other of the proudest items in the Plan. William Stoneman of the Chicago *Daily News* at one time obtained from over-communicative local officials exact figures showing that prisoners outnumbered free laborers on the construction end of Magnitostroi and a series of other projects. William Henry Chamberlin of the *Christian Science Monitor*, who traveled widely through newly industrialized areas, wrote: "I could testify from personal observation that tens of thousands of such prisoners, mostly exiled peasants who had been guilty of no criminal offense, were employed at compulsory labor at such places as Magnitogorsk, Cheliabinsk, and Berezniki." Indeed, whatever differences there may have been in our estimates of the number in G.P.U. peonage, the existence of such peonage was accepted in Moscow as normal, matter-of-course, and indisputable.

The blossoming of the G.P.U. into a "vast industrial organization" began with the liquidation of the kulaks in 1930. The police suddenly found themselves in charge of enormous masses of raw labor—herded deliberately into harsh sections of the country where free labor could not be lured. Subsequent mass arrests in city and country alike expanded this labor force, and the influx of engineers and specialists by the tens of thousands gave the G.P.U. a terrorized technical personnel as well. Specific industrial jobs were therefore assigned to this "educational institution," particularly in the Far North, the Central Asiatic wilderness, and the more inhospitable sectors of Siberia. When the civilian economic authorities could not cope with a particularly difficult industrial task—certain chemical enterprises in the sub-Arctic territory, for instance—it was taken over by the G.P.U. and administered with compulsory labor by "educational" methods which included brutal beatings, a diet of garbage, a fearsome mortality rate, a regime that shriveled the spirit and withered the body of the victims and degraded the masters no less than the slaves.

Only the most hardened fanatic can read the stories of the Tchernavins and Kitchin without a shudder of horror. Not the blandest of apologists can deny the essential accuracy of those accounts; only a literary genius the peer of Dante could have conjured brutality in such meticulous detail from his own imagination. It happens that, like others who lived in Russia during the Five Year Plan era, I have talked to dozens of people who had survived those "educational" purgatories. What they told fitted so perfectly into the Tchernavin and Kitchin stories that there is no room for doubt.

I am not inveighing against labor by prisoners. I simply question the "revolutionary" pretensions of a society which counts its prisoners by the million, subjects them to hideously inhumane conditions, then seeks to fool the world into accepting the monstrosity as an "educational institution." I question the "building of socialism" by slaves. I question the unprecedented hypocrisy that would rally the noblest instincts of the outside world, the soaring hopes inspired by the Russian Revolution, in blind support of human degradation and organized sadism.

II. Bernard Shaw in Moscow

GEORGE BERNARD SHAW swept down on Moscow that August, his white whiskers and coat-tails and wisecracks flying—Lady Astor holding on breathlessly to the coat-tails, the American correspondents scrambling desperately for the wisecracks, the Russians gazing goggle-eyed at the strange antics. Lord Lothian and Lady Astor's handsome and sensible son, David, were in the party and grateful for the shadows while the other two held the limelight. From the first, the Irish bard was surrounded and cut off from contaminating contact with Russian facts by British and American yes-men for the Soviets and by Russian functionaries. They had a simple job of it. The great G.B.S. was more interested in being seen than in seeing, in being heard than in hearing. He exhibited himself at banquets, in a factory or two, on a hand-tooled collective farm, astride the Napoleon cannon in the Kremlin, wherever cameramen could get good shots of him and he could deliver better shots.

We wondered at the time that a playwright wise in the tricks of stage effect should be taken in so completely by his hosts and guides. Then we understood that he was not taken in, but himself collaborating in the deception, with the world at large as the common dupe. The Kremlin was too good an eminence from which to thumb his nose at the conventional capitalist world, and Shaw evidently had decided not to miss the chance. At first, Soviet officialdom was uneasy: the incorrigible oldster might play a few pranks on them. He might pry into their closets for skeletons of forced labor, valuta arrests, concentration camps, or make nasty remarks about the hard-worked and undernourished proletariat. He might demand statistics on political prisoners. But their fears were quickly allayed. Shaw was clearly in his most expansive and playful mood and would praise everything Soviet if only to annoy dear Nancy Astor. She mothered him, and the least he could do was to act the bad boy. (Mrs. Shaw had warned her to see to it that G.B. did not neglect his beard; Lady Astor made sure by washing it herself.)

Shaw did twit the Bolsheviks a bit on their ignorance of socialism, and shocked them with a few quips at Lenin's expense. But that was nothing, as long as his main preoccupation was to make faces at the decaying bourgeois world through Soviet windows.

It was a fortnight of clowning that ran us ragged. Since I reported for British United Press as well as the mother agency, I could not afford to miss a Shavian wheeze or sneeze. My secretary camped in the Metropole lobby, someone else trailed the party on its sight-seeing trips. Deftly Shaw skimmed the surface, careful not to break through the lacquer of appearances; if Lady Astor asked too many questions he neatly slapped her wrist. He judged food conditions by the Metropole menu, collectivization by the model farm, the G.P.U. by the model colony at Bolshevo, socialism by the twittering of attendant sycophants. His performance was not amusing to the Russians, I happen to know. It was macabre. The lengthening obscenity of ignorant or indifferent tourists, disporting themselves cheerily on the aching body of Russia, seemed summed up in this cavorting old man, in his blanket endorsement of what he would not understand. He was so taken up with demonstrating how youthful and agile he was that he had no attention to spare for the revolution in practice.

His seventy-fifth birthday took place while he was in Moscow and the celebration was staged at the old Nobles' Club, in the immense chamber with its ghosts of many farcical demonstration trials. It was at this gathering that Shaw achieved the apex of cynicism. In any other man it might have been ignorance or stupidity; in Shaw it was cold and calculated taunting of the audience. Shaw could not have failed to know that Russia was suffering acute food shortage. Rations were growing shorter; some foodstuffs had disappeared altogether; scant quotas of milk and butter were reserved for children only, and were available only at long intervals; food prices had just been doubled. All the hopes and thoughts of the overwhelming mass of Russians were centered on this fearful shortage. And in the face of all this, the rosy-cheeked self-satisfied foreigner stood on a platform and mocked the Soviet hardships.

"When my friends learned that I was going to Russia," he said, "they loaded me with tinned food of all sorts. They thought Russia was starving. But I threw all their food out of the window in Poland before I reached the Soviet frontier." He laughed like a mischievous schoolboy.

The vision of good English food thrown away in Poland was mockery of the underfed audience. Shaw's listeners gasped. One felt the convulsive reaction in their bellies. A tin of English beef would provide a memorable holiday in the home of any of the workers and intellectuals at that gathering—and those tins lay scattered in Poland. Even before he reached Russia, Shaw assured them, he knew that this talk of food difficulties was poppycock. Why, he had been overstuffed ever since he reached Moscow (forced wry laughter). Forty-eight food specialists had been shot last year in one clip to explain the lack of food, and international "plots" had been woven by the secret service to explain it. Shaw, however, knew it to be poppycock through his superior intuition and his full stomach.

He talked at length that night. Others loaded him with praise second only to the praise he loaded on himself. But his cynical tale of throwing away food was the one memory that remained deeply chiseled into a thousand minds when the celebration dispersed.

At a luncheon in the Metropole next day, Mrs. William Henry Chamberlin remarked to Shaw that Russians were sorry he did not wait to throw away his food on Soviet soil. Shaw looked around the restaurant and asked cutely, "Where do you see any food shortage?" Mrs. Chamberlin tried to tell him.

"I have a four-year-old daughter," she said. "As a foreigner I can buy all the milk she needs, but if I were dependent on the Russian milk rations my little girl would suffer terribly."

"Why don't you nurse her yourself?" Shaw retorted.

"But she's four, she's too old. . . ."

"Nonsense! Certain Eskimos nurse their children till the age of twenty."

Shaw wrote and spoke extensively on Russia after he got home. His every sentence carried the proof that he had seen nothing and learned nothing in his Soviet visit. In broadcasting on the

Russian theme to the United States, he addressed American listeners with some such greeting as "Hello, boobs!" Perhaps he knew more about Russia than he let on.

Bernard Shaw made a large contribution toward the myth of a happy, prospering, enthusiastic socialist Russia being built up in the outside world, especially among a certain type of intellectual. For the Webbs and people like them, there is at least the excuse of wishful thinking: they were eagerly molding a make-believe Russia close to their own heart's desire. Shaw had already attained his heart's desire. His humanitarianism was a self-indulgence rather than an ideal, or he would have revealed some slight twinge of awareness of the Russian humanity.

In a book published five years later by an Italian refugee from Mussolini's penal colony on Lipari Island (*Road to Exile*, by Emilio Lussu), he tells how the small library collected by the prisoners was suppressed:

> Hundreds of volumes were confiscated as dangerous to the regime; every book on the French and Russian Revolutions, all works by Russian writers and all works by free-thinkers such as Voltaire, Mazzini, and Anatole France. Only Bernard Shaw was respected. It was a bad moment for his admirers.

Shaw's clowning in Russia was no less a bad moment for his admirers in Moscow. Nor is it without significance that those who take Bolshevik excesses in their stride find it equally easy to take fascist enormities in their stride. It is no accident that Shaw has praised Hitler, too.

2

It was at a party in honor of the guests given by the British Embassy that the one exciting news story in the whole Shaw-Astor show developed. I was standing near Maxim Litvinov, Commissar of Foreign Affairs, on the small terrace leading from the house into the embassy garden when Lady Astor came toward us. She was followed by a few correspondents who had smelled excitement. A telegram fluttered in her hand. The commissar's fleshy face changed color as Lady Astor, with a grand gesture, kneeled before him and held out the telegram.

"As in days of yore," she declaimed for all to hear, "I present a petition to your government on bended knee. Most humbly I pray you in the name of humanity to save this suffering family."

Litvinov's fingers trembled and his jaws worked nervously as he took the telegram and read through it hastily. Then he shoved it back at her.

"This matter is not within my jurisdiction," he said gruffly, without troubling to conceal his anger, and walked away.

The correspondents took possession of the telegram. It was a story, and an "American-angle story," if ever there was one. The message, addressed to both Shaw and Lady Astor, was signed by a Professor Krynin, of Yale University, and begged for their intercession to get his family out of Russia. Some years previously, he had left Russia and for reasons of his own had been afraid to return. Now he was under sentence of death, like all who failed to obey an official summons to come back. Whatever his political sins, his wife and his children were innocent. They were in Moscow now. For years the professor had been trying to get them to America. A request by the eminent Britishers, he thought, might obtain the release of his family.

We all hopped to it. The message gave Mrs. Krynin's address, and thither we raced. The poor woman nearly collapsed with fright and excitement when the reporters descended on her. She knew nothing of her husband's desperate cable and was in no way responsible for it. Fearful that this move would only make her position worse, she at first refused to speak. Under pressure, she admitted that she lived only to care for her children and in the hope of some day joining their father. But she uttered not a word of criticism of the Soviet government.

With Shaw and Lady Astor in Moscow, the censors could scarcely interfere with the sending of our dispatches, and the story was a three-day sensation in the American press. Lady Astor did not accept Litvinov's refusal but carried the matter to other officials, including the G.P.U.; in particular, she used publicity through the correspondents in the hope of forcing action. She was stalled with promises. The Soviet government, she was assured, had no desire to keep a wife and children from their husband and father. But by the time she left, nothing had been done. And after she left, of course, the matter was forgotten.

Four or five months later, I received a cable from Roger Baldwin, director of the American Civil Liberties Union, asking me to ascertain if possible the whereabouts of Mrs. Krynin. Her husband was in despair, he indicated, having failed to hear from her or about her since his ill-advised message to the English party.

At the address where we had seen Mrs. Krynin before, the people who opened the door of her apartment pretended that they had never even heard the name. "No, no, there's no such person," they said and shut the door in my face in a panic. Going down the steep stairs I ran into a boy of ten.

"Do you live here?" I asked him.

"Yes."

"Well, then, maybe you know what apartment Citizen Krynin lives in?"

"She doesn't live here any more."

"She doesn't?" I pretended surprise. "Then where does she live?"

"How should I know?" the child replied. *"They came and took her* a long time ago."

So I knew. "They" came and took her. How many others who disappeared in these years had been taken by "them"? Every night the big "black Marias" moved through the stillness collecting another load of undesirables. Coming home from a late party, we often saw these wagons—immense closed-in trucks like American long-distance furniture moving vans, with a row of perforations near the top for air. Late one night, I rang the outer gate to a courtyard, having been persuaded to attend a social gathering despite the late hour. A sleepy *dvornik* (concierge) came to the door rubbing his eyes.

"And I thought it was the wagon again," he mumbled complainingly. "Almost every night they come for somebody."

"They" had come for the Krynin mother and children. Lady Astor's spirited intercession had landed the family in some secret exile, where correspondents would never again write embarrassing stories about them.

The same train that brought the Shaw-Astor party also brought one of my chiefs, the late Robert J. Bender, news editor and Vice-president of the United Press, and with him young Jack Howard, the son of Roy W. Howard. Their lively presence made the chore of covering the English party harder but brightened our lives all the same. If Shaw had half the good sense and one-quarter the honesty of Jack Howard in observing Russia, the world would have been spared a chunk of misinformation wrapped in the cellophane of Shavian paradox.

It was in the spirit of gentlemen from Missouri, who had to be shown, that both Bender and Jack confronted the over-publicized Russia. They stood in queues with the Russians, and took walks into less manicured sections of the city, and supplemented the official information with such off-record data as even a tourist can obtain if really interested. I was no longer a volunteer propagandist for the Soviet idea and the views these two carried away were less tinctured with my synthetic optimism than those carried away by Jack's father and other United Press people who had come under my guidance in former years.

Bernard Shaw's frolicsome clowning gave the pitch for that year's visitors and for years to come. Besides the individual tourists, there were groups, shepherded by alleged specialists in Soviet affairs—the blind leading the halt. Many of these leaders had a professional stake in the fashion for a watered-down version of communism: annual tours, books, lectures. They could not afford to have the doors of the U.S.S.R. shut against them by a wayward word, and many of them were as honestly and high-mindedly eager as their flocks to avoid upsetting truths. Professors or liberal clergymen, they were deeply disturbed by the shattered economic and social orthodoxies in which they were raised; if they lost their compensating belief in Russia life would become too bleak to endure.

Their belief was plastic enough. In 1929 and 1930 they celebrated the "equality" of all Soviet citizens. From 1931 onward they were no less earnestly enamored of piece work, differentiated wages to speed up production, the "realism" of Stalin which recognized that all men were not, after all, created equal. In 1931 they saw in the Bolshevik "Puritanism," in the prohibition of dancing and gypsy music, etc., the token of a new world. In

1935 they were to see the same token in the fox-trots and other resurrected amusements. Faith moves mountains of paradox.

The building of the Russian myth required no machiavellian propaganda tricks. The outside world in depression years had need of it as a fixed beacon in the storm of doubt. As Voltaire said of God—if there were no socialist Russia mankind was ready to invent one. It was fashioned in the image of men's hopes.

III. Ambulance and Motor-Cars

CONSIDERED in the most cold-blooded engineering spirit, with Leninist-Stalinist firmness and no petty bourgeois humanitarian nonsense, the practical wisdom of placing machines before medicines is still open to grave question. Broken-down factory workers cause breakdowns in machinery and impaired office workers retard the pace of operation. Except in agitational concoctions on the stage, even the firmest Stalinist develops a touch of bourgeois weakness when the missing medicines are needed for someone whose life he values.

One of the most callous of the orthodox brethren—a Checkist, a civil war veteran, a liquidator of kulaks—smiled grimly at our concern for the life of Rachelle Ossipovna. The Five Year Plan, he assured us, would not be affected in the slightest by the lady's passing. Despite this, I pulled official wires to obtain certain deficit medicaments, and used incoming Americans to fill prescriptions in Berlin; Billy canvassed our foreign friends to find citrous fruits and other things which might help sustain Rachelle's strength.

Much later I watched this hard-boiled Checkist when disease struck in his own household. His hard-boiledness did not reach all the way down. The victim was his sister-in-law, as useless to the *Piatiletka* as Rachelle had been. But his efforts to outdistance the galloping tuberculosis were as heroic as any he put forth in the Ukrainian civil wars.

We were to remember Rachelle's last illness as a gruesome epitome of Russian indifference to human life, of the primitive hygienic methods under the statistical triumphs of social health, and of sheer Russian carelessness. While millions of dollars were being poured into the purchase of machinery and raw materials and technical services, the government never could find the means to buy the elementary drugs and equipment for fighting disease. There was money to buy spare parts for everything but men and women out-of-order. Only the Kremlin Hospital, serving the most important strata of Moscow's hierarchy, had any of a long list of medicinal ingredients. These supplies were inaccessible to 99% of the Moscow population.

A disease of her gums which, with proper care and medicines, might have been cured, infected Rachelle's jaw. Her husband was a big enough fish in his own pond, but a mere minnow in the communist ocean. He did not rate the Kremlin Hospital. Home treatment seemed preferable to the overcrowded, understaffed, and unhygienic hospitals available to the proletariat. But when her condition became dangerous, Rachelle was rushed to one of these places. We visited her there—an ill-smelling, grimy barracks of a hospital, run in the most haphazard style, bed crowded upon bed.

It was in this hospital that Rachelle Ossipovna caught cold, which developed into pneumonia, of which she died in a few days. She was killed by the hospital as surely as though it had administered arsenic.

We came, unluckily, to know a lot more about Soviet medical practice than most of our colleagues. Like the "stable" currency and the wonderful educational methods, the socialized medicine under the official statistical surface was a snarl of contradictions, shortages, and ineptness. Doctors and dentists regarded their obligatory work for the state as an exaction and depended on private practice for their real income. The more famous medical specialists did not budge for less than fifty or a hundred rubles; often it required "pull" to get their services at any price. The public health service was by all odds inferior to the free public and charitable health services available to the poor in cities like New York or Chicago.

Russian medicine was doing significant work in theoretical research, but it was at a pitifully low level in ordinary everyday curative and preventive practice. I had the professional opinion of leading physicians in Moscow to confirm my own impression on this point. The gaping gulf between abstract research and practical application, between grandiose planning and messy execution, ran through every department of Russian life, but it seemed particularly horrifying in relation to medicine. The difference between the care open to the upper few and to the gray swarms of humanity below seemed particularly startling.

Despite the political leverage I could manipulate as a foreign correspondent, despite my American income and contacts, illness was fearful as it had never been under more civilized conditions. I could not help thinking how hopeless it must be for Soviet citizens without my advantages.

During the winter after our return from America, Billy was taken sick. Formal letters from the Foreign Office and hours of waiting to obtain ordinary drugs. Frenzied telephone calls to high officials for their intercession in getting an out-of-the-ordinary prescription filled. Finally, a panicky campaign to obtain an ambulance to transport her to the Botkinsky Hospital—regarded as second only to the Kremlin Hospital. Three doctors in consultation had diagnosed acute appendicitis. We thought an operation might be necessary any minute.

The day of Billy's transfer to the hospital was the quintessence of nightmare. It took hours of work, official influence, and more hours of waiting to obtain an ambulance. I sat by Billy's side as the rickety contraption bounced over the ice-mounds and cobblestones, every jolt sending the patient into paroxysms of excruciating pain. The half hour's ride seemed half a century. But finally we drove through the gates of the Botkinsky.

"We've arrived, darling," I consoled her. "You'll be comfortably in bed in a minute."

The ambulance stopped at a small structure about a quarter of a mile from the main building. Several orderlies began to remove the patient. Frantically I protested that we were not yet at our destination.

"But first we must register the patient here," the idiots insisted.

"Never mind the registration," I shouted. "My wife's in agony. She must first be taken to the hospital and made comfortable. To hell with your red-tape!"

Over my violent protests, however, Billy was dragged from the ambulance and carried into a drafty office. There, with the patient on the floor, moaning, tears rolling down her cheeks, a nurse drew out a long questionnaire form and proceeded to ask endless questions.

"Get her to the hospital first," I pleaded, "and I promise to fill out all the questionnaires you wish."

"But those are the rules—"

"Never mind the rules, my wife's dying," I shouted. "You must send her to the hospital immediately."

"But first we must examine her," the nurse insisted, and, good as her word, began to unwrap Billy in this room, with gusts of the icy wind blowing into the place every time the door was opened.

"Over my dead body! I'll tear the place up, if you keep her here another minute."

By this time, a few other employees had gathered. They stared at the barbarian foreigner who would not fill out forms, or allow a suffering woman to be unwrapped and examined in a drafty and unsanitary office. But for once the rules were shattered. For once the relief of human pain took precedence over red-tape.

By the time I had won my fight in the office, the ambulance disappeared. Billy was now packed into an open sled—an open sled in sub-zero weather!—which two men pulled to the main building. There I fought another battle with attendants to prevent her going through a regulation bath in a large, ill-smelling, filthy bathroom.

"You'll have to wash her in bed," I insisted. "Her strength will give out if you torture her any more."

"But the rules—" The astonished women, in gray aprons, lifted their eyebrows at such goings-on.

The first night Billy was kept in a sort of general ward, where the screams of accident patients and the constant comings and goings of divers people tore right through the sedatives. Next day she was transferred to a quieter room. The label "appendicitis" remained on her bed throughout her stay, although the diagnosis was adjudged erroneous almost from the beginning. Another indicated that she was entitled to "special feeding"—a privilege accorded to the more influential patients. Black soggy bread was the chief ingredient of the special feeding. Several times a day a porter came through the corridor dragging a wooden box filled with chunks of bread, and tossed a chunk with grimy fingers toward every table. The whole hospital echoed with the rasping sounds of that box being dragged.

Billy improved rapidly, despite the special care, and was soon well enough to watch the conduct of that hospital by way of sociological diversion. If I had not been there day after day and seen some of the primitive and careless procedure myself, I should have thought the details she told me were the effects of delirium. Only a few of the women were trained nurses—the others were ignorant girls of the servant type. They stomped up and down corridors and banged doors and called for one another in loud voices. Except under unusual circumstances, bed linens were changed once a week. The blankets were not washed but merely disinfected, so that they were crusted with the dirt and vomit of previous patients. The precious rules prohibited the bringing of linens, blankets, or other accessories from outside. But by devious means I smuggled in everything Billy needed, and doctors, nurses, patients came to her ward to inspect and exclaim over the fleecy American blankets; the hospital buzzed with the news of a foreigner who changed her sheets, her nightgown, and even her pillow-cases, every day.

The doctors, Billy thought, were capable but overworked. I succeeded—again by outraging the blessed rules—in having our own physician, who was familiar with her case, treat her. As soon as she could be moved safely she returned home.

Ever after, the glowing reports of socialized medicine in Russia in American books and magazines have been a source of amusement to us. Always we have wished their authors only one punishment—a week or so as patients in the second-best hospital in Russia.

2

I rode with Boris Andreyevich Pilnyak, that cumbersome and lovable blond bear, from Leningrad to Moscow in a shiny and gaily painted two-seater. Not in vain his journey to America, since it had netted the brilliant Russian novelist an automobile, apogee of Soviet daydreams.

The reunion of Boris Andreyevich with his Chevrolet on the docks of Peter's city which is now Lenin's city was most touching. He patted it and dusted it and fed it rationed gasolene. When he parked the creature outside a beer-hall, the leading writers of the city came reverently to admire, and they scrupled not to show their envy. Boris Andreyevich drove through this street and that, tooting the American-accent horn, like a little boy with a kiddy-car. His acquisition of the car was by all odds the literary event of the year, and I, sitting by his side in the triumphal march upon Moscow, shared in the glory.

Though the highway is the most traveled in the land and one of the few tolerably smooth roads, the Chevy cut a wide swathe of excitement in the peasant humanity between the old capital and the new. Men and women rushed from their huts to stare after us, horses shied, dogs went wild, little boys threw stones, and Boris Andreyevich blew his horn continuously, as though we were traveling on horn-power alone. Wherever we paused in our three days of leisurely driving, the entire village population soon gathered to marvel and to interrogate.

In one village where we stopped to eat, paying in Leningrad bread for fresh warm milk only slightly soiled, the name of the novelist had percolated down to one peasant youth, who quickly spread the news that a writer in the flesh was in their midst. The presence of an American started another widening circle of excitement—not so much my inconsequential corporeal self, as the attachments thereto, such as the fabrics of my clothes, my shoes, fountain-pen, wrist-watch and glasses. But neither a writer nor a foreigner could compete with the central object of scrutiny, the car. The younger and bolder men tapped its ribs with timid knuckles and felt its upholstery and tried its horn. A very old and gnarled woman with dragging skirts went round and round the contraption looking for the secret.

"But how does it run, just like that, all by itself?" she wanted to know.

Boris Andreyevich wiped the milk from his lips and strode to the machine with the manner of a full-fledged necromancer.

"Simple as potatoes," he said. "Come in, *babushka*, and I'll show you."

She needed a lot of coaxing by neighbors and assurances by the driver, and her blue head-kerchief framed a terrorized lot of wrinkles as the Chevy raced up the road and down again.

"To think that I lived to see this day," *babushka* muttered as she alighted, and there was that in her voice which implied that she still did not quite believe it.

In the next hour nearly every man, woman and child tasted a first ride in an automobile, with Boris Andreyevich as cheerful and perspiring as any shock-brigadier in a poster. There is at least one village in Russia where everyone can talk of automobiles from personal experience.

While my companion educated the villagers, I pushed those relentless sociological researches which distinguish the foreigner in Russia even more than his clothes. I listened to a long catalogue of complaints, ranging from loss of land to lack of calico and boots. The city people get everything while we in the village get nothing but work and taxes. Our horses plowed better than the tractors; besides, our village hasn't got any tractor. We're getting poorer every day working for the government and only the private peasants who take their produce to the towns live well. After a lot more of this, I felt a tug at my sleeve. A boy of fourteen or fifteen indicated that he wished to talk to me alone.

"Don't believe them, they're all kulaks!" he whispered in great agitation. "We liquidated twelve households in this village, but all of them deserve to be liquidated, all without exception. . . . They're dark people and oppose progress."

"Why are you afraid to talk?"

"It's hard enough living among them as it is," the boy sighed. "As for me, I shall leave them behind and go to the city and be a proletarian, that's what I'll do. The darkness of these people chokes me."

"And are they really all kulaks? I mean, do they all have cows and land?"

"No, they're poor as mice. Most of them are in the *kolkhoz*. But they think like kulaks and they should be liquidated. The Soviet power isn't firm enough with them, that's what. If I had my way—"

If he had his way, the whole of his native village, not excepting his own family, would be in the Northern forests chopping wood. Just who would then cultivate the *kolkhoz* the boy could not quite say. Not himself, certainly, since his hopes were fixed on escape to the city.

In a dozen other villages I tried to probe. The inclination of the peasants in talking to a stranger was clearly to lay the gloomy colors on with a spade. Questioned by Boris Andreyevich, they often admitted exaggeration and admitted particularly that the past, before the revolution, was even worse. But they were not consoled. The peasant who defended collectivization seemed to me everywhere the exception; he spoke of necessity in the future tense and was often jeered by the others. I recall the definite impression that the countryside was sullen and bitter; and coupled with that a sense of the obduracy, the ignorance, and the enmity of the peasant material which the Kremlin was forcing into new economic molds.

"Peasants always complain," Boris Andreyevich said. "They keep on whining, from the time they're born till the day they die. It has always been thus with us in Russia."

The first night we slept in the city of Novgorod. Like a very old and chipped icon, its colors faded and its figures archaic, but beautiful with the nostalgic beauty of ancient things. Novgorod was a brilliant and wealthy capital when Moscow was still a provincial town. Many of its moldering churches and monasteries were now inscribed with the names of Soviet institutions, in big red letters. A medieval convent was now used in part as a hotel and for the rest as a vacation resort for young girls. The arrival of the shiny car set the nuns' cells (filled with vacationing girls) aflutter. A few of the girls fluttered outdoors to exclaim over the car and its occupants until a stern directress came to drive them back.

"Just like nuns," a plump little girl with thick straw-colored braids complained.

But before yielding to discipline she slipped a scrap of paper into my hand. "My address, in Leningrad, and you must let me know when you are in Leningrad again. You're the first foreigner I ever talked to."

The second night we slept in Tver. But "slept" is an exaggeration. All the bedbugs in the province were holding a convention in the bed assigned to me. Next morning I mentioned the matter to the unshaven fellow at the hotel desk. He registered honest astonishment—the first such complaint he had ever had.

For years after that trip I was privy to every phase of the biography of the two-seater: its illnesses and miraculous recoveries; its missing parts the replacement of which sometimes required months of conniving; its mobilization for military service in the annual maneuvers. The car was sign and proof of the affluence of popular writers in the U.S.S.R. It set Boris Andreyevich off from the common run of man even more than his talents and temperament.

3

Blow, trumpet! Hail, Stalin! for now the Lyons family, too, rolls through the capital of approximate socialism in an automobile of its own. Thenceforth the family would designate chronology for its Russian period as B.F. and A.F.: before and after the Ford. Let censors dig their homes at the end of the world, let news explode in the most distant aerodromes, let the Press Department issue its mimeographed smudges at ungodly hours! Such B.F. torments lost their sting A.F. Thenceforth, transportation was no longer a lowly private vexation but a lofty public problem, like housing, liquidation of illiteracy, or differentiation of wages. Thenceforth, mystical interviews with eloquent average Muscovites in street-cars would be composed without the disturbing memories of stench and bruises.

Semichasov, the chauffeur, sat as proudly at the wheel as though it were a Rolls Royce; the social distance between car owners and the trolley rabble was so great that the class distinctions between different makes of cars counted not at all. Nor was there anything absonant in a Ford with a chauffeur. The care of an automobile under Moscow conditions required the full time and attention of at least one person. Gasoline rations must be obtained at specified distributing points. Garage space (at a cost twice as big as the average Soviet worker's total wages) must be located, if found at all, at a point ten miles from one's home. The slightest repair job necessitated days or weeks of routine grief.

Besides, driving in the rutted streets, thick-packed with the humanity that overflowed sidewalks, zig-zagging among the slow-moving peasant carts, required the nonchalance and the Slavic instincts of a Semichasov. There was a magnificent optimism in the way Russian chauffeurs cut through crowds at top speed, trimming toes and shaving beards and scattering bundles but incredibly, miraculously, killing no one. If there was in it a shattering contempt of the Russian mob, there was a profound understanding as well. Foreign drivers inched their way through mobs where Russian chauffeurs stepped on the gas to get through.

Now that we had a car, it was hard to imagine how we had managed without one. Three-quarters of the physical difficulties of living in Moscow fell away automatically. It is almost impossible to convey to people who have not experienced it on their own flesh and nerves the hardships of transportation in Russia, just as one cannot convey the reality of the housing situation. It was fitting that a few years later the construction of a gaudy subway in Moscow (though it had no perceptible effect in solving the transportation problem) should be raised to a symbol of the glories-to-come.

I was the last of the working foreign newspapermen to acquire a car, partly because I could not convince my bosses in New York to pay for one; even more so because I felt it faintly disreputable to drive around in public view while Muscovites fought for a foothold on the rims of tramcars. To the very end of my stay it seemed to me a little like flaunting one's health by doing handsprings in a hospital for cripples. I was not alone in this senseless self-consciousness; I know other foreigners who harbored a sense of guilt in publicly enjoying advantages which Soviet officials enjoyed without blinking an eyelid.

4

Soviet newspapers that winter were writing a great deal about an "aero-sled" of domestic invention. A motor-driven sled with a rear propeller, it was said to achieve a speed of some two hundred kilometers an hour on flat snow-covered ground. Ever enthusiastic over new mechanical toys, Russians foresaw an important future for this invention in covering immense spaces in the wintertime for purposes of commerce and in the event of war.

One day all foreign correspondents were invited to a demonstration of the aero-sled. Most of us accepted. It was one of those Russian days when the frost seems to be a ferocious beast lurking outside your door, ready to snap its teeth shut on your nose. But we bundled up and rode to the very end of a car-line, and there found a group of Soviet officials, and the engineer-inventor of the propeller sled. Having inspected the two sleds and interviewed the inventor, we were offered rides.

In batches of three or four, we crowded into the open sleds. At two hundred kilometers an hour, in a cold about thirty below zero, the drive was no picnic. Always demons for speed, and now intent upon demonstrating their new toy, the Russian chauffeurs forgot all caution, or perhaps never had known it. They darted into the open fields with the speed of arrows, flashing around an occasional stone or tree, while those who watched, including confirmed atheists, prayed for the passengers. A few of the foreigners had the courage of their doubts and declined the ride. It takes a brave man to admit fear, and my own valor did not suffice.

I climbed into the aero-sled, buried myself as deeply as I could in my clothes and waited for the worst to happen. For three or four minutes I found out what it would be like to ride a torpedo. It was with a feeling of deep and heart-warming relief that I stepped out. On the way home I found that all the others had the identical feeling.

Three days later a black-bordered item in all the newspapers announced the death of the engineer-inventor and several others. Even before we had reached the warmth of our homes, the men we had interviewed were dead. Having disposed of the correspondents, they piled into the sleds for another ride, were smashed up and most of them killed.

IV. Gold Mining in Torture Chambers

THE miracle of white bread: crisp little loaves in a glowing heap on the Torgsin counter. Not the sand-gray bread that passed, at double prices, for white in the ruble stores, but luminously real. At the other end of the long angular shop was the jewelry department. Its litter of rubies and diamonds for foreign buyers had not half the radiance of the white loaves; precious stones shine with a cold inner glitter, whereas white loaves are prisms to reflect fascination in the eyes of hungry Russians. There was butter, too, and cheeses, bland Volga salmon and great flanks of blood-dripping meat. But the white bread outshone them all—at once substance and symbol of desire.

Russians moved shyly in the glow of that miracle, as though in an art gallery. They spoke softly, placatingly, to the clerks, and asked for prices in apologetic tones. This was the one shop where trade was encouraged, because it was paid for in valuta. But the habit of meekness in buying, fixed by these years of shortage, was strong upon them. They remained grateful for the right to buy and self-conscious when their purchases seemed too large.

The shop windows of Torgsin were the most exciting episode in Moscow's life since the demise of Nep. The announcement of the Five Year Plan had not caused nearly so much talk, so much envy, so many daydreams. Commissar Ordzhonikidze's figures for heavy industry in the second quarter of the third year of the Plan were for economists and professional communists. But the shimmering bread loaves set in a windowful of other foodstuffs, the fashionable shoes and shirtwaists and chic hats—these were for Ivan, Stepan, and Marusya, who stood spellbound for long minutes.

A peremptory doorman kept the rabble out. With one hand he opened the door obsequiously for foreigners and well-dressed Russians, while with the other he shooed off the ragged peasants and poorly dressed workers. Oh, you couldn't fool him! One look and he knew a valuta customer. If your dress was unprepossessing, you must exhibit the proofs of valuta: an actual foreign banknote, a gold coin, a credit slip in foreign denominations.

Torgsin was started solely for commerce with resident foreigners and tourists, to gather in their dollars before the half-illicit currency bootleggers got them. The word Torgsin, in fact, is an abbreviation for "trade with foreigners." But some financial genius (several claimed credit for the idea) suggested to the government that many Russians, too, possess valuta, and that others had friends and relatives abroad who would send them valuta once a place to spend it was provided. The store was therefore opened late in 1931 to all the lucky ones and its business instantly skyrocketed. Additional Torgsins were opened in other parts of the city, then in other cities, and soon its network of stores, its mail order business, its foreign package business, turned Torgsin into the most lucrative trading organization in the land. The Kremlin had discovered the "internal foreign market," and was to exploit it until 1936.

Prices were reckoned in rubles, but payment was accepted only in the gold equivalent. Those who had actual foreign money paid directly and got their change either in a handful of assorted currencies, or in a credit slip. Others took their gold—tsarist coins, spoons, trinkets, wedding rings, old dental plates—to an assay counter, obtaining a credit slip in return. Russians receiving money from abroad got their Torgsin credits directly from the bank. Later, special Torgsin coupons in many denominations were issued to facilitate the business, and became, in effect, a superior currency, from thirty to sixty times more valuable than the official currency.

Though the authorities sought to assure people that no questions would be asked, and no record of their identity made, Russians entered the place with beating hearts, many of them only when driven by hunger or despair. They feared secret arrest if branded as persons possessing valuta. And, in fact, despite the assurances, the G.P.U. kept a sharp look-out and got thousands of its "leads" to valuta owners through Torgsin. More cautious or less naive Russians (unless their money came from abroad through the banks) did not venture into the Torgsin. Dozens of times Billy and I, like every other foreigner, made purchases for Russians who dared not call attention to their pitiful affluence by entering the place.

Nevertheless, millions of dollars were collected for the government's coffers every month. Millions of rubles in tsarist gold pieces, it appeared, were still in private possession, and these now rolled in turbulent streams into the Torgsin stores, chiefly in exchange for food. The choicest products in the land—white flour, fruit, canned food, cotton goods, etc.—were diverted to the valuta emporia. After some months the flood of gold subsided, and Torgsin began to accept silver. Mountains of silver tableware, trinkets, picture frames—things snatched somehow from the maw of revolution and treasured these fifteen years—were gathered. Still later, when the silver had been drawn off, precious stones were added to the media of exchange, and finally any other valuables (furs, pictures, icons, antiques) which had a ready market abroad.

In working this "internal foreign market," the government was as conscienceless as the most heartless pawn-broker. Acute shortage and semi-starvation had destroyed the Russian's sense of value. Gratefully, he gave the government his last silver cup for a few pennies' worth of butter, his wedding ring for a lemon, a diamond for a few pairs of stockings. I remember calculating the cost of a series of Torgsin items in silver and learning that a pair of shoes cost twice its weight in silver. A hundred dollars sent by an American relative bought perhaps ten or twenty dollars' worth of goods. The government robbed its citizens twice in one transaction—first in its arbitrary valuation of the proffered jewels or other valuta, and then in its steep prices. Meanwhile, the secret agent stood in his corner marking off victims for the final kill by the Valuta Department of the G.P.U.

Only a few of Russia's teeming millions, of course, could have any dealings with Torgsin. For the rest, these stores filled with food luxuries only emphasized the general poverty. At moments of sharpened shortage, when food rations were reduced and prices raised, the Torgsin windows in every large city of Russia must have seemed deliberate mockery.

To a foreigner it was inexplicable that the obvious resentments never boiled over in violent action. In the center of famine districts in the Ukraine in 1933, when wagons went around collecting the day's corpses, Torgsin windows flaunted bread and butter and sausage, and it occurred to none of the starving to smash the windows and seize another day of life. In any Western city there would have been riots; the brow-beaten, bovine Russians merely stared and sighed and suffered. Had the Soviet people had a spark of real rebelliousness in their make-up, the revolution would inevitably have taken a different course. It was, paradoxically, the absence of the revolutionary instinct upon which the Russian revolution rested. Opposition, when it did assert itself, was negative in character—a sullen, do-nothing non-coöperation such as was now spreading among the peasantry, and isolated, unorganized acts of desperation.

The stifled laughter filled with tears quickly took Torgsin into its orbit. Jokes about these stores multiplied. One of them caricatured the usurious prices. A young husband, it went, wishing to present his bride with some unusual gift, took his one silver spoon to Torgsin and obtained a credit slip for twenty-three kopeks. In vain he searched for an item within that figure. Finally he went to the director of the shop. "I have twenty-three gold kopeks," he said, "and want to know what I can buy for it." The kindly director looked through his price lists and after a while exclaimed cheerfully: "There it is! Exactly twenty-three kopeks—one aluminum spoon."

The most popular and biting anecdote of all had it that there was a special room in every Torgsin where, for a fat fee in valuta, you were allowed to sing the old Russian national hymn, *God Save the Tsar!* The implication, of course, was that the Kremlin was selling its revolutionary ideals for gold.

2

Words have a life of their own, overtones of meaning and depths of emotion, that no dictionary definition can convey. The Russian Revolution has thrown many words into sharp relief, charged them with intimate significances unintelligible to strangers. Words like *kulak*, *vredityel* (wrecker), *udarnik* (shock-brigadier), *liquidatsiya* (liquidation), have their individual careers; a literal translation may give their body but no indication of their soul.

But of all the words lifted to eminence none can compare with *valuta*, syllables electric with wonder and with danger. By 1931, all the works of Marx and Lenin, all the speeches of Kaganovich and Kalinin, were outweighed in the scales of Russian consciousness by this one word. Valuta shops, valuta restaurants, valuta arrests, valuta tortures, valuta whores: just a few dimensions of that inexhaustible word. To record that it means "real values," such as foreign money, precious metals and jewels, does not begin to explain it.

The revolution that was to free the human spirit from its economic fetters began, perhaps unavoidably, by concentrating all its attention on those fetters, reducing all mortal values to the common denominator of economics. Industrialization under Stalin carried that simplification to paranoiac extremes, scrapping its socialist conscience, every shred of humaneness, for economic values: production, factories, canals, mines, shimmering statistics. And the common element in all of those was valuta. Valuta bought machines and brains, arms and munitions, all the essentials that cheap labor alone could not obtain. Valuta was the concept of money refined to its quintessential core of pure hard value.

The world economic depression heightened the importance of valuta by reducing the income from Soviet exports. In the first half of 1931, for instance, the country sent out more goods, by 754,000 tons, than in the same months of the preceding year, but received for it $63,730,000 less in money. The government's desperate yearning for valuta began to blot out all lesser appetites.

The entire tourist business was placed strictly on a valuta basis, and the main hotels, catering to foreigners, were put on a foreign currency footing. Taxis and such other services as could conveniently be withheld from foreigners if they did not pay in some currency other than rubles were put in the valuta category.

The central symbol of the valuta-snaring fever seemed to me the Hotel Metropole, now remodeled to match the Russian conception of foreign taste. The perspiring musicians in their marble tower at the Grand Hotel, still grinding away at *Hallelujah*, saw the foreign ingredient in the gala night audiences dwindle to almost nothing. The Metropole was the new social center for the bourgeois colony. Its main restaurant was a Russian peasant's dream of capitalist splendors—immense candelabra, oversized lights, heavy furniture, a jazz band of symphony orchestra proportions. The place always made me think of the Grand Central Station turned into a Rotarian banquet hall. The chief pride of the restaurant, its ultra-bourgeois touch, was a great circular pool where lights and rather proletarian-looking fishes played. On grand occasions, the chef in cap and apron emerged from his sanctum with a net over his shoulder and captured a fish for a special valuta client. The dancing couples rotated around the pool, and sometimes an unsteady customer joined the fishes to the great delight of the assembled crowd.

That restaurant was a lonesome and rococo bourgeois island in the limitless ocean of Bolshevism. Gypsy music was forbidden throughout the land, but a large gypsy chorus was salvaged from the social garbage heap and installed here to entertain the valuta guests. It was a very fine chorus, too, if a bit out of practice.

In the beginning, admission was restricted to valuta-paying customers, which, in effect, meant foreigners earning non-Soviet wages and willing to squander them on the fantastic Metropole price scale. The island was very scantily patronized. I remember evenings when a jazz band of twenty men and a gypsy chorus of thirty-odd did their stuff for an audience of four or five couples. A gloomier and more depressing place can scarcely be imagined outside a cemetery or a prison.

After a few months of this pathetic emptiness, the hall was opened to the Russian citizenry, or that portion which could pay five rubles * for a plate of *borsch* and twenty-five rubles * for a portion of chicken. Two menus were available, one in dollars, the other in rubles. On the dollar menu, the same soup could be had for 15 cents and the same chicken for 85 cents. Russians were handed, as a matter of course, the ruble bill-of-fare. Foreigners were asked pointedly whether they wished the dollar menu. The difference was not alone in price, but in service. For a valuta customer, the very circumambient air changed its flavor; the waiters, old-timers with tender memories of tsarist banquets and grand-ducal tips, instantly became more ingratiating, the soup came warmer and the chicken more succulent. White bread, of course,

* The official rate at this time was about 1 ruble 13 kopeks to the dollar; the unofficial rate in general use, acknowledged by the government in these valuta and non-valuta menus, was from 30 to 50 rubles to the dollar; for the average Russian, of course, 5 rubles was the equivalent of a day's labor.

was served to dollar clients only, and the bar (high stools, foot-rail, highly rouged barmaids, amiable bartender, and all the trimmings even unto soggy potato chips) was open to valuta-payers only. Even the Russians who had the wherewithal and the boldness to visit the Metropole never dared enter the barroom, the occupants of which looked into the main room as though from a distant hilltop. . . .

The piece-work system, higher payment for technical work, and a slight release in the tension under which intellectuals lived, tended to enlarge the Metropole's clientele. With the abandonment of the unbroken work week, and the establishment of a uniform day of rest every sixth day, *pered-vikhodnoy*, "the eve of the free day," became the big night at the hotel. Whatever remained of fashion and affluence in the capital congregated here every sixth night for a big feed, vigorous dancing, and a brief release from drabness. For the Russians who could safely indulge it, an evening at the Metropole was the next best thing to a trip abroad. What if the place was honeycombed with spies, marking off (for a little intimate interrogation sooner or later) the big spenders and those too chummy with foreigners? What if one evening's entertainment cost a week's wages? What if it called for a little discreet embezzling of official funds, an offense soon made punishable by death? There were enough Russians risking it to crowd the bourgeois island to capacity.

Yet another device for raising valuta was soon developed, which to this day is netting the Soviet government a handsome profit. My dispatch announcing the innovation described it as "the export of human beings to help balance the foreign trade budget," a statement which did little to endear me to the censors' hearts. I might, however, have said worse and described the process more accurately by calling it a ransom system.

The Kremlin one day announced that Russians could buy their way out of the Soviet land by paying a passport fee of five hundred gold rubles if they were proletarians, and one thousand gold rubles if non-proletarians. Russians who had so much valuta hidden away did not dare admit it, knowing that less pleasant ways of extracting it would be employed than the issuance of a passport. In effect, therefore, the new dispensation meant that friends and relatives abroad could arrange passports for Russians by paying the specified ransom.

The government travel bureau, Intourist, was made the channel for this unsavory transaction, and it added insult to injury by charging a steep service fee—in valuta—for its intercession. Intourist offices abroad advertised their bargain sale on ransomed Soviet citizens; in America, in particular, they did a brisk business, thousands of Russian-Americans having fought in vain for years to bring aged, decrepit, persecuted, or merely disgruntled relatives out of their native land.

The Soviet authorities themselves determined whether an applicant for emigration was proletarian or not—that is to say, whether to demand one thousand gold rubles or content themselves with half the amount. The number among the departing citizenry who qualified as low-price proletarians was consequently very small. Moreover, the deposit of the ransom valuta was no guarantee that the hostage would be released. The government judged every applicant individually to decide whether he merited escape. Anyone whose economic value at home was larger than a thousand rubles in valuta was not allowed to leave; anyone articulate enough to prove a possible influence for anti-Soviet propaganda was likewise kept at home.

Notwithstanding these limitations, the ransom system sent a wave of hope through certain sections of the urban population, particularly the disfranchised millions and the Jews who were being systematically tormented by the G.P.U. on suspicion of concealing valuta. In the months after this announcement, tens of thousands of letters were sent by Russians to acquaintances and blood relations in all parts of the capitalist world begging to be bought out. In many instances, Russians who had the necessary ransom money smuggled it out to acquaintances abroad, with instructions to make the arrangements at the nearest Intourist office.

3

These were open means of slaking the government's thirst for valuta. Beyond them, furtive and sinister, talked of in whispers even among foreigners who had nothing to fear personally, was the organized extortion of valuta by a special division of the G.P.U.

I approach the subject fearfully, because the hurt of it is fresh and raw on my mind, and because I realize that the reader will find it hard to believe me. No other episode in the entire history of the revolution has been so carefully and so successfully hidden from the world. To write about it is to touch moral slime. But the valuta tortures did more to color and toughen my reaction against the Bolshevik way than any other single element in my experience; a record of the experience that omitted or slurred over that element would falsify the whole narrative.

Long before I learned the details of the process, I heard casual and veiled references to the "sweat room," the "lice room," the "conveyor," "cold treatments," and other refined tortures. I heard them from the lips of boastful G.P.U. agents whose tongues had been loosened by too much vodka, in half-ribald allusions here and there, in political jokes whose full import I did not gather at the time. The first specific incidents came to my notice late in 1930. An acquaintance who showed up after a period of unexplained disappearance gave me under pledge of absolute secrecy a hair-raising account of his ordeal. He had been arrested on suspicion of possessing dollars, and had been put through revolting forms of torture before he convinced his tormentors that the suspicion was unfounded.

"I envied those who really had something they could give away," he told me. "They held out for a week or two, then they confessed where the stuff was hidden and they were through. But I had nothing to confess, so I remained on and on for months. 'You're lying! Where is it?' they bellowed at me; 'back to the *parilka!* Back to the conveyor! We can wait until you make up your mind!' I don't know how I survived it."

The worst of it, he said, was that he was still under suspicion, and might be returned to that purgatory any minute. From several other directions I got substantially the same story. One woman after a few days of torment gave up a gold watch and other trinkets which were gifts from her dead husband. "Even when the children were without bread," she said, "I did not sell them. They seemed to me a part of my dear Kolya. Now they've sweated them out of me, the fiends! the robbers!" Those who were made to disgorge signed formal statements in grandiloquent language "contributing" their valuta to "help the Five Year Plan." Whether they had anything to bequeath to the Plan or not, they were warned never to mention to anyone, not even their families, what they had seen and suffered, on pain of being returned to the torture chambers.

I could not bring myself to believe that the heads of the G.P.U. and the heads of the Communist Party knew about such things or countenanced them. Only as the evidence piled up, month after month and year after year, was I driven to recognize that the practice was nation-wide, deliberate and systematized. In the end I came to know the conduct of the "gold mining" department of the G.P.U. in all the ripeness of its corruption.

The extortions went under the euphemism of "mobilization of hidden valuta resources," and were, in effect, an unwritten adjunct of the Five Year Plan. "Income" from that source was earmarked for specific valuta obligations of the Kremlin. Like any other branch of the economic apparatus, the G.P.U. had its "control figures" for the year: a rigid plan or commitment to extract specific sums from the population. Every regional and local branch was assigned a quota and no questions were asked about the arguments used to persuade gold-bearing citizens to "contribute." If a few people died of suffocation or pain, if most of the unfortunates were broken physically for life, if the minds of men and women snapped—well, slag and dross were to be expected in any ambitious mining operation.

The human ore for G.P.U. smelting was gathered from many groups and classes, and ranged from servant girls with a single gold piece in their possession to former millionaires with caches of jewels. Nepmen and pre-revolutionary merchants who might logically have salted away remnants of their former opulence. Jewelers, watch-makers, dentists, others whose trades in freer days made it likely that they had saved leavings and scourings of gold. Outstanding professional men and women—physicians, engineers, writers, etc.—known to have earned large sums during the years when the ruble was stable and legally convertible into other currencies. Persons whose standard of living was above their visible sources of income. Above all, Russians who had been receiving remittances from relatives in America and other countries.

Besides its own sensitive nose for valuta, the G.P.U. depended upon anonymous denunciations and denunciations under pressure; the Valuta Department assumed shrewdly that anyone having foreign money would probably know others similarly cursed, and drew that information from him along with his cash contribution to the *piatiletka*. As far as possible, it sought to make its every victim a spy as well, often as the price of personal immunity to further "mining." An acquaintance in Kharkov had been on the valuta rack three times at intervals of a month or two. He seemed to have grown twenty years older in the year since I had seen him; his cheeks had fallen in and his hands trembled. Had he been ill? I asked. "Worse, much worse," he said, "but let's not talk about it." And Russian-wise he proceeded to talk for hours; every moment of his weeks in the torture chambers were sharply etched in his memory.

"The first two times," he said, "I gave them money. But the third time I had no more to give. And God knows when I will be called again. I can no longer sleep or eat or work"—he held a fairly responsible job in the food trust—"just waiting for the horror to begin again. They have made me an offer. They will let me alone, but at a terrible price, as terrible as the tortures."

"What's the price?"

"That I become an informer on all my friends in Kharkov! I stand well in the Jewish community, and it's mostly Jews they're after. They think that I can smell out who has valuta and where it is hidden, and who has rich relatives in America to be exploited. If I do that, they won't touch me; otherwise—back to the *parilka*. But I won't do it. I'll die first. I think of nothing but suicide. If it weren't for the children . . ."

The great majority of the victims were Jews, since Jews predominated among the former Nepmen and among those who received money from American relatives.

"Do you think the thing is an expression of anti-Semitism?" I asked one victim, a highly intelligent Jewish physician.

"No, I think not," he said. "They pick up non-Jews just as readily. It simply happens that our race is hardest hit by the valuta arrests. On the other hand, there is no doubt at all that the

G.P.U. agents in charge of this work are deeply anti-Semitic and do their dirty work with great enjoyment. They're Black Hundred men and *pogromshchiks* at heart, and the word *zhid* is always on their tongues, along with all the other filth, in terrorizing the valuta suspects. *Zhid*, parasite, *zhidovskaya morda* are commonplaces in the yelling and cursing along the conveyor."

Once I was told how a patriarchal Jew held in Moscow as a valuta suspect was forced by jeering torturers to drink his own urine. I have never been able to erase that ghastly image from my mind. At the most unlikely moments—listening to Premier Molotov in the Kremlin Palace, going through some model Soviet institution, listening to the hallelujahs of some American enthusiast for Bolshevism—this image had a way of obtruding itself. What were all the statistical boasts and models and enthusiasms against the gray-bearded old man choking on his own urine—in the fourteenth year of the revolution, with the strongest government on the face of the earth in charge of the obscenity!

On the day I heard this story, from a person whose honesty I could not doubt, I turned to the famous passage in *Brothers Karamazov*, where Dostoievsky discusses sadistic cruelty through the mouth of Ivan Karamazov. I underlined the passage where Ivan, speaking to his brother Alyosha, says:

> "Tell me yourself, I challenge you, answer! Imagine that you are creating a fabric of human destiny with the object of making men happy in the end, giving them peace and rest at last, but it was essential and inevitable to torture to death only one tiny creature—that baby beating its breast with its fist, for instance—and to found that edifice on its unavenged tears, would you consent to be the architect on those conditions? Tell me, and tell me the truth."
>
> "No, I wouldn't consent," said Alyosha softly.

4

When I write of tortures, I use the word in its literal sense. There was moral degradation, the erasure of all human dignity and self-respect—the entire system was nicely calculated to reduce the strongest men and women, whether janitors or celebrated professors, to the common level of slobbering fear. "You just forget that you're human, that there are still people who are not wild beasts, that somewhere sometimes you heard of music and poetry and civilization," one woman tried to explain it to me.

But the basic mechanism and chief reliance of the extortion artists were physical torture. In every city the Valuta Department might develop its own sadistic specialties, but apparently several basic techniques were common to them all.

The *parilka*, or sweat room, has been described to me so often that I feel as though I had seen it with my own eyes. I can see it now with my mind's eye. Several hundred men and women, standing close-packed in a small room where all ventilation has been shut off, in heat that chokes and suffocates, in stink that asphyxiates, one small bulb shedding a dim light on the purgatory. Many of them have stood thus for a day, for two days. Most of them have ripped their clothes off in fighting the heat and the sweat and the swarming lice that feed upon them. Their feet are swollen, their bodies numbed and aching. They are not allowed to sit down or to squat. They lean against one another for support, sway with one rhythm and groan with one voice. Every now and then the door is opened and a newcomer is squeezed in. Every now and then those who have fainted are dragged out into the corridor, revived and thrown back into the sweat room . . . sometimes they cannot be revived.

The so-called "conveyor" has been graphically described by Professor Tchernavin in his book, *I Speak for the Silent*. His description coincides substantially with the accounts I have heard myself from victims who had been through the torture. Examiners sit at desks in a long series of rooms, strung out along corridors, up and down stairways, back to the starting point: a sort of circle of G.P.U. agents. The victims run at a trot from one desk to the next, cursed, threatened, insulted, bullied, questioned by each agent in turn, round and round, hour after hour. They weep and plead and deny and keep running. . . . If they fall they are kicked and beaten on their shins, stagger to their feet and resume the hellish relay. The agents, relieved at frequent intervals, are always fresh and keen, while the victims grow weaker, more terrorized, more degraded.

From the *parilka* to the conveyor, from the conveyor to the *parilka*, then periods in ugly cells when uncertainty and fear for one's loved ones outside demoralize the prisoner . . . weeks of this while the "hidden valuta resources" are being "mobilized" by the G.P.U. in a thousand cities of the socialist fatherland. I am aware of my impotence to translate more than a hint of the Gehenna into words. One must hear it from the mouth of a haggard, feverish victim fresh from the ordeal to grasp the hellishness of it.

If physical torture failed to break down someone who, the G.P.U. was convinced, actually had a lot of valuta, members of his family were brought in and tortured under his eyes. I heard the detailed story of a former merchant who insisted for weeks that he had nothing, absolutely nothing left. Only when one of his children, a little boy, was thrown into the *parilka* with him and kept there for three days did he remind himself that he did have a box of jewels buried in his back yard. Then another child was brought for torture, and he admitted to more valuta in another hiding place. His whole family was on the rack before he was stripped clean of his surreptitious wealth.

A Russian-American businessman came as a tourist to visit his aged parents in Kiev. For years he had been sending them a monthly remittance, which was their only support. Completely distressed by the squalid poverty in which his father and mother lived, he tried in vain to arrange for them to leave the country; this was before the valuta ransom racket was inaugurated. He did the next best thing and found them a better room to live in by paying American dollars to the trust which controlled the tenement house. He outfitted them at Torgsin and paid for large stocks of food. And before departing he left them four or five hundred dollars in cash.

That gift was tantamount to a sentence of torture for the father. No sooner had his son left than the old man was dragged away to the torture chambers. He immediately relinquished the few hundred dollars. The very alacrity with which he did it convinced the agents that it could not be all, that he must have more than he admitted. (Seasoned victims knew the danger of yielding too soon and thereby exciting the doubts and cupidity of their tormentors; one victim warned another to take the medicine of torture before capitulating if he wanted to be believed.) So he was kept for weeks, and for at least a year to my personal knowledge was taken in custody at regular intervals for another installment of "persuasion."

A routine practice was to force Soviet citizens to write to relatives abroad begging for large sums of money. The letters, dictated by the G.P.U., usually made frantic appeals for specified amounts, explaining vaguely that it was "a matter of life and death." When the money arrived, it was, of course, instantly "contributed" to the Five Year Plan. Jews in particular were subjected to this racket on the theory that blood ties are strong in Jewish families and a tragic plea for cash would not be ignored by well-off American sons and uncles.

As late as the summer of 1934, when I was working in Hollywood, a Russian émigré came to see me. For years, he explained, he had been receiving strange, almost incoherent, requests for money from a brother in a certain Soviet city. He could afford it and did not grudge the money, but he was mystified by the secrecy with which his brother surrounded the vague matter of life and death that needed periodical sums to save him. He showed me one of the missives and I recognized it instantly as a typical G.P.U. extortion letter.

5

In the sum total of anguish incident upon the revolution, the valuta episode may not bulk large. Its victims must be counted by the tens of thousands, while those of liquidation, concentration camps, and man-made famine run into millions. But its cruelty was naked and unprovoked, without a shadow of "revolutionary" rationalization, its victims drawn from all classes. None of the stock alibis for brutality applied: a dictatorial state merely captured its subjects secretly and bled them white for a paltry few million dollars. There was not even the formality of a decree to sanctify the procedure; *the victims with few exceptions had come by their valuta legally, and even under the Soviet law had every right to it;* the hocus-pocus of a "voluntary contribution" through torture somehow added depths of ugliness to the ghastly business.

In Dostoievsky's imagined torture of a child, it was assumed to be "essential and inevitable" in creating a noble fabric of human destiny. It is this unavoidable necessity that apologists for official *Schrecklichkeit*, whether under Bolshevism or fascism, urge to excuse brutality. But the planned torture for valuta cannot easily be twisted to appear essential and inevitable. It achieved nothing except to hasten the collection of a few million dollars, most of which would have come into the coffers of the state anyhow sooner or later, though more slowly, through Torgsin and other non-violent methods of collection. The private robber and highwayman takes certain chances—the law may catch up with him. This lawlessness by the Bolshevik state lacked even that redeeming feature of sportsmanship. Its perpetrators worked with impunity.

Socialist thinking had always placed human life above property. Now the Kremlin was placing property far above human life. The net proceeds of its steam rooms and conveyors and exotic inquisitions probably did not suffice to pay for one more factory in the hundreds erected.

It was because of the starkness of this episode, its apparently frivolous exercise of a talent for inflicting pain, its offhand indulgence of an appetite for the macabre, that the Soviet authorities guarded this secret more desperately than any other. From 1931 forward, it was the most gruesome and shameful of the skeletons in the Kremlin's closet. Some of the foreign correspondents knew more about the valuta tortures than others, depending on the extent of their contact with Russians; but not one was totally ignorant of it. A thousand times we talked about it among ourselves. It was the supreme taboo in a land teeming with political taboos. For a correspondent to write about it would have amounted to open declaration of war against his official hosts; and probably futile, since he would not only elicit violent official denials but would very likely be let down by his colleagues.

Our reticence was deepened by the fear of getting Russians close to us into trouble. (Even in writing this chapter, far off in time and in space from the Moscow of the early thirties, I am constrained to edit myself carefully to protect Russians; I omit tell-tale details in the dread that they may point toward my sources of information.) The nearest I came to touching the subject—the only time, I believe, that the subject was even hinted at by any American correspondent while on Soviet soil—was in a general article about a new wave of arrests. Having listed many varieties of victims, I added that "there is a category of arrests never mentioned in the press," namely, valuta suspects; and that they "are held under conditions none too pleasant" until they agree to part with their valuta. The article was published in the New York *Herald Tribune*, and in dozens of other papers. But only the *Jewish Daily Forward* of New York understood the hint, picked up the seemingly casual sentence and made it the basis of an editorial.

Only the Jewish press of the world, in fact, seemed aware of the valuta horrors. An international Jewish committee, headed by the Hebrew poet, Bialik, had gathered hundreds of letters smuggled out by Russians to relatives abroad giving harrowing details of their experiences in torture chambers.

None of the standardized alibis for brutality, as I have said, suffice to explain, let alone explain away, the valuta episode. It could have happened only under a regime which had lost even the memory of respect for human life and suffering; one in which the guinea-pig theory of humanity as inert raw stuff for experimental purposes has conquered all natural instincts. It was a symptom of something pathological: whether the atrophy of the instinct of human compassion, or worse—a positive relish for inflicting pain.

The suspicion that a sort of collective sadism had been evoked in Russia by long years of brutality, ripened in my mind. It made explicable for me aspects of the revolution which otherwise were baffling. That the brutality may at times have been "essential and inevitable," or forced upon the regime in its struggle for power, makes little difference so far as the fact itself is concerned. I saw the pathological streak dignified in the official rhetoric as "Bolshevik firmness" or "Stalinist ruthlessness." I saw it reflected in the semi-official apologetics of foreigners who found it in their conscience to treat the vast network of concentration camps as an "industrial" enterprise and an "educational institution" without so much as a suspicion that their emotional arteries were hopelessly hardened.

I could never again completely drive out of my own mind the gnawing awareness of the valuta tortures as long as I was in Russia. They remained in the background of my consciousness to cast their shadow on the industrial triumphs about which I wrote every day. The thought that only a few blocks away, on Liubianka Square, men were gasping in the *parilka* or staggering on the conveyor was under the surface of my mind: the counterweight to all the boasts and promises and revolutionary pretensions that filled the press, the billboards, the speeches, and the plans.

V. Culture in a Straitjacket

COVERING a "beat" the size of the Soviet Union single-handedly for a high-powered American press association against energetic competition, induces a fellow-feeling for ancient galley slaves, not untinged with envy. It is no job for a lazy man. Stories might break in any of the twenty-four hours or all of them. They didn't, of course; but the mere possibility kept you forever tethered to a telephone in nervous expectancy. You might be watching a ballet, flirting with a ballerina, or competing with a Russian in the annihilation of vodka and *zakuski*—but never with all your mind and senses. Part of you was tensed to spring when that impending story broke. Denying the dispatches of your colleagues took as much labor as working up your own mistakes—but was much more fun. It became second nature to scan the talk and the faces around you for hints of news.

Right on the stage in Moscow, in magnificently distorted versions of American plays like *Front Page* and *Chicago*, handsome newspapermen careened adventurously, living and loving and cussing at high tension; by all fictional indices, foreign correspondents, in particular, lived expansively and dangerously. But here we were, perspiring and unromantic. We chewed the cud of our daily statistics, adventured among Five Year Plan percentages, and hacked our way heroically through the jungles of interminable speeches. Digging through the day's newspapers, which is the larger half of a Moscow correspondent's job, was about as thrilling as digging ditches. The daily doses of economic and political facts would shape up as exciting history in the perspective of time, and some had the skill to inject a premonition of that excitement into current dispatches. But on the whole they made a dull enough routine.

My own deep concern with the meanings of economic and political developments, luckily, invested the routine with a good deal of intellectual excitement. I felt a little as though I were watching a tense chess game, even if the moves were painfully slow. But there were among us newspapermen who neither knew nor cared for that sort of chess: alert police reporters in search of spot news, sensations, front-page stuff. Their frustration and boredom were sad to behold. The swashbuckling correspondent was quickly reduced to quiescence by the censorship and the lack of anything worth swashbuckling over.

One moved carefully, fearfully, between the Scylla of exacting editors and the Charybdis of the Russian Press Department, with an eye always alert for the maneuvers of competing correspondents. One sweated to trace down a piece of news, then sweated some more to convoy it safely past the rocks where Charybdis-Umansky belched the waters of his idealogical wrath. Terse inquiries from home reported sensations about Russia, emanating from Moscow itself or neighboring capitals, and ended with the one word, "How?". You didn't know "how," probably never would know "how"; the reporters who started the sensation themselves didn't know "how." The censors whom you woke out of their sleep or disturbed at their tea drinking, you were well aware, would not know "how," and would not confide in you if they did know.

Or equally terse orders demanded immediately the "official reaction" to some international event. The nearest you got to the Kremlin was, most likely, a sleepy censor in a shabby bathrobe, and he figured in the resultant dispatch as "official circles" or "high quarters" or "sources close to the government." Usually these one-man circles and sources "expressed astonishment" or "made vigorous denials" or "refused to dignify the report by a formal denial."

All these things taken together kept one busy enough. My days were crowded with work, my nights rarely uninterrupted by urgent "hows" and untimely summonses from the Foreign Office. The interstices of leisure were amply filled with sacred and profane activities ranging from dancing or stud poker to symphony concerts or theater, though which were sacred and which profane I shall not attempt to decide here.

I record these facts lest I have left a false impression that I spent all my time bewailing the fate of Marxism in Russia. An emotional experience distilled in a chapter or two of summary, of course, sounds more intense than the original experience spread over years and diluted by the million diversions of everyday existence. Firewood for that huge and omnivorous oven in our kitchen and a supply of American cigarettes claimed precedence over the horrors of Solovyetsky or the glories of Magnitostroi. For my Russian neighbors, too, the chores of daily life overshadowed the larger Soviet problems about which books (including this one) are written.

Once upon a time, living under the capitalist system which I despised and which I labored earnestly to overthrow, I had managed to wring a full measure of personal satisfaction out of each day notwithstanding. Now, living under the hammer and sickle and profoundly aware of social facts which distressed me, I managed likewise to find personal joys and amusements notwithstanding. Between work and play, both of which I relish, I had small margin of time left for making melancholy faces at myself in the mirror of my thoughts.

My deepening disapproval of the Bolshevik way certainly cannot be attributed to personal discomforts. With a big house, a car, servants, an American salary and the innumerable privileges attaching to my status as a correspondent, we lived on a level considerably higher than ever before, and pretty thoroughly insulated against the physical shocks of Soviet conditions. Far from being roused to resentment by living conditions, a foreign correspondent was more likely to be lulled into conformity. The environment of general poverty and shortage, whatever its moral effects, made our plane of existence seem even higher than it was. Foreigners with jobs maintained standards that, relatively speaking, compared with a life of affluence in the outside world.

2

I tried to follow the more significant plays, movies, books, magazines—but no longer with the expectation of encountering an original thought. There might be vigor and beauty of form, but the content was just boresome repetition of a few prescribed and over-simplified ideas. In scientific fields where heresy hunters found the going pretty hard—geological research, let us say, or Arctic exploration—a spirit of bold investigation could still be detected. But in anything that bordered on pure thought, anything that might open vistas of scientific skepticism or might encourage "dangerous" curiosity, there was an intellectual reign of terror.

What passed as history was a calculated distortion of facts to match the latest Kremlin edicts. Anthropology must goose-step on the policy line in relation to minority races. Psychology must be twisted to conform to Stalinist assumptions (the whole Freudian psychology, for example, was taboo; not because any Bolshevik had disproved it, but because it was contrary to the "Party line"). As to philosophy, it was more dangerous to question dialectic materialism according to Stalin in present-day Moscow than it had been to question the flatness of the earth in Rome of the Dark Ages. Even in the natural sciences, there was plenty of grotesquery about "Leninist surgery" and "Stalinist mathematics" and ideological deviations in biology.

Intellectual life was depressed to a dead level of conformist mediocrity. Charlatanism and mental prostitution were the easiest paths to artistic success. In the final analysis, a thick-headed secret service man or bureaucratic censor was judge, jury, and lord high executioner on every product of the human mind. Suppression was the least of this official's weapons; he could remove scientists from their laboratories, deny writers the privilege of print, or condemn the intellectual culprits to exile or prison.

I was not unmindful of the successful campaign to teach people to read and write. Elementary education for children was now almost universal. Specialized technical education was being pushed on a wholesale scale in speed-up style. Physical and military training was at levels undreamed of in old Russia.

For some reason, every totalitarian state hastens to teach its subjects to read, while suppressing free thought, straitjacketing the press, and putting its artists in uniforms. In Italy I saw the same drives for literacy. Perhaps the maximum effectiveness of a censored press and literature requires a literate population. The need for industrialized states to encourage technical education and for militarist states to encourage physical prowess is self-evident. The spokesmen of all such states seek to palm off this utilitarian education as proof of their "culture" and progress.

An approach to genuine culture, an approximation of intellectual liberty, however, require fearless creative investigation by scientists; fearless creative production by artists. And such things were unthinkable, impossible, suicidal in Russia at this time. Even in France before the Revolution, there was a measure of relative liberty—but who can imagine a Soviet Voltaire or Diderot attacking the accepted mores of the Soviet era? Even in Russia of the tsars, there was a measure of this liberty—but where is a Soviet Tolstoy or Turgenyev or Saltykov to criticize the *status quo?* To dare even to describe that *status quo* accurately? A Soviet writer with one-tenth the critical boldness of a Voltaire or a Lev Tolstoy would be lucky to escape with a ten-year term in Siberia. Tsarist censorship was placated if the artist or thinker took a neutral attitude and merely avoided politics. To the Soviet censor, neutrality is one of the deadliest sins—every artist and scientist must show proof of active support of the official dogmas. The tsars, moreover, did not concern themselves with every sphere of intellectual and esthetic effort from dancing to astronomy like their successors in the Kremlin, so that there were a few sanctuaries for man as a thinker and an artist.

At a moment when the strain of the *Piatiletka* seemed almost unbearable, Moscow was shocked by the Second Moscow Art Theater production of Alexei Tolstoy's daring *Peter I.* In a series of sharply etched scenes out of Peter the Great's life, the first-night audience saw the Bolshevik effort in historical replica. They saw Peter imposing Western industrial methods upon a backward nation against its will, contemptuous of the cost in life and resources. They saw him driving the peasantry with a whip along new social paths, building factories and cities with armies of forced labor. In his very Westernism, Peter appeared most Asiatic, brutally indifferent to the sufferings of millions of individuals in an obsessed devotion to the larger destiny of the state. The non-communist intelligentsia of the capital tittered inwardly, pretending not to notice the remarkable analogy. Communists were scandalized. It was generally assumed that the play would be swept off the boards and Tolstoy disciplined. But nothing of the sort happened. Joseph Stalin himself saw the production and—another Petrine touch!—commanded that it remain. Remain it did, a bold political parable in the midst of rigid censorship.

The recurrent patterns in Russian history, such as this one

dramatized by Alexei Tolstoy, were for me a continuous source of amazement. Among the second-hand volumes in a Moscow book-shop, I picked up *The Mainsprings of Russia*, by Maurice Baring. In it I read of a Russian leader that "he accelerated to an extent, which seems little short of miraculous, the natural progress of the country; he accomplished in a few years the work of many generations; he sketched the outlines of a gigantic plan, which still remains to be filled in to this day; the violence and fury with which he compelled a reluctant people to adopt his changes had, of course, its drawbacks."

It is not to Joseph Stalin that Baring referred, but to Peter the Great. The book was published in 1914! It is far easier to relate the career of Stalin to Peter than to Karl Marx.

3

At a certain point in their drinking, Pyotr and Lyova brushed away the ornate little glasses Billy had picked up in a commission shop, brushed them away with a gesture of disdain, and poured the vodka into deep tumblers which they drained with one noisy swallow. They were no longer humdrum economic officials—the years rolled back and they were again iron Chekists back in their Ukrainian city, dispensing death and crushing enemies. The ecstasy of that bloody period when men killed and died and life wasn't worth a copper kopek was fresh in their minds.

"Remember?" Lyova exulted. "I strangled them with these bare hands to save bullets! My fingers are like iron pincers. Here, feel them, Gene. . . ."

"Do I remember!" Pyotr snorted. "And the time we lined up five of them and finished them off with one bullet . . . fell neatly, like pushing over a row of tin soldiers, *do, re, mi, fa* . . ."

In his sober incarnation as a factory director, Pyotr's hands trembled and he seemed a little scatter-brained. But vodka had a way of steadying his nerves and his brain. The drunker he got the more proudly certain he was of his beautiful sobriety. He filled the tumbler to its uttermost brim, until the surface was a tight silken film, and he lifted it to his lips without spilling a drop.

"After the killing of our chief, Lavrov," he said, "we ordered the shooting of every tenth prisoner to put the fear of the Cheka in their rotten hearts. Lyova was with me—weren't you, Lyova? —and also Isaak Lazarovich, when we went down to the cellars. We lined them up single file and counted—eight, nine . . . *you* . . . eight, nine . . . and *you*. . . . That was a girl, a Jewess. 'But, Isaak Lazarovich,' she wailed, 'you wouldn't shoot me, would you? We were in school together, you kissed me once.' 'You're a goddam *boorzhoika* now,' says Isaak. But he would have spared her if he weren't ashamed of being soft-hearted in our presence. It was very funny."

Both Pyotr and Lyova were about my own age, so that they could scarcely have been more than twenty when they served together in the Cheka of their city. Ordinarily it was hard to imagine them as pitiless dictators of a whole region. Lyova, in particular, could be tender and compassionate, and he looked too much like a poet for such sanguinary business. But when they were far gone in liquor I no longer could doubt their melodramatic past. Something strong and sharp as steel came into their eyes: an intoxication deeper than any that resides in vodka. They were again fanatics, avenging spirits, the relentless revolution personified.

"With these ten fingers I strangled them to save bullets," Lyova repeated. It was the refrain to all his alcoholic reminiscences. The horror of windpipes cracking like eggshells in his grip had seared his nerves.

Sometimes they retold the story of "Petrova," a celebrated actress of their city, and how she came to beg permission to go to Rumania for herself and her company. She showed a letter from a theater there, inviting them to put on a season of Russian plays.

"We told her to go and good riddance," Lyova said. "And how many are there in her company of players? I asked her. 'Twenty-two,' she says. 'Twenty-two,' Pyotr says, 'that's a lot, but we Bolsheviks aren't beasts. We don't keep artists against their will.' So we made out a permit.

"A week or so later all the twenty-two were having a great party to celebrate their departure. It was in Petrova's mansion on the Naberzhnaya. Champagne and *zakusky* and roast duck. They were clinking their glasses and weeping tears of joy because they would be leaving Russia. The doors were locked and the windows shuttered, and every now and then they all stood up and sang, *God save the Tsar!*"

And in the midst of the drunken, sentimental celebration, in the midst of the patriotic singing behind the shutters—*bang! bang! bang!*—Pyotr struck the table with his tumbler by way of illustration—a company of Chekists with drawn revolvers pushed in the door and joined the party.

"I looked around," Pyotr took up the narrative, "and sure enough—there were Petrova and her husband, and twenty of the richest men and women in the city. 'So this is your company of actors?' I laughed. 'You, Matvei Borisovich, will play Hamlet, I suppose, or is it Boris Godunov?' Matvei Borisovich owned the largest department store in town. 'And you,' I said to another, 'what role have you selected?' It was very funny. We shot all twenty-two that night, every one of them, including Petrova."

"They paid her a thousand gold rubles each to join her company and escape on the permit," Lyova explained. "Their trunks were marked 'costumes' and were filled with jewels and valuables, and their clothes were lined with gold pieces and brilliants. But we got wind of the trick. Petrova was a great actress, though she was getting old. That was her last play though, and she never got any older."

Almost at random, Lyova and Pyotr thus reached into the storehouse of their recollections and drew out stories of death and terror. There were punitive expeditions to peasant villages which had harbored White fugitives, when every man, woman and child was slaughtered and the whole village set on fire. There were fearful atrocities against the Reds, and a fearful vengeance wreaked against the next batch of *boorzhooyi* that came to hand.

Sometimes their drunken reminiscences took them to the civil wars. There was really no front, just guerilla fighting. A dozen times the Whites and the Reds rolled over the city. Once the Petliurists came and slit a lot of Jewish throats. The air was as thick with down as though it were snowing. It was an ancient *pogrom* amusement, ripping open pillows and featherbeds.

"They made our people dig their own graves and climb in and they made their comrades cover them with earth and trample on the graves," Lyova said. "But we knew as many amusing tricks as they did. And when there were not enough bullets, I strangled them with my own hands. Remember, Petya?"

"Do I remember?" Pyotr snorted, and downed another tumblerful of vodka.

And as they talked I became sharply conscious of the bloody nightmare of remembrance under the humdrum surface of Soviet life. Pyotr, Lyova, thousands like them, old Chekists, guerilla fighters, G.P.U. executioners, carried a staggering burden of memories. They were pinned under the weight, hostages of their past. They dared not question the rightness of what they had done and suffered. Every prompting of conscience was an awesome threat to their peace of mind, their very sanity. To doubt for a moment the revolutionary sanctions of their cruelties—would turn them into fiends in their own eyes.

The ordeal of these men was to live with themselves. They were condemned to a lifetime of Bolshevik firmness. The minute they stopped being their own heroes, the minute they stopped regarding themselves as Revolutionary Fate incarnate, they would change into monsters. The only true reassurance lay in continuing to play the mystic role of Fate, contemptuous of individual lives. None of my prejudices against brutality could possibly touch them; to admit the dignity or sanctity of life would have meant spiritual suicide for these men—it would have turned their heroism into sordid crime.

They must measure their acts by their own yardsticks, not mine. The more I understood these compulsions under which such people lived, the less I could trust them. I realized that their emotions were warped, must remain warped. They were prisoners of their memories and could not even dream of escape.

VI. Fog of Skepticism over Russia

A CRUSADE for God or country may be conducted on an empty stomach—but not so easily a crusade for earthly goods: bread and boots and bathtubs. Having planted its materialist faith, the Kremlin lacked the material things which alone can fertilize such a faith. Therein lay the paradox of the Soviet effort. How nurture a coldly "scientific" religion of economic improvement in the here and now on self-abnegation and vague promises for better times in the hereafter? Why, indeed, should a Russian drilled in economic determinism logically be expected to accept an ascetic regimen of disciplined labor, food rations and unquestioning obedience? By what right could a collective of peasants taught to glorify tractors and material advancement be expected to give up the products of the tractors for the sake of an abstract socialized future? Acceptable answers could be made only with a whip.

The groundswell of enthusiasm evoked by the launching of the *Piatiletka* had fallen away to a murky trickle by the time the Plan entered its final year in 1932. Surviving in the inflated rhetoric of speeches, slogans and bombastic statistics, it had withered in the heart of the Russian people. That enthusiasm, after all, had derived from a naively literal reading of the official propaganda. In the ordinary Russian's mind it had shaped up as a short-term investment: "We shall work hard and sacrifice for five years—then everything will be better, freer, ampler." But now, approaching the end of the Plan, the Kremlin called upon its citizens to contemplate the triumphs of electrification by the dim glimmer of anemic bulbs prescribed for household use; to celebrate the mechanization of coal-mining while a drastic reduction in fuel rations was being enforced; to glory in the fulfillment of the oil industry's five-year-plan in two and a half years while freezing on kerosene queues. A judicious selection of statistics might do for political window-dressing, but for the population the proof of the planned pudding was in the eating—and they weren't eating.

I watched skepticism spread like a thick wet fog over Russia, soaking into the flesh and spirits of men and women. It chilled the hearts of the leaders no less than of the masses. Men who publicly spent all their time pumping up optimism, talked bitterly in private of the planlessness of the Plan, the terrible wastage of substance and energy, the dislocation of a national economy swollen in some of its limbs and shrunken in the rest. Doubts of the efficacy of enthusiasm were expressed in a constantly greater stress on cash rewards at one pole and harsh punishment at the other. Technical specialists, "emancipated" after the long persecution, now acted as consultants to half a dozen trusts at once and drew half a dozen salaries; high earnings were again respectable and shrewd conniving citizens (the same breed largely which thrived under Nep) began to prosper again. New "commercial" stores and cafés were opened in ever larger number to stimulate the newly enfranchised profit motives. At the same time Draconic decrees were minted almost weekly to discipline and repress the common workers. One of them made a single day's absence from work punishable by loss of job, bread book, and living space: tantamount to a sentence of slow death.

The physical proofs of industrial growth in electric power stations, new factories, strange new machines, could not disperse the fog of doubt. They merely spread more fundamental doubts as to the wonder-working power of machinery. The bitter-sweet humor of political cynicism was filled with ribaldries about milking the tractors to provide milk and mating the tractors to provide meat. The most widely repeated anecdote was the one about a naked man on a train; when amazed and scandalized passengers remonstrated, he seemed astonished. "But, comrades," he said, "I come from Minsk where we have already completed our Five Year Plan!" Another represented President Kalinin as rebuking workers for complaining about the lack of clothes, and suggesting that they look at the Hottentots who live happily though nude. "Ah," a worker commented, "the poor Hottentots must have had communism even longer than we."

The leaders juggled statistics to maintain appearances, but were themselves deeply aware of the deceptions. They boasted of "over-fulfillment" of plans for investment, knowing that the "victory" reflected the inflation of currency and the inordinately high cost of production. They shouted hallelujah over the abolition of unemployment, knowing full well that the swollen labor forces reflected the low productivity of labor.

That drain on labor resources meant, in reality, that millions of women and young people had given up their care of the family, or their leisure, for jobs on construction sites, in mines, and in mills. It meant that father, mother, and all the grown children worked where father alone formerly earned the family's keep. Unless carrying hods up and down ladders is an end in itself (a theory hotly sustained by intellectuals who have never tried hod-carrying) there was little cause for thanksgiving in the labor shortage. The family's total income might be greater than before, but its total purchasing power and purchasing possibilities were generally smaller.

Meeting for the first time since 1928, the All-Union Congress of Trade Unions this spring indicated that average annual wages had risen from 702 rubles in 1928 to 1,101 rubles in 1931; and would rise again to 1,202 rubles by the end of this year. The average income per person, in other words, had jumped from about 15 rubles a week to about 24 rubles. This touted "victory" was nonsensical, of course, in the light of an inflation that reduced the ruble in the same period from 50 cents to 3 or 4 cents—or, making allowances for rations and other government privileges, to 10 or 12 cents at best. It was at this time that a well-meaning American communist who had not been in Russia since 1926 published a thick volume on "how the Soviet worker lives," all based on the absurd assumption that a ruble was still 50 cents!

Exceptionally impressive achievements in isolated branches of the national economy were not unmixed blessings. The astounding expansion of the petroleum industry, for instance, placed an undue burden upon transportation facilities from which other industries naturally suffered. Completion of Dnieprostroi or some other electric station in record time at a cost of record sacrifices made fine editorial matter, but meant little when the plants to use the power were not yet built. A four-fold overfulfillment of the plan for agrarian socialization, to cite the most dismal triumph of all, was positively disastrous, since the mechanical power for such an area was unavailable and the animal power had been destroyed in the course of forcible collectivization.

Dramatization of individual constructions was perhaps good politics. Turksib Railroad finished! Dnieprostroi finished! Four blast furnaces under way in Magnitogorsk! The "Ford" factory in Nijni-Novgorod opened as a New Year's present to the Infallible Leader! But it was not necessarily good economics. In the haste to open Turksib the small matter of repair shops to keep it in operation was overlooked. The hurried completion of the Nijni-Novgorod plant was followed by a total break-down of production three months later. The blast furnaces were idle most of the time because of faulty construction and inexpert handling. In fact, the straining for political effect, for "giants" and startling "tempos," was responsible for much of the defective work, diversion of materials and men from less spectacular but no less essential jobs—a fictitious speed paid for sooner or later in accidents and general dislocation. Good showmanship and good economics do not always go together.

The neatest trick of totalitarian braggadocio was the averaging of results. Certain industries were ahead of the plan and others behind, so that "average" achievement was statistically satisfactory. Such arithmetical triumphs were in sober fact economic monstrosities. One might as well say (as an American writer has pointed out) that a cross-eyed person averaged up to normality; or that a cripple with one leg overlong and the other too short averaged all right. In a speech claiming satisfactory average progress, Stalin, casually almost, asserted that the backwardness was to be found in coal, steel, transportation, and the productivity of labor—as though any major industry could function averagely when it lacked these essentials! A factory 72% completed is quite as useless as though it had never been started—and costs more. A machine which does not earn its own keep by commensurately raising production per worker and lowering unit costs is scarcely a victory, however shiny it may be.

2

There is, it seems to me, a fundamental fallacy in systematic sacrifice. The most dangerous people have always been those ready to sacrifice their lives for a cause, for the first expression of that disrespect for life is a readiness to sacrifice the lives of others. But leaving aside such philosophical considerations, sacrifice on the plane of economics is a costly form of national romanticism. Russia sacrificed light industry for heavy industry, peace manufactures for war manufactures, quality for quantity, food for machines, men for statistics. But men and machines, food and productivity of labor, quality factors as well as quantity, light industry and its heavy brethren all depend one on the other. The integrated economy is no stronger than its weakest link.

Sacrifice is a postponement, not a solution—the disbalance is paid for in immediate suffering, higher costs, ultimate stalling of the economic machine. Lack of food undermines the workers, causes a fearsome turnover of labor, saps the morale of the people. Lack of nails holds up house-building as surely as lack of brick. The fantastic striving for bigger and better statistics, at whatever cost in human degradation and disjointed economy, more and more socialization at whatever cost in peasant opposition, led to such facts as these: more tractors spoiled and gathering rust than tractors in operation; automobiles leaving the belt as "finished" products without headlights, brakes, or some other vital organ; mountains of goods rotting and rusting in factory yards for lack of transportation; expensive machines, bought with the torture-money called valuta, standing idle for lack of repair parts. And all this was paid for by the masses in accumulating shortages, deprivations, losses of basic rights.

The sacrificial fallacy, which only an all-powerful state dictatorship can enforce, makes for the relinquishment of political no less than economic values in the interests of some larger theoretical good. In the name of the Five Year Plan one socialist objective after another was sacrificed. In my own Soviet years, I saw the control of workers over their own jobs and destinies whittled away to the *reductio ad absurdum* of whittling: a good round zero, the perfection of nothingness. A more balanced and integrated economy and political regime would probably have had less spectacular objects to boast about, but certainly fewer horrors to conceal.

The inexperience and native sloth of the Russians did not seem to me, watching the process at close range, a sufficient or honest explanation of the disbalance. I came to believe that its causes lay much deeper, in the very assumptions of the Soviet regime, particularly the assumptions that the sacrifice of human beings did not matter in the achievement of human happiness, that the sacrifice of socialist ethics were of no account in the building of socialism, and—most important and most Russian of all—that anything could be accomplished by brute force.

Panicky with fear or consumed by political ambition, officials piled up factory output to fulfill and overfulfill plans, so that quality suffered. Construction projects must be driven to the goal line by May Day or November 7 even if they would collapse a month later. It seemed more important to provide a good report than a good product. The Russian department at the University of Birmingham once calculated that the 1928-29 output of galoshes in the new Russia, officially given as 48% above 1913, was actually 29% below 1913 if the factor of durability was taken into consideration. Nor was it all due to native inefficiency. Much of the blame must fall on the government's policies, which assumed that logic and organic development could be "heroically" and "ruthlessly" substituted by decrees and threats.

By 1932, it was clear to all but the most frenzied partisans of "Bolshevik ruthlessness" that force does have its limitations. Absolutism, too, has frontiers beyond which it is without jurisdiction. A dictatorship could squeeze its people, force through industrial projects at a superhuman pace with involuntary labor. But it could not create industrial skills or train efficient managers with the knout. It could impose almost overnight an alien way of life upon a hundred million peasants, but it could not remold the mind and instincts of those peasants, and must therefore contend with "kulak collectives" precisely as it had contended with individual kulaks.

The triumphs of the Five Year Plan were largely in the externals of an industrialized society. The essence—a harmonious economy, a fairly contented people, etc.—was farther off than ever. The good will of the workers, which is an enormous economic leverage in any society, had been squandered through hard-boiled contempt for their immediate needs. Practically the whole peasantry had been turned to sullen opposition by excessive doses of force. The technical intelligentsia had been outraged and persecuted and emasculated. The whole spirit of the Soviet enterprise in these years bred bureaucrats concerned with the prestige of fine plans and fine statistical fulfillments, regardless of cost or quality, intent upon protecting their own official posts and skins, while passing the economic buck to others.

The romantic conception of state planning as a magic formula transcending logic was in disrepute at home. Abroad, too, it lost some of its force. In the beginning of 1931, the specters of Soviet dumping threw the world into a panic. Hastily many governments erected legal barriers against the expected torrents of cheap Soviet goods. A year later those specters were fading out. Soviet competition lost most of its terror. Far from dominating the world market for foodstuffs, Soviet grain exports ceased and internal food difficulties grew more acute. In 1931, coal production was 66 million tons instead of the planned 77 million; iron totaled 5 million tons instead of 8,300,000; steel likewise 5 million instead of 8,800,000. The realization grew that Soviet industry would not become the formidable giant which capitalism feared in one five-year plan or three; it would need decades and generations to meet its own needs, however political showmanship might dress up its statistical face.

Ominous symptoms of the industrial dislocation appeared in sporadic strikes against feeding conditions. Nothing about these appeared in the press, of course. Yet much of it leaked out. We could not write about it—and few of us had any inclination to do so—because we could only match our assertions against the violent denials of the government. An American specialist in industrial psychology, a liberal who analyzed and prescribed for the illnesses of factory-personnel relations, arrived in Russia. He heard of the strikes and offered to help the employers—that is, the government—straighten them out. A little investigation, however, punctured his fervor. He found that the cause was lack of food and his system of cure had no specific for that disease. A technician from the Red Putilov factory in Leningrad, a show place of the Soviet industrialization and the heart of the 1917 uprising, told me the story of a brief "sit-down" strike there. By a sort of common impulse the workers had laid down their tools and ceased work. The authorities rushed many truckloads of foodstuffs to the Putilov, distributed them liberally, and the strike was over. In the following days one after another of the suspected ring-leaders and agitators was called out by the G.P.U.

They never returned. I made a half-hearted attempt to cable the story but was quickly squelched by the censors.

With difficulties multiplying on all sides, the prospect of a second and surely no less exacting Five Year Plan did not draw sparks of enthusiasm from the Russian people. The various commissions set up to plot new charts of industrial progress worked in an atmosphere hushed, apathetic, puzzled, and hostile. The population was adjusting itself with ill grace to the realization that at the end of the *Piatiletka* it would be rewarded only by another *Piatiletka*. No one had really expected the Five Year Plan to accomplish the miracle of turning a primitive, half-starved country into a comfortable and prosperous place. Yet most of the popular appeal of the Plan lay precisely in the definiteness and brevity of the period. It set a term upon suffering.

It was not an easy thing, therefore, for the Soviet people to pretend ardor for a second plan, though pretend they must in resolutions and demonstrations. Had the Kremlin been able to declare a dividend on its promises, in terms of better living conditions, a little of the sullenness might have been dissipated. But it could not; on the contrary, it must pile on new burdens of discipline, exactions by coercive internal loans, forcible seizure of grain stocks. Even the least politically literate Russians knew that no let-up in pressure was possible.

Ever more frequently I heard middle-aged and even younger Russians say, "Our generation is doomed. Our children . . . perhaps . . ."

VII. Planned Chaos

STALIN'S six-point program and the plethora of decrees growing out of it aimed to inject individual responsibility within the framework of the state's economic monopolies. This unleashing of private initiative for public purposes had some fantastic results.

A managerial job still involved great personal risks. The frenzied baiting of specialists had subsided, but failure to fulfill plans still might bring punishment. The borderline between deliberate and accidental mistakes was as hard to find as ever. Three successive directors of one small building coöperative erecting additional stories on old houses, I happened to know, ended in concentration camps before the work was completed. The construction of the Moscow subway had scarcely gotten under way, but already many of its engineers were under arrest and at least one, it was generally understood, had been shot.

Cautious, level-headed men with executive ability continued, in the main, to avoid responsibility like the plague. They feared that the new authority conferred upon yesterday's class enemies might be only additional rope for their eventual hanging. I knew that my friend Pavel Semionovich, for instance, was dodging responsible executive work, preferring to eke out a meager livelihood through occasional technical articles. Like thousands of others he felt that genuine safety lay, in the final analysis, in obscurity. Even in the Foreign Office, a crawling swamp of careerism, there were men who kept themselves carefully in the background; one, to my knowledge, wriggled out of promotions repeatedly, making way cheerfully for younger and less able men.

But there were others for whom authority was a tempting and heady beverage. Born tradesmen and schemers, they rushed greedily for the power, the sense of importance, the material rewards. For the first time since the suppression of Nep the natural go-getters, the breed of *entrepreneurs*, had scope for their talents.

The years of persecution had killed off or disabled tens of

thousands of experienced men, so that the shortage of directorial personnel was sharp. Men who normally would not have qualified as managers of a single store found themselves lifted to supreme command of city-wide or nation-wide trading trusts. Men who ordinarily might have attained a foremanship, not infrequently were put in charge of construction jobs involving tens of millions of rubles and tens of thousands of workers.

Appetites for economic conniving starved by long denial were suddenly let loose. Money, prestige, promotion, the sheer joy of bargaining and scheming, moved this type of official or engineer (engineer is a vague and all-inclusive word in its Russian usage) to miracles of accomplishment. He found deficit building materials where there were none, pulled technical personnel out of his cap, produced transportation where others could not find it. They were not always healthy accomplishments: the deficit materials were as likely as not filched from some other urgent undertaking; the technicians "stolen" from other trusts; the diversion of railroad cars left other goods to rot.

Each man seemed concerned only with making a good showing on his own restricted job, and the devil take the hindmost. An enormous amount of off-record barter developed. The manager of a construction project, let us say, had an extra carload of radiators but not enough window glass. He traded the extra radiators for nails. He did not need nails himself but knew that they were in great demand and could be exchanged sooner or later for glass. The word that described this curious type of business promotion was *kombinatsya*—literally, a "combination" or scheme. *Kombinatsya* solved seemingly insoluble problems.

Vasya, a dark young man with small shifty eyes and a broad streak of vulgarity, was a veritable genius at *kombinatsya*. He took an artist's pride in his skill in arranging, manipulating, smoothing out difficulties; every now and then he told me gloatingly of some extravagant scheme in progress as though exhibiting a masterpiece. He had acquaintances at key points, not excluding the G.P.U., and paid favor for favor. His talents made him an asset to any economic organization, and if he drew four or five salaries simultaneously as "technical consultant" to as many enterprises, he earned every one of them.

Somehow Vasya had food delicacies for his family when even

commissars went without them; somehow he managed to buy valuta products for rubles. His pockets bulged with "documents" that admitted him to all sorts of places, gave him all sorts of privileges, and recommended him warmly to divers influential people. Whatever the problem of the trust to which he was accredited consultant, he had a document and a *kombinatsya* which he mixed and juggled to produce a magical solution. Ultimately, Vasya ended up with a ten-year term of exile—the best-laid *kombinatsya* may go awry—but that's another story; even in exile he found a *kombinatsya* that took him legitimately to Moscow at frequent intervals!

Illicit barter, economic log-rolling, excessive zeal in small matters to the detriment of larger state interests, quickly developed into a stubborn problem for the Kremlin. Decrees were issued making such things illegal; demonstrative arrests and trials were staged. But objective conditions turned the decrees into dead letters. The hazard of falling down on the plan was normally greater than the hazard of being tangled in a *kombinatsya*. Beneath the varnished externals of official plans there was this proliferating grab-as-grab-can planlessness.

This nether world of unplanned, harshly competitive enterprise under the surface of the Five Year Plan seems to have escaped the notice of foreign students of Soviet economy. Like currency inflation and other concealed elements in the economic set-up, it did not show up in the formal statistics and interviews. One might almost assert that "dialectically" the pressure of planned economy under a political dictatorship was creating its extreme opposite: a chaotic and furtive economy of desperate adjustments.

What applied to deficit materials and services applied also to deficit labor forces and brain power. While the Kremlin was exerting itself to hold down the fearful turnover of labor, many a factory director did not scruple to divert workers from other establishments to his own, sometimes by spreading rumors of better feeding conditions, sometimes by offering transportation and better wages. Directors were constantly complaining that some other office or trust had "lured" its technicians by promises of advantages.

In the sphere of the food supply, too, large-scale socialization by fiat and centralized economic control evoked their very opposites: a disordered and hectic and futile attempt of individuals and small groups to raise food for their own immediate needs. Truck gardening and poultry culture had been practically exterminated with the suppression of private farming. Unable to feed its population, the government now tossed the responsibility back to the people. It ordered and exhorted them to raise their own food.

Yesterday, private farming was considered a petty bourgeois leftover; today, it was a patriotic duty for every Soviet citizen who had access to a few square yards of arable soil to plant vegetables, raise pigs and breed rabbits. Factory workers achieved publication of their faces by raising a record crop of cabbage in their back yards. Great machine shops and coal mines and tractor plants as a side-line now went in for truck gardening and rabbit breeding to help feed their own employees! The press echoed with propaganda for this self-help; industrial leaders were reprimanded for their failure to raise carrots and their ineptitude at breeding porkers.

Only the growing pathos of food shortage—now rolling ever faster towards the calamitous winter of 1932-33—made it impossible to smile at the absurdity and wastage of the situation.

2

The rabbit had emerged as a national hero (or rather heroine, since her fecundity was at the bottom of the new fame) in 1931. It was the successor, in that role, of an even less fastidious if less proliferous animal: the pig, which in 1930 had been counted upon to provide the Soviet Union with the meat killed off by forcible collectivization. The pig failed, failed dismally, despite all the arrests and punishments for sabotage of the pig-breeding campaign. Orders therefore came through from on high that where the ungrateful porker had failed, the rabbit must succeed! The female bunny was cast in the role of Joan of Arc!

Those unfamiliar with Soviet ballyhoo in full blast cannot even imagine the celebrity that came to the rabbit. To this humble creature, innocent of birth control and not too finicky about housing and diet, was assigned the task of replenishing the meat supply. Its picture was in the papers and on the billboards. Academicians wrote learned papers about its habits and nutritional values.

Bawdy jokes about its love life multiplied. Economists and planners provided elaborate charts and figures showing how one pair of rabbits, given a proper chance, could in short order fill the land with their progeny. It was all very simple.

If the rabbit, too, failed in its mission, it was certainly not for lack of encouragement. A whole nation was cheering. But fail it did. By the summer of 1932 its reputation was pretty definitely forfeit. Somehow, the creatures did not multiply as expected in the cages at steel mills and in the courtyards of the city folks. Somewhere, there was a kulak taint in them—they simply lost their libido in all-Soviet surroundings, and developed cantankerous diseases; they forgot how to breed and began to die off as fast as class enemies in concentration camps. The fact that one official sent the male rabbits to one city and the females to another explains only the failure in those two places. Lack of proper food and the blundering ways of steel mill workers with rabbits may account for the failure elsewhere. A few forlorn bunnies now still lingered on billboards and a few arrests for disrupting the rabbit breeding program were still being made—great campaigns die slowly. But the rabbit was through, like the pig before him.

Before the end of this summer, mammals were abandoned in a huff, and faith pinned on a fungus: mushrooms, that great national resource, until now shamefully neglected, came into their own. The same Academicians now published articles—articles were very well paid—proving that mushrooms are a first-rate substitute for meat. Editorials and radio speeches proved that there were enough ungarnered mushrooms in the country to feed every man, woman, and child; anyone who starved was therefore clearly a lazy lout who deserved to starve. Mushroom collection parties were organized everywhere on the free days. School children by the hundred thousand picked the fungi in shock brigades.

But the mushroom craze died even more quickly than the rabbit hope. A half-hearted and rather shamefaced campaign was then started for the snail; a front-page story one day apprised the Soviet citizenry that Frenchmen, admittedly the most cultured of races, not only eat snails but thrive on them, and the Academicians in following issues cashed in with a new series of articles. The snails, however, never quite took hold of the propaganda machine, by this time exhausted from the extravagant promotion of pigs, rabbits, and mushrooms.

It is hard to believe that the Kremlin leaders seriously expected amateur gardening and rabbit breeding by hard-worked proletarians to solve the food problem. My own surmise at the time, to which I still adhere, is that in investing tons of paper, ink and lung power on such economic horse-play the authorities intended merely to maintain popular morale by raising hope of an immediate food supply: pig, rabbit, mushroom, snail were the successive carrots dangled in front of the plodding donkey's nose.

The recalcitrance of the rabbits, incidentally, calls to my mind a curious conversation with an American specialist on a related subject. We met on the train going from Moscow to the frontier. When I introduced myself, he said without prelude:

"This here country ain't gonna solve its food troubles until its horses and cattle begin to make love again."

"Say that again," I smiled, suspecting a hoax. "I'm afraid I don't get you."

"Sure you don't," he said with a serious mien; "what you bozos who write articles out of your heads don't know is that Russian animals don't make love any more. They've lost interest in life, I might say. Especially the horses. The Russians buy the best bulls and stallions in Argentina and Canada and places and pay a lot of dough for 'em, but soon after they get here they pay no more attention to females than they would to you and me. And the females plain ignore their husbands. It's the lousy fodder and not enough of it. See?"

I was beginning to see. The American was a specialist in stock raising, working at one of the largest of the *sovkhozes* devoted to animal breeding. This was his first trip "out" in more than a year. And a most disgusted citizen he was.

"We gotta use artificial tricks to breed 'em," he went on, and for a half hour described those tricks. "But artificial impregnation don't always work; if the animal ain't up to snuff physically they drop the calves and colts before time or stillborn. No, siree, they can't lick this thing until the peasants and the chemical industry begin to deliver good rich food for the animals."

3

It was at the railroad station at R., while on a trip into the country, in the summer of 1932, that I witnessed a scene which was to prove more significant than I guessed at the moment—a tiny symptom of the shattering tragedy engulfing southern Russia. An old peasant, with a shaggy head and matted beard, wearing a burlap coat, patched trousers and reed shoes (*lapti*) was weeping aloud, unashamedly, and pleading with the station-master through his sobs. The peasant was holding a large heavy sack.

"You can go on the next train, tomorrow morning, yes," the station-master said, not unkindly, "but not your bundle. Law is law—no bread can be transported without a license."

"But, citizen station-master, dear one," the old man repeated, "how can I return to the village with empty hands? Without the money and without bread? Tell me, dear one, how shall I face the village? They await my return and their bellies are empty. Now I have spent all their money—no bread, no money. . . ."

The station-master shrugged his shoulders. He had been listening to this refrain for hours: since his men ordered the shaggy peasant and his sack off the train. The peasant now turned to me and several other spectators.

"Some of us in the village"—he mentioned a province in Ukraine—"got together. We threw our money in one pot, and they chose me to go north, where money could buy bread. I paid a fortune for what I have in this sack. And now they won't let me take it to the village. And why? Others in nearby villages did the same, and they had bread to eat for weeks. They feasted. Why were they allowed but not I? Is that Soviet justice? Citizen station-master, whom will it harm if I take this bag on a train? I shall keep it on my lap and creep into a corner on the topmost shelf."

"It will do you no good, citizen," the station-master said. "You'll be chucked off at some other station. Law is law."

Several weeks earlier I had read the decree forbidding the transport of bread and other food products without a license. The purpose, the papers explained dishonestly, was to prevent the further overcrowding of trains. I had wondered whether the decree deserved a line by cable, and decided against it.

The weeping old peasant hit by the decree, unable to understand why he should not be permitted to bring bread to his family and his neighbors, personalized that law for me. Always, anywhere, it is easier to accept news in the abstract, in cold print, than in its warm human form. For months I forgot this incident. Then, as the horrors of famine began to pile up, the scene came to life again in my mind, its every lineament sharply etched. Not all the sophistries of my communist friends explaining and justifying the famine could erase this old man in his burlap coat.

Conditions in agrarian Russia were shaping up for disaster. Late in 1931, the government was obliged once again to resort to undisguised coercion in collecting grain from the peasants—this time, be it noted, from socialized farmers as well as individual growers. Notwithstanding the baptism of forcible socialization, the peasants were unregenerate at the core. In collectives they behaved as before: wherever possible they distributed the surplus production among the members, who promptly buried it for a rainy day. After paying the "tractor station" 20 or 25% of the crop for the use of its machinery, and paying the state banks an installment for cash loans, and paying the government for its advances in seed, there was little enough surplus to divide. The state exactions, thinly camouflaged as government "purchases," seemed to ninety-nine out of a hundred peasants outright robbery.

And why, in the name of Marx and Engels, should they have relinquished the products of their labor for paper money that could buy nothing? A government which ridiculed compassion and prided itself on callousness could scarcely expect the peasants to behave like philanthropists. Socialization based almost entirely on brute force could expect to maintain itself only by continued use of brute force. Renewed coercion, and particularly the confiscation of cattle for meat collection arrears, started another wave of slaughter of livestock. The situation was complicated, moreover, by the partial crop failure of 1931.

An inkling of the peasant tragedy came to the world in the first months of 1932 in dispatches out of Bucharest. Rumanian frontier guards began to discover the bullet-riddled bodies of Moldavian peasants from the Soviet side on the frozen river Dniester which separated the two countries at this point. There were days when the corpses totaled into hundreds. Soviet soldiers were using machineguns to shoot down peasants trying to escape the country.

Bucharest newspapermen went to the border and returned with harrowing details of a mass flight from threatening hunger and official oppression. For every peasant who succeeded in crossing the line it was obvious that several had been killed in the attempt. Moscow made the expected denials, but Soviet representatives in Rumania were of necessity more frank. They took part in a Soviet-Rumanian commission which sought to identify the corpses and arranged for burial. From Poland and other contiguous countries came similar accounts of flight and death.

Soon the government ordered a halt to coercive seizure of farm products and published the same old promises to obey its own laws—the oft-repeated pattern of broken faith with the peasant masses. It went farther and reduced grain collection quotas for the new year by 20% and gave the peasants, individual farmers and collectives alike, the right to bring their produce to the open market for sale at open-market prices, twenty and thirty times higher than the official prices.

The retreat was too late. Already many agricultural districts were petitioning the central authorities for food relief. Those who had hidden stocks were afraid to bring them into the open. Distrust of the government was by now second nature.

It required no sociological clairvoyance to recognize that the country's agriculture was heading for catastrophe in this, the final year of the tragic Five Year Plan, tragic alike in its successes and in its failures. It was no accident that the growing peasant "recalcitrance" was greatest in just those areas where the "success" was greatest. The ultimate disaster, ranking with the greatest catastrophes in modern times, occurred in precisely those provinces that had been declared "100% collectivized," precisely where the "liquidation of kulaks" had been announced as 100% perfect, namely, the Ukraine and North Caucasus. Where the force was greatest, the reaction was greatest; the tragedy was in direct proportion to the "successes."

Four years of pressure had squeezed the last drop of active opposition out of the peasantry. Violent expressions of dissatisfaction were increasingly rare. A more terrible, less palpable opposition had arisen—a supine despair manifest in indifference, laziness, neglect. The richest grain areas were suddenly over-run with weeds so luxuriant that they broke the teeth of mechanical reapers. *Pravda* and *Izvestia* began to write more candidly about crops rotting unharvested on the fields. Angry opposition had given way to lackadaisical non-coöperation.

What the Webbs were to call the "rebelliousness" of the peasants was nothing of the sort; rebellion can be dealt with by a powerful government. How deal with an animal-like indifference, a weariness of the spirit and body so profound that even the prospect of death by starvation could not stir them into activity? The Soviet government, in the last year of its Plan, faced those final unanswerable Asiatic arguments: silence and inactivity and prostrate hopelessness. The world had seen an expression of these Asiatic arguments in India, in the non-coöperation movement; but the Indian apathy was more conscious. Russia's peasant masses adopted the tactics of passive resistance almost unconsciously, through a sort of torpor and sluggishness and bottomless hopelessness.

Half-heartedly, they raised enough food for themselves, hazily aware, and scarcely caring, that the government might take it from them. Torpidly, they ate their seed allotment, not enough vitality left in their spirit to wonder what next. The British and American literature of apologetics which in later years "blamed" the peasants for the famine that killed millions of them was either cynical or stupid. One might as well blame draught animals for collapsing under the excessive load. The paralyzing indifference of the Russian peasantry that brought the greatest crop of weeds in recorded history and left bread crops to rot while men and women starved was not a rebellious "plot"—forty million people do not easily conspire together. None of it was by design. It was an expression of ultimate hopelessness, a natural catastrophe of the human spirit, a non-coöperation movement that was akin to mass suicide.

In Moscow, the encroaching tragedy was manifest in a hundred symptoms, over and above the verbal reports by people who had been in the highly collectivized regions and those with relatives there. The throngs of refugees around the railroad stations grew always bigger. Street beggary grew. A continuous stream of beggars came to our kitchen door. There was a timid knock; you opened the door and faced a ragged peasant, man or woman, on his knees pleading for a piece of bread. A friend who worked in the post office told me that the number of packages being sent by parcel post to villages in the Ukraine and North Caucasus was growing constantly larger—bread and other foodstuffs being sent to relatives in the regions that once fed not only Russia but half of Europe.

About half a dozen correspondents went to see the great Dnieper dam in construction, now being rushed to completion. An official of Dnieprostroi conducted us over the site and stocked us up with boastful statistics. I had a letter of introduction to a General Electric engineer from his chief in Moscow. As I sat with him discussing the dam—and his off-record version was less optimistic than the statistics in my pocket—I heard a door at the rear of the house opening and closing at intervals of a few minutes. The sounds distracted my attention.

"Oh, that?" the engineer smiled wryly when I asked about the noise. "Come and I'll show you."

He led me to the kitchen. A wicker basket near the door was half-filled with slices of black bread. A grimy peasant woman was being given a slice by the servant as we entered.

"All day long these poor people come begging for bread," the engineer explained. "I have a basketful ready for them. Most of them are peasants from the surrounding country, but a good many of them are workers on the construction whose rations are not enough for their large families. I suppose some of them are hoarding against the future, but I'd rather be played for a sucker than turn away a hungry beggar."

"I'm afraid you are lacking in Bolshevik ruthlessness," I said.

"I suppose I am," he laughed. "So, as I was saying, these turbines should be ready for the test in three or four months. . . ."

In August, we sent our first reports of executions for the theft of socialized property. Members of a collective farm helping themselves to the grain they had themselves raised were subject to capital punishment. It was not easy to cure the peasant of the mistake that he could take a few bushels of the grain from the land that he and his family had worked on. The decree also applied to theft of socialized property of any other kind, whether in the city or on the land. Since practically everything in the U.S.S.R. except one's personal clothes and furnishings was socialized property, the decree in effect made all stealing a capital crime.

Thus, in the fifteenth year of Bolshevism, in the last year of the *Piatiletka*, the Russian people were presented with the harshest law since the advent of the revolution. Shrill editorials boasted of the implacability of revolutionary justice, and newly minted communists in New York applauded.

VIII. The End of RAPP

AND another of those "revolutions" from above came to pass in this spring of 1932, this time in the realms of arts and letters. With a single and resounding whack, Joseph Stalin did shatter and disperse the phalanxes of embattled "proletarian" writers, poets, dramatists, painters and musicians. His one imperial *ukase* was enough to send all the enthroned nonentities, their generals and their camp-followers, sprawling in the mud. Brusquely Stalin informed them that their vaunted "conquest of power in art" for the proletariat had blighted Soviet letters and turned Russian art into a desert.

Out with the bureaucrats of literature, the time-servers of art! Out with the cliques and the "left vulgarizers" of esthetics! A decree on April 23, 1932, dissolved RAPP and its sister organizations and commanded that all writers be made eligible to a broader, less politically orthodox society, the Union of Soviet Writers.

It would be less than human for Soviet authors not to relish the sight of yesterday's literary dictators crawling on their bellies in the mire, the spectacle of piddling poets and second-rate journalists, who had set up as orthodox judges of art, now scampering back to their dusty holes. The chief trouble with the politicians of art, Stalin now proclaimed, was that they produced no art, contenting themselves with loud conferences, pompous programs, and attacks on the talented. And Stalin's parrot press, which on April 22 failed to note any flaw in the system of art by terror, on April 24 proceeded to kick and pommel the fallen Napoleons with all the fury of long-suppressed desire. All of this made a brief holiday for artistic and intellectual circles in Moscow.

Within a few months, no one even remembered the names of the Auerbachs and Chumandrins, of all the whilom tsars of proletarian literature, Bolshevized criticism, Leninist painting and the rest of it—proof enough of the emptiness of their pretensions. Nothing remained to mark their reign except a litter of pronunciamentos and the ashes of artists whom they had hounded to suicide and broken on the rack of persecution.

If, for most of the leaders and hangers-on of RAPP, the "conquest" of art had been a convenient path to careers, there were others who had brought themselves honestly to believe their own twaddle. They were really convinced that the G.P.U. was the final authority on esthetics and that a text from Stalin outweighed the accumulated beauty of human genius. Uninspired bookkeepers of literary sins and virtues like Sergei Dinamov, fervent sloganeers in verse like Bezimensky, ambitious writers of editorials in four acts like Kirshon, were blinded by bewilderment under Stalin's sudden blow. They must not only accept humiliation, but must kiss the knout publicly and pretend that they "recognized their mistakes."

It is not pleasant to hear people shouting, "Down with us! Kick harder, O brethren!" Not even when they deserve it.

How unrelated Stalin's edict was to inner forces in the nation's life may be judged from the astonishment it caused. The blow fell while the ink was still wet on the most elaborate of the pontifical RAPP programs for the development of proletarian culture. The *Literary Gazette*, mouthpiece of the whole proletarian art movement, in its groggy bewilderment, failed to cry "Amen!" loud enough to the decree that ended its power, and was duly disciplined. In the next issue, the editors beat their breasts and begged indulgence. In the very act of bestowing a counterfeit freedom upon the arts, the Kremlin made a show of its absolutist power over creative thought. For intelligent artists it was not a victory but a deep insult.

Abroad, too, in all the little magazines of the communist movement, in the literary circles where esthetic proletarianism had become the fashion, there was confusion and humiliation.

But the sycophants and hosanna-singers everywhere quickly regained their poise. Without a word of apology for their own antics, they hailed the Stalin *ukase* as a masterpiece of dialectic leadership. They managed to find some esoteric wisdom in Stalin's failure or refusal to understand the depredations of the heresy-hunters in the arts until this spring of 1932, when Soviet intellectual life was a blighted desert. Again his tragic lateness was invested by the faithful with a higher wisdom surpassing the understanding of infidels.

I was close enough to the edges of artistic circles, through a dozen or two friends, to share their gleeful feeling of sated revenge. But I was close enough, also, to share their sense of frustration and shame. With a wink of his little finger, Stalin had done what the whole community of Russian artists in years of grumbling and sacrifice and heartbreak had failed to do. They were pleased with the cutting down of RAPP but they could scarcely take any joy in this new demonstration of the helplessness and subserviency of the arts.

The new freedom, whatever it might be worth in practice, was given to artists as a royal gift, and the same omnipotence which today chose to be benevolent might be doubly malevolent tomorrow. The change in the domain of art was in no way intrinsic —it was itself an act of violence. The artists whom it ostensibly liberated could feel no sense of personal fulfillment; their hands remained tied behind their backs.

Once, when I was in my 'teens, I sweated over a short story of the ambitious psychologizing sort dear to undergraduate fiction writers. I started with a man unjustly condemned to prison. All his brooding and outraged innocence focus on a dream of escape. Only freedom by the strength of his own wit and courage could square accounts with the system that robbed him of human dignity. This dream sustains him in his confinement. But suddenly the end of his term comes so close that he can see it and the prospect horrifies him. To be let out with a pat on the shoulder by the hated keepers seemed to him only an added indignity. He feels ever more sharply that in accepting freedom as a gift, instead of wresting it from unwilling keepers, he would be acknowledging their right to dispose of his life. And at the last moment, to ward off that humiliation, he attempts a hopeless jail-break, is subdued and given a new sentence—more time to plot a successful escape.

Soviet writers liberated from the yoke of RAPP, by the same external and arbitrary power which put the yoke of their necks, felt something of the revulsion which hurt my imaginary prisoner even more than prison itself.

2

Behind Stalin's sudden fit of good sense in regard to art, some people detected the guiding hand of Maxim Gorky. Despite his adherence to the Bolshevik group since its beginning, and despite his friendship with Lenin, Gorky had opposed Bolshevik methods after the revolution on humanistic grounds. But from about 1929 forward he yielded to the philosophy of ruthlessness. In the late spring of 1931 he gave up his home in Sorrento, Italy, and settled permanently in Moscow.

Until then a favorite Soviet conundrum ran: "Who lives well in the U.S.S.R.? Answer—Gorky in Sorrento." Now the conundrum was obsolete. He was known to have become one of Stalin's most intimate associates, his word weighing heavily in the scales of the dictator's decisions. On those rare occasions when Stalin showed himself in public, the stooped, shaggy figure of the great writer was usually by his side.

Gorky, the universally acknowledged father of proletarian literature, became the Kremlin's author-laureate. His articles on cultural matters, and even on economic and political themes, were regarded more and more as the authentic voice of the Kremlin. They showed increasingly a tendency to pontificate, instruct and rebuke younger writers.

There is no doubt that on the whole Soviet literature had a friend at court in Gorky. More than once he saved erring writers from the official boot; several times to my own knowledge he obtained for Soviet artists the supreme boon of a trip abroad. There may even be some basis for the theory (advanced after his death) that Gorky, in swallowing Stalin's personal dictatorship and its attendant brutalities, had deliberately compromised with his conscience in the hope of mitigating the harshness of the regime.*

Nevertheless, writers and artists resented deeply Gorky's surrender to the temporal powers after a long lifetime of struggle

* Recent disclosures strengthen the picture of Gorky as a champion of greater tolerance, playing on Stalin's vanity to obtain more humane treatment of non-communist intellectuals. He is known to have argued so vehemently against the terror which followed Kirov's assassination that he incurred Stalin's disfavor for a period. In 1935, the breach reached a point where Gorky tried to leave the country—and was denied an exit visa!

for the dignity of the human spirit. His influence at court might be useful, but it was a compromising role and one incongruous with his entire career. That eloquent voice of Gorky, which had rung out so long and so lustily for the persecuted and the disinherited, now joined every official chorus of blood hate. In his diatribes against the chosen victims of political persecution, one expected at least a touch of compassion, an echo of the old Gorky who hated suffering and bloodshed, but one found only obbligatos to the slogans in the editorial columns and official theses. The man who wrote *My Childhood* and *The Lower Depths* never got around to speaking up for the innocent children of "class enemies," never once protested against the deepening horror of concentration camps and valuta tortures, the indignity of the new internal passport system, the hounding of pre-revolutionary intellectuals of his own generation.

Outwardly, at least, it seemed that Gorky had capitulated—that the crusading rebel had turned into an irascible old reactionary. In return for honors such as had rarely before come to any great literary man in his own lifetime, he had consented to act as cultural window-dressing for a dictatorship that betrayed every humane and cultural element in his own literary legacy. Gorky, an old and sick man, weary in body and spirit, was placing the seal of his intellectual respectability on every crime perpetrated by the Kremlin. He applauded when the forty-eight professors were put to death without trial; he called for death and vengeance, in almost the same hysterical words as *Pravda* and *Izvestia*, every time another batch of men was brought to a demonstration trial on charges compounded by the secret service.

The newer generation of Soviet writers, many of whom had been brought up in adoration of Gorky's compassionate humanism and uncompromising devotion to truth, felt let down. To question any word of Gorky's had become as dangerous almost as questioning a word of Stalin's or Kaganovich's—the loved story-teller had been transfigured into an untouchable Pooh-Bah of literature. But privately, among trusted friends, I have heard him assailed as a renegade to his own past. Writers whom Gorky invited to his "at homes" were flattered and thrilled. There they were sure to find the mighty of the land, sometimes Stalin Himself. But in their own minds they did not confuse the enthroned Gorky of his last few years with the earlier, the true Gorky of deathless fame in the history of the human spirit.

The apotheosis of Gorky was to take place in September of this year, 1932, when the Soviet government celebrated forty years of his literary activity. The Bolshoi Theater was the scene. All the important political leaders, from Stalin down, were on the platform; all the *kosher* men of letters, the goose-stepping artists, and successful flatterers were there. It was there decreed that the ancient city of Nijni-Novgorod, scene of Gorky's boyhood sufferings, should thereafter carry his name. Tverskaya, which is Moscow's Main Street, was renamed Gorky Street. The Moscow Art Theatre, though its tradition is forever linked with the name of Anton Chekhov, was renamed for Gorky—an indignity Gorky himself deplored. Everything that an all-powerful dictatorship could do to exalt and flatter and overawe the shaggy and rather pathetic old man was done.

It was a sort of solemn interment of the revolutionary Gorky; what remained was a mummified and sanctified old man. Perhaps he felt this. When he rose to speak his voice was curiously sad, deprecating. "No mortal man," he said, "could possibly deserve all this." But he did not find in himself the strength to utter words like "freedom" and "idealism" and "beauty"—words that were the keynotes in the symphony of his genius.

3

The future American ambassador to the U.S.S.R., William C. Bullitt, came to Moscow that spring on an unofficial errand, presumably for the future President of the United States. "Franklin Roosevelt will be the next President," he assured me at our first meeting, "and American recognition of the Soviet government will be one of the first acts of his administration." The mission, whatever it was, apparently was not proceeding too smoothly. Commissar Litvinov, whom Bullitt was particularly anxious to see, was not in Moscow. The casual manner in which Bullitt was received is sufficiently clear from the fact that Intourist stuck him into the worst of the tourist hotels, the New Moscow, on the other side of the river. The food there was not agreeing with him, and our Shura's cooking saved another American from the gastronomical blues.

Sentimental to the core, Bullitt felt that he could not leave Moscow without placing flowers on the grave of his friend John Reed, whose widow, Louise Bryant, he married some time after Reed's death. Reed's ashes were buried on Red Square, just outside the Kremlin wall, along with other native and foreign heroes of the revolution. The graves are within easy view but not within easy approach, being surrounded by an iron fence. The decoration of the grave therefore came down to the eternal problem of obtaining a *propusk*, a permit to go behind the fence. George Andreychine,* whom I had visited in Leavenworth Prison thirteen years ago, and who since then had tasted a lot of Soviet prison, was now an official of Intourist. His efforts through that organization, seconded by my own through the Foreign Office, finally elicited the *propusk*.

Early one morning, Bullitt, Andreychine, and I drove to Red Square. Two of us watched from the distance while Bullitt, carrying a large wreath, walked solemnly toward Reed's grave. We saw him place the flowers on the stone and stand there with bowed head for many minutes. When he returned to the car, tears were rolling down his cheeks and his features were drawn with sorrow. No one said a word as we drove to the New Moscow Hotel.

I talked a great deal with Bullitt during his visit. His conception of the new Russia was deeply colored by the romanticism of the earliest period, when he made his memorable trip to Moscow for President Wilson during the Versailles peace negotiations. He was thoroughly informed, of course, about the physical changes that had taken place in the intervening thirteen years, but wholly innocent of the far greater changes in the mood of the revolution—the hardening of its emotional arteries, its callousness and unromantic "realism." He was still seeing Russia through the fresh ardors of the John Reeds and the Rhys Williamses. I remember saying to Billy after a long evening of talk, "Bullitt's enthusiasm for Russia, I'm afraid, wouldn't survive a long residence

* Exiled again by the Soviet authorities about 1935.

here. . . . It's based on romantic assumptions that no longer hold good. . . ." I was a better prophet than I guessed at the time.

Cecil B. DeMille typified another side of foreigners' uncritical enthusiasm for the Soviet experiment. He was thrilled by its sheer exoticism, its swarming and ripe-odored backwardness. He had watched the gray mass pouring through Red Square in a parade, lost himself in the tangle of Moscow's crowded sidewalks, and was impressed with the pictorial challenge of this crowded humanity. "Feet . . . marching feet . . . millions of them marching endlessly," he tried to explain his feeling to me. "If ever I do a picture about the new Russia, that would be its *motif* . . . feet in leather and feet in rags and bare feet, but all marching, moving, flowing . . . Feet!"

There was, of course, nothing particularly new and Bolshevik in these feet. What the gifted DeMille, a mystic to his fingertips and sensitive to the drama and pathos of mankind in the mass, felt was the ant-hill abundance of this Russian people, and its picturesque poverty. He would have reacted in exactly the same way twenty years earlier, in the tsar's Russia. John Reed the poet, *before 1917*, before he dreamed of being a communist, had written: "Russian ideals are the most exhilarating; Russian thought the freest, Russian art the most exuberant; Russian food and drink are to me the best, and Russians themselves are, perhaps, the most interesting human beings that exist!" Later Reed was to read Marxist enthusiasms into his esthetic feeling for the age-old backwardness.

DeMille and a thousand other foreigners now read "the new Russia" into that backwardness. Shall I ever forget the shock of a passage in Waldo Frank's book about Russia in which he recounted his mystical transport as he walks through the streets of Leningrad? He could not eat, he wrote with a singular lack of humor, because he wanted to sing; this at a time when the drab population which caused his mystical anorexia could not eat for other and less lyrical reasons.

DeMille never made that picture on the new Russia, though he toyed with the idea for years. Possibly he discovered that swarming feet were not specifically Russian—what interested him most in Russia, in other words, was its human element, not its Soviet trimmings. He urged me to give him a story on which he might do a picture. Billy and I were to dine with him and the gracious Mrs. DeMille on their last evening in Moscow. I had not thought about a story. That afternoon Billy, who has a better "story mind" than I, helped me to work out a plot: we imagined a crowded Moscow apartment, conveniently stocked with different types of Soviet human beings, and nicely scrambled in political and emotional tangles.

At dinner, in the Hotel Metropole, DeMille asked for the story. I explained that I had an idea, but very much in the rough. "All right, let's hear it," he said. I began the narrative hastily concocted a few hours earlier. As I talked, however, DeMille's face took on a strangely quizzical expression, somewhere between amusement and astonishment. I was disconcerted but decided to plow right ahead to the bitter end. When I had finished the story DeMille looked me in the eyes:

"Tell me, Gene," he said, "have you read the play just written by Walter Duranty and Maurice Hindus?"

"No, I haven't. I knew they were writing a play but haven't the slightest idea what it's about."

"That's extraordinary! Almost uncanny," DeMille said. "They gave me the play to read, and I just finished it. Well, this story you have just told me is almost the identical story in their play!"

It was my turn to be astonished. But perhaps the thing was not as strange as it seemed at first blush. All of us had had approximately the same experience and in attempting to convey that experience in fictional terms chose the obvious story.

IX. Living Space

ASKED to list the cities she had learned to know intimately in her ten crowded years of life, our Genie replied without hesitation, "New York, London, Paris, Berlin, Moscow, and Klyasma." The Klyasma thus bracketed with more notable metropoli outweighed, at the moment, the others in importance. Its broad muddy avenues and rowdy children and nude bathing, its easy and earthy ways, must have impressed Genie as pleasantly exciting after the trim orderliness and hushed respectability of Lichterfelde in Berlin where she was being schooled.

Klyasma, where we spent the summer of 1932, lay on a meandering river of the same name, about thirty miles outside of Moscow. It retained the externals of its former character as a summer resort and suburban residential town for middle-class Muscovites; roomy houses, each with its plot of ground and shrubbery, sat well back behind tinted picket-fences. But it had a frayed look and a somewhat strained and nervous atmosphere. The more elaborate structures were being used as official vacation places and sanatoria; a good many had been taken over by government organizations for their officials. But many of the houses were still in private hands. Those who had managed to hang on to a private home through fifteen years of revolution, never certain of their rights or tenure and tentative in their sense of ownership, were responsible for the nervous overtones of Klyasma; they were chiefly in-between people socially, walking the tight-rope of political respectability.

A block or two from us, in a ramshackle clapboard house of many rooms and dark corridors and rickety stairways, Jimmy Abbe, the quixotic American photographer, was installed with his family. Besides the diminutive bald-headed papa Abbe, his attractively buxom Polly, and the three children who were destined to celebrity through their book *Around the World in Eleven Years*, the menage included the four children of Dr. Hecker, an assortment of house guests, a dog or two. A Sanger Circus on the Klyasma, as it were, noisy and hectic and irresponsible—far more Russian in these respects than any Russian household. The Abbe hospitality was exuberant and most catholic; another ill-assorted dozen guests to share the food (bought with borrowed rubles) meant nothing at all. Ivy Litvinov, wife of the Commissar, and their adopted daughter were there often; Dr. Alcan Hirsch's Rolls Royce, brought from America each time he came to give the Russians his well-paid advice on matters chemical, was parked there frequently; stray Russians and less routine tourists came and went.

Spencer Williams, an ex-newspaperman in charge of the American-Russian Chamber of Commerce, and his wife, Caroline, were also summering in Klyasma; an enthusiastic motion picture amateur, Spencer came out of Klyasma with the most intimate record of nude bathing available anywhere. The Chamberlins, a few other Americans, and several Viennese families were scattered through the town. Our own household entertained transient Americans, among them, I recall, Henry Luce, proprietor of *Time* Magazine; Stanley High, preacher and publicist; and Alfred Stern, head of the Rosenwald Foundation, with his charming wife, the daughter of Julius Rosenwald. All in all, the inhabitants of Klyasma that summer had a close-up view of foreigners and their foibles such as few Russian towns could boast.

We shared our house, for our sins, with the director of a trust and his family: one Panteleyev, pot-bellied and unctuous, his ecclesiastical hair and beard (a carroty red in color and silken in texture) trimmed to a stage version of the Old Bolshevik. The company of these Panteleyevs, father, mother and son, was far from edifying. But as a sociological study they were useful and fascinating. Perfect laboratory specimens, they were, of the newly entrenched bourgeoisie profiteering on the revolution: loud, vulgar, and self-centered people, greedily garnering comforts and advantages for themselves in the name of the proletariat. Even the oily obesity of all three seemed symbolic. The house ostensibly belonged to the trust, freshly seized for its "workers," but it was occupied in expansive ease by the Panteleyevs. The automobile that took him to and from the city, and stood always ready, chauffeur and all, for his bidding, likewise belonged to the trust.

And the sacks of potatoes with which he filled the cellar, at a time when his "workers" were standing in queues for them, presumably also belonged to the trust. Eventually socialism would give every worker a summer home, an automobile and plenty of potatoes; for the present, as a beginning, Panteleyev enjoyed such things in their name.

We rented the *dacha* sometime in May or June from its original owner, a lanky and ineffectual old man named Kalishnik, who held a semi-technical job in one of the commissariats. His wife was a fluttery, old-fashioned little woman, as dried up as an old pea. Both of them, trailed by an elongated son of fifteen, showed us over the premises, every potted plant and faded armchair spotlessly clean. The house was their little world; they had lived in it these thirty years or more.

Having signed the lease entitling us to occupy the ground floor during the summer, and having paid the rental, we considered the matter settled. But nothing in Russia happens quite so smoothly. In a few weeks we were privileged witnesses to one more "liquidation."

The Kalishniks, it appeared, had negotiated with a state trust for the sale of the house. They would receive in exchange an apartment in the city and a sum in cash. The deal, clearly, had been dictated by these people's fear of losing their home without compensation. A preliminary and unsigned draft agreement was drawn up. In the meantime, however, the government had taken a more liberal tone toward private owners. The Kalishniks took heart and called off the deal.

But they were reckoning without Comrade Panteleyev, director of the trust. One night he arrived with his family and belongings and installed himself in the house, over the hysterical protests of the owners, with nothing but the preliminary agreement to justify the forcible occupation. Even for Russia, such direct action seemed extreme. Had the offender been an ordinary mortal, the police would have dislodged him as a matter of course. But this was a communist, a "responsible worker" with a histrionic coiffure, so the local police preferred not to budge him.

The Kalishniks had recourse to the courts. Either the agreement was in effect, in which case the trust should provide them with a city apartment and the specified cash consideration, or it was ineffective, in which case the intruders would be expelled. In the simplicity of their own hearts the Kalishniks knew that these were the only alternatives; and in the simplicity of my own logic I agreed with them.

It was in the rough-and-ready courtroom of the neighboring town of Pushkino that I had my first view of the oleomarginous Panteleyev. He was holding forth when I arrived, in the flowing periods of a practiced demagogue, and the three judges, one of them a young kerchiefed girl, seemed deeply impressed. Listening to him it was hard to surmise that he was fighting to retain a pleasant *dacha* for his fat wife and roly-poly boy. It was a *dacha* for the "workers" of his trust that he was defending, and the miserable Kalishniks were just bourgeois creatures with an exaggerated notion of private property rights. Poor Kalishnik, tremulous and a little incoherent, was a sorry sight by comparison. Where Panteleyev was prepared nobly to enjoy the house in the name of the state, Kalishnik was trying to enjoy it and care for it in his own name.

The court took the problem under advisement. A few days later it confirmed Panteleyev in his "expropriation" of the property for the "workers" of his trust. It confirmed the validity of the tentative and unsigned agreement, but made it enforcible only on one side. The Kalishniks were not even to receive the promised city apartment and cash. In short, they were liquidated. By the time we moved in, Panteleyev's influence had succeeded in placing the owners in prison. The technical charge against the withered old woman, we learned, was that she harbored an "anti-Soviet mood," as evidenced presumably by her hysterical objections to the loss of the only home she possessed. Against her husband, Panteleyev had dug up a faded charge dating back to the civil war days—true or false, the charge was just a convenient pretext for removing his melancholy face from the vicinity.

Only the boy Kolya and his dog remained, living in a sort of outhouse, and dependent on such food as Billy gave them. A family had been broken and scattered, a commissariat had been robbed of one of its minor technical workers, and a boy born and raised under the hammer and sickle had been forever embittered, in order that the "revolutionary" Panteleyev and his ménage might have a desirable *dacha!*

Our landlord was therefore a state trust, as personified in a hairy ball of fat. Panteleyev was nobody's fool. Many of the friends who came to share the comforts of his *dacha* wore the leather coats and slick boots that were almost a uniform of the secret service. Many of them arrived in automobiles which they were using for private recreation as proxies for their respective groups of workers. Panteleyev chose his friends carefully; his kind chooses its friends from the ranks of the privileged under any system that has ever been devised. He waited only for the end of the summer to be rid of the embarrassing American witnesses to his maneuvering. Then he would remain in sole and complete possession of public property, where private property had been shown its place.

One day, representatives of the *Finotdyel*, the finance department of the government, arrived and made a careful inventory of the property on the premises; every broken-down chair and threadbare carpet was listed. The personal belongings of the Kalishniks had been confiscated for the proletariat along with their house. This or some other Panteleyev would soon be using them for the glory of Karl Marx.

Panteleyev was not left in doubt as to what his American tenants thought of his unctuous hijacking. He began with a campaign of petty persecutions which I squelched quickly enough by using some of my own influence—influence is as efficacious a commodity under totalitarian bureaucracy as money under capitalism. He thereupon changed his technique and tried to make friends of us. Possibly he had become alarmed at the likelihood of such a public record of his methods as these pages. Once he asked me point-blank why I didn't like him. I told him point-blank.

Watching the Panteleyevs at lordly ease on the lawn Mrs. Kalishnik had tended for thirty-odd years was an ordeal to the end of that summer. A stout servant plied them with appetizing morsels, the silken beard flowed gently in the country breeze, the proletarian chauffeur waited for hours for their orders—the revolution had triumphed over another bourgeois family and all was well with the Panteleyevs' world.

2

Among our regular guests at Klyasma, and after we returned to town, were several American Negro boys and girls, the cynosure of all Russian eyes wherever they went. These were the sorry wreckage of a politico-artistic project that foundered on the rocks of the higher diplomacy. The project, greatly ballyhooed in the American Negro press, had envisioned a superfilm of Negro history: a sort of cavalcade of the colored race in America, its exploitation, and its stirring to proletarian class consciousness. To this end, twenty-two American Negroes, mostly from New York's Harlem, were engaged and shipped to Moscow, all of them actors and actresses of extremely amateur standing. As may be supposed, they were for the most part members or sympathizers of the Communist Party. The whole undertaking seemed to them token of the new world dawning in Russia—in Hollywood the Negroes were sentimental mammies or clowning comics, but Moscow would do justice to the epic tragedy of a race in bondage.

The arrival of the Negro group in Russia was an occasion for editorial handsprings on the theme of minority races and their eventual emancipation by the Comintern. A German film director who had done a picture about Africa was selected to direct the new film—his familiarity with African savages, by Russian logic, equipped him to interpret Mississippi and Harlem. I read an outline of the scenario and it seemed to me replete with absurdity, profoundly ignorant of the American Negro, his psychology and his problems. Nevertheless, it might have produced some vigorous pictorial symbolism.

When news of the project reached the American press, all the professional friends of the Soviet Union were horrified. They acted to avoid the political catastrophe. Here they were trying to cement Soviet-American friendship, trade and diplomatic relations, and Moscow theorists were spoiling everything by hitting white United States in the most tender area of its social anatomy, the Negro problem! Such a thing was patently undiplomatic.

The Kremlin saw the point instantly. The whole undertaking was canceled. The public—and the disgruntled Negroes—were fed lying statements which first pretended that it was merely a postponement of the project, then blamed the abandonment upon defects in the scenario. It was perfectly clear, however, that the retreat was diplomatic. The interests of the U.S.S.R. as a functioning state among states had collided with the interests of the U.S.S.R. as the vanguard of world revolution. The real needs of a real state received preference over the hoped-for revolution.

The majority of the twenty-odd Negroes were simply bewildered by the bankruptcy of their plan. The disciplined communists among them meekly took orders, signed the statements drafted for them, and scouted around for jobs. But a minority made no secret of its sorrow. Four of them sat in my office, sizzling with indignation, feeling themselves insulted and betrayed.

"American race hatred has reached across the ocean and hit us in the face," one of them exclaimed. "Even in Soviet Russia hatred of our people has caught up with us."

This was the disillusionment they carried back to America, where a few were outspoken enough on the matter. More opportunist members of the party decided that there was no use quarreling with a powerful government, whatever its revolutionary slogans. They remained in Moscow, working or studying. One of these was a slim, light-colored, and very attractive young Negress from Harlem. Communist politics were above her head, but the admiration and flattery of individual communists quite understandable. The competition for her company was keen and undisguised, with a prominent novelist and a prominent official of the Foreign Office among the more eager wooers. Even a few white Americans made a strong bid. It is to the girl's credit that her popularity did not go to her head; she played one admirer against the other and ultimately left them all in the lurch when she went back to Harlem.

3

The domestic spaciousness in which we had lived and entertained in Moscow, that spaciousness so widely envied, so celebrated in the folklore of the foreign colony, came to an abrupt end in the fall of 1932. No more bourgeois amplitude and quiet and cleanliness; now the broad corridors and marble staircase were slimy with Moscow's mud, now a hundred voices outshouted each other and doors banged and strangers dashed into our living room and sleeping room, now the field-like ballroom upstairs was crowded with desks, and Shura's lordly domain turned into a factory kitchen. Worst of all, the overgrown bathtub was liquidated, the bathroom converted into a lunch counter.

In short, the *Moscow Daily News*, English-language newspaper, was suddenly moved in on us at the Hammer mansion, and thereafter until we left Russia it blanketed our lives.

It took nearly as large a staff and ten times as much noise to produce this amateur four-page newspaper as it does to get out the New York *Times*. Both the noise and the staff flowed in turgid streams past our doors and overflowed our thresholds. The *Moscow Daily News* was a haven of economic refuge for the more literate Americans and Britishers wishing to remain in the Soviet capital. Now and then, a professional journalist like Harvey O'Connor or Millie Bennett joined the staff, and in the higher reaches of its special writers were a few capable people like Anna Louise Strong; but in overwhelming majority the staff consisted of assorted British-American incompetents, with Michael Borodin, the Colonel Lawrence of the Chinese Revolution, in charge.

My objections, however, were not to the quality of the journal but to the fact that it was quartered upon us. In justice, it must be attested that the *Moscow Daily News* felt that the United Press and the Lyons family were quartered upon them. Dr. Hammer had negotiated the transfer of the premises in great secrecy and had undertaken rashly and in so many words to remove us from the place. In return he received a large apartment elsewhere and divers other considerations. But I refused to move, for the simple and sufficient reason that I had no place to move to. The hotels were far beyond my means and tenting on the sidewalks a bit awkward.

Generalissimo Borodin blustered and threatened in a manner quite unbecoming to a Historical Personage famed for diplomatic finesse and the long view. Forcible eviction seemed in the cards, and American cameramen stood prepared to photograph the scene for posterity. I sent long communications to the Foreign Office and to *Ogoniok*, the publishing trust which issued the *Moscow Daily News*, offering to vacate just as soon as they found me a roof but not until then.

In the end, the ponderous Borodin organization decided that

half a house was better than none, and for some eighteen months we lived together, each the despair of the other. We were restricted to the two small rooms on the lower floor and the cubicle which served as United Press office. Day and night, the thunder of a newspaper aborning and the lightning of Borodin's irascible generalship crackled all around us. We were an exposed and unprotected islet of domesticity in the midst of a clamorous Soviet enterprise.

Many members of the staff were our close friends, and sought sanctuary occasionally on our islet. We listened to their plaints and their gossip and were privy to the complicated intrigues and angers and editorial fits of temper in which the English-language daily had its being. A bevy of oversexed American females and homosexual Englishmen had found harborage on the *Moscow Daily News* (a tragically futile combination); a complex struggle for power went on among the Russian functionaries; English-speaking technicians and tourists flocked with complaints and schemes; and through it all pulsed the querulous basso of Borodin. Despite placards marked "PRIVATE," a lot of the backwash of that churning disorder penetrated my office and my home. In all the months in which we shared the mansion on Petrovsky Pereulok, I did not step into Borodin's acreage more than four or five times. But I could not stop Americans, having told their tales of woe to the *Daily News*, from repeating them to the United Press on the way out.

It was impossible to believe that my nervous and unmannerly neighbor was the same Borodin who had helped to shape Chinese history. In the preceding years I had met him socially now and then, and been sufficiently impressed by his chunky body, his walrus mustache, and decisive voice. I knew him at second-hand not only from books and articles about the Chinese Revolution, in which he had acted as Moscow's emissary, but through the admiration of the Chen children, Anna Louise Strong, and others who had shared his Chinese experience. And now I marveled: was this the same man who had guided the destiny of China and organized the forces of an epochal revolution? The idea seemed preposterous and incredible. I could only assume that the Borodin of 1932 was the empty shell of the Borodin of 1927, broken-down, bitter, and petty.

Our bathing facilities were now reduced to cold sponging in our narrow corridor. Gone were the days when we invited friends to bathe in our house; now it was our turn to beg a bath from others. I became a regular client of the public baths and can claim a more intimate knowledge of the male Russian anatomy than any other correspondent. You left your clothes on a bench in a cold anteroom, wondering what you would do if they disappeared while you steamed yourself. A brass check costing a ruble entitled you to a vigorous soaping and drubbing; you brought your own soap, of course, and retrieved the remainder; my foreign brands always plucked admiring sibilants from the "rubbers." You gasped for breath on the lowest level in the steam-room, marveling at the fortitude of Russians who remained for hours on the uppermost shelf, whipping themselves with twigs and dousing the red-hot oven wall to thicken the steam.

My chief amusement in the Russian bath—a kind of private game—was to try to identify the men's social status in their nakedness. Often I picked out the G.P.U. officers: even in the altogether their manner implied a leather jacket and puttees. Recognizing the bureaucrats was no trouble at all; I could practically see the phantom brief-case under their naked wings, along with a paunch, a trimmed beard, and a self-important gait.

In the steam-room one day, his voice coming from the fog as though from a great distance, a Russian friend who was frequently my bathing companion told me a famous story of Anton Chekhov's. That story had a bathhouse for setting and ran as follows:

Among the men on the upper shelf of the steam chamber was an agent of the *Okhranka,* the tsar's spy system. Though he was off duty, his trained ear caught suspicious inflections in the voice of one obese bearded individual. The suspect, commenting on life and its problems, used a tone which seemed to the agent faintly unorthodox, if only because the language was above his thick agent's head. "Aha!" the spy decided, "this customer will bear watching." When the suspect left, the agent followed. From a corner of the dressing room he watched his quarry getting slowly into clothes, and—horror of horrors!—it turned out to be a priest. Conscience-bitten that he should have suspected a priest, the spy approached him, bowed low, and apologized. "Forgive me, Father," he said, "but *I thought you had ideas!*"

The Chekhov story was almost worth the loss of a bathtub. Thereafter, when the G.P.U. took some intellectual of my acquaintance into custody for questioning, when an office "wall paper" directed its irony against some hapless old man of doubtful social origin, when the press assailed some leader on the skids, I was able to say sagely, "Forgive them, Father, but *they think he has ideas.*"

4

Borodin and his associates waited for me to clear out as for a deliverance. My infidel bourgeois presence was an embarrassment. More important, my "living space" was needed as the staff grew from day to day. On my part, I was no less anxious to end the enforced propinquity.

Opportunity knocked at my door. A group of Moscow's foremost literary men were building a coöperative apartment on Nashchokinsky Pereulok. The work was slowed up by lack of transportation. If only they had a few auto-trucks, one novelist sighed, they could rush the job. There and then a *kombinatsya* was born: I would provide them with enough American money to import a truck, maybe two, and they would give me an apartment in the coöperative house. My apartment would be ready for occupancy, I was assured, by the November holidays, by the end of the year at the latest.

Actually it was not completed until the spring of 1934; I was not fated to occupy it. But I had the doubtful privilege of watching over its construction. The sum discussed was fifteen hundred dollars; I was maneuvered into paying twenty-five hundred, just enough to buy two American trucks through Torgsin. Having accepted my money, the literary coöperative evidently felt that the transaction was completed. From that point forward, for nearly eighteen months, my every plea for action in building the apartment and reasonable quality in construction was treated as an intrusion. A dozen times I was held up for more valuta; materials that I bought for my apartment out of my own pocket were nonchalantly diverted to other apartments; specifications solemnly agreed to in the presence of Foreign Office witnesses were instantly forgotten; every ounce of progress I paid for in tons of heartache.

Starting as a simple bargain, the thing became as involved as the Five Year Plan, with the Foreign Office, the Workers and Peasants Inspection, and the G.P.U. taking a hand in the matter. A detailed account of the juggling, struggles, negotiations and compromises that went into the making of the home I never occupied—weeks stretching into months, months into years—would require a book in itself. Luckily I was able to shift most of the burden on the strong shoulders of a brilliant and hard-headed young California engineer, Zara Witkin.

Having laid out the interior of the apartment for me, and touched by my gullible helplessness in the practiced hands of the coöperative bureaucrats, Zara assumed full charge of the proceedings. While engaged upon rationalizing construction activities for the entire Soviet Union, or supervising the construction of a great aviation school or chemical plant, he made the time to inspect the Lyons home in progress. No trick of faking in materials or workmanship escaped his trained eye. Bolder, more pugnacious, and more optimistic than I, Zara made this apartment a test case of rationalization and honesty in construction. He forced the builders to tear down walls that were ill made, watched the mixing of paints, insisted on elementary principles of decent workmanship. The very sight of this calm, business-like American engineer gave the bureaucrats the jitters.

He would listen to a long harangue of pyramided alibis, pretend that he did not understand a word, and remark coolly, "*Khorosho!* Now tear up this floor and do it right!" And ultimately it *was* torn up.

The United Press, which now occupies that apartment, may take pride in the fact that the mind which supervised the building of the Hollywood Bowl and some two hundred other outstanding California structures also supervised the building of its Moscow headquarters.

5

Mine was not the only housing crisis—and decidedly the least tragic. The chronic housing hardships by the end of that year were to take a malicious turn. Some fifty million Russians, the entire urban population, would be questioned, classified, weighed in the social balance in the most far-reaching residential purge in Russian history, carried through with a frightful indifference to human suffering.

For truthlessness on the grand scale, the process ranked with liquidation of the kulaks, though the rest of the world, inured by now to wholesale brutality, seemed scarcely aware of the thing. Our dispatches on the edict and its pitiless enforcement never made the front pages: editors and the public alike never quite grasped the meaning of this nation-wide reshuffling of population. To this day I find Americans otherwise well-informed on Soviet affairs, including people who earn their livelihoods as Russian experts, who seem totally unaware that an internal passport system far more stringent than the tsar's was announced at the end of the Five Year Plan, introduced in the following months, and is still in force. The Stalin Constitution adopted in 1937 failed to revoke that scourge. I have searched in vain for a mention of this system in supposedly objective apologia for Stalinism written by foreigners. (The fabulous Webbs in their 1143 pages have exactly one reference to it—and an erroneous one—in a footnote!)

The announcement of the revival of the internal passport system shocked the Soviet people, who by this time were not easily shocked. For fifteen years the revolution had boasted of the abolition of passportization as one of its great accomplishments. The boast was chiseled in large letters on the base of many a revolutionary statue. The official Soviet Encyclopaedia described passports as "a practice of the tsarist government forcibly to segregate the population, unknown in the Soviet Union."

Now the hated instrument was restored and made more onerous. Not since the establishment of serfdom had a Russian government ventured to tie its subjects so securely to their places of employment; indeed, one has to go back to the Middle Ages for a European parallel. Under the Romanovs, every subject had a passport merely for identification, to assure effective police control. It did not restrict their right to travel or change their residence within the Russian frontiers—except for the Jews, most of whom were confined in the so-called Pale of Settlement.

The new Soviet passport decree went much further. It turned every locality into a "pale" for all its inhabitants, beyond which they could not move without the government's explicit sanction. The passport now issued fixed the domicile of its holder. No *con-*

cierge or relative could give him shelter for more than three days without a special permit. Anyone found outside his prescribed area could be summarily ordered to return; those harboring the straying culprit were subject to punishment.

The purge was not applied to the entire country at once. The process required nearly a year. Beginning in the largest cities, it was extended after a while to less important cities, then to entire provinces and finally to the whole nation. The "undesirables" were thus pushed ever farther from the more habitable regions, like animals at bay surrounded by a tightening circle of hounds. Passport commissions in every neighborhood interrogated the residents and decided, on the basis of class origin and other fixed standards, whether they were entitled to live in that city. Refusal of a passport meant, after a few days allowed for an appeal, loss of housing space and migration to some unpassported district. When the purge reached that new district, the victims might be obliged to move again, until they were pushed into some territory so undesirable that everyone obtained a passport.

Moscow, Leningrad, Kharkov, Odessa, Vladivostok, and a few other key cities were the first to undergo the cleansing. No one bothered to explain what the "undesirables" were to do if they had no place to go to and no funds to get them there. The code of Bolshevik firmness made it "unfriendly" and counter-revolutionary to raise such a "private" problem. "We can't stop to worry about such sentimental nonsense," communist acquaintances said. "They'll get there, one way or another, or they'll blow out their brains. We have enough to worry about without that."

Panic swept through every street in Moscow. Hundreds of thousands who had adjusted themselves after years of travail must again justify their warrant to remain alive. They knew that neighbors with influence, perhaps on the passport commission itself, coveted their corner of "living space." The city's population was rapidly approaching the four million mark. The new houses going up did not even suffice to make up for deterioration of old structures. It was the announced purpose of the government to expel a million, and it actually did drive out several hundred thousand: in effect a wholesale exile. The passport officials were pitiless, arbitrary, autocratic, sparing neither the very aged nor the very young, not even bed-ridden invalids.

An epidemic of suicides spread through the capital. Naturally the press said nothing about this, but communists privately estimated them in the hundreds. Scarcely a day passed but I heard the details of some family denied a passport and choosing death as the only remaining alternative. What was true of Moscow was true in a hundred other cities.

My friend Isaak Lvovich came to me one day in utter despair. Though he was a highly paid technician in an important trust, he had been denied a passport by his local commission. His household, besides a wife and four young children, included a father of nearly eighty and a crippled niece. His was the taint of Nepmanism eight or nine years back.

"Unless my appeal is granted," he said, "I must move them all somewhere—God knows where or how. . . . In what city can I possibly find housing for my family? It seems easier to end it all . . . eight bullets and my problem is solved. . . . My Nep past has little to do with it. We have three rooms and a separate kitchen. Someone with influence wants that space."

Only one in a hundred ever obtained a reversal of the commission's decision. Because Isaak Lvovich was extremely valuable to his trust, and its director happened to be a courageous communist, he was that one in a hundred. A few days lated he phoned to invite us to a party. He was celebrating the receipt of a passport, as though it were a commutation of the death sentence. His joy was well-nigh hysterical.

Passportization, coinciding with the sharpened food shortage everywhere and the beginning of famine in south Russia, with another stringent purge of the Communist Party ranks, and the worst record for industrial production of any year since 1923 (8½% instead of the 37% planned), provided a most inauspicious background for the launching of a second *Piatiletka.*

Indeed, the moment was far more critical than anyone outside the highest circle of power suspected; disclosures in the next five years have made this clear. Half the country was starving, as we shall see; the rest was on extremely short rations. No amount of bluster could speed up the workers, since sheer physical debilitation was at the root of the trouble. Secret anti-Stalin documents were being passed from hand to hand among important communists; one of these, written by the well-known communist Riutin in prison, boldly called for Stalin's removal. Among more idealistic young people in the Comsomol organization there was guarded talk of terror against tyrants. The diary of Nikolaiev, the young communist who assassinated Kirov on December 1, 1934, has never been published; but one who read it has revealed that it reflects the desperate mood of a large portion of youth as the Plan drew to its tragic conclusion. Subsequent charges of terrorism and anti-Stalin conspiracy which in 1936-37 were to bring dozens of Old Bolsheviks and military leaders, as well as hundreds of rank-and-file communists, before the firing squad, grew in the main out of the crisis at this juncture.

"This was the end of 1932, when the situation in the country was similar to 1921—the time of the Kronstadt rebellion," an Old Bolshevik was to write in a letter smuggled out and published anonymously abroad.* "In 1932, it is true, there were no actual revolts, but many believed that it would have been better if the government had had to deal with actual revolts."

On December 27, 1932—in the very last week of the Plan, that is—it was decreed that every Soviet worker surrender his passport or other identification documents to the administration; in case of a "disciplinary" dismissal—for one day's absence from work, for instance—the administration must inscribe that fact on the document. No other state institution was allowed to employ a worker with such a black mark for six months after his dismissal; in the meantime he lost his rations and sometimes his home. The proletarian's role by the end of the Five Year Plan had been reduced to silent obedience, with starvation as the only alternative.

* *Letter of an Old Bolshevik*, Rand School Press, New York, 1937.

X. American Tragedies

BECAUSE of the absence of diplomatic relations between the U.S.A. and the U.S.S.R., every American correspondent, to his infinite annoyance, became an unofficial diplomat in the eyes of Americans in trouble. I was constantly being maneuvered into interceding for Americans who had lost their passports, or were being forcibly detained on Soviet soil, or were trying to pull a Russian wife out of the country. An ill-gained repute for tender-heartedness won me more than my normal share of these problems. More hard-boiled colleagues were inclined to shunt troublesome countrymen—unless they were countrywomen endowed with pulchritude—to Petrovsky Pereulok. And on occasion, if the truth be told, I wished such annoyances on some colleague. The technique was to assure the frenzied petitioner modestly that Duranty or Barnes or Fischer, as the case might be, was a person of much greater influence in high quarters and could consequently help more effectively. By way of insurance, it was best to add: "But you'd better not tell him I sent you. . . ."

The fact is that none of us was a match for the devious and illogical ways of bureaucracy. The most we could do was to employ the threat of publicity in the American press in breaking through the barricades of rules and regulations.

One morning, for instance, I received a yard-long cablegram from a friend in New York, invoking my help in the following circumstances. An American furniture manufacturer while touring the Soviet Union met a personable young lady in Odessa and fell in love with her; the furniture he manufactured being exceedingly modernistic, he may be forgiven this romantic deviation. His love brought him back to Russia and Odessa for a second visit, and on this occasion he married the girl and applied for an exit visa for her. Local officials stalled him week after week with vague promises and finally he had to return alone. He continued the efforts to get her out for months by long distance, without success. Meanwhile it appeared that he had left his wife in what used to be called "an interesting condition." The gentleman was naturally much distressed and begged that I "do something."

Upon making certain inquiries in Odessa, I discovered that the Russian bride, soon after the American's departure, had been arrested for reasons that I could not ascertain. Reasons are not important in Russia anyhow—the circumstance that she was of bad birth (that is, good birth old-style) and had associated with a foreigner may have had something to do with it.

I thereupon consulted my typewriter and what emerged was a cable dispatch about love and passports. The gist of it was that the Russian bride of an American business man, a bride who would soon be a mother, languished in prison while the heartbroken bridegroom and father-to-be fought for her release. This lugubrious tale I laid with a straight face upon the desk of his highness the censor. The censor read it and blanched in the two spots on his face not covered by beard. This decidedly was not the sort of story he cared to have spread on record in the American newspapers.

I pretended astonishment at his astonishment. "Why, this is just an innocent little human-interest yarn of the sort dear to the American heart. No one denies you have a right to jail Soviet citizens even if they're pregnant and married to Americans."

He looked at me in a way that made further discussion superfluous. "Just leave it with me, Mr. Lyons, and we'll ascertain the facts." Next day I telephoned to inquire whether the facts had been ascertained, ditto the day after that. On the third day the censor's voice had an optimistic lift to it.

"I'll have some news for you on that story, I think, in a few hours."

That afternoon he phoned to say that the story was untrue; the lady had been released from jail and had, in fact, been given an exit visa. I had never had the slightest intention of cabling that story, of course.

The news that Russia had liquidated unemployment and was in dire need of labor power brought hundreds of foreign job hunters to Moscow. Most of them arrived as third-category tourists, lived lordly tourist lives for the five or ten days specified, then found themselves penniless, homeless and jobless in the citadel of socialism. Even where they had specific mechanical trades, only one in a hundred managed to cut through the jungles of red-tape around Soviet jobs. Many of them had sold their last belongings to make the trip, certain that the new society waited for them with open arms.

By 1931-32, these hordes of stranded Americans became a real problem. There was an American worker who had come with a young son to start life anew in his socialist fatherland. His last dollar was gone. At the time the correspondents learned of their plight, they had been sleeping in corridors for ten days and gone without food for days at a time, shuttling in despair between one Soviet office and another, begging work. Others were quartered upon already overcrowded American homes—one woman came to spend a night at the Lyons ménage and remained for eight months!

Ralph Barnes of the New York *Herald Tribune*, whose journalistic courage was always a notch or two higher than the Muscovite average (a fact that did not make him too popular in certain official areas), was the first to write a dispatch about the American derelicts on Soviet shores. Other correspondents followed his lead. These stories led the government to issue the sensible order that all tourist tickets must be round-trip and Soviet agents abroad were instructed to make it clear that no one arriving on a tourist visa could remain in the U.S.S.R. to work.

An increasing number of Russian-Americans, also, found themselves virtual prisoners in the land of their birth, and turned hopefully to the correspondents for help. The victims were almost always humble, meek, friendless individuals whose failure to return to the land of their adoption was not likely to excite American public opinion. Not a single instance came to my knowledge of an American of Russian origin with money, education and influential friends in the U.S.A. being claimed as a Russian by the Soviet government. Those naturalized Americans whose passports were summarily confiscated were poor, simple, scared workers.

Legally and technically, the Soviet authorities were apparently well within their rights. American naturalization does not wipe out the prior claim of a person's native land. This issue has often arisen in relation to alien-born Americans in other countries and has been adjusted in some instances in special treaties. In Russia, there were a number of themes strictly taboo for reporters who cared to live on more or less amicable terms with the authorities, and "captured" Americans was one of them. A large proportion of the profitable tourist trade consisted of Americanized Russians returning for a glimpse of their homelands. Publicity about confiscated passports would have endangered this lucrative trade and the Press Department made it clear that such stories would be considered "unfriendly" acts. For years I tried, as did one or two others, to elicit a clear-cut statement of policy in this respect. If the Soviet government stood four-square on its rights to claim every Russian-born American at will, we argued, it was our duty as correspondents to report the fact, if only as a warning to Russian-Americans. Our efforts came to nothing.

The taboo was finally broken through as a result of a particularly tragic case of such citizen-snatching. A California machinist born in Russia but raised in America since boyhood accepted a job in Russia. Being a widower, he brought two American-born children with him. His passport was taken up on arrival and his every attempt to regain possession failed. After a year or so of procrastination, he was informed that he was considered a Soviet citizen. Perpetual exile from America had been no part of his intention in accepting Soviet employment, and the prospect of his children—typical American youngsters—growing up as Russians appalled him. The fellow had more than ordinary courage, and raised a howl heard by all the correspondents. The refusal of Russian officials to grant exit visas for the American-born children, in particular, riled us.

Several of us took the matter up with the Foreign Office but got no satisfaction. I thereupon proposed to Duranty's temporary substitute that for once we send stories on the subject. Being less of a diplomat than his boss, he saw the facts in newspaper terms as "a swell story," and by agreement we mailed our dispatches to London, whence they were cabled to America. The American passport was restored soon thereafter.

The most pathetic category of Americans held in Russia against their will were those who had voluntarily given up American citizenship through communist patriotism, then changed their minds. Most of them were Russian by birth, but a few were native-born

Americans or natives of other European nations. Having escaped the iniquitous capitalist world and embraced the socialist dream, they threw away American citizenship—joyously, defiantly—as though casting off chains. The period of disillusionment ranged from two weeks to a year, and the embittered regrets were in direct proportion to the fervor of the original renunciation. It was the finality of their act, the realization that they were trapped and held and could never leave Russia again, which worked on these people, even more than their disillusionment with the U.S.S.R. They would come to my office, or the office of some other American, and weep bitter tears. We could offer them nothing but sympathy.

When an American Embassy was eventually opened, its first and largest headache was the adjustment of hundreds of these passport cases.

The love element in our amateur diplomatic work was provided by the American engineers, resident salesmen for American manufacturers, and others who had acquired Russian wives only to find, when the moment for departure came, that they could not take those wives along. A few foreigners of exceptionally influential standing managed to obtain exit visas for their Russian loves, but the average mortal could not. Americans, without an embassy to intercede for them, were especially helpless under such circumstances.

I could fill a book with the strange tales of Russian-American romances in which a most unromantic Soviet passport office figured as the villain of the piece. I knew several cases in which lonesome Americans took women into their homes knowing that they were little more than prostitutes and spies, but took them in time into their hearts as well, married them, and fought long and tragic battles to extricate them from the U.S.S.R.

Why the Soviet regime in the Stalin era has been, and still remains, so uncompromising in its determination to prevent its subjects from emigrating has never been clear to me. I have heard all the semi-official explanations and guesses, but they sound unconvincing. The most common alibi is that the emigrants might be unable to find work and become a burden on some foreign nation. This solicitude is hard to swallow; it is particularly unconvincing in relation to tens of thousands with families abroad eager to care for them. Another explanation offered is that the U.S.S.R. could not spare labor power—a strange reason, certainly, for holding thousands of aged and decrepit people eager to join relatives abroad, or tens of thousands of disfranchised persons who were not given the right to work.

More candid officials did not resort to such palpably lying explanations. They admitted that if the gates of their country were opened, hundreds of thousands and possibly millions would leave. They would naturally be the most dissatisfied elements and would therefore be a potential source of anti-Soviet propaganda. The myth of a happy, busy, socialist nation and an enthusiastic population might be punctured. A communist friend whom I pressed on the subject finally blurted out:

"Why should the bastards who hate us be allowed to get out of our control? And why should they be exempted when the rest of us are starving and suffering for the future? They'll stay right here and suffer with us!"

Whatever the reason for locking the Russian people into their country, it seemed to turn the U.S.S.R. into a dungeon. It helped to make "abroad" the most glamorous word, the greatest gift within the power of the Kremlin.

2

The point of poor Larry's experiences in Russia is blurred unless one knows Esther, the wife who remained behind in America. Larry is a chirping and pleasant little man, very intelligent in an academic fashion but a little helpless in practical matters. Esther, being a large and capable and energetic female, complements him completely. It was Esther who supported the family when I first met them, while Larry studied engineering; that was when she worked with me for the Sacco-Vanzetti defense in Boston. I saw them at long intervals in the following years and she was still the generalissimo of the family.

They are both "idealists"—their common interest in righting the wrongs of the world, indeed, is one of the strongest bonds between them. Their ideals, like themselves, are on different planes, Esther's rather professional and Larry's on a more rarefied level. Even the study of civil engineering had its idealistic overtones for them. True, it would enable him to make a living and one must eat. But that was incidental. The important consideration was that the Russian revolution had need of trained technical minds and his profession would enable him to make a "valuable contribution" to the great cause.

While he was still in school, back in 1921, this vision of helping Russia invested the studies with a deeper social significance. Just as soon as he was eligible he joined the various societies for technical aid to the Soviet government and wrote weighty papers on engineering under socialist conditions. The troubles the revolution was having with its technical personnel (to a degree which obliged the Kremlin to shoot and jail thousands of them, mind you) only strengthened Larry's and Esther's certainty that in preparing a trustworthy revolutionary engineer for Russia they were doing their important bit for humanity.

But for one reason and another—lack of money, the arrival of babies—Larry didn't actually get to the U.S.S.R. in construction until the Five Year Plan was far under way. He made his contract with Amtorg in New York and set off joyously to consummate the dream of a lifetime. Esther remained in America with the babies on the understanding that as soon as he was nicely settled in Moscow they would join him. Meanwhile, he would send them part of his earnings. The contract gave him five hundred rubles a month, an apartment and other privileges. Surely he would not need all of $250 a month (that's how he thought of the rubles) and a large slice would go to Esther.

I heard that Larry was in Moscow, and though I pretended to be amused by his failure to visit me I was a bit hurt underneath. But I could understand his shyness. After all I was a bourgeois correspondent, and had the "wrong attitude" toward the revolution. Personal friendships must be sacrificed to the cause.

Four or five weeks after he had reached the Soviet land, however, lo and behold! Larry was on my threshold, the same diminutive, chirping and helpless Larry we had known in Boston. There was that forbidden-fruit look on his face that other American communists wore when impelled by distress or affection to enter a home contaminated by bourgeois ideology. Larry began on a note of affection but soon shifted to his distress. He didn't tell me all his troubles at once, obviously hoping that some of them would be dissipated. But he returned frequently and soon I was privy to all his worries, and there were plenty of them.

"You see, Gene, the five hundred rubles aren't as much as I supposed. Of course, I'd read articles by a lot of counter-revolutionaries like yourself that talked of inflation, but I knew that was just capitalist propaganda. The Soviet journals ridiculed any suggestion that the ruble was worth less than fifty cents. The fact is"—he lowered his voice and looked around for eavesdroppers—"that in purchasing power my salary is really less than ten bucks a month. . . . But naturally you know that. It's even worse than that: I can't send a penny of it home, because it seems rubles can't be exported and wouldn't be worth anything if they were exported."

"But, Larry, didn't you know that much about Russia? You—a close student of Soviet affairs!"

"I studied those affairs too much in the columns of the *Daily Worker*, the *New Masses*, the *New Republic*, and *The Nation*, I'm afraid," he sighed.

His promised "apartment" did not materialize, and he was living in a filthy barracks, in a room with half a dozen Russian technicians working with him in the railroad commissariat. A corner in a private home for which he negotiated would have cost him more than half his entire salary!

"The real trouble," he said, "is that they somehow won't treat me like a foreigner. The engineers who are here for the money, as out-and-out bourgeois specialists, get attention, and most of them had sense enough to make contracts in dollars. But I'm a communist, one of their own people so to speak, and they treat me like a Russian."

"Well, why don't you tell them to go fly a kite and return to New York?"

And then he told me the most serious disaster. It seems that he was Russian-born and had received strong hints that his American passport, which had been taken up by the authorities when he first arrived, might never be returned. He had met several other Russian-American enthusiasts who had been trying for months and years to regain possession of their American passports. Technically he was a Russian, and if his Soviet hosts were that way minded he might never be allowed to leave their hospitality. The possibility threw him into a panic.

"I want to make a confession, Gene, and a humble apology," he suddenly interrupted himself. "God knows, I owe it to you. It's no secret to you what your radical friends in America are saying about you. They think that you're a renegade, that you're lying about conditions in Russia. You might as well know that I was one of the most outspoken in the attacks on you. It seemed to me that you were betraying the revolution.

"Well, I've been here more than two months now, and I can testify that you are in fact a liar, a lot more so than I suspected. But you're lying *for* Russia, not *against* it. The things you write are mild and pussyfooting compared with the truth that I am seeing with my own eyes."

"How does Esther take your disappointments?"

Larry went pale. He wrung his hands. Among his multitudinous troubles, Esther was by all odds the most serious.

"Esther doesn't know about it," he said. "I realized right away that all my incoming letters are being read, and I've learned enough to suspect that the same applies to outgoing mail. With my passport in their hands and all, I don't dare write the truth. Maybe it's nerves, but they have me completely scared. Poor Esther can't understand why I write so little—she sends me a letter every day!—and why I don't answer the thousand questions she asks about life here. And I can't tell her. . . . I just keep on repeating that everything is all right and it's wonderful to be in the Soviet Union at last and that sort of thing. . . . I'm sure the poor girl can't make out what's happened to her Larry. It's all perfectly terrible."

One day he arrived greatly upset, to show me a cablegram from Esther, received several days earlier. She was not the woman to be dillydallied with. She wanted to know immediately when she should start out for Moscow. She was all ready.

"You know Esther," Larry said in a choking voice, "she'll sell our last belongings and come over. For all I know she's on her way now!"

"Well, why don't you wire her not to budge?"

"I did, but she cabled right back wanting to know why—and I couldn't tell her."

When he left, he was calmer. We had drafted a message warning her not to do anything until she got his next letter. I undertook to send that letter out in the diplomatic pouch of a friendly courier, and Larry at last was able to tell his Esther the whole truth.

He now had only one purpose in life—to obtain his passport and a permit to depart. In a few months, he achieved this. Whether he risked ostracism by his friends, all of them communists and near-communists, by telling them why he did not work out his contract or import his family I have no way of knowing. Perhaps, back home in depression America, he drifted back into the hosanna-singing fraternity.

3

I have mentioned Zara Witkin. There was little in our first meeting to hint that our paths would run parallel for two years and that I should become involved emotionally in his soul-searing experience. That experience was intensely personal, yet it came to have for me, and for him too, a symbolic quality in relation to the whole Soviet scene.

In the forefront of Zara's life in Russia was his fantastic tug-of-war with the Soviet bureaucracy, a struggle in which Stalin himself at one point took a hand. Behind that was the stranger secret drama of his love affair with his Dark Goddess. And behind these were depths upon depths of intrigue: vast unseen and unfeeling forces playing with human lives as though they were pebbles. Somehow this intricate pattern of one man's experience—cold engineering, feverish romance, and an impersonal and pervasive cruelty—seemed an epitome of Bolshevik Russia.

A dark, chunky, broad-shouldered young man with a warm smile and tanned, open features, Zara came to me one day in the spring of 1932 with a letter of introduction. He had come to Russia to give himself unreservedly to the task of Soviet construction. He had given up a position as chief engineer of one of the largest American building firms for that purpose. But because he offered his knowledge and talents without demanding gold, the Soviet officials looked askance at him. In this land presumably translating an ideal into reality, nothing was more suspect than idealism. It seemed to them incredible and even suspicious that an American engineer should give up a good income at home for the sheer joy of helping build a new world. A perverted materialism had bitten so deeply into their minds that disinterested devotion to a cause looked to them like quixotic sentimentality.

In the end, however, he found work. Then began his fight against the bureaucrats. Entrenched officials resented his advice, which cut too deeply into their pretenses and inefficiency. His plans were side-tracked. Month after month he struggled to introduce a measure of elementary good sense into the construction process, to rescue his plans from pigeon-holes, to save the government millions of rubles by rationalizing various technical procedures.

Before he was through, part of the press was tugging on his side of the rope, and finally Stalin himself added his not inconsiderable weight on the American's side. Zara was entrusted with drawing up a plan for the rationalization of the entire construction industry of the Soviet Union: the most important assignment given to any single foreign specialist. At the same time he was made consultant on a number of the most critical building jobs in the aviation industry and other branches of the national defense.

Not even *Izvestia* and Stalin could budge the entrenched bureaucracy more than a few inches. Tens of thousands of incompetents were too deeply rooted in their places to give way; their survival depended on the continuation of an intricate system of inefficiency. But it was a lusty battle which I followed closely and in which I sometimes took a part.

Parallel with this struggle, becoming eventually a part of it, was the engineer's amazing love affair. Not until we had met a dozen times or more did he confide to me his love for the woman whom he called the Dark Goddess. He had never met her!

Several years before he had seen a Soviet motion picture in which Russia's best-known cinema actress, Emma Cessarskaya, had a role. Emma is beautiful with that healthy, earthy, peasant beauty one sees occasionally in Russian paintings: a vital, deep-bosomed and fertile beauty beyond mere comeliness. Zara fell in love with her. He wrote to her but received no reply.

Long before this he had dreamed of going to the Soviet land and of working for the joy of it rather than profit. That dream now acquired a new dimension of passionate consecration. This woman seemed to him the new Russia incarnate. He never doubted that he would find her and that she would respond to his love.

His instincts were correct. Billy and I helped him to meet Emma, and they became inseparable companions. From Emma's love he drew the strength for his fight against the bureaucrats—he was doing it for her country. He taught her English and together they read the letter he had sent her from Los Angeles—it had been unopened all these years!

Often they were at our house. Emma grew very fond of Billy. It was pleasant to see Zara and his goddess together; he so solemn and protective in his happiness, Emma gay and full of the devil. Occasionally the two of them called me into serious conference. They were planning ways and means of joining the strands of their lives forever—in America. On those occasions there was an undercurrent of fear and sadness which not all of Emma's gaiety could disperse. They knew, as I did, that larger forces must be propitiated. Moscow would not willingly give up its greatest cinema actress to a foreigner and to America.

It is almost blasphemous to tell the story so briefly. But suffice that the enemies Zara had made in insisting upon bringing a little order into the chaos of the construction industry struck back at him through Emma. After some eight months during which they met daily, Emma was snatched away from him. His every effort to get to her was frustrated. Several times he talked to her by telephone. She begged him in a panic not to call her, to accept the inevitable. He understood that she was under some terrific fear, and helpless.

For months thereafter he remained in Moscow, in the grip of a deep despair. (Ultimately he and I returned to the United States together.) The G.P.U. exploited his tragedy in an unsuccessful attempt to inveigle him into its network of spies. His plan for the rationalization of construction, other work done with the knowledge and encouragement of Stalin, all turned out so much futile flailing of water.

XI. Persian Entr'acte

I WAS talking to Billy by long-distance telephone to Berlin, where she awaited my arrival. I was all packed for a vacation.

"Hello, darling," I said, "I am leaving tomorrow—"

"That's swell!"

"Hold on. Not so swell. . . . I'm leaving tomorrow, but not for Berlin. I'm going to Persia."

"Going where?"

"To Persia—Teheran."

I repeated it twice more before she grasped the direction of my sudden assignment.

"And listen," I said. "Keep this thing under your hat. We don't want any of the opposition to get wind of it. My instructions are to get there, get there quick, and get there first."

Late that night Billy called me back.

"That Persia secret of yours," she said, "is all over town here. I no sooner stepped into the Adlon bar than the whole gang wanted to know about your trip to Persia. I had to pretend it was all news to me. Lucky thing I'm a first-rate liar!"

The Shah of Persia, that swashbuckling trooper who ousted an old dynasty and made himself King of Kings, had just canceled the D'Arcy Concession under which the Anglo-Persian Oil Company operated its Persian fields. With its prestige in the Near East threatened, the British lion was obliged to do some lusty roaring. Its fleet east of the Suez was maneuvered suggestively and the London press talked of war-like measures.

Whether or not this bellicose show impressed His Majesty at Teheran, it impressed their majesties of the United Press sufficiently to rush their Moscow correspondent to the Persian capital. On the map, Persia is deceptively near Moscow, though a reporter flying from Paris or Rome could have gotten there sooner. Of course, there was a distinct Soviet angle to the story. The Russian bear and the British lion had shared dominance of Persia between them before the war, and were still sparring for advantages. In some London quarters, the question was asked whether Moscow might have encouraged the Shah to defy the British.

In the interests of their political health, many governments, Persia among them, made it a rule not to issue visas in Russia to non-Russians. My friends in the Persian Legation declared themselves helpless against this rule; that necessitated cables among Moscow, London, New York, Washington, and Teheran, which multiplied in geometrical progression but summed up to precisely nothing. I left for Baku without a visa and exacted one by sheer force of desperation from the local Persian consul, just in time to catch the weekly boat across the Caspian Sea to Enzeli (now Pahlevi).

The three days' trip from Moscow to Baku was raucous with Soviet culture. Radios had been installed on this important railroad line; loud speakers in the corridor flooded our lives and drowned our thoughts with classic caterwauling and distorted lectures. In the coupé adjoining mine, an Armenian member of the government (his beribboned insignia of office as large as an usher's at a ball) set up a gramophone in competition to the radio. He played three cracked records of ancient dance tunes hours on end. Before the trip was over, I succeeded in switching this official's enthusiasm from Western music to Armenian cognac by the simple expedient of sharing it with him. This not only helped to silence his gramophone but fortified my nerves against the overdose of corridor culture.

Our train went through an area already in the tightening grip of hunger, and even important government dignitaries, if mellowed by native cognac, allow themselves caustic comments on the trend of national affairs. The morale of the Russian people was clearly at its lowest ebb in this final month of the Five Year Plan. What one sensed, cutting diagonally across the country, pausing at stations, talking guardedly to people on the train, was something far more depressing than discontent—physical and moral debilitation, hopelessness, impotence, and sickly despair. There was none of the eager and angry argument in excited knots of people that I had watched in my first trip through this general area four years earlier. Where there had been ferment, I now found flatness. Where peasants had clamored to sell food, they now begged weakly for a hand-out. The restaurant counters in station waiting-rooms offered only anemic tea and gritty, fly-specked biscuits at absurdly high prices. Construction jobs, of which we saw many, seemed forlorn and lackadaisical.

From Baku to the Persian coast was an overnight journey due south. Enzeli, on the northern brim of Persia, is a sleepy down-at-heel place. What struck me at first sight, after Russia, was the incredible abundance of food: pomegranates and lemons, stacks of flat bread disks, goat cheese and mutton. The madness of a world where children languish with hunger a night's distance from such abundance!

At the customs house, at the damp and chilly hotel, everywhere, I looked into the strong, unsmiling face of the self-made Shah; his picture was as ubiquitous here as Stalin's in Russia. Always he was shown in the semi-profile that emphasized his large eagle-beak nose and beetling eyebrows. The hope of interviewing Riza Shah Pahlevi, the royal dictator of this ancient empire, had been born in my mind the moment I received the assignment. I knew that he had not submitted to an interview by an out-and-out newspaper reporter since he mounted the Peacock Throne. The hope seemed so remote that I did not mention it to my editors, but it was the obbligato to my thoughts. I remembered reading how Larry Rue and Richard Halliburton and other distinguished colleagues had fought for such an audience and failed, and trusted that my luck might outweigh their skill.

Between Enzeli and Teheran are the majestic Elburz Mountains, with one defile that mounts gradually to a snow-covered plateau more than eight thousand feet above the Caspian level. I hired a dilapidated car driven by a taciturn and most unprepossessing chauffeur. Toward sunset we reached the flattened peak: a limitless world of shimmering white, snow and sky. We were in luck; the road, which had been blocked by snowdrifts, was passable. Soon we were in the picturesque, unreal streets of Kavsin, and toward midnight we passed through a gate in the mosaicked wall of Teheran.

Despite the hour, the American Minister, Charles D. Hart, insisted that I visit the Legation residence immediately. I found him charming and generously helpful. The soft rugs, the cheerful fire in the grate, and a few tall drinks thawed the pessimism induced by the wearing mountain journey, and I confided my hope of talking to the Shah. Himself a former Washington correspondent, Mr. Hart was sympathetic but advised against wasting my energies in reaching for the moon.

The next few weeks were crowded with work. The only full-fledged American correspondent on the scene, I made the most of the opportunity. The Persian events had meanwhile been pushed off the front pages, but that only made the need for out-of-the-ordinary stories more pressing. I obtained the only interview on the oil controversy with His Highness Mohammed Khan Foroughi, Minister of Foreign Affairs (later Premier)—an urbane black-bearded gentleman who spoke an excellent English. I talked with British oil executives, foreign diplomats, Persian journalists. Quickly enough, I discovered that the whole dispute—the annulment, threats and posturings on both sides—amounted to a haggle over the government's royalty percentages on the oil profits; the shouting and rug-waving about Persian independence was political decoration of very secondary importance.

Few things in life give me more joy than the feeling of putting my mental teeth into a new situation, trying to crack its shell of appearances for the meat of reality. If I crack my teeth instead, what of it? My very ignorance of Persian affairs made the attempt more exciting. I picked up a keen-witted and energetic secretary-interpreter named Musa: a Persian Jewish lad educated in the American schools run by Christian missions and a convert to the new religion of Bahai. My genuine interest in his lectures on salvation through Bahai won Musa's heart, and he worked with me cheerfully night and day.

The country is still semi-feudal. Entire villages and districts are owned and ruled by hereditary lords. Though Riza Shah has done much to undermine the power of tribal chieftains, the feudal relationship has not been broken. On top of this feudal society, however, the government is imposing modern industrialization, subsidizing manufacture, building mills and railroads with the help of foreign technical specialists. In talking to officials and "Westernized" Persians, I was continuously impressed by the essential parallel of their enthusiasms with those I knew in Russia. It was not of Iranic art and traditions that they boasted, but of the new cement mixing plant erected outside Teheran, the new railroad mileage added by the Shah, and the progress in unveiling their women. The urge to industrialize was no Leninist invention. The whole East felt it, finding local slogans to express the self-same desire for the West's machines and comforts. For Western democratic government, too, Persians expressed a high enthusiasm, though—as the President of the *Medjlis,* or parliament, put it to me—"Democracy is a luxury we Persians cannot as yet afford."

2

The possibility of interviewing the Shah seemed more remote the closer I came to Persia and its leaders. The mere suggestion shocked officials. His Majesty's Minister of the Court, Timur Tash, had been, ever since the Kadjar dynasty was kicked off the throne, the closest adviser of the new ruler. He was a Grand Vizier in the ancient tradition: wise, magnificent, powerful. When he consented to see me, I felt that the first big step towards the Shah was already accomplished. At the appointed hour, I arrived at Timur Tash's palace, but His Highness was not there. The explanation that he had suddenly taken sick seemed to me a low and transparent alibi. His secretaries were embarrassed and flustered. They shrugged their shoulders and assured me that the Minister was not only sick but would remain sick at least for some months. Indignantly I drove to Timur Tash's residential estate, half an hour outside town, to insist on my journalistic pound of flesh, only to receive the same evasive apologies.

The fact was that his agreement to receive me was the Grand Vizier's last official act. That night he was placed by his master under house arrest. If I lost my conference with him, at any rate I was the first foreigner to learn of his downfall, and to report it to the outside world. Subsequently Timur Tash was transferred to prison, where he died under mysterious circumstances some six months later.

Only the Minister of Foreign Affairs, it now seemed, might force a path for me to His Majesty. H. H. Foroughi was sympathetic but not encouraging. After a week or so of trying, he announced formally and definitely that the Shah-an-Shah would not talk. It was then that I resorted to an obvious and therefore neglected technique: the same technique that had helped me into

Stalin's presence. I went directly to the Shah. With Musa's assistance, I wrote a letter to His Majesty, as flowery and humble as an *Arabian Nights* petition, and took certain measures to assure its safe delivery at the Pahlevi Palace.

Then I made arrangements to return to Moscow. Two days before my scheduled departure H. H. Foroughi informed me that His Majesty had graciously changed his mind and would receive me in audience after all.

The interview was set for ten in the morning. For nearly forty-eight hours I worried myself into a nervous state over the "protocol" of royal audiences in the Orient. I could borrow the formal clothes from friendly diplomats, but where could I borrow the skill to bow as the protocol described, the forms of address, and —most frightening of all—the art of backing out from the royal presence? Anyone who thinks backing out is easy need only try it! By chance I dined with Prince Amir Esmail Malek Monsour Kadjar, a member of the "liquidated" dynasty, first cousin of the last Kadjar Shah, on the evening before my interview. Persian liquidations being less thorough than in the neighboring Russia, Prince Esmail was not only alive but lived in a run-down and depressing palace next-door to the new Shah who had kicked his family off the throne. When I mentioned casually, over the rice-and-mutton, that I was to visit Shah Pahlevi next morning, the prince and his friends became as excited as schoolboys.

Far from harboring any grudge against the interloper, they seemed loyal subjects of the new Shah. Prince Esmail began by reminiscing about his life at his cousin's court as a boy, and ended by instructing me in the protocol. There was a rich piquancy in the spectacle of a Kadjar prince instructing an American reporter how to back out gracefully from the self-made Shah's presence. Over an ornate French mantelpiece, brought from his celebrated European trip by Prince Esmail's grandfather, the Shah Nasr ed Din who reigned for forty-eight years, hung a portrait of that ruler. Perhaps "grandpa," as the prince called him, did not mind that lesson in homage to his upstart successor, but it seemed to me that his enormous mustaches bristled angrily.

When I arrived at the palace in a gorgeous car with the words "FOR HIRE" on its hood in immense red lettering, I brought with me the court photographer, who turned out to be a pretty Rumanian Jewess. But His Majesty turned thumbs down on the plan to photograph the interview. The best I could get was a picture of the correspondent in the royal gardens, flanked by the Court Master of Ceremonies and the Minister of Foreign Affairs.

That Master of Ceremonies, Amir-Nezam, led me up a marble stairway and suddenly he was genuflecting in the royal presence. Clumsily I followed suit. I was still trying to remember the next step in the protocol when the King of Kings was upon me, smiling pleasantly and extending the royal palm for a firm handshake. Then he pulled over a chair toward the fireplace and motioned for me to sit down. Sitting in the imperial presence was nowhere in the protocol. I could see that H. H. Foroughi, who was already in the chamber to act as interpreter, was horrified by the informality of the proceedings. When the Shah asked him, too, to be seated the Minister complied reluctantly; he sat on the edge of the chair and, never, I am sure, quite touched it.

The Shah is tall and broad-shouldered, quite unlike most Persians in this respect. He seemed a rough-hewn, simple man, cut out by nature for action rather than words; he sounded decisive rather than eloquent. He wore a sort of Russian blouse, khaki-colored, and belted in the Russian manner, and his full-length trousers ended incongruously over bedroom slippers. Like all Moslems, he wore a hat—the inverted dishpan head-gear prescribed for all Persians. The only decorative touches were two tiny gold crowns in silhouette on his shoulders and the silver tassel on the short string of amber beads in his strong hands.

The questions and answers arranged in advance were disposed of in a few minutes. His Majesty reiterated his claims in the Anglo-Persian dispute, indicated his anxiety for a peaceable settlement, and took occasion to transmit a warm message of friendship to the American people. These chores done with, I discovered that the King of Kings was more than willing to protract the visit. To the surprise of his Foreign Minister, his guest, and possibly himself, the interview continued on an easy informal basis for nearly fifty minutes, where five minutes had been scheduled. Unprepared for this generosity, I asked questions at random, many of them so impertinent that I would scarcely have included them in a prepared catechism. I alluded, for instance, to His Majesty's humble origin. His rise from a Cossack trooper under

Russian officers to the throne of Cyrus and Xerxes, I said, had touched the imagination of the world and his personality had evoked the greatest curiosity.

"To what elements in your own character," I asked, "do you attribute your amazing achievement?"

He thought for many seconds and said earnestly:

"It is not easy to answer. But if I were to summarize my own explanation I would say this: I am a soldier, just a simple soldier, and I love my task."

Before leaving I apologized for the frankness of my interrogation. "I'm no diplomat, but a reporter," I said. The Shah laughed. "I, too, am no diplomat," he assured me.

Not until I was out in the sunshine again did I remember that I had completely forgotten to back out!

The news of the interview, a one-day curiosity for the world press, was a sensation in Teheran itself. The pleased astonishment of Mr. Hart was my best reward. By a freak of luck, I was now the first man to have interviewed two Eastern monarchs, Stalin and Shah Riza Pahlevi. Two men born only a few hundred miles apart and within less than a decade of one another, one the son of a cobbler and the other the son of poor farming folks, they became absolute rulers of their respective nations. One is called King of Kings and sits on the Peacock Throne; the other veils his majesty under the title of Comrade. One exercises his control with the candid despotism of a Genghis Khan, the other surrounds it with the hocus-pocus of a proletarian dictatorship. But these differences are externals. In essentials—the vastness of their power, the quality of the adulation with which they are inundated, their rise to the heights on waves of revolutionary sentiment—the two men are remarkably alike. Even in their manner of speech and their restrained simplicity, I thought, they resembled one another. And both of them are, under different political slogans, instruments of the historical impulse which is spreading Western industry Eastward.

I filed my interview and set off for home: across the Elburz peak, from Enzeli by boat to Baku, and back to Moscow. It makes a great deal of difference whether one enters Russia from Europe or from the Near East. Coming from Persia, there is no shock of novelty—Russia seems a natural and easy transition stage toward Europe. After the authentic East, with its rags and smells, its beggars and swarming poverty, the Russian equivalents seem natural. Moscow, so exotically un-European after Berlin and Warsaw, seemed European enough after Teheran. And it took a journey into Asia to make me realize how completely I had adjusted myself to Moscow. I had the feeling of a homecoming, more poignantly than on my return to New York two years before.

XII. Upon Sodom and Gomorrah Brimstone and Fire

THE Soviet land presented a tragic picture at the beginning of 1933. The Five Year Plan was ended. Instead of an ampler existence along socialist lines it had brought undernourishment bordering on hunger; a scheme for fixed residences amounting to restoration of feudal disciplines; laws prescribing death for theft; destruction of the last semblance of popular control of working conditions; deepening discontents in the communist ranks; fascist reactions in the outside world; lop-sided and chaotic development of the planned economy. The national supply of livestock had dropped 50 to 60% below 1928. Grain exports, resumed in 1930 and large enough in 1931 to alarm the international markets, had ceased abruptly. The political police had become the largest single employer of labor, and inquisitional methods were being used to scrape up gold still in the possession of the citizenry.

But of all the misfortunes that afflicted the country the most disastrous for the common people was the circumstance that the last months of 1932 coincided with the end of the *Piatiletka*. The hopes and enthusiasms blown up at home and abroad with the bellows of propaganda made face-saving the most compelling motive in shaping the Kremlin's policies. Candor and compromise might have been considered at any other time. They could not be made to jibe with the paramount *political* need of this juncture, which was to claim a "successful" completion of the Plan with a straight face.

No sacrifice in life or suffering seemed exorbitant for the maintenance of appearances. The prestige of the ruling oligarchy was at stake. An inviolable Party line, an infallible leader, an omniscient Central Committee, can be maintained only on a diet of bigger and better "successes." Where none of the power is shared with the populace, none of the responsibility can be shared either. The consequences of brute force must be covered with more brute force. As *Pravda* kept repeating, this was no time for "weak nerves."

Food difficulties in southern Russia were fast reaching famine proportions. Admission of this fact would have made celebration of the completion of the Five Year Plan impossible. Ruthlessness in killing doses was therefore prescribed for the Ukraine and Northern Caucasus, an area with some forty million inhabitants, the area of "100% collectivization." It would be futile to argue whether these millions were themselves to blame for their fate. The mentality which presumes to judge and punish forty million human beings operates in a dimension beyond mortal logic—in the mystic clouds of a mad god of vengeance. For all the sophistries of wishful thinking "friends" of the U.S.S.R. and cynical apologists, forty million people can never be either "innocent" or "guilty" but rather the creatures of forces beyond their control.

No one at this time advanced the theory of guilty millions responsible for their own impending doom. That was a post-mortem theory, a cynical coroner's verdict of mass suicide brought forward by the Webbs and others much later, when the famine was over and the debris of corpses removed. At the moment common sense on a mortal level could not compass the possibility of Jehovah-like vengeance against regions as large as half a dozen European countries put together. The New York *Times* * correspondent cabled that if conditions did not improve, the Soviet leaders still had an alternative:

> They can either import food and other needed commodities from abroad either on credit, where they can get it, or by using a part of the gold reserve. Or they can follow Lenin's example and back-pedal in favor of private enterprise.

* By an ironic accident of personalities, the conservative New York *Times* had become (in defiance of all Marxist laws of economic determinism) the mouthpiece of the Kremlin abroad. Its Moscow correspondent in November, however, was obliged to devote a series of articles to the food shortage. With an optimism sadly contradicted by events in the next eight months, he declared that "it is a mistake to exaggerate the gravity of the situation; the Russians have tightened their belts before to a far greater extent than is likely to be needed this winter." Soon enough he was forced to swallow these words with an estimate of at least two million dead through "malnutrition," though later he tried crudely to deny his own estimate. In any case, the *Times* was alone in its optimism, and inordinately wrong.

Like the *Times*, I assumed that the government would import food. The markets of the world at the moment were glutted with grain. A few million dollars would have bought enough bread in Canada and elsewhere to head off the famine. A very minor diversion of money from machines to food would have saved millions of lives.

But the Kremlin was not thinking on the level of common sense. Ordinary logic could not follow the reasoning in the rarefied reaches of its delusions. It neither imported food nor permitted an appeal to the world's charitable instincts as Lenin had done in another famine emergency, nor back-pedaled in favor of private enterprise. It merely took extreme measures to conceal the disaster from the world and thus save face for the fabled Plan. The decision made Stalin and his underlings as directly responsible for every death from typhus, every bloated baby stomach, every wagonload of corpses in the following months as if they had strangled the victims with their own hands.

My lingering scruples against speaking out about Soviet realities were badly shaken up by the impact of this supreme cruelty. It was increasingly difficult to make high-minded excuses for silence and formulas of evasion. Inertia, procrastination, a conscious anxiety to hold on to my job a little longer—the same forces which were silencing many of my colleagues—provide the essential explanation. I wrote just enough of the facts to placate my conscience—and to infuriate my official hosts—but not enough to break the conspiracy of silence that now enshrouded the Soviet Union.

Inwardly I was deeply ashamed of the goose-stepping into which the press corps had been maneuvered, and I know that other correspondents shared that shame. We talked of little else than the hunger and the terror about which we did not write or wrote in misty circumlocutions. Looking back upon that period I find it impossible to make honest apologies for myself or for them, except the pseudo-Marxist apology of economic determinism. I can only make amends, as a few others are doing.

Against this background of muted despair, the celebration of the official opening of Dnieprostroi, in the heart of the district soon to be devastated by man-made famine, had an edge of the grotesque. Several carloads of foreigners and high government officials went in a special train from Moscow to the new hydroelectric station. Practically all the resident foreign correspondents, and a batch arrived on special assignment, were in our party. Malcolm Muggeridge of the *Manchester Guardian* has, in his book *Winter in Moscow,* an unforgettable chapter on that journey; though done as broad caricature that chapter conveys the essential truth (which is the function of good caricature): the insanity of a junket to hungerland, the correspondents chaperoned by official hallelujah-shouters, to dedicate a mechanical mammoth among wheatfields abandoned to weeds; of a holiday to glorify an electric station built in large part with coerced labor and producing electric power for factories not yet in existence.

Muggeridge himself was among the most gullible on this journey, having only just arrived from London, with all the preconceptions about Russia fostered by the paper he represented and other well-meaning liberal publications. I remember how he and another young Londoner defended their dream against the doubts and cynicisms of the more seasoned correspondents. The other Englishman died in Moscow in a tramcar accident with his illusions intact. Muggeridge lived to record his disillusionment; much of the bitterness of his brilliant book is clearly a revenge against his own imported certainties.

The graceful curve of the Dnieper dam, the tamed jungle of masts and wiring, the giant dynamos provided a luscious feast for a modern photographer like the personable Margaret Bourke-White. Whether in the Ukraine or Muscle Shoals, machinery is impressive and lends itself naturally to the rhetoric of camera and typewriter. Neither the striking photographs of Miss Bourke-White nor the striking statistics in our dispatches touched the core of the curious rite of machine-worship in a stricken land.

On the evening of our arrival we were moved to ecstasy by the beauty of this great station looming against the star-studded skies. The next morning was chill, overcast and gloomy, but a residue of that ecstasy remained with us. The mass of people in the grandstand, however, had been on the scene too long to be thrilled by the strident poetry of machines. Meekly they applauded the speeches; but there was no warmth of conviction in them. Kalinin and Ordzhonikidze and a dozen others made dully repetitious speeches; a number of Russians and Americans were awarded beribboned badges; and the holiday was dispersed.

Immense signs proclaimed that SOVIET POWER PLUS ELECTRICITY

EQUALS SOCIALISM, and no one asked aloud whose power? what kind of socialism? There was grim fitness in the fact that the most publicized object in the whole Plan, completed punctually in the final months of the Plan, should be located in the region which was paying the most gruesome price for the whole undertaking.

Nor was it accidental that a renewed purge of the Party ranks should be ordered almost at the same moment that Dnieprostroi was declared opened. The drive for orthodoxy was but another symptom of the mounting difficulties; heresy hunting always thrives in moments of crisis. The Kremlin aimed for absolute conformity of minds.

As many as a million communists, it was announced, must be expelled. Since the Party numbered about three millions, every member felt that he faced a one-to-two chance of expulsion. No matter how cautious and tight-mouthed he had been, he might be denounced as a heretic, stripped of his membership card, his job, his Soviet respectability. For tens of thousands it would mean beginning again at the bottom of the ladder in that climb to preferred positions to which they devoted their lives. Through the disgrace of one man many others might be dragged into outer darkness: relatives, intimate friends, those who owed their political preferment to his influence.

The purge set for January first—to continue throughout the new year—thus spread a panic of fear, not only among the Party members but in widening circles to millions of others. The cleansing, in the final analysis, is a device for disciplining the Party, for weeding out those of incomplete faith. The time for the purge was shrewdly chosen. At this moment when the cumulative mistakes of the Stalin leadership were providing a harvest of hunger and discontent, it was a warning to communists that the whip was poised over their backs.

In the symphony of fears the purge was a strong *motif*.

2

In a play then popular in Moscow, Alexander Afinogenyev's *Fear*, an Old Bolshevik woman, Klara Spasova, recalls the horrors of Russia's past. "Entire villages of rebellious serfs were whipped," she exclaims.

In January, 1933, the rulers of Russia's present, too, whipped rebellious villages. They packed all the inhabitants of three Cossack towns in the Kuban, North Caucasus, into cattle cars and shipped them to the Arctic forests. All men, women, and children, innocent and guilty alike, young and old, sick and sound, were torn up by their roots and dumped in the wilderness.

Their fate was to serve as an object lesson to the rest of the Kuban.

Reading of it, I recalled that when the Lord's wrath was about to be loosed from the heavens upon Sodom and Gomorrah, the patriarch Abraham pleaded with Jehovah, saying, "Wilt thou consume the righteous with the wicked?" Finding the God of Wrath amenable to reason, Abraham did a little Oriental haggling. Would Jehovah spare the cities if they harbored fifty of the righteous, or even fifty-less-five, finally bargaining down to ten. And Jehovah said, "I will not destroy it for the ten's sake." Even when "Jehovah rained upon Sodom and Gomorrah brimstone and fire from Jehovah out of heaven," He spared Lot.

There was no Abraham to plead and bargain for the Kuban towns: he would instantly have been convicted of "rotten liberalism" and "petty bourgeois idealism" and forced to share the doom of the Cossack sinners. The Bolshevik gods of wrath in the North Caucasus, moreover, had none of Jehovah's Trotskyist strain. On the contrary, they boasted in the Rostov and other local newspapers that no one, not a solitary Lot, was spared, and the righteous were indeed consumed with the guilty as a warning to other districts which loved not collectivization. They boasted of it in eight-column headlines, and told how Red Army veterans would be quartered upon the land and in the houses from which the owners had been driven.

By chance I saw those newspapers. A European journalist under instructions to "play ball" with the Soviet leaders and therefore unable to send the story himself, turned the papers over to me. For five years, the Press Department had insisted that anything published in the Soviet press was by that fact alone exempt from censorship. I therefore wrote the story and submitted it to Comrade Umansky. He was exceedingly distressed that the Kuban atrocity should have reached the ears of a foreign correspondent. Yet he could not see his way clear to forbidding the cable; I had the Rostov clippings with me. For many minutes he scratched his long hair and gritted his golden teeth—and suddenly he saw a way out.

"But, Mr. Lyons," he smiled, "you say that 40,000 are involved in this mass deportation. Where do you get the figure?"

"That's simple. I looked up your latest official census. The population of the three *stanitzas* [settlements] as given there totals about 40,000. In fact, my dispatch cites the official source for the figure."

"All the same, I'm sorry, I can't let you use that figure. That was the population two or three years ago. How do you know what it is today?"

"All right—*you* tell me how many were deported! Surely someone in your government knows."

"No, your cable can't go unless you eliminate the figure. Just say that the inhabitants were exiled, without specifying how many."

I was willing to compromise for fifteen or twenty thousand to get it by, but refused to send the story without some approximate figure—which was precisely what the censor wanted to accomplish. There was the glint of victory in the golden fangs.

A few days later I was in Berlin, on the vacation trip that I had postponed for the Persian assignment. I discussed the censored story with Fred Kuh, head of our Berlin Bureau, and he agreed that it was too important a piece of news to be suppressed. He filed it for me from Berlin. The world was horrified by the story. More than the generalized talk of peasant troubles, this concrete instance of many thousands of human beings exiled *en masse*, without regard to individual guilt or innocence, dramatized the Soviet agrarian tragedy.

Questioned by their editors, all Moscow correspondents were obliged to corroborate my facts, though there were different guesses as to the number affected. My own editors showered me with congratulatory messages on the "clean scoop." Two Moscow colleagues, Ralph Barnes of the New York *Herald Tribune* and Bill Stoneman of the Chicago *Daily News*, were emboldened by the interest stirred up by my Kuban scoop to make a surreptitious journey into Ukraine and North Caucasus. They were picked up by the G.P.U. and ordered back to Moscow, but not before they had been surfeited with horror in close-up. Barnes' account of the trip began with ominous words about "hunger and terror stalking southern Russia." Correspondents being an imitative clan, others were led to write more daringly of the facts we all knew.

My Kuban story, it thus transpired, started the first serious breach in the conspiracy of silence around the famine. The Soviet authorities, I had reason to learn, never forgave me.

At the same time, a series of mail stories that I had written in Moscow began publication all over the world. In these I summarized the cumulative increase of official pressures amounting together to a new reign of terror. I referred to the passport system; the recent death decrees; the new "Political Departments"—in effect, G.P.U. detachments—established throughout agrarian districts with unabridged authority over the peasant millions; the renewed drive against non-conformists in the Communist Party.

None of this was news. We had all cabled these things in brief, isolated dispatches. Drawn together in one series of articles, however, they could not be so easily lost upon the outside world. Any one of these things might be explained away; taken together they revealed a state of crisis at the end of the Five Year Plan. The sin of my Kuban dispatch was thus made a hundredfold more culpable. Several of the German newspaper clients of the United Press were featuring the series, and word was conveyed to me that the Soviet Embassy in Berlin was boiling over with indignation.

3

I was still in Berlin on January 30, the day Adolf Hitler assumed power. Several of us were loitering at the Adlon bar, rolling poker dice with toothpicks for chips, when one of the players was summoned to the telephone. He emerged from the booth in great excitement. "Hitler's just been made Reichskanzler," he threw over his shoulder as he rushed to his office. A little later four or five of the American correspondents foregathered for lunch. Their talk seethed with fateful questions.

The "impossible," the ludicrous had come to pass—the half-hysterical Austrian, the fantastic *opéra bouffe* Napoleon, was actually at the head of Germany's government. Did that mean full-blown fascism? Did it presage a personal dictatorship? Was it merely another brief episode in the country's travail? Despite the millions of votes accumulated by his mongrel National Socialism (the very name a political hybrid of incompatibles), seasoned reporters had refused to believe that he would succeed in strangling the Republic. Even on this day of his triumph, in fact, I still heard correspondents of international repute scoff at the notion of a Nazi dictatorship. Was not the democratic machinery still in force? they asked. Were there not von Papen and von Hindenburg as brakes on Nazi ambitions?

They moderated their skepticism long before midnight. That evening they watched Hitler and Hindenburg reviewing the Nazi victory parade. The aged President seemed a pathetic supernumerary in that show, as uniformed Nazi battalions by the hundred thousand marched past the balcony on the Wilhelmstrasse yelling "Heil Hitler!" The genie released from the bottle could never be stuffed back again. Thereafter events moved with the swiftness of catastrophe—the providential fire, the suppression of all civil liberties, and the abdication of the Reichstag in favor of the brown-shirt dictatorship; lawlessness enthroned and sadistic orgy haloed by nationalist and racial phobias.

Less than five months earlier, the Comintern, in a resolution on the international situation, had hailed its phantom "successes" everywhere, including Germany. Solemnly it had attested the imminence of proletarian revolution in Spain and Poland—and Germany! The machiavellism inspired by the Kremlin had begun by duping others and ended by duping itself. In Germany, as elsewhere in the world, it had erected a *papier-mâché* "movement" of sonorous names for make-believe organizations: the "united front from below." Moscow wanted its foreign creatures uselessly occupied with noisy toys, with Red-This and Proletarian-That, so that it might build socialism in one country without the additional bother and responsibility of revolutionary movements abroad. A hollow intransigence made the most noise and involved the least likelihood of practical action. All communists of any but the exact brand sanctioned by Moscow were therefore "renegades" and "the chief danger of the present period." All labor leaders and socialists were "social fascists" and therefore worse than the unsocial fascists of the Hitler stripe.

While the Nazi movement was rolling up strength, Moscow's policies continued to splinter the labor and liberal opposition.

German communists who recognized the danger and begged for a strategy dictated by German realities rather than Russian sectarianism were expelled and pilloried as enemies of the proletariat. Instead of rallying to the defense of the Republic, the official communists, their emissaries shuttling between Moscow and Berlin, joined the Nazi attack on democracy, had actually voted with the Hitlerites in Prussia, and used their chief strength against the Social-Democrats and more conservative labor groups.

The exact measure of Moscow's responsibility for the German tragedy will be argued for generations and will never be settled. Only two things seem to me too clear to be doubted—and infinitely important in judging communist effort in other countries:

First: At every point in Germany's history in the years preceding Hitler's victory, communist policy and tactics were decided in Moscow, with the specific interests of Soviet Russia, rather than the interests of Germany or the larger interests of the international labor movement, in mind. The rationalization of this state of affairs is clear enough: Russia *is* the world revolution and its practical needs must take precedence. But the rationalization is mendacious sleight-of-mind. As long as the Communist International is little more than another name for Russia's political power, as long as the Russian tail wags the international dog, the sacrifice of the proletariat in one country or two dozen countries will seem small enough price for some immediate political advantage to the Soviet regime. The International is simply a helpless instrument of Soviet statecraft, a "stooge" for the Kremlin.

Second: The Communist propaganda against democracy *per se* as a bourgeois deception, its cavalier attitude toward civil rights, its ridicule of humanistic squeamishness over mass slaughter and organized brutality, all played directly into the hands of the Hitler legions. By its very need to defend *Schrecklichkeit* in Stalin's domain, the official Communist Party provided the justification for *Schrecklichkeit* in Hitler's domain.

By implication the Comintern subsequently admitted at least the second of these facts. Too late—and glorying as always in the superior wisdom of its lateness—it began in the next few years to recognize virtues in the capitalist brand of democracy. Too late—and swinging characteristically to the opposite extreme—it discovered the need for a united front from above, as far above as possible, with practically anybody willing to unite except Trotskyists and other non-conformist communists. Russia itself, until then proudly contemptuous of democracy, was scared by the German debacle into a panicky revision of its views on government (not, alas, its behavior!) to make them more acceptable to democratic nations. None of this post-factum wisdom, however, could undo the evil in Germany or slacken the momentum of the fascist advance.

Despite three years of world depression, unemployment and capitalist despairs, communism internationally had made no headway. Instead, Germany was in the grip of Hitler, and fascist tendencies were dominant in half a dozen other European countries. Moscow's dictatorship over the revolutionary movement of the world had shown itself a pathetic failure. More communists were outside the Comintern fold than inside. Whatever strength the movement had was hopelessly splintered.

The Soviet consulate in Berlin, for the second time in my experience, held up my visa for Moscow. Having left my passport as usual, I returned for it in a few hours, which in the past had sufficed. A minor functionary spoke out of turn. "Visa for Lyons?" he said; "oh, but that is not yet decided. It is being discussed at this very moment inside there." When I called the following afternoon I was ushered into the office of one of the Embassy secretaries.

On his desk lay a stack of clippings of my articles. He fingered them, shook his head sadly, shrugged his shoulders.

"Ah, such things," he sighed, "such things are very bad, especially now. They help the Hitler cause."

"Precisely," I agreed. "That's one reason why I object to such things. The sooner Moscow quits them the better for everybody, especially correspondents."

The "things" to which he referred, however, were my articles rather than the Soviet facts they embodied. Apparently the Stalin regime had every right to "rain upon Sodom and Gomorrah brimstone and fire from Jehovah out of heaven," consuming "the righteous with the wicked;" it could slaughter its peasants and imprison its heretics. The Kremlin was blameless. But a correspondent who reported such triumphs of monolithic madness was grievously at fault. The secretary could not see that Stalin's crime in deporting the Kuban peasants was at least as serious as mine in recording the fact. Or, who knows? Perhaps he did see it. I have never envied Soviet spokesmen at home or abroad their unsavory job.

The mild reprimand having been administered, my visa was duly issued. In Moscow the second installment of the reprimand awaited me. Comrade Umansky took a friendly-sarcastic tack, one of his most practiced roles. Apparently I had been mischievous . . . correspondents will be correspondents . . . and he, for one, would like to guard me against the wrath of his government.

"But what can I do?" he asked, pursing his lips in a cherubic expression of impotent philanthropy. "You have placed the Press Department in a position where we cannot intervene in your behalf if certain other branches of the government decide to take action against you."

"What action? Are you hinting at expulsion for that story of the deported Kuban *stanitsas?*"

"I cannot tell what they might do."

"Well, I'm prepared to take my medicine. Nobody questions the truth of the story. You have confirmed it yourself. After all, I didn't deport them—you did."

I transmitted the gist of this conversation to the United Press in New York. I told them that an order for my expulsion for the story that elicited the congratulatory cables was not out of the question. When the order finally did not come, I was surprised. My sojourn in the land of the Five Year Plan, however, was from this time forward on sufferance only. I had broken a taboo by giving the outside world a peep into the official closets where skeletons were stored. The miracle is that I survived nine months longer.

XIII. Did the First Five Year Plan Succeed?

MOUNTAINS of statistics have been piled up, sorted and re-sorted, tunneled and dynamited in attempts to ascertain whether the Five Year Plan "succeeded." There is no amateur economist so humble that he has not ventured an analysis. Under the compulsion of my trade, I have myself dabbled in billions and tried to unscramble the many different monetary measures—pre-war rubles, 1926 rubles, "rubles of respective years," etc. I have wondered what to do with clean-cut statistical triumphs which somehow showed up in frightful disaster all around me. I have puzzled over mysterious hiatuses in the official figures and low-quality correctives and sectors of the original Plan which were sunk and forgotten in transit.

In my heart of hearts, I have always felt the futility and the ghoulish cynicism of reducing these years of travail to arithmetic. Fine mathematical successes in agriculture had no place for the famine cadavers, liquidations, death edicts, the conquest and pacification of a hundred million peasants. Try as I would to marshal figures, I could not be thrilled by furnaces and electric stations *per se,* without reference to the human beings who built them and worked in them. The forms of political and economic power, the happiness and dignity of the myriads of men, men and children, outweighed for me those mountains of statistics.

Was the first Five Year Plan a "success"? For whom and for what? Certainly not for the socialist dream, which had been emptied of human meaning in the process, reduced to a mechanical formula of the state as a super-trust and the population as its helpless serfs. Certainly not for the individual worker, whose trade union had been absorbed by the state-employer, who was terrorized by medieval decrees, who had lost even the illusion of a share in regulating his own life. Certainly not for the revolutionary movement of the world, which was splintered, harassed by the growing strength of fascism, weaker and less hopeful than at the launching of the Plan. Certainly not for the human spirit, mired and outraged by sadistic cruelties on a scale new in modern history, shamed by meekness and sycophancy and systematized hypocrisy.

If industrialization were an end in itself, unrelated to larger human ends, the U.S.S.R. had an astounding amount of physical property to show for its sacrifices. Chimneys had begun to dominate horizons once notable for their church domes. Scores of mammoth new enterprises were erected. A quarter of a million prisoners —a larger number of slaves than the Pharaohs mobilized to build their pyramids, than Peter the Great mobilized to build his new capital—hacked a canal between the White and the Baltic Seas; a hundred thousand survivors of this "success" were digging another canal just outside Moscow as the second Plan got under way. The country possessed 32 blast furnaces and 63 open hearth furnaces that had not existed in 1928, a network of power stations with a capacity four times greater than pre-war Russia had, twice as many oil pipe lines as in 1928. Hundreds of machines and tools formerly imported or unknown in Russia were being manufactured at home and large sections of mining were mechanized for the first time. The foundations were laid for a new industrial empire in the Urals and eastern Siberia, the impregnable heart of the country. Two-thirds of the peasantry and four-fifths of the plowed land were "socialized"—that is, owned and managed by the state-employer as it owned and managed factories and workers. The defensive ability of the country, in a military sense, had been vastly increased, with new mechanical bases for its war industries.

Measured merely for bulk, the Plan achieved much, though it fell far short of the original goals. On the qualitative side, the picture is much less impressive. Here, we find reflected the low caliber of the human material through which the Plan was necessarily translated from paper to life. Overhead costs were greater all along the line than expected—all construction allowed 50% for overhead, compared with 12% allowed in America. Error and spoilage surpassed the worst fears of the Kremlin. A Conference on Quality Production in 1933, for instance, disclosed officially that spoilage in textile mills ranged between 13 and 47%. The productivity of labor did not rise as expected, so that twice as many men and women as planned had to be drawn from leisure or agriculture to make up the difference. The costs of the Plan, reckoned in any terms, were tragically exorbitant, more so than even the keenest Soviet enemies had prophesied.

These costs were not merely bookkeeping tragedies. They were paid for in hunger, terror, privation, epidemic diseases.

But let us look at the Plan in its most mechanistic aspect.

Speaking at a Party conference in January, Stalin claimed a quantitative fulfillment of 93.7%. The figure—close enough to 100% for all practical purposes—remains the Kremlin's formal estimate of the results.

At the start of the final year, 1932, it was officially announced that the Plan would be carried out fully if a growth of production by 37% were achieved. In point of fact, as Molotov has stated, the growth that year was only 8½%. Simple arithmetic shows that when it requires a 37% increase to finish a job, and only 8½% is attained, the job is no more than 79% complete. This is *prima facie* evidence that Stalin's figure of 93.7 is suspiciously optimistic.

How did he reach that figure? The government's summary showed a gross output for "census industry" in 1932, the last year of the Plan, of 34.3 billion rubles' production in the values of 1926-27. The Plan allegedly called for a total of 36.6 billion rubles in the concluding year. That is where Stalin got his percentage.

But the statistical method involved is open to question. Stalin's figure assumes that the Plan started from scratch and reached 93.7% of what it aimed to accomplish. In sober fact, the Plan started with an output of 15.7 billion rubles in the year preceding its launching. What was actually aimed at was an *increase* of 20.9 billions; the *increase* achieved was 18.6 billions, so that the margin of non-fulfillment was 11%, instead of the 6.3% cited by Stalin.

This statistical method deserves a little consideration, since it is typical of jugglery such as an American income-tax chiseler might well envy. The sleight-of-mind is so deft that I followed this method myself for years, until Zara Witkin, whose engineering mind is proof against statistical magic, pointed it out to me.

Throughout its figures, the Kremlin compares *total results* with the planned totals, instead of comparing the *actual* increase with the *planned* increase. A consideration of the figures for the steel industry, for instance, will illustrate the difference:

Steel output in 1928 was 4.2 million tons. The Plan foresaw an increase of 6.1 millions, for a total of 10.3 millions. Actual production in the final year was 5.9 millions. This meant an increase of 1.7 millions over 1928, or 28% of the increase planned. The Kremlin, however, says: "We aimed at 10.3 and got 5.9, therefore our plan was fulfilled by 57%." On that basis, if production had not increased a single ton, if it had remained at 4.2 millions, the plan would have been carried out by 42%—extraordinary statistical progress while standing still and marking time!

When this cute piece of arithmetical legerdemain is "liquidated," many of the Kremlin's proudest boasts are strangely deflated. Steel output instead of increasing by 57%—in itself a sad failure considering the staggering investments—shows up as only 28%. New housing, with an official credit of 84% increase, actually increased only by 44% (the need for new housing, at the same time, grew by several hundred percent because of the increase of urban workers). The mileage of railroads in operation, instead of reaching 89% of the plan as claimed, showed an increase of only 44%. Petroleum production, manufacture of steam turbines and a very few other items actually exceeded the quantitative totals of increase called for by the Plan. The margins of failure in important branches of national economy may be judged from the following percentages of increase compared with the 100% planned: tractors, 28%; automobiles, 13%; brick, 28%; cement, 37%; lumber, 40%; electrification, 77%.

2

It is not without interest that the official Soviet summary of the fulfillment gives no production figures for such important industries as non-ferrous metals (copper, zinc, lead, aluminum), although tremendous amounts of capital had been poured into those industries. It omits output in the textile industry, sugar, rubber shoes, salt and many other branches catering to the everyday needs of the people. These omissions may reasonably be assumed to reflect a breakdown in those sectors.

The disastrous conditions in transportation and the railway system were not denied by the government spokesmen. But these were the funnels through which the entire industrial program must of necessity filter. The insistence on "success" when transportation has all but collapsed is, to say the least, extraordinary. By a little judicious juggling the impression is created that the very success of the plan, in overtaxing the transport facilities, was to blame. One of the major failures is thus revamped into a counterfeit proof of success. The fact, however, is that transportation was not only badly planned, but even those defective plans were not carried out. The *Piatiletka* called for the completion of 17,000 kilometers of new railway. Only 6,500 kilometers were accomplished. In the ten preceding years, 1918-28, despite civil war and without the bloodshed and ballyhoo of the Five Year Plan, there had been completed 18,500 kilometers, or nearly three times as much as during the Plan.

The failure in steel, cement, lumber and brick is particularly significant. Certainly new construction, the essential factor in the whole Plan, could not go beyond the construction materials available. Stalin's claim of 93.7% fulfillment is illogical and patently "doctored" when the increase in construction materials needed for that fulfillment ranges between 28 and 40%.

The doctoring evidently can be traced to the confusion in ruble values on which Stalin's figure rests. The official publication of the Five Year Plan gave 1928 production in census industry (to which alone Stalin has reference) as 8.1 billion *pre-war* rubles. The equivalent in 1926 rubles is given as 15.7 billions. The government thus recognized the 1926 rubles as about one-half the value of the *pre-war* ruble. The same published Plan gave the planned production for the final year as 21 billion *pre-war* rubles. On the same ratio this would be about 42 billions in 1926-27 rubles. Strangely enough, however, the planned production is set down arbitrarily as 36.6 billions in 1926 values, or some five billions less than it should be according to the government's own valuations.

Reducing the whole business to *pre-war* rubles, in which we are merely following the method of the original Plan, the actual increase of 18.6 billions in 1926-27 rubles cited by Stalin amounts to 9.3 billions in *pre-war* rubles. This means only 72% of the scheduled growth—a far throw from the 93.7% claimed by Stalin.

Even that figure is vastly inflated, since it takes no cognizance of quality factors, increased cost per unit, inadequate production per man. My personal estimate—and I make no pretensions as an economist—is that the Five Year Plan, in terms of production, was only *half* fulfilled.

Colleagues more qualified to judge statistical mysteries regard that as a conservative estimate. In any event, it is a more responsible figure than Stalin's in relation to the official statistics for available construction materials. It is also more nearly in logical relation to the power resources in actual use. The Plan called for an increase of power by 3.5 million kw. capacity; the actual increase was only 2.7 million kw. or 77%; while there are no reliable statistics as to what portion of this new power capacity was utilized, no competent observer claims that more than three-quarters of it was in use; three-quarters of 77%, the most optimistic reckoning, gives a 58% increase in power—much more nearly in line with a claim of half fulfillment than with Stalin's claim of almost complete fulfillment.

In agriculture—and there is a nauseating cold-bloodedness about measuring the agrarian tragedy statistically—we have the Kremlin's own figure of 699 million centners of grain in 1932, the last year of the Plan. This compares with 801 million centners in 1913 and 733 in 1928. The area under grain increased, but the unit output fell (1913—8.4 centners per hectare; 1932—7 centners per hectare; a decline of about 20%), despite the abolition of the strip system, the staggering cash investments, the immense accretion of farm machinery and the sacrifice of millions of human lives. The tragic failure in the domain of livestock—which can be translated as food, leather, draught power, etc.—was too evident to be denied or juggled arithmetically.

Agriculture, standards of living, housing facilities were as much a part of the Five Year Plan as production in census industry to which Stalin limits himself. When these are considered as part of the whole set-up, when the costs in life and suffering and political terror are added, the Plan must be regarded as one of the most startling failures in all human history. One searches the records of mankind in vain for a more miserable return on a vast investment.

That the Plan has been accepted even by hostile capitalist economists as on the whole "successful" shows the gullibility and naivete of those who deal in cold figures instead of living realities. Parrotwise the world has repeated rhetorical exaggerations about "decades of industrial progress crowded into a few years"—I shudder to think how much such loose rhetoric I have floated myself!

The second *Piatiletka* was sketched in broad strokes at the same time that the claim of "success" was advanced for the first one. The details were not to be filled in for more than a year; the building was more than a fifth erected before the architects finished the designs. The rough sketch, however, showed clearly enough that there would be no let-up in the killing tempos. Still panting and out of breath from the harrowing effort of the first plan, the Russian people were confronted, early in 1933, with a second and no less strenuous one. The loud official enthusiasm awoke no echoes in the breasts of the masses. They were too intimately aware of the obstacles and sacrifices to be thrilled by the road ahead. But by this time the popular reaction counted for less than ever before: there were harsh decrees, passports, a new concept of factory management, the revivified profit motive to take the place of enthusiasm.

Viewed in sufficient perspective, so that the human factor fades out, the launching of the new plan occurred under propitious circumstances. The high pageant of Soviet economic and social daring was dramatically set off by the world-wide economic crisis. The foreign press and bourgeois economists were too completely demoralized by the ghastly shambles of their own economic scene to be critical of Soviet claims. Soviet leaders were not behindhand in bringing the contrasts home to the humblest of their wards and the most distant of their deaf villages. In the domain of mass propaganda, in forging simple slogans, they have no peers anywhere. Every newspaper and billboard and factory bulletin in the land carried a schematized reminder of capitalist troubles: *Over There* and *Over Here*, with the items listed selected arbitrarily and with small regard for completeness. This international scoreboard was etched on the consciousness of the Soviet population with all the acids of press, radio, screen and school. The Soviet state was represented as marching forward resolutely while the rest of the world groped through fog banks of depression. The gods who manage such things had provided a setting for the new plan as effective as though made to order for the Kremlin.

But at closer range the moment was not nearly so auspicious. The world crisis itself had had strong repercussions on Moscow's economic plans. It undermined the foreign markets through which Russia must pay for imported machinery, equipment, and brains. If the second Five Year Plan must rely almost entirely on domestic machinery and native brains, it was not altogether a free choice. Despite all its international scoreboards, the U.S.S.R. was as eager to overcome the world depression as any other nation.

Even more important, the concluding year of the first plan had turned out the most difficult. Defects and failures are no less cumulative than successes. Notwithstanding the barrage of alibis (many of them true ones), the ordinary citizen judged the plan just ended in personal terms, in meat and herrings and shoes and personal freedoms rather than in kilowatt-hours or ton-kilometers. His private balance of the plan was not nearly as cheerful as Stalin's.

The resolution on the new plan adopted by the Party conference at which Stalin spoke undertook nothing less than *the actual introduction of socialism*. The first plan, it asserted, had laid the foundations for socialism—the second would erect the final edifice:

> The conference holds that the chief political task of the Second Five Year Plan is to do away with the capitalist elements and with classes in general; to destroy fully the causes giving rise to class distinctions and exploitation; to abolish the survivals of capitalism in economy and in the consciousness of the people; to transform the whole working population of the country into conscious and active builders of a classless society.

Having redefined socialism to mean merely state monopoly of all branches of economy—a feudalistic serf "socialism" undreamed of by socialist theorists and philosophers and agitators before the Soviet era—Stalin's conference thus attested its impending triumph. In due time it would announce that the triumph was completed.

To explain the palpable failures and hardships despite claims of such towering achievements, Stalin resorted, as usual, to the machinations of foreign and internal enemies. He warned that espionage and sabotage were rife. "A strong and powerful dictatorship of the proletariat," he exclaimed, "that is what we must have now in order to shatter the last remnants of the dying classes and to frustrate their felonious designs." Forgetting utterly that the state was to have evaporated as socialism triumphed, he called for a stronger, more ruthless, more arbitrary state even while announcing the triumph of socialism.

The G.P.U. took up his challenge. Scapegoats were found. Again the arrests were counted by the score and the hundred. In March, thirty-five agrarian specialists, among them high officials of the agricultural commissariat, were shot at one sweep. Posthumous charges even more incredible than those against the forty-eight similarly shot in 1930 were advanced. Perhaps there was an element of truth in these charges, but the accused were safely dead and could not refute them. And on the very day after this wholesale execution which was to symbolize the difficulties in agriculture, half a dozen Englishmen and several dozen Russians were arrested on similar charges in relation to industry. The second plan, like the first, began with a demonstration trial.

XIV. Britishers on Trial

ON MARCH 12, 1933, a "free day" in the Soviet six-day week, Linton Wells, then representing the International News Service, came into exclusive possession of one of the biggest news stories in many a Russian year. Lunching at the British Embassy that day, he learned that six Englishmen, as well as a few dozen Russians, employed by the Metropolitan-Vickers Company on its projects in the U.S.S.R. had been arrested and were being kept incommunicado. They were apparently charged with high crimes against the Soviet state. G.P.U. agents had rounded up the Metro-Vickers people the night before and the Embassy had not as yet been permitted to see any of them. It was the first time since the Shakhty affair in 1928 that a group of foreigners had been arrested and was certain to stir up intense interest throughout the world.

Linton did the most heroic thing that any newspaperman can possibly do—risking life is a minor matter by contrast. He called all the British and American correspondents to his apartment and shared his information with us. We were too excited by the news to be properly grateful. With capital charges facing six foreigners, some of whom were his friends, Linton placed their interests above his own professional glory. Only a reporter can appreciate the mettle of that heroism.

We sent a test dispatch to the home of censor Mironov and apprised him that we would be up to see him with our final stories at a definite hour; this gave him time to check up on the facts. At the appointed hour more than a dozen of us climbed the long flights of stairs and presented our cables.

"I am sorry, gentlemen, very sorry," Mironov smiled the smile that brought his nose within a few centimeters of his protruding chin. "The story can't go. This is, as you know, a free day. We cannot obtain confirmation. As far as I'm concerned, I know nothing about such arrests."

For the first time in all my Moscow years the entire press corps was acting together. Even Duranty spoke up boldly; being an Englishman himself he could scarcely do less. This story did not concern six million Russians, but six Britishers. The unanimity and grimness of our protest yanked Mironov's nose from his chin. He did some frantic telephoning to mysterious places. Finally he emerged with instructions to pass brief dispatches giving no more than the bare fact of the arrest. The "united front" of Anglo-American journalism scored a victory of a sort.

Most of us rounded out the victory by telephone. Since telephone communications with Berlin and London had been opened, the correspondents had fallen into the habit of evading the censorship occasionally. Technically we were expected to get the Press Department's consent before transmitting anything by telephone; in practice the censors winked at the procedure. Several of my colleagues, indeed, used the telephone exclusively and for all practical purposes considered the censorship liquidated.

The news of the arrests created a great sensation throughout the world. We were pressed for additional information. The chief of the Metro-Vickers operations in the U.S.S.R., Allan Monkhouse, was released next day. We interviewed him and obtained the first graphic story of the raid, the search of the Britishers' homes and the initial interrogations.

The Press Department refused to pass our stories of this interview. It was "investigating" the matter and would let us know later. The correspondents thereupon adjourned for a council of war. The unanimous decision was to send the interview by telephone. With a group of foreigners already in prison and opinion abroad aroused, Moscow could scarcely offend the whole world by expelling the whole press corps. We each returned to our homes and sent the Monkhouse account without benefit of blue-pencil.

Late that evening, we were advised that with certain changes we could cable the interview. Umansky in person would be at his office to censor the dispatch. Apparently Umansky waited and waited in vain—only the *Times* correspondent showed up with the story. The rest of us, having transmitted the interview without Umansky's blessing, naturally did not come to ask for it. This strange boycott finally puzzled the number one censor and he decided to telephone one of the correspondents to solve the mystery. For my heavy sins, he picked on me.

"Gene," he said, "why aren't you sending the Monkhouse interview? I am now in a position to pass it."

"Because I have already filed it—by telephone."

"Mr. Lyons! Please come to see me immediately."

And so, though all but one of the correspondents had offended equally, the full force of Comrade Umansky's indignation was loosed on my head. Umansky in a classic rage was a comic sight: Mickey Mouse in a leonine temper. The scene did not sweeten the atmosphere in which I had my infidel being since I broke the story of the mass deportations from the Kuban towns.

The following weeks were lurid and electrical with developments in the Metro-Vickers case. The arrests caused a storm of patriotic anger in England, and other countries whose nationals were engaged on Soviet industrial projects were alarmed in varying degrees. All but one of the accused Britons were freed on bail—a privilege never granted to Soviet citizens. The British government demanded the immediate release of its citizens and, failing to receive satisfaction, placed a total embargo on trade with the U.S.S.R. (Butter suddenly became more plentiful in Moscow because of this embargo.) Sir Esmond Ovey, the Ambassador, was recalled demonstratively to make a personal report, and reaching London he proceeded to lambast the Soviet Union and all its institutions with rather undiplomatic vigor. A batch of English newspapermen arrived especially to cover this story. The stage was set for one of the trials of the century.

Sir Esmond's flaming indignation was particularly distasteful to the Moscow government. He was a diplomat of liberal persuasions who had arrived for his task with typical liberal preconceptions about the great Soviet experiment. At his former post, in Mexico City, he had watched Dwight Morrow, the American banker, in the role of good-will Ambassador, and seemed determined to play the same role for his own country in relation to the land of Soviets. For a while he was the lone "Bolshevik" in the diplomatic corps, apologizing and explaining everything Soviet as stoutly as any *Manchester Guardian* emissary. Then he turned—and in his apostasy grew as sharply critical as any *Manchester Guardian* emissary in reverse. His case was just one more justification for Moscow's canny distrust of the liberal breed. It had learned from sad experience that a militantly pro-Soviet diplomat or correspondent was a dangerous gamble. A frankly capitalist representative, without illusions, was at least proof against disillusionment. Small wonder that many months later the Kremlin, outwardly pretending satisfaction over the appointment of William C. Bullitt as the first American plenipotentiary, actually viewed him with dire misgivings, only too well borne out by his subsequent withdrawal in a mood of tight-lipped disappointment. Mr. Bullitt's successor, a corporation lawyer with lots of money, unencumbered by pro-Soviet leanings, was far more to the Kremlin's taste.

Whatever else the Metro-Vickers case was expected to accomplish, it succeeded in diverting attention abroad, and to some extent at home, from the expanding catastrophe in the villages. Not until the trial was over and forgotten did any of us bother again with the famine.

2

Two of the six Englishmen tried in the Metropolitan-Vickers case wrote and signed elaborate confessions of espionage, sabotage, and bribery during their interrogation by the G.P.U., in which they involved many of their fellow-countrymen. One of them, W. H. MacDonald, adhered to his confession at the trial, and the other, Leslie Thornton, repudiated his effusion. Even the theory that they were guilty does not suffice to explain their confessions, since every consideration of self-interest and professional reputation, of loyalty to their friends and patriotism to their government, should have prompted them to deny the charges.

It was not as though they had been confronted with incontrovertible proofs of guilt and obliged to accept the inevitable. Not one tiny scrap of independent evidence to support their admissions was offered by the government, though all foreigners are under constant surveillance and a thorough search had been made of the Britishers' homes and offices. Had they insisted that they were innocent, it would have pitted their word against the word of their Soviet employees and associates, and the world's public opinion unquestionably would have been on their side.

Whatever it may have been that induced these men to tar themselves and their colleagues, it was not disclosed by the trial.

More than that: their confessions went beyond the claims of the prosecution. The Soviet court itself exonerated completely one of the defendants, A. W. Gregory, who was implicated in those confessions and at least one of the twenty-seven men listed by Thornton as spies was in the courtroom as a spectator. The failure of the G.P.U. to arrest him was at least an implied admission of his innocence. To this day, though all the Britishers are free and have small reason to protect the reputation of the G.P.U., no tenable explanation for those confessions has been forthcoming. Both MacDonald and Thornton, moreover, have remained in the employ of the Metropolitan-Vickers Electrical Company despite the "betrayal," thus adding another element of mystery to the whole business.

I sat through every session of that trial and studied the published record of the proceedings afterwards. I read the book written by Allan Monkhouse, one of the chief defendants. But I am as much at sea as any casual newspaper customer. Only of this I feel sure: that the real story, the real compulsions, were located far behind the scenes. What transpired in the improvised courtroom at the former Nobles Club seemed to me little more than a shadow play on a screen. The tantalizing margin of mystery was as wide in this trial as in any that preceded it—perhaps wider, in view of the enormous support that these men had from their government.

MacDonald, it is true, remained in the hands of the G.P.U.—practically incommunicado from the moment of his arrest. No Britisher was given access to him. During the trial, while the other five Britishers were free on bail between sessions and in constant touch with the British Embassy people, MacDonald was led off to his prison cell. A thin, nervous man of twenty-eight, with a close-cropped goatee and weak, pallid features, a cripple from boyhood, he made an unpleasant impression. Watching his twitching fingers and glazed eyes, we all felt that he was putty under the manipulating fingers of the Secret Police.

But Thornton had been released from prison eight days before the trial started. He was constantly with William Strang, the British *chargé d'affaires* and with Anglo-American correspondents as eager as Mr. Strang to demonstrate that the whole case was a frame-up. However, though he sought to withdraw his fulsome confession and referred vaguely to "moral pressure," he failed to supply a wholly satisfactory reason for that document.

The conviction that grew in my mind at the time and has been deepened since then was that immense unseen forces were at work. The G.P.U. and the prosecution, I came to feel, had a club over the heads of some of the Britishers. British guilt was involved (whether of the British Intelligence Service or of individual Britishers, I dare not surmise), but that guilt referred to matters which were not even mentioned at the trial. If that theory has any validity, it was not the first time that men and governments have accepted responsibility for lesser crimes to conceal larger ones.

Another element in the complicated case to which the correspondents could only hint darkly is the possibility that several of the Englishmen were protecting people whom they loved. Most of them had lived in Russia the greater part of their lives and spoke the language fluently. Monkhouse had been in the country fairly continuously since 1911. Thornton's family, I believe, had been in business in Russia long before the revolution. The friendships and intimacies developed in many years may have enabled the G.P.U. to apply its practical technique of keeping victims in line by threats against people for whom they cared.

Before the trial started, the Press Department called me in and gave me "inside information" about the love life of Anna Kutusova, Russian secretary in the Metropolitan-Vickers office who was among the eleven Russian defendants, and of another woman who did not appear at the trial. Whether the same information was offered to other correspondents I do not know. The transparent purpose was to shock Puritan public opinion in England. I refused, of course, to send such rubbish. The likelihood that one or more of the Britishers were protecting the lives and the reputations of these women, and to that extent under official duress, is certainly not excluded.

As for the Russians who sat in the dock with the foreigners, they were true to the monotonous pattern drawn in former demonstration trials. With one or two negligible exceptions, they were panic-stricken, half-hysterical penitents collaborating with the G.P.U. and the prosecution. The contrast provided by several blunt and self-assured Britons made the belly-crawling of the Russian group that much uglier and more pathetic.

A blundering, demoralized little man named Gusev, director of the electrical plant at Zlatoust, confessed to gathering military information and wrecking machines at his own plant and concealing alleged defects in English equipment, all for a bribe of three thousand rubles—about fifteen pounds sterling in real money! Another Russian engineer, Kotlyarevsky, testified that he turned over to MacDonald important secret plans, wrecked a turbine and hid defects in imported machinery for the munificent bribe of one thousand rubles, worth perhaps five pounds. The sole witness not himself under arrest, a certain Dolgov, testified to receiving from Thornton a bribe of five thousand rubles. Both Thornton and Monkhouse insisted it was a loan ultimately written off as a gift when Dolgov failed to repay it. Against the seriousness of the sabotage and espionage in question, these sums were ludicrously small. There were few foreigners in Russia who had not loaned or even made gifts of a few thousand of the inflated nearly worthless rubles to Russian friends in distress.

The dreary and repetitious confessions of the Russians provided the background for the trial. All of them watched for the flick of Prosecutor Vishinsky's whip and obeyed with the frightened alacrity of trained animals. In their "last words" they begged for their lives and promised to do penance in the tones and the words that had become a familiar refrain since the Shakhty trial.

The real interest centered around the Englishmen. There was the morning when Monkhouse stepped to the microphone and in a clear, precise voice charged that "this trial is a frame-up against Metropolitan-Vickers engineers based on evidence of terrorized prisoners." But he failed signally in the following days to substantiate that charge. There was the sensational moment when the pallid, limping MacDonald, as though awaking from a long trance, suddenly withdrew his confession. A short recess was called after this sensation, during which MacDonald was removed along with the Russians. When court resumed, MacDonald seemed to have relapsed into his stupor of hopelessness—again he attested the truth of the confession.

A fiery little Welshman, the red-headed Gregory, talked to the Soviet judges and the prosecutors as they had never been talked to before. He kept exploding with his sense of insulted innocence. But the state never really pressed its accusations against him. John Cushny, a tall, swarthy, stolid fellow, was firm and impressive in his denials. Nordwall, too, would not be shaken in his repudiation of all the charges.

Few of us pretended to understand the convolutions of this trial, staged at a critical moment to show the Soviet population and the world at large why Russian industry was still so ineffective and living conditions so low though the Five Year Plan was finished. Those who had the key to the mystery did not use it, have not used it to this day. But that the case was not proved against either the Russians or the foreigners seemed plain enough. There were defense lawyers, Soviet citizens all, timorous pre-revolutionary gentry frightened for their own skins; but there was no defense. The most amateur of American or British criminal lawyers could have shattered the proceedings by asking questions that were never asked—questions that would focus general charges down to specific dates, places, sums; questions that would pursue relentlessly the teeming contradictions in the testimony. The line-up of beards at the defense counsel table, a very museum of beards, was most impressive; but the accused were left to stumble and flail through the trial without real guidance and without coördinating their testimony. And as always in these ballyhooed political trials, the case ended as it began, with confessions and confessions only, unsupported by external and unimpeachable proofs.

The presiding judge was Comrade Ulrich. I had seen him a year ago baiting and brow-beating and taunting a half-imbecile boy, Judas Stern, whom he was about to condemn to death for shooting at a German Embassy car. In Ulrich's round podgy face the gods had modeled a mask of impish, gloating cruelty. His flushed, overstuffed features were twisted continuously into a grimace of brutal sarcasm. The muscles of his mouth seemed incapable of anything suggesting a judicial expression: that melon-face hovering above the trial, sneering and jeering, was a caricature of the very idea of justice. Ulrich's snarl and grimace had taken the place of Krylenko's in demonstration trials. In a judge they were infinitely more obscene than in a prosecutor.*

* Ulrich later achieved international notoriety as presiding judge in the Zinoviev-Kamenev, Radek-Piatakov, and Tukhachevsky trials.

3

A former dining hall of the Nobles Club, holding perhaps three hundred spectators, was the scene of the Metro-Vickers show. The blue walls, the Ionic columns, a frieze of dancing figures at the ceiling line, gave the proceedings an incongruously frivolous setting. The elaborate broadcasting and photographic arrangements of previous trials were absent. But the international character of the case gave the court a resonance that carried to the farthest corners of the earth. A number of prominent London journalists had arrived to cover the trial, and the American press was also keenly interested. The diplomatic corps was well represented. All of us came and went constantly; our messengers rushed back and forth with dispatches; the atmosphere was informal and almost sociable. The fact itself that defendants on trial for such grave crimes were free between sessions set this demonstration off sharply from all previous ones. To the Russians such official largesse was beyond belief.

The lobby outside the courtroom was given over chiefly to the press. A small room off the lobby was used by the censors; it was labeled "Doctor" and was the place, we wisecracked, where they performed surgical operations on our dispatches.

Competition among the Anglo-American newspapermen was extremely sharp. The press agency men especially were working at an ungodly tension. Every split second was important in the fantastic race which had developed for priority in transmitting testimony. In retrospect that struggle for a few seconds' advantage in reporting what Monkhouse or Cushny or Vishinsky said seems sufficiently grotesque, but at the time it was all very earnest. I blame upon this tension the farcical climax of the competition. Those chiefly responsible were genuinely ashamed of what happened and one by one proffered sheepish apologies to me in the days after the trial. Whether or not the Metro-Vickers firm was implicated in a plot, there was at least a full-sized plot among the Anglo-American correspondents.

Through a few lucky accidents, and perhaps because I was able to follow the testimony without benefit of interpreters, I had scored a long series of scoops. In England, where the British

United Press was distributing my dispatches, I had been pretty consistently ahead of Reuters. Although Reuters had sent in a brilliant journalist, John Fleming (brother of the much-traveled Peter Fleming), he was at a disadvantage because of language barriers and lack of familiarity with the Soviet scene. In any case, my puny triumphs had gotten under the skin of immediate competitors to an extent that I never suspected.

Came the night of the verdict. The judges were deliberating. It was the last lap in our absurd race against time—speed in flashing the verdict was of immense importance to every one of us. In the lobby I noticed the American and English reporters whispering mysteriously. Never suspecting that the whispering had any relation to my humble self, I approached. Complete and embarrassed silence . . . Late that night the judges filed in. We were tensed to act on the verdict, like runners waiting for the pistol shot.

I had made no special arrangements for the final dispatch, knowing from past experience that there were no short-cuts. But instead of remaining in the courtroom, I waited in the censors' room, listening to the proceedings through a pair of earphones. As soon as the verdict was announced, I scribbled it on a cable blank; Billy took it down to our chauffeur who rushed it to the cable office.

It was only later, over highballs at the National bar, that I learned of the plot against me. That afternoon there had been a council of war in a hotel room, with all the agency representatives and most of the special correspondents present. A solemn decision was reached to "gang up" on the United Press, which had had too many scoops to be permitted the final coup. All of them, it was decided, would work together to defeat Lyons.

All contingencies were discussed and arranged for. The verdict would be relayed from the court to the corridor. Even the time for running downstairs would be saved—envelopes weighted with sand were prepared and they would be thrown from the window to conspirators waiting on the sidewalk. A telephone line would be kept open between the courthouse and the telegraph building, with a conspirator stationed at either end. Another would take instant possession of the second phone. Everything was prepared for the collective defeat of my unsuspecting self.

At the last moment, of course, everything went wrong. The

window jammed. The telephone connection was cut off. An incoming call from London tied up the second phone. The collapse of the strategy meant a last-minute scramble, every man for himself, with consequent loss of time. By a fluke of luck, that incoming call was for a Russian secretary covering the trial on the side for a minor British agency, and he was able to beat us all. I was second, by a good fat margin on all the others. In America, I was first. Without any special effort—helped rather than hindered by the plot—I had beaten the gang.

At the bar a few hours later I could not resist exhibiting a batch of congratulatory messages, specifying the time by which I had scooped Reuters in London and the opposition agencies in America. The conspirators looked at one another, shook their heads sadly, and proceeded to disclose the plot that failed. I had not the slightest hesitancy in standing drinks on that story.

All but one of the Russians were given prison sentences. Thornton and MacDonald received three- and two-year terms, respectively. Gregory was acquitted and the other three were condemned to expulsion from the country. To millions of Russians whose supreme dream was escape from the country, that "punishment" must have sounded slightly bizarre.

Dictatorship under an infallible leader calls for a system of scapegoats. Between the first and the last demonstration trials that I attended, the Shakhty case and the Metro-Vickers case, I saw that system shaped toward perfection. Pre-revolutionary engineers, professors, Mensheviks, foreign technicians had been condemned and punished to explain difficulties, but the difficulties were not thereby ended. Not even those among us who were most critical of the sacrificial rites would have guessed that the system would be refined further, to the point where by 1936-37 it was destroying revolutionary military heroes and the fathers of the Bolshevik revolution themselves.

XV. The Press Corps Conceals a Famine

"THERE is no actual starvation or deaths from starvation but there is widespread mortality from diseases due to malnutrition."

This amazing sophistry, culled from a New York *Times* Moscow dispatch on March 30, 1933, has become among foreign reporters the classic example of journalistic understatement. It characterizes sufficiently the whole shabby episode of our failure to report honestly the gruesome Russian famine of 1932-33.

The circumstance that the government barred us from the afflicted regions may serve as our formal excuse. But a deaf-and-dumb reporter hermetically sealed in a hotel room could not have escaped knowledge of the essential facts. Reporting, as we did daily, industrial victories in the Baikal region or Tajikistan without personal investigation, we had small warrant for withholding and minimizing and diluting the famine story because we were prohibited to make personal investigation. Whatever doubts as to the magnitude of the disaster may have lingered in our minds, the prohibition itself should have set at rest.

The episode, indeed, reflects little glory on world journalism as a whole. Not a single American newspaper or press agency protested publicly against the astonishing and almost unprecedented confinement of its correspondent in the Soviet capital or troubled to probe for the causes of this extraordinary measure.

The New York *Times,* as the foremost American newspaper, is automatically selected for investigation in any test of American reporting. But it was certainly not alone in concealing the famine. The precious sentence quoted above was prefaced with its correspondent's celebrated cliche: "To put it brutally—you can't make an omelette without breaking eggs." A later dispatch enlarged upon the masterpiece of understatement and indicated how the eggs were being broken. Asserting that "in some districts and among the large floating population of unskilled labor" there "have been deaths and actual starvation," he catalogued the maladies of malnutrition as "typhus, dysentery, dropsy, and various infantile diseases." The maladies, in short, that always rage in time of famine.

Not until August 23 did the *Times* out of Moscow admit the famine. "It is conservative to suppose," it said, that in certain provinces with a total population of over 40,000,000 mortality has "at least trebled." On this basis, there were two million deaths more than usual. In addition, deaths were also "considerably increased for the Soviet Union as a whole." This dispatch came one day behind an uncensored cable to the New York *Herald Tribune* by Ralph Barnes, in which he placed the deaths in his ultra-conservative fashion at no less than one million. The Barnes story was front-paged and the *Times* could no longer ignore the subject. Its own admission followed, raising Barnes' ante. By a singular twist of logic, the *Times* story introduced the admission of famine with this remarkable statement:

> Any report of a famine in Russia is today an exaggeration or malignant propaganda. The food shortage which has affected almost the whole population in the last year and particularly in the grain-producing provinces—the Ukraine, North Caucasus, the lower Volga region—has, however, caused heavy loss of life.

The dividing line between "heavy loss of life" through food shortage and "famine" is rather tenuous. Such verbal finessing made little difference to the millions of dead and dying, to the refugees who knocked at our doors begging bread, to the lines of ragged peasants stretching from Torgsin doors in the famine area waiting to exchange their wedding rings and silver trinkets for bread.

These philological sophistries, to which we were all driven, served Moscow's purpose of smearing the facts out of recognition and beclouding a situation which, had we reported it simply and clearly, might have worked up enough public opinion abroad to force remedial measures. And every correspondent, each in his own measure, was guilty of collaborating in this monstrous hoax on the world. Maurice Hindus, though among the most industrious apologists for Stalin, was kept waiting nearly a month for a visa during the famine and finally was admitted on condition that he should not go outside of Moscow. During his 1933 visit, therefore, he did not go to his native village as in the past. In his books, articles and lectures, curiously, he does not allude to that enforced omission and its causes.

The very next day after the *Times'* half-hearted admission from Moscow, its representative in Berlin, Frederick T. Birchall, talked to a group of foreigners just returned from the famine territory, among them a reputable American. "The revelations of what they have seen in the last few weeks," Birchall cabled, "indicate that the recent estimate of four million deaths due indirectly to malnutrition in agricultural Russia in recent months may be rather an understatement than an exaggeration." The word "malnutrition" had, by dint of repetition, taken hold even outside Russia—a clean triumph for planned censorship.

All of us had talked with people just returned from the famine regions. Jack Calder, as honest a man as ever drew a Soviet paycheck, returned from a long tour of Kazakstan with stories to curdle one's blood. Perched on a high stool at the Metropole valuta bar, we listened to his graphic description of Kazakstan roads lined with stiff corpses like so many logs. Most of us saw the pictures taken by German consular officials in the Ukraine showing scenes of horror reminiscent of the Volga famine of 1921. Few of us were so completely isolated that we did not meet Russians whose work took them to the devastated areas, or Muscovites with relatives in those areas. Around every railroad station in the capital hundreds of bedraggled refugees were encamped, had we needed further corroboration; they gathered faster than the police could clear them away.

The truth is that we did not seek corroboration for the simple reason that we entertained no doubts on the subject. There are facts too large to require eyewitness confirmation—facts so pervasive and generally accepted that confirmation would be futile pedantry. There was no more need for investigation to establish the mere existence of the Russian famine than investigation to establish the existence of the American depression. Inside Russia the matter was not disputed. The famine was accepted as a matter of course in our casual conversation at the hotels and in our homes. In the foreign colony estimates of famine deaths ranged from one million up; among Russians from three millions up. Russians, especially communists, were inclined to cite higher figures through a sort of perverse pride in bigness; if it called for Bolshevik firmness to let a million die, it obviously called for three times as much firmness to kill off three million. . . .

The first reliable report of the Russian famine was given to the world by an English journalist, a certain Gareth Jones, at one time secretary to Lloyd George. Jones had a conscientious streak in his make-up which took him on a secret journey into the Ukraine and a brief walking tour through its countryside. That same streak was to take him a few years later into the interior of China during political disturbances, and was to cost him his life at the hands of Chinese military bandits. An earnest and meticulous little man, Gareth Jones was the sort who carries a note-book and unashamedly records your words as you talk. Patiently he went from one correspondent to the next, asking questions and writing down the answers.

On emerging from Russia, Jones made a statement which, startling though it sounded, was little more than a summary of what the correspondents and foreign diplomats had told him. To protect us, and perhaps with some idea of heightening the authenticity of his reports, he emphasized his Ukrainian foray rather than our conversation as the chief source of his information.

In any case, we all received urgent queries from our home offices on the subject. But the inquiries coincided with preparations under way for the trial of the British engineers. The need to remain on friendly terms with the censors at least for the duration of the trial was for all of us a compelling professional necessity.

Throwing down Jones was as unpleasant a chore as fell to any of us in years of juggling facts to please dictatorial regimes—but throw him down we did, unanimously and in almost identical formulas of equivocation. Poor Gareth Jones must have been the most surprised human being alive when the facts he so painstakingly garnered from our mouths were snowed under by our denials.

The scene in which the American press corps combined to repudiate Jones is fresh in my mind. It was in the evening and Comrade Umansky, the soul of graciousness, consented to meet us in the hotel room of a correspondent. He knew that he had a strategic advantage over us because of the Metro-Vickers story. He could afford to be gracious. Forced by competitive journalism to jockey for the inside track with officials, it would have been professional suicide to make an issue of the famine at this particular time. There was much bargaining in a spirit of gentlemanly give-and-take, under the effulgence of Umansky's gilded smile, before a formula of denial was worked out.

We admitted enough to soothe our consciences, but in roundabout phrases that damned Jones as a liar. The filthy business having been disposed of, someone ordered vodka and *zakuski*, Umansky joined the celebration, and the party did not break up until the early morning hours. The head censor was in a mellower mood than I had ever seen him before or since. He had done a big bit for Bolshevik firmness that night.

We were summoned to the Press Department one by one and instructed not to venture out of Moscow without submitting a detailed itinerary and having it officially sanctioned. In effect, therefore, we were summarily deprived of the right of unhampered travel in the country to which we were accredited.

"This is nothing new," Umansky grimaced uncomfortably. "Such a rule has been in existence since the beginning of the revolution. Now we have decided to enforce it."

New or old, such a rule had not been invoked since the civil war days. It was forgotten again when the famine was ended. Its undisguised purpose was to keep us out of the stricken regions. The same department which daily issued denials of the famine now acted to prevent us from seeing that famine with our own eyes. Our brief cables about this desperate measure of concealment were published, if at all, in some obscure corner of the paper. The world press accepted with complete equanimity the virtual expulsion of all its representatives from all of Russia except Moscow. It agreed without protest to a partnership in the macabre hoax.

Other steps were taken to prevent prying. Until then, foreigners arriving at the frontier received their passports as soon as the train got under way. Now the passports were retained by the authorities until just before the train pulled into Moscow—thus guaranteeing that no foreigner would drop off en route for unchaperoned research.

When M. Herriot, the liberal French statesman, arrived in Russia at Odessa, the one French correspondent in the country,

M. Lusiani, demanded the right to meet him. The Press Department finally gave its permission—on Lusiani's solemn undertaking to remain with the official party and not to stray into the countryside. M. Herriot, conducted along the prescribed road between Odessa and Moscow, completely surrounded by high functionaries, was able to say honestly when he returned to Paris that he had not personally seen any famine. Neither had Lusiani.

2

I was not the first Moscow observer to remark that God seems to be on the side of the atheists. What the Kremlin would have prayed for, had it believed in prayer, was perfect weather, and that is what it received that spring and summer: perfect weather and bumper crops. The fields had been planted under the aegis of the newly established *Politotdyels* (Political Departments) with unlimited authority over the peasants. Food rations barely sufficient to sustain life had been distributed only to those actually at work in the fields. Red Army detachments in many places had been employed to guard seed and to prevent hungry peasants from devouring the green shoots of the new harvest. In the midst of the famine, the planting proceeded, and the crops came up strong and plenteous. The dead were buried—for the living there would be bread enough and to spare in the following winter.

Belatedly the world had awakened to the famine situation. We were able to write honestly that "to speak of famine *now* is ridiculous." We did not always bother to add that we had failed to speak of it or at best mumbled incomprehensibly *then*, when it was not ridiculous. Cardinal Innitzer, Archbishop of Vienna, made the first of his sensational statements about Soviet agrarian conditions on August 20, when those conditions were already being mitigated. Certain anti-Soviet newspapers in England and America began to write about the famine at about the time it was ended, and continued to write about it long after it had become history: their facts were on the whole correct, but their tenses were badly mixed. The most rigorous censorship in all of Soviet Russia's history had been successful—it had concealed the catastrophe until it was ended, thereby bringing confusion, doubt, contradiction into the whole subject. Years after the event—when no Russian communist in his senses any longer concealed the magnitude of the famine—the question whether there had been a famine at all was still being disputed in the outside world!

In the autumn, the Soviet press was exultant. Lazar Kaganovich was given most of the credit for the successful harvest. It was his mind that invented the Political Departments to lead collectivized agriculture, his iron hand that applied Bolshevik mercilessness. Now that a healing flood of grain was inundating the famished land, the secrecy gradually gave way. Increasingly with every passing month Russian officials ceased to deny the obvious. Soviet journalists who had been in the afflicted areas now told me personally such details of the tragedy as not even the eager imaginations of Riga and Warsaw journalists had been able to project. They were able to speak in the past tense, so that their accents were proud boasts rather than admissions.

The Kremlin, in short, had "gotten away with it." At a cost in millions of lives, through the instrumentalities of hunger and terror, socialized agriculture had been made to yield an excellent harvest. Certain observers now insisted in print that the efficacy of collectivization had been demonstrated; nothing, of course, had been demonstrated except the efficacy of concentrated force used against a population demoralized by protracted hunger.

There were few peasant homes in the worst of the famine districts which had not paid a toll in life for this harvest. In hundreds of villages half the population was gone: some had been killed by the "diseases of malnutrition" and others had fled to seek food. In September and October, Chamberlin, Duranty, and others who visited southern Russia still found half-deserted villages. It would be years before the memory of this fearful time would lose its poignancy in the Ukraine and North Caucasus, in Kazakstan and Lower Volga. And there were those who believed, as I did, that the memory was indelible and would rise to plague those who had decided in cold blood to let the villages starve. But in the cities, at least, a new optimism was born.

The attitude of the professional friends of the U.S.S.R. on the famine went through a curious cycle. First, while the disaster was under way, they made furious denials. Since then, they have tended to admit the facts but to explain them away as unavoidable, and as a just and proper punishment meted out to a "rebellious" peasantry. "Why harp on something that is by now history?" sums up their reproachful objection to a reminder of the period. But all great social crimes, given time, become history. By that fantastic logic, time has wiped out the guilt of those who perpetrated the Inquisition and the St. Bartholomew's Night massacres, the World War and the fascist destruction of Vienna's socialist housing, the Reichstag fire and the fascist attack on democratic government in Spain. The Kremlin had foreseen the famine and permitted it to run its course of death and horror for political reasons. The philosophy which made such a decision possible, the mad arrogance of rulers condemning millions to death, are not justified by the fact that the dead are buried and the survivors being fed.

How many millions actually died will never be known accurately. It is not generally understood abroad that the Soviet government *stopped the publication of vital statistics for the period in question*, although such statistics were published as a matter of routine in previous years; otherwise it would be a simple matter to compare the death-rate for the winter and spring of 1932-33 with the normal death-rate.

Estimates made by foreigners and Russians range from three to seven millions. Chamberlin, after his journey through the devastated districts, described in detail in his *Russia's Iron Age*, placed the cost in life at four million. Duranty, after a similar journey, withdrew his previous estimate that the death-rate had increased threefold as far as the North Caucasus was concerned but stated that "he is inclined to believe that the estimate he made for the Ukraine was too low." A more than trebled death-rate in the Ukraine would bring the famine deaths in that one area alone to a million and a half. Maurice Hindus, after years of vagueness on the subject, finally settled on "at least three million" as his estimate.

Southern Russia, after many months of total news blockade, was opened to foreign correspondents in easy stages. The first to be given permission to travel in the forbidden zones were the technically "friendly" reporters, whose dispatches might be counted upon to take the sting out of anything subsequent travelers might report. Duranty, for instance, was given a two weeks' advantage over most of us. On the day he returned, it happened, Billy and I were dining with Anne O'Hare McCormick, roving correspondent for the New York *Times*, and her husband. Duranty joined us. He gave us his fresh impressions in brutally frank terms and they added up to a picture of ghastly horror. His estimate of the dead from famine was the most startling I had as yet heard from anyone.

"But, Walter, you don't mean that literally?" Mrs. McCormick exclaimed.

"Hell I don't. . . . I'm being conservative," he replied, and as if by way of consolation he added his famous truism: "But they're only Russians. . . ."

Once more the same evening we heard Duranty make the same estimate, in answer to a question by Laurence Stallings, at the railroad station, just as the train was pulling out for the Polish frontier. When the issues of the *Times* carrying Duranty's own articles reached me I found that they failed to mention the large figures he had given freely and repeatedly to all of us.

XVI. Forebodings

LIKE the proverbial candle about to expire, my reputation in official eyes flared up again brightly before it was snuffed out utterly. My attitude toward the trial of the Britons threatened briefly to restore me to the good graces of the Soviet powers. Almost alone among the Anglo-American reporters I had taken an undeviating stand on the right of the Soviet government to try foreigners accused of crimes within its frontiers. London's peremptory demands for immediate surrender of its citizens seemed to me to smack of extraterritoriality. The trial itself, at least as far as it applied to the accused foreigners, seemed to me a closer approximation of justice than any previous demonstration trial.

Outwardly correct, the British Embassy crowd soon made me feel that my point of view was not to its liking. Certain of the Embassy officials were outspoken in their criticism of my dispatches, which were being widely used throughout the British Empire. I was permitted to attend the general press conferences but carefully excluded from the more intimate Embassy gatherings. I was never invited, for instance, to lunch with the defendants between sessions as were several other Americans and all the British reporters.

Soon after the trial, several communist friends brought me the same message in almost the same words. Government circles, they said in mysterious undertones, were fully cognizant of the British hostility toward me and greatly impressed with my handling of the trial. Comrade Umansky himself began to look at me less venomously. Everyone was in a mood to forgive past recalcitrance; they were only watching to see whether the change was permanent or a passing whim.

Let no one suppose that official favor is a small thing in the atmosphere of an authoritarian state. In a hundred ways life becomes simplified, mellowed, warmed by an inner sense of strength. Over and above the physical and professional advantages is the feeling of being integral with power. Think of the glow in which Americans who have made themselves spokesmen for the Soviets to their countrymen march through each day, feeling themselves monitors of communist respectability. Think of their heart-warming illusion, as they join the political shop-talk of local pomposities, that they are in some measure architects of a new world.

The real medium of exchange in Moscow, buying that which neither rubles nor dollars can touch, was power. And power meant Comrade Stalin, Comrade Umansky, the virtuoso of *kombinatsya*, the fellow whose uncle's best friend has a cousin on the collegium of the G.P.U. To be invited to exclusive social functions, to play bridge with the big-bugs, to be patted on the back editorially by *Pravda*, to have the social ambitions of one's wife flattered: such inducements are more effective in bridling a correspondent's tongue than any threats. The sense of importance that comes with being accepted tacitly as an accredited interpreter for an entire government weighs heavily in the scales of mundane judgment in deciding how to phrase an embarrassing piece of news or whether to transmit it all. By the same token, the consciousness of being rejected by the new environment (and dictatorial governments are past masters in the art of salting the wounds of ostracism) is not easy to bear.

Whether in Moscow or Berlin, Tokyo or Rome, all the temptations for the practicing foreign reporter are in the direction of conformity. It is more comfortable and in the long run more profitable to soft-pedal a dispatch for readers thousands of miles away than to face an irate censor and closed official doors. The simplest formula for judging contradictory information sent by any two correspondents from a dictated capital is this: The correspondent less "friendly" to the ruling group, less eager to give the dictators the benefit of every doubt, is likely to be more dependable. There may be exceptions to this rule, of course. But there can be no doubt that every leverage of self-interest works in the dictators' favor.

It would be useless to pretend that such considerations had no effect upon me. If anywhere in these pages I have unwittingly implied that my armor of righteousness was impervious, I renounce the implication. The sudden easing of tension in my relations with the authorities was more than welcome. If I relapsed again all too quickly into waywardness it was despite myself. Some pestiferous element in my make-up—call it a social conscience or some less polite name—led me astray. Instead of resting content with the manicured mendacities provided in daily instalments by the press, it incited me to probe precisely where probing was *verboten*.

And I did probe assiduously. Of necessity I remained cautious and diplomatic in my writing, but I stored up forbidden knowledge. I managed to talk at length with people who had spent many years in prison camps and "isolators." From eyewitnesses I garnered details of the horrors in famine areas. From heartsore communists I learned the magnitude and depth of the shams and fears and toe-licking sycophancy that soiled the inner life of the ruling Party.

I had shed the last of the veils of political inhibition in searching out the facts behind the formulas. In retrospect I now recognized how painstakingly I had fooled myself in the earlier years —how I had been wont to take long detours in my observations and longer ones in my thinking to avoid truths that hurt too much. The need for evasion to spare my own feelings had fallen away.

Increasingly I sensed the strength of the underground currents directed against the government; not the monarchists or Mensheviks or vengeful kulaks of the editorials but communists and ex-communists were the people whom these currents touched. Unorganized, isolated, desperately afraid, they were conscious, all the same, that they were not alone. In meeting communists I could often sense whether their basic loyalties were toward the revolution as such or toward the Kremlin clique on whom their jobs depended.

In America in the following years, watching the process of the liquidation of the revolution, I was not surprised, therefore, to find that those told off by the Kremlin for destruction were almost all communists. The process, first unmistakably manifest in the abolition of the Society of Old Bolsheviks, led inevitably to the physical annihilation of most of the remaining leaders of the 1917 revolution. It led to the purging of the G.P.U. of the "Chekist" elements, whose psychological commitments were to the original revolution rather than to the present incumbents of the Kremlin. It led to the killing off of military leaders whose careers stemmed from the pre-Stalin years.

These things were still in the future. But sensing them as I did, a genuine reconciliation with the powers-that-be was out of the question.

2

Karl Bickel, President of the United Press, arrived for his second visit to Russia during my incumbency. Fully aware of the hardships of covering a "beat" like mine, he seemed on the whole perturbed by the change that had come into his correspondent's relations with the Soviet authorities since his visit four years earlier. The first and irreducible need of a press agency is for the most cordial relations possible with all governments. An individual newspaper might refuse to play with obdurate dictatorships, but an agency cannot afford the luxury of independence. It must accept the rules of the game set by a Mussolini or Hitler or Stalin, since it must cover the entire map all the time. It is geared, moreover, for instantaneous reporting in which a margin of a few minutes is of crucial competitive importance. If that margin must be paid for with an occasional reticence, the price does not seem unreasonable.

Americans who suppose that editors are inclined to cheer their correspondents in the fearless pursuit of truth have a naively idyllic view of modern journalism. They forget that the principal commodity of the newspaper is news, not truth, and the two do not always coincide. A newspaperman with a crusading streak will soon be out of a job. The correspondent who gets himself expelled or even disliked for talking out of turn puts his employers to great expense and, more important, endangers their sources of information.

Bickel realized that I was no longer happy on my Moscow post. He realized, too, that the man who survives six years under a dictatorship without becoming a messenger boy for the ruling dynasty has something of an achievement to his credit. He sounded out whether I was interested in taking over the management of the Tokyo Bureau; but the Tokyo assignment at the time called for more executive work than straight reporting, and I declined the tentative offer.

Bickel was one of those rare press agency titans with a genuine interest in world affairs aside from their commercial value as news.

A thoroughgoing liberal by nature, the Russian revolution touched his imagination from the very beginning. He watched its evolution with sympathy which often bordered on enthusiasm. On this visit, too, he was indefatigable in gathering views and facts. The interview that impressed him most was with Karl Radek, the Puck of the communist revolution. We remained with Radek in his penthouse home overlooking the Moscow river for more than an hour. The conversation ranged freely in time and space. The scope of Radek's information was little short of miraculous: he could discuss the local politics of Chicago with as intimate knowledge as the politics of Moscow. There was a gargoyle quality in Radek's face, a sort of fascinating ugliness. His features, in a frame of unkempt brownish hair, seemed curiously out of focus; his teeth charred and uneven; his eyes very much alive behind thick glasses, like frisky pups behind plate glass. Aside from his looks, Radek's personality was memorable not because of his astonishing erudition but because that erudition was coupled with a sparkling sense of humor. We left his presence feeling as though we had watched a one-man circus crowded with incredible feats of intellectual agility.

The larger part of that summer I spent with my family in San Remo, soaking in Italian sunshine. This time we took Genie back to Moscow with us. The school in which she had spent four years was still permitted by the Hitler dictatorship to carry on, but only after its progressive tradition of several generations had been crushed. After some investigation we placed Genie in one of Moscow's model schools, on Pimenovsky Pereulok, where the two young children of Stalin were her schoolmates.

The modernistic experiments in education which had won the hearts of the John Deweys had by this time been thrown out. The children now sat with their hands behind their backs, took regular examinations, and concentrated on the three R's. The classrooms —fifty to sixty pupils to one teacher—reminded me of my own elementary school days in New York thirty years before: from an extreme of Daltonesque modernism the Soviet school system had apparently swung to the opposite extreme of stodginess.

Genie's celebrity in the school overshadowed that of the Stalin children. She was an *Amerikanka,* from the fabulous land of skyscrapers and wondrous machines on the other side of the world—her foreign clothes, her outlandish accent, her long Germanic braids, and straight long-limbed loveliness endlessly exciting to her classmates. Our daughter's scrambled American-German-Russian education worked havoc with her curriculum, but it enriched her mind far beyond the average child's, and physically she had developed into a tall, graceful and finely coördinated specimen of girlhood.

3

I sloshed through the October muds of Leningrad, from institute to institute and museum to museum, interviewing bearded professors and moth-eaten curators and eager young people who talked even of paleozoic fossils in terms of the *Piatiletka.*

I had undertaken the ambitious job of a journalistic survey of scientific research in progress and found that the center of gravity in this domain was located in the old capital, where the Academy of Science had its headquarters, where the venerable Professor Pavlov conducted his experiments in conditioned reflexes. Perhaps because I was concentrating my attention on museums and laboratories, the curious illusion grew upon me that the whole city was a sort of museum and laboratory combined. Social experiment and vivisection amidst the petrified remnants of the old life. The battered survivors of the *ancien régime* seemed more in evidence in this city which had been the center of fashion and power than in the Soviet capital. The spires of Peter and Paul, the majestic Neva, the brackish canals, the old official buildings in pastel shades, had failed somehow to adjust themselves to the new life.

My mind was now made up to leave Russia as soon as I could. The feeling that I was seeing Leningrad for the last time gave the crowded visit an emotional obbligato. Billy and I took in the theaters and ballet and dined at the Hotel Astoria, which was to Leningrad what the Metropole was to Moscow: a fake-bourgeois retreat from the Soviet world. An extraterritorial jazz band filled the tinselly restaurant with strange versions of Western dance music and self-conscious Russians fox-trotted and blackbottomed jerkily in a style all their own. Waiters of pre-revolutionary vintage in soiled jackets showed an archaic obsequiousness to valuta customers. The furtive desperation that made the counterfeit gaiety of the Metropole so pathetic was even more poignant here.

A few old-world creatures sat uneasily in the deepest corners, as though poised for flight at the first sign of danger; museum pieces, they seemed, of another epoch.

A good deal of this haunting and slightly tragic museum quality attached to the palatial home of Alexei Tolstoy, the great novelist, at Dyetskoye Selo. Almost alone among Russians, Tolstoy lived in baronial style in a rambling many-roomed old mansion stocked with rich antiques. Around his table, the night we visited him, were some thirty people, and there was little in the snow-white embroidered linens, the silverware, the crystal, the many vintages and abundant food to remind one of the clamorous slogans and liquidations outside. Tolstoy himself, fat and expansively hospitable, looking a little like G. K. Chesterton, seemed an old-fashioned *barin* out of Turgenyev's pages, surrounded by his family and guests and retainers. The conversation, the musicale after the dinner, the whole atmosphere of ripe old-world culture seemed a throw-back to a nearly forgotten period. In his work-room upstairs, that nostalgic character was even more distinct. A death-mask of Peter the Great (one of three such masks in existence) struck the keynote in an ivory tower seemingly remote in time and space from the raucous Soviet existence—a chamber spacious, mellowed, insulated; a window set into the angle of a gable framed an immemorial Russian winter scene of huddled cottages and church cupolas.

"This," he said, "is where I work on my trilogy on the life of Peter. One of my ancestors, you know, was a power in Peter's court."

Returning far past midnight from the Tolstoy mansion, the crisp snow crunching under the wheels of an Astoria Hotel valuta car, I felt as though I had visited a perfectly preserved section of Nineteenth Century Russia.

Leningrad is a city of lurid memories. This swampland turned into a modern city by the ferocious will of one Asiatic despot, the flesh and blood of a hundred thousand serfs kneaded into its foundations, has known more of orgy and extravagance, of autocratic blood-letting and popular fury, than the rest of the country put together. The name of Lenin has been pasted on it, but it is still essentially the city of the fabulous Peter, that savage in Western garb. Under the drabness of the city's latest incarnation there is a teeming ghost world of purple and crimson shadows. Exploring its by-ways, strolling along its embankments, inspecting the dungeons under the old fortress, I had the sense of nearness to the past—the feeling that the Soviet episode is but a moment in the long life of Peter's hand-tooled capital.

My scientific prowling was cut short by an urgent summons from Moscow. President Roosevelt had invited President Kalinin to discuss the resumption of diplomatic relations between their governments and I had to take the next train back to Moscow. The hasty retreat from Leningrad meant the cancellation of an interview scheduled with the "Stalin of the North," Sergei Kirov, a member of the Politburo and one of the strong men of the ruling Party. Kirov had never been interviewed; few foreigners had even seen him. He had promised to receive me in the next few days. A year later, when Kirov was killed by a young communist, I had additional cause to regret the chance that had deprived me of a close-up view of the man.

The establishment of diplomatic relations with the United States was the consummation of the Soviet Union's most cherished political dream. Regardless what we felt about Soviet internal affairs, we were gratified by this sensible American move. Anything which helped to break down Russia's isolation, which made the Kremlin more concerned with the public opinion of the outside world, seemed to me urgently desirable from the vantage point of the Russian masses. The deeper Russia was driven into its own Asiatic skin, the less hope there seemed to me of salvaging the gains of the revolution.

For the American colony in Moscow, and for the correspondents in particular, there were rounds of receptions, interviews with Soviet leaders, a new friendliness. But personally I knew that my assignment was nearing its close. With recognition, a quiet but persistent purge of "recalcitrant" American correspondents was in the cards. Practically all the American newspapermen in Moscow—Chamberlin, Barnes, Wells, Stanley Richardson, myself—were destined to leave, for one reason or another, in the months after the Soviet-American *rapprochement.* Those who came to take their place could know the horrors of the "Iron Age" only at second hand.

BOOK 5

REDEDICATION

I. My Recall from Moscow

IN THOSE narrow circles in America where purblind Soviet fanaticism feeds upon self-deception, every defection from the ranks of the faithful is instantly matched by a standardized explanation. It is simpler and psychologically more satisfying to annihilate the critic than to deal with his criticism.

For years the *Christian Science Monitor* representative, Chamberlin, was held in high esteem in those circles. When he turned critical, an easy explanation was hatched by alarmed American believers. The story was spread industriously that he had been misled by the Russian Princess to whom he was married. The "princess" was only a New York schoolteacher of Russian-Jewish extraction whom Chamberlin married before he went to Russia, but fables are more stubborn things than facts.

"Unfriendly" reports by correspondents were explained airily on the basis of economic determinism—hirelings of the kept press doing the bidding of their capitalist masters. But "friendly" reports by no less capitalistic reporters were exempted from this Marxist law.

Every returning engineer who hinted that all was not rose-tinted in the land of Soviets was obviously an incompetent giving vent to his private grudges. But engineers who joined in the hallelujahs at Friends of the U.S.S.R. banquets, though they were making fortunes out of Soviet contracts, were high-minded gentry in no wise affected by crass considerations of self-interest.

Around my own recall from Moscow, and my decline from official grace, that inclement fanaticism has woven a dark saga of intricate absurdity. Years after the event, new fantasies continued to be embroidered on the somber fabric. Ever so often the echoes of some new and more extravagant fable reached me, by way of accounting for my views on the Bolshevik land. Such legendry thrives on its own grotesqueness, each new absurdity sprouting a dozen sustaining absurdities in the hopeless groping for the foundation that is not there.

The American move for recognition of the U.S.S.R., toward the end of 1933, it was generally assumed in both Washington and Moscow, was motivated in large measure by President Roosevelt's anxiety over the war danger in the Far East. It was felt that a sign of American friendship would act as a brake on the ambitions of the Japanese military party. The Soviet press made all the political capital it could out of the impending Russian-American *rapprochement*. The United States was pictured as a great peace-loving republic which, with the sturdy Soviet republic by its side, would help preserve international peace.

The world at this time seethed with talk of war in the Far East. Huge armies were deployed on both sides of the Soviet-Manchurian frontier, and mutual charges of violating that frontier flew like sparks from the respective capitals. All the tinder was piled up for a conflagration and any one of those sparks might ignite a war. Border incidents with loss of life were taking place constantly, and it was an open secret that some of those clashes were more serious than the press dared reveal.

Early in November the Soviet press charged Japanese war planes with flying over the Soviet border. Tokyo papers countered with similar charges against Russian planes. Probably both sides were telling the truth; it was only to be expected that each army would reconnoiter the other's terrain, at the risk of being shot down as intruders. There were also charges of equivalent violations on the rivers and the sea. Tokyo talked of Soviet coastal batteries having fired on Japanese fishing trawlers. Despite the formal denials, Russians close to military affairs chuckled knowingly; the "fishing trawlers," they hinted, were disguised naval reconnoitering parties and they only got what was coming to them.

The annual November parade in Moscow was, more than ever before, a pointed military demonstration, climaxed by an unprecedented turn-out of war planes that blackened the skies over Red Square. Instinctively, all of us on the reviewing stands turned our eyes toward the Japanese military and naval attachés as the planes roared overhead, and the Soviet newsreels a few days later cut in significant glimpses of these foreign observers as the tanks and cavalry divisions and airplanes were shown.

At the formal reception to the diplomats and correspondents on the evening of November 7, at the Spasso-Peskovsky palace that later became the American Embassy, the whispered talk revolved around the dangerous situation in the Far East. Several diplomatic acquaintances spoke to me of the reports going the rounds about serious incidents in the Far East.

It was at this reception, incidentally, that I first met Alexander Troyanovsky. When I confronted him with the news that he was scheduled to go to Washington as his country's first Ambassador, the tone of his denial only confirmed the correctness of my information. That very evening I cabled that Alexander Troyanovsky was the likely choice for Washington, pointing out the fact that his long experience in Tokyo gave a fine political point to his choice.

Litvinov had left for the United States, accompanied by several other officials, among them Comrade Umansky. For reasons that surpassed our understanding, or possibly from an ingrained habit of mystery, their departure was treated as a major state secret. The entire press corps was therefore on the station to watch them going off. Umansky, characteristically, went out of his way to throw us off his trail, under a comic illusion that his movements were of international moment. At a banquet given by Intourist, he took the trouble to announce publicly that he was on his way to Spain, so that no one was surprised when he showed up in New York.

On the evening of November 9, I had several guests at my home, among them a Japanese newspaperman. Inevitably the Far Eastern incidents—particularly the airplane and fishing vessels episodes—were mentioned. No one doubted the authenticity of the reports, least of all my Japanese colleague. His attitude suggested, indeed, that he knew more about it than he cared to discuss. I did not dream of cabling those reports, of course.

Several days later, I was preparing to go to a concert. Just then two Russian friends, both of whom I knew to be well connected in the higher circles of the G.P.U., arrived for an unexpected visit. I told Billy to go on to the concert alone, while I entertained the guests. Even today, when the whole strange business is surely known to the Soviet authorities in its minutest details, I am inhibited against using the names of these guests. I shall refer to them as Ivanov and Petrov.

They were both in exceptionally gay spirits—not a little heightened, it is true, by vodka. I inquired the cause of their exalted mood and they proceeded to tell me, interrupting one another to add gleeful details to the recital. Their hilarity, it seemed, derived from the stinging lesson their military forces had given to Japanese intruders in Soviet territory in recent weeks.

"The sons of she-dogs will be more careful about poking around where they're not wanted," Ivanov exclaimed.

And Petrov, slapping his thighs and smacking his lips, confirmed this conviction. Between them they presented me in startling detail a complete account of the two Far Eastern episodes that were being so widely discussed in the capital. Japanese bombing planes which had penetrated far into Siberian territory had been shot down by Soviet anti-aircraft batteries. Prowling Japanese naval boats had been destroyed by the coast guards. They even described how the Japanese bodies removed from the airplane wreckage had been returned to the Manchurian side.

I never doubted the truth of their stories. Everything they said fitted perfectly into what I had heard elsewhere. They provided the missing pieces for the jigsaw puzzle of reports and rumors. But I wondered why they were speaking to a correspondent so freely and fully on a matter of grave international importance. Not in all my Soviet years had critical information been conveyed to me by responsible communists quite so candidly.

"This is sensational news you are giving me," I said; "aren't you afraid I might use it? You've confirmed what many of the correspondents have picked up in the last few days from other sources. You know, it's a great temptation to cable the story. . . ."

Normally, the hint of publication gives Soviet citizens the jitters. Neither Ivanov nor Petrov, however, bothered to caution me against using their information. On the contrary, even after I suggested that I might do so, they continued to add color to the picture. Afterwards, when I became the center of a major scandal, the foreign colony, including most of the American correspondents, were convinced that I had been "framed." Possibly I allowed myself naively to be taken in. The simple fact is that I got the specific impression that *they wanted me to send the story of the Far Eastern incidents,* that their primary purpose in visiting me that evening was to encourage me to send this news.

It seemed to me logical at the moment, moreover, that Moscow should want these incidents known to the outside world. The tension in the Far East was one of Litvinov's best cards in his negotiations with Roosevelt. Obviously, I thought, Moscow wants this story sent in order to impress Americans with the seriousness of the Far Eastern situation and the boldness of Japanese aggression. There were flaws in this logic no doubt, but it seemed crystal clear to me that evening. Like the man who walked through a plate-glass window, I could only say afterwards that "it seemed to me a good idea at the time."

When Ivanov and Petrov left, I typed out a brief dispatch on the subject of their disclosures. It was carefully couched in the subjunctive mood and described the information as "unconfirmed reports" having wide currency in high quarters. Both governments, I added, would be certain to deny these reports, having reached a tacit agreement not to make a public issue of the incidents. Having written the dispatch, I laid it aside. My better judgment told me that it was loaded with dynamite and that I ought to let it alone, even if the Soviet authorities did seem eager to have it transmitted.

My better judgment, however, was not equal to the occasion. As hard luck would have it, a long-distance call came through from the London office of the United Press, on a totally different matter. At the end of the conversation, the voice at the other end said:

"Anything new in Moscow, Gene?"

And I yielded to the temptation, the temptation only a newspaperman can fully appreciate, of scoring a scoop.

"Yes," I said, "lots of news. Take down this dispatch."

I dictated the brief message about the two Far Eastern incidents.

Even as I dictated it, I felt that I was making a blunder. Almost as soon as I dropped the receiver, I regretted having been maneuvered into filing a story that could only bring official denials and leave me "holding the bag." In less than an hour I had London on the phone again, with the purpose of "killing" the dispatch.

But a press agency works too fast for that. The startling news had already gone around the world.

2

A few hours later, hell broke loose, and its fires of fury played around my hapless head for weeks. I found myself at the dizzy center of a whirlpool of intrigue, lies, fears, some of which are still spinning.

The subjunctive mood of my dispatch got lost in the shuffle. The careful qualifications were for the most part shed in transit and my story, as published on the world's front pages, gave as specific facts what I had sent as unconfirmed reports. The Moscow correspondents were being pelted with urgent inquiries by their editors and the entire press corps assailed poor Comrade Podolsky, *pro tem* director of the Press Department. Both the Soviet and the Japanese Foreign Offices issued vigorous denials. Litvinov, in a righteous rage, issued statements in Washington implying that I had been used as cat's-paw in a Japanese plot to wreck the recognition negotiations. Tokyo, in a no less righteous rage, insisted that I had been used as a cat's-paw in a Soviet plot to help those negotiations.

Meanwhile, the United Press clamored to know immediately and specifically the sources of my information. My chief mistake at that juncture, now that I can judge the affair in ample perspective, was probably in not disclosing those sources. But I was convinced that any mention of Ivanov and Petrov would get them shot. Even if they had acted under instructions in talking to me, I felt, the Soviet government would be obliged to punish them once their names became known. For the protection of the two men, and with full knowledge that I was sacrificing myself for their safety, I therefore asserted that I had obtained the reports from "trustworthy foreign diplomatic sources, confirmed by well-informed Russians." Beyond this formula, I refused to commit myself.

Angry, insistent, cajoling cables from the U.P. chiefs poured in on me. London telephoned me continuously for hours and days. Ignorant of the Moscow atmosphere, they could not understand why I should withhold the names of my informants.

"At least," Webb Miller in London pleaded, "at least tell us off-record. We will agree not to publish the information."

"Don't you understand that there is nothing off-record here?" I tried to explain. "We are being listened to at this very moment. Anything I say or cable will be instantly known. I can't reveal any more without endangering Russian lives. Do what you wish about it. I can't say any more."

The year that had begun for me with a threat of expulsion because of the Kuban story thus ended with a much worse offense. Litvinov and Umansky in America made peremptory demands that I be recalled. If I were not withdrawn peaceably, Litvinov stormed, his first act on returning to Moscow would be to expel me. For a while the United Press held out. In six years of reporting I had not let them down once; Bickel, Bender, and others were convinced (as they told me later) that I had acted in good faith and that my story was substantially correct. But in the end they yielded. With the two countries entering a new era of diplomatic friendship, they could scarcely do less.

The fact that neither Ivanov nor Petrov was punished for his indiscretion on a military matter gave color to the widespread supposition in Moscow that I had been hoaxed by the G.P.U. for purposes of its own. The identity of everyone I had talked to on the critical evening could scarcely have remained a secret to the authorities. But such suppositions, however logical they might sound, did not seem to me justification for seeking personal exoneration by endangering the lives of others.

The very day after I dictated the offending story, Ivanov visited Zara Witkin at his lodgings. Aware of my difficult position, Zara put the matter squarely to the Russian. He pointed out that both the Moscow and Tokyo governments had denied his facts, and the correspondent was caught between two fires.

"Naturally," Ivanov said, apparently unperturbed, "official denials in such cases are purely formal. They really confirm the facts."

Then he proceeded to give Zara even more specific military and technical details of the Far Eastern episodes. When Zara reported the conversation to me, he gave it as his solid conviction that my dispatch was not only justified but probably a watered-down version of the truth.

I hunted up Ivanov and Petrov. I explained to them that while they had not given me explicit authority to use their information, they had not warned me against using it. Their permission was at least implicit. Now I was "in a pickle," and so, I presumed, were they. They seemed curiously placid about the whole affair.

"Everything we told you is true," Ivanov said, "though I am sorry you sent it abroad. But all the official rage is just make-believe, and there is no cause to worry."

A Russian acquaintance who had been for years in the G.P.U. service in France and now resided in Leningrad came to see me. He was fully informed on my troubles. Not only was my story correct, he said, but it had actually appeared in certain Soviet newspapers in the Far East, before the government ordered the story suppressed. What is more, he had himself seen the published account in the Leningrad library and volunteered to clip it for me. He was leaving for Leningrad next day and when he returned he would have the documentary proof of the airplane and naval incidents for me.

At the railroad station next day, just before the Leningrad train pulled out, this fellow was arrested—his wife brought me the news—and he was not released until after I left Russia several months later.

Ed L. Keen, Vice-President of the United Press in charge of Europe, apprised me that he was coming to Moscow. He had been instructed by New York to break the news of my recall to me personally so as to soften the shock. I looked up Ivanov.

"Keen will be here in a day or two," I said. "He is doubtless coming to make a personal check-up on this whole mess."

"That's fine," Ivanov smiled. "I shall be glad to meet him and to confirm all the facts. You might as well know that I have seen the G.P.U. archive on the matter. There are many clippings from our own Far Eastern papers that tell the story exactly as I have told it to you."

When Keen arrived, I tried in vain to find Ivanov. During all the time Keen was in Moscow, Ivanov was in hiding. When I ran into him again weeks later he looked at me apologetically and shrugged his shoulders. There was no need for words. Higher authorities had evidently decided to let me "hold the bag." In a hundred ways I attempted in the following months to lay hands on tangible proofs of the story, the essential correctness of which I have never doubted. At every turn I was frustrated.

I remained in Moscow eight or nine weeks longer, to tie up loose ends in my personal affairs, and particularly to dispose of my newly built and as yet unoccupied apartment. That apartment represented practically everything I had managed to save in my six years in Moscow; in terms of cash I would be starting from scratch when I returned home—scratch is a well-worn groove for all newspapermen.

Officially, no one let on that I had been recalled at Litvinov's angry insistence. I had made no secret of my plans to give up the Moscow post soon, even before the recall took the initiative out of my hands. Before I left, the Press Department gave an official luncheon in my honor and we parted on a basis of polite if strained cordiality.

II. Farewell to Russia!

A YOUNG Russian whom I had not seen for more than three years came to me one day in great agitation. His overcoat collar and a thick woolen scarf hid his face; not until he was sure I was alone in my office did he reveal himself.

"In coming here I am risking my life," he said. "If they find out that I have told you what I'm going to tell you, my life isn't worth this . . ." and he snapped his fingers.

I knew who "they" were. Even a pronoun referring to the G.P.U. is electric with terror on a Russian tongue.

"But I am here because I love you"—Russians use words like love more easily than Americans—"and because I believe you are an honest man. I want to warn you to be careful—and to get out of Russia as soon as you can. Don't ask me how I know. But I do know. I heard 'them' discuss you. They're cooking up a frame-up on you. They're afraid of what you'll say when you get back to America."

"What sort of a frame-up?" I asked.

"I don't know. All I know is that they are determined to discredit you. What bothers them is that you're leaving with a clean record. One of them said that they'd tried to draw you in five years ago, soon after you came to our country, but that you refused to see them."

"Well, what in the world can I do about it? I can't possibly leave for another month or more. I have about three thousand dollars invested in an apartment I bought from the Writers' Housing Coöperative. I must at least rent it to someone before I clear out."

The Russian shrugged his shoulders, in genuine distress.

"My only thought was that if you knew, you would be more careful," he said. "The only advice I have is that you should suspect everyone and trust no one, not even your best Russian friends. They've had to report on you like we all report on foreigners, and they may be forced to try to get you involved in trouble. Be careful. Don't commit yourself on anything. Above all, don't sign anything."

He got up, kissed me warmly on both cheeks, Russian fashion, and put up his collar again. At the door he paused.

"And, dear Gene, only one thing I ask of you. That will be my reward for risking my neck by warning you. When you are out in the free world—tell the truth about Russia—tell them what we would tell if we dared."

He peeped out into the corridor. The coast was clear, and he hurried away.

That this Russian was close enough to the G.P.U. to overhear secrets of the sort he conveyed to me was not a surprise. Long ago I had ceased being surprised to learn that gentle, inoffensive people were inveigled into the network of spying. I pretended not to be aware that men and women whom I saw frequently were "reporting" on me. I bore them no ill will, knowing that they had been forced into the service and hated it.

Once after a Russian acquaintance left me I found a piece of paper he had dropped accidentally. On it were notations all too clearly intended for the G.P.U. For a minute I smiled at the idea of returning it to him and watching his discomfiture. Then pity for the man and his compulsory avocation overcame me. I destroyed the scrap of paper and never mentioned it to him.

There was one occasion when the chauffeur of a borrowed car stopped a good two blocks from the address I had given him. He blushed with embarrassment.

"Mr. Lyons," he said, "do you mind dismissing me here and walking? I don't want to know where you are going."

"But I'm only going to see a dentist," I laughed.

"Oh, in that case . . ." and he stepped on the gas.

Espionage and surveillance were the element in which we lived, part of the air we breathed. In the first years I continued to be surprised when Russians inadvertently showed familiarity with some phase of my private affairs that they could know only by eavesdropping on my conversation or mail, but in the end this experience became too commonplace. A show-off streak in his character led one Russian to mention casually intimate details of my own or Billy's activities, watching us slyly for the inevitable expression of astonishment.

That sort of thing, in any event, helped to keep one on the straight and narrow path. We lived under floodlights in glass houses equipped with loud speakers. . . .

Whether the warning I had received was justified or not, I shall never know. The fact that I was thoroughly alarmed is scarcely an index of a guilty conscience. I had seen too many demonstration trials to dismiss the Soviet frame-up artists lightly. The *agent provocateur* has been an instrument of Russian statecraft for centuries. I became tight-lipped and circumspect with all my Russian acquaintances, an abrupt change in my free-and-easy attitude which must have seemed inexplicable to them. Only one incident may have had a direct relation to the dramatic warning. The same "Petrov" who helped embroil me in the unfortunate Japanese airplane story telephoned one afternoon to invite me urgently to his home.

"But I'm terribly busy," I apologized; "why not make it some other day?"

"Because I have a friend here, who's eager to meet you . . . *a very important person.*"

"In that case, I certainly am too busy to come."

"All right, Gene, I'll be frank with you. You are leaving the country soon. Why shouldn't we separate as friends? You can help us—and we can help you."

"Well, you tell your friend, no matter how important he is, that there is nothing he can do for me, and even less I can do for him."

I never heard about the matter again. But several friends talked to me in terms too parallel to have been quite accidental. They sought to impress upon me the wisdom of silence. One put his plea on a personal basis; anything derogatory that I might write would reflect on the "loyalty" of those who were close to me. A Russian newspaperman put the argument on a professional footing:

"After all you can't afford to make an enemy of our government," he said. "You will undoubtedly remain in journalism. A war is coming. Think what it will mean to your career to be able to cover the war from the Soviet lines, with your knowledge of Russian and your experiences here!"

Day after day, the counsel of silence was pressed on me in almost the same words. I no longer doubted that it was an inspired campaign. The appeal to professional cupidity did not touch me: I was too seriously compromised in the Kremlin's eyes to reconquer a "friendly" label by keeping my mouth closed. The danger of embarrassing the scores of Russians with whom I had associated in the course of six years, on the other hand, did impress me. It was to be the most effective curb on my candor. Even in these uninhibited pages it has served as a brake on eloquence.

2

Parting with a beloved city is like parting with a beloved friend; in the sentiment of separation one forgives much and idealizes much. My experience had been sufficiently galling. It is not pleasant to feel your hope changing inexorably into despair. But at least I had lived on a high emotional level; Moscow would be forever associated for me with heights and depths. Those who dwell on a humdrum level of apathy and intellectual comfort can never know that it is the intensity of the years, not their quality of pleasure, that makes them precious. The thought that I might have remained an ignorant confederate in the horrors I witnessed is frightening. Distressing as my experience has been, I treasure it.

The knowledge that I was leaving Moscow, perhaps forever, made me look at the city and its people with a sharper vision. Things were suddenly focused more clearly, and I allowed the image to soak into my consciousness. In the outer chambers of my mind I was pleased, on the whole, by the impending change. But at its core I felt already premonitory twinges of homesickness. I knew for a certainty that I should never again touch Russian music, Russian pictures, Russian memories, without a gnawing nostalgic pain.

I have no need to reconcile my detestation of the soul of Bolshevism—its cruel, morbid, jesuitical soul—with my affection for Russia and the Russians. People who hated the pogrom-mongering tsarist autocracy, too, often found it possible to love Russia, sometimes impossible not to love it. Much of my resentment against the organized brutality that I witnessed derived, as a matter of fact, from my affection for the Russians. More and more with every passing year, I had identified myself psychologically with them. I rejected the assumption underlying the condescending "objectivity" of certain foreign observers that the Russians are a peculiar breed set aside by destiny for sacrificial rites and laboratory experimentation. To this day, nothing riles me more than the placid acceptance of Russian "sacrifices" by comfortable "friends of Soviet Russia" in the spirit of vivisectionists.

I was parting from Moscow in its huddled, mysterious winter embodiment, precisely as I had first made its acquaintance. It was a white city of brief days and long enshrouding nights, whose life was hidden away deep within its many garments of fear and intrigue. In every city there is a world below the surface, beyond the reach of the five senses; anyone who has sought to know more intimately New York or London, Paris or Rome, has become aware of this elusive nether reality. But in Moscow the secret seems more profoundly buried. The absence of a free press, the all-powerful secret service, the outlawry of all independent thoughts and feelings, the tom-tom monotony of surface slogans —all these things that have been the country's portion for a thousand years seem to have driven the Russian people underground: their essential life seems subterranean, a life of secret thoughts, unspoken hopes, vague dreads, clandestine satisfactions.

If this sounds mystical the fault is with my lack of skill in expressing the idea. It is a real, almost a physical essence to which I refer. Every Russian man and woman lives automatically a double existence, has lived it for numberless generations: one public and obviously conformist, the other private and untrammeled. For a moment, in the throes of revolution, the inner existence broke through the surface restraints—then it was driven back to its lair. The fissures have now been completely filled and sealed and the outer life is again policed by the ancient threats and compulsions.

These people whom I was leaving behind—my heart reached out to them in sympathy. Some were pariahs, hiding in corners, disguising their voices and their faces. Others were adjusted to the new system, but living in continuous dread of a new persecution. The mass of workers had had a moment of intoxicating glory, when they marched and shouted and waved flags and felt themselves masters. Now they were under the heel of arbitrary power again, terrified by teeming threats: loss of bread ration, loss of passport, loss of their squalid "living space." The peasants —still the great majority in the nation—had won their land only to lose it again; were being chastised with flaming sword for preferring their instinctive way of life; felt themselves in their frustration indentured laborers slaving for absentee landlords in the Kremlin. Every liquidation disclosed another class needing to be liquidated, and the flaming sword was being whetted on the prostrate body of the Russian population. At the top, new privileged classes had emerged, with power of life and death over their fellows, using that power with the ferocity of cynical indifference or the more dreadful ferocity of fanaticism; a parvenu aristocracy based on raw and naked power.

Above all, I had the sense of leaving behind me *a nation trapped*. Trapped physically, with bloodhounds and machineguns and death sentences guarding the frontiers to prevent people from escaping, with a passport system to prevent them from moving freely inside the frontiers, with endless *ukases* and threats to regulate their existence. Trapped intellectually, with every thought prescribed and mental curiosity punished as heresy; the new literacy seemed an additional taunt, sharpening the appetite while denying it sustenance. Trapped spiritually, through the need of pretending enthusiasm for the knout, genuflecting to hateful images and practicing hypocrisy as the first law of survival. In the past, the word freedom had been whispered in secret caves, but now punishment was too swift and too deadly. There was no longer even the solace of martyrdom for the defiant; a technique had been evolved for breaking their spirit and dragging them into the limelight for slobbering confessions of guilt.

The fact that these things had come to pass under the banners of "socialism" only made them more ghastly. The word socialism, the eternal dream of equality and justice, was also trapped.

The parting was not "such sweet sorrow." It was tinctured with gall. For months, I had been planning to leave, and I was vexed that recall should have come before resignation. Ever since I was threatened with expulsion early in the year, I knew that my tenure was highly uncertain; the Kremlin would use the first plausible alibi for ridding itself of my comment on its affairs. It was not astonishing that a dispatch which would have been condoned in a "friendly" correspondent should be turned instantly into a jack for prying me out of my journalistic post. The Soviet objection clearly was not to this one dispatch but to the whole tenor of my reporting. I was mortified, therefore, that I had enabled Litvinov and Umansky to convert what was a divergence in principle into a petty squabble over the authenticity of one story among the thousands I had written.

I was saddened, too, by this parting on a note of rancor. The memory of the exalted mood of consecration to a cause in which I began my assignment in the Russian Utopia was still fresh in my mind. The collapse of the mood, the slow crumbling of the assumptions on which it had fed, was a personal tragedy. From the wreckage I was desperately anxious to save my basic emotional investment: the faith that a juster and happier world was worth fighting for. For the world, too, the tragedy of the Russian debacle is that it may impugn the value of all social striving; that by mocking ideals it threatens idealism as such with bankruptcy.

I felt that the Russian revolution has a symbolic validity which not all its horrors can extinguish. It marks a high moment on the plains of time, a moment of release and challenge and daring. Whatever its course inside Russia, it signalized the end of the divine rights of capital even as the French revolution, which also degenerated into a new despotism in its own day, signalized the end of the divine rights of kings. The original ideals of the Russian revolution are in the stream of human thought: not a million Stalins and G.P.U.'s can change that. Increasingly, I am convinced, they will become the unquestioned axioms of mankind's thinking, regardless of their fate in any one country, precisely as the philosophical concepts of the French revolution became axiomatic for the civilized world in the Nineteenth Century. What happened in Russia twenty years ago will remain a frontier in time, token of the deepening twilight of the capitalist era.

The Russian revolution gave wings to earthbound hopes. My problem, the moral and intellectual problem of millions who know that the revolution has been betrayed and perverted, was to disown the perversions without clipping those wings.

3

The last day of January, 1934, my last day in Moscow, remains in my memory with a peculiarly sharp-edged vividness. A day of gray light filtering through wet snow, of farewells that seemed as final as death, of pathetic farce and tragic episode.

My family had left for Berlin about a week earlier. My personal belongings had been shipped off. Only the debris of a long residence remained: odds and ends too trivial or decrepit to be given away. A fantastic competition for these leavings developed that day. People who came to say good-by and were genuinely grieved by my departure, nevertheless eyed a discarded pair of shoes or a chipped cup covetously. I gave them *carte blanche* to help themselves, a little ashamed of the poverty which made people so tremulously acquisitive at an almost solemn moment. Then I discovered that my generosity was working havoc with Shura's temper. As our housemaid and cook for so many years she considered herself justifiably the heiress presumptive to all left-over property!

A well-known Russian cornered me for a last-minute appeal to hold my peace when I emerged from his country; and if I must talk, at least never to mention his famous name.

Nathalie's last chore as my secretary was to wrench from *Glavlit,* the literary censorship office, the delayed permit for my notes, clippings and other materials; no written words may leave the country without that bureau's authority.

Long and weary months of waiting were about to bring the *Moscow Daily News* their reward. Borodin and his lieutenants had looked hungrily at the space occupied by the United Press and its correspondent. They regarded my going as a divine deliverance and scrupled not to show their jubilation. But their joy was not undiluted by apprehensions. What if my successor, or some other influential foreigner, seized the coveted area, what, indeed? But not while the mind that directed an epochal revolution in China, a revolution whose echoes will thunder down the ages, was still capable of strategy! Generalissimo Borodin stationed guards in the corridors, and even the limping old doorman was mobilized, all under instructions to apprise the commander-in-chief as soon as an enemy was sighted. The arrival of a large suitcase nearly precipitated hostilities, until I explained that I was taking it with me to Europe and that it did not foreshadow a new tenant.

And everywhere that last morning the city's life was disrupted. Unexpected orders had come through for a "spontaneous" mass parade in the afternoon, so that work in offices was all but suspended. The endless formalities incident to leaving the country, many of them postponed to the last day, were therefore snarled in alibis. Papers, tickets, permits, were in the end obtained only by heroically hacking through the wild disorder. Every messenger returned with a tale of procrastination, elusive functionaries, and helpless apology. A parade and routine business were not miscible.

"But what's the parade about?" I asked.

Semichasov, my chauffeur, thought he knew. It was, he opined, in honor of the brave airmen who had gone up in a stratosphere balloon the previous day. The morning's papers headlined the fact that they had set a new world's record in altitude, surpassing the record established by a previous balloon earlier in the year. Others made the same surmise. But few people seemed to know specifically what triumph was to be celebrated, what sudden and spontaneous sentiment was to be demonstrated. . . .

It was not, alas!, the stratosphere flight. The foreign correspondents, like a few others in Moscow, knew of the gruesome tragedy in which the record-making flight had ended. Having reached and reported an unprecedented height, the balloon's radio suddenly went dead. Hours later the spherical, gaily painted gondola and the shattered bodies of its occupants were found. The facts were already spread on the front pages of the outside world—but they were being concealed from the Soviet people in order not to dampen the spirit of the parade. In reporting the flight and hiding its catastrophic climax, the Soviet press was deliberately lying to its readers. As always, "news" was doled out to the people like bread rations, or suppressed altogether in the interests of the higher truth.

By the time the parade got under way, of course, the marchers knew that they were displaying their unbounded enthusiasm for the Party conference in progress at the former Nobles' Club. The prepared banners were clangorous with panegyrics of Stalin and his Party and his Central Committee and his unmatched genius.

I had seen parades in these years that had in them the throb and the lift of holiday. But this, my last parade in Russia, was a funereal and leaden-footed thing: weary men and women by the hundred thousand dragging their own weight under soggy banners for hours through a gloomy dusk.

Even before the hall door was closed, I saw Borodin's stalwarts rushing to take possession of the rooms we had occupied. Great tears rolled down Shura's chapped cheeks as I shook her calloused hand. Timidly she had given me a parting gift: a large lacquered Palekh box with the picture of a Ukrainian peasant girl on the cover. I remember wondering through all the excitement how such a thing had come to her, since it could be bought only at Torgsin for valuta; two years later, reading E. E. Cummings' book on Russia, I learned in its pages that he had presented it to her.

The entire press corps and a batch of diplomats were at the Alexandrovsky railroad station to see me off. This mass turn-out for foreigners going "out" is a Moscow tradition. A few more intimate Russian friends were there, timidly keeping their distance from the untouchable foreigners. Two or three of them wept softly. Several who said they would be at the station obviously could not muster the courage for such a public demonstration of their friendship with a foreigner.

At the moment when the train begins to pull out of Moscow, one feels more sharply than ever the great gulf between Russia and the surrounding world. Could it really be that this train touches an incredible world where people speak their minds, where bread is plentiful; a world without G.P.U.'s and *Piatiletkas* and food queues and censorship? The newspapermen, the diplomats knew how flimsy is that freedom, how uneven that plenitude. But for Russians, to whom a trip across the frontier is as fantastically impossible as a trip to the moon, the forbidden world glowed with the rainbow colors of their dreams.

Farewell to Moscow! Farewell to the city of desperations and enthusiasms, beauty and squalor. The thought that I might never see it again was a vise, every turn of the train wheels closing its arms more painfully on my heart.

III. A Tour of Tyrannies

BEFORE returning to the United States, I spent several months (February-April, 1934) in intensive travel and investigation on the European continent, in the stimulating company of Zara Witkin. An assignment from *Cosmopolitan* Magazine for several political articles gave my trip a purposive cohesion which a random tour cannot have. But I really needed no such external discipline. I was impelled by a harsh inner drive that fixed the direction of my journey and, even more so, the direction of my thought. In a sense I was still exploring Russia.

The questions plowed up in my consciousness by the Soviet experience pursued me through Germany and Austria, Italy and Spain, clamoring for clear and honest answers. They howled down every attempt at pettifogging. Equivocation and compromise might do the trick for strangers: you balanced the brutalities of the G.P.U. against those of the Gestapo; you wrote off the valuta tortures by reference to anti-Semitism in Poland and Germany; you let the horrors of the destruction of Vienna tenements cancel out the horrors of liquidation. But in the secret mind where a man must live with himself, you rejected this spurious bookkeeping. You were obliged to total up the iniquities instead of checking them off against one another.

In Germany, the hectic inhumanities of the first months were settling down to more routine cruelties. In Vienna, we saw the Social-Democratic workers trapped and killed in their communal houses by bravos who called themselves Christian Socialists: as cynical an insult to the name of Christ—and the name of socialism—as has ever been perpetrated. Poland squirmed under the camouflaged dictatorship of Marshal Pilsudski, jammed in between Hitlerism and Stalinism. In Italy, we were weighed down by the quiet as of a vast prison in which force and fear are the keepers. The Spanish people looked down shudderingly into an abyss of civil war. In Switzerland and France, where democratic government still held on with bleeding fingers, totalitarian insanities were being shouted from both Right and Left.

Everywhere we saw hordes of the outlawed and declassed cower in corners. Ordinary conversation was sunk to a whisper. The fumes of prejudice, distrust and desperation hung over Europe in thick fogs. Everywhere sadistic minorities, disciplined under an arbitrary autocrat, working their will upon the patient, suffering, inarticulate masses. Everywhere—and that is what impressed us most, exploring Russia beyond its own frontiers—the autocrats using almost the identical slogans, wielding the selfsame "sword of history" for class or race or nation.

Everywhere independent thinking was called unpatriotic, counterrevolutionary, heretical, and a new generation was being reared to believe that it was inheriting a monopoly of ultimate truth beyond the need for reason. War was being idealized again—the terrors of the last war carefully concealed from those who must fight the next one. Just twenty years after a holocaust swept the world, devouring a generation of men and laying waste entire nations, charring the earth and littering the floor of the seas with corpses of men and their ships, Europe was once again arming to its teeth. The stench of scorched flesh was still in the air, and already nations were jockeying for position in a struggle that nobody wanted and everybody expected.

Isolated scenes, like so many snapshots, remain in my mind:

A lanky, nervous individual, with a wisp of brown tobacco-stained beard and a pained smile full of black teeth, talked to us in a Warsaw café. My knowledge that he carried terrible war wounds was an overtone to his earnest voice.

"We're the Belgium of Eastern Europe," he was saying. "No matter who fights whom, we Poles get caught in between. We've got the Nazis on one side and the Bolsheviks on the other—nice little Polish sandwich, eh? Can you imagine us inviting Comrade Budenny's armies onto Polish soil? They'd never get out again. And if Germans ever enter, as friends or foes, there's just as little chance of their leaving again."

As he spoke, the enormous military display in his country began to make sense. Abundant gold braid; droves of long-waisted officers, a touch of the operatic in their elegance—signs not of strength but of fear. And other fears, minor patterns on the main design, came into view. A young newspaperman joined us, red-haired, excitable, Semitic. He was lambasting the extreme Rights.

"A monarchist party without a candidate for monarch!" he shouted. "They are just envious of Hitler and aching for some juicy pogroms of their own."

"There you have it," the Polish friend who had introduced us to these people made the résumé. "There you have it. Pszemitsky is afraid of the Bolos. Guterman is afraid of anti-Semitic outbreaks. This fellow is scared of the Nazis. All of us are afraid of war and trouble and sure they're coming, plenty of it. As long as the cussing colonel—Pilsudski, I mean—sits on the lid there is some hope. But when he's gone, God help Poland! Oh, well, there's a new Mickey Mouse playing today, which is something in a confused world."

Berlin and Hamburg reverberated with atrocity stories. The German husband of a lovely Jewish woman of our acquaintance was taken off a train in the provinces and beaten to a pulp. A Jewish boy of eleven came home weeping bitterly while we drank tea one day with his parents; all his life he had played in the neighborhood park, but today the Gentile boys, his own friends, chased him off the soccer field. All the Nazi arguments—and they were retailed to me for hours by otherwise normal Germans—shriveled to nothing in the heat of one child's outraged soul.

A former Social-Democratic Deputy consented to meet us in a café on the Kurfuerstendam; and one of the world's greatest architects, outlawed because of his modernistic style, though he was as Aryan as Streicher racially, received us in his home. After Moscow, these men seemed to us startlingly daring. Political outlaws under the hammer and sickle would never have dared meet foreign investigators so openly. But these were differences in the age and temper of the two dictatorships, rather than differences in kind.

"They're putting gables on all the fine houses I have built," the architect smiled wryly. "Flat roofs are taboo—Judaeo-Bolshevik roofs these maniacs call them . . ."

Outside the G—— restaurant, Berlin was caught up in an emotional frenzy. Parades, harangues, ballyhoo, *Heil Hitler!* Brown uniforms, black uniforms, the staccato of marching men and the eternal rattle of collection boxes. But inside this restaurant there was an oppressive quiet. The enveloping excitement seemed to make the silence here slightly unreal, like an exaggerated set on a modernist stage. A little like a homey dugout with war raging all around—an illusory quiet and safety. To a foreigner the people in this place looked like some more Germans. But the Germans had disowned them. They were men and women without a country: German Jews.

It was a tangible presence—their common disaster. Nearly all of them, if asked, would describe themselves as patriotic Germans. They know no other *Vaterland*. Many of them are devout Christians. Now they all huddled together, for human warmth, for fear of humiliation in other places. Already they were in a psychological ghetto, ringed by walls of insult, hatred, discrimination more confining than the physical walls that ringed the ghettos of their ancestors in the Middle Ages.

A gawky, sandy-haired lad in brown uniform, awkward in his shirt sleeves, with a swastika on his arm, entered the restaurant. He rattled a collection box, apparently unaware that he had intruded on a Jewish corner. An embarrassed hush fell on the place as the boy went from table to table. A few sheepishly dropped some coins into his box. The others bent their heads over their plates in sudden concentration. I saw face muscles twitch.

The communal tenements for workers built by a socialist government in Vienna were celebrated around the world as an example of what enlightened coöperation could achieve. Zara had often spoken of visiting the Austrian capital especially to see these blocks of houses. And now, at last, he was seeing them—as a shambles of brick and mortar and human flesh. In many places we had no need for doors, but walked through the shellholes in walls made by Christian Socialist artillery.

We reached the city on the last day of fighting. I rushed to the scene with some of the American correspondents and wrote a piece about what I saw: the last thing I did for the United Press. Soldiers still patrolled the area and machineguns were trained on the battered houses. There were few men in the tenements, but many women and children wandered through the ruins like ghosts in search of bodies. In a kindergarten we saw toys and picture books in a congealed pool of black blood. On one of the house-fronts a sculptured figure of Peace had escaped injury and presided ludicrously over the wreckage.

Through a shellhole we stepped into the remains of a kitchen. Its windows were a tangle of splintered wood and metal. The opposite wall was mostly a great ragged wound. And there, in the debris, in this room without walls or windows, an old woman was sitting close to the cold stove, gnarled hands clasped in her lap. It was grotesque, the woman sitting there so still, as though waiting for company, in the ruin of a kitchen. A half-eaten meal, clearly several days old, was on the table.

"What are you waiting for?" I asked, more to cover my embarrassment over the intrusion than to elicit information.

She did not answer, only seemed to shrink more deeply into her crumpled garments. Her eyes were staring and lusterless. Suddenly she spoke:

"I am not waiting. I am home. This is the only home I have."

Had the word "home" ever been applied more inappropriately? Nothing had been touched since the bombardment. Broken glass and plaster lay around in heaps. To our surprise the woman spoke again, as if to herself rather than to her uninvited visitors.

"I was in the cellar when the shooting went on," she said. "So was Frau Mueller and the Platkin children, all of us. Karl was killed the first day. Karl is my husband. They wouldn't let me look at him. He was so horribly broken. But at night I went up. I made supper for my sons. They made me go down again. I knew I should have stayed—look, they never finished supper."

"Where are your sons now?"

"How should I know? Maybe dead, or arrested, or hiding."

She shrugged and forgot us. We tiptoed out, feeling guilty. Ashamed for the human race.

After the fighting, it was good to be back in the Ring, the inner core of Vienna, where life went on as usual. The city of *Gemütlichkeit. The Blue Danube.* Strauss. The charm of Vienna's café life. Over the coffee cups and their little mounds of whipped cream I heard details of that day's executions. One man condemned by the court-martial was horribly wounded, but he was dragged from a hospital cot to the gallows.

In the next days I listened to the diminutive Chancellor Dollfuss, and to the robust Prince von Starhemberg. They both talked of God. They both had divine sanction for wrecking the life of the old woman sitting by a cold stove in a home without walls or windows.

As we stepped off the train in Zurich in the evening, we heard shooting somewhere beyond the station. My nerves still taut after the days of blood-letting in Vienna, I jumped to conclusions. Another revolution! A man-sized riot at the least. I felt a bit flattered by the way the gods were apparently timing affairs to my journalistic convenience.

We rushed to the street, only to find that the shooting came from the park, where colored fireworks were being exploded. Zurich was celebrating carnival that night. The main street was ankle-deep in confetti. Masked women tickled us with feather dusters and tooted horns in our ears. After the shambles in Austria, I could not adjust myself at once to the loud, friendly holiday mood here. I could not drive from my mind's eye the sights of death and ruin. Vienna was real—it was this city of fireworks and confetti and carnival spirits that must be askew. How could both be real on the same planet, a few hours' distance from one another?

An American functionary working for the League of Nations conducted us through the building in Geneva. An ominously clean, quiet, somnolent place. He pointed with pride to the efficient system for distributing documents to affiliated governments, and to the tall shiny files everywhere. Geneva itself is a spick-and-span file where conferences are stuck away one after another—and forgotten.

Unconsciously we talked in whispers, as people do in a cemetery. He told us how the League was making progress in the matters of opium and white slavery and succeeding in minor things. Only in its larger objectives it was failing. Germany and Japan were out, but the League was still patronized by the authors of universal calendars and the like—there are special files for every variety of crank, our guide boasted. There is an international mind, he reassured us, and the League may still be the rallying point for peace forces.

And then he added seriously: "At the moment, of course, it's as flat as a pancake."

The Italian fascists have a corner on swagger. Trumpeters tore down the streets of Rome on motorcycles blowing shrill triumph. Announcing some fascist victory? Summoning all good patriots to the colors? Not at all. Merely the advance guard of a Sunday morning bicycle outing of the Fascist Youth. In Italy, officers toss the ends of their capes with the gestures of toreadors defying bulls. Revolver holsters slap sleek hips in rhythm to a strut. The very infants and toddlers are decked out in black uniforms with meters of white braid like old-fashioned curtain cords.

The gangling, aristocratic-looking Angelina, whom I knew from San Remo sojourns, was an enthusiastic fascist. She volunteered to act as our guide. A *dopolavora* headquarters, strangely like the workers' clubs in Moscow. A model dispensary, and a lecture on social hygiene; medical help gratis for all citizens. A model children's home. "The fascist regime," Angelina explained, "looks first of all to its new generation." Statistics on the successful fight against illiteracy. I whispered to my companion, "At least the weather is different from Moscow."

Barcelona and Madrid were immeasurably charming; to the untrained eye a life mellowed by time, crusted with tradition. But under their picturesqueness we found a social tension, a tremulous expectancy. Spain was a country walking a tight rope. Count Romanones, many times Premier, led us through his musty palace, filled with works of art—mostly paintings of grandee ancestors. Alone among the aristocrats he had dared to speak up in the Cortes for the ousted monarchs. A broad, stunted man, limping through the gloomy place, all his features oversized and a little disordered, he seemed a caricature of the *ancien régime*.

"This is a lull. The revolution in Spain did not end with the expulsion of the Bourbons," he said. "They've started something they won't be able to stop."

Largo Caballero, the head of the socialist and trade-union movements, likewise prophesied civil strife. He was a large, quiet, stolid-looking person; there was something incongruous between the calm of his appearance and the impending violence of which he spoke to me. The civil war, to him, was not a possibilitv but an unavoidable fact.

The same assurance of disaster was voiced to me next day by young Primo de Rivera, son of the former dictator. A slim, handsome young man, gentle in speech and manner, only the accident of his name placed him in a role of leadership in the fascist camp. Two years later he was to die at the hands of the Loyalists.

"You see," an old Parisian explained, "the asphalting of our streets has struck a serious blow to social revolution. How is one to build barricades without cobblestones? Two months ago, in the February fighting, though, our resourcefulness was vindicated. Despite the width of our new streets and despite the absence of the romantic cobblestones, we did raise barricades. Oh, yes, it was a sort of dress rehearsal for what is still to come. Do not be misled by the calm exterior, my friend. It is class against class, and next time it may be a show-down. Who knows? This isn't peace. It's an armed truce."

Such was the atmosphere of Europe in the spring of 1934, such were its moods of desperation. We searched for the glint of a silver lining on the lowering clouds and found only the reflection of sharpened steel. The very word "revolution," hallowed by what happened in America in 1776, in France in 1789, in Russia in 1917, had been commandeered by the reaction. Young de Rivera and the blustering Starhemberg spoke of their "revolutions." Nazis baiting Jews and Christian Socialists bombarding workers' homes boasted of their "revolutions" and exterminated their "counter-revolutionaries." Instead of describing a break towards liberty, the word had been distorted to cover a stampede back into the Dark Ages.

2

We traveled especially to Switzerland to talk to Romain Rolland. As boys, both Zara and I had cut our spiritual teeth on *Jean Christophe*. For Zara in particular, the grand old man of European letters towered above the moral landscape of his epoch as the champion of freedom, justice, the human spirit. We were too recently from Russia and Germany to use such words, even in the privacy of our thoughts, without a certain embarrassment. Such ideas and ideals had lost intellectual caste, had been tarred and feathered and made ridiculous. But in relation to Rolland there were no other words. Our Jean Christophe had spoken up, often alone, against the mass madness of war and the vengeance of the victors.

Could he, knowingly, condone wholesale brutalities anywhere? Was it possible that Jean Christophe had donned the uniform of denominational partisanship and ruthless fanaticism? Could the Rolland who wrote rhapsodically of Gandhi and the non-coöperation movement consent knowingly to the extermination of millions of Russian peasants as punishment for their passive Gandhi-like resistance? To forced labor on an unprecedented scale? To the world's largest army of political prisoners? As far back as 1930, I had been tragically let down by Romain Rolland's refusal to protest against the execution of the forty-eight food specialists. The execution of thirty-five more only a year ago had again failed to draw his lightning.

Perhaps, we thought, Jean Christophe had a magic explanation for having joined the conspiracy of silence. . . . Zara wrote him from Germany that two Americans, profoundly hurt by long residence in the Soviet land, wished to talk to him frankly and fully about their quandary, and he replied immediately inviting us to visit him.

We found Rolland in his sunny retreat at Villeneuve, on Lake Geneva. Tall, erect, in a blue suit of military cut and a high clerical collar, a blanket over his frail shoulders, with a beautifully chiseled face and bright, almost feverish, green-blue eyes, Rolland measured up physically to our rather romanticized expectations. A priest without a church, in a religion of goodness and justice without any ceremonial. Rolland was ill, he spoke in a low, nervous voice, aflutter with a sort of passionate helplessness.

We tried to speak of Russia. But Rolland would not listen. Tremulously, in genuine panic, he shied away every time, switching the talk to Germany, France, the war and the peace. I stared in unbelieving consternation—not in all my thirty-six years had

I seen a clearer show of intellectual and moral diffidence. Here were two earnest young men, reasonably intelligent, who had lived and worked for many years in Russia—who were eager to save a little of the faith they had brought with them to Russia. At the very least, Rolland might have made some inquiries about conditions in that country; about the truth or falseness of the famine reports, the direction in which that nation was tending and the temper of its humanity. He asked nothing and looked distressed each time Zara or I tried to drag the conversation back to Russia.

When we forced him to speak by point-blank questions, Rolland limited himself to a few threadbare formulas about the Soviet Union's hostile surroundings: the self-same formulas we had been fed by Nazis and fascists and spokesmen for Dollfuss. "Russia," he said in a pained voice, "is in a state of war"—rubber-stamped slogans clipped from communist editorials. But he neither said nor asked anything about the Russian people on their farms, in their factories, about the millions cutting timber in the North and digging canals in Central Asia. Jean Christophe was strangely disinterested in the Russian people and went off on a tangent whenever the talk threatened to touch those people.

His Soviet Russian wife, young, petite, attractive, was on the alert to divert the discussion to safer channels whenever the American visitors in meek bewilderment alluded to their Russian years. Possibly I was mistaken—I hope I was—but the conviction grew upon me that Rolland's young wife was deliberately and industriously shielding him against an understanding of the Soviet Union. In appraising that interview later, Zara and I were driven to the unpleasant suspicion that Mme. Rolland, apparently an ardent communist of the Stalinesque brand, was acting as a buffer between the famous Frenchman and the infamous phases of Russian life. She felt, perhaps, that in guaranteeing his uncritical friendship for the Kremlin she was making her contribution to the cause. If our suspicion was uncharitable, part of the blame must attach to the communist jesuitism we had seen in action in Moscow. We knew too intimately that nothing, literally nothing, was morally too devious to be embraced by the formula of the end justifying all means. It may well be, of course, that the lady was only trying to spare her husband the pain and bruises of a knowledge of Russia.

"People say there is no artistic freedom in Russia," Rolland said in a quivering, almost pleading voice, "yet they publish my writings in Moscow, though I am not a communist. They say there is no personal freedom, yet I correspond with a Tolstoyan in Russia. He writes me frankly about everything. . . ."

That was the nearest Rolland approached the subject all that afternoon. The fathomless naïveté of his plea left no room for discussion. It bespoke a total and infantile ignorance of the political pressures, the pervasive fears, the doctrinal obscurantism of present-day Russia. The fact that some of his own works are published in the U.S.S.R. veiled from his sight the multiple censorships, the continuous purgings of the arts, the muzzling of scores of writers adjudged heretical. The "Tolstoyan" who wrote him "frankly about everything" might have been a suicidal maniac or someone assigned to the job by the higher authorities. The personal freedom accorded to Tolstoyans has been sufficiently described by the great writer's daughter, Alexandra Tolstoy, after she escaped from Russia.

Rolland was guarding a beautiful idealized vision of a Russia that does not exist and shrank from anything that might mar its lovely contours. It was the solace of his old age in a world that was going mad. It was a blanket to warm his chilled spirit.

He must have sensed my disappointment at his failure to face issues fearlessly. As we were parting toward dusk, he put his delicate hand on my shoulder.

"I must fight the evil that is nearer and greater," he said, softly. "I am fighting Hitlerism. . . ."

It was not an explanation. It was an apology and I was unreasonably sorry for the old man. Jean Christophe, I said to myself, had capitulated. Jean Christophe was accepting the lesser evil. Once, when he was younger and stronger, he would have refused to compromise with evil on any terms. We left Villeneuve like men crushed. Romain Rolland had no magic explanation. He lived by self-deception, like any American tourist buying a hand-me-down religion from the Soviet travel bureau. A year later, when Rolland visited Russia, and was feted and lionized, I watched carefully for his statements. Unless the Soviet press misrepresented him, he delivered himself of platitudinous eulogies of everything Soviet in the style of a *Moscow Daily News* interview with a third-category tourist.

3

We had gone to Russia believing there were good dictatorships and bad. We left convinced that defending one dictatorship is in fact defending the principle of tyranny. As long as the Rollands and G. B. Shaws and Barbusses condoned political murder and mass exile and the crushing of human decencies in one place and for one cause, they were supporting those methods in all places and for all causes. Everything else was sophistry and deception.

The European journey strengthened that conviction. The answers that I sought were implicit in the questions. The common denominator in all that we saw, it seemed to me, was the decadence of the moral sense in mankind, the attrition of ethical vales. That decadence showed itself in an indifference to suffering and a callous disrespect for the stuff of life. *The moral collapse of Europe was far more terrible than its economic collapse.* Until the World War, even the narrowest philosophies of progress decked themselves in the feathers of humanism: greater freedom, happiness and security for individual men and women, were the end-purposes advanced by all leaders who dared hope for a following. Now individual human beings were being degraded, brutalized, tortured, and murdered for the glorification of some abstraction of class or race. Whatever its pseudo-scientific justifications, every specialized phobia was like the other in that it began by nullifying the individual. Not one of them has room in its scheme of salvation for individual liberties and happiness; for all of them life is plentiful—and worthless.

It could not be claimed that the contempt for men and women as such derives from the philosophy of Hitlerism or fascism or communism, since that is their *common element.* Precisely the reverse seemed to me the case: these philosophies all radiated from that common center. Nor are they the last of its radiations; at this very moment it is sprouting new ones in Spain, Austria, Japan, China. To destroy any of these philosophies is futile, since the disease that afflicts our epoch is at the core, in its repudiation of those humanistic values nurtured through centuries. Until the dignity of life, the importance of human happiness, a respect for truth, and a horror of slavery under any guise are restored as motivating ideals if not as functioning realities, the economic or racial or national Utopias will remain inhuman monstrosities.

Without these values, what is socialism but a society of regimented slaves and regimented slave-drivers, in which private exploitation has been supplanted by public exploitation? Without these values, what is to distinguish socialism according to Stalin from socialism according to Mussolini as soon as Italy has nationalized the last of its industries and turned the owners into responsible directors? What is the essential differentiation between state socialism for Russia according to the Politburo and state socialism for Germany according to the Nazis of the extreme Left?

I felt this increasingly the longer I lived in Russia. Every visit to fascist countries, and the long "tour of tyrannies" that I undertook after I left Russia, deepened that feeling. The "coming struggle"—and it is not coming, it is already here—is not between communism and fascism. It is the struggle for the moral and ethical ideals which have been renounced by both those movements.

Once upon a time, socialism in any of its varieties was automatically associated with the whole heritage of mankind in terms of liberty and human dignity. Its chief argument against the economic relations under capitalism was that they were incompatible with that heritage. Socialization of the means of production was not an end in itself, but only a means for making the higher end-purposes of human progress possible. The socialist economy was regarded only as the bare framework on which a free, democratic society of equals would be built. Socialism, in short, was not merely an economic formula but an ethical system of ideals.

The crime of Bolshevism is that it tore down the whole ethical structure, retaining only the economic framework. Because it was born in a land where the democratic and humanist ideals were practically unknown, in a land still feudalistic in its thinking, Bolshevism merely adapted the mechanism of socialist economy to its old slave psychology. The result was at best a sort of feudal socialism.

As a boy on the East Side, as a man fighting the iniquities of the society in which I lived, I was drawn to socialism by an outraged sense of justice. I have yet to meet anyone in the radical movement who was attracted to socialism in any of its versions solely through the mind by the hard, cold logic of Marx or some other "scientific" prophet. The first impulse was always emotional —a search for justice or a reaction to injustice. It is the ethical content of socialism that is accepted first, and its "scientific" logic follows as a rationalization. Marx himself was a rebel against the iniquities of the world long before he systematized his indignations into a theory of historical development. Lenin was moved to hatred of the society that killed his brother long before he translated that hatred into Bolshevik dogma.

That is why socialism emptied of its humanitarian impulses and "prejudices" is not only barren but reactionary. It can advance no argument which fascism cannot duplicate. Already it has brought the idea of socialism into disrepute by cutting off all its associations with the accumulated treasures of human freedom. A mechanistic, dehumanized socialism based on dictatorship, systematic brutality, regimented robots working for an impersonal state administered by a privileged caste of bureaucrats has only the virtue that it is different from capitalism. But that is a virtue it shares with the social system of the African savages or feudalism in its pre-capitalist forms. Those who defend such a socialism, no matter how noble their motives, are essentially reactionary.

I left Russia and Europe convinced that the immediate task—for those who have the urge to participate consciously in the historical processes of their lifetime—is to defend the basic concepts of freedom, humaneness, intellectual integrity, respect for life. The triumph of any new economic system will be an empty victory, a tragic retrogression, if these concepts are insulted and expunged in the process. They must be defended from Bolshevik onslaughts no less than fascist or capitalist onslaughts. If the certainty of a full belly is to be made the only goal of socialism (and Russia, or any other country, may attain that goal in time) then the inmates of Sing Sing and Leavenworth Penitentiary are already living under socialism.

IV. To Tell or Not to Tell

MY FAMILY had sailed for home while I prowled among the European desperations. In April, I followed them, into an America of the New Deal, N.R.A., industry codes, brain trusts, legal liquor. It was an America vastly different from the one I left behind in 1931; the "rugged individualism" of which Secretary Stimson had talked to me had become a vaudeville joke; the state's obligation to feed, clothe, and house its population was no longer disputed.

But the differences were microscopic when measured on the scale of social and moral distances separating our life from life in Germany or Russia. The talk of New Deal regimentation sounded absurd against my experience of totalitarian practices. Though I had given many years to the defense of political prisoners and civil liberties in America, I now found myself angered by glib and offhand denunciations of American democracy by people who could not even imagine what total annihilation of democratic processes and civil rights meant.

In drawing up an indictment of American civilization, of its racketeering profit system, its political corruptions, its pious hypocrisies, its shrieking contrasts of wealth and poverty, I could enter competition with the *Daily Worker*. All the same, being back in America gave me a sense of physical expansion. The tensions of authoritarian Europe were suddenly released; the commonplace freedoms of press, speech and assembly no longer seemed commonplace—like long-lost friends, I was excited to have them back despite their obvious imperfections. And I was shocked by the cavalier fashion in which certain Americans seemed ready to trade in these hard-won rights for a mess of slogans. They needed to be reminded, I felt, that these liberties, for all their limitations and blemishes, were wrenched from unwilling masters and are treasures to be guarded.

Mass meetings, picketing, minority newspapers, magazines of

protest, communists on the radio, unionization of workers—the mere scope for open struggle, for free discussion, for public indignations was intoxicating in my first year or two of America. Before Russia I had been contemptuous of voting, of the bill of rights, of the judicial procedure as bourgeois snares and delusions. Now I derived an almost sensuous pleasure from watching and taking part in democratic processes. For the first time in my life I accepted jury service; and the memory of demonstration trials, death sentences behind closed doors, mass executions without trial gave that task a peculiar relish. Crude as the system of justice might be, the accused at least had a sportsmanlike chance to defend themselves. In the presidential campaign of 1936, I became the publicity director of the American Labor Party in New York State and knew the elation of political freedom. I saw all the forces of organized wealth go down in thundering defeat before the popular will.

The indictment against our racketeering civilization still stands, but there are basic rights and values which must be saved in any reconstruction of that civilization, otherwise we shall have a successful operation—and a dead patient.

The interview in Villeneuve became increasingly significant as time went on. Romain Rolland's panicky acceptance of the Russian brand of socialism—a socialism divested of all progressive ideals, all "democratic prejudices," and divesting itself rapidly of its internationalist prejudices as well—was typical of the acceptance I saw around me in America. With teeth clenched, eyes shut tight, minds barricaded, American radicals (except some despised "renegades") were holding on to the lesser evil.

Exaggerated faith in the Soviet experiment had become the intellectual fashion. The more openly the Stalin regime moved away from socialism, the more ardently these latterday communists championed the "socialist fatherland." They were obliged to assimilate so many blows to their human sensibilities, as the Kremlin piled enormity upon enormity, slaughter upon slaughter, that the process became a sort of conditioned reflex; every new brutality, every new liquidation of Bolshevik leaders, automatically stiffened their know-nothing faith.

It would have been polite and socially profitable to bolster up eager misconceptions. I needed only to fall into step to be received by the intellectual elite, and the temptations were strong enough. But the imprint of what I had seen in Russia was too deep upon my nerves. I could not bring myself to play the intellectual stooge.

Yesterday's liberals, in particular, were resentful of the truth. They had turned into "communists" of the Russian brand just when the Russians ceased pretending that their brand was communist. But they had not the courage to match their new convictions. They asked questions about the U.S.S.R. but ran off horrified when my answers were not to their acquired taste. It seemed to me that these men and women, insulted to their marrow by the iniquities of bourgeois society, were wiping out the insult in Japanese style by committing mental hara-kiri. They might survive as "revolutionaries" (until, at least, a revolution came along to destroy them) but they were committing suicide as reasoning creatures.

I marveled at their mental agility. In the same book, sometimes in the same paragraph, they could celebrate the *real* democracy of the Soviet system, as against the bogus democracy of the parliamentary governments—and the abandonment of that real democracy for the bogus kind. They could excoriate a political purge in one country on the same page where they boasted of a political purge of vastly larger scope in Russia, without seeming so much as aware of the inconsistency. Though they had pity for the sharecroppers of our South and for suffering peasants in Patagonia, they had not a sigh to spare for the millions deliberately starved to death by the Kremlin in southern Russia.

Inevitably, I drifted into arguments—Russia could not be discussed, it must be argued. Try as I would to keep the squabbles within reasonably factual limits, they degenerated instantly into sprawling swamps of generalization. We trudged knee-deep in slogans, through a jungle of dialectics, ideologies, deviations, and formulas. We detoured into morasses of citations, mostly a little vague at the edges, from Marx, Lenin and lesser prophets even unto Browder and Duranty.

As we argued, the everyday Russia I knew receded farther and farther into the background; soon it was forgotten altogether. The one hundred and sixty million flesh-and-blood Soviet citizens were displaced by heroic or villainous abstractions of poster quality. A great deal was said about a contraption labeled Dictatorship of the Proletariat, but nothing about who dictated to whom. Industrialization bulked large, but nary a word was permitted about actual working conditions, trifles like forced labor, passportization, real wages.

An extraordinary importance attached, above all, to the insurmountable limitations of petty bourgeois minds—specifically, my own—when watching history in flux: in distinguishing, for instance, between black and white, hunger and satiety, misery and boundless joy. The counts on which my testimony was invalidated amounted roughly to this:

I was too close to the Russian picture for a proper perspective and too isolated in the foreign colony to get close enough to the picture, while afflicted with a Petty Bourgeois Mentality that prevented me from grasping the true dialectic inwardness of outward phenomena and so conditioned by my revolutionary background as to overlook whole sectors of reality. Further, I failed to take the long view prescribed for others, while refusing to admit the exigences that forced a short view upon a regime trying to get along in a difficult world. I had managed to remain in Moscow for so many years because I was a willing tool of the kept capitalist press, and I did not manage to remain any longer for the same reason. I was clearly a hireling of Wall Street apprenticed to the Nazis, not to mention Trotsky. Obviously I knew too much about Russia for a clear judgment—couldn't see the forest for the trees, you know; besides, I didn't know enough about Russia, having been too deep in the forest to see the trees, which, in fact, had changed shape and foliage anyhow since I was unable to see them.

Should this bill of particulars leave a few shreds of credibility on my Soviet experiences, more violent methods were at hand. The ethical no-man's land in which everything is fair, once restricted to love and war, had been extended to embrace disagreements on Russia. No holds were barred, least of all strangleholds on personal character. I was familiar with the fantastic whispering campaigns against others whose Russian opinions were "undesirable"; now I saw such a campaign spread around my own character. It grew more fanciful with every article I published. Interesting reports about my villainy, rather flattering in their assumptions of my staggering capacity for evil, reached me—always in the same words, as though emanating from one source. Sometimes I stared in wide-eyed admiration at the opulence of the creative lying.

The irresponsible libels all had the same advantage for those who resented my views; they made it superfluous to discuss those views. Having demolished my character, the disputed facts could be dismissed with a superior shrug.

2

One day I was invited to a staff luncheon of the *New Republic*. Billy went with me. Presumably the staff were interested in obtaining my fresh reactions to Russia. I was given an opening to denounce those books which had told too much about Russia. The G.P.U. had just been "abolished," being converted into a Commissariat for Internal Affairs. By stretching my conscience, I might have consoled that congregation of high-minded editors with hopes of a new era of liberalism dawning for the Russians. But I sacrificed the chance for reconcilation. Instead I alluded to the famine and a few other unpleasantnesses.

Immediately a chill came over the luncheon. The eyes of the *New Republic* were glued to the plates, and I knew that nevermore would I be invited. I was guilty of the most heinous offense: puncturing noble delusions. The Olympian irony of the scene—and I could not help smiling at it inwardly—is that they, their exact kind, were being stamped out in the Soviet Union like so many obnoxious insects. They fitted perfectly into the hated category of pre-revolutionary intellectuals who must hide in dark cracks, praying only for the boon of invisibility.

Of my former friends among communist leaders, only one had the urge or the audacity to face the shameless backslider. If this traffic with an untouchable becomes known, the daring young man may still be punished; unless he had the dialectic foresight to obtain a dispensation for this one brief interview with an infidel. Tom (though that is not his name) and I had been young and ardent together once, and this was our first confrontation since 1931. My memory of the meeting ranks second only to the meeting with Rolland among the tragi-comic scenes of my retreat from Moscow.

"You must believe me, Gene," Tom began, in the dim light of a Greenwich Village ex-speakeasy, "that I have not joined the chorus of abuse against you. I know you too well to doubt that your views are honest. That's why I decided to talk to you. . . ."

We talked. I warmed up to the theme. Page by page I turned the book of my Russian observations. I skipped over the most somber pages because my friend seemed so distressed. I paused consolingly to interject a standardized apology for the Kremlin which, after all, was neck-deep in problems and helplessly fenced in by centuries of backwardness. But even at that the story was not too cheerful.

Tom listened—and drank whiskey. Could it really be, he asked—and threw down a few more "straights." How awful, he said—and ordered another bottle. Tom is not a heavy drinker ordinarily. This sudden thirst was plainly psychological.

"If I thought half of what you tell me to be true," he said weakly, "I would come out openly against it. Believe me I would."

I was startled by this blasphemy. "You can't mean that . . . you would then be giving ammunition to the reactionaries, just as I am supposed to be doing."

"There is such a thing as intellectual integrity," Tom murmured, as though arguing with himself. "This is not the kind of communism I am giving my life to. . . ." He was now flushed with drink.

Our conversation had a conspiratory edge—the dim lights, Tom's disconsolate embarrassment, his unconscious anxiety to wash out doubts with alcohol. It was silly of me to go on, but I was too wound up to stop of my own accord. And at the precise point where the logic of the talk demanded conclusions and decisions, Tom collapsed, literally collapsed across the table, snoring drunk. His deliverance, I am sure, was induced by spiritual anguish more than by whiskey.

We carried him out of the impious rendezvous and delivered him home. Presumably he awoke from that stupor with his faith wholly repaired. I never heard from him again and his writing on Soviet themes remained as spotlessly "official" as ever before.

I threw together some vignettes of Soviet life for a book called *Moscow Carrousel.* Every sketch had been written under the direct impact of some actual event or experience. But before submitting it to the publishers, I went through the manuscript carefully and deleted words, phrases, entire sections which might offend communist sensibilities too sharply. I was still under compelling psychological pressure to save face for the revolution. There was scarcely a hint in the book of the towering horrors which I have recounted in the present volume. More than that, I wrote in pages of apology, putting them into the mouths of fictitious Russians, to blunt the effect of "unfriendly" passages. The book stands as a monument to my indecision and cowardice; I soon came to feel ashamed of its mealy-mouthed evasions.

But carefully as I had edited it, the "liberal" reviewers were appalled (what the communist reviewers did to me can well be imagined!). The daily book critic of a New York paper, for instance, left the implication that my "difficulties with the censors" were in large part responsible for my acid pictures of Soviet everyday life. Thus neatly he disposed of facts too harsh for his stomach.

I wrote him, pointing out that 90% of *Moscow Carrousel,* having been written before the "difficulties" to which he alludes, could hardly be credited to that event. "My feelings on the Bolshevik methods of procedure have nothing to do with personal difficulties," I assured him. "It was the other way around—the difficulties came because of my feelings. And, in sober fact, there were no difficulties. I lived comfortably and on the whole received better treatment than most other correspondents." To which the critic replied with this curious and revealing explanation:

> I think that any newspaperman who lived for years in Moscow seems to acquire a certain morbidity of mind, which expresses itself in various ways. Your book seemed to me to suggest that you had suffered less from it than might have been anticipated.

The "undesirable" conclusions about the U.S.S.R. of foreign newspapermen thus boils down to a mental ailment! I cite this critic only as typical of the self-consolatory thinking about Russia then in vogue. He did not stop to analyze *why* Moscow gives normal newspaperman "a certain morbidity of mind." Evidently it did not occur to him to seek the causes in the Moscow realities rather than in private difficulties with censors. Like the *New Republic* editors, he preferred the soothing thought that the fault was not with the Kremlin but with some mysterious aberration in the correspondent's mind or character.

At a house party one day I was introduced to a mother and her sixteen-year-old daughter. The girl had read something of mine in a magazine and seemed thrilled to meet an author in the flesh. There was real enthusiasm in her voice.

"Eugene Lyons?" she exclaimed. "I know you—why, *I've cursed you!*"

On that foundation we quickly became good friends that evening. Russia for her was not a real place with real people. It was the never-never land of her burgeoning idealism. Except for their more expert and more desperate rationalization, it was the land which she shared with the Rollands, the Webbs, my friend Tom, the legions of intellectuals who had bartered logic and their entire heritage of libertarian and humanistic ideals for a solid faith backed up by a Red Army and a G.P.U. Inquisition.

More sharply than ever I faced the dilemma: *to tell or not to tell.* Now, I first realized how powerful a brake my residence in Russia, the professional need to keep the Soviet doors open, had been upon my writing. But there were other brakes. The desire to "belong," not to be a political dog in the manger, was a constant inducement to cautious understatement. And in six years I had sunk roots in the Russian soil. I loved Russia and its people. Yet I knew for a certainty that the Soviet gates, inscribed with the slogan, "Workers of the world, unite, you have nothing to lose but your chains," would be closed to me if I did not chain my tongue.

These personal considerations I settled easily enough. The decision, indeed, was automatic, a moral reflex action. The same impulses that had taken me from college into movements for the defense of political prisoners, now forced me to disregard these private interests.

The social considerations, however, were not so easy to appraise or to act upon. Forces of reaction and fascism, of anti-Semitism and know-nothingism, were unquestionably at work in America. The new Russia, rightly or wrongly, had come in myriad minds to symbolize the opposition to these forces. The symbol was grotesquely unlike the reality I had seen and felt and tasted. But was it not more desirable, perhaps, to leave the symbol intact?

Intellectually, I answered the question in the negative. I had come to believe that every defense of Stalin's methods was a defense of fascist methods, on which reaction fattened and grew stronger. Psychologically, however, I had not quite freed myself from old inhibitions. The diluted, pussyfooting *Moscow Carrousel* is proof enough. Facing an audience of earnest, hopeful Americans, workers and middle class people, I still could not bring myself to speak with a whole mouth. I shrank from hurting those of my listeners who had invested all their hopes and all their faith in the new Russia. They cursed me as a renegade for the little I did tell them, never guessing how carefully I wrapped facts in soft words to dull the blow. I could not even resent their curses—my sympathies were entirely on their side.

It was more than a year before I overcame those inhibitions. An article in *Harper's* Magazine, which I called *To Tell or Not to Tell,* signalized that inner victory. During that year I had become more deeply certain that in defending Soviet brutalities, the communists were fertilizing the American ground for brutalities of an opposite order. The shrill oh-and-ah enthusiasm for Russia which I found among the well-to-do in their penthouses and duplex apartments was a dangerous parlor game. Here, as in Germany before Hitler, the Bolsheviks were propagating a type of thinking—a disdain for human life, a contempt for truth, a glorification of brute force—which was essentially fascist, totalitarian. In helping Americans to conquer their "democratic prejudices" and their respect for individual freedom, the communists were opening for them an easy path to fascism. Leftist fascism—looking to an absolute state that planned and controlled all economy—was a large element in putting both Mussolini and Hitler in power; it figured also in the ideology thrown up hastily by Franco in Spain. The fascist approach to human problems, the moral putrescence that stripped the socialist hope of its ethical and progressive associations, must be fought under whatever labels they paraded; indeed, a Marxist label made the poison more deadly.

Two lectures at the Community Church forum in New York, one soon after my arrival, the other late in 1935, are a measure of the new courage which I drew from these convictions. That forum is largely patronized by men and women on the periphery of the communist movement. In the first talk I pulled my punches, feeling like a fraud when I did it. In the second I dared speak my thoughts. I was roundly abused, of course, from the floor. But I left that hall buoyed by the feeling that in a few minds at least I had broken down the blockade against independent thinking.

3

The international communist movement is soaked through and through with a fetid machiavellism that lies to its own adherents and to the rest of the world. Rationalized in terms of duty and ultimate goals, prevarication becomes a lop-sided virtue instead of a fault—just one more weapon in the "final conflict" that will "free the human race." Thomas Mann, speaking in New York in April, 1937, warned eloquently against this mentality; against a kind of man who has "here and there attained absolute power," who "without scruple . . . commits or approves crimes, provided they serve his advantage, or what he calls his advantage; he has no dread of falsehood, but reckons falsehood as high as truth, provided only that it is useful in his sense of the word." Communist leaders have lost self-consciousness in the matter and even take pride in their skill in sleight-of-mind. Devious thinking has become for them, as for their psychological blood-brothers in the fascist camp, normal and habitual, so that straightforward truth-telling seems shocking and perverse in their eyes.

One must understand this, if he is to make any sense out of such phenomena as fervent denials of the obvious; ardent "confessions" to palpable lies in open court; suppression and adjustment of statistics; hysterical attacks on persons who tell tales out of the Soviet school; books about the U.S.S.R. so far from the flesh-and-blood Russians that they might as well refer to some country on the other side of the moon.

The whole movement is committed to a theory of multiple truths, each diluted and doctored for the palate and stomach of the recipient, beginning with a "true" truth for the uppermost layer of leaders and graduated down to downright lies for the masses. In between are synthetic mixtures for special groups: a truth for the initiated officialdom whose self-interest helps them digest harsher morsels; a specially perfumed truth for Fabians, intellectuals, artists, who are known to be allergic to the bloodier ingredients.

The American sector of the communist world seemed to me rotten with this machiavellism. The springs of natural idealism were dammed up, and a flow of arbitrary "directives" from Moscow headquarters took their place. Endless fake organizations were hatched, each dressed up with a respectable false front of complacent or innocent clergymen, social workers, befogged millionaires, journalists living a dual capitalist and communist life under different names. All these organizations were in effect different names for the same clique of small-time Napoleons. The revolutionary pig-Latin of "Party lines" and "fronts" and dialectics had displaced connected thinking and open discussion. Literary blackmail and logrolling for "proletarian art" had displaced honest Left criticism. The superior logic which castigated radicals and trade-unionists of the wrong denominations as "social fascists" managed to take under its wing everything from Utopian pacifism to religious maniacs in Harlem. The ease with which yesterday's slogans were cast out and new ones, often diametrically opposite, adopted overnight showed how expert the movement had become in mental jiu-jitsu.

American communism had need for its charlatanism, because its fundamental assumption was make-believe. It was a militant proletarian party without proletarians in its ranks. Having failed to find a base in the working masses, it came to rest on the more muddled members of other classes—petty bourgeois and intellectual elements distressed by the sorrows of the world, especially their own economic uncertainty, and sorely in need of a faith safely beyond logic. For some of these "communists," caviar and vodka took the place of the hammer and sickle as emblems of the proletarian revolution. Already they had assumed a little of the manner of commissars and dictators. These recruits were in evidence at official Soviet consular and diplomatic functions, at banquets of self-styled friends of the new Russia, and mutual admiration parties thrown by well-to-do Left intellectuals. They pressed every last drop of titillation from their status as capitalist anti-capitalists.

In my own mind these economic masochists figured as "penthouse Bolsheviks." This private christening derived from an exclusive penthouse party—exclusive in the sense that only true-blue admirers of the Soviets were invited. The opulence of the setting, the abundance of caviar and champagne, the well-heeled guests and well-groomed Soviet diplomats in attendance, even the incongruous presence (for atmosphere) of a few unkempt specimens of the genuine article, composed into a delightful burlesque on revolution. They were celebrating the "inevitable" collapse of their social system in warm comradeship up there above the New York skyscrapers. . . . It was all so cozy. Once, not long after I reached New York, I found myself in a stiff-shirted evening-gowned company in one of the swankiest hotels; chiefly wealthy people with arty and intellectual hobbies. When Russia was mentioned I discovered that I was in a minority of one—they were all "communists"!

I pilloried their breed in an impolite article and the phrase "pent house Bolsheviks" gained wide currency.

Depending for its support so extensively upon middle-class folk, American communism was unavoidably more parsimonious with the "true" truth than communists, let us say, in France or pre-Hitler Germany. It was a mythical Russia which had "already entered the stage of true socialism," a Russia of "the world's most democratic constitution," the "happy life" and "classless society" that was being entrenched in the American mind. So many weary or bored or panicky Americans had made their spiritual homes in its wonder-chambers that anyone who threatened to undermine its foundations was treated as a shameless vandal. Perhaps he was.

Way back in the years when I was sending American news to Tass in Moscow I knew that only a small fraction, the "safe" and "desirable" information, would be passed on to ordinary Russian readers; the rest would be circulated for the private enlightenment of leaders who rated the "true" truth. The sifting is even more careful with information about Russia allowed to percolate to the outside world. In this task the Kremlin has the perfervid collaboration of whole battalions of wishful-thinking foreigners;

we have seen them in these pages, trooping gaily amidst the horrors, intent on the pretty colors of their own illusions. These are the amateurs.

In addition every nation has its contingent of professional interpreters of Russia who have made it their life's career to maintain appearances for the U.S.S.R. as Utopia-in-construction. With few exceptions they are a high-minded crew, coloring and concealing things with the noblest motives. Devotees of the theory of multiple truths, they speak more candidly than they write, and they think more candidly than they speak. They would as soon give the undiluted truth to their politically backward countrymen, whether readers of The *Nation* or the comic strips, as they would administer poison to children. Theirs is the logic of old-fashioned mothers who lie about sex to pubescent daughters—the American public, in their view, is simply too young, politically speaking, for the facts of Russian life. A few of them, I know, have inner qualms; the rest, on the contrary, feel positively heroic, strong in their ability to dispense with petty bourgeois prejudices about truth and mass brutality.

I decided, for myself, that I must tell the truth as I saw it. The decision in time assumed the magnitude of a pressing moral obligation.

V. Adventure in Idealism

DEVELOPMENTS in the Soviet Union since my departure have confirmed and deepened the conclusions forced upon me by my six years of personal observation.

The international alignment called for Soviet gestures to soothe the sensibilities of democratic nations which are potential allies in the looming war. The new Party line of united popular fronts, embracing all anti-fascist groups except communists disowned by Stalin, likewise demanded a pretense of democracy. Policy inside the country, however, remained stubbornly totalitarian. Prisons and "isolators" remained crowded with political dissenters; communists who strayed from the catechism continued to be dumped in Siberia and the Far North. The purges, in fact, grew bloodier.

Every new wave of hope for the liberalization and humanization of the Kremlin regime broke sickeningly on crags of terror. The G.P.U. was "abolished" by being rechristened Commissariat for Internal Affairs. The applause of the desperate optimists was still reverberating through the world when the assassination of Sergei Kirov evoked a saturnalia of vengeance. The "abolished" G.P.U. under its new name had lost none of its sadistic appetites.

Immediately after the promulgation of "the world's most democratic constitution" came the panicky annihilation of leading Old Bolsheviks—Kamenev, Zinoviev, Piatakov, Smirnov, Serebriakov, a dozen others—and the arrest of thousands more. The closest collaborators of Lenin were killed off in obscene haste after demonstration trials that were a mockery of the new constitutional guarantees. "Confessions" by demoralized prisoners to incredible accusations sown with self-evident lies, unsupported by documents or other independent evidence, without the formality of a credible defense, were made the excuse for wholesale extermination of the men who made the Bolshevik revolution. The fathers of the Soviet revolution were forced to paint themselves abjectly as depraved monsters, degenerates, allies of the most reactionary governments in the world. The whole story reeked with the crude melodrama of the police mind. To believe any portion of it—other than that these founders of the Soviet Union despised Stalin and his regime as counterrevolutionary usurpers—would be to believe that the revolution was corrupt at its roots from the beginning. One man or a dozen may prove to be perverted arch-criminals, but that nearly *all* those who stood in the highest places in the first years of the Soviet revolution were of this stamp is too great a strain on credulity. And even if they were traitors ten times over—*especially* if they were men of such low moral caliber—why should they suddenly turn against themselves, besmirch their records as Bolsheviks, bare their villainy for all to see? The working of dreadful pressures is so clear that only the desperation of unreasoned faith or the cynicism of self-interest can compass credence in the trials.

Immediately thereafter came the sensational executions of a large number of the highest ranking leaders of the Red Army, among them newly created Field Marshals, national heroes of the civil war period, the heads of the mammoth civilian military training organizations: men like Tukhachevsky, Putna, Yakir. A wave of suicides engulfed leaders of the governments in constituent Soviet Republics, veteran revolutionists like Tomsky, key personalities in the Kremlin hierarchy like Vice-Commissar of War Gamarnik. No dependable facts beyond the standardized charges in the official communiqués are available and it may be decades before the truth of the bloody debacle in high quarters will be known, if ever.

Neither can anyone do more than guess at the truth behind the routine charges of "banditry," Trotskyism, collaboration with Hitler and Japan, lodged against former Premier Alexei Rykov; Nikolai Bukharin; Jacob Doletzky, for some fifteen years chief of the official Soviet news agency; outstanding Soviet journalists like Vladimir Romm and Lapinsky; the heads of the Jewish colonization effort in Biro-Bidjan; practically all the important leaders of the trade unions; the key people in nearly every important department of Soviet life. The charges are not mere political disputation—they spell ruin, imprisonment, exile, suicide, capital punishment for the thousands involved. Even those who were in direct control of the atrocities to which I was witness—yes, the very G.P.U. chieftains who prepared the information on which

Old Bolsheviks are being destroyed—are under arrest, accused not only of counterrevolution but of ordinary embezzlement.

The whole tragic process is shrouded in mystery. The only certainty is that on the eve of the twentieth birthday of the Bolshevik state, treachery and horror and violent death are daily commonplaces. Taking the official version of the orgiastic liquidations at face value, we still have the spectacle of fearsome discontents, maniacal hatreds, and desperate disillusionment precisely among those who have sacrificed most and achieved most for the revolution. Unlimited terror has bred constantly new terrors through the years. The only certainty is that the Kremlin stands neck-deep in blood. The very basic elements of the Leninist-Trotskyist-Stalinist methods of revolution are in disrepute. The cumulative and gigantic sacrifice may be justified ultimately, when history's record is clearer, chiefly as an object lesson *how not to make revolutions.*

One after another, at the same time, the remaining progressive and idealistic elements in the Soviet system have been liquidated. Old ranks and titles were restored. The enlightened attitudes toward birth control and family relations, which won for Russia more liberal and radical adherents than its economic innovations, were abandoned. The wage and class differentiations adopted out of necessity were, by 1936, sanctified by neo-Marxist labels. Everything modern or advanced or experimental in music, architecture, literature, pedagogy was ostracized as "bourgeois Leftism," loaded with ridicule, proscribed by arbitrary edict.

Any one of these things in itself may be unimportant. Some of them may be defensible. Taken together, their meaning seems to me beyond dispute: evident to the naked intelligence not blinded by fanaticism. The central fact of these last Russian years has been the intense entrenchment of the new ruling political and economic groups on a basis of thoroughgoing conservatism. There has been a constantly stronger reaction against modernism in every department of Soviet life. The *status quo* of socialism-in-construction, with its bureaucracy, its sharply stratified population, its contrasts of poverty and ease, its renunciation of that mood and temper which may be called, for lack of a better word, advanced, has emerged as fixed, static, one of the great forces for conservatism in the present-day world. Other impulses may hammer down this system, but every ounce of the Kremlin's energy is now invested in establishing and maintaining a world equilibrium. The logic of Russia's struggle for survival as a state, coupled with absolutist government, has landed it in the camp of desperate and militant conservatism.

Underlying Moscow's new conservatism in every branch of its existence is the tacit admission that the present Soviet system will remain unaltered as long as its rulers can stave off change. The "transition period" has been accepted for all practical purposes as permanent.

It requires no special perspicacity to recognize that certain groups in the Soviet population by this time have large stakes in the "transition period," and that the normal conservatism of human nature—product of habit and fear of change—is operative. I refer not merely to the infinitesimal minority in the Kremlin, that small, closely-knit governing oligarchy, but its millionfold foundation of inter-dependent officials: the bureaucrats, large classes of privileged military and police officials, administrators, better-paid technical workers, the new Soviet-made intelligentsia.

The revolutionary driving force had petered out long ago, and in the last few years we have been watching the rebound. Those radicals who prefer to fool themselves with the old slogans and shut their eyes to the actualities are in fact supporting a reaction which with every month brings the Soviet state closer in essence to the fascist states in Germany and Italy.

The new Russian chauvinism, this or that decree, the liquidation of this composer or that novelist, a thousand other expressions of the reaction may each be argued or defended in itself. But the defense, assuredly, cannot rest on "revolutionary" grounds; no matter how impressive the arguments, they are tory arguments unrelated to the original philosophy and the original impetus of the revolution. The attitude which we normally associate with a revolutionary nature—an attitude of scientific skepticism, defiance of established authority, freedom from intellectual bondage, healthy doubt of the infallibility of dead or living prophets, courageous defense of unorthodox views—are more alien to Stalin's party than to Stanley Baldwin's or Herbert Hoover's. The U.S.S.R.

no longer has any room for agitators and innovators, whether in government, economy, or the arts. Its ideals, like the ideals of every ruling clique, are stability, productivity, conservatism.

Sooner or later, the fervid friends of the U.S.S.R the world over will have to separate in their minds the economic innovations (state ownership of all the means of production and distribution) from the cultural and human reaction; an economic set-up that has in it the germ of the world's future from a political set-up that is wholly of the past; the Marxist formulas from the Stalinist actualities. They will have to distinguish between Russia and the socialist dream.

Until they make that adjustment they will continue to defend every form of injustice and obscurantism, every reactionary thought and act, every insult to their larger hopes, merely because these are stamped "Made in the U.S.S.R." Though tormented in their private conscience, they will continue to stand up for such parodies of justice as the Zinoviev-Radek trials; for the degradation of the human spirit, the sycophancy, the one-man rule through one controlled party, which are increasingly the marks of old Russia in its new habiliments.

2

Stalin stands as the symbol of the "permanent transition" which has taken the place of the permanent revolution once basic in socialist thinking. The purity of his motives and his fitness for the job are of only academic interest. Like his Romanov predecessor, Stalin works his will through governmental machinery: a Politburo, a Cabinet, a Central Committee, an impotent legislature. What is crucially important is the restoration of a single, personal incarnation of the state. The ancient Russian symbol of absolutism, the "Little Father," is again enthroned.

The glorification of Stalin must be seen to be believed. I quote at random from Soviet newspapers on my desk:

> Our own, our passionately beloved, our great leader, Comrade Stalin. . . . The unmatched genius and courage and brilliant wisdom of the great and beloved Stalin. . . . To you, Comrade Stalin, whose marvelous leadership brings us still more socialist triumphs. . . . Long live the great Stalin, leader and inspirer of the working classes of the

whole world. . . . The great and glorious Stalin, head and brilliant theoretician of the world revolution. . . . Stalin, the great and beloved. . . .

As recently as 1928 or 1929, it was still possible to find an unadorned reference to the "boss" (as communist officials call him in private) simply as Comrade Stalin. Today, the name is never mentioned publicly without a profound verbal genuflection. The continuous hosannas depend on repetition rather than originality for their effect. The adjectives and qualifying phrases in which the ineffable name is cushioned are fairly standardized. Innovations, even in the direction of juicier flattery, are dangerous. A new adjective needs the sanction of usage in the columns of *Pravda* or in the mouth of some impeccable grand vizier like Kaganovich before it is woven into the routine litanies of praise.

Currently the words most used are *veliki i liubimi*—"great and beloved." They are so continuously attached to his name that they have lost their original contours and merged with Stalin, like a part of his name or a prescribed title. The most casual mention in a public gathering is the signal for a demonstration—every speaker automatically pauses for the ovation, just as a trained comedian pauses for his laugh. In printed matter, the worship has been standardized to a point which to an outsider is not without humor. Other objects worthy of enthusiasm are followed in the stenogram by the one word "applause." When the occasion is the mention of Stalin or anything pertaining to Stalin the parentheses record "thunderous applause" or "stormy applause," and sometimes add, "everybody rises and sings the *International*." A wisecrack from any less elevated source may be followed in the record by the word "laughter." A witticism by Stalin is invariably followed by "hilarious laughter." In a published photograph where Stalin appears with other leaders, the line underneath identifies the figures in the picture by listing Stalin first, regardless where he may be located in the line-up, then going back to the left to list the others. His name in an editorial is always printed in larger letters than the rest of the text, just as the name of deity is capitalized in Western print.*

* Recently, in 1937, a curb was ordered on the verbal adulation of Stalin, but the substance, in his deification, remains unchanged.

The fawning exaltation of the man is official and largely synthetic. The Russian people do not know him. The glorification is almost impersonal. Not a real, living, human Stalin, but the figure carefully molded by Party politicians and publicists is the recipient of the adulation. The character of that synthetic figure changes: at the height of the Iron Age it was a symbol cast in iron; now it is increasingly a benevolent leader kissing a little child. . . .

The worship is exaggerated but not exuberant. It is vast but neither deep nor soaring. The newspapers and orators and poets who sing paeans of praise to Stalin are official newspapers, official orators, and official poets. Possibly this apotheosis is not wholly his own doing. He may have been convinced that for his subjects, conditioned by centuries of autocracy at one end and slavery at the other, power must be personified in one man. When I left Russia, I was sure that the exaltation of a mortal creature could not be carried any further. I was mistaken. The Soviet press bulges with proofs that the human animal's capacity for groveling sycophancy is literally boundless.

Powerful beyond any medieval tsar in his own domain, the "great and beloved" is also acknowledged pretender to an international throne as dictator of the Comintern. Millions in all nations of the world bring him unquestioning obedience as the incarnation of their hopes, recognizing no fatherland but his Russia. Underground in places like Japan and Germany, aboveground in most countries, the viceroys of Stalin, leaders of their respective communist sections, are ever alert for the snap of his whip, the accent of his wishes. The pseudo-scientific movement which he has broken to his will has been raised to a pitch of mystic consecration, so that he is at once emperor and pope, general and infallible oracle, comrade and master.

Stalin is without the cool genius of a Lenin, without the flamboyant talents of a Mussolini, without the hysterical fervor of a Hitler. An uninspired practical politician, this slow-moving, slow-thinking but implacable Caucasian has hoarded and organized power slowly through his years and made himself the strongest person on the face of the earth. Reckoned by the numbers who willingly or under coercion bring him allegiance, Stalin's temporal empire dwarfs Caesar's and Napoleon's, and it has a spiritual content theirs did not possess.

Thus the collectivist idea has come to fruition in the apotheosis of an individual. Absolutism reigns in the name of a collectivist philosophy. One man is regent for Demos—which, come to think of it, was precisely the role of the "tyrants" in ancient Greece. History has again played one of its gruesome jokes and the cosmic bellylaugh will echo through endless generations.

3

In my six years in the Soviet Union there was little of the spectacular. There were routine difficulties without end and buzzing annoyances and occasional half-hearted threats of expulsion. There were intense moments of purely professional achievement or failure, isolated episodes bordering on drama, and a vast number of human contacts touched with high color.

But I can inflate none of these experiences into major personal risks in the do-and-dare tradition of newspaper legend. At no time did I endanger life or limb or face any more serious hazard than a bruised conscience or a reprimand from the home office. As for the shrill little triumphs and defeats of competitive journalism, they seem petty enough in retrospect.

Even at the time, these five-minute scoops and ten-minute beatings were edged with absurdity. Against the background of desperation and enthusiasm and pitiless bigotry, against the life-and-death struggles amidst which we foreigners had our sheltered alien being, the breathless race of American newspapermen to file an emasculated blue-penciled little dispatch ninety seconds before a rival was, in sober fact, grotesque. When the dispatch, as so often happened, dealt in mealy-mouthed fashion with some decree that snapped the props from under millions of human existences, that race for a few seconds' advantage was almost obscene.

No, there was no melodrama in my foreign assignment. The surveillance to which we were subjected had nothing in common with the terror which, as I saw a thousand times over, turned strong men and women into whimpering wretches, bled them white of all dignity and self-respect. We lived in relative spaciousness in the midst of ghastly overcrowding, and never lacked cake when bread was a luxury to 90% of our neighbors.

Yet the six years are in my mind like some great and continuous adventure, crowded with vivid excitement and suffused with deep feeling. Though I was myself never hurt, the memory is filled with pain. Though my function was merely to cable news developments tersely and inexpensively, the memory is touched with elations and flaring hopes. It seems a stretch of turbulence marked off by the calmer years that preceded and the quiet since my return.

When I try to trace that turbulence to its source, I discover that it flows from the things that happened to Russia and its people rather than to me.

The adventure was real enough. But I lived it on an intellectual and emotional plane rather than a physical level. The feelings stirred in my blood by the first mass demonstration on Red Square, by the unfoldment of the Shakhty trial, by my first view of the *Tzik* in session, by the epic tragedies of the peasant revolt and the man-made famine are woven into that intense spiritual adventure. The mental anguish and searching and desperate rationalizations as my imported certainties crumbled under the hammering of everyday impressions, likewise, are in the intricate design of that memory.

The material events were all outside myself. All the promptings of personal comfort and career were in the direction of casual and uncritical acceptance of the Soviet scene as raw stuff for reportorial dispatches—picturesque, titillating, but without inner relation to my own life. All the pressures of friendship, of respectable conformity within my own social group, were for unreasoned hosanna-singing or, failing that, a synthetic enthusiasm.

Had I been differently constituted, therefore, the Soviet years might easily have flowed over me without leaving any deep marks. When I record that I did take the Soviet reality closely to heart and did become emotionally and mentally involved in the processes I was reporting, I am neither boasting nor apologizing. The "objectivity" which accepts the revolution, its promises and its disappointments, as just so much grist for the journalistic mills was simply beyond me. I had too large an investment of personal hope and faith at stake.

4

My conscience has stood behind me, looking over my shoulder as these pages were written. Again and again, it forced me to go back and re-assay my judgments. Repeatedly, it protested against the sharpness of a phrase, the finality of a conclusion. Even more often it pulled me short when I seemed minded to accept the shadow for the substance or to flatter the self-deceptions of the believers. It would not permit me to compromise with that cumulative memory.

And now its voice is more insistent than ever. Have your dreams, it demands, been a silly delusion? Horror has seared your nerves, but has it burned out all hope? Were it not better, perhaps, to bury your knowledge in your own heart instead of carrying it to others? Because an adventure in idealism in one place has ended in a new reaction, because a fight for economic freedom has ended in a new form of slavery, shall you—and millions like you—yield utterly to despair? Shall you sink your dreams in the muddy morass of disillusionment, and join the "practical" men in ridiculing the utopists, the visionaries, the prophets of all time?

To which I reply: I despair only because I lack the skill and the eloquence to translate my deepest feelings for other men's minds. I wish I were able to convey to them that the Russian experience has been for me less a disillusionment than a rededication. It has forced me to pitch my hopes above the merely nutritive, to recognize that man lives not by bread alone. In the knowledge of the Russian experiment I am able once more to affirm without shame the value of such things as justice, humaneness, truth, liberty, intellectual integrity, and human dignity. From the Russian mistakes I have drawn the strength to assert that without these things social systems can only be variations on the old injustice.

I have seen that movements for economic change are worthless, even dangerous, as soon as they throw off respect for life, for liberty, for justice. The very fact that such an assertion, which would have sounded axiomatic in the past, now has a quixotic ring is a measure of the distortion in our mass thinking. Our epoch is gangrened by a contempt for the protoplasm of society: the individual human being. It is steeped in a machiavellism that styles itself "scientific" and hurls all fundamental human values indiscriminately into the retorts of its "experiments." Perhaps it is the revenge of the machine age; its insensitive gods of statistical efficiency have spawned monstrous mechanistic religions in which people are mere cogs and digits. The gangrene set in with the

World War and has been eating more deeply into the flesh of the race. It is a stench in the nostrils of mankind in Russia and Germany, on the battlefields of Ethiopia and Spain. It has turned leaders and nations into cynical vivisectionists. However the rotting flesh may be disguised with slogans about race and class and nation, the horror shows through in prisons and concentration camps and wholesale slaughters of human beings, in ugly fears and uglier propitiations of flattery.

I, too, was infected by that disease. I was ready to liquidate classes, purge millions, sacrifice freedoms and elementary decencies, arm self-appointed dictators with a flaming sword—all for the cause. It was a species of revenge rationalized as social engineering. Then I saw these things in full swing and discovered that the revenge was being wreaked on the very masses who were to be saved by that cause. I found that the means are more real than the professed end; that they harden into a system of power and privilege which must postpone the end in order to maintain itself. Having seen the putrescence where the disguise was most convincing, I have found the courage to declare that I am a humanitarian, that I respect truth and that I abhor the vivisection of human beings for their own good.

I am convinced that any philosophy of human progress which does not rest uncompromisingly on respect for life, no matter how honest its original intentions, becomes brutalized and defeats its own professed purposes. A socialism that offers to fill the bellies of its people but retains the privilege of slitting those bellies at will is reactionary; it cancels out ages of struggle and costly victory in the domain of the human spirit. On those terms, indeed, competitive capitalism too can make the same offer to fill the bellies of its robots; the bargain has already been struck in Germany and elsewhere. The economic security of a prison or a military barracks—the "ideal" for which our epoch seems ready to barter all the human values accumulated through the ages—seems to me the most repulsive ever foisted upon mankind. It is the *reductio ad absurdum* of a dehumanized materialism.

Precisely today, when such words and such concepts are being spat upon, it is important that those for whom they still have some meaning should defend liberty and honesty and justice. The gangrene cannot be fought in one country and allowed to fester in another. No plan for economic salvation must be accepted if it is diseased with disdain for life. Ultimately, Russia will not be judged by how much bread it has given its people—by that standard other countries and other systems may be far more successful—but by how much freedom, self-respect, justice, equality, truth, and human kindness it has brought into the world.

I know only too well that those who elect to stand on this bedrock of human decencies and cherished freedoms will be exposed to the sneers of their more "practical" fellow-men. They will be pelted with sophistries and insults and under the temptation always to turn "practical" likewise and put on some denominational uniform—to defend one set of horrors against another instead of fighting them all. They will be taunted because they cannot provide scientific definitions: "What is this truth, this liberty, this justice of which you prate? What is its color, how much does it weigh, where have you seen it in its pure form?" As though we should worship ugliness because no one has succeeded in defining beauty, or darkness because no one has succeeded in marking the boundaries of light. . . .

But I know also that through changing systems, through conflicting programs, those undefined values have survived and will survive as the ultimate tests of all systems and all programs.

No set-back can end the adventure in idealism. That adventure began with the dawn of the race and will continue when the slogans and phobias of our own day will have been forgotten.

Index